W9-BWK-261

The Waite Group's

# Microsoft® C

## Programming for the PC

## HOWARD W. SAMS & COMPANY
### HAYDEN BOOKS

# Related Titles

**The Waite Group's C Primer Plus, Revised Edition**
*Mitchell Waite, Stephen Prata, and Donald Martin*

**The Waite Group's Advanced C Primer++**
*Stephen Prata*

**The Waite Group's C++ Programming (Version 2.0)**
*Edited by The Waite Group*

**The Waite Group's Essential Guide to ANSI C**
*Naba Barkakati*

**The Waite Group's Essential Guide to Microsoft® C**
*(forthcoming)*
*Naba Barkakati*

**The Waite Group's Microsoft® C Bible**
*Naba Barkakati*

**The Waite Group's QuickC™ Bible**
*Naba Barkakati*

**The Waite Group's Essential Guide to Turbo C®**
*The Waite Group*

**The Waite Group's Turbo C® Bible**
*Naba Barkakati*

**The Waite Group's Turbo C® Programming for the PC, Revised Edition**
*Robert Lafore*

**The Waite Group's Inside the Amiga® with C, Second Edition**
*John Berry*

**The Waite Group's MS-DOS® Bible, Second Edition**
*Steven Simrin*

**The Waite Group's MS-DOS® Developer's Guide, Revised Edition**
*John Angermeyer, Kevin Jaeger, et al*

**The Waite Group's Understanding MS-DOS®**
*Kate O'Day and John Angermeyer*

**The Waite Group's Tricks of the MS-DOS® Masters**
*John Angermeyer, Rich Fahringer, Kevin Jaeger, and Dan Shafer*

**The Waite Group's Discovering MS-DOS®**
*Kate O'Day*

---

For the retailer nearest you, or to order directly from the publisher, call **800-428-SAMS**. In Indiana, Alaska, and Hawaii call 317-298-5699.

The Waite Group's
# Microsoft® C
## Programming for the PC

*Revised Edition*

Robert Lafore

*HOWARD W. SAMS & COMPANY*

*A Division of Macmillan, Inc.*
*4300 West 62nd Street*
*Indianapolis, Indiana 46268 USA*

©1989 by The Waite Group, Inc.

SECOND EDITION
FIRST PRINTING—1989

All rights reserved. No part of this book shall be reproduced, stored
in a retrieval system, or transmitted by any means, electronic,
mechanical, photocopying, recording, or otherwise, without written
permission from the publisher. No patent liability is assumed with
respect to the use of the information contained herein. While every
precaution has been taken in the preparation of this book, the
publisher and author assume no responsibility for errors or
omissions. Neither is any liability assumed for damages resulting
from the use of the information contained herein.

International Standard Book Number: 0-672-22661-8
Library of Congress Catalog Card Number: 88-64064

**From The Waite Group, Inc.**
Development Editor: *Mitchell Waite*
Editorial Director: *James Stockford*
Managing Editor, Revised Edition: *Scott Calamar*
Content Editor, Revised Edition: *Kay Nelson*

**From Howard W. Sams & Company**
Acquisitions Editor: *James S. Hill*
Development Editor: *James Rounds*
Manuscript Editor: *Don MacLaren, BooksCraft, Inc., Indianapolis*
Production Coordinator: *Marjorie Hopper*
Illustrators: *William D. Basham, Ralph E. Lund, and T. R. Emrick*
Cover Artist: *Ron Troxell*
Indexer: *Northwind Editorial Services*
Electronic Coding Processor: *Automated Business Services*
Compositor: *Shepard Poorman Communications Corp.*

*Printed in the United States of America*

**Trademarks**

All terms mentioned in this book that are known to be trademarks or
service marks are listed below. In addition, terms suspected of being
trademarks or service marks have been appropriately capitalized.
Howard W. Sams & Company cannot attest to the accuracy of this
information. Use of a term in this book should not be regarded as
affecting the validity of any trademark or service mark.

CodeView debugging program is a registered trademark of Microsoft
Corporation.

IBM AT is a registered trademark of International Business Machines
Corporation.

Microsoft is a registered trademark of Microsoft Corporation.

MS-DOS is a registered trademark of Microsoft Corporation.

PC-DOS is a trademark of International Business Machines
Corporation.

UNIX is a registered trademark of Bell Laboratories.

*This book is dedicated to RWL, GGL,
and all the gang at 10 Rose Hill Road.*

# About the Author

 Robert Lafore has been involved in the computer industry since 1965, when he learned assembly language on the DEC PDP-5. He holds degrees in mathematics and electrical engineering; founded Interactive Fiction, a software games company; and has served as managing editor of The Waite Group. Mr. Lafore is author or co-author of the books *Soul of CP/M*, *Assembly Language Primer for the IBM PC*, *Microsoft Macinations*, *Turbo C Programming for the IBM*, and *Peter Norton's Inside OS/2*. Mr. Lafore has also been a petroleum engineer in Southeast Asia, a systems analyst at the Lawrence Berkeley Laboratory, and has sailed his own boat to the South Pacific.

# Acknowledgments

I'd like to thank Mitchell Waite of The Waite Group for his dedicated and painstaking editing (complete with humorous asides and subliminal suggestions) and Harry Chesley, co-author of *Supercharging C* (Addison-Wesley), for his expert advice.

I am also indebted to the following individuals at Howard W. Sams & Company: Jim Hill for having the faith to buy this book idea, Damon Davis for publishing it, Jim Rounds for nursing it into the system, and Wendy Ford and Marjorie Hopper for overseeing its production.

I would also like to thank Doug Adams for his technical edit; Bruce Webster of *Byte* magazine, Ray Duncan, Herbert Schildt and Kay Nelson for reviewing the final manuscript; and Don MacLaren of BooksCraft for his painstaking and skilled copy editing.

# Contents

# Foreword

### by Ray Duncan

In just a decade, C has made the transition from an obscure Bell Laboratories house language to the programming language of choice for professionals. C has been used successfully for every type of programming problem imaginable —from operating systems to spreadsheets to expert systems—and efficient compilers are available for machines ranging in power from the Apple to the Cray. On the new wave of the windowing, graphics-intensive 68000-based personal computers such as the Macintosh, Amiga, and Atari, C is the de facto standard for serious developers.

Why has C met with such success when other languages, born in the same time frame and designed with similar objectives, have gained only limited acceptance or have faded from view altogether? C's intimate association with UNIX, and the penetration into academia that was made possible by Bell Laboratory's broadminded licensing plans for universities, must be partly responsible. But the largest measure of C's success seems to be based on purely practical considerations: the portablility of the compiler; the standard library concept; a powerful and varied repertoire of operators; a spare, elegant syntax; ready access to the hardware when needed; and the ease with which applications can be optimized by hand-coding isolated procedures.

The increasing dominance of C for both systems and applications programming has created a tremendous market for C books. I must confess that I am a compulsive buyer of computer books of every sort: an addiction based on curiosity, on a desire to learn from the approaches and styles of other authors, and on a continual search for excellent new books to recommend to readers of my column in *Dr. Dobb's Journal*. While indulging this pleasant but somewhat expensive habit over the last few years, I have built up quite a collection of C tutorials and reference works, but I have found nearly all of the introductory C books to be unsatisfying. The authors either have difficulty discussing C without blurring the issues with UNIX-specific details, or they succumb to a fascination with clever C tricks, or they simply progress so quickly from elementary concepts to lengthy, complex example programs that they leave the reader behind.

When Mitchell Waite asked me if I would like to review Robert Lafore's manuscript for this book, I was surprised but gratified. I have long considered Robert's *Assembly Language Primer for the IBM PC and XT* (New American Library) to set the standard of quality in its category, and I hoped that his C primer would be equally well organized, lucid, and complete. I certainly was not disappointed! I believe the book you are holding in your hands is the most accessible book on C that has yet been published. The material is presented in Robert's usual clear, forthright style, and the pace is steady but not intimidating. Best of all, the example programs are short but interesting, clearly demonstrate the concepts under discussion, and are relevant to everyday programming problems on the IBM PC—you don't need to speak UNIX or buy your own VAX to reap their benefits.

*Ray Duncan is a software developer and columnist for* Dr. Dobb's Journal. *He is also author of* Advanced MS-DOS.

# Foreword

## by Douglas Adams

Before reading this book, I asked myself if there was really a need for yet another book on C programming. I now feel the answer is a ringing yes. Robert Lafore has done an outstanding job of presenting information for C programmers who use the hardware of IBM and compatible personal computers and want to understand the specifics of the Microsoft C compiler.

Because of the unique approach of this book it will be useful both to beginning and advanced C programmers. The C programming language was really designed for use with the UNIX operating system on minicomputers. Compiler writers and Microsoft in particular have gone to a great deal of effort to provide a powerful tool for personal computers. Other books on the topic tend to ignore the PC-DOS/MS-DOS operating system and personal computers. If this is your working environment, you need this book. There are three major advantages to this book; I will mention each in turn.

First, the latest version of Microsoft C is now considered to be the most powerful and efficient C compiler for personal computers. It has been developed over a period of years by Microsoft, which used C to compile many of its successful programs. Its libraries are unusually complete and it generates very compact and efficient code. It also includes a source code debugging tool, which is usually a costly extra with other compilers. It is thoroughly up-to-date and includes most of the proposed ANSI enhancements. Microsoft continues to improve the compiler, while offering program updates at a modest cost. If you own another C compiler, this is still a fine book with which to learn C programming.

Second, this book carefully makes clear how the C language is best used with PC-DOS. With nominal understanding of PC-DOS/MS-DOS, you will be able to begin C programming with a minimum of effort. The book, as well as the compiler, supports the PC-DOS/MS-DOS operating system very well. It is well known that Microsoft is always working on improving the operating system; you can rest assured that as the operating system is improved, the C compiler will also be upgraded.

Third, and perhaps most important of all, this book delves into how the IBM hardware works. While there are several books treating these topics for the assembly language programmer, this is the first book devoted to accessing hardware for the C programmer. This is important since assembly language is not necessary for most programming. Since C is much easier to understand, maintain, and enhance, most early programs written in assembler are now being rewritten in C by software developers.

The monochrome display and graphics display treated here are not discussed in other books. Finally, the chapter on PC-DOS files is indispensable, since a program that cannot store data on a disk file is of little value. Most of this information has previously been available only in Microsoft's technical reference manuals. These are not the free manuals that came with your computer, but are special publications that are very expensive and difficult to obtain.

The book is fun. The explanations are clear. The programming examples which you are encouraged to try out are interesting and useful. Questions and exercises follow the chapters, with the answers supplied. This is a good book for programming classes and an outstanding book for you to use to learn on your own.

*Douglas Adams' 18 years of computing experience includes the development of programs in C for AT&T, which it is using nationwide. He is president of Century System Corp., a consulting firm in San Francisco.*

# *Introduction*

This book has two interconnected goals: to teach the C programming language, and to show how C can be used to write serious programs on the IBM family of computers—the PC, XT, AT, and PS/2 series—and compatible machines from other manufacturers.

The Microsoft C Optimizing Compiler is the most widely used professional software development tool for the IBM. QuickC, which is included in the Optimizing Compiler and can also be purchased separately, is an easy-to-use integrated development environment, ideally suitable for those learning C. This book works with both the Optimizing Compiler and QuickC.

## Who This Book Is For

Almost anyone who has used a computer for any length of time has developed an idea for a new program or an improvement to an existing one. If you've had such an idea and would like to transform it into a working, marketable program for the IBM, this book will show you how. If you're a student interested in learning C, with an IBM computer at your disposal, this book will provide an easy-to-follow but thorough introduction to the language. It is suitable for use in school and university computer science courses.

## What's Different about This Book?

Many introductory books on C present the language either in a UNIX-based environment or in a theoretical context, ignoring the machine the language is running on. This book uses a different approach: it teaches C in the context of IBM computers and the PC-DOS (or MS-DOS) operating system. This method offers several advantages.

First, concentrating on a specific machine makes learning the language easier and more interesting. C running in a UNIX environment generally does not have access to graphics or other hardware-related peripherals. Therefore programming examples must concentrate on simple text-based interaction. In the IBM world, on the other hand, we can make use of such features as graphics characters, program control of the cursor, and color graphics—capabilities that can enliven program examples and demonstrations.

Also, as we move on to more complex aspects of the C language, C constructs that might otherwise seem theoretical and mysterious—such as **far** pointers and unions—can be explained by relating them to actual applications on the IBM.

Finally, if your goal is to write programs specifically for the IBM, then learning C in the IBM environment, with examples using specific aspects of the IBM hardware, will give you a head start in the creation of practical programs.

## Learn by Doing

We have used a hands-on approach in this book. We believe that trying things yourself is one of the best ways to learn, so examples are presented as complete working programs, which can be typed in and executed. In general, we show what the output from the examples looks like, so you can be sure your program is functioning correctly. Very short examples are given at the beginning of the book, working up to longer and more sophisticated programs at the end.

## Illustrations and Exercises

We've also tried to make this a visual book. Many programming concepts are best explained using pictures, so wherever possible we use figures to support the text.

Each chapter concludes with a set of questions to test your general understanding of the material covered, and programming exercises so you can be sure you understand how to put the concepts to work. Answers to the questions and exercises can be found in the back of the book.

# Why Use C?

In the last several years, C has become the overwhelming choice of serious programmers on IBMs. Why? C is unique among programming languages in that it provides the convenience of a higher-level language such as BASIC or Pascal, while allowing close control of hardware and peripherals, as assembly language does. Most operations that can be performed on the IBM in assembly language can be accomplished—usually far more conveniently—in C.

C has other advantages as well. The better C compilers (the Microsoft compiler in particular) can now generate amazingly fast code. This code is so efficient that it is often difficult to produce significant speed increases by rewriting it in assembly language. C is also a well-structured language; its syntax makes it easy to write programs that are modular and therefore easy to understand and maintain. The C language includes many features specifically designed to help create large or complex programs. Finally, C is more portable (programs can be converted to run on a machine other than that originally intended) than most languages.

# What You Should Know Before You Read This Book

Before you read this book, you should probably have at least some experience with a higher-level language, such as Pascal or BASIC. It is certainly possible to learn C as your first computer language. However, C is geared more to the experienced programmer. Its syntax is not—at least at first glance—as easy to understand as BASIC, and it incorporates some concepts that a beginning programmer might find difficult. So we will assume that you have had some experience with a higher-level language and that you are familiar with such concepts as variables, looping, conditional statements, and functions (called procedures or subroutines in other languages).

You should also be familiar with PC-DOS (called MS-DOS on non-IBM computers) or OS/2 and how it works. You should be able to list directories and create, execute, copy, and erase files, and you should also be familiar with tree-structured directories and be able to move about in them.

# What Equipment You Need to Use This Book

You can use this book with a variety of hardware and software configurations. Here's what you'll need.

## Hardware

You should have access to an IBM PC, XT, AT, or PS/2, or a compatible machine. Either a monochrome or color monitor will work fine for most of the book. (We'll mention the exception in a moment.)

You'll need either dual floppy drives or a fixed (hard) disk drive with a single floppy drive. Most modern C compilers are so large that juggling disk space becomes a problem on floppies, and floppies are also much slower. A student can probably get by with a floppy system, but if you want to develop your own programs, you'll save so much time with a fixed disk that it is almost an essential investment.

Chapters 11 and 12, on color graphics, require the use of a color monitor. Almost any color monitor will work for the bulk of these chapters, since most of the examples work with CGA graphics modes. You'll also need a CGA graphics adaptor board. A few examples need EGA and VGA graphics, so an EGA or VGA board, and a monitor to match, is preferable.

Finally, while it's not absolutely essential, you'll probably want a printer to generate program listings and record program output.

## Software

You should use the MS-DOS or PC-DOS operating system, version 2.0 or greater. You can also run the Optimizing Compiler version 5.1 in OS/2 protected mode and QuickC in the OS/2 compatibility box. (However, some example programs will not run in OS/2 protected mode.)

You'll need either the Microsoft C Optimizing Compiler or QuickC.

QuickC supports all the examples in this book. Optimizing Compiler versions 3.0, 4.0, 5.0, and 5.1 are all compatible with almost all the examples in this book. The exception is the Microsoft graphics library, described in Chapter 12, which is supported only by versions 5.0 and later of the Optimizing Compiler. Future releases of these products will probably continue to be compatible.

Actually, much of the material in this book is applicable no matter which compiler you're using. However, the descriptions of the installation procedures, debuggers, and editors are specific to the Microsoft products. Also some library functions, notably graphics, are Microsoft-specific, and some other library functions have minor variations between compilers.

QuickC has its own built-in editor, which is described in Appendix I. However, if you're using the Optimizing Compiler, you'll need a text editor to write the source files for your programs. Many of the common word processors can be used for this purpose. In some, such as WordStar and WordPerfect, you'll need to save the text in a special ASCII format so it will not contain control characters that the compiler can't digest.

Many professionals use special editors designed for writing programs, such as BRIEF, VEDIT, Epsilon, the Norton Editor, and so on. Version 5.1 of the Optimizing Compiler includes such an editor, called "Microsoft Editor." You can also use QuickC to generate source files, then save them to disk and compile with the Optimizing Compiler.

## The Optimizing Compiler vs. QuickC

Should you use the Optimizing Compiler or QuickC with this book? The Optimizing Compiler is the most widely used professional software development tool for the IBM. It generates highly optimized code, can accommodate very large and complex programs, contains an excellent run-time library, and comes with a rich assortment of utilities. As *Dr. Dobbs Journal* put it after comparing 18 different C compilers, "Microsoft's C compiler is the best MS-DOS development environment value today."

QuickC does not generate code that is as highly optimized, and it lacks other features of the Optimizing Compiler, including the powerful CodeView debugger. QuickC's strength is the ease of use of its integrated environment: the edit-compile-link-execute cycle is far faster and more convenient than that in the Optimizing Compiler (or other traditional compilers).

You can certainly use QuickC for all the examples in this book. As you grow in experience, and as your programs grow in complexity, you may find QuickC too limiting. At this point, you can switch to the Optimizing Compiler. Or you can start right off with the Optimizing Compiler. This book supports both approaches.

## What Version of C?

The C language was created by Dennis Ritchie at Bell Laboratories in the early 1970s. (Its predecessor was a language called B.) In 1978 Brian Kernighan and

Dennis Ritchie published a book, *The C Programming Language,* which until recently served as an effective definition of the language. Now a new standard is emerging from the American National Standards Institute, the ANSI-standard C. Some compilers, including Microsoft's Optimizing Compiler and QuickC, attempt to adhere to this new standard as much as possible.

In this book, since we'll be basing our examples on the syntax acceptable to the Optimizing Compiler and QuickC, we'll be following the ANSI standard.

## How This Book Is Organized

The first seven chapters of this book cover the fundamentals of the C language. In the first chapter you'll write a very simple C program, compile it, link it, and run it. This will give you an idea of what the language looks like and how it's used. The second chapter discusses some preliminaries you'll need to know before moving on to larger programs: variables, simple input/output statements, and operators, such as ( = ) and ( + ). Again, programming examples are used to demonstrate the various topics. Chapters 3 and 4 cover the most basic of C constructs: loops and decisions. Chapter 5 describes functions, Chapter 6 covers arrays, and Chapter 7 explains pointers, a construct widely used in C but unknown or little used in many other languages.

At this point the focus shifts from C to the IBM. In Chapter 8 we look closely at how the keyboard and the display work, and how C can be used to gain control of these devices. Chapter 9 discusses the advanced C constructs of structures and unions, and shows how unions are used in accessing the important set of routines built into the IBM's hardware: the Read-Only Memory Basic Input/Output System (ROM BIOS). Chapter 10 covers the monochrome display, and Chapter 11 shows how to create color graphics using ROM BIOS routines and directly accessing video memory. Chapter 12 describes the Microsoft graphics library.

Chapter 13 covers files and their use with floppy and fixed disk systems in the PC-DOS environment. Chapter 14 explores a variety of topics that are useful with larger and more complex programs, and Chapter 15 concludes the book with a discussion of some of the finer points of using variables.

A number of appendices are also provided to help you learn C and to make the book easier to use as a reference. The first appendix summarizes the syntax of the major C constructions. If you've forgotten whether to use a colon or a semicolon in the **switch** statement, for example, you can look it up there. Appendix B contains a number of programs that are too large or too complex to fit in the main part of the book. These programs give an idea of how larger programs can be constructed out of smaller building blocks and demonstrate some new programming techniques. Appendix C explains the hexadecimal (base 16) numbering system. Hexadecimal is used at various points in the book and is useful for a thorough understanding of the IBM system. Appendices D and E consist of a bibliography and a table of the character codes used on the IBM. Appendix F describes the operation of the Microsoft CodeView debugging utility. Appendix G describes the debugging features built into QuickC, Appendix H explores the QuickC editor, and Appendix I summarizes the Microsoft graphics functions described in Chapter 12.

## Typographical Conventions

In the text sections of this book (as opposed to program listings) all C keywords, such as **if**, **while**, and **switch**, will be shown in boldface to better distinguish them from the ordinary usage of these words. Likewise, all C library functions, such as **printf()**, **gets()**, and **lseek()**, will be in bold as will user-written functions. Variable names will also be in bold to distinguish them from normal text.

Where string constants are used in the text they will be set off by double quotes, just as they are in the C language itself: "Good morning" and "Fatal error". Character constants will be set off by single quotes, again following the convention of the C language: 'a' and 'b' are characters.

Operators, which often consist of a single character, will be surrounded by parentheses for clarity: ( + ) and ( / ).

Keyboard keys, such as [Ctrl] and [Return], are enclosed in square brackets.

Program names are not in bold, but include the file extension, such as .c and .obj in myprog.c, yourprog.c, myprog.obj.

## Good Luck, Lieutenant

This book covers a lot of territory—from simple one-line programs to complex graphics and telecommunication applications. We intend to make the exploration of this territory as easy as possible, starting slowly and gradually working up to more challenging concepts. We hope we've succeeded and that you have as much fun reading this book as we had writing it.

## Note on the Second Edition

This revised edition of *Microsoft C Programming for the IBM* includes considerable new material designed to bring the book up to date with the latest releases of Microsoft C products. There are three major additions:

First, a new chapter and appendix have been added to cover the new library of Microsoft graphics functions.

Second, the text has been revised to include the installation and operation of QuickC, and appendices have been added to describe QuickC's editor and debugging features.

Third, the example programs have been revised to reflect the new American National Standards Institute (ANSI) prototyping approach to function usage.

There are other, less major, changes as well. For example, material on the VGA graphics standard has been added.

# Getting Started

- Compiling and linking
- Setting up the programming environment
- Files used in C programs
- Structure of C programs
- Writing a simple program
- The **printf()** function

# 1

This chapter has several goals. First, for those of you who are not familiar with compiled languages, we will explain something about the compilation process. (If you're an old hand at a compiled language like Pascal, you can probably skip this first section.) Next, we want to help you get your system—the Optimizing Compiler or QuickC—up and running. To this end, we'll discuss the various files that come with your C compiler, how they are arranged, and how they communicate with each other. Finally, with these preliminaries out of the way, we'll plunge into the C language itself: you'll write your first C program and learn something about the structure of C programs in general, and, in particular, about the **printf()** function.

## Compiling and Linking

If your programming experience is restricted to BASIC or other interpreted languages, you may find the operation of the C compiler somewhat mysterious. In this section we'll explain briefly what a compiler does, why another program called a "linker" is necessary, and how different files represent your program at various stages of the development process.

### Human to Machine

You write a computer program with words and symbols that are understandable to human beings. To run on a computer, the program must be translated into binary numbers understandable to the computer's Central Processing Unit (CPU). These binary numbers are called "machine language," since the computer understands them.

It is the job of a compiler program to translate the human-readable version of the program into the machine-readable version. Using a word processor or text editor, you type in the program lines, creating a file called the "source file." The compiler then uses this file to generate another file consisting of machine language.

## Linking

It would be simple if that were the end of the story, and now you just executed this new compiler-generated file to run your program. However, there's another step involved in most compiled languages, including C: a process called "linking."

Linking is necessary because you may not want to compile all of your program at the same time. For instance, you may be writing a large program, with parts of it working and debugged while other parts are under development. Since it may take a fairly long time to compile a large program (from seconds to many minutes, depending on the size), you may want to recompile each time only those parts of the program that are under development.

Also, many compiled languages (C is a prime example) come with library routines that can be added to your program. These are routines written by the manufacturer of the compiler to perform a variety of tasks, from input/output to mathematical functions. The manufacturer could provide source code files of these functions, and require the user to compile them at the same time the user's program is compiled, but it is far more efficient to provide the previously compiled machine-language versions of the functions and have the user link them to the machine-language version of the user's program. Thus you need a way to link together previously compiled library and program files with recently compiled files to produce a complete program.

For this reason the compiler generates an intermediate kind of file called an "object file." This is a machine-language file that is incomplete: it needs to be connected to other object files before it can work. Library files consist of groups of object files. The linker combines all the necessary object files, both library and user-written, to produce a final, executable program. The relationship of compilation to linking is shown schematically in Figure 1-1.

Even if only one file is to be compiled it must still be compiled and linked in two separate steps. However, almost all C programs use at least one library function, thus requiring the linking of the user's program and the library file.

## Program File-Naming Conventions

In most versions of C, you must give your source file the .c file *extension,* as in "myprog.c". The intermediate object files are automatically given the .obj extension by the compiler, and the executable program files are given the .exe extension by the linker. (The compiler and linker may also generate various other kinds of files, but we'll ignore them for the moment.) The operating system recognizes files with the .exe extension as executable programs.

> The text editor produces .c (source) files, which go to the linker, which produces .obj (object) files, which go to the compiler, which produces .exe (executable) files.

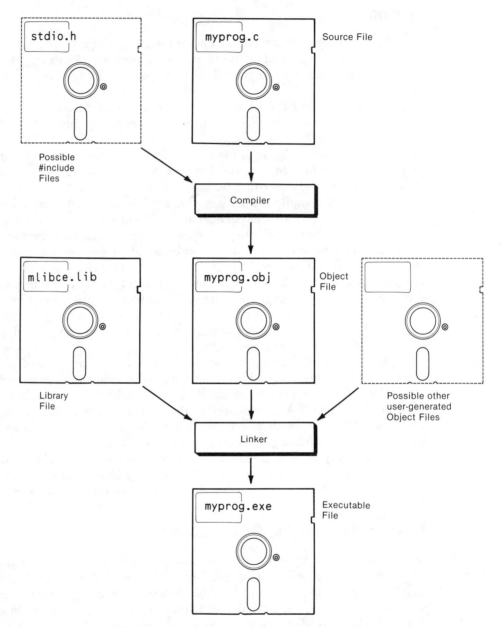

Figure 1-1. Relationship of Compiler and Linker

Both the Microsoft C Optimizing Compiler and QuickC hide this two-step compile-link process to some extent. Both can compile and link with a single command, which gives the impression that only one process is involved. Also, QuickC generally does not generate .obj and .exe files on the disk. They are kept (in altered form) in memory (although QuickC can generate these files when necessary).

Even if it is somewhat disguised, the process of compiling source files into object files, and linking these to create an executable file, is the underlying basis for creating C programs.

We'll examine compiling and linking in more detail after we've seen how the development system is organized.

# Setting Up Your System

You install your system by running a utility program called SETUP. This program creates directories, copies files to them, generates library files, and performs various other tasks.

Some versions of Microsoft's setup programs, such as those in C 5.0 and QuickC 1.0, require that information be supplied from arguments on the command line. In newer versions, such as in C 5.1, the program queries the user once it starts running. Regardless of format, you'll need to know what to tell the program. We won't provide step-by-step instructions for running SETUP; the manuals that accompany it do that. Rather, we'll provide an overview that should make the setup process less mysterious. Don't be discouraged if setting up your system seems complicated. Although many advanced topics are involved, an intimate understanding of them is not necessary to perform the setup process.

## Directory Structure

When you run SETUP you need to specify a directory for your entire C development system. This will be the master directory, which in turn will hold subdirectories. Usually you'll specify a directory in the root directory, using a pathname like C:\C5, C:\QC, or C:\MSOFT.

In this master directory SETUP will install several subdirectories, such as BIN, INCLUDE, LIB, and TMP. (There may be a few others as well.) Let's see what sorts of files go in these subdirectories.

## The BIN Subdirectory

The programs that actually do the work of compiling your program, linking it, and carrying out other tasks are stored in a subdirectory named BIN.

The most important file is the compiler itself. If you have the Optimizing Compiler, this consists of the file CL.EXE, which you invoke to compile (and usually to link) your program. There are several other files, such as C1.EXE and C2.EXE, that CL.EXE calls as it performs different phases of the compilation. There are other support files for CL as well, such as CL.ERR, which contains error messages, and CL.HLP, which contains help messages.

If you're using QuickC, fewer files are associated with the compiler. There's QuickC itself, QC.EXE, and it's support files, such as QC.HLP, and QC.OVR, for other QuickC activities.

The BIN directory in both the Optimizing Compiler and QuickC also contains utility programs for specialized situations. LINK.EXE links files in special cases when CL or QuickC won't work. LIB.EXE manages library files. MAKE.EXE automates the management of files with multiple source files. QuickC contains an alternative compiler, QCL.EXE, for situations that are too complex for the normal QuickC program, QC.EXE. There may be other utility programs as well, but you won't need to worry about these until later in your study of C. Most of the example programs in this book can be compiled and linked with QC.EXE if you're using QuickC or CL.EXE if you're using the Optimizing Compiler.

## The INCLUDE Subdirectory

The INCLUDE subdirectory contains *header files* (also called "include files"). These files all have the .h file extension. Header files are difficult to explain until you've actually programmed in C and seen how they're used, but a brief description may give you a rough idea of their purpose.

The compiler often needs to be told things about specific functions or told the names and values of constants. This information would be tedious to type into your program every time you used a particular function. To save typing it for a particular group of functions, the information is grouped together in a separate file. By inserting a single line into your program listing you can cause this entire file to be included in the source code of your program.

Including a header file in your program this way is similar to the way a secretary using a word processor keeps files of standard headings for business letters. The secretary calls up a header, inserts it at the beginning of the letter, and starts the body of the letter below it.

In C, many programs include the header file STDIO.H, which contains definitions for such standard input/output functions as **printf()**.

We'll talk more about header files as we go along. At this point, remember that they are text files like the ones you generate with your editor, and they can be combined with your program before it is compiled.

## The LIB Subdirectory

We've already mentioned the existence of library files, which are groups of routines for performing a variety of specific tasks, such as I/O, math, or data conversion. Library functions are precompiled routines that are added to your program by the linker. C is especially rich in the number and variety of these routines. Many activities that in other languages are built into the definition of the language (such as input/output statements) are handled in C by library functions.

In recent versions of Microsoft C, library files have become more complicated because the files that come on your disk are not (usually) the files that end up in your LIB directory. We'll learn more about this in the section on combined libraries.

## The TMP Subdirectory

While the compiler is working it generates temporary files. When the compilation process is complete, these files are erased, but in the meantime the compiler needs a place to put them. The TMP directory serves this purpose. When you investigate it with DIR you'll almost always find it empty, but if you remove it the compiler won't work.

## Other Subdirectories

Some additional subdirectories may be produced during the setup process. These can hold example programs, among other items.

You'll need to create your own subdirectories to hold your program files. It's usually convenient to place these in the main directory with the rest of your C system; for example, in C:\MSOFT\MYPROGS. You can develop programs anywhere in your system, however.

## Combined Libraries

The SETUP program will ask you several questions about libraries. To answer these, you should have a rough idea of what SETUP does with library files. This requires a very brief background in two topics: memory models and floating point emulation. (We'll explore memory models more thoroughly in Chapter 14.)

### Memory Models

The architecture of the Intel 8086 family of chips used in MS-DOS computers imposes a fixed *segment size* on programs and data. A segment is 64K (65,536) bytes. Many programs use the small memory model and are limited to one segment of data and one of code. By using the other memory models, programs can be created with more data segments (the compact model), or more code segments (the medium model), or both (the large model). These programs will not execute as fast as the small model, so a trade-off is involved.

A different library of routines is required for each memory model. When you set up your system, you need to specify which memory model (or models) you will be using, so the correct routines can be combined with your system. For the programs in this book, you should specify the small model if you're using the Optimizing Compiler. If you're using QuickC, you should specify the medium model, which is QuickC's default.

### Floating Point Routines

A different set of math routines must be used for *floating point* (or *real*) numbers than for integers. Because executing floating point arithmetic operations is comparatively time consuming, several alternative ways of carrying them out have been developed.

If you have a math coprocessor chip (an 8087, 80287, or 80387) in your computer, you can use special routines that take advantage of this chip to carry out floating point operations. This is by far the fastest approach. However, not all computers have a math coprocessor.

For computers without a coprocessor, a different, slower, set of floating point routines is available. These use software to "emulate" the operation of the math chip. These will work on machines with a math coprocessor as well.

The Optimizing Compiler includes another floating point option: the *alternate* math package. This is similar to the *emulation* package, but it generates code that is faster although less accurate than the emulator's.

A different set of library routines is used, depending on which routines you want to use for floating point operations. In this book we'll assume that you specify the emulator.

### Building Combined Libraries

The distribution disks that come in your system contain *uncombined library* files. Usually the SETUP program combines an appropriate selection of these files, depending on the memory model and floating point option you choose, to form a single *combined library* file. Let's look for a moment at the uncombined files.

The bulk of all the library routines go in files called SLIBC.LIB, MLIBC.LIB, CLIBC.LIB, and LLIBC.LIB. One of these four files is used, depending on which memory model you choose. Parts of the floating point routines are in model-specific files called SLIBFP.LIB, MLIBFP.LIB, and so on. Other parts are in 87.LIB if you're using the math coprocessor or in EM.LIB if you're using the emulator.

You can link these individual files to your program directly (this is called using uncombined libraries), but the linking process is speeded up significantly and made more convenient if these files are merged into a single combined library file. This is one of the major tasks of the SETUP program. For instance, if you've specified the small model and emulation, SETUP will combine SLIBC.LIB, SLIBFP.LIB, EM.LIB (and perhaps a few other odds and ends) into a single library file called SLIBCE.LIB. The first letter in SLIBCE reflects the memory model (S, M, C, or L), and the last character reflects the emulation mode (E for emulation or 7 for the math coprocessor). For the Optimizing Compiler, SETUP should construct SLIBCE.LIB. For QuickC, which uses the medium memory model, it should make MLIBCE.LIB.

### The Graphics Library

Another question you will need to answer for the SETUP program is whether you want to include the graphics library in your combined library. You should include this file, since in Chapter 12 we'll be writing example programs that call the functions in this library. These routines are in the uncombined library file GRAPHICS.LIB and will be automatically added to your combined library file if you so specify.

## Files and More Files

We've talked about many kinds of files in many different directories. Why does C use so many different files?

Dividing its various aspects into separate files gives the language more flexibility. By keeping the input/output routines in separate library files, for instance, it's easier to rewrite C to work on a different computer: all you need to change are the files containing input/output functions; the language itself remains the same. The multiplicity of library files also means that the routines used with a particular program can be tailored to that program's needs: if you don't need the large memory model, for example, you won't need to use the complex routines that go with it.

Don't worry at this point if the purpose of the various kinds of files still seems a bit obscure. Once you've had some experience with the language itself you'll be better able to see how they fit together.

## The STARTUP.BAT File

The SETUP program generates a file that can replace (or be combined with) your existing STARTUP.BAT file.

The STARTUP.BAT file needs to contain two kinds of commands. One tells DOS where the compiler is, so you can compile programs no matter which directory you're in. The other command sets up equivalencies between symbolic names known to the compiler and linker and the actual pathnames in your system, so the compiler and linker can find the files they need. Let's look at the necessary commands.

### The PATH Command

To make the compiler and linker visible in the directory you are using to develop programs, SETUP uses the DOS command PATH in the STARTUP.BAT file. This command causes DOS to search in a specific directory for any files it doesn't find in the current directory. Let's assume you chose a directory in the C: drive called C:\MSOFT as the master development directory. The SETUP program then puts CL.EXE (or QC.EXE, if you're using QuickC) and associated files in the BIN subdirectory of your master directory. SETUP instructs DOS to look for these files there with the command

```
PATH=C:\MSOFT\BIN
```

Now, suppose we're in a directory with the pathname C:\MSOFT \MYDIR. To compile and link a program in this directory, we can use a command like

```
qc myprog
```

even though QC.EXE is in the BIN directory.

### The SET Command

The compiler and linker always look for header files using the pathname INCLUDE and for library files using the pathname LIB. These are not the correct pathnames, however. In the present example, we are assuming that header and library files are in C:\MSOFT\INCLUDE and C:\MSOFT\LIB, respectively. It is therefore necessary to translate the pathnames the compiler and linker are using into the actual pathnames for a particular system.

The PATH command makes a directory visible in all other directories, while the SET command causes one phrase in a DOS command to be substituted for another.

The DOS command SET performs this function by creating a sort of dictionary, equating a name with a pathname. When DOS is given a name that is in this dictionary, it substitutes the pathname supplied earlier by the SET command. In our case, we use SET to equate the word INCLUDE with the actual directory name, C:\MSOFT\INCLUDE, and LIB with the directory name C:\MSOFT\LIB, using the commands

```
SET INCLUDE=C:\MSOFT\INCLUDE
SET LIB=C:\MSOFT\LIB
```

The compiler also needs to access the directory for temporary files; it looks for it under the name TMP. This requires another command:

```
SET TMP=C:\MSOFT\TMP
```

## Using a Batch File for DOS Environment Commands

It would be an inconvenience to have to type these PATH and SET commands to DOS every time you start up your system, so SETUP places them in a batch file. You could execute this batch file to set up the system, but it's more convenient to incorporate the commands from this file into the AUTOEXEC.BAT file, where they'll be executed each time the system is booted up. The resulting file looks like this:

```
PATH=C:\MSOFT\BIN
SET INCLUDE=C:\MSOFT\INCLUDE
SET LIB=C:\MSOFT\LIB
SET TMP=C:\MSOFT\TMP
```

If you already have an AUTOEXEC.BAT file you can insert these commands in it.

The program environment described above is shown schematically in Figure 1-2.

## The CONFIG.SYS File

When an MS-DOS or PC-DOS computer system is booted up, the operating system first looks for the CONFIG.SYS file. If it is present, this file tells DOS various things about how to configure the system, including how many files can be open at one time and how many data buffers are available.

### Files and Buffers

The Optimizing Compiler and QuickC require that DOS be able to open up to 20 files and that there be 10 buffers (temporary storage areas in memory) for holding I/O data. Thus there must be a CONFIG.SYS file in the root directory with lines like this:

```
FILES=20
BUFFERS=10
```

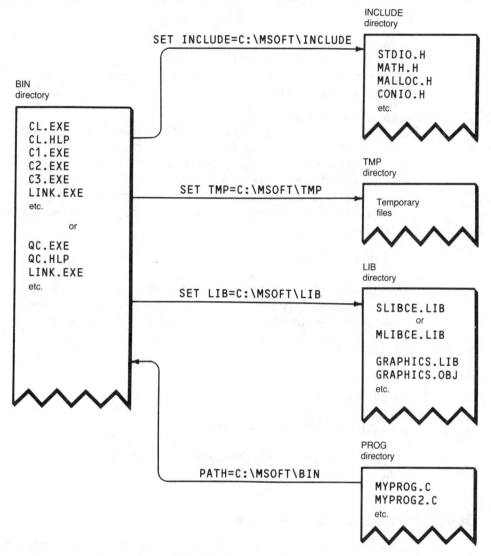

Figure 1-2. The Program Environment

The SETUP program generates a file that contains these lines. You can place it in the root directory and rename it to CONFIG.SYS, or you can copy the lines into your own CONFIG.SYS file.

### The ANSI.SYS File

In order to use the cursor control commands, which we'll be discussing in Chapter 8, it's necessary for the operating system to replace the standard keyboard I/O routines with those in a file called ANSI.SYS, provided as one of the utilities on the operating system disk. To do this, first install the ANSI.SYS file in the root directory. Second, add the following line to the CONFIG.SYS file:

```
DEVICE=ANSI.SYS
```

With this arrangement, the ANSI.SYS driver will be loaded into place every time you start up your system.

### Environmental Space

The SET and PATH commands (described above in the section on the AUTOEXEC.BAT file) become part of the operating system's *environment*. This environment has a fixed size (160 bytes in DOS 3.2), so it may not be able to hold all the commands you want to place in it. If this happens, you'll get the DOS error message "out of environment space" when you boot up your system.

To fix this, you can expand the environment space by adding this line to your CONFIG.SYS file:

```
SHELL C:\COMMAND.COM /E:400 /P
```

This tells DOS that COMMAND.COM is the shell (user interface) for the system. (It was anyway, but that's not why we're using this command.) The /E option specifies the new size of the environment: in this case 400 bytes. You may need the /P option to cause the AUTOEXEC.BAT file to be executed. Thus the complete CONFIG.SYS file should look like this:

```
FILES=20
BUFFERS=10
DEVICE=ANSI.SYS
SHELL C:\COMMAND.COM /E:400 /P
```

If you already have statements in a CONFIG.SYS file, you'll need to combine these statements with them.

# Developing Your First Program

We'll assume that you've sucessfully negotiated the installation process and that the appropriate files are arranged in their proper places in the system. How do you write, compile, link, and execute a C program?

## Writing the Source File

The first step is to write a source file containing the program listing. We discussed the issue of which editor to use in the introduction, so we'll assume you're ready to write.

Type in the following short program:

```
main()
{
```

```
    printf("I charge thee, speak!");
}
```

We won't talk about what this means now; instead, we'll concentrate on transforming this source code into an executable program. Make sure the program is entered exactly as shown: pay attention to the paired braces, parentheses, and quotes and don't forget the semicolon. Spelling and capitalization are also important.

## Compiling and Linking with the Optimizing Compiler

If you're using the Optimizing Compiler, save this file from your editor to disk, using the file name oneline.c. Exit from the editor to DOS. Now you can compile and link the program in one step, by entering the command

```
C>cl oneline.c
```

If you examine the directory containing your source file, you'll find there are now two additional files: oneline.obj and oneline.exe. The CL utility has successfully compiled oneline.c into an object file, ONELINE.OBJ, and linked this file into the executable file, ONELINE.EXE.

To run the program, type its name on the command line, as you would with any other executable file. You should see the phrase (from Act I of Shakespeare's *Hamlet*) printed out:

```
C>oneline
I charge thee, speak!
C>
```

## Compiling and Linking in QuickC

In QuickC you do all your work in the QuickC environment, without returning to DOS. When you've typed the program into the view window, select Start from the Run menu. Your program will be compiled, linked, and executed automatically. The display will switch to the output window, and you'll see the program's output immediately following the line in which you called up QuickC:

```
C>qc
I charge thee, speak!
Program returned (21). Press any key
```

When you press a key, you'll find yourself back in the QuickC view window. To see the output again, select Output Screen from the View menu. To save the source file to disk, select Save from the File menu.

Unless you specifically request it, QuickC will not create permanent object or executable files, so you won't see these when you return to DOS. (You won't see the source file either, unless you've saved it, but you're prompted to do this when you exit.)

### *Making a Permanent Executable File*

You may want to create a permanent executable file, so you can run your program without calling up QuickC. To do this, you'll need to compile and link in a different way. Select Compile . . . from the Run menu. When the options window appears, select the Exe entry in the Output Options list. Then select Build Program. When this process is finished (after some clicking and whirring from the disk) you can exit from QuickC. You'll see that the ONELINE.OBJ and ONELINE.EXE files have been created. You can run the ONELINE.EXE file directly from DOS.

# The Basic Structure of C Programs

When most people first look at a C program they find it complicated, like an algebra equation, packed with obscure symbols and long program lines. Uh oh, they think, I'll never be able to understand this. However, most of this apparent complexity is an illusion. A program written in C is really not much more complicated than one written in any other language, once you've gotten used to the syntax. Learning C, as is true with any language, is largely a matter of practice. The more you look at C programs, the simpler they appear, until at some point you wonder why you ever thought they looked complicated.

We'll introduce C in a carefully graded progression, so that each example appears as simple as possible. We want to avoid suddenly confronting you with a program so complicated that it looks like the blackboard scribblings of a mad scientist, making your eyes turn glassy. (If the examples seem *too* simple, don't worry; they won't stay that way long.)

We'll start by examining our oneline.c program in some detail.

## Function Definition

First, note the term "main." All C programs are divided into units called "functions." A function in C is similar to a subroutine in BASIC or a function in Pascal. We'll have more to say about functions in Chapter 5; for now, the thing to note is that **main()** is a function. Every C program consists of one or more functions; this program has only one. No matter how many functions there are in a C program, the **main()** function is the one to which control is passed from the operating system when the program is run; it's the first function executed.

> C programs consist of functions. The function called **main()** is the one to which control is passed when the program is executed.

Thus our program begins the way all C functions do: with a name, followed by parentheses (which may or may not be empty; we'll learn more about that later). The name followed by parentheses signals the compiler that a function is being defined.

## Delimiters

Following the function definition are braces that signal the beginning and ending of the body of the function. The opening brace ( { ) says, "a block of code that forms a distinct unit is about to begin." The closing brace ( } ) directly below it terminates the block of code. Braces in C play a similar role to BEGIN and END statements in Pascal, which also delimit a section of code.

Braces are used to delimit other blocks of code as well as functions: they are used in loops and decision-making statements, for example. We'll find out more about that in the next few chapters.

Do you think that the basic structure of C programs looks fairly easy and that you could never make a mistake in putting it together? We'll bet that at some point in your programming career you will either (1) forget the parentheses after **main** or (2) forget one or both braces.

## Program Statements

The line in the program

```
printf("I charge thee, speak!");
```

is an example of a program *statement*. This is an instruction to the compiler to create machine-language code in order to perform a certain action. In this case, this action is executing the function **printf()**.

An important thing to notice about this statement is the semicolon at the end. Every complete statement in C must be terminated with a semicolon. Note (especially if you're a BASIC programmer) that it's the semicolon that terminates the line, not the carriage return you type after the semicolon. C doesn't pay any attention to carriage returns in your program listing (except those used inside quotes as parts of strings). In fact, the C compiler doesn't pay any attention to any of the "whitespace" characters: the carriage return, the space, and the tab. You can put as many or as few whitespace characters in your program as you like; they all look the same to the C compiler.

While we're on the subject of semicolons, we'll make another bet: at some point you'll forget to use one at the end of a C statement.

Figure 1-3 shows the points of program structure discussed above.

## Program Style, Round One

Since you can put as many whitespace characters as you want in your program, it is an almost universal practice to use these characters to make the program easier to read. This is done by conforming more or less to the style guidelines used by Kernighan and Ritchie in *The C Programming Language* (see the Bibliography). For instance, you could write the oneline.c program above as

```
main(){printf("I charge thee, speak!");}
```

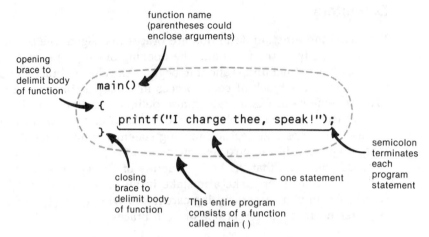

Figure 1-3. Structure of a Simple Program

The compiler wouldn't know the difference. However, stretching the code out vertically results in a more comprehensible program, and aligning matching braces vertically makes it easier to ensure that each opening brace is matched by a closing brace.

> The whitespace characters (space, tab, newline) are invisible to the compiler.

Indentation of blocks of code enclosed in braces is an important aspect of making C programs readable. In Figure 1-3 the program line is indented 3 spaces; that will be our standard indent throughout this book. Indenting the line of code isn't critical in this short example, but when there are many sets of nested braces in a program, indentation becomes an important way to increase the readability of programs.

## The *printf()* Function

The program line

```
printf("I charge thee, speak!");
```

causes the phrase in quotes to be printed on the screen. The word "printf" is actually a function name, just as "main" is a function name. Since **printf()** is a function, it is followed by parentheses. In this case, the parentheses are not empty, but contain the phrase to be printed, surrounded by quotes. This phrase is a function *argument*—information passed from **main()** to the function

**printf()**. We won't dwell too much on arguments and the formal aspects of functions at this point; we'll save that for Chapter 5. Note, however, that when we mention function names such as **printf()** and **main()** we'll usually include the parentheses just to make it clear that we're talking about a function and not a variable or something else.

## Strings

"I charge thee, speak!" is an example of a *string*; that is, a string of characters. In C, string constants such as this are surrounded by quotes; this is how the compiler recognizes a string. We'll be using and discussing strings as we go along, and we'll really dig into their complexities in Chapter 6.

## Library Functions

Here's something else to notice about the **printf()** function. We've used this function in our program; that is, we called it, just as we would call a subroutine in BASIC or a function in Pascal. However, there is no code for the function in the source file of our program. Where is the function itself stored?

If you're using the Optimizing Compiler, the code for the function is in the library file SLIBCE.LIB. The **printf()** file is extracted from this library file and automatically connected to your program during linking. A similar process is followed for all C library functions.

If you're using QuickC, the code for **printf()** is actually stored in memory as part of QuickC itself, in the so-called "core library," not in a separate library file. The result is much the same, however: the code for the function ends up being linked to your program.

## C Is Case Sensitive

One other aspect of our sample program deserves mention: the fact that the program (except for the I in the string) is written entirely in lowercase. Unlike some programming languages, C distinguishes between upper- and lowercase letters. Thus the functions **PRINTF()** or **Printf()** are not the same as the function **printf()**. A practice often followed in C is to keep pretty much everything in lowercase, for ease of typing. However, many programmers use both lower- and uppercase when naming functions and variables.

# Syntax Errors and Debugging

If you've made a typing mistake in a program, the compiler will detect this and inform you of a *syntax error*. For example, suppose you type the oneline.c program, but forget the last set of quotes, so the program looks like this:

```
main()
{
```

```
        printf("I charge thee, speak!);
    }
```

This will not compile correctly and will generate error messages. The way these errors are displayed depends on whether you're using the QuickC or Optimizing Compiler.

## Syntax Errors in QuickC

In QuickC, when you attempt to compile and run your program by selecting Start from the Run menu, an error window will appear on the bottom of your screen. This window holds only one error at a time. In this case, it will say

```
error C2001 : (1 of 2)
newline in constant
```

The number C2001 refers to compiler error 2001, which you can look up in the "Error Message Reference" appendix in the QuickC programmer's guide. Since the closing quotes are missing, the compiler thinks that the newline at the end of the line is part of the quoted string—an illegal construction.

In many cases, one typing mistake leads the compiler to report several errors, and that's the case here. To see the second error message in QuickC, select Next Error from the Search menu or type [Shift] [F3]. The second error will be displayed in the error window:

```
error C2143 : (2 of 2)
syntax error : missing ')' before '}'
```

The compiler thinks the closing parenthesis is part of the string constant and not part of the program, so it reports it as missing when it gets to the closing brace.

In a multiline program, the cursor in the view window automatically moves to the program line containing the error, so it's easy to correlate the message in the error window with the appropriate place in the program.

Correct the error by changing the offending program line in the view window, and then select Start from the Run menu again. When you've fixed all the errors, the program will run, instead of displaying error messages.

## Syntax Errors in the Optimizing Compiler

When you run CL to compile and link your program you'll see the same two error messages, but in this case they're printed on the normal DOS screen:

```
oneline.c(4) : error C2001 : newline in constant
oneline.c(4) : error C2143 : syntax error: missing ')' before '}'
```

The number in parentheses is the line number in the program where the compiler detected the error. You'll need to jot down the error messages, or print them out, and then get back into your editor to see the offending program lines. Once in the editor you can make the necessary changes. Then exit the editor and compile again with CL.

## More Serious Bugs

Your program may compile and link without generating error messages, but perform in unexpected ways when you execute it. Sometimes such errors can be discovered by examining the listing and trying mentally to execute each program line. When this approach fails, a debugger program can save the day. A debugger permits you to single-step through your program, to watch the values of variables change as the program runs, and to diagnose your program in other ways.

We won't discuss debuggers in detail at this point, since your knowledge of C is still rudimentary. However, as you learn more about C and write longer and more sophisticated programs, you'll find more reason to use a debugger. The Optimizing Compiler comes with a powerful stand-alone debugger called CodeView. We describe its operation in Appendix F. In QuickC the debugging features are built in. We describe how to use these features in Appendix G. If you skim through the appropriate appendix now, you'll get a feel for the debugger's features. You can return to it later for a more detailed look when you find yourself with a program that, despite all your powers of mental analysis, still doesn't behave as it should.

# Link Errors

Another category of errors may arise during the linking process. The most common of these is caused by using the wrong name for a library function. For example, suppose you mistype the oneline.c program this way:

```
main()
{
    printx("I charge thee, speak!");
}
```

There is no "printx" library function, so the linker will be unable to connect oneline.obj to it. If you're using the Optimizing Compiler, you'll see this error message:

```
LINK : error L2029: Unresolved externals:
_printx in file(s):
ONELINE.OBJ (oneline.c)
```

In QuickC you'll find a similar message in the error window:

```
error C2175: (1 of 1)
'printx' : unresolved external
```

The solution to this problem is to spell the name of the function correctly. (The linking process is described in more detail in Chapter 14.) If the problem persists, you probably don't have your system set up correctly.

### Non-Core Library Functions in QuickC

This same link error may arise for a different reason in QuickC: the function you called is a valid library function, but is not in the core library that QuickC keeps in memory. You won't encounter this problem until later in this book, but you should be aware of it so you'll be ready when the time comes. So skim over this section now, but remember where it is. (This problem does not occur with the Optimizing Compiler, since this compiler always uses the SLIBCE.LIB (or similar) file, which contains all the library functions.)

The common functions, such as **printf()**, are part of QuickC's core library; but many functions, including mathematics functions, exist only in MLIBCE.LIB. Incorporating non-core functions into a QuickC program involves the creation of a *program list*.

### Setting Up a Program List

Let's say you're trying to use QuickC to compile a program called getsin.c that uses the **sin()** library function. This function is not in the QuickC core library, so when you try to link getsin.c you'll get the "unresolved external" message. To fix the problem, you must create a program list to tell QuickC you want to link with other files. The program list will specify the two files you want to link: your program getsin.c and the library file MLIBCE.LIB. The program list is actually a file with the extension .mak. It usually has the same name as the program, so in this case it's getsin.mak.

To create this file, select Set Program List from the File menu. Enter the name getsin.mak in the window provided. Answer "yes" to whether you want to create the file. The screen will change automatically to one titled Edit Program List. In the box provided, enter getsin.c, which should also appear in the list at the bottom of the screen. Now type mlibce.lib; it should also appear on the list. Select Save List. This process automatically generates the getsin.mak file. Now you'll find that you can compile and run your program successfully by selecting Start from the Run menu.

## Exploring the *printf()* Function

The **printf()** function is a powerful and versatile output function. It's the workhorse output statement in C and we'll be using it extensively throughout the book. We're going to spend the remainder of this chapter exploring it.

The **printf()** function uses a rather unique format for printing constants and variables. For a hint of its power let's look at another example:

```
main()
{
```

```
        printf("This is the number two: %d", 2);
    }
```

Can you guess what message will be printed if you compile (using the name, printwo), link, and run this program? Here's the output:

```
C>printwo
This is the number two: 2
C>
```

Why was the digit 2 printed, and what effect does the %d have? The function **printf()** can be given one or more arguments. In the previous example we gave it only one: the string, "I charge thee, speak!" Now, however, we're giving it two: a string ("This is the number two: %d") on the left and a value (2) on the right. These arguments are separated by a comma. The **printf()** function takes the value on the right of the comma and plugs it into the string on the left. Where does it plug it in? Where it finds a *format specifier* such as %d.

## Format Specifiers

The format specifier tells **printf()** where to put a value in a string and what format to use in printing the value. In this example, the %d tells **printf()** to print the value 2 as a decimal integer. We could use other specifiers for the number 2. For instance, %f would cause the 2 to be printed as a floating point number, and %x would print it as a hexadecimal number.

Why not simply put the number 2 into the original string?

```
        printf("This is the number two: 2");
```

In this example, the output would not differ, since 2 is a constant. As we'll see in the next chapter, however, variables can be used in the **printf()** function as well as constants, giving it the capability to change what it prints while the program is running.

## Printing Strings

We can also print string constants using format specifiers. Here's an example that shows both a string and a number being printed:

```
main()
{
    printf("%s is %d million miles\nfrom the sun.", "Venus", 67);
}
```

The output of this program will be:

```
Venus is 67 million miles
from the sun.
```

The **printf()** function has replaced the %s symbol with the string "Venus" and the %d symbol with the number 67, as shown in Figure 1-4.

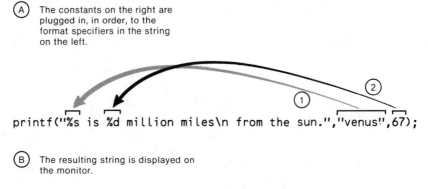

(A) The constants on the right are plugged in, in order, to the format specifiers in the string on the left.

```
printf("%s is %d million miles\n from the sun.","venus",67);
```

(B) The resulting string is displayed on the monitor.

Figure 1-4. The **printf()** Function

The above example also includes a new symbol, the '\n'. In C, this means "newline" and stands for a single character which, when inserted in a string, has the effect of a carriage return and linefeed; that is, following a '\n' character, printing is resumed at the beginning of the next line. The newline character is actually stored in memory as a single character—a linefeed—but it has the effect of both a carriage return and linefeed.

## Printing Characters

In our final example in this chapter we'll show how **printf()** can be used to print a single character.

You might think that a character is simply a string with only one character in it, but this is not the case in C; characters and strings are separate and distinct entities. Here's a program that prints a character and a string:

```
main()
{
    printf("The letter %c is ", 'j');
    printf("pronounced %s.", "jay");
}
```

Here we've made two program lines, each with a **printf()** function. The output of this program will be:

```
The letter j is pronounced jay.
```

In this program 'j' is a character and "jay" is a string. Notice that 'j' is surrounded by single quotes, while "jay" is surrounded by double quotes. This is how the compiler tells the difference between a character and a string. The format specifier %c is used to print the character 'j'.

Also note that even though the output is printed by two separate program lines, it doesn't consist of two lines of text. The **printf()** function does not automatically print a newline character at the end of a line; if you want one, you must insert it explicitly.

## Summary

In this chapter you've learned how your system is organized, and how to write, compile, link, and run C programs. You've learned what simple C programs look like and that even the main part of a C program is a function. You know some of the potential of the **printf()** function, including how to print number, character, and string constants; how to use format specifiers; and the purpose of the newline character. At this point you should be able to write one- or two-line C programs that display various phrases on the screen.

In the next chapter we'll continue our exploration of the **printf()** function and look at other input and output functions. We'll also look at two other important C building blocks: variables and operators.

## Questions

1. Linking permits the following to be combined with your program:
   a. header files
   b. library functions
   c. batch files
   d. previously compiled functions

2. After the source file for a C program has been written, it must be
   c_____, l_____, and e_____.

3. The library files that come with the C programming system contain:
   a. functions that perform input and output
   b. a text editor for program development
   c. functions for advanced math and other purposes
   d. the compiler and linker

4. In a C program, statements are combined into basic building blocks called
   _____.

5. What is the purpose of the parentheses following the word **main** in a C program?

6. The braces that surround the code in a C program:
   a. delimit a section of code

b. show what code goes in a particular function

c. separate the code from the constants

d. separate the source file from the object file

7. True or false: a carriage return must be used at the end of every C program statement.

8. What's wrong with the following C program?

```
main
(
print"Oh, woe and suffering!"
)
```

9. What two sorts of things can go in the parentheses following the function **printf()**?

10. What is the output of the following program?

```
main()
{
    printf("%s\n%s\n%s", "one", "two", "three");
}
```

## Exercises

1. Write a two-statement program that will generate the following output:

```
Mr. Green is 42,
Mr. Brown is 48.
```

Use string constants to represent the names and integer constants to represent the ages.

2. Write a program that will print the phrase:

```
a, b, and c are all letters.
```

Use character constants to represent the letters.

# 2

# *C Building Blocks*

- Variable types
- The **printf()** output function
- The **scanf()** and **getche()** input functions
- Special characters
- Arithmetic operators
- Relational operators

# 2

Before you can begin to write interesting programs in C you need to know at least some of the fundamentals of the language. In this chapter we present a selection of these basic building blocks.

Three important aspects of any language are the way it stores data, how it accomplishes input and output, and the operators it uses to transform and combine data. These are the three kinds of building blocks we'll discuss in this chapter. Of course, in a single chapter we can't present every aspect of each of these topics; much will remain to be said in later chapters. However, what we cover here will be enough to get you off the ground.

In the following chapters we'll put these building blocks to use exploring the control statements of the language: loops, decisions, and functions.

## Variables

Variables may be the most fundamental aspect of any computer language. A variable is a space in the computer's memory set aside for a certain kind of data and given a name for easy reference.

Variables are used so that the same space in memory can hold different values at different times. For instance, suppose you're writing a program to calculate someone's paycheck. You'll need to store at least the hourly rate and the hours worked. If you want to do the calculation for more than one employee, you will need to use the same program and the same spaces in memory to store similar data for additional employees. A variable is a space in memory that plays the same role many times, but may contain a different value each time.

What different kinds of variables does the language recognize? How is this data stored? How do you tell the computer what sort of data you want to store? These are the questions we'll be exploring in this section.

## Constants and Variables

In Chapter 1 we showed how the **printf()** function can be used to print constant numbers, strings, and characters. For example, this program

```
main()
{
    printf("This is the number two: %d", 2);
}
```

printed the constant 2, plugging it into the format specifier, %d:

```
This is the number two: 2
```

Of course this is not very useful, since we could more easily have written:

```
main()
{
    printf("This is the number two: 2");
}
```

to achieve the same result. The power of the **printf()** function—indeed, the power of computer languages in general—comes from the ability to use variables—which can hold many different values—in program statements. Let's rewrite the program above to use a variable instead of a constant:

```
main()
{
    int num;
    num = 2;
    printf("This is the number two: %d", num);
}
```

This program gives the same output as before, but it has achieved it in quite a different way. It creates a variable, **num**, assigns it the value 2, and then prints out the value contained in the variable.

This program contains several new elements. In the first program statement,

```
int num;
```

a variable is declared: it is given a name and a type (type **int**, which we'll examine soon).

In the second statement,

```
num = 2;
```

the variable is assigned a value. The assignment operator ( = ) is used for this purpose. This operator has the same function as the ( = ) operator in BASIC or the ( := ) operator in Pascal. (We'll have more to say about assignment operators in the last section of this chapter.)

In the third statement of the program, the variable name, **num**, is used as one of the arguments of the **printf()** statement, replacing the constant 2 used in the example in Chapter 1.

## Variable Declarations

The statement

```
int num;
```

is an example of a *variable declaration*. If you're a Pascal programmer you'll be familiar with this sort of statement; BASIC doesn't use (or at least doesn't need to use) variable declarations. The declaration consists of the *type* name, **int**, followed by the name of the variable, **num**. In a C program all variables must be declared. If you have more than one variable of the same type, you can declare them all with one type name, separating the variable names with commas:

```
int apples, oranges, cherries;
```

Declaring a variable tells the compiler the *name* of the variable, and the *type* of variable. Specifying the name at the beginning of the program enables the compiler to recognize the variable as "approved" when you use it later in the program. This is helpful if you commit the common error of misspelling a variable name deep within your program; the compiler will flag the error, whereas BASIC would simply assume you meant a different variable. Declaring variables also helps you organize your program; collecting the variables together at the beginning of the program helps you grasp the overall logic and structure of your program.

All variables must be declared to specify their name and type.

When you declare a variable, the compiler sets aside an appropriate amount of memory to store that variable. (There's a subtle distinction between the terms "declare" and "define" that's relevant here, but we won't worry about it until later.) In the present case we've declared a variable of type **int**. Most variables in Microsoft C always occupy the same memory space, but the number of bytes occupied by type **int** changes, depending on the computer being used. (Nothing is ever simple.) For 8088-, 8086-, and 80286-based computers, type **int** occupies 2 bytes (16 bits), while for 80386-based machines it's 4 bytes (32 bits). This corresponds to the data path of the computer: it's the size that can be read and written most efficiently. Figure 2-1 shows how an integer looks in memory.

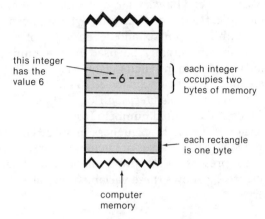

Figure 2-1. An Integer in Memory

The value of two-byte integers can vary from −32,768 to 32,767, while four-byte integers can vary from −2,147,483,648 to 2,147,483,647.

If you want to guarantee a two-byte variable, regardless of the type of machine, use type **short**, which means short integer. If you want to guarantee a four-byte integer, use type **long**. This is a useful size for representing numbers like the purchase price of a home in Marin County, California. Usually type **int** is preferred, unless you know its value will exceed the limit for two-byte integers, in which case you'll need to use type **long**.

Note that the amount of memory used for any of the C data types is not specified in the C language itself, but rather by the particular compiler and machine being used.

There are, of course, other types of variables besides integers. We'll summarize them here and then give examples of the uses of the more common types.

## Variable Types

Most variable types are numeric, but there is one that isn't: the *character* type. You've already met character constants; you know that they consist of a letter or other character surrounded by single quotes. A character variable is a one-byte space in memory in which the character constants, such as 'a' or 'X', can be stored. The type name for a character is **char**. Thus, to declare two character variables, called **ch1** and **ch2**, you would use the statement:

```
char ch1, ch2;
```

There are also two kinds of *floating point* variables. Floating point numbers are used to represent values that are *measured,* like the length of a room (which might have a value of 145.25 inches) as opposed to integers, which are used to represent values that are *counted,* like the number of rooms in a house. Floating point variables can be very large or small. The most usual type of floating point variable, type **float**, occupies four bytes and can hold numbers from about $10^{38}$ to $10^{-38}$ with between six and seven digits of precision. (Precision means how many digits can actually be used in the number; if you attempt to store a number with too many digits, such as 2.12345678, in a floating point variable, only six digits will be retained: 2.12345.)

A monster *double-precision* floating point variable, type **double**, occupies eight bytes and can hold numbers from about $10^{308}$ to $10^{-308}$ with about 15 digits of precision. (The slight vagueness in specifying these limits of precision arises from the fact that variables are actually stored in the computer in binary, which does not represent an integral number of decimal digits.)

Figure 2-2 shows these variable types as they would look in the computer's memory.

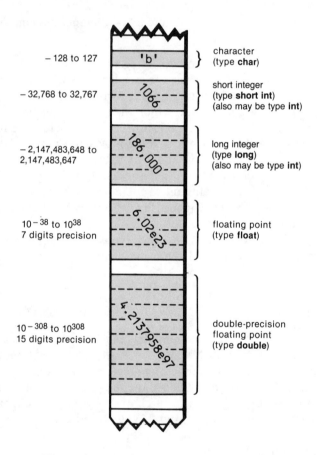

Figure 2-2. Variable Types in Memory

The character type and the integer types also have **unsigned** versions (type **unsigned char**, **unsigned short**, **unsigned int**, and **unsigned long**) which change the range of numbers the type can hold. For instance, the **un-**

**signed int** type holds numbers from 0 to 65,535, rather than from −32,768 to 32,767 as the regular **int** type does. These unsigned types can be useful in special circumstances, but are not used as often as the signed versions.

You may be wondering why we haven't mentioned a string type. The reason is simple: there is no string variable type in C. Instead, strings are represented by arrays of characters. We've shown some examples of string constants already. For string variables, we'll have to wait until Chapter 6.

Let's look at a program that uses character, floating point, and integer variables. We'll call this program event.c.

```c
main()
{
    int event;
    char heat;
    float time;

    event = 5;
    heat = 'C';
    time = 27.25;
    printf("The winning time in heat %c", heat);
    printf(" of event %d was %f.", event, time);
}
```

Here's the output of this program:

```
C>event
The winning time in heat C of event 5 was 27.250000.
```

This program uses the three most common variable types: **int**, **char**, and **float**. You'll notice that we've used a new format specifier, %f, to print out the floating point number. We'll discuss this and other format specifiers soon, in the section on input/output. For now, remember that %f is used to print floating point numbers the same way that %d is used to print integers and %c is used to print characters.

## Floating Point Variables

Floating point numbers are different from integers in that they are stored in memory in two parts, rather than one. These two parts are called the "mantissa" and the "exponent." The mantissa is the value of the number, and the exponent is the power to which it is raised.

Scientists and engineers use a similar technique for representing numbers: it's called "exponential notation." For example, in exponential notation the number 12,345 would be represented as 1.2345e4, where the number 4, following the e, is the exponent—the power of 10 to which the number will be raised—and 1.2345 is the value of the number. The exponent can also be negative: .0098765 is represented in exponential notation as 9.8765e−3. The idea in exponential notation is to transform every number, no matter how large or how small, into a value with only one digit to the left of the decimal point, followed by the appropriate power of 10. In effect, the exponent represents how many places you need to move the decimal point to transform the number into this standard form.

Exponential notation permits the storage of far larger and far smaller numbers than is possible with integers. However, arithmetic and other operations are performed more slowly on floating point numbers, so an integer variable is preferable unless the larger capacity of floating point numbers is necessary.

In Microsoft C on the IBM, a floating point number of type **float** is stored in four bytes; one for the exponent, and three for the value of the number, as shown in Figure 2-3.

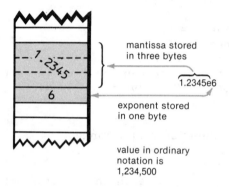

Figure 2-3. Floating Point Variable

The format is actually not quite the same as the exponential notation used by humans, since the value of the number and the exponent are stored in the computer's memory in binary rather than decimal. However, the effect is the same. The one-byte exponent is large enough to hold exponents between 38 and −38. For instance, the number 123,456,000,000,000,000,000,000,000,000,000,000,000.0 (which has 38 digits following the 1) is close to the largest number that can be stored; it would be represented in exponential notation as 1.23456e38.

Since only three bytes are available for holding the value of the number, only six or seven digits of precision are available in floating point variables. Thus, you can write numbers like 4345345.8476583746123, but the computer will store only 4.345345e6.

Just because a floating point variable is stored in the computer in exponential notation doesn't mean it must print out that way or that you need to type it in using exponential notation. In the event.c program shown earlier, the %f format specifier causes the number to be printed in the normal way with a decimal point. However, as we'll see in the next section, you can force **printf()** to print in exponential notation or even to make a choice between decimal and exponential.

## Initializing Variables

It's possible to combine a variable declaration with an assignment operator so that a variable is given a value at the same time it's declared. For example, the event.c program could be rewritten as:

```
main()
{
    int event = 5;
    char heat = 'C';
    float time = 27.25;

    printf("The winning time in heat %c", heat);
    printf("of event %d was %f.", event, time);
}
```

The output is just the same, but we've saved some program lines and simplified the program. This is a commonly used approach.

# Input/Output

It's all very well to store data in the computer and make calculations with it, but you also need to be able to type new data into the computer and print out the results of your calculations. In this section we'll continue our examination of the ouput function **printf()**, and we'll introduce two input functions: **scanf()**, a versatile function that can handle many different kinds of input, and **getche()**, a specialized input function that tells your program which character you've typed the instant you type it.

## The *printf()* Function

We've been using **printf()** up to now without too much explanation of all its possibilities. Let's take a closer look.

### Format Specifiers

As we saw from Chapter 1, a format specifier (such as %d or %c) is used to control what format will be used by **printf()** to print out a particular variable. In general, you want to match the format specifier to the type of variable you're printing. You would, for example, usually use a %d specifier to print an integer, and you'd use a %c format specifier to print a character (although there are exceptions to this rule).

We've already used four of the format specifiers available with **printf()**: %d to print integers, %c to print characters, %s to print strings, and %f to print floating point numbers. While these are by far the most commonly used, there are others as well. Here's a list of the common format specifiers for **printf()**:

%c    single character

%s    string

%d    signed decimal integer

%i    signed decimal integer

%f    floating point (decimal notation)

%e    floating point (exponential notation)

%g    floating point (%f or %e, whichever is shorter)

%u    unsigned decimal integer

%x    unsigned hexadecimal integer (uses "abcdef")

%o    unsigned octal integer

l    prefix used with d, u, x, o, and i, to denote long integer, and before %f, %e, and %g to denote double precision (examples: %ld, %lf)

h    prefix used with d, u, x, o, and i to denote short integer

'E' and 'G' used in place of 'e' and 'g' will cause the letter 'e', denoting the exponential in the number, to print out as 'E'. Also, 'X' in place of 'x' will cause uppercase letters "ABCDEF" to be used in hex numbers.

### Field-Width Specifiers

The **printf()** function gives the programmer considerable power to format the printed output. Let's see how this is done.

In our event.c program the floating point variable **time** was printed out with six digits to the right of the decimal, even though only two of these digits were significant:

```
The winning time in heat C of event 5 was 27.250000.
```

It would be nice to be able to suppress these extra zeros, and **printf()** includes a way to do just that. We'll rewrite the event.c program, inserting the string ".2" (period 2) between the '%' character and the 'f' in the second **printf()** statement:

```
main()
{
    int event;
    char heat;
    float time;

    event = 5;
    heat = 'C';
    time = 27.25;
    printf("The winning time in heat %c", heat);
    printf(" of event %d was %.2f.", event, time);
}
```

Here's the output of this program:

```
The winning time in heat C of event 5 was 27.25.
```

As you can see, a number *following* the decimal point in the field-width specifier controls how many characters will be printed following the decimal point.

A digit *preceding* the decimal point in the field-width specifier controls the width of the space to be used to contain the number when it is printed. Think of this field width as an imaginary box containing the number. An example (with integer values) is shown in Figure 2-4.

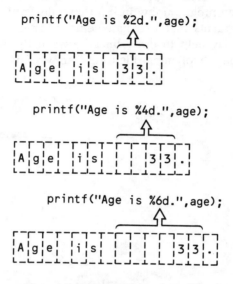

Figure 2-4. Field-Width Specifier

Specifying the field width can be useful in creating tables of figures, as the following program demonstrates.

```
main()
{
    printf("%.1f %.1f %.1f\n", 3.0, 12.5, 523.3);
    printf("%.1f %.1f %.1f\n", 300.0, 1200.5, 5300.3);
}
```

Here's the output:

```
3.0 12.5 523.3
300.0 1200.5 5300.3
```

Even though we used spaces in the format strings to separate the numbers (the spaces in the format string are simply printed out as spaces in the output) and specified only one decimal place with the ".1" string, the numbers don't line up and so are hard to read. However, if we insert the number 8 before the decimal place in each field-width specification we can put each number in a box eight characters wide. Here's the modified program:

```
main
{
    printf("%8.1f%8.1f%8.1f\n", 3.0, 12.5, 523.3);
    printf("%8.1f%8.1f%8.1f\n", 300.0, 1200.5, 5300.3);
}
```

We should acknowledge the cluttered appearance of the **printf()** statements. Instant legibility is not one of C's strong points (at least not until you've been programming in it for a while). Although you know the purpose of all the elements in these statements, your eye may have trouble unraveling them. It may help to draw lines between the individual format specifiers to clarify what's happening. Figure 2-5 shows this format string dissected.

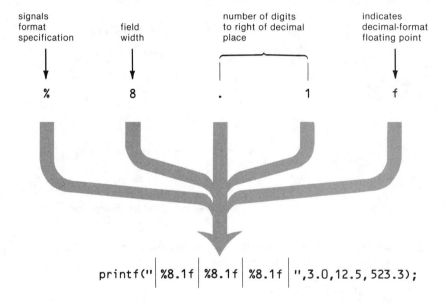

Figure 2-5. *printf()* Format String

The format specifier in **printf()** determines the interpretation of a variable's type, the width of the field, the number of decimal places printed, and the justification.

Here's the output of the program, showing that, although the format specifiers may be hard to read, the output is a model of organization:

```
    3.0    12.5    523.3
  300.0  1200.5   5300.3
```

A minus sign preceding the field-width specifier will put the output on the left side of the field instead of the right. For instance, let's insert minus signs in the field-width specifiers in the program above:

```
main
{
    printf("%-8.1f%-8.1f%-8.1f\n", 3.0, 12.5, 523.3);
    printf("%-8.1f%-8.1f%-8.1f\n", 300.0, 1200.5, 5300.3);
}
```

the output will be lined up on the *left* side of the fields, like this:

```
3.0     12.5    523.3
300.0   1200.5  52300.3
```

This format may be useful in certain circumstances, especially when printing strings.

The various uses of the format specifier are summarized in Appendix A.

### Escape Sequences

We saw in Chapter 1 how the newline character, '\n', when inserted in a **printf()** format string, would print the carriage return-linefeed combination. The newline character is an example of something called an "escape sequence," so called because the backslash symbol ( \ ) is considered an "escape" character: it causes an escape from the normal interpretation of a string, so that the next character is recognized as having a special meaning. Here's an example using the newline character and a new escape sequence, '\t', which means "tab."

```
main()
{
    printf("Each\tword\tis\ntabbed\tover\tonce");
}
```

Here's the output:

```
C>tabtest
Each    word    is
tabbed  over    once
```

C tabs over eight characters when it encounters the '\t' character; this is another useful technique for lining up columns of output. The '\n' character causes a new line to begin following "is."

The tab and newline are probably the most often used escape sequences, but there are others as well. The following list shows the common escape sequences.

| \n | Newline |
|---|---|
| \t | Tab |
| \b | Backspace |
| \r | Carriage return |
| \f | Formfeed |
| \' | Single quote |
| \" | Double quote |
| \\ | Backslash |
| \xdd | ASCII code in hexadecimal notation (each d represents a digit) |
| \ddd | ASCII code in octal notation (each d represents a digit) |

The first few of these escape sequences are more or less self-explanatory. The newline, which we've already seen, has the effect of both a carriage return and linefeed. Tab moves over to the next eight-space-wide field. Backspace moves the cursor one space left. Formfeed advances to the top of the next page on the printer.

Characters that are ordinarily used as delimeters—the single quote, double quote, and the backslash itself—can be printed by preceding them with the backslash. Thus, the statement

```
printf("Dick told Spot, \"Let's go!\"\n");
```

will print

```
Dick told Spot, "Let's go!"
```

## Printing Graphics Characters

What's the purpose of those last two escape sequences, \xdd and \ddd?

As you probably know, every character (letters, numbers, punctuation, and so forth) is represented in the computer by a number. True ASCII (an acronym for American Standard Code for Information Interchange) codes run from 0 to 127 (decimal). These cover the upper- and lowercase letters, digits from 0 to 9, punctuation, and control characters such as linefeed and backspace.

IBM computers use an additional 128 characters, with codes running from 128 to 255. These additional characters consist of foreign-language symbols and graphics characters. IBM has also redefined a few characters below ASCII code 32 to be graphics characters. The entire set of IBM character codes is listed in Appendix E.

We've already seen how to print ordinary ASCII characters on the screen using characters or strings in **printf()**. We also know how to print certain special characters with a backslash escape sequence. But graphics and other nonstandard characters require a different approach; they can only be printed by sending the backslash and the number representing their character code.

The number can be represented in either octal or hexadecimal notation. Traditionally, octal has been used in UNIX-based systems, and to some extent this has carried over into C implementations on IBM computers. However, the rest of the IBM world, including all operating system and assembly language programming, speaks hexadecimal; so that's what we'll do in this book. There is no way to use decimal numbers as part of escape sequences—evidence of C's genesis in the world of systems programmers, who tend to think in terms of octal or hexadecimal, rather than decimal. (If you're not familiar with the hexadecimal system, consult Appendix C.)

Let's look at a program that prints a simple graphics character, a small rectangle:

```
main()
{
    printf("Here's the character: \xDB");
}
```

The output of this program is shown in Figure 2-6.

Here is the character: ■

Figure 2-6. Printing a Graphics Character

We've used the hexadecimal number DB (219 in decimal), which represents a solid rectangle, as can be seen in Appendix A.

Here's another example of the use of graphics characters:

```
main()
{
    printf("\xC9\xCD\xBB\n");
    printf("\xC8\xCD\xBC\n");
}
```

This program, which prints nothing but graphics characters, displays a box on the screen, as shown in Figure 2-7.

Graphics characters are printed using their hex code in an escape sequence, such as '\xB0'.

These graphics characters are specific to the IBM world, so programs using them cannot be ported to UNIX or other systems without modification. However, graphics characters offer an easy way to create graphics images on the IBM

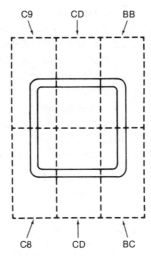

Figure 2-7. Box Made with Graphics Characters

monochrome screen. Programs using this form of graphics can be run on any IBM system, even those without color graphics capabilities, making this the most universal form of graphics in the IBM world. While not as versatile as color graphics, graphics characters can be used in many applications where simple graphics are required. In Appendix B, for example, you'll find a maze-drawing program that makes use of them.

We'll use other examples of graphics characters in programming examples in later chapters.

## The *scanf()* Function

You already know about C's most-used *output* statements, **printf()**. In this section we're going to introduce an important *input* function, **scanf()**. C has a bewilderingly large collection of input and output functions, but **printf()** and **scanf()** are the most versatile in that they can handle all of the different variables and control their formatting.

Here's a program that uses **scanf()**. You can give it the file name age.c:

```
main()
{
    float years, days;
    printf("Please type your age in years: ");
    scanf("%f", &years);
    days = years * 365;
    printf("You are %.1f days old.\n", days);
}
```

Besides **scanf()**, this program introduces two new symbols: the arithmetic operator for multiplication ( * ), and the address operator, represented by the ampersand ( & ). We'll talk about both of these later in the chapter. For the moment, simply note the surprising fact that **scanf()** requires the use of an ampersand before each variable name.

A typical interaction between the program and a precocious youngster might look like this:

```
C>age
Please type your age in years: 2
You are 730.0 days old.
```

Since we're using floating point we can also input decimal fractions:

```
C>age
Please type your age in years: 48.5
You are 17702.5 days old.
```

As you can see, the format for **scanf()** looks very much like that for **printf()**. As in **printf()**, the argument on the left is a string that contains format specifiers. In this case there is only one, %f. On the right is the variable name, **&years**.

The format specifiers for **scanf()** are similar to those for **printf()**, but there are a few differences. The following table shows them side-by-side for comparison:

| Format | printf() | scanf() |
|---|---|---|
| single character | %c | %c |
| string | %s | %s |
| signed decimal integer | %d | %d |
| signed decimal integer | %i | |
| decimal, hex, or octal integer | | %i |
| floating point (decimal notation) | %f | %f or %e |
| floating point (exponential notation) | %e | %f or %e |
| floating point (%f or %e, whichever is shorter) | %g | |
| unsigned decimal integer | %u | %u |
| unsigned hexadecimal integer (uses "ABCDEF") | %x | %x |
| unsigned octal integer | %o | %o |

As we noted earlier, the first four type characters are the most commonly used.

In **scanf()** [unlike **printf()**] %e can be used in place of %f; they have the same effect. You can type your input using either exponential or decimal notation; either format is accepted by both %e and %f. The %g specifier, which allows **printf()** to choose exponential or decimal notation, whichever is shorter, is not necessary with **scanf()**, because the user makes the decision.

Like **printf()**, **scanf()** uses a prefix letter 'l' following the percent sign and before the letters 'd', 'i', 'o', and 'u' to denote long integers, and the letter 'h' to denote short integers. (Older versions of C used capital letters 'D', 'I', 'O', and 'U' with **scanf()** for this purpose, but they are no longer supported.) The 'l' can also be used before 'f' to denote a double-precision floating point.

The **scanf()** function can accept input to several variables at once. To demonstrate this, let's revise our event.c program to use input from the user, rather than assigning values to the variables within the program:

```
main()
{
    int event;
    char heat;
    float time;

    printf("Type event number, heat letter, and time: ");
    scanf("%d %c %f", &event, &heat, &time);
    printf("The winning time in heat %c", heat);
    printf(" of event %d was %.2f.", event, time);
}
```

Here's the output:

```
C>event2
Type event number, heat letter, and time: 4 B 36.34
The winning time in heat B of event 4 was 36.34.
```

How does **scanf()** know when we've finished typing one value and started another? Let's look at the process. As we type our three input values, 4, 'B', and 36.34, we separate them by spaces. The **scanf()** function matches each space we type with a corresponding space between the conversion type characters in the **scanf()** format string "%d %c %f". If we had tried to separate the values with another character—a dash or comma, for example—this would not have matched the space in the format string. The space we type serves as a delimiter because it matches the space in the format string. This process is shown in Figure 2-8.

Actually, we can use any whitespace character (space, newline, or tab) as a delimiter when we type in our input values; each will match the space in the format string. Here's a sample using the [Return] key, which sends a '\n' to **scanf()**:

```
C>event2
Type event number, heat letter, and time:
7
A
49.2
The winning time in heat A of event 7 was 49.20.
```

And here's an example using the [Tab]:

```
C>event2
Type event number, heat letter, and time: 3       A        14.7
The winning time in heat A of event 3 was 14.70.
```

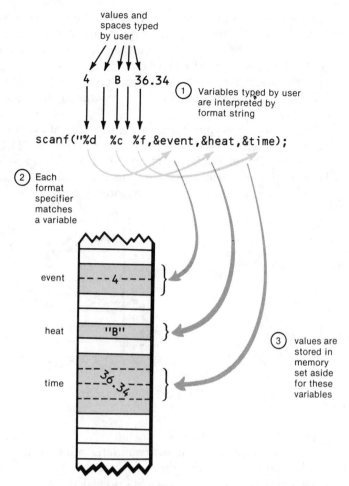

Figure 2-8. Using *scanf()* with Multiple Inputs

There are other, more complex ways of handling the formatting of input to **scanf()**, but we won't be concerned about them now.

## The Address Operator ( & )

The **scanf()** function in the age.c and event.c programs above used a new symbol: the ampersand ( & ) preceding the variable names used as arguments.

```
scanf("%f", &years);
scanf("%d %c %f", &event, &heat, &time);
```

What is its purpose? It would seem more reasonable to use the name of the variable without the ampersand, as we did in **printf()** statements in the same programs. However (for reasons which will be clearer in the chapter on point-ers), the C compiler requires the arguments to **scanf()** to be the *addresses* of variables, rather than the variables themselves. This peculiarity of **scanf()** is one of C's least user-friendly characteristics; it is close to certain you will forget the ampersands before the variables in **scanf()** at least once. However, the idea of *addresses* is the key to one of C's most powerful and interesting capabilities, so let's explore it further.

The memory of your computer is divided into bytes, and these bytes are numbered, from 0 to the upper limit of your memory (524,287, if you have 512K of memory). These numbers are called the "addresses" of the bytes. Every variable occupies a certain location in memory, and its address is that of the first byte it occupies. Figure 2-9 shows an integer with a value of 2 at address 1367.

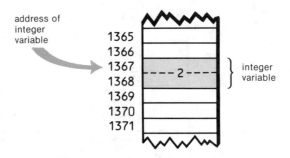

Figure 2-9. Address of Variable

Suppose we have declared an integer variable, **num**, in a program, and assigned it the value 2. If the program later refers to the name of the variable, **num**, the compiler will give the *value* stored in that variable, or 2. However, if you refer to the name of the variable preceded by the ampersand, **&num**, the compiler will give the *address* where **num** is stored.

Here's a program that demonstrates this operation:

```
main()
{
    int num;
    num = 2;
    printf("Value=%d, address=%d", num, &num);
}
```

And here's the output:

```
Value=2, address=3536
```

On our particular computer, the address where the variable **num** is stored is 3536. In another computer it would almost certainly be different, because of variations in the size of the operating system and other factors. In any case, knowing where a variable is stored will turn out to be very important in C programming, as we'll learn when we get to the chapter on pointers.

In the meantime, all you need to remember about the address operator is that in using **scanf()** you need to precede variable names with the ampersand (except in the case of strings, which we're coming to soon).

## The *getche()* Function

For some situations, the **scanf()** function has one glaring weakness: you need to type a [Return] before the function will digest what you've typed. But we often want a function that will read a single character the instant it's typed, without waiting for [Return]. For instance, in a game we might want a spaceship to move each time we pressed one of the cursor-control (arrow) keys; it would be awkward to type [Return] each time we pressed an arrow key.

We can use the **getche()** function for this purpose. The "get" means it gets something from the outside world; in other words, it's an input function. The "ch" means it gets a character, and the "e" means it echoes the character to the screen when you type it. (There is a similar function, **getch()**, which does not echo the typed character to the screen.) Another function, **getchar()**, is better known to programmers working on Unix systems, but in Microsoft C **getchar** is *buffered*, which means it doesn't pass the character typed by the user to the program until the user hits [Return].

Here's a simple program that uses **getche()**:

```
main()
{
    char ch;
    printf("Type any character: ");
    ch = getche();
    printf("\nThe character you typed was %c.", ch );
}
```

And here's a sample interaction:

```
C>getche
Type any character: x
The character you typed was x.
C>getche
Type any character: T
The character you typed was T.
```

If you run this program, you'll notice that the phrase "The character you typed was" is printed immediately when you press any character key; you don't have to press the [Return] key.

Another point to notice is that the function itself takes on or "returns" the value of the character typed. It's almost as if the function were a variable that assigned itself a value; the function becomes the character typed. This is considerably different from the technique used in **scanf()**, where the value returned was placed in a variable that was one of **scanf()**'s arguments. Figure 2-10 shows the operation of the **getche()** function.

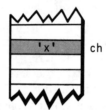

Figure 2-10. Operation of *getche()*

There is a downside to using **getche()**; if you make a mistake, you can't backspace to correct it, since as soon as you type a character, it's gobbled up by your program.

We'll see how useful **getche()** can be in the next chapter, when we learn such skills as how to count characters in phrases typed in by the user.

There is more to say about input/output, and we'll be returning to the topic throughout the book.

# Operators

Operators are words or symbols that cause a program to do something to variables. For instance, the arithmetic operators ( + ) and ( − ) cause a program to add or subtract two numbers. There are many different kinds of operators; to list them all here would be to invite debilitating ennui. Instead we'll mention the most common: arithmetic and relational operators, and the less well-known (to non-C programmers) increment/decrement operators and arithmetic assignment operators. (Operators are summarized in Appendix A.)

## Arithmetic Operators

In the age.c program we used the multiplication operator ( * ) to multiply two numbers together. C uses the four arithmetic operators that are common in most programming languages, and one, the remainder operator, which is not so common.

+   addition
−   subtraction
*   multiplication
/   division
%   remainder

Here's a program that uses several arithmetic operators. It converts temperatures in Fahrenheit to centigrade.

```
main()
{
    int ftemp, ctemp;

    printf("Type temperature in degrees fahrenheit: ");
    scanf("%d", &ftemp);
    ctemp = (ftemp-32) * 5 / 9;
    printf("Temperature in degrees centigrade is %d", ctemp);
}
```

Here's some sample interaction with the program:

```
C>ftemp
Type temperature in degrees fahrenheit: 32
Temperature in degrees centigrade is 0
C>ftemp
Type temperature in degrees fahrenheit: 70
Temperature in degrees centigrade is 21
```

This program uses the standard formula for converting degrees Fahrenheit into degrees centigrade: subtract 32 from the Fahrenheit temperature and multiply the result by five-ninths.

```
ctemp = (ftemp-32) * 5 / 9;
```

There are several things to note about this statement. First, you'll see that we've surrounded some of the operators, the ( * ) and the ( / ), with spaces but have not used spaces around the minus sign. The moral here is that the C compiler doesn't care whether you use spaces surrounding your operators or not, so you're free to arrange your expressions however they look best to you. If you don't like the way the spaces are arranged in the example, you can arrange them however you like when you type in the program.

### Operator Precedence

The second point to notice about the ftemp.c program is that we've used parentheses around (ftemp − 32). For those of you who remember your algebra the reason will be clear; we want the 32 subtracted from **ftemp** *before* we multiply it by 5 and divide by 9. Since multiplication and division are normally carried out before addition and subtraction, we use parentheses to ensure that the subtraction is carried out first.

The fact that ( * ) and ( / ) are evaluated before ( + ) and ( − ) is an example of *precedence*; we say that ( * ) and ( / ) have a higher precedence than ( + ) and ( − ). We'll be returning to this idea of precedence when we discuss different kinds of operators.

### The Remainder Operator

The remainder operator (sometimes called the modulo operator) may be unfamiliar to you; it is used to find the remainder when one number is divided by another. ("Modulo" is the correct spelling.) For example, in the statement below, the variable **answer** will be assigned the value 3, since that's the remainder when the 13 is divided by 5.

```
answer = 13 % 5;
```

We'll find uses for all the arithmetic operators as we go along, but the remainder operator is useful in unexpected ways.

### Expressions versus Variables

Where can you use expressions containing arithmetic operators? We've already shown examples of their use in assignment statements, such as

```
days = years * 365;
```

It's also possible to include expressions involving arithmetic operators (and other kinds of operators as well) directly into **printf()** and other kinds of statements. For example, the following usage is just fine:

```
main()
{
    int num = 2;
    printf("Number plus four is %d."; num + 4);
}
```

When this program is executed the following phrase will be printed out:

```
Number plus four is 6.
```

Instead of a constant or a variable, **printf()** has printed out the value of the expression

```
num + 4
```

An "expression" is simply a combination of constants, variables, and operators that can be evaluated to yield a value. Since the variable **number** had the value 2, the expression evaluates to 6, and that's what is printed out. So you can use an expression almost anyplace you can use a variable. This is done more often in C than it is in most languages; we'll see examples as we go along.

An entire expression can be used almost anyplace a variable can be used.

While we're on the subject of arithmetic operators, we should mention two kinds of operators that you may not have encountered before in other languages: arithmetic assignment operators and increment/decrement operators. Both are widely used in C, and both help to give C source listings their distinctive appearance.

### Arithmetic Assignment Operators

If you compare a C program with a program with a similar function written in another language, you may well find that the C program is shorter. One reason for this is that C has several operators that can compress often-used programming statements. Consider the following program fragment:

```
total = total + number;
```

Here the value in **number** is added to the value in **total**, and the result is placed in **total**. In C this statement can be rewritten:

```
total += number;
```

The effect is exactly the same, but the expression is more compact, as shown in Figure 2-11.

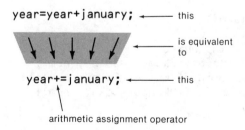

Figure 2-11. The Arithmetic Assignment Operator

Here's a program that makes use of this "plus-equal" operator:

```
main()
{
    int total = 0;
    int count = 10;
    printf("Total=%d\n", total);
    total += count;
    printf("Total=%d\n", total);
    total += count;
    printf("Total=%d\n", total);
}
```

And here's the output, showing the results of repeatedly adding the value of **count**, which is 10, to **total**.

```
Total=0
Total=10
Total=20
```

All the arithmetic operators listed earlier can be combined with the equal sign in the same way:

+ =   addition assignment operator

– =   subtraction assignment operator

* =   multiplication assignment operator

/ =   division assignment operator

% =   remainder assignment operator

There are assignment versions of some other operators as well, such as logical operators and bit-wise operators, but we'll ignore these for now.

## The Increment Operator

C uses another operator that is not common in other languages: the increment operator. Consider the following program:

```
main()
{
    int num=0;
    printf("Number=%d\n", num);
    printf("Number=%d\n", num++);
    printf("Number=%d\n", num);
}
```

Here's the output:

```
Number=0
Number=0
Number=1
```

How did the variable **num** get to be 1? As you can guess by examination of the program, the ( + + ) operator had the effect of incrementing **num**; that is, adding 1 to it. The first **printf()** statement printed the original value of **num**, which was 0. The second **printf()** statement also printed the original value of **num**; then, *after* **num** was printed, the (+ +) operator incremented it. Thus the third **printf()** statement printed out the incremented value. The effect of **num(+ +)** is exactly the same as that of the statement

```
num = num + 1;
```

However, **num** ( + + ) is far more compact to write, as shown in Figure 2-12. It also compiles into more efficient code.

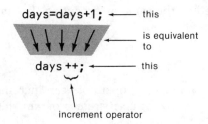

Figure 2-12. The Increment Operator

Let's rewrite the program, making a subtle change:

```
main()
{
    int num=0;
    printf("Number=%d\n", num);
    printf("Number=%d\n", ++num);
    printf("Number=%d\n", num);
}
```

What did we do? We moved the ( + + ) operator to the *beginning* of the **num** variable. Let's see what effect this has on the output:

```
Number=0
Number=1
Number=1
```

Now the variable **num** in the second **printf()** statement is incremented *before* it is printed.

Since there's an increment operator you can guess there will be a decrement operator as well. Let's modify our program again, using ( – – ), the decrement operator.

```
main()
{
    int num=0;
    printf("Number=%d\n", num);
    printf("Number=%d\n", num--);
    printf("Number=%d\n", num);
}
```

Now instead of being incremented, the **num** variable is decremented: reduced by 1.

```
Number=0
Number=0
Number=-1
```

The effect is just the same as executing the statement

```
num = num - 1;
```

> The ( + + ) and ( − − ) operators can increment and decrement a variable without the need for a separate program statement.

The ability to increment (or decrement) a variable deep within an expression, and to control whether it will be incremented before or after it is used, is one of the features that makes a single line of code so powerful in C. We'll see many examples of the use of these operators as we go along.

## Relational Operators

In the next two chapters we'll be dealing with loops and decisions. These constructs require the program to ask questions about the relationship between variables; is a certain variable greater than 100? If so, stop looping. Is the character the user just typed equal to a space? If so, increment the count of the number of words.

Relational operators are the vocabulary the program uses to ask questions about variables. Let's look at an example of a relational operator, in this case the "less than" ( < ) operator.

```
main()
{
    int age;

    age = 15;
    printf("Is age less than 21? %d", age < 21 );
    age = 30;
    printf("\nIs a less than 21? %d", age < 21 );
}
```

```
Is age less than 21? 1
Is age less than 21? 0
```

In this program the **printf()** statements take the whole expression

```
age < 21
```

and print out its value. What is its value? That depends on the value of the variable **age.** When **age** is 15, which *is* less than 21, a 1 is printed out. When **age** is 30, which is *not* less than 21, a zero is printed. It would seem that 1 stands for true, and 0 stands for false. This turns out to be the case. In C, true is represented by the integer 1, and false is represented by the integer 0. In some languages, such as Pascal, true and false values are represented by a special variable type called "boolean." In C, there is no such data type, so true and false values are represented by integers. The operation of the relational expression is shown in Figure 2-13.

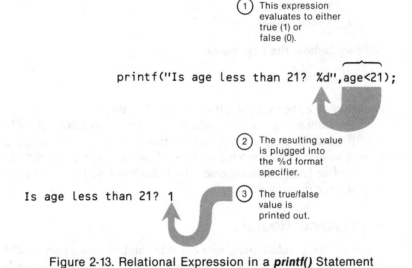

(1) This expression evaluates to either true (1) or false (0).

```
printf("Is age less than 21? %d",age<21);
```

(2) The resulting value is plugged into the %d format specifier.

```
Is age less than 21? 1
```

(3) The true/false value is printed out.

Figure 2-13. Relational Expression in a *printf()* Statement

The relational operators in C look much like those in other languages. There are six of them:

| | |
|---|---|
| < | less than |
| > | greater than |
| <= | less than or equal to |
| >= | greater than or equal to |
| == | equal to |
| != | not equal to |

Note that the relational operator "equal to" is represented by *two* equal signs. A common mistake is to use a single equal sign as a relational operator. For reasons that we'll learn later, the compiler doesn't notice that this is an error, so it can be a particularly frustrating bug to track down.

Here's an example using the equal-to ( = = ) operator (sometimes called the "equal-equal" operator).

```
main()
{
    int speed;

    speed = 75;
    printf("Is speed equal to 55? %d", speed == 55 );
    speed = 55;
    printf("\nIs speed equal to 55? %d", speed == 55 );
}
```

Here's the output of the program.

```
Is speed equal to 55? 0
Is speed equal to 55? 1
```

Note again how the expression

```
speed == 55
```

evaluates to either a false (0) or a true (1) value.

An interesting point to notice about true and false values is that, although C will generate a 1 when it means true and a 0 when it means false, it will recognize *any* nonzero value as true. That is, there are a lot of integers that C thinks of as true, but only one—0—it thinks of as false. We'll make use of this fact in later programs.

## Precedence, Round II

What will be printed out if you execute the following program? Remember that **true** is the integer 1 and **false** is the integer 0. These values can be used just like any other integer values.

```
main()
{
    printf("Answer is %d", 2+1 < 4 );
}
```

If you guessed "Answer is 1" you're right. First 2 + 1 is evaluated to yield 3, then this is compared with 4. It's less, so the expression

```
2+1 < 4
```

is true. True is 1, so that's what's printed.

Now watch closely: we're going to try something a little tricky. What will this program print?

```
main()
{
    printf("Answer is %d", 1<2 + 4 );
}
```

Did you guess "Answer is 5"? If so, you probably decided that 1<2 would evaluate to true, or 1, and 1 added to 4 would give 5. Sorry, this is plausible but incorrect. We misled you with the use of spaces in the expression 1<2 + 4. Here's how we should have written it:

```
1 < 2+4
```

There are two lessons here. First, as we mentioned before, the compiler doesn't care where you put spaces; both forms of the expression compile into the same program. Second, arithmetic operators have a *higher precedence* than relational operators. That is, in the absence of parentheses, the arithmetic operators are evaluated *before* the relational operators. In the expression above, the arithmetic operator ( + ) is evaluated first, yielding a value of 6 from the expression 2+4. Then the relational operator ( < ) is evaluated. Since 1 is less than 6, the value of the entire expression is true. Thus, the output of this program will be

```
Answer is 1
```

> Arithmetic operators have a higher precedence—that is, are evaluated before—relational operators.

All operators in C are ranked according to their precedence. We have not encountered many of these operators yet, so we won't pursue the subject of precedence further here. It will, however, arise from time to time as we learn more about C. Precedence is a more important issue in C than it is in some languages because of the complexity of the expressions that are routinely created. Appendix A includes a table showing the precedence of all the C operators.

# Comments

It's helpful to be able to put comments into the source code file that can be read by humans but are invisible to the compiler. Here's a revision of our age program, with comments added:

```
/* age.c */
```

```
/* calculates age in days */
main()
{
    float years, days;                    /* initialize variables */

    printf("Please type your age in years: "); /* print prompt */
    scanf("%f", &years);                /* get age in years from user */
    days = years * 365;                   /* calculate age in days */
    printf("You are %.1f days old.\n", days);  /* print result */
}
```

A comment begins with the two-character symbol slash-asterisk ( /* ) and ends with an asterisk-slash ( */ ). These two-character symbols may seem awkward to type, especially in comparison to BASIC, where a single apostrophe ( ' ) at the beginning of the comment is all that's necessary. It also doesn't contribute to fast typing that the slash is lowercase while the asterisk is uppercase. As with other endeavors, however, if you type enough comments, it will start to seem easy.

In this example we've used two full-line comments to name the program and to say what it does. We've also placed comments on the lines with the program code. The only problem with comments that share lines with code is that it's easy to run out of space. C's long program statements, and the fact that they are indented, combine to reduce the number of character spaces available on a line.

Although a lot of comments are probably not necessary in this program, it is usually the case that programmers use too few comments rather than too many. Comments should be added anyplace there's a possibility of confusion. We'll refrain from repeating the standard lecture on how an adequate number of comments can save hours of misery and suffering when you later try to figure out what the program does.

Since C ignores whitespace characters it's perfectly possible for comments to flow over two or more lines:

```
/*
This is
a multiline
comment
*/
```

Often asterisks are placed at the beginning of each line in a multiline comment. This is for aesthetic reasons; the asterisks are not comment symbols themselves and are ignored by the compiler.

```
/* This is a fancier
 * multiline
 * comment
 */
```

This is a common usage in C.

It is illegal to *nest* comments. That is, you can't say

```
/* Outer comment /* inner comment */ more outer comment */
```

This restriction can be annoying when you're debugging a program and you want to cause part of it to be invisible to the compiler by "commenting it out" (surrounding it with comment symbols). If the section of code you're commenting out contains comments, you'll be in trouble.

It's easy to make errors with comment symbols, and the results of such errors can be particularly baffling to debug. For instance, if you forget the close-comment symbol ( */ ) at the end of a comment, the compiler will assume that your entire program from then on is a comment. It will not compile it and it also won't issue any error messages, or at least any messages that relate specifically to comments. Tracking down this sort of bug can be a major inconvenience, so be careful that every begin-comment operator is matched with a close-comment operator.

We've included a C program called "comcheck.c" (for "comment check") in Appendix B. It will look through your source program and verify that each open-comment symbol is matched with a close-comment. If you have trouble with comments you might want to try this program. There are also programs available commercially that check the syntax of your C program in a more general way before it's compiled; these can also spot mismatched comment symbols.

## Summary

In this chapter we've introduced some of the more fundamental parts of C: variables, input/output, and operators.

You've learned that there are five major variable types in C: character, integer, long integer, floating point, and double-precision floating point. You've learned how to declare and initialize variables and how to use them in assignment and other kinds of statements.

Among input/output functions, you've learned about format and field-width specifiers in the **printf()** function, about escape sequences, and about how to print graphics characters. You've been introduced to the **scanf()** and **getche()** input functions, and seen how **scanf()** is good for a variety of input and can handle multiple variables, while **getche()** returns any character typed in.

We've covered two major categories of operators, arithmetic operators and relational operators, and mentioned two less important but very "C-like" operators, the arithmetic assignment statement and the increment/decrement operator. We've also discussed comments and operator precedence.

With these fundamentals under your belt you should be ready to wade into the next few chapters, where we discuss program structures such as loops, decisions, and functions.

## Questions

1. Declaring variables is advantageous because it:

    a. helps organize the program

    b.  helps the compiler work efficiently

    c. avoids errors from misspelled variable names

    d. simplifies the writing of very short programs

2. The five major data types in C are

    c_____

    i_____

    f_____

    l_____

    d_____.

3. Which of these C statements are correct?

    a. int a;

    b. float b;

    c. double float c;

    d. unsigned char d;

4. True or false: two variables can be declared in one statement.

5. Type **float** occupies _____ times as many bytes of memory as type **char**.

6. Type **int** can accommodate numbers from _____ to _____.

7. Which of the following is an example of initializing a variable?

    a. num = 2;

    b. int num;

    c. num < 2;

    d. int num = 2;

8. True or false: type **long** variables can hold numbers no larger than twice as big as type **int** variables.

9. Floating point variables are used instead of integers to:

    a. avoid being too specific about what value a number has

    b. make possible the use of large numbers

c. permit the use of decimal points in numbers

d. conceal the true value of the numbers

10. What do the escape sequences '\x41' and '\xE0' print?

11. Express the following numbers in exponential notation:

    a. 1,000,000

    b. 0.000,001

    c. 199.95

    d. − 888.88

12. Express the following numbers in decimal notation:

    a. 1.5e6

    b. 1.5e − 6

    c. 7.6543e3

    d. − 7.6543e − 3

13. What's wrong with this program?

```
/* age.c */
/* calculates age in days */
main()
{
    float years, days;
    printf("Please type your age in years: ");   /* print prompt */
    scanf("%f", years);                           /* get input */
    days = years * 365;                           /* find answer */
    printf("You are %f days old.\n", days);       /* print answer */
}
```

14. A field-width specifier in a **printf()** function:

    a. controls the margins of the program listing

    b. specifies the maximum value of a number

    c. controls the size of type used to print numbers

    d. specifies how many character positions will be used for a number

15. True or false: a function can have a value.

16. Which of the following are arithmetic operators?

    a. +

    b. &

c. %

d. <

17. Rewrite the following statement using the increment operator:

```
number = number + 1;
```

18. Rewrite the following statement using arithmetic assignment statement:

```
usa = usa + calif;
```

19. What is the meaning of the characters '\t' and '\r'?

20. The function **scanf()** reads

    a. a single character

    b. characters and strings

    c. any possible number

    d. any possible variable type

21. True or false: you need to press [Return] after typing a character in order for **getche()** to read it.

22. A relational operator is used to:

    a. combine values

    b. compare values

    c. distinguish different types of variables

    d. change variables to logical values

23. Are the following expressions true or false?

    a. 1 > 2

    b. 'a' < 'b'

    c. 1 = = 2

    d. '2' = = '2'

24. Precedence determines which operator:

    a. is most important

    b. is used first

    c. is fastest

    d. operates on the largest numbers

25. Is the following a correctly formed comment?

```
/* This is a
/* comment which
/* extends over several lines
*/
```

## Exercises

1. Modify the age.c program to print the age in minutes instead of days.

2. Write a program that prints the square of a number the user types in. (The square is the number times itself.) Use floating point.

3. Rewrite the box.c program so it draws a similar box, but one that is four characters wide and four characters tall.

# 3

# *Loops*

- **for** loop
- **while** loop
- **do while** loop
- nested loops
- values of functions and assignment statements
- **break** and **continue** statements

# 3

In the last chapter we introduced variables, input/output functions, and operators. With these programming elements we could write programs that were almost useful: converting from Fahrenheit to centigrade, for example. However, the programs were limited because, when executed, they always performed the same series of actions, in the same way, exactly once.

Almost always, if something is worth doing, it's worth doing more than once. You can probably think of several examples of this from real life, such as going to the movies and eating a good dinner. Programming is the same; we frequently need to perform an action over and over, often with variations in the details each time. The mechanism that meets this need is the "loop," and loops are the subject of this chapter.

There are three major loop structures in C: the **for** loop, the **while** loop, and a cousin of the **while** loop called the **do** loop (or **do while** loop). We'll discuss each of these in turn. We're going to start with the **for** loop because it has close analogies in both BASIC and Pascal, whereas—at least in old-style BASIC—there is no equivalent to the **while** loop. Also, the **for** loop is conceptually easy to understand, although the details can get complicated. This is true because all its elements are stated explicitly at the beginning of the loop. In the other loops, the elements are scattered throughout the program.

## The *for* Loop

It is often the case in programming that you want to do something a fixed number of times. Perhaps you want to calculate the paychecks for 120 employees or print out the squares of all the numbers from 1 to 50. The **for** loop is ideally suited for such cases.

Let's look at a simple example of a **for** loop:

```
/* forloop.c */
/* prints numbers from 0 to 9 */
main()

{
   int count;
   for (count=0; count<10; count++)
      printf("count=%d\n", count);
}
```

Type in the program (you can call the source file forloop.c) and compile it. When executed, it will generate the following output:

```
C>forloop
count=0
count=1
count=2
count=3
count=4
count=5
count=6
count=7
count=8
count=9
```

This program's role in life is to execute a **printf()** statement 10 times. The **printf()** prints out the phrase "count=" followed by the value of the variable **count**. Let's see how the **for** loop causes this to happen.

## Structure of the *for* Loop

The parentheses following the keyword **for** contain what we'll call the "loop expression." This loop expression is divided by semicolons into three separate expressions: the "initialize expression," the "test expression," and the "increment expresssion." Figure 3-1 shows the structure of the **for** loop.

| Expression | Name | Purpose |
|---|---|---|
| 1) count = 0 | Initialize expression | Initializes loop variable |
| 2) count < 10 | Test expression | Tests loop variable |
| 3) count + + | Increment expression | Increments loop variable |

The variable **count** occupies a key role in this **for** loop. In conjunction with the three parts of the loop expression, **count** is used to control the opera-

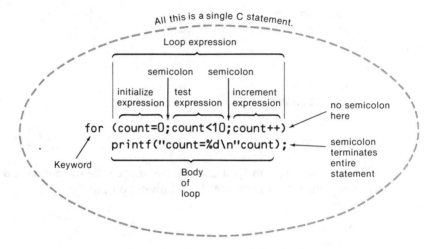

Figure 3-1. Structure of the *for* Loop

tion of the loop. Specifically, it keeps track of how many times we've been through the loop.

Let's look in more detail at the three parts of the loop expression and how they operate on the variable **count**.

### The Initialize Expression

The initialize expression, **count = 0**, initializes the **count** variable. The initialize expression is always executed as soon as the loop is entered. We can start at any number; in this case we initialize **count** to 0. However, loops are often started at 1 or some other number.

### The Test Expression

The second expression, **count < 10**, tests each time through the loop to see if **count** is less than 10. To do this, it makes use of the relational operator for "less than" ( < ). If the test expression is true (**count** *is* less than 10), the loop will be executed. If the expression becomes false (**count** is 10 or more), the loop will be terminated and control will pass to the statements following the loop (in this case, there aren't any, so the entire program terminates).

Here the test expression becomes false when **count** becomes 10, so the program terminates at that point, without executing the body of the loop (the **printf()** statement).

### The Increment Expression

The third expression, **count + +**, increments the variable **count** each time the loop is executed. To do this, it uses the increment operator ( + + ), described in the last chapter.

The loop variable in a **for** loop doesn't have to be increased by 1 each time through the loop. It can also be decreased by 1, as we'll see later on in this chapter, or changed by some other number, using an expression such as:

```
count = count + 3
```

In other words, practically any expression can be used for the increment expression.

### The Body of the for Loop

Following the keyword **for** and the loop expression is the body of the loop: that is, the statement (or statements) that will be executed each time round the loop. In our example, there is only one statement:

```
printf("count=%d\n", count);
```

Note that this statement is terminated with a semicolon, whereas the **for** with the loop expression is not. That's because the *entire combination* of the **for** keyword, the loop expression, and the statement constituting the body of the loop, are considered to be a single C statement.

In a **for** loop, don't place a semicolon between the loop expression and the body of the loop, since the keyword **for** and the loop expression don't constitute a complete C statement.

## Operation of the *for* Loop

Let's follow the operation of the loop, as depicted in Figure 3-2. First the initialization expression is executed, then the test condition is examined. If the test expression is false to begin with, the body of the loop will not be executed at all. If the condition is true, the body of the loop is executed and, following that, the increment expression is executed. This is why the first number printed out by our program is 0 and not 1; printing takes place *before* **count** is incremented by the ( + + ) operator. Finally the loop recycles and the test expression is queried again. This will continue until the test expression becomes false—**count** becomes 10—at which time the loop will end.

We should note here that C permits an unusual degree of flexibility in the writing of the **for** loop. For instance, if separated by commas, more than one expression can be used for the initialize expression and for the increment expression, so that several variables can be initialized or incremented at once. Also, none of the three expressions actually needs to refer to the loop variable; a loop variable isn't even essential. In many cases, the **for** loop is used roughly as we've shown it in the example, but we'll see an instance of mulitiple initialization in the next example.

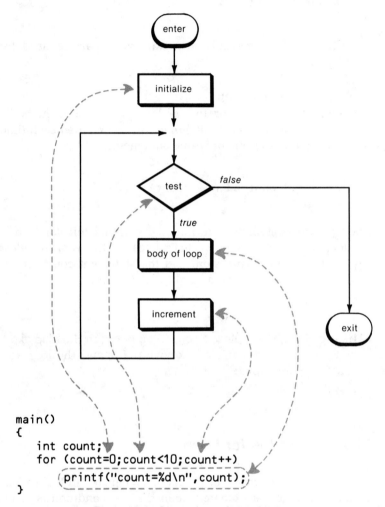

```
main()
{
    int count;
    for (count=0;count<10;count++)
        printf("count=%d\n",count);
}
```

Figure 3-2. Operation of the *for* Loop

## Multiple Statements in Loops

The preceding example used only a single statement in the body of the loop. Two (or more) statements can also be used, as shown in the following program:

```
/* forloop2.c */
/* prints numbers from 0 to 9, keeps running total */
main()
{
    int count, total;
    for (count=0, total=0; count<10; count++)
        {
        total += count;        /* same as total=total+count; */
```

```
        printf("count=%d, total=%d\n", count, total);
        }
    }
```

Type the program in (call it forloop2.c) and compile it. This program not only prints the numbers from 0 to 9, it also prints a running total:

```
C>forloop2
count=0, total=0
count=1, total=1
count=2, total=3
count=3, total=6
count=4, total=10
count=5, total=15
count=6, total=21
count=7, total=28
count=8, total=36
count=9, total=45
```

Truly, a performance to make any power user envious.

The most important new feature of this program is the use of braces ( { and } ) to encapsulate the two statements that form the body of the loop:

```
    {
    total += count;
    printf("count=%d, total=%d\n", count, total);
    }
```

There are two points to remember about this multistatement loop body. The first is that the whole package—the opening brace, the statements, and the closing brace—are treated as a single C statement, with the semicolon understood. This is often called a "compound statement" or a "block." Thus, you don't need to type a semicolon after the last brace. The second point is that each statement within the block.is also a C statement and must be terminated with a semicolon in the usual way. Figure 3-3 shows the operation of the **for** loop with multiple statements in the loop body. This figure is similar to that for the single-statement loop body; we've included it here partly to facilitate comparison with the operation of the **while** loop in the next section.

Another point to note about the program is that we've used the (+ =) arithmetic assignment operator to add the value of **count** to the value of **total** in the expression:

```
    total += count;
```

As we saw in Chapter 2, we could just as well have written:

```
    total = total + count;
```

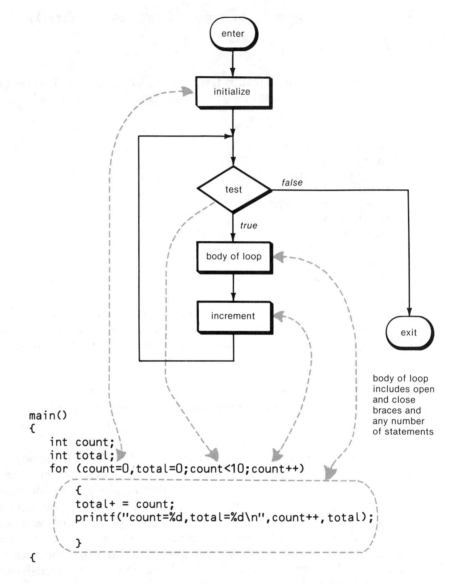

Figure 3-3. Multiple Statements in *for* Loop

## Loop Style Note

Many C programmers, including the venerable Kernighan and Ritchie (referred to in Chapter 1), handle braces in a somewhat different way than we've shown above. They put the opening brace on the same line as the loop expression:

```c
for (count=0, total=0; count<10; count++) {
   total += count;
   printf("count=%d, total=%d\n", count, total);
}
```

This has the advantage of saving a line in the listing. However, the compiler doesn't care which way you choose, and we feel that aligning the matching braces vertically makes it easier to ensure that each opening brace is matched by a closing one and helps to clarify the structure of the program. Both approaches are common. For ease of learning we'll use the one-brace-per-line approach for most of this book, but in the final chapters we'll switch to the more compact format.

## Multiple Initializations in the *for* Loop

Another subtlety we've introduced into the forloop2.c program is that the initialization expression in the **for** loop contains *two* statements, separated by a comma: **count = 0** and **total = 0**. As we mentioned, this is perfectly legal syntax.

```
for (count=0, total=0; count<10; count++)
```

In this particular program we didn't really need to put the initialization of **total** within the loop; we could also have said:

```
total = 0;
for (count=0; count<10; count++)
```

but we wanted to show how two (or more) statements can be used in the initialization expression, and we saved a line of code—a desirable end in the eyes of most C programmers.

As we noted, multiple statements can also be used in this way in the increment expresssion; that is, you can increment two or more variables at the same time. However, only one expression is allowed in the test expression, since a single condition must determine when the loop terminates.

The use of multiple statements in the initialization expression also demonstrates why semicolons are used to separate the three kinds of expressions in the **for** loop. If commas had been used (as commas are used to separate the arguments of a function, for example), they could not also have been used to separate multiple statements in the initialization expression, without confusing the compiler. The comma is sometimes called the "sequential evaluation operator," since it serves to separate a list of similar items that will be evaluated in turn. Items separated by commas are evaluated from left to right.

## An ASCII Table Program

Here's a program that uses a **for** loop to print out a table of ASCII codes. As you learned in Chapter 2, in the IBM PC family each of the numbers from 0 to 255 represents a separate character. From 0 to 31 are control codes (such as the carriage return, tab, and linefeed) and some graphics characters; from 32 to 127 are the usual printing characters, and from 128 to 255 are graphics and foreign language characters.

```
/* asctab.c */
/* prints table of ascii characters */
main()
{
    int n;
    for (n = 1; n < 256; n++)      /* codes from 1 to 255 */
        printf ("%3d=%c\t", n, n); /* print as number and as char */
}
```

A section of the output is shown below:

```
 41=)   42=*  43=+  44=,   45=-   46=.   47=/   48=0  49=1   50=2
 51=3   52=4  53=5  54=6   55=7   56=8   57=9   58=:  59=;   60=<
 61==   62=>  63=?  64=@   65=A   66=B   67=C   68=D  69=E   70=F
 71=G   72=H  73=I  74=J   75=K   76=L   77=M   78=N  79=O   80=P
 81=Q   82=R  83=S  84=T   85=U   86=V   87=W   88=X  89=Y   90=Z
 91=[   92=\  93=]  94=^   95=_   96='   97=a   98=b  99=c  100=d
101=e  102=f 103=g 104=h  105=i  106=j  107=k  108=l 109=m 110=n
111=o  112=p 113=q 114=r  115=s  116=t  117=u  118=v 119=w 120=x
```

This program uses the tab character ( '\t' ) in the **printf()** statement. This causes the next item printed to start eight spaces from the start of the last item. In other words, it divides the screen into columns eight characters wide. On an 80-column screen then, we have room for 10 items. (In the listing above the columns are actually only six spaces wide; we compressed it so the printout would fit on the page.) The **printf()** function also uses a field-width specifier of 3 so that each number is printed in a box three characters wide, even if it has only one or two digits.

### The printf() *Function as a Conversion Device*

The **printf()** statement in our asctab.c program is performing a complex task with a minimum of fuss: printing both the character and its ASCII code. In most languages, this would require a separate conversion function to change the number **n** into the character whose ASCII value is **n.**

In C, we can use the same variable, **n,** for both number and character; only the format specifier changes: %c prints the character, while %d prints the number.

```
printf ("%3d=%c\t", n, n);
```

Format specifiers can interpret the same variable in different ways.

What's actually stored in the computer's memory is an integer, **n,** as specified in the type declaration statement. The %d format specifier prints the decimal representation of **n**, while the %c format specifier prints the character whose ASCII code is **n**.

## Drawing a Line with a Graphics Character

In Chapter 2 we introduced a graphics character representing a rectangle (ASCII code DB hexadecimal). Let's use this character and a **for** loop to draw a line across the screen. Here's the program:

```
/* line.c */
/* draws a solid line using rectangular graphics character */
main()
{
    int cols
    for (cols=1; cols<40; cols++)
        printf("%c", '\xDB');
}
```

Each time through the loop another rectangle is printed, creating a solid line of rectangles. The process is shown in Figure 3-4.

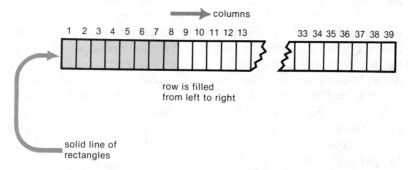

Figure 3-4. Operation of the line.c Program

## Nested *for* Loops

It is possible to nest one **for** loop inside another. To demonstrate this structure, we'll concoct a program that prints out the multiplication table:

```
/* multab.c */
/* generates the multiplication table */
main()
{
    int cols, rows;
    for(rows=1; rows<13; rows++)          /* outer loop */
```

```
        {
        for(cols=1; cols<13; cols++)      /* inner loop */
            printf( "%4d", cols * rows ); /* print product */
        printf("\n");                     /* new line */
        }
    }
```

When you run this program, you'll get the following output:

```
C>multab
   1   2   3   4   5   6   7   8   9  10  11  12
   2   4   6   8  10  12  14  16  18  20  22  24
   3   6   9  12  15  18  21  24  27  30  33  36
   4   8  12  16  20  24  28  32  36  40  44  48
   5  10  15  20  25  30  35  40  45  50  55  60
   6  12  18  24  30  36  42  48  54  60  66  72
   7  14  21  28  35  42  49  56  63  70  77  84
   8  16  24  32  40  48  56  64  72  80  88  96
   9  18  27  36  45  54  63  72  81  90  99 108
  10  20  30  40  50  60  70  80  90 100 110 120
  11  22  33  44  55  66  77  88  99 110 121 132
  12  24  36  48  60  72  84  96 108 120 132 144
```

In this program the inner loop steps through 12 *columns*, from 1 to 12, while the outer loop steps through 12 *rows*. For each row, the inner loop is cycled through once; then a newline is printed in preparation for the next row. Each time through the inner loop—that is, at each intersection of a column and a row—the product of the row number (**rows**) and the column number (**cols**) is printed by the **printf** function. For instance, if the variable **cols** was 8, meaning we're on the eighth column, and **rows** was 4, meaning we're on the fourth row, then the program multiplies 8 by 4 and prints the product at the intersection of this row and column. Since we used the "less than" operator ( < ), the loop variables **cols** and **rows** never reach the limit of 13; the loops both terminate at 12.

To ensure that the columns line up, we use a field-width specifier of 4 in the **printf()** function.

### Indentation and Nesting

As you can see, the body of the outer **for** loop is indented, and the body of the inner **for** loop (in this case a single line) is further indented. These multiple indentations make the program easier to read and understand. Although invisible to the compiler, some form of indentation is employed by almost all C programmers.

The actual multiplication of **cols** times **rows** takes place inside the **printf()** function:

```
    printf( "%4d", cols * rows );
```

We could have used another variable, say **product** (which would need to be declared), and written the inner loop:

```
{
product = rows * cols;
printf ( "%4d", product );
}
```

However, as we've noted, C programmers usually try to telescope statements in order to achieve compactness and eliminate unnecessary variables.

## The fill.c Program

Here's another example of the nested **for** loop construction. This one looks like the multiplication table example, but instead it fills a box-shaped area of the screen with a solid color. It's actually an extension of the line.c program: fill.c repeatedly prints lines of rectangles to create a solid area. Here's the listing:

```
/* fill.c */
/* fills square area on screen */
main()
{
    int cols, rows;
    for (rows=1; rows<=22; rows++)        /* outer loop */
       {
       for (cols=1; cols<=40; cols++)     /* inner loop */
          printf("\xDB");                 /* print rectangle */
       printf("\n");                      /* new line */
       }
}
```

As in the multab.c program, fill.c uses an outer **for** loop to control the rows and an inner **for** loop to control the columns. That is, the inner loop cycles through the columns to write a single row of rectangles, then the outer loop increments to go on to the next row. Figure 3-5 shows what the ouput of the program looks like while the program is in progress.

We've used a new relational operator in this program, the ( < = ) operator, meaning "less than or equal to." This means that the numbers used in the test expressions in the **for** loops, 22 and 40, are actually reached by the variables, as shown in Figure 3-5. In earlier programs the variables stopped one short of these limits, because the "less than" ( < ) operator was used.

Notice also that since '\xDB' is a character, and a character can be part of a string, we've put '\xDB' directly into the **printf()** format string, making it a one-character string. We could have written

```
printf("%c", '\xDB');
```

as we did in the line.c program, but the representation used in fill.c is simpler.

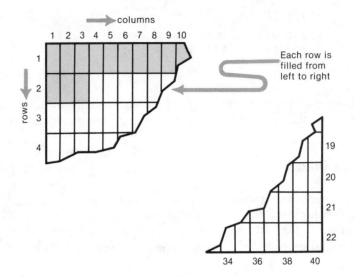

Figure 3-5. Output of the fill.c Program

## The *while* Loop

The second kind of loop structure available in C is the **while** loop. Although at first glance this structure seems to be simpler than the **for** loop, it actually uses the same elements, but they are distributed throughout the program.

Let's try to compare, as directly as possible, the operation of the **for** loop and the **while** loop. The following program uses a **while** loop to reproduce the operation of our earlier forloop2.c program, which printed the numbers from 0 to 9 and gave a running total.

```
/* wloop.c */
/* prints numbers from 0 to 9, keeps running total */
/* uses while loop */
main()
{
    int count = 0;          /* initialize count */
    int total = 0;          /* initialize total */
    while ( count < 10 )    /* loop until count is 10 */
        {
        total += count;     /* same as total = total + count */
        printf("count=%d, total=%d\n", count++, total);
        }
}
```

As before, this program produces the following table:

```
C>wloop2
count=0, total=0
count=1, total=1
```

```
count=2, total=3
count=3, total=6
count=4, total=10
count=5, total=15
count=6, total=21
count=7, total=28
count=8, total=36
count=9, total=45
```

Certainly the expression in parentheses following the keyword **while** is simpler than the three-part expression in the **for** loop. It dispenses with the initialization and increment expressions, retaining only the test expression:

```
count < 10;
```

The resulting structure is shown in Figure 3-6.

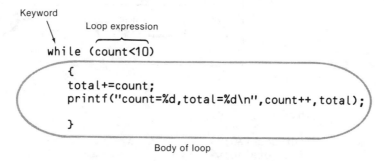

Figure 3-6. Structure of the *while* Loop

If the expressions that initialize and increment the counting variable are not in the **while** loop expression itself, where did they go?

The initialization step is now included in a variable declaration:

```
int count = 0;
```

The incrementing of the count variable can be seen in the **printf()** statement, which includes, instead of the variable **count** you might expect, the expression **count + +** instead. This means that, as soon as **count** is printed, it is incremented.

Notice how easily we were able to increment the variable. In most other languages we would have needed a separate statement:

```
count = count + 1;
```

following the **printf()** statement; in C the expression **count + +** has the same effect.

The operation of the **while** loop is shown in Figure 3-7.

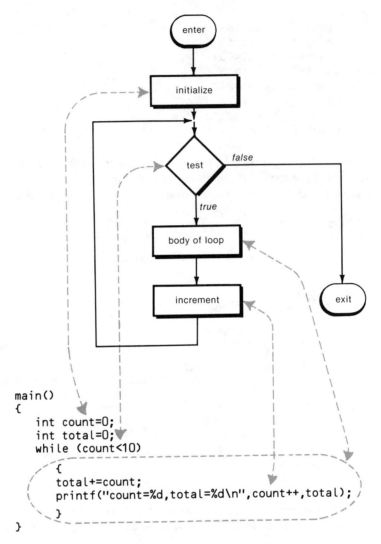

```
main()
{
    int count=0;
    int total=0;
    while (count<10)
    {
    total+=count;
    printf("count=%d,total=%d\n",count++,total);
    }
}
```

Figure 3-7. Operation of the *while* Loop

The loop variable **count** is initialized outside the loop in the declaration **int count = 0**. When the loop is first entered, the condition **count < 10** is tested. If it's false, the loop terminates. If it's true, the body of the loop is executed. The increment expression is buried in the body of the loop. When the **printf()** statement which forms the loop body has finished printing, **count** is incremented by the ( + + ) operator.

## The Unexpected Condition

In situations where the number of iterations in a loop are known in advance, as they are in the wloop.c example, **while** loops are actually less appropriate. In this case the **for** loop is a more natural choice, since we can use its explicit initialize, test, and increment expressions to control the loop. So, when is the **while** loop the appropriate choice?

The **while** loop shines in situations where a loop may be terminated unexpectedly by conditions developing within the loop. As an example, consider the following program:

```
/* charcnt.c */
/* counts characters in a phrase typed in */
main()
{
    int count=0;
    printf("Type in a phrase:\n");
    while ( getche() != '\r' )
        count++;
    printf("\nCharacter count is %d", count);
}
```

This program invites you to type in a phrase. As you enter each character it keeps a count of how many characters you've typed, and when you hit [Return] it prints out the total. Here's how it looks in operation:

```
C>charcnt
Type in a phrase:
cat
Character count is 3

C>charcnt
Type in a phrase:
Knowledge rests not upon truth alone, but also upon error.
Character count is 58
```

(This last phrase is from Carl Jung, and considering that it was written before the invention of computers, it is surprisingly applicable to the art of programming.)

> **While** loops are more appropriate than **for** loops when the condition that terminates the loop occurs unexpectedly.

Why is the **while** loop more appropriate in charcnt.c than a **for** loop? The loop in this program terminates when the character typed at the keyboard is the [Return] character. There's no need for a loop variable, since we don't have to keep track of where we are in the loop, and thus no need for initialize or increment expressions, since there is no loop variable to initialize or increment. Thus the **while** loop, consisting only of the test expression, is the appropriate choice.

Let's look more closely at the loop expression in the **while** loop:

```
( getche() != '\r' )
```

This incorporates the function **getche()**, which, as we saw in Chapter 2, returns the value of a character the instant the character is typed. As you also learned, this function takes on or "returns" the value of the character typed, so the function can be treated like a variable and compared with other variables or constants. In this program we compare it with the constant '\r', the carriage return character that **getch()** will return when the user presses the [Return] key. The evaluation of the loop expression is shown in Figure 3-8.

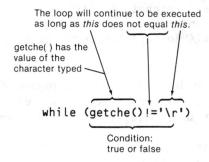

Figure 3-8. A Function Has a Value

Since we use the "not equal" operator ( != ), the **while** loop will continue to be executed as long as it does *not* encounter a '\r'. When it does encounter it, the loop will terminate and the total number of characters typed will be printed out.

### Using Functions as Elements in Expressions

Putting the **getche()** function into the **while** loop expression certainly makes for unusual looking syntax (at least that's how it strikes non-C programmers). Do we really need to do this? Doesn't it complicate things unnecessarily? As Will Rogers said when someone complained of the evils of old age, consider the alternative. We'll rewrite the program to use an explicit variable, **ch**, in the **while** expression, instead of the **getche()** function:

```
/* charcnt2.c */
/* counts characters in a phrase typed in */
main()
{
    int count = -1;
    char ch;

    printf("Type in a phrase:\n");
    ch = 'a';
    while ( ch != '\r' )
        {
```

```
        ch = getche();
        count++;
        }
    printf("\nCharacter count is %d", count);
}
```

Now the **while** loop expression is simplified, but look at the effect of this change on the rest of the program. We now have an extra variable **ch**. We need to initialize **ch** to avoid the possibility (remote though it may be) that it would start out with the value '\r'. We have an extra statement in the body of the **while** loop. And, **count** must be initialized to an odd-looking –1 value because checking to see which character is read now occurs *after* the loop is entered instead of before. Altogether, it appears that including the **getche()** function in the **while** expression is a good idea. It's also a very popular sort of construction in C.

## ASCII Revisited

The expression used in the **while** loop expression in the charcnt.c program was relatively complex, but loop expressions can also be very simple. As an example, consider the following program:

```
/* ascii.c */
/* finds ascii code of a character */
main()
{
    while (1)
    {
        char ch;
        printf("Enter a character: \n");
        ch=getche();
        printf("\nThe code for %c is %d.\n", ch, ch);
    }
}
```

This program asks the user to type a character and then prints out the ASCII code for the character. It will do this over and over. It's sort of a shorthand version of the asctab.c program shown earlier, but it's more useful if you only want to check the ASCII codes for one or two keyboard characters, without looking at the entire table. Here's some sample output:

```
C>ascii
Enter a character:
a
The code for a is 97.
Enter a character:
b
The code for b is 98.
Enter a character:
```

```
A
The code for A is 65.
```

Here the only purpose of the **while** loop is to keep recycling indefinitely, asking the user over and over to enter a character. Since 1 is by definition always true, the **while** expression will never be false.

Are we stuck then in an infinite loop? In MS-DOS (PC-DOS) systems the key combination [Ctrl] [c] will terminate most programs that use keyboard input routines such as **getche()** or screen-printing routines such as **printf()**; this is a commonly used method for returning to the operating system. So terminating the program is an easy matter: hold down [Ctrl] and type [c]. The infinite loop is somewhat less than infinite after all!

Since the **getche()** function is no longer included in the **loop** test expression, it has become part of an assignment statement:

```
ch = getche();
```

(We could also have used the **getche()** expressions in the **printf()** statement, eliminating the **ch** variable altogether, but this would have made for a lengthy program line.)

The **printf()** function, as in the asctab.c program, prints both the character version of **ch**, and the numeric version, using the %c and %d format specifiers. Note that we can print a numerical value of **ch** even though at the start of the program it was declared a variable of type **char**. This demonstrates a useful feature of C; character variables can be interpreted as *either* characters or numerical values (with a range of −128 to 127).

## Nested *while* Loops

Just as **for** loops can be nested, so can **while** loops. The following program shows such nesting:

```
/* guess */
/* lets you guess a letter */
main()
{
    char ch;
    while ( 1 )
        {
        printf("\nType in a letter from 'a' to 'e':\n");
        while ( (ch=getche()) != 'd' )
            {
            printf("\nSorry, %c is incorrect.\n", ch);
            printf("\nTry again.\n");
            }
        printf("\nThat's it!\n");
        }
}
```

This program lets you guess a lowercase letter from 'a' to 'e' and tells you if you're right or wrong. The outer **while** loop keeps cycling until you exit the program by typing [Ctrl] [c]. The inner loop determines whether your guess is correct. If not, it loops again, asking you to make another try. When you do guess correctly (which should take you no more than five tries, if you're on your toes) the inner loop terminates. The correct answer is always 'd' (unless you modify the program).

Here's a sample interaction:

```
Type in a letter from 'a' to 'e':
a
Sorry, a is incorrect.

Try again.
c
Sorry, c is incorrect.

Try again.
d
That's it!
```

As in the nested **for** loop example, each of the loops is indented to help clarify the operation of the program.

## Assignment Expressions as Values

The most radical aspect of the guess.c program is the use in the inner **while** loop test expression of a complete *assignment expression* as a value:

```
while ( (ch=getche()) != 'd' )
```

In the charcnt.c program we saw that a *function* could be used as if it were a variable; here the idea is carried to even greater lengths. How is this loop expression interpreted? First the function **getche()** must return a value. Say it's the character 'a'. This value is then assigned to the character variable **ch**. Finally, the entire assignment expression

```
ch=getche()
```

takes on the value of **ch**, which is 'a'. This value can then be compared with the character 'd' on the right side of the not-equal relational operator ( != ). Figure 3-9 shows this process. The use of assignment expressions as values is a common idiom in C.

### Precedence: Assignment versus Relational Operators

Note that there is an extra set of parentheses around the assignment expression in the test expression of the inner **while** loop discussed above.

```
while ( (ch=getche()) != 'd' )
```

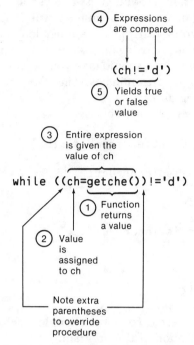

Figure 3-9. An Assignment Expression Has a Value

If the parentheses weren't there, the compiler would interpret the expression like this:

```
while ( ch = (getche() != 'd') )
```

This of course isn't what we want at all, since **ch** will now be set equal to the results of a true/false expression. The reason we need the parentheses is that the precedence of the relational operator ( != ) is greater than that of the assignment operator ( = ). (This is shown in the table of operator precedence in Appendix A.) So, unless parentheses tell the compiler otherwise, the relational operator ( != ) will be evaluated first. By inserting the parentheses we ensure that the expression is evaluated correctly.

## A Mathematical *while* Loop

Before we leave the subject of **while** loops, let's look at one more example. This one calculates the factorial of a number. As you no doubt remember from Mr. Klemmer's high-school math class, the factorial of a number is the number multiplied by all the numbers smaller than itself. Thus the factorial of 4 is 4*3*2*1, or 24.

Here's the listing:

```
/* factor.c */
/* finds factorial of number typed in */
main()
{
    long number, answer;
    while (1)
        {
        printf("\nType number: ");
        scanf("%D", &number);
        answer = 1;
        while ( number > 1 )
            answer = answer * number--;
        printf("Factorial is: %ld\n", answer);
        }
}
```

Here's a sample of interaction with the program:

```
Type number: 3
Factorial is: 6

Type number: 4
Factorial is: 24

Type number: 7
Factorial is: 5040

Type number: 16
Factorial is: 2004189184
```

As in the guess.c program, factor.c uses an outer **while** loop to recycle until the [Ctrl] [c] keys are pressed. The inner loop uses the decrement operator to reduce the variable **number**—which starts out at the value typed in by the user—by 1 each time through the loop. When **number** reaches 1 the loop terminates.

A new wrinkle in this program is the use of long integers. Because factorials grow so rapidly, even an initial value of 8 would have exceeded an integer variable's capacity of 32,767. Long integers provide an improvement in that they can hold numbers up to 2,147,483,647, as you learned in Chapter 1. To use long integers, we have used the variable type **long** in the declaration statement, used the uppercase 'D' in the format specifier in the **scanf()** function, and modified the format specifier to "ld" in the **printf()** function.

## Using *while* Loops and *for* Loops

Now that we know how to write two different kinds of loops, how do we decide which one to use in a given situation?

Generally speaking, if at the time you enter the loop you already know how many times you want to execute it, you're probably better off with the **for** loop. If, on the other hand, the conditions for terminating the loop are imposed by the outside world, such as the user typing a certain character, then you're better off with the **while** loop.

We'll use numerous examples of both kinds of loops throughout this book.

## The *do while* Loop

The last of the three loops in C is the **do while** loop. This loop is very similar to the **while** loop—the difference is that in the **do** loop the test condition is evaluated *after* the loop is executed, rather than before.

Here's our familiar program that prints the numbers from 0 to 9 and a running total, revised to use a **do** loop:

```
/* doloop.c */
/* prints numbers from 0 to 9, keeps running total */
/* uses do loop */
main()
{
    int count = 0;
    int total = 0;
    do
        {
        total += count;
        printf("count=%d, total=%d\n", count++, total);
        }
    while ( count < 10 );
}
```

The output is the same as in previous versions of the program:

```
C>doloop
count=0, total=0
count=1, total=1
count=2, total=3
count=3, total=6
count=4, total=10
count=5, total=15
count=6, total=21
count=7, total=28
count=8, total=36
count=9, total=45
```

The **do** loop, unlike the other loops we've examined, has *two* keywords: **do** and **while**. The **do** keyword marks the beginning of the loop; it has no other function. The **while** keyword marks the end of the loop and contains the loop expression, as shown in Figure 3-10.

An important detail to note is that this loop, unlike the **for** and **while**

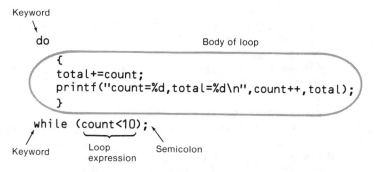

Figure 3-10. Structure of the **do** Loop

loops, is terminated with a semicolon; that is, the test condition in the parentheses following **while** ends with a semicolon.

The operation of the **do** loop is sort of an upside-down version of the **while** loop. The body of the loop is first executed, then the test condition is checked. If true, the loop is repeated; if the test condition is false the loop terminates, as can be seen in Figure 3-11. The important point to notice is that the body of the loop will always be executed at least once, since the test condition is not checked until the end of the loop.

Pascal programmers might want to note that the **do** loop is similar to the "repeat until" loop in Pascal, except that it continues to loop *while* the test condition is true, while "repeat until" loops *until* the test condition is true.

When would you use a **do loop**? Any time you want to be sure the loop body is executed at least once. This situation is less common than that where the loop might not be executed at all, so the **do** loop is used less often than the **while** loop. When in doubt, use the **while** loop; the operation of the program is clearer if the test condition is set forth at the beginning of the loop. If you find yourself writing a lot of **do** loops, you might want to try restructuring your program to turn some of them into **while**s.

## Revised Guessing Game

Here's an example of a situation that calls for a **do** loop. Suppose we want to play our guess-the-letter game, but now, instead of assuming you want to continue playing until you press the [Ctrl] [c] key combination, we want to know if you want to play again after each game. To achieve this effect we can rewrite the program as follows:

```
/* guessdo.c */
/* lets you guess a letter */
/* uses do loop to ask if new game wanted */
main()
{
    char ch;
    do
```

```
       {
   printf("\n\nType in a digit from 'a' to 'e':\n");
   while ( (ch=getche()) != 'c' )
       {
       printf("\nSorry, %c is incorrect.\n", ch);
       printf("Try again.\n");
       }
   printf("\nThat's it!\n");
   printf("\nPlay again? (Type 'y' or 'n'): ");
       }
   while ( getche() == 'y');
   printf("\nThanks for playing!");
}
```

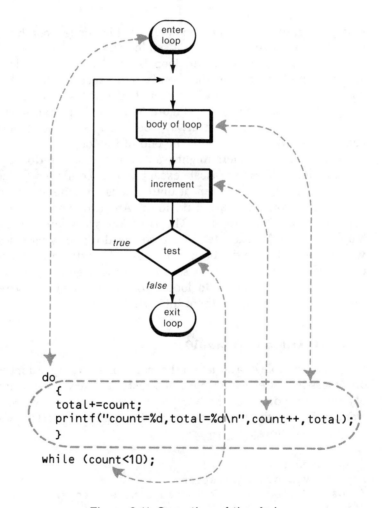

Figure 3-11. Operation of the *do* Loop

Here's a sample session with the guessdo.c program:

```
Type in a digit from 'a' to 'e':
b
Sorry, b is incorrect.
Try again.
c
That's it!

Play again? (Type 'y' or 'n'): y

Type in a digit from 'a' to 'e':
d
Sorry, d is incorrect.
Try again.
c
That's it!

Play again? (Type 'y' or 'n'): n
Thanks for playing!
```

Notice that the body of the **do** loop will always be executed once. If you called up the program in the first place, we can assume that you want at least one game. After the first game, we ask if you want to continue. It is this situation, in which something must be done once before we ask if it should be done again, that is properly implemented with a **do** loop.

> The **do** loop is useful when the body of a loop will always be executed at least once.

## The *break* and *continue* Statements

To round out our discussion of loops we should mention that C has two statements which can be used with any of the loops described above: **break** and **continue**.

The **break** statement bails you out of a loop as soon as it's executed. It's often used when an unexpected condition occurs; one that the loop test condition is not looking for. We'll see examples of this statement later.

The **continue** statement is inserted in the body of the loop, and, when executed, takes you back to the beginning of the loop, bypassing any statements not yet executed. **Continue** is a bit suspect in that it can make a program difficult to read and debug by confusing the normal flow of operations in the loop, so it is avoided by C programmers whenever possible.

## Summary

This chapter has focused on the three C loops: **for**, **while**, and **do while**. You've learned how to create these and use them in a variety of situations. You've also learned how to nest one loop inside another, and how to use variables, functions, and assignment statements with relational operators in the loop expression. In short, you're ready to do things again and again.

## Questions

1. The three parts of the loop expression in a **for** loop are

   the i_____ expression

   the t_____ expression

   the i_____ expression.

2. A single-statement **for** loop is terminated with a

   a. right bracket

   b. right brace

   c. comma

   d. semicolon

3. A _____ is used to separate the three parts of the loop expression in a **for** loop.

4. A multiple-statement **while** loop is terminated with a

   a. right bracket

   b. right brace

   c. comma

   d. semicolon

5. Multiple increment expressions in a **for** loop expression are separated by _____.

6. A **while** loop is more appropriate than a **for** loop when:

   a. the terminating condition occurs unexpectedly

   b. the body of the loop will be executed at least once

   c. the program will be executed at least once

   d. the number of times the loop will be executed is known before the loop is executed

7. True or false: the initialize expression and increment expression are contained in the loop expression in a **while** loop.

8. An expression contains relational operators, assignment operators, and

arithmetic operators. In the absence of parentheses, they will be evaluated in the following order:

a. assignment, relational, arithmetic

b. arithmetic, relational, assignment

c. relational, arithmetic, assignment

d. assignment, arithmetic, relational

9. The more deeply a loop is nested, the more _____ it should be indented.

10. An assignment statement can itself have a _____, just like a variable.

11. The advantage of putting complete assignment statements inside loop expressions is:

a. to avoid awkward program constructions

b. to simplify the flow of control in the program

c. to reduce the number of program statements

d. to clarify the operation of the program

12. True or false: in almost every case where a variable can be used, an increment or decrement operator can be added to the variable.

13. A **do while** loop is useful when:

a. the body of the loop will never be executed

b. the body of the loop will be executed at least once

c. the body of the loop may never be executed

d. the body of the executed loop was found by the butler

14. The **break** statement is used to exit from which part of a loop?

a. beginning

b. middle

c. end

d. none of the above

15. True or false: a **continue** statement causes an exit from a loop.

## Exercises

1. Write a program that prints the squares of all the numbers from 1 to 20. (Perhaps you can adapt a similar exercise from the last chapter.)

2. Rewrite the charcnt.c program so that it counts characters until a period ( . ) is typed, rather than [Return].

3. Write a program that repeatedly calculates how many characters separate two letters typed in by the user, until terminated with [Ctrl] [c]. For instance there are *two* characters ( 'b' and 'c' ) between 'a' and 'd'. Take advantage of the fact that the arithmetic operators work on character variables just as well as they do on numbers.

# 4

# Decisions

- The **if** statement
- The **if-else** statement
- The **else-if** construct
- The **switch** statement
- The conditional operator

# 4

We all need to be able to alter our actions in the face of changing circumstances. If the forecast is for rain, then I'll take my raincoat. If the freeway is under construction, then I'll take the back road. If, when I propose, she says yes, I'll buy her a ring; if she says no, I'll start dating Gladys.

Computer languages, too, must be able to perform different sets of actions depending on the circumstances. C has three major decision-making structures: the **if** statement, the **if-else** statement, and the **switch** statement. A fourth, somewhat less important structure, is the **conditional operator**. In this chapter we'll explore these four ways a C program can react to changing circumstances.

## The *if* Statement

Like most languages, C uses the keyword **if** to introduce the basic decision-making statement. Here's a simple example:

```
/* testif.c */
/* demonstrates if statement */
main()
{
    char ch;
    ch = getche();
    if ( ch == 'y' )
        printf("\nYou typed y.");
}
```

You can no doubt guess what will happen when this program is executed:

```
C>testif
y
You typed y.
```

```
C>testif
n
C>
```

If you type 'y', the program will print "You typed y." If you type some other character, such as 'n', the program doesn't do anything.

Figure 4-1 shows the structure of the **if** statement. This structure is surprisingly similar to that of the **while** statement described in Chapter 3. The keyword is followed by parentheses, which contain a conditional expression using a relational operator. Following this, there is the body of the statement, consisting of either a single statement terminated by a semicolon, or (as we'll see shortly) multiple statements enclosed by braces. In fact, the only difference between the structure of the **if** statement and that of the **while** is that the words "if" and "while" are different.

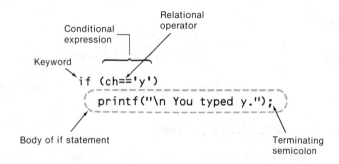

Figure 4-1. Structure of the *if* Statement

Notice too that there is no "then" keyword following the conditional expression, as there is in Pascal and usually is in BASIC.

There is no "then" keyword in C.

The **if** statement is similar to the **while** statement in operation as well as format. In both cases the statements making up the body of the statement will not be executed at all if the condition is false. However, in the **while** statement, if the condition is true, the statement (or statements) in the body of the loop will be executed over and over until the condition becomes false; whereas in the **if** statement they will be executed only once. Figure 4-2 shows the operation of the **if** statement.

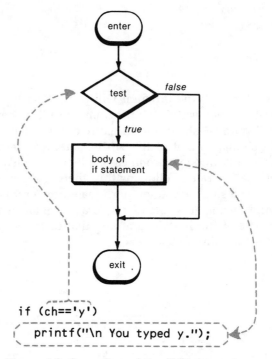

Figure 4-2. Operation of the *if* Statement

## A Word-Counting Program

In the last chapter we included a program, charcnt.c, which counted the number
of characters in a phrase typed by the user. Here's a slightly more complex
program that counts not only the number of characters, but the number of
words as well:

```
/* wordcnt.c */
/* counts characters and words in a phrase typed in */
main()
{
    int charcnt=0;
    int wordcnt=0;
    char ch;
    printf("Type in a phrase:\n");
    while ( (ch=getche()) != '\r' ) /* read character and */
        {                           /* quit loop on [Return] */
        charcnt++;                  /* count character */
        if ( ch == ' ' )            /* space? */
            wordcnt++;              /* then count word */
        }
    printf("\nCharacter count is %d", charcnt);
    printf("\nWord count is %d", wordcnt+1);
}
```

This program figures how many words there are by counting the number of spaces. (It could be fooled by multiple spaces between words, but we'll ignore that possibility.) Here's some sample interaction with the program:

```
C>wordcnt
Type in a phrase:
cat and dog
Character count is 11
Word count is 3

C>wordcnt
Type in a phrase:
This sentence actually uses nine words and sixty-five characters.
Character count is 65
Word count is 9
```

A tip of the hat to Douglas Hofstadter and his book *Metamagical Themas* (Basic Books, 1985) for the second phrase, which is the sort of example that is hard to type correctly the first time.

This program is similar to the charcnt.c program. The major addition is the **if** statement:

```
if ( ch == ' ' )
    wordcnt++;
```

This statement causes the variable **wordcnt** to be incremented every time a space is detected in the input stream. There will always be one more word than there are spaces between them (assuming no multiple spaces), so we add 1 to the variable **wordcnt** before printing it out. (We could also have used + +**wordcnt**).

## Multiple Statements with *if*

As in the case of the various loop statements, the body of the **if** statement may consist of either a single statement terminated by a semicolon (as shown in the example above) or by a number of statements enclosed in braces. Here's an example of such a compound statement:

```
/* testif2.c */
/* demonstrates multiple statements following if */
main()
{
    char ch;
    ch = getche();
    if ( ch == 'y' )
        {
        printf("\nYou typed y.");
        printf("\nNot some other letter.");
        }
}
```

In both testif.c programs we could have embedded the **getche()** function in the **if** expression, as we did in similar situations with the **while** loop in Chapter 3:

```
if ( getche() == 'y' )
```

This is more C-like, but we thought using it would make what the **if** statement was doing a bit less clear. However, in this next example, which is a program that reads two characters from the keyboard, we'll use this more compact construction.

## Nested *if* Statements

Like the loop statements of the last chapter, **if** statements can be nested. Here's a simple example:

```
/* nestif.c */
/* demonstrates nested if statements */
main()
{
    if ( getche() == 'n' )
        if ( getche() == 'o' )
            printf("\nYou typed no.");
}
```

Nesting here means that one **if** statement is part of the body of another if statement. In the example above, the inner **if** statement will not be reached unless the outer one is true, and the **printf()** statement will not be executed unless both **if** statements are true, as the following interaction with the program shows:

```
C>nestif
x                  ← a non 'n' to start with terminates the program
C>nestif
nx                 ← a non 'o' as the second letter does likewise
C>nestif
no                 ← only 'n' followed by 'o' gets to the printf()
You typed no.
C>
```

The operation of nested **if** statements is shown in Figure 4-3.

## The *if-else* Statement

The **if** statement by itself will execute a single statement, or a group of statements, when the test expression is true. It does nothing when it is false. Can we execute a group of statements if and only if the test expression is *not* true? Of

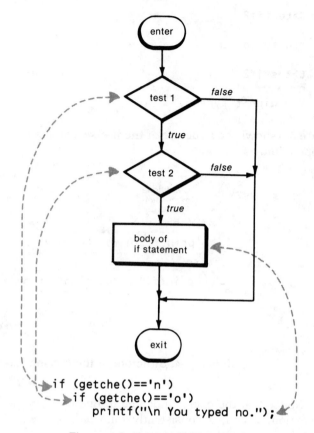

Figure 4-3. Nested *if* Statements

course. This is the purpose of the **else** statement, which is demonstrated in the following example:

```
/* testelse.c */
/* demonstrates if-else statement */
main()
{
   char ch;
   ch = getche();
   if ( ch == 'y' )
      printf("\nYou typed y.");
   else
      printf("\nYou didn't type y.");
}
```

Typing 'y' elicits one response, while typing *anything else* elicits a different response.

```
C>testif2
y
You typed y.

C>testif2
n
You didn't type y.
```

Figure 4-4 shows the structure of the **if-else** statement and Figure 4-5 flowcharts its operation.

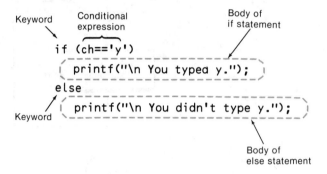

Figure 4-4. Structure of the *if-else* Statement

Notice that the **else** is indented to line up with the **if**. This is a formatting convention, which, if consistently followed, will enable you to better understand the operation of your program.

> For clarity, each **else** should be indented the same amount as its matching **if**.

## Character Graphics and the Checkerboard

As an example of the **if-else** statement at work, consider the following program, which prints a checkerboard on the monochrome screen.

```
/* checker.c */
/* draws a checkerboard on the screen */
main()
{
    int x, y;
    for (y=1; y<9; y++)              /* stepping down */
        {
        for (x=1; x<9; x++)          /* stepping across */
            if ( (x+y) % 2 == 0 )    /* even numbered square? */
                printf("\xDB\xDB");  /* print filled square */
```

```
    else
        printf("  ");          /* print blank square */
    printf("\n");              /* new line */
    }

}
```

Try out the program so you can see what it does. Figure 4-6 shows roughly what you'll see.

This program is similar to those in Chapter 3 that drew a line and a rectangle, in that it uses the graphics character '\xDB' and nested loops to scan part of the screen. Here, however, the **if-else** construction gives the program the power to alter its operation, depending on which part of the screen it's about to write on.

How does this program work? The outer **for** loop (the variable **y**) moves down the screen one row at a time. That is, **y** marks what row we're on, starting at **y** = 1 for the top row, and moving down to **y** = 8. The inner loop (the variable **x**) moves across the screen one column at a time. That is, **x** marks what column we're on, starting at **x** = 1 for the left-most column and moving across until **x** = 8.

Actually, each of the columns pointed to by **x** is two characters wide. This glitch in the program is necessary because the characters on the IBM screen are

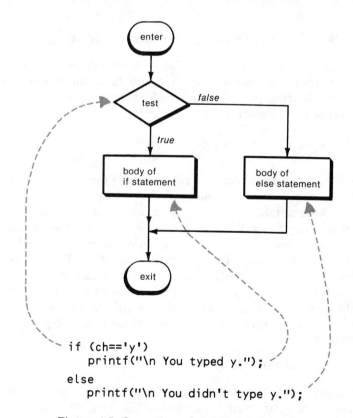

Figure 4-5. Operation of the *if-else* Statement

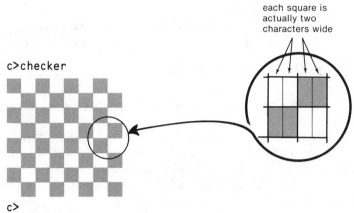

each square is
actually two
characters wide

c>checker

c>

Figure 4-6. Output of the Checker Program

about twice as high as they are wide, so to create a correctly proportioned checkerboard each square must consist of two characters side-by-side: either two spaces or two solid rectangles. The purpose of the two **printf()** functions is just this: one prints two spaces, the other prints two solid rectangles using the '\xDB' character.

## Getting Even with the Remainder Operator

How does the program decide when to print a square and when not to? In effect, the program numbers the squares and then colors only the even-numbered squares, leaving the odd-numbered squares blank. It determines whether a square is odd or even in the statement:

```
if ( (x+y) % 2 == 0 )
```

Each square is numbered, as shown in Figure 4-7. The number is obtained by adding the **x** and **y** coordinates of the square: **x+y**.

These numbers are not unique (more than one square has the same number) but they do exhibit the desired alternation between odd and even.

How then does the statement shown above reveal when a number is odd and when it is even? The remainder operator ( % ), which we mentioned in Chapter 1, is used for this purpose. With a divisor of two, the remainder will be 0 if the dividend is even, and 1 if the dividend is odd. The **if-else** statement can then determine whether to print two colored rectangles or two spaces for a given square (that is, for a particular value of **x** and **y**).

## Drawing Lines

As another example of character graphics and the **if-else** statement, let's look at a pair of programs that draw lines on the monochrome screen. Actually, "line" may be too strong a word; it's really more of a diagonal "staircase" pattern.

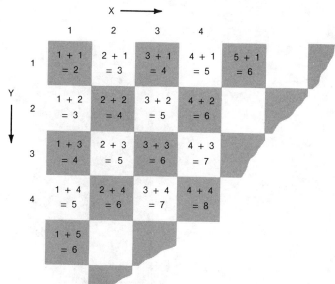

Figure 4-7. Numbering Squares on the Checkerboard

Here's the first program:

```
/* lines.c */
/* prints diagonal lines on screen */
main()
{
    int x, y;
    for (y=1; y<24; y++)          /* step down the screen */
        {
        for (x=1; x<24; x++)      /* step across the screen */
            if ( x == y )         /* are we on diagonal? */
                printf("\xDB");   /* yes, draw dark rectangle */
            else
                printf("\xB0");   /* no, draw light rectangle */
        printf("\n");
        }
}
```

This program is similar to the checkerboard program, except that instead of printing on even-numbered squares, it prints wherever the **x** coordinate and the **y** coordinate are equal. This will create a diagonal line extending from the upper left corner of the screen, where **x** = 1 and **y** = 1, down to the bottom of the screen, where **x** = 23 and **y** = 23.

Where the line is *not* drawn, the background is filled in with a light gray. For this purpose the program uses another graphics character, '\B0'. This is the same size as the solid rectangle created by '\DB', but consists of a pattern of tiny dots, creating a gray effect. Part of the output of the program is shown in Figure 4-8.

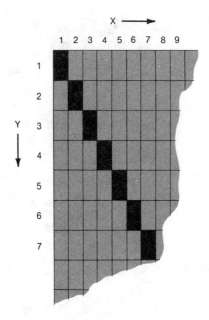

Figure 4-8. Output of the lines.c Program

In this program we have not attempted to compensate for the aspect ratio of the characters on the screen as we did in the checkerboard program. As a consequence, each of the rectangles making up the line is twice as high as it is wide, and the line, which should appear to be at a 45-degree angle, actually slopes downward more steeply than that.

## Nested *if-else* Statements

It is perfectly possible to nest an entire **if-else** construct within either the body of an **if** statement or the body of an **else** statement. The latter construction, shown in the following example, is quite common.

```
/* lines2.c */
/* prints two diagonal lines on screen */
main()
{
    int x, y;
    for (y=1; y<24; y++)            /* step down the screen */
        {
        for (x=1; x<24; x++)        /* step across the screen */
            if ( x == y )           /* NW-SE diagonal? */
                printf("\xDB");     /* print solid color */
```

```
      else
         if ( x == 24 - y )        /* SW-NE diagonal? */
             printf("\xDB");       /* print solid color */
         else
             printf("\xB0");       /* print gray */
      printf("\n");                /* next line */
      }
   }
```

This program is similar to the last one, except that it draws two lines on the screen, as shown in Figure 4-9. The first line is the same as in the last program. The second line goes in the opposite direction, from upper right to lower left. Thus the two lines create a dark X shape in the middle of a gray rectangle.

Note how the second **if-else** construction, which draws the second line, is nested inside the first **else** statement. If the test expression in the first **if** statement is false, then the test expression in the second **if** statement is checked. If it is false as well, the final **else** statement is executed. The process is shown in Figure 4-10.

You can see in the listing how each time a structure is nested in another structure, it is also indented for clarity. This is similar to the way nested loops are indented.

There are several alternatives to this nested **if-else** structure. One involves a format change, one involves a new C statement, **switch**; and the third involves *logical operators*. We'll look at this last alternative in a moment. First, however, let's examine a possible pitfall in the use of nested **if-else** statements.

## Which *if* Gets the *else*?

Consider the following program, which looks as if it would respond with an appropriate comment when the user types in the temperature (in degrees Fahrenheit).

```
/* temper.c */
/* makes remark about temperature */
main()
{
   int temp;
   printf("Please type in the temperature: ");
   scanf("%d", &temp);
   if ( temp < 80 )
      if ( temp > 60 )
         printf("Nice day!");
   else
      printf("Sure is hot!");
}
```

Suppose **temp** is 32. What will be printed when this program is executed? Would you guess nothing at all? That seems reasonable: the first **if** condition

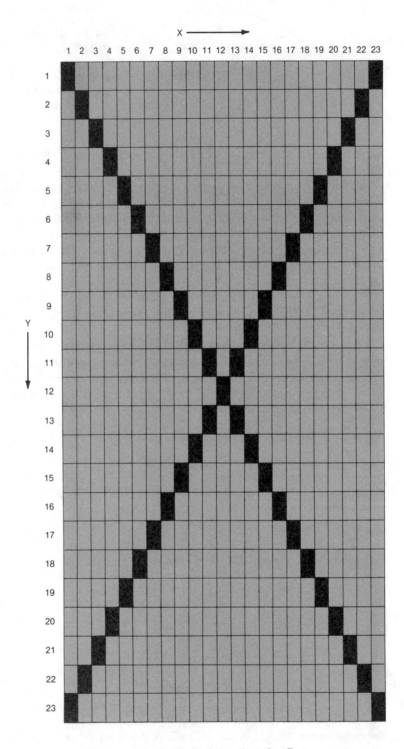

Figure 4-9. Output of the lines2.c Program

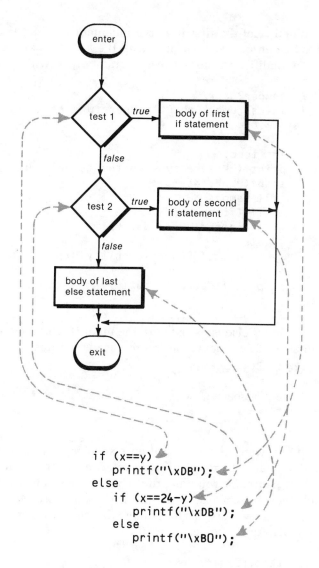

```
if (x==y)
    printf("\xDB");
else
    if (x==24-y)
        printf("\xDB");
    else
        printf("\xB0");
```

Figure 4-10. Nested *if-else* Statements

( temp < 80 ) will be true, so the second **if** condition ( temp > 60 ) will be evaluated. It will be false, so it looks as if the program will exit from the entire nested **if-else** construct.

However, we have attempted to mislead you by altering the indentation. You may have been fooled, but the compiler won't be. Here's what happens:

```
Please type in the temperature: 32
Sure is hot!
```

The problem is that the **else** is actually associated with the **if** immediately preceding it, not the first **if** as the indentation would lead you to believe. The rule is that an **else** is associated with the last **if** that doesn't have its own **else**. Here's a modified version of the program which will operate correctly:

```
/* temper2.c */
/* makes remark about temperature */
main()
{
    int temp;
    printf("Please type in the temperature: ");
    scanf("%d", &temp);
    if ( temp < 80 )
        if ( temp > 60 )
            printf("Nice day!");
        else
            printf("Sure is chilly!");
    else
        printf("Sure is hot!");
}
```

Here the inner **else** is paired with the inner **if**, and the outer **else** is paired with the outer **if**. The indentation in this case is not misleading.

An **else** is associated with the last **if** that doesn't have its own **else**.

If you want to ensure that an **else** goes with an earlier **if** than the one it would ordinarily be matched with, you can use braces to surround the intervening **if** structure. Surrounding the **if** with braces makes it invisible to the **else**, which then matches up with the earliest nonbraced **if**. We've modified the example to show how this looks (note that this program doesn't print anything if the temperature is colder than 60).

```
/* temper3.c */
/* makes remark about temperature */
main()
{
    int temp;
    printf("Please type in the temperature: ");
    scanf("%d", &temp);
    if ( temp < 80 )
        {                             /* these braces make */
        if ( temp > 60 )              /* this "if" */
            printf("Nice day!");      /* invisible */
        }                             /* to */
    else                              /* this "else" */
        printf("Sure is hot!");
}
```

## Logical Operators

We can simplify the lines2.c program from earlier in this chapter by using an operator we have not yet encountered: the *logical operator*. Logical operators are a powerful way to condense and clarify complicated **if-else** structures (and other constructions as well). Let's see what effect a logical operator, in this case the OR operator, represented by two vertical bars ( ¦¦ ), will have on the program. Then we'll explore logical operators in general.

```
/* lines3.c */
/* prints two diagonal lines on screen */
main()
{
    int x, y;
    for (y=1; y<24; y++)
       {
       for (x=1; x<24; x++)
          if ( x==y || x==24-y )   /* if either condition */
              printf("\xDB");       /* is true, print solid box */
          else                      /* otherwise */
              printf("\xB0");       /* print gray box */
       printf("\n");
       }
}
```

This program yields the same output as the previous example—a pair of crossed diagonal lines, but does so in a more elegant way. The logical OR operator ( ¦¦ ) means if *either* the expression on the right side of the operator (x==24-y), *or* the expression on the left (x==y) is true, then the entire expression ( x==y ¦¦ x==24-y ) is true.

Note that the logical operator ( ¦¦ ) performs an *inclusive* OR. That is, if either the expression on one side of the operator, or the expression on the other, or *both* expressions, are true, then the entire expression is true. (An *exclusive* OR, by contrast, would provide a *false* result if the expressions on both sides were true; C does not have an exclusive OR operator.)

There are three logical (sometimes called "Boolean") operators in C:

¦¦    logical OR

&&    logical AND

!    logical NOT

Here's a program that uses the logical AND operator ( && ):

```
/* digitcnt.c */
/* counts characters and numerical digits in a phrase */
main()
{
    int charcnt=0;
```

```
int digitcnt=0;
char ch;
printf("Type in a phrase:\n");
while ( (ch=getche()) != '\r' )     /* until [return] typed */
   {
   charcnt++;                       /* count character */
   if ( ch > 47 && ch < 58 )        /* if ch is digit */
      digitcnt++;                   /* count digit */
   }
printf("\nCharacter count is %d", charcnt);
printf("\nDigit count is %d", digitcnt);
}
```

This program is a modification of our earlier charcnt.c and wordcnt.c programs. In addition to counting the characters in a phrase, it also counts any of the numeric digits 0 through 9 which are part of the phrase. Here's an example:

```
C>digitcnt
Type in a phrase:
He packed 4 socks, 12 shirts, and 1,000 hopes for the future.
Character count is 61
Digit count is 7
```

The key to this program is the logical AND operator ( && ). This operator says: if *both* the expression on the left (ch > 47) and the expression on the right (ch < 58) are true, then the entire expression ( ch > 47 && ch < 58 ) is true. This will only be true if **ch** is between 48 and 57; these are the ASCII codes for the digits from 0 to 9.

There are several things to note about these logical operators. Most obviously, they are composed of double symbols: ( ¦¦ ) and ( && ). Don't use the single symbols: ( ¦ ) and ( & ). These single symbols also have a meaning (they are bitwise operators, which we'll examine later), but it isn't the meaning we want at the moment.

Perhaps it is not so obvious, though, that the logical operators have a lower precedence than the relational operators, such as ( == ). It's for this reason that we don't need to use parentheses around the relational expressions x == y, ch > 47, and so on. The relational operators are evaluated first, then the logical operators. (We'll summarize operator precedence in a moment.)

Logical operators have lower precedence than relational operators.

Although we don't make use of the fact here, you should know that logical operators are always evaluated from left to right. Thus, if you have a condition such as:

```
if ( a<b && b<c )
```

you know that (a < b) will be evaluated first. Also, in this case, C is smart enough to know that if the condition to the left of the && is false, then there's no point in evaluating the rest of the expression, since the result will be false anyway.

The third logical operator is the NOT operator, represented by the exclamation point ( ! ), and sometimes called the "bang" operator. This operator reverses the logical value of the expression it operates on; it makes a true expression false and a false expression true.

The NOT operator is a unary operator: that is, it takes only one operand. In this way it's similar to the negative sign in arithmetic: the ( – ) in –5 also takes only one operand.

Here's an example of the NOT operator applied to a relational expression.

```
!(x < 5)
```

This means "not x less than five." In other words, if **x** is less than 5, the expression will be false, since (x < 5) is true. We could express the same condition as (x > = 5).

The NOT operator is often used to reverse the logical value of a single variable, as in the expression

```
if( !flag )
```

This is more concise than the equivalent

```
if( flag==0 )
```

### Operator Precedence, Revisited

Since we've now added the logical operators to the list of operators we know how to use, it is probably time to review all of these operators and their precedence. Table 4-1 summarizes the operators we've seen so far. The higher an operator is in the table, the higher its precedence. (A more complete precedence table can be found in Appendix A.)

### Table 4-1. Operator Order of Precedence

| Operators | Type |
|---|---|
| ! – | unary: logical NOT, arithmetic minus |
| * / % | arithmetic (multiplicative) |
| + – | arithmetic (additive) |
| < > < = > = | relational (inequality) |
| == != | relational (equality) |
| && ¦¦ | logical AND and OR |
| = + = – = * = / = % = | assignment |

Unary operators—those which act on only one value—have the highest priority. Then come arithmetic operators; here multiplication and division have higher precedence than addition and subtraction. Similarly, those relational operators that test for inequality have a higher precedence than those that test for equality. Next come the logical operators and finally the assignment operators. As you know, parentheses can be used to override any of these precedence relations.

## The *else-if* Construct

We've seen how **if-else** statements can be nested. Let's look at a more complex example of this arrangement:

```
/* calc.c */
/* four-function calculator */
main()
{
    float num1, num2;
    char op;
    while (1)
        {
        printf("Type number, operator, number\n");
        scanf("%f %c %f", &num1, &op, &num2);
        if ( op == '+')
            printf(" = %f", num1 + num2);
        else
            if (op == '-')
                printf(" = %f", num1 - num2);
            else
                if (op == '*')
                    printf(" = %f", num1 * num2);
                else
                    if (op == '/')
                        printf(" = %f", num1 / num2);
        printf("\n\n");
        }
}
```

This program gives your computer, for which you spent thousands of dollars, all the raw power of a four-function pocket calculator. You first type a number, then an operator—which can be any of the arithmetic operators ( + ), ( – ), ( * ), or ( / )—and finally a second number. The program then prints out the answer.

Here we've used **scanf()** to read in the first number, the operator, and the second number in a single statement. As we discussed in Chapter 1, the white spaces between the variables in the format string in the **scanf()** statement permit you to separate the variables you type in with any sort of whitespace characters: spaces, tabs, or newlines. Actually, it's not even necessary to type any whitespace character in this example; **scanf()** will know we've finished typing the first number when it sees a non-numeric character, and it will then wait for the second number. Here are examples of different approaches used with the calc.c program:

```
C>calc.c
Type number, operator, number
3 + 3                                    ← separated by spaces
 = 6.000000
Type number, operator, number
1
/                                        ← separated by newlines
3
 = 0.333333
Type number, operator, number
1000*1000                                ← no separation
 = 1000000.000000
Type number, operator, number
1000000/3
 = 333333.333333
```

As in previous examples, we escape from the program by typing [Ctrl] [c].

Structurally, the important point to notice about this program is how the **if-else** constructs are nested. Since there are so many, the nesting and the resulting indentation gets quite deep, making the program difficult to read. There's another way to write, and think about, this situation. This involves the creation of a sort of imaginary construct called "else-if." We reformat the program, but not in a way the compiler will notice:

```
/* calc2.c */
/* four-function calculator */
main()
{
    float num1, num2;
    char op;
    while (1)
        {
        printf("Type number, operator, number\n");
        scanf("%f %c %f", &num1, &op, &num2);
        if ( op == '+')
            printf(" = %f", num1 + num2);
        else if (op == '-')
            printf(" = %f", num1 - num2);
        else if (op == '*')
            printf(" = %f", num1 * num2);
        else if (op == '/')
            printf(" = %f", num1 / num2);
        printf("\n\n");
        }
}
```

This operates exactly as before, but we've rearranged the whitespace to make the program easier to read. By simply deleting spaces and the newline, each **if** is moved up next to the preceding **else**, thus making a new construction: **else-if**. We think of **else-if** as meaning, "if the test expression that follows is true, execute the statement in the body of the **else-if** (in this case a **printf()** statement) and go to the end of the entire **else-if** chain; otherwise, go to the next **else-if** statement in the chain." Figure 4-11 shows this process in a flowchart.

> The **else-if** construction is a reformatting of nested **if-else** statements.

## The *break* Statement

In the next section we'll look at the **switch** statement, which provides an alternative to the **else-if** construct. However, the **switch** statement relies on another statement, **break**. So we'll digress briefly to see how **break** is used to escape from a loop; then we'll go on to explore the role it plays in the **switch** statement.

We'll demonstrate **break** with a guessing game program. In this game the user picks a number between 1 and 99 and the program tries to guess what it is. The user replies to the computer's guesses by saying whether the guess is higher or lower than the number the computer is thinking of. Here's the listing:

```
/* numguess.c */
/* program guesses number user is thinking of */
main()
{
    float guess, incr;
    char ch;
    printf("Think of a number between 1 and 99, and\n");
    printf("I'll guess what it is. Type 'e' for equals,\n");
    printf("'g' for greater than, and 'l' for less than.\n");
    incr = guess = 50;              /* two assignments at once */
    while ( incr > 1.0 )            /* while not close enough */
        {
        printf("\nIs your number greater or less than %.0f?\n",
                                                        guess);
        incr = incr / 2;
        if ( (ch=getche()) == 'e' )  /* if guessed it already */
            break;                   /* escape from loop */
        else if (ch == 'g')          /* if guess too low, */
            guess = guess + incr;    /*    try higher */
        else                         /* if guess too high, */
            guess = guess - incr;    /*    try lower */
        }
    printf("\nThe number is %.0f. Am I not clever?", guess);
}
```

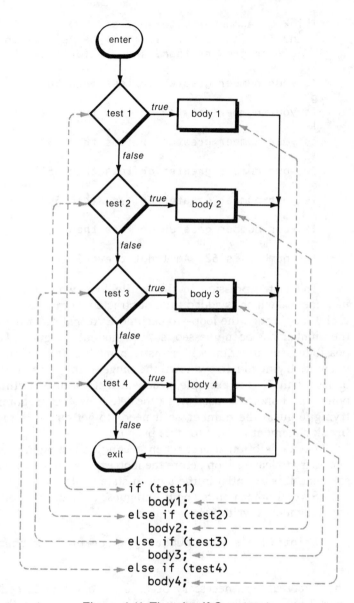

Figure 4-11. The *else-if* Construct

The strategy employed by numguess.c is to ask questions that cut in half the range in which the number might lie. Thus the program first asks if the number is greater or less than 50. If the number is greater than 50, the program asks if the number is greater or less than 75, while if it's less than 50 the program asks if it's greater or less than 25. The process continues until the program deduces the number. Here's a sample interaction, with the user thinking of the number 62:

```
Think of a number between 1 and 99,
  and I'll guess what it is. Type 'e' for equals,
  'g' for greater than, and 'l' for less than.

Is your number greater or less than 50?
g
Is your number greater or less than 75?
l
Is your number greater or less than 63?
l
Is your number greater or less than 56?
g
Is your number greater or less than 59?
g
Is your number greater or less than 61?
g
The number is 62. Am I not clever?
```

The test expression in the **while** loop waits for the variable **incr** (for increment)—which is added to or subtracted from **guess** and then divided by 2 each time through the loop—to become 1. At that point the program knows that the number has been guessed, so it prints out the guess. However, there is the possibility the program will actually print the number the user is thinking of when it's trying to narrow down the range; it might ask if the number is greater or less than 75, for example, when in fact the user is thinking of 75. At this point, the honorable user will type 'e'. Now the program knows it can stop trying to guess the number, so it needs to get out of the loop right away. The **break** statement is used for this purpose.

**Break** is often useful when a condition suddenly occurs that makes it necessary to leave a loop before the loop expression becomes false. And, as we'll see next, it is essential in the **switch** statement.

Several other points about numguess.c should be noted. First, the following statement is written on two lines:

```
printf("\nIs your number greater or less than %.0f?\n",
                                                guess);
```

This linebreak was necessary because the one line exceeded the width of the page. The C compiler doesn't mind if you break a line in the middle this way, as long as you don't break it in the middle of a string.

Second, in the statement

```
incr = guess = 50;
```

we've assigned two variables a value using only one statement. This is possible because an assignment statement itself has a value (as we mentioned in Chapter 3). In this case, the statement

```
guess = 50;
```

takes on the value 50, and the variable **guess** can then be set equal to this value.

## The *switch* Statement

Now that we know how the **break** statement works, we're ready to move on to **switch**. The **switch** statement is similar to the **else-if** construct but has more flexibility and a clearer format. It is analogous to the **case** statement in Pascal; there is no equivalent in BASIC. Let's rewrite our calc2.c program to use **switch:**

```c
/* calc3.c */
/* four-function calculator */
main()
{
    float num1, num2;
    char op;

    while (1)
        {
        printf("Type number, operator, number\n");
        scanf("%f %c %f", &num1, &op, &num2);
        switch ( op )
            {
            case '+':
                printf(" = %f", num1 + num2);
                break;
            case '-':
                printf(" = %f", num1 - num2);
                break;
            case '*':
                printf(" = %f", num1 * num2);
                break;
            case '/':
                printf(" = %f", num1 / num2);
                break;
            default:
                printf("Unknown operator");
            }
        printf("\n\n");
        }
}
```

Structurally, the statement starts out with the keyword **switch**, followed by parentheses containing an integer or character variable which we'll call the "switch variable" (although it can also be an expression, like $a+b$). The structure of the **switch** statement is shown in Figure 4-12.

Following each of the **case** keywords is an integer or character *constant*. (It can be a constant expression, like 'a' + 2, but it must evaluate to a constant; variables are not allowed here.) This constant is terminated with a colon (not a semicolon). There can be one or more statements following each **case** keyword.

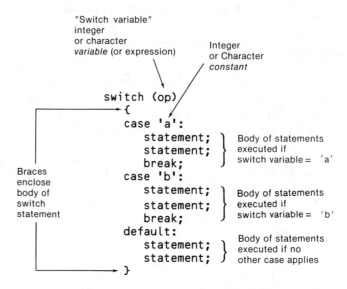

Figure 4-12. The Structure of the **switch** Statement

These statements need not be enclosed by braces, although the entire body of the **switch** statement—all the **case**s—is enclosed in braces.

When the **switch** is entered, the switch variable should already have been set to some value, probably the value of one of the integer or character constants that follow the **case** keywords. If so, control is immediately transferred to the body of statements following this particular **case** keyword. The operation of the **switch** statement in the calc3.c program is shown in Figure 4-13.

If the **switch** variable does not match any of the case constants, control goes to the keyword **default**, which is usually at the end of the switch statement. Using the **default** keyword can be a great convenience; it acts as a sort of master **else** statement, saying in effect, "if none of the above, then do this." (If there is no **default** keyword, the whole **switch** statement simply terminates when there is no match.) In the example above, if the user has typed a character that isn't one of the four for which there is a **case** constant, then control will pass to the statements following the **default** keyword. Here's how that possibility looks in operation when an illegal operator symbol is typed:

```
Type number, operator, number
2 q 2
Unknown operator
```

The **break** statements are necessary to terminate the **switch** statement when the body of statements in a particular case has been executed. As it did in the numguess.c example earlier, the **break** statement has the effect of immediately taking the program out of the structure it finds itself in: a loop in numguess.c and a **switch** here.

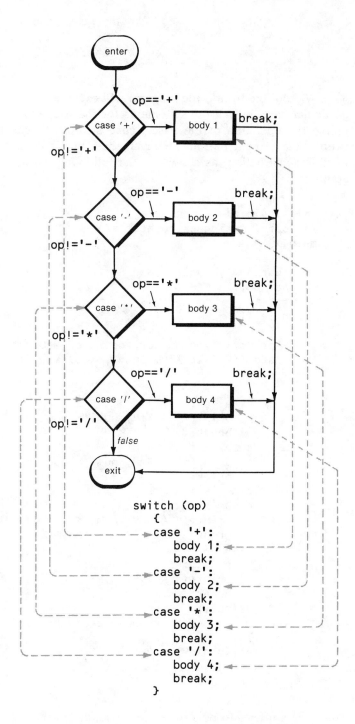

Figure 4-13. Operation of the *switch* Statement

If no **break** statement is used following a **case**, control will fall through to the next **case**.

Without the **break**, the program will execute not only the statements for a particular case, but all the statements for the following cases as well. (This is unlike the operation of the Pascal **case** statement.) Needing to write all the **breaks** may sound like an inconvenience, but it actually makes for a more flexible construction, as shown in the following variation of the calc3.c program:

```c
/* calc4.c */
/* four-function calculator */
main()
{
    float num1, num2;
    char op;

    while (1)
        {
        printf("Type number, operator, number\n");
        scanf("%f %c %f", &num1, &op, &num2);
        switch ( op )
            {
            case '+':
                printf(" = %f", num1 + num2);
                break;
            case '-':
                printf(" = %f", num1 - num2);
                break;
            case '*':
            case 'x':
                printf(" = %f", num1 * num2);
                break;
            case '/':
            case '\\':
                printf(" = %f", num1 / num2);
                break;
            default:
                printf("Unknown operator");
            }
        printf("\n\n");
        }
}
```

This program tries to be a little more friendly to the user by dealing with the instances when the user types an 'x' instead of a '*' to mean multiply, or a '\'

instead of a '/' to mean divide. Since control falls right through one **case** to the **case** below in the absence of a **break** statement, this construction makes it easy for several values of the **switch** variable to execute the same body of code.

Note that, since the backslash is already the escape character, we must type '\\' to indicate the backslash itself.

Here's what happens when you type the new operators:

```
C>calc4

Type number, operator, number
2 \ 3
  = 0.666667

Type number, operator, number
10 x 10
  = 100.000000
```

## The Conditional Operator

We'll finish off this chapter with a brief look at one of C's stranger constructions, a decision-making operator called the "conditional operator." It consists of two operators used on three different expressions, and thus it has the distinction of being the only ternary operator in C. (Ternary operators work on three variables, as opposed to the more common binary operators, such as ( + ), which operate on two expressions, and unary operators, such as ( ! ), which operate on only one.) The conditional operator has the form: *condition ? expression1 : expression2.*

The conditional operator consists of both the question mark and the colon. *Condition* is a logical expression that evaluates to either true or false, while *expression1* and *expression2* are either values or expressions that evaluate to values.

Here's how it works. The condition is evaluated. If it's true, then the entire conditional expression takes on the value of expression1. If it's false, the conditional expression takes on the value of expression2. Note that the entire conditional expression—the three expressions and two operators—takes on a value and can therefore be used in an assignment statement.

Here's an example:

```
max = (num1 > num2)  ?  num1 : num2;
```

The purpose of this statement is to assign to the variable **max** the value of either **num1** or **num2**, whichever is larger. First the condition (**num1** > **num2**) is evaluated. If it's true, the entire conditional expression takes on the value of **num1**; this value is then assigned to **max**. If (**num1** > **num2**) is false, the conditional expression takes on the value of **num2**, and this value is assigned to **max**. This operation is shown in Figure 4-14.

This expression is equivalent to the **if-else** statement:

```
if (num1 < num2)
    max = num2;
else
    max = num1;
```

But it is more compact than the **if-else;** since the entire statement takes on a value, two separate assignment statements are not needed. This operator can be used very elegantly in the right sort of situation.

Here's another example:

```
abs = (num < 0) ? -num : num;
```

This statement evaluates to the absolute value of **num**, which is simply **num** if **num** is greater than zero, but – **num** if **num** is less than zero.

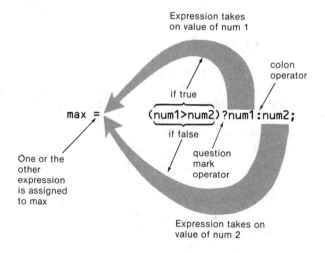

Figure 4-14. The Conditional Operator

## Summary

You now know a good deal about the major elements of decision-making in C. You've learned about the three major decision-making statements—**if, if-else,** and **switch**. You've seen how **if** statements and **if-else** statements can be nested and how a series of **if-else** statements can be transformed into the **else-if** construction. You've learned the elements of the **switch** statement: the switch variable, switch constants, and the **case** and **default** keywords. You've also learned about the three logical operators NOT ( ! ), OR ( ¦¦ ), and AND ( && ) and about the **break** statement, which causes an immediate exit from a loop or **switch** structure. Finally, you learned about the conditional operator, which returns one or the other of two values, depending on whether a condition is true or false.

# Questions

1. In a simple **if** statement with no **else**, what happens if the condition following the **if** is false?

   a. the program searches for the last **else** in the program

   b. nothing

   c. control "falls through" to the statement following the **if**

   d. the body of the **if** statement is executed

2. Is the following a correct C program?

```
main()
{
    if ( getche() == 'a' ) then
        printf("\nYou typed a.");
}
```

3. True or false: nesting one **if** inside another should be avoided for clarity.

4. The main difference in operation between an **if** statement and a **while** statement is:

   a. the conditional expression following the keyword is evaluated differently

   b. the **while** loop body is always executed, the **if** loop body only if the condition is true

   c. the body of the **while** statement may be executed many times, the body of the **if** statement only once

   d. the conditional expression is evaluated before the **while** loop body is executed but after the **if** loop body

5. The statements following **else** in an **if-else** construction are executed when:

   a. the conditional expression following **if** is false

   b. the conditional expression following **if** is true

   c. the conditional expression following **else** is false

   d. the conditional expression following **else** is true

6. Is this C program correct?

```
main()
{
    if(getch()=='a') printf("It's an a"); else printf("It's not");
}
```

7. True or false: the compiler interprets **else-if** differently than it does an equivalent **if-else**.

8. The statements following a particular **else-if** in an **else-if** ladder are executed when:

   a. the conditional expression following the **else-if** is true and all previous conditions are true

   b. the conditional expression following the **else-if** is true and all previous conditions are false

   c. the conditional expression following the **else-if** is false and all previous conditions are true

   d. the conditional expression following the **else-if** is false and all previous conditions are false

9. Which **if** in a program does an **else** pair up with?

   a. the last **if** with the same indentation as the **else**

   b. the last **if** not matched with its own **else**

   c. the last **if** not enclosed in braces

   d. the last **if** not enclosed in braces and not matched with its own else

10. The advantage of a **switch** statement over an **else-if** construction is:

    a. a default condition can be used in the **switch**

    b. the **switch** is easier to understand

    c. several different statements can be executed for each case in a **switch**

    d. several different conditions can cause one set of statements to be executed in a **switch**

11. Is this a correct **switch** statement?

```
switch(num)
   {
   case 1;
      printf("Num is 1");
   case 2;
      printf("Num is 2");
   default;
      printf("Num is neither 1 nor 2");
   }
```

12. True or false: a **break** statement must be used following the statements for each **case** in a **switch** statement.

13. Is this a correct **switch** statement?

```
switch (temp)
   {
   case temp<60:
      printf("It's really cold!");
      break;
   case temp<80:
      printf("What charming weather!");
      break;
   default:
      printf("Sure is hot!);
   }
```

14. The purpose of the conditional operator is to

    a. select the highest of two values

    b. select the more equal of two values

    c. select one of two values alternately

    d. select one of two values depending on a condition

15. If num is −42, what is the value of this conditional expression?

    ( num < 0 ) ? 0 : num*num;

# Exercises

1. Write a program that will ask the user how fast he or she drives, and then print out what response a police officer would make to the following speed ranges: >75, >65, >55, >45, <45. Use nested **if-else** statements.

2. Modify the checker.c program to draw a checkerboard where each square, instead of being one row high and two columns wide, is three rows high and six columns wide.

3. Modify the lines2.c program to draw four lines, the first two the same as in lines2.c, the third a vertical line passing through the center of the rectangle (where the first two lines cross) and the fourth a horizontal line passing through the center of the rectangle. The effect is something like a British flag. Use the **else-if** ladder construction (no logical operators).

4. Change the program in example 3 to work with logical operators, eliminating the **else-if** ladder.

5. (Extra credit) Write a program to draw a quarter circle on the screen, with a radius of 20 characters, centered at the upper-lefthand corner of the screen. Make use of the formula for plotting circles:

$$rs = x*x + y*y$$

where rs stands for radius squared (which will be 400). Interpret this formula as being correct if x*x + y*y is within 20 of rs.

# 5

# *Functions*

- Functions
- Returning a value from a function
- Sending values to a function
- Arguments
- External variables
- Preprocessor directives

# 5

No one can perform all of life's tasks personally. You may ask a repairperson to fix your TV set, hire someone to mow your lawn, or rely on a store to provide fresh vegetables rather than growing your own. A computer program (except for a very simple one) is in much the same situation; it cannot handle every task alone. Instead, it calls on other programlike entities—called "functions" in C—to carry out specific tasks. In this chapter we'll explore the topic of functions. We'll look at a variety of ways functions are used, starting with the simplest case and working up to examples that demonstrate some of the power and versatility of functions in C.

At the end of the chapter we'll explore another area of C that ties into the idea of functions in several ways: that of "preprocessor directives."

## What Do Functions Do?

As we noted in Chapter 1, a function in C serves a similar purpose to a subroutine in BASIC and to functions or procedures in Pascal. Let's examine in more detail why a function is used.

### Avoiding Unnecessary Repetition of Code

Probably the original reason functions (or subroutines, as they were first known) were invented was to avoid having to write the same code over and over. Suppose you have a section of code in your program that calculates the square root of a number. If, later in the program, you want to calculate the square root of a different number, you don't want to have to write the same instructions all over again. Instead, in effect, you want to jump to the section of code that calculates square roots and then jump back again to the normal program flow when you're done. In this way, a single section of code can be used many times in the same program. The saving of code is depicted in Figure 5-1.

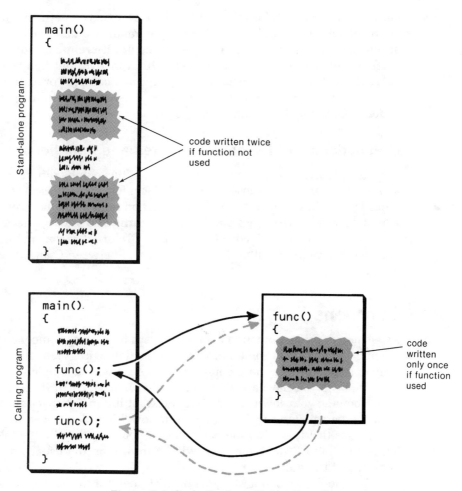

Figure 5-1. Code Savings Using Function

## Program Organization

This is all the early subroutines did, and is still all the subroutine construction does in BASIC. However, over the years it was found that using the subroutine idea made it easier to organize programs and keep track of what they were doing. If the operation of a program could be divided into separate activities, and each activity placed in a separate subroutine, then each subroutine could be written and checked out more or less independently. Separating the code into modular functions also made programs easier to design and understand.

## Independence

As this idea took hold it became clear that there was an advantage in making subroutines as independent from the main program and from one another as possible. For instance, subroutines were invented that had their own "private" variables; that is, variables that could not be accessed from the main program or the other subroutines. This meant that a programmer didn't need to worry about accidentally using the same variable names in different subroutines; the variables in each subroutine were protected from inadvertent tampering by other subroutines. Thus it was easier to write large and complex programs. Pascal and most other modern programming languages make use of this independence, and C does too, as we'll find out soon.

### C Functions and Pascal Procedures and Functions

For Pascal programmers, we should mention at this point a difference between C and Pascal that might cause some initial confusion. In Pascal, functions and procedures are two separate entities. A function in that language returns a value, whereas a procedure carries out a task or returns data via arguments. In C these two constructs are combined: a C function can return data via arguments and can also return a value. We'll note other differences between C and Pascal as we go along.

## Simple Functions

As we noted, using a function is in some ways like hiring someone to perform a specific job for you. Sometimes the interaction with such a person is very simple; sometimes it's more complex. Let's start with a simple case.

Suppose you have a task which is always performed in exactly the same way—mowing your lawn, say. When you want it done, you get on the phone to the lawn person and say, "It's time, do it now." You don't need to give instructions, since that task is *all* the person does. You don't need to be told when the job is done. You assume the lawn will be mowed in the usual way, the person does it, and that's that.

Let's look at a simple C function that operates in the same way. Actually, we'll be looking at two things: a program that "calls" or activates the function (just as you call the lawn person on the phone) and the function itself. Here's the program:

```
/* textbox.c */
/* puts box around text */
void line(void);                 /* prototype for line() */

main()
{
   line();                                /* draw line */
   printf("\xDB TITUS ANDRONICUS \xDB\n");  /* message */
   line();                                /* 2nd line */
}

/* line() -- this is function definition */
/* draws solid line on screen */
void line(void)              /* function declarator */
```

```
{
    int j;                      /* counter */

    for (j=1; j<=20; j++)       /* print block 20 times */
        printf("\xDB");         /* solid block */
    printf("\n");               /* print carriage return */
}
```

This program draws a box around the words "TITUS ANDRONICUS" (one of the lesser-known Roman emperors). Figure 5-2 shows what the output looks like.

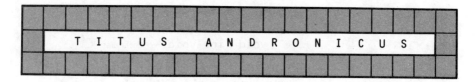

Figure 5-2. Output of textbox.c

To achieve this effect we've first drawn a line of rectangles across the screen (using the graphics character '\xDB'), then printed the emperor's name—preceded and ended by a rectangle to form the ends of the box—and finally drawn another line. However, instead of writing the code to draw the line twice, we made it into a function, called **line**.

## Structure of Functions

The textbox.c program looks almost like two little programs. Actually, it contains two functions: the first is called **main()** and the second is called **line()**. As we saw in Chapter 1, **main()** is a function, so it's not surprising that **line()**, which is also a function, looks like it. The only thing special about **main()** is that it is always executed first. It doesn't even matter if **main()** is the first function in the listing; you can place other functions before it and **main()** will still be executed first.

In this example, **main()** calls the function **line()**. "Calls" means that it causes it to be executed. To draw the two lines of boxes, **main()** calls **line()** twice.

There are three program elements involved in using a function: the function *definition*, the call to the function, and the function *prototype*. Let's look at each of these in turn.

### The Function Definition
The function itself is referred to as the function definition. The definition starts with a line that includes the function name, among other elements:

```
void line(void)             /* note: no semicolon */
```

This line is the *declarator* (a name only a lexicographer could love). The first **void** means that **line()** doesn't return anything and the second means that it takes no arguments. We'll examine return values and arguments later in the chapter; for now, just be sure to include these voids. They're both necessary.

Note that the declarator does *not* end with a semicolon. It is not a program statement, whose execution causes something to happen. Rather, it tells the compiler that a function is being defined.

The function definition continues with the *body* of the function: the lines of code that do the work. Figure 5-3 shows the declarator and the function body that make up the function definition.

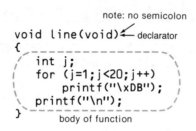

Figure 5-3. Function Definition

The body of the function is enclosed in braces. Usually these braces are placed at the left margin, as we have seen already in numerous examples of the function **main()**.

### Calling the Function

As with the C library functions we've met, such as **printf()** and **getche()**, our user-written function **line()** is called from **main()** simply by using its name, including the parentheses following the name. The parentheses are needed for the compiler to know you are referring to a function and not a variable or something else. Calling a function like this is a C statement, so it ends with a semicolon.

```
line();      /* function call -- note semicolon */
```

This function call causes control to be transferred to the code in the definition of **line()**. This function draws its row of squares on the screen, and then returns to **main()**, to the statement following the function call.

### Function Prototype (Declaration)

There's a third function-related element in the textbox.c example. This is a line before the beginning of **main()**:

```
void line(void); /* function prototype -- note semicolon */
```

This looks very much like the declarator line at the start of the function definition, except that it ends with a semicolon. What is its purpose?

You've already seen many examples of *variables* in C programs. All the variables were declared by name and data type at the beginning of the function in which they were used. A *function* is declared in the same way at the beginning of a program. The function declaration (or prototype—the terms mean the same thing) tells the compiler the name of the function, the data type the function returns (if any), and the number and data types of the function's arguments (if any). In this case, the function returns nothing and takes no arguments.

Notice that the prototype is written *before* the **main()** function. This causes the prototype to be visible to all the functions in a file. We'll learn more about this when we talk about external variables later in this chapter.

The key thing to remember about the prototype is that the data types (the two uses of **void** in this example) must agree with those in the declarator in the function's definition. If they don't, you'll get unhappy messages from the compiler.

A *prototype* declares a function.
A *function call* executes a function.
A function *definition* is the function itself.
A function *declarator* (in the definition) names the function and specifies its return type and arguments.

## Local Variables

The variable **j** used in the **line()** function is known only to **line()**; it is invisible to the **main()** function. If we added this statement to **main()** (without declaring a variable **j** there):

```
printf("%d", j);
```

we'd get a compiler error because **main()** wouldn't know anything about this variable. We could declare another variable, also called **j**, in the **main()** function; it would be a completely separate variable, known to **main()** but not to **line()**. This is a key point in the writing of C functions: variables used in a function are unknown outside the function. The question of which functions know about a variable and which don't is called the "visibility" of the variable. A local variable will be visible to the function it is defined in, but not to other functions.

A local variable used in this way in a function is known in C as an "automatic" variable, because it is automatically created when a function is called and destroyed when the function returns. The length of time a variable lasts is called its "lifetime." We'll have more to say about visibility and lifetime in Chapter 15, when we discuss storage types.

## A Sound Example

Let's reinforce our understanding of functions with another example. This one uses the special character '\x7', which is called BELL in the standard ASCII code. On the IBM, printing this character, instead of ringing a bell, causes a beeping sound. Here's the program:

```
/* beeptest.c */
/* tests the twobeep function */
void twobeep(void);             /* function prototype */

main()
{
   twobeep();                   /* function call */
   printf("Type any character: ");
   getche();                    /* wait for keypress */
   twobeep();                   /* function call */
}

/* twobeep() function definition */
/* beeps the speaker twice */
void twobeep(void)              /* function declarator */
{
   long j;

   printf("\x7");               /* first beep */
   for (j=1; j<100000; j++)     /* delay */
      ;                         /* (null statement) */
   printf("\x7");               /* second beep */
}
```

This program first calls a subroutine, **twobeep()**, which does just what its name says: sounds two beeps separated by a short silent interval. Then the program asks you to strike a key; when you do, it sounds the two beeps again.

Note how the delay is constructed: A **for** loop is set up to cycle 100,000 times. However, there is no body of program statements in this loop. Instead, there is a statement consisting of only the semicolon. This constitutes a "null" statement: a statement with nothing in it. It's only role is to terminate the **for** loop.

# Functions that Return a Value

Let's look at a slightly more complicated kind of function: one that returns a value. An analogy can be made here with hiring someone to find out something for you. In a way, you do this when you dial 767-8900 to find out what time it is. You make the call, the person (or computer) on the other end of the line gives you the time, and that's that. You don't need to tell them what you want; that's understood when you call that number. No information flows from you to the phone company, but some flows from it back to you.

A function that uses no arguments but returns a value performs a similar role. You call the function, it gets a certain piece of information and returns it to you. The function **getche()** operates in just this way; you call it—without giving it any information—and it returns the value of the first character typed on the keyboard.

Suppose we wanted a function that returned a character as **getche()** does, but that also automatically translated any uppercase characters into lowercase. Such a function, with a calling program that uses a **switch** statement to create a rudimentary menu program, is shown below:

```
/* getlower.c */
/* tests getlc function */
char getlc(void);      /* function prototype */

main()
{
    char chlc;              /* char returned */

    printf("Type 'a' for first selection, 'b' for second: ");
    chlc = getlc();    /* get converted character */
    switch (chlc)         /* print msg, depending on char */
        {
        case 'a':
            printf("\nYou typed an 'a'.");
            break;
        case 'b':
            printf("\nYou typed a 'b'.");
            break;
        default:
            printf("\nYou chose a non-existent selection.");
        }
}

/* getlc */
/* returns character */
/* converts to lowercase if in uppercase */
char getlc(void)
{
    char ch;                /* char from keyboard */

    ch = getche();          /* get character */
    if ( ch>64 && ch<91 )   /* if it's uppercase, */
        ch = ch + 32;       /* add 32 to convert to lower */
    return (ch);            /* return character to caller */
}
```

Our new function, **getlc()** (for "get lowercase"), is called from the main program with the statement:

```
chlc = getlc();
```

Just as in the case of **getche()**, the function itself appears to "take on the value" it is returning. It can thus be used as if it were a variable in an assignment statement. In getlower.c the value returned (a lowercase character) will be assigned to the variable **chlc**, which is then used in the **switch** statement to determine which message will be printed. Here's an example of output from the program:

```
C>menu
Type 'a' for first selection, 'b' for second: a
You typed an 'a'.
C>menu
Type 'a' for first selection, 'b' for second: A
You typed an 'a'.
C>menu
Type 'a' for first selection, 'b' for second: c
You chose a nonexistent selection.
```

Notice how the capital 'A' typed by the user is successfully converted to lowercase. (We should mention that Microsoft C includes library functions for case conversion: **toupper()** and **tolower()**.)

## The *return* Statement

In the textbox.c and beeptest.c programs shown earlier the functions returned (jumped back to) the calling program when they encountered the final closing brace ( } ) which defined the end of the function. No separate "return" statement was necessary.

This approach is fine if the function is not going to return a value to the calling program. In the case of our menu.c program, however, we want to return the value of the character read from the keyboard. In fact, we want to return one of two possible values: the character itself, if it is in lowercase already, or a modified version of the character, if it is in uppercase. So we use the **if** statement to check if **ch** is in uppercase (uppercase letters run from ASCII 65 to 90). If so, we add 32 (the difference between ASCII's 'A' = 65 and 'a' = 97) to **ch**. Finally, we return to the calling program with the new value of the character, by placing the variable name between the parentheses following **return()**.

The **return()** statement has two purposes. First, executing it immediately transfers control from the function back to the calling program. And second, whatever is inside the parentheses following **return** is returned as a value to the calling program.

Figure 5-4 shows a function returning a value to the calling program.

The **return** statement need not be at the end of the function. It can occur anywhere in the function; as soon as it's encountered control will return to the calling program. For instance, we could have rewritten the **getlc()** function like this:

```
/* getlc() */
```

```
/* returns character */
/* converts to lowercase if in uppercase */
char getlc(void)
{
    char ch;
    ch = getche();          /* read character */
    if ( ch>64 && ch<91 )   /* if uppercase, */
        return (ch+32);     /*    return converted value */
    else                    /* otherwise, */
        return (ch);        /*    return original value */
}
```

Here different **return** statements will be used depending on whether **ch** is uppercase or not.

The **return** statement can also consist of the word "return" used alone. When this is the case, no value is returned to the calling program.

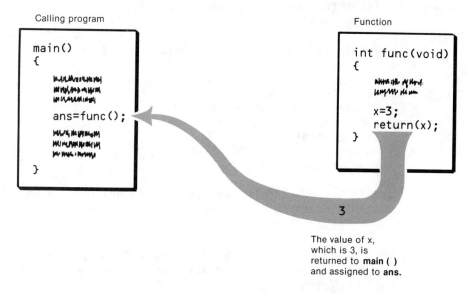

Figure 5-4. Function Returning a Value

The **return** statement in **getlc()** returns the value of the variable **ch**, which is type **char**. This must be reflected in both the prototype for **getlc()** and in the declarator in the function definition. The prototype is

```
char getlc(void);
```

The declarator is the same but has no semicolon. The type specifier **void**, used to indicate the return value in previous examples, meant that no value was returned from the function. In getlower.c this specifier has been replaced with the specifier **char** to indicate that the function returns a value of that type.

## Hours and Minutes

Here's another example of a function that returns a value. This one, called **getmins()**, gets a time in hours and minutes from the user and converts it to minutes. The main program uses this function to calculate the difference in seconds between two times:

```
/* intimes.c */
/* calculates difference between two times */
int getmins(void);                          /* func prototype */

main()
{
    int mins1, mins2;                       /* minutes */

    printf("Type first time (form 3:22): ");
    mins1 = getmins();                      /* get minutes */
    printf("Type second (later) time: ");
    mins2 = getmins();                      /* get minutes */
                                            /* find difference */
    printf("Difference is %d minutes.", mins2-mins1 );
}

/* getmins function */
/* gets time in hours:minutes format */
/* returns time in minutes */
int getmins(void)
{
    int hours, minutes;

    scanf("%d:%d", &hours, &minutes);   /* get user input */
    return ( hours*60 + minutes );      /* convert to minutes */
}
```

Essentially, what the function **getmins** does is to accept a time in hours and minutes from the user and convert it into minutes by multiplying the hours by 60 and adding the minutes.

Note that the **getmins()** function returns a value of type **int**. This is reflected in the prototype for the function:

```
    int getmins(void);
```

Again, the declarator is the same, but without the semicolon. The **void** in parentheses does not change, since the function takes no arguments.

### New Wrinkle in scanf()

If you are very attentive you may have noticed something new in the **scanf()** statement: there is a *colon* between the two format specifiers, %d and %d, rather than a space as in the past.

```
    scanf("%d:%d", &hours, &minutes);
```

This has the effect of requiring the user to type a colon between the two numbers for the two %d's, rather than permitting only whitespace characters (space, tab, newline). Thus, the user can type the time in standard hours and minutes format, using a colon to separate them. Here's a sample session with intimes.c:

```
C>intimes
Type first time (form 3:22): 6:00
Type second (later) time: 7:45
Difference is 105 minutes.
```

You may notice that **scanf()** is not a very forgiving function; if you type anything but a colon, **scanf()** will terminate immediately without waiting for the minutes to be typed and without giving you any warning that it's doing so. A truly user-friendly program would add some code to give better feedback to the user.

### Limitation of *return()*

There is a key limitation in the use of the **return** statement: it can return only one value. If you want your function to return two or more values to the calling program, you need another mechanism. In the following sections we'll see how, using arguments, it's possible to pass more than one piece of information *to* a function. However, getting more than one piece of information back will be a topic for a later chapter, since it requires a knowledge of the concepts of addresses and pointers.

> Using a **return** statement, only one value can be returned by a function.

## Using Arguments to Pass Data to a Function

So far the functions we've used haven't been very flexible. We call them and they do what they're designed to do, either returning a value or not. Like our lawn person who always mows the grass exactly the same way, we can't influence them in the way they carry out their tasks. It would be nice to have a little more control over what functions do, in the same way it would be nice to be able to tell the lawn person, "Just do the front yard today, we're having a barbecue out back."

The mechanism used to convey information to a function is the *argument*. (The word "parameter" is often used as a synonym for "argument.") You've already used arguments in the **printf()** and **scanf()** functions; the format strings and the values used inside the parentheses in these functions are arguments.

Here's an example of a program in which a single argument is passed to a function:

```
/* bargraph.c */
/* draws bargraph, demonstrates function arguments */
void bar(int);              /* function prototype */
```

```
main()
{
    printf("Terry\t");        /* print name */
    bar(27);                  /* draw line 27 chars long */
    printf("Chris\t");        /* print name */
    bar(41);                  /* draw line 41 chars long */
    printf("Reggie\t");       /* and so on */
    bar(34);
    printf("Cindy\t");
    bar(22);
    printf("Harold\t");
    bar(15);
}


/* bar() */
/* function draws horizontal bar, 'score' characters long */
void bar(int score)           /* function declarator */
{
    int j;

    for(j=1; j<=score; j++)   /* draw 'score' number of */
        printf("\xCD");       /*     double-line characters */
    printf("\n");             /* newline at end of bar */
}
```

This program generates a bargraph of names and bars representing, say, the scores in a spelling test. The output of the program is shown in Figure 5-5.

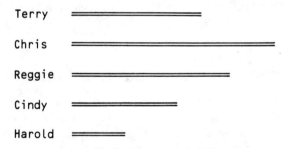

Figure 5-5. Output of the bargraph.c Program

In this program the purpose of the function **bar()** is to draw a horizontal line, made up of the double-line graphics character ('\xCD') on the screen. For each person (Terry, Chris, etc.), the main program prints the name and then calls the function, using as an argument the score received by that person on the test.

## Structure of a Function Call with Arguments

There are a number of things to notice about this program. First, in the main program, the number we want to pass to the function **bar()** is included in the parentheses following "bar" in the function call:

```
bar(27);
```

We could have used a variable name instead of the constant 27; we'll see an example of this shortly.

In the declarator at the beginning of the function **bar()**, the variable name **score** is placed inside the parentheses, along with its data type:

```
void bar(int score)    /* declarator */
```

See how the value of **score** is transferred, as if by magic, to the function. The value placed in the parentheses in the call to the function is automatically assigned to the corresponding variable in the function when the function is called. In the first call to the function, the value 27 will be assigned to **score**. This is shown schematically in Figure 5-6. The second time **bar()** is called, the value 41 will be assigned, and so forth.

The prototype reflects the data type of the argument:

```
void bar(int);    /* prototype */
```

Note that the prototype differs from the declarator in that no variable name is used for the argument in the prototype, only the data type. (A name can be used here, as we'll see soon, but it's optional.)

Because the function **bar()** doesn't return anything, its return type is **void**.

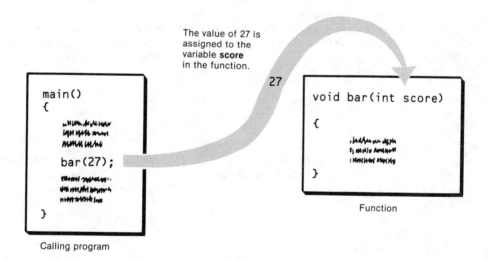

Figure 5-6. Passing a Value to a Function

The variable **score** in the function **bar()** is not declared the same way normal variables are. Nonetheless, it is declared; its inclusion in the function declarator serves not only to specify that it is a function argument, but to declare it as well. It can be used like any other variable in the function; the only difference is that it is passed an initial value from the calling program when the function is first called.

The definition of a function with an argument is shown in Figure 5-7.

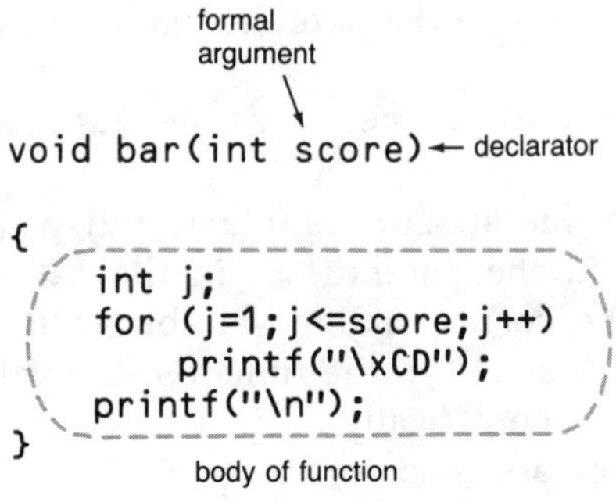

Figure 5-7. Structure of Function with Argument

## Passing Variables as Arguments

In the example above we passed *constants* (such as the number 27) as arguments to the function **bar()**. We can also use a *variable* in the calling program, as this variation on the bargraph.c program demonstrates:

```
/* bargr2.c */
/* draws bargraph, demonstrates function arguments */
void bar(int inscore);          /* function prototype */
                                /*     with identifier */
main()
{
    int inscore;

    while (1)
        {
        printf("Score=");       /* prompt the user */
        scanf("%d", &inscore);  /* get score from user */
        bar(inscore);           /* draw line */
        }
}

/* bar */
/* function to draw horizontal bar */
void bar(int score)
{
    int j;

    for(j=1; j<=score; j++)     /* draw 'score' number of */
        printf("\xCD");         /*     double-line characters */
    printf("\n");               /* newline at end of bar */
}
```

In this program the function **bar()** is the same as before. The prototype is also the same. However, the main program has been modified to accept scores from the keyboard. Figure 5-8 shows a sample of interaction with the program.

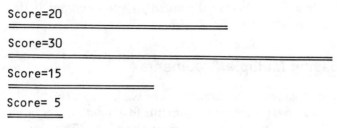

Score=20

Score=30

Score=15

Score= 5

Figure 5-8. Output of the bargr2.c Program

Since the scores we pass to **bar()** are no longer known in advance, we must use a variable to pass them to the **bar()** function. We do this in the statement:

```
bar(inscore);
```

Now, whatever value the user types is recorded by **scanf()** and assigned to the variable **inscore**. When **bar()** is called, this is the value passed to it as an argument. Figure 5-9 shows this process.

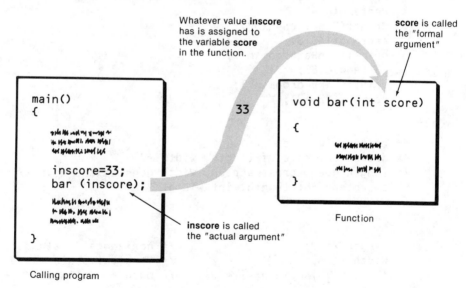

Figure 5-9. Variable Used as Argument

Different names have been assigned to the arguments in the calling and called functions: **inscore** in the calling program and **score** in the function. Actually, we could have used the same name for both variables; since they are in different functions, the compiler would still consider them to be separate variables.

Note that the argument in the calling program is referred to as the "actual argument," while the argument in the called function is the "formal argument." In this case, the variable **inscore** in the calling program is the actual argument, and the variable **score** in the function is the formal argument. Knowing these terms will not help you program better, but it may impress people at parties.

## Passing Multiple Arguments

We can pass as many arguments as we like to a function. Here's an example of a program that passes two arguments to a function, **rectang()**, whose purpose is to draw variously sized rectangles on the screen. The two arguments are the length and width of the rectangle, where each rectangle represents a room in a house.

```
/* roomplot.c */
/* tests the rectang function */
void rectang(int, int);              /* function prototype */

main()
{
    printf("\nLiving room\n");    /* print room name */
    rectang(22,12);               /* draw room */
    printf("\nCloset\n");         /* etc. */
    rectang(4,4);
    printf("\nKitchen\n");
    rectang(16,16);
    printf("\nBathroom\n");
    rectang(6,8);
    printf("\nBedroom\n");
    rectang(12,12);
}

/* rectang function */
/* draws rectangle of length, width */
/* length goes across screen, width goes up-and-down */
void rectang(int length, int width)
{
    int j, k;

    length /= 2;                  /* horizontal scale factor */
    width /= 4;                   /* vertical scale factor */
    for (j=1; j<=width; j++)      /* number of lines */
        {
        printf("\t\t");           /* tab over */
        for (k=1; k<=length; k++) /* line of rectangles */
            printf("\xDB");       /* print one rectangle */
        printf("\n");             /* next line */
        }
}
```

This program prints the name of a room and then draws a rectangle representing the dimensions of the room. A sample of the output from the program is shown in Figure 5-10.

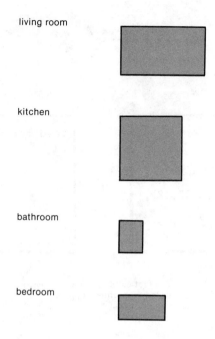

living room

kitchen

bathroom

bedroom

Figure 5-10. Output of the roomplot.c Program

The operation of the function is very much like that of the rectangle-drawing program in Chapter 3. Our new wrinkle here is the use of scale factors. These are necessary so the room dimensions can be expressed in feet. The function divides the length (the horizontal dimension on the screen) by 2 and the width (the vertical dimension) by 4. This makes it possible for a series of typical rooms to fit on the screen, and also compensates for the fact that a character on the screen is twice as high as it is long. To make a square room look square, we must divide its vertical dimension by twice as much as its horizontal dimension. The division operation for the scale factors is carried out using an assignment operator. As we saw in Chapter 2, the statement

```
length /= 2;
```

is equivalent to

```
length = length / 2;
```

The process of passing two arguments is similar to passing one. The value of the first actual argument in the calling program is assigned to the first formal argument in the function, and the value of the second actual argument is assigned to the second formal argument, as shown in Figure 5-11.

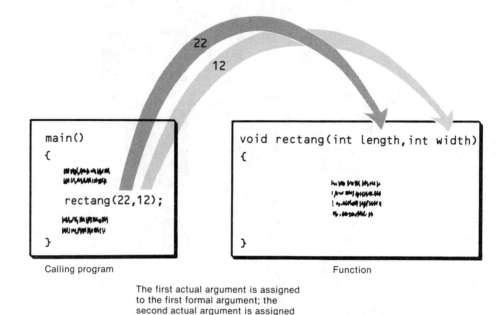

Figure 5-11. Multiple Arguments Passed to Function

Of course, three or more arguments could be used in the same way.

## Identifiers in the Prototype

Here's another wrinkle in the use of the prototype: you can use names as well as data types for the arguments. For instance, instead of saying

```
void rectang(int, int);
```

you could say something like

```
void rectang(int length, int width);
```

The advantage in using names is that the prototype can convey information about the purpose of the arguments. In this case, we make it clear to anyone looking at the prototype which of the two arguments is the width and which the length. Note that these names in the prototype have nothing to do with the names of the variables used later as the actual arguments when the function is called; they are merely a convenience to the person looking at the listing. We'll use them occasionally in program examples.

# Sending and Receiving

We've seen examples of functions that return a value and of functions that accept arguments from the calling program. Let's look at a function that both accepts an argument and returns a value. For variety, we'll use the floating point data type for both the argument and return value.

In this program the **main()** function asks the user for the radius of a sphere and then calls a function named **area()** to calculate the area of the sphere. It sends the radius as a floating point argument. The **area()** function returns the area of the sphere as a floating point number.

```
/* sphere.c */
/* calculates area of a sphere */
float area(float);     /* prototype */

main()
{
   float radius;

   printf("Enter radius of sphere: ");
   scanf("%f", &radius);
   printf("Area of sphere is %.2f", area(radius) );
}

/* area() */
/* returns area of sphere */
float area(float rad)
{
   return( 4 * 3.14159 * rad * rad );
}
```

You'll see that the function prototype and the declarator reflect the **float** data type for both the argument and the return value of **area()**. Since the function uses floating point numbers, the format specifier %f has been used in the **scanf()** and **printf()** functions. In **printf()** the .2 in the specifier restricts the output to two decimal places.

Here's a sample of interaction with the program:

```
C>sphere
Enter radius of sphere: 10
Area of sphere is 1256.64
C>sphere
Enter radius of sphere: 4000
Area of sphere is 201061760.00
```

The last interchange calculates the approximate surface area of the earth: a little over 200 million square miles. With so much space available it's surprising people are willing to pay such high prices for land in Manhattan.

# Using More than One Function

You can use as many functions as you like in a program, and any of the functions can call any of the other functions. There is an important difference here between C and Pascal. In Pascal, a function (or a procedure), call it Alpha, can be defined *inside* another function, Beta, so that it is not visible to other functions, like Gamma, that are not in Beta. In C, however, all functions are visible to all other functions. This situation is shown in Figure 5-12.

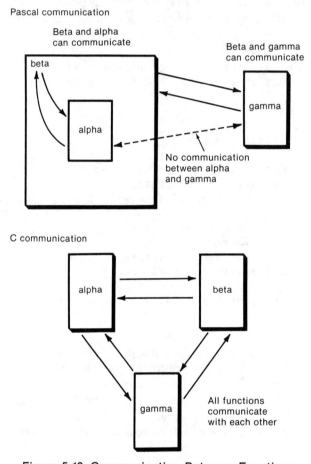

Figure 5-12. Communication Between Functions

In this respect, C is more like BASIC, where it is impossible to nest or "hide" one subroutine inside another.

> In C, all functions, including **main()**, have equal status and are visible to all other functions.

Which approach is better? Being able to nest functions, as in Pascal, does provide some added flexibility in certain situations—you could use the same function name for two different functions, for example, which might be advantageous in large programs. However, the C approach—all functions are equal—is conceptually easier and usually doesn't result in any inconvenience to the programmer.

Let's look at a program involving several functions. This program calculates the sum of the squares of two integers typed in by the user. The program actually uses three functions as well as **main()**. The first function does the actual calculation, while **main()** simply gets the numbers from the user and prints out the result. The second function returns the square of a number (the number multiplied by itself), and the third function returns the sum of two numbers.

```
/* multifun.c */
/* tests sumsqr() function */

int sumsqr(int, int);              /* function prototypes */
int sqr(int);
int sum(int, int);

main()
{
    int num1, num2;                /* user-supplied values */

    printf("Type two numbers: ");   /* gets two numbers, */
    scanf("%d %d", &num1, &num2);   /* prints sum of squares */
    printf("Sum of the squares is %d", sumsqr(num1,num2) );
}

/* sumsqr function */
/* returns sum of squares of two arguments */
sumsqr(int j,int k)
{
    return( sum( sqr(j), sqr(k) ) );
}

/* sqr function */
/* returns square of argument */
sqr(int z)
{
    return(z * z);
}

/* sum function */
/* returns sum of two arguments */
sum(int x, int y)
{
    return(x + y);
}
```

Notice that none of the functions is nested inside any other. In Pascal, we could have placed, for instance, the **sum()** and **sqr()** functions inside the **sumsqr()** function. In C, all the functions are visible to all other functions. The main program, for instance, could call **sum()** or **sqr()** directly if it needed to.

Another point to note is that functions can appear in any order in the program listing. They can be arranged alphabetically, in the order in which they are called, by functional group, or any other way the programmer wishes. Arranging the functions in an order that makes them easier to refer to can be a real advantage for the programmer, especially in larger programs with dozens of functions. Note too that the **main()** function does not need to be the first one in the program, although it usually is.

# Prototypes versus Classical K and R

When Kernighan and Ritchie defined the C language in their 1978 book (see the Bibliography), they did not include prototypes. Prototypes are a refinement introduced by the evolving ANSI standard. The ANSI standard has generally been adopted by all the leading compiler vendors, including Microsoft, so all programs should be written using prototypes. However, since many existing programs were written using the older K and R approach, you should have at least some familiarity with it. Also, comparing the prototype system with the classical K and R approach helps to clarify the advantages of prototypes.

## Examples of the Two Approaches

Let's look at two versions of a simple program. The first uses the prototype approach:

```
/* proto.c */
/* uses prototyping */
void func(int);                 /* function prototype */
main()
{
    int actarg = 1234;

    func(actarg);               /* function call */
}

/* func() */
/* function prints out value of argument */
void func(int formarg)          /* function declarator */
{                               /*     and variable declaration */
    printf("Argument is %d", formarg);
}
```

There should be no surprises here. The **main()** function passes a value to **func()**, which prints it out.

Now let's look at the older K and R approach, without prototypes:

```
/* noproto.c */
/* program doesn't use prototyping */
main()                                  /* no prototype */
{
    int actarg = 1234;
    func(actarg);                       /* function call */
}


/* func() */
/* function prints out value of argument */
func(formarg)                           /* function declarator */
int formarg;                            /* declare argument */
{
    printf("Argument is %d", formarg);
}
```

Although it uses the obsolete format, this program will compile and run in Microsoft C. The ANSI standard, to which Microsoft adheres, allows the old-style approach so that older source files can be compiled.

There are two major differences between this and the prototype approach. First, as its name suggests, noproto.c does not use a prototype. This works, provided the function doesn't return anything or returns type **int**. If the function returns some other type, like **float**, then it must be declared. However, the declaration need not include the data types of the arguments. (A full prototype always includes the data types of the arguments or **void**.)

Second, in the function, the function declarator and the declaration of the argument are on separate lines. This works the same as the single-line format although it does make the listing longer. The single-line format is favored in the prototype approach so that the prototype and the declarator have a similar format.

If no prototype is used, the compiler constructs one for its own use from the first reference to the function it comes across, whether it is a call to the function or the function definition.

## Advantages of Prototyping

Why were prototypes adopted for the ANSI standard? The major advantage is that the data types of a function's arguments are clearly specified at the beginning of a program. A common error has been to call a function using the wrong data type for an argument; **int**, for instance, instead of **long**. If the function call and the function definition are in different files this led to program failure in a way that was difficult to debug. (We'll explore the use of different files in C programs in Chapter 14.) When a prototype is used, however, the compiler knows what data types to expect for the function, and it is always able to flag a mismatch as an error. Also—as in declaring variables—the prototype clarifies for the programmer and anyone else looking at a listing what each function is and what its arguments should be.

The ANSI standard also introduced the type **void** for a function that doesn't return anything. Previously, a function with no return value was considered to be type **int**, an inconsistent and potentially confusing approach. ANSI also introduced type **void** with a second usage, to indicate that the function takes no arguments.

## External Variables

So far, the variables we have used in our example programs have been confined to the functions using them; that is, they have been "visible" or accessible only to the function in which they were declared. Such variables, which are declared inside a particular function and used only there, are called "local" (or "automatic") variables. While local variables are preferred for most purposes, it is sometimes desirable to use a variable known to *all* the functions in a program rather than just one. This is true when many different functions must read or modify a variable, making it clumsy or impractical to communicate the value of the variable from function to function using arguments and return values. In this case, we use an "external" variable (sometimes called a "global" variable).

Here's an example of a program that uses an external variable:

```c
/* extern.c */
/* tests use of external variables */
void oddeven(void);                  /* function prototypes */
void negative(void);

int keynumb;                         /* external variable */

main()
{
    printf("Type keynumb: ");
    scanf("%d", &keynumb);
    oddeven();                       /* function call */
    negative();                      /* function call */
}

/* oddeven() */
/* checks if keynumb is odd or even */
void oddeven(void)
{
    if ( keynumb % 2 )               /* reference external var */
        printf("Keynumb is odd.\n");
    else
        printf("Keynumb is even.\n");
}
```

```
/* negative() */
/* checks if keynumb is negative */
void negative(void)
{
    if ( keynumb < 0 )                    /* reference external var */
        printf("Keynumb is negative.\n");
    else
        printf("Keynumb is positive.\n");
}
```

In this program, **main()** and two other functions, **oddeven()** and **negative()**, all have access to the variable **keynumb**. To achieve this new global status for **keynum** it was necessary to declare it *outside* of all of the functions, including **main()**. Thus it appears before the definition of **main**.

Here's a sample interaction with the program:

```
C>extern
Type keynumb: -21
Keynumb is odd.
Keynumb is negative.

C>extern
Type keynumb: 44
Keynumb is even.
Keynumb is positive.
```

As you can see, **main()** is able to place a value in the variable **keynumb**, and both **oddeven()** and **negative()** are able to read the value of the variable.

There is more to be said about the visibility of variables to various functions and the related question of how long a variable lasts: its *lifetime*. These questions relate to another important topic: C's capability of combining separately compiled object files together at link time into a single executable program. We'll return to these topics in Chapter 15.

We should, however, point out the dangers of indiscriminate use of external variables. It may seem tempting to simplify things by making all variables external; BASIC programmers in particular tend to fall victim to this practice. However, there are several reasons why it is not a good idea. First, external variables are not protected from accidental alteration by functions that have no business modifying them. Second, as we'll see in Chapter 15, external variables use memory less efficiently than local variables. The rule is, variables should be local unless there's a very good reason to make them external.

# Preprocessor Directives

At this point, we'll shift gears a little and explore a topic which at first glance might not seem to have much to do with functions: the use of *preprocessor directives*. Preprocessor directives form what can almost be considered a language within the language of C. This is a capability that does not exist in many other higher-level languages (although there are similar features in assembly language).

To understand preprocessor directives, let's first review what a compiler does. When you write a line of program code

```
num = 44;
```

you are asking the compiler to translate this code into machine-language instructions which can be executed by the microprocessor chip in the computer. Thus, most of your listing consists of instructions to the microprocessor. Preprocessor directives, on the other hand, are instructions *to the compiler itself.* Rather than being translated into machine language, they are operated on directly by the compiler before the compilation process even begins; hence the name *preprocessor.*

> Normal program statements are instructions to the microprocessor; preprocessor directives are instructions to the compiler.

Here we'll examine two of the most common preprocessor directives, **#define** and **#include**. There are others, some of which we'll look at in Chapter 14.

Preprocessor directives always start with a number sign ( # ). The directives can be placed anywhere in a program, but are most often used at the beginning of a file, before **main()**, or before the beginning of particular functions.

## The *#define* Directive

The simplest use for the **define** directive is to assign names (such as DAYS_ YEAR or PI) to constants (such as 365 or 3.14159). As an example, let's modify the sphere.c program from earlier in the chapter. In its original incarnation, the constant 3.14159 appeared in this program in the **area()** function in the line

```
return( 4 * 3.14159 * rad * rad );
```

Here's the modified program:

```
/* sphere2.c */
/* calculates area of a sphere */

#define PI 3.14159                    /* #define directive */
float area(float);                    /* prototype */

main()
{
    float radius;
```

```
    printf("Enter radius of sphere: ");
    scanf("%f", &radius);
    printf("Area of sphere is %.2f", area(radius) );
}

/* area() */
/* returns area of sphere */
float area(float rad)
{
    return( 4 * PI * rad * rad );      /* use of identifier */
}
```

In this new version the preprocessor first looks for all program lines beginning with the number sign ( # ). When it sees the **#define** directive, it goes through the entire program, and at every place it finds PI it *substitutes* the phrase 3.14159. This is a mechanical process: simply the substituting of one group of characters, "3.14159" for another, "PI." It's very much like a "global search and replace" using a word processor. Figure 5-13 shows the structure of the **#define** directive.

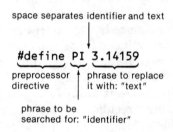

Figure 5-13. Structure of the **#define** Directive

The phrase on the left (PI), which will be searched *for*, is called the "identifier." The phrase on the right (3.14159), which will be substituted for it, is called the "text." A space separates the identifier from the text. By convention, the identifier (in this case, PI) is written in all caps. This makes it easy when looking at the program to tell which parts of the program will be altered by **#define** directives.

### Why Use #define?

Perhaps you wonder what we've gained by substituting PI for 3.14159 in our program. Hopefully, we've made the program easier to read. Although 3.14159 is such a common constant it is easily recognizable, there are many instances where a constant does not reveal its purpose so readily. For example, as we'll find out later, the phrase "\x1B[C" causes the cursor to move one space to the right. But which would you find easier to understand in the middle of your program, "\x1B[C", or "CURSOR_RIGHT"? Thus, we would use the **#define** directive

```
#define CURSOR_RIGHT "\x1B[C"
```

Then whenever CURSOR_RIGHT appeared in the program it would automatically be replaced by "\x1B[C" before compilation began.

There is another, perhaps more important reason for using the **#define** directive in this way. Suppose a constant like 3.14159 appears many times in your program. Further suppose that you now decide you want an extra place of precision; you need to change all instances of 3.14159 to 3.141592. Ordinarily, you would need to go through the program and manually change each occurrence of the constant. However, if you have defined 3.14159 to be PI in a **#define** directive, you only need to make one change, in the **#define** directive itself:

```
#define PI 3.141592
```

The change will be made automatically to all occurrences of PI before compilation begins.

### Why Not Use Variable Names?

Couldn't we use a *variable* for the same purpose as a **#define** directive? A variable could also provide a meaningful name for a constant and permit one change to effect many occurrences of the constant. It's true, a variable can be used in this way. However, there are at least three reasons why it's a bad idea. First, it is inefficient, since the compiler can generate faster and more compact code for constants than it can for variables. Second, using a variable for what is really a constant encourages sloppy thinking and makes the program more difficult to understand: if something never changes it is confusing to make it a variable. And third, there is always the danger that a variable will be altered inadvertently during execution of the program, so that it is no longer the "constant" you think it is.

In other words, using **#define** can produce more efficient and more easily understood programs. It is used extensively by C programmers—you'll see many examples as we go along.

## Macros

The **#define** directive is actually considerably more powerful than we have shown so far. This additional power comes from **#define**'s ability to use *arguments*. Before we tackle this, let's look at one more example of **#define** without an argument to make the transition clearer. In this example we show that **#define** can be used, not only for constants, but to substitute for any phrase we like. Suppose your program needs to print the message "Error" at several places in the program. You use the directive:

```
#define ERROR printf("\nError.\n");
```

Then if you have a program statement such as

```
if (input > 640)
    ERROR
```

it will be expanded into

```
if (input > 640)
    printf("\nError.\n");
```

by the preprocessor before compilation begins. The moral here is that an identifier defined by **#define** can be used as an entire C statement.

Now let's look at an example of **#define** with an argument. If you've ever
thought that the **printf()** function makes you go to a lot of trouble just to print a
number, consider this alternative:

```
/* macroprn.c */
/* demonstrates macros, using printf() statement */
#define PR(n) printf("%.2f\n",n);
main()
{
    float num1 = 27.25;
    float num2;

    num2 = 1.0 / 3.0;
    PR(num1);
    PR(num2);
}
```

Here's the output of the program:

```
C>macroprn
27.25
0.33
```

You can see that our abbreviated version of the **printf()** statement, **PR(n)**,
actually prints out the two numbers.

In this program, whenever the preprocessor sees the phrase "PR(n)" it
expands it into the C statement:

```
printf("%.2f\n",n);
```

> A **#define** directive can take arguments, much as a function does.

However, that's not all it does. In the **#define** directive, the **n** in the identifier
**PR(n)** is an *argument* that matches the **n** in the **printf()** statement in the text.
The statement **PR(num1)** in the program causes the variable **num1** to be
substituted for **n**. Thus, the phrase **PR(num1)** is equivalent to:

```
printf("%.2f\n", num1);
```

Figure 5-14 shows how this process works.

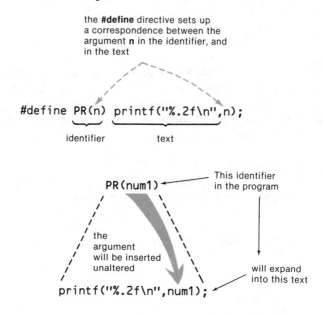

the **#define** directive sets up a correspondence between the argument **n** in the identifier, and in the text

```
#define PR(n) printf("%.2f\n",n);
```

identifier       text

PR(num1)

This identifier in the program

the argument will be inserted unaltered

will expand into this text

```
printf("%.2f\n",num1);
```

Figure 5-14. Arguments Used in the **#define** Directive

A **#define** directive that uses arguments in this way is called a "macro." Macros have some of the characteristics of functions, as will be made clearer in the next example.

Syntax note: whenever you use a **#define** directive you shouldn't use any spaces in the identifier. For instance,

```
#define PR (n) printf("%.2f\n",n);
```

would not work, because the space between PR and (n) would be interpreted as the end of the identifier.

### Macros and Functions

Macros and functions can actually perform many of the same tasks. For instance, let's modify our sphere.c program from earlier in the chapter to use a macro, instead of the function **area()**, to do the actual calculation of the area of a sphere. Here's the revised program:

```
/* sphereM.c */
/* calculates area of a sphere */
/* uses a macro */
#define PI 3.14159                /* definition of PI */
#define AREA(X) (4 * PI * X * X)  /* macro for area of sphere */
main()
{
```

```
    float radius;
    printf("Enter radius of sphere: ");
    scanf("%f", &radius);
    printf( "Area of sphere is %.2f", AREA(radius) );
}
```

Here the preprocessor will substitute the text

```
(4 * 3.14159 * radius * radius)
```

for the identifier AREA(radius). Note that we've used an identifier within an identifier: first AREA(radius) is expanded, then the PI within it is changed to 3.14159.

### Use of Parentheses in Macros
Liberal use of parentheses in a macro can save considerable grief. Why? Suppose your program contains the following lines:

```
#define SUM(x,y) x + y
- - - - -
ans = 10 * SUM(3,4)
```

what value will **ans** be given when you run the program? You might think 3 would be added to 4, giving 7, and that result, when multiplied by 10, would yield 70. Wrong. Look at the expansion of the assignment statement. **SUM(3,4)** turns into simply **3 + 4**. Thus, the entire statement becomes:

```
ans = 10 * 3 + 4
```

Multiplication has a higher precedence than addition, so the result will be 30 + 4, or 34. This is different enough from the correct answer of 70 to suggest that we have a problem. The solution is to put parentheses around the entire text part of the **#define** directive:

```
#define SUM(x,y) (x + y)
```

Now the assignment statement is expanded into

```
ans = 10 * (3 + 4)
```

which yields the correct result.

Even enclosing the entire text in parentheses, however, does not solve all possible problems. Consider a macro that does multiplication:

```
#define PRODUCT(x,y) (x * y)
- - - - -
ans = PRODUCT(2+3,4)
```

Here the programmer was rash enough to use an expression, 2+3, as an argument for the macro. One might hope that this would yield an answer of 20 (2+3 is 5, multiplied by 4). However, look what happens in the expansion:

```
ans = (2+3*4).
```

The multiplication will be done first, so we'll have 2 + 12, or 14. Here, the solution is to enclose *each argument* in parentheses. For clarity, we did not do this in the examples above, but we should have. Suppose in the sphereM.c program we had used an expression such as **rad+3** as an argument to the AREA(radius) macro. It would have been expanded to (4 * PI * rad + 3 * rad + 3) or (4*PI*rad + 3*rad + 3), which is no way to calculate the area of a sphere of radius rad+3.

> For safety's sake, put parentheses around the entire text of any define directive that uses arguments and also around each of the arguments.

Thus, to be sure your macros will do what you want, enclose the entire text expression in parentheses and each variable in the text expression, as well.

### When to Use Macros

Macros often can be used more conveniently than functions, as our example above demonstrates. Of course, the task to be carried out by the macro must not be too complex, as a **#define** statement is limited to one line in the Microsoft compiler. (Some compilers permit more, but most programmers try not to excede this limit anyway.) Assuming such a simple task however, when should you use a macro and when a function?

Each time a macro is invoked, the code it generates is actually inserted in the executable file for the program. This leads to multiple copies of the same code. The code for a function, however, only appears once, so using a function is more efficient in terms of memory size. On the other hand, no time is wasted calling a macro; whereas, when you call a function the program has to arrange for the arguments to be transferred to the function and jump to the function's code. So a function takes less memory but is slower to execute, while a macro is faster but uses more memory. You have to decide which approach suits your particular program better.

> A macro generates more code but executes more quickly than a function.

Excessive use of macros can also make a program difficult to read, since it requires constant reference back and forth between the **#define** directives at the beginning of the program and the identifiers in the program body. Deciding when to use a macro and when not to is largely a matter of style.

## The #*include* Directive

The second preprocessor directive we'll explore in this chapter is **#include**. The **#include** directive causes one source file to be included in another.

Here's an example of why you might want to do such a thing. Suppose you write a lot of math-oriented programs that repeatedly refer to formulas for calculating areas of different shapes. You could place all these formulas, as macros, in a single separate source file. Then, instead of having to rewrite all the macros every time you wrote a program that used them, you could insert them into the .c source file using the **#include** directive.

Such a separate source file might look like this:

```
#define PI 3.14159
#define AREA_CIRCLE(radius) (PI*radius*radius)
#define AREA_SQUARE(length,width) (length*width)
#define AREA_TRIANGLE(base,height) (base*height/2)
#define AREA_ELLIPSE(radius1,radius2) (PI*radius1*radius2)
#define AREA_TRAPEZOID(height,side1,side2) (height*(side1+side2)/2)
```

This is not something you would want to type over and over again if you could avoid it. Instead, you type it in once with your word processor and save it as a file. You might call the file AREAS.H. The .h extension is commonly used for "header" files, which this is: a group of statements that will go at the head of your program.

When you write your source file for a program that needs to use these formulas, you simply include the directive

```
#include "areas.h"
```

at the beginning of your program. All the statements shown above will be added to your program as if you had typed them in.

This is very similar to a word processor or editor being used to read, say, a standard heading into a business letter. In fact in this particular instance you could have used your word processor to read the file AREAS.H into your source file; the effect would have been similar.

There are actually two ways to write **#include** statements. The variation in format tells the preprocessor where to look for the file you want included.

The variation shown above

```
#include "areas.h"
```

shows the filename surrounded by quotes. This causes the preprocessor to start searching for the AREAS.H file in the directory containing the current source file. If it doesn't find it there it will look in other directories.

The other approach is to use angle brackets:

```
#include <areas.h>
```

This format causes the preprocessor to start searching in the standard header directory, which we'll discuss next.

## Prototypes for Library Functions

The astute reader may have noticed an inconsistency in our approach to functions. We use prototypes for user-written functions; but where are the prototypes for library functions? For instance, if we call the function **getche()**, shouldn't there be a line like

```
int getche(void);
```

at the start of our program? The answer is, yes there should. If we insert a prototype for each library function used in our program, the compiler will be able to detect mismatches in the data types and the number of arguments we send to the function and the data type the function returns. This is an obvious advantage.

However, we don't need to write these prototypes ourselves. They're grouped together in header files, which are all in the INCLUDE directory, as we discussed in Chapter 1. To cause one of these files to be included in our program, we can use the #**define** directive.

For instance, the header file that contains the prototype for **printf()** is in the header file STDIO.H (along with many other prototypes and various definitions and macros). You can find the appropriate header file by looking up the function in the Microsoft run-time library reference manual. To include this file in the source file for our program we need only place this line at the beginning of our listing:

```
#include <stdio.h>
```

Using header files in this way is highly recommended. In many programs in this book we leave off these #**include** directives in the interest of brevity. In writing your own program, however, do as we say, not as we do. Include the appropriate header file for every library function you use. For instance, here's a program with appropriate header files:

```
/* header.c */
/* demonstrates correct use of header files */
#include <stdio.h>      /* for printf() */
#include (conio.h>      /* for getche() */
main()
{
    printf("Type 'y' or 'n': ");
```

```
    getche();
}
```

## What about *main()*?

We've discussed the use of prototypes for user-written functions and library functions. What about the **main()** function? It's not necessary to use a prototype for **main()** (although you can). In some cases it may help to clarify **main()**'s operation if you use a complete declarator for it:

```
void main(void)
```

Arguments can be used for **main()**, as we'll see later, so this usage makes it clear they're not being used in a particular circumstance.

## Macros in Header Files

Some entities that look like functions are actually macros that are defined in header files. For example, **getchar()** and **putchar()**, which are used as if they were functions to read a character from the keyboard and place a character on the screen, are actually macros. To use them, you must include stdio.h in your program; otherwise the linker will flag them as "unresolved externals."

It's interesting to browse through the header files. They're source files, so you can look at them with the TYPE command or with your editor. (Be careful not to change them, of course.) They contain some features we haven't discussed yet, but the broad outline of what they contain should be clear.

# Compiler Warning Levels

You can use compiler warnings to guard against mistakes in using prototypes and header files. Until now you've probably been using the default warning level when you compiled your program. At this level you receive some warning messages, in addition to actual error messages (which keep your program from compiling). However, other, more nit-picky, warnings are not reported.

Warning levels run from 0 to 3. At level 0 you get no warnings, and at level 3 you get them all. Level 1 is the default. If you want your program to be as correct as the compiler can possibly make it, you can request level 3.

On the Optimizing Compiler this is done using a switch in the command line. Invoke CL this way:

```
C>cl /W3 myprog.c
```

In QuickC, select 3 from the Warnings list in the window that appears when you choose Compile from the Run menu.

If you use warning level 3 this way you'll find out immediately if you've used prototypes incorrectly. You'll also get messages if you haven't used prototypes at all; this will happen if you don't include the appropriate header file for a library function. You'll even get warnings if you haven't used a declarator for **main()**, as discussed above.

Many programs work correctly even when they generate level 2 and level 3 warnings. However, such warnings can be a symptom of incorrect operation or of bad programming style. It's a good idea to try compiling with level 3 to see what the warnings reveal.

### Pragmas

Preprocessor directives tell the compiler to do something *before* compiling the program. Another kind of instruction to the compiler, the *pragma*, tells the compiler to do something *during* compilation. Pragmas often tell the compiler to start doing something (such as loop optimization or stack checking) at some point in the program listing and to stop doing it at another point.

Pragmas start with the number sign and the word "pragma." Here's a pragma that activates pointer checking:

```
#pragma check_pointer(on)
```

Many pragmas apply to advanced C features we won't be exploring in this book.

## Summary

In this chapter you've learned how to use functions: how to write them, how to use them to return values, and how to send them information using arguments. You've learned that a function commonly uses local variables which are visible only within the function itself and not to other functions. You've learned, too, to use external variables, which are visible to all functions. Finally you've learned about the preprocessor directives **#define**, which can be used to give names to constants or even whole C statements, creating a functionlike capability, and **#include**, which causes one source file to be included in another.

## Questions

1. Which of these are valid reasons for using functions?
   a. they use less memory than repeating the same code
   b. they run faster
   c. they keep different program activities separate
   d. they keep variables safe from other parts of the program

2. True or false: a function can still be useful even if you can't pass it any information and can't get any information back from it.

3. Is this a correct call to the function **abs()**, which takes one argument?

```
ans = abs(num)
```

4. True or false: to return from a function you must use the keyword **return**.

5. Write a prototype for a function called **foo()** that returns type **char** and takes two arguments of type **float**.

6. Is this a correctly written function?

```
void abs(int num);
{
    if(num < 0)
        num = -num;
    return(num);
}
```

7. Which of the following are differences between Pascal and C?

   a. Pascal uses functions and procedures, C only functions

   b. there is no way to return from a Pascal function as there is in C

   c. functions can be nested in Pascal but not in C

   d. Pascal functions are all of type **int**

8. True or false: the variables commonly used in C functions are accessible to all other functions.

9. Which of the following are valid reasons for using arguments in functions?

   a. to tell the function where to locate itself in memory

   b. to convey information to the function that it can operate on

   c. to return information from the function to the calling program

   d. to specify the type of the function

10. Which of the following can be passed to a function via arguments?

   a. constants

   b. variables (with values)

   c. preprocessor directives

   d. expressions (that evaluate to a value)

   e. functions (that return values)

11. Is the following a correctly structured program?

```
void type(int);
main()
{
    int three=3;
    type(three);
}
void type(float num)
{
    printf("%f", num);
}
```

12. Which of the following is true?

    a. C functions are all equal

    b. C functions can be nested within each other

    c. C functions are arranged in a strict hierarchy

    d. C functions can only be called from **main()**

13. External variables can be accessed by _____function(s) in a program.

14. An external variable is defined in a declaration

    a. in **main()** only

    b. in the first function that uses it

    c. in any function that uses it

    d. outside of any function

15. An external variable can be referenced in a declaration

    a. in **main()** only

    b. in the first function that uses it

    c. in any function that uses it

    d. outside of any function

16. What is a preprocessor directive?

    a. a message from the compiler to the programmer

    b. a message to the linker from the compiler

    c. a message from the programmer to the compiler

    d. a message from the programmer to the microprocessor

17. The **#define** directive causes one phrase to be _____ for another.

18. Is this a correctly formed **#define** statement?

```
#define CM PER INCH 2.54
```

19. In this **#define** directive, which is the identifier and which is the text?

```
#define EXP 2.71828
```

20. What is a macro?

    a. a **#define** directive that acts like a function

    b. a **#define** directive that takes arguments

    c. a **#define** directive that returns a value

    d. a **#define** directive that simulates **scanf()**

21. A variable should not be used to store values which never change because

    a. the program will run more slowly

    b. the program will be harder to understand

    c. there is no such data type

    d. the value of the "constant" might be altered

22. Will the following code correctly calculate postage that is equal to a fixed rate times the sum of the combined girth and height of a parcel?

```
#define SUM3(length,width,height) length + width + height
postage = rate * SUM3(l,w,h)
```

23. The **#include** directive causes one source file to be _____ in another.

24. A header file is

    a. a file which must precede all source code files

    b. a source code file

    c. a file that can be **#include**d in other source code files

    d. a source code file containing various definitions and macros

25. Standard header files can be found in the _____ directory.

# Exercises

1. Write a program that prints out the larger of two numbers entered from the keyboard. Use a function to do the actual comparison of the two numbers.

Pass the two numbers to the function as arguments, and have the function return the answer with **return()**.

2. Rewrite the intimes.c program from this chapter so that instead of working only with hours and minutes, it works with hours, minutes, and seconds. Call this program times.c.

3. Write a program that will swap two external variables. The variables should be typed in by the user, printed out, swapped, then printed out again. Use a function to do the actual swapping.

4. Rewrite the times.c program from exercise 2 to use a macro instead of a function. Getting the data from the user must take place in the main program, but the conversion from hours-minutes-seconds to seconds should take place in the macro.

# 6

# *Arrays and Strings*

- Arrays
- Initializing arrays
- Multidimensional arrays
- Arrays as function arguments
- Strings
- String functions

# 6

You might wonder why we have placed the topics of arrays and strings together in one chapter. The answer is simple: strings *are* arrays: arrays of type **char**. Thus to understand strings we need to understand arrays. In this chapter we'll cover arrays first and then move on to strings.

We should note that, in many C books and courses, arrays and strings are taught at the same time as pointers. We feel it is clearer to introduce these topics separately. Pointers will be a new concept for many readers, and it seems unfortunate to complicate the discussion of arrays and strings, which are not really that different from their counterparts in other languages, by introducing pointers at the same time. We'll get to pointers soon enough: they're the subject of Chapter 7.

## Arrays

If you have a collection of similar data elements you may find it inconvenient to give each one a unique variable name. For instance, suppose you wanted to find the average temperature for a particular week. If each day's temperature had a unique variable name, you would end up reading in each value separately:

```
printf("Enter Sunday temperature: ");
scanf("%d", &suntmp);
printf("Enter Monday temperature: ");
scanf("%d", &montmp);
- - - - -
```

and so on, for each day of the week, with an expression for the average such as this:

```
(suntmp + montmp + tuestmp + wedtmp + thutmp + fritmp + sattmp)/7
```

This is an altogether unwieldy business, especially if you want to average the temperatures for a month or a year.

Clearly we need a convenient way to refer to such collections of similar data elements. The array fills the bill. It provides a way to refer to individual items in a collection by using the same variable name, but differing *subscripts*, or numbers. Let's see how we'd solve our problem of averaging the temperatures for a week using arrays:

```
/* temp.c */
/* averages one week's temperatures */
main()
{
    int temper[7];                  /* array declaration */
    int day, sum;

    for (day=0; day<7; day++)       /* put temps in array */
        {
        printf("Enter temperature for day %d: ", day);
        scanf("%d", &temper[day]);
        }

    sum = 0;                        /* calculate average */
    for (day=0; day<7; day++)
        sum += temper[day];
    printf("Average is %d.", sum/7);
}
```

This program reads in seven temperatures, stores them in an array, shown symbolically in Figure 6-1, and then, to calculate an average temperature, reads them back out of the array, adding them together, and dividing by 7. Here's a sample run:

```
C>temp
Enter temperature for day 0: 74
Enter temperature for day 1: 76
Enter temperature for day 2: 77
Enter temperature for day 3: 77
Enter temperature for day 4: 64
Enter temperature for day 5: 66
Enter temperature for day 6: 69
Average is 71.
```

(Meteorology buffs will notice that temperatures rose slowly during the first part of this particular week in August and that a cold front passed through on Wednesday night.)

There's a lot of new material in this program, so let's take it apart slowly.

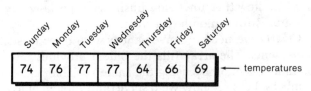

Figure 6-1. Symbolic Representation of an Array

## Array Declaration

An array is a collection of variables of a certain type, placed contiguously in memory. Like other variables, the array needs to be declared, so the compiler will know what kind of array, and how large an array, we want. We do that in the example above with the line:

```
int temper[7];
```

Here the **int** specifies the type of variable, just as it does with simple variables, and the word **temper** is the name of the variable. The **[7]**, however, is new. This number tells *how many* variables of type **int** will be in our array. (Each of the separate variables in the array is called an "element.") The brackets tell the compiler that we are dealing with an array. Figure 6-2 is a schematic representation of what the array looks like.

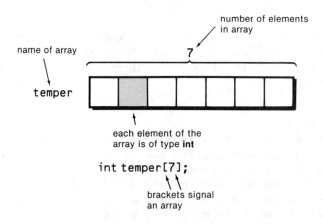

Figure 6-2. Array Declaration

# Referring to Individual Elements of the Array

Once the array has been established, we need a way to refer to its individual elements. This is done with subscripts, the numbers in brackets following the array name. Note, however, that this number has a different meaning when *referring* to an array element than it does when *declaring* the array, when the number in brackets is the size of the array. When referring to an array element, this number specifies the element's position in the array. All the array elements are numbered, starting at 0. The element of the array with the number 2 would be referred to as:

```
temper[2]
```

Note that, because the numbering starts with 0, this is *not* the second element of the array, but the third. Thus the last array element is one less than the size of the array. This arrangement is shown in Figure 6-3.

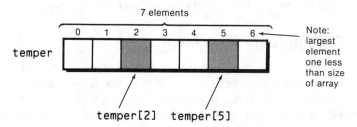

Figure 6-3. Array References

In our program we are using an integer *variable*, **day**, as a subscript to refer to the various elements of the array. This variable can take on any value we want and so can point to the different array elements in turn. This ability to use variables as subscripts is what makes arrays so useful.

```
temper[day]
```

## Entering Data into the Array

Here's the section of code that places data into the array:

```
for (day=0; day<7; day++)        /* put temps in array */
    {
    printf("Enter temperature for day %d: ", day);
    scanf("%d", &temper[day]);
    }
```

The **for** loop causes the process of asking for and receiving a temperature from the user to be repeated seven times. The first time through the loop, **day** has the value 0, so the **scanf()** statement will cause the value typed in to be stored in array element **temper[0]**, the first element of the array. This process will be repeated until **day** becomes 6. That is the last time through the loop, which is a good thing, because there is no array element **temper[7]**.

> The first element in an array is numbered 0, so the last element is 1 less than the size of the array.

This is a common idiom in C for dealing with arrays: a **for** loop that starts with 0 and goes up to, but does not include (note the "less-than" sign), the size of the array.

In the **scanf()** statement, we've used the address operator ( & ) on the element of the **&temper[day]** array, just as we've used it earlier on other variables ( **&num**, for example) to be read in by the **scanf()** function. In so doing, we're passing the *address* of this particular array element to the function, rather than its value; this is what **scanf()** requires.

## Reading Data from the Array

The balance of the program reads the data back out of the array and uses it to calculate an average. The **for** loop is much the same, but now the body of the loop causes each day's temperature to be added to a running total called **sum**. When all the temperatures have been added up, the result is divided by 7, the number of data items.

```
sum = 0;                         /* calculate average */
for (day=0; day<7; day++)
    sum += temper[day];
printf("Average is %d.", sum/7);
```

## Using Different Variable Types

Although the example above used an array of type **int**, an array can be of any variable type. As an example, let's rewrite temp.c to be of type **float**:

```
/* fltemp.c */
/* averages one week's temperatures */
main()
{
    float temper[7];             /* array declaration */
    float sum;
    int day;

    for (day=0; day<7; day++)    /* put temps in array */
        {
        printf("Enter temperature for day %d: ", day);
        scanf("%f", &temper[day]);
        }

    sum = 0.0;                       /* calculate average */
    for (day=0; day<7; day++)
```

```
        sum += temper[day];
     printf("Average is %.1f", sum/7.0);
  }
```

This program operates in much the same way as temp.c, except that now it can accept numbers with decimal fractions as input and so can calculate a more precise average. Here's a sample run:

```
C>fltemp
Enter temperature for day 0: 80.5
Enter temperature for day 1: 78.2
Enter temperature for day 2: 67.4
Enter temperature for day 3: 71.4
Enter temperature for day 4: 74.6
Enter temperature for day 5: 78.3
Enter temperature for day 6: 80.1
Average is 75.8
```

We had a cooling trend in the middle of the week, with ideal beach temperatures on the weekends.

We've changed the array (and the variable **sum**) to type **float**, and we've altered the format specifiers in the **scanf()** and **printf()** statements accordingly.

## Reading in an Unknown Number of Elements

So far we've worked with a fixed amount of input, requiring a data item for each of the days of the week. What if we don't know in advance how many items will be entered into the array? Here's a program that will accept any number of temperatures—up to 40— and average them:

```
/* fltemp2.c */
/* averages arbitrary number of temperatures */
#define LIM 40
main()
{
   float temper[LIM];               /* array declaration */
   float sum=0.0;
   int num, day=0;

   do                               /* put temps in array */
      {
      printf("Enter temperature for day %d: ", day);
      scanf("%f", &temper[day]);
      }
   while ( temper[day++] > 0 );

   num = day-1;                     /* number of temps entered */
   for (day=0; day<num; day++)      /* calculate average */
      sum += temper[day];
```

```
        printf("Average is %.1f", sum/num);
}
```

Here's a run in which only three temperatures are entered:

```
C>fltemp2
Enter temperature for day 0: 71.3
Enter temperature for day 1: 80.9
Enter temperature for day 2: 89.2
Enter temperature for day 3: 0
Average is 80.5
```

As you can see, we've replaced the **for** loop with a **do while** loop. This loop repeatedly asks the user to enter a temperature and stores the responses in the array **temper**, until a temperature of 0 or less is entered. (Clearly, this is not a program for cold climates.) When the last item has been typed, the variable **day** will have reached a value 1 greater than the total number of items entered. This is true because it counts the 0 (or negative number), which the user entered to terminate the input. Thus to find the number of items entered, **num**, we subtract 1 from **day**. The variable **num** is then used as the limit in the second **for** loop, which adds up the temperatures, and it's also used as the divisor of the resulting sum.

There's another change in the program as well. We've used a **#define** directive to give the identifier LIM the value of 40:

```
#define LIM 40
```

We then used LIM in the array declaration. Using a **#define**d value as an array size is common in C. Later, if we wish to change the size, all we need do is change the 40 in the **#define** statement, and the change will be reflected anywhere this value appears. In this particular program the number is only used once, but we'll soon see examples in which the array dimension occurs repeatedly in the program, making the use of the **#define** directive a real convenience.

## Bounds Checking

We've made the size of the array to be 40 in the **#define** directive. This is large enough to hold one month's temperatures, with some left over. But suppose a user decided to enter *two* months worth of data? As it turns out, there probably would be Big Trouble. The reason is that in C there is no check to see if the subscript used for an array exceeds the size of the array. Data entered with too large a subscript will simply be placed in memory *outside the array*: probably on top of other data or the program itself. This will lead to unpredictable results, to say the least, and there will be no error message to warn you that it's happening.

C does not warn you when an array subscript exceeds the size of the array.

The solution, if there's the slightest reason to believe the user might enter too many items, is to check for this possibility in the program. For instance, we could modify the **do-while** loop as follows:

```
do
   {
   if ( day >= LIM )                 /* beyond array end? */
      {
      printf("Buffer full.\n");
      day++;                         /* won't be incremented later */
      break;                         /* exit loop */
      }
   printf("Enter temperature for day %d: ", day);
   scanf("%f", &temper[day]);
   }
while ( temper[day++] > 0 );
```

Now if the loop is entered with **day** equal to 40, which is 1 past the end of the buffer at 39, the message "Buffer full" will be printed and the **break** statement will take us out of the loop to the second part of the program. (We need to increment **day** since the **while** statement won't be executed.) Here's a run showing the last few lines before the user oversteps the bounds:

```
Enter temperature for day 38: 73.4
Enter temperature for day 39: 62.2
Buffer full.
Average is 75.1
```

As you can see, the temperature for day 39 is accepted, but then the program realizes that one more item would be one too many, prints the message, and **break**s out of the loop.

## Initializing Arrays

So far, we've shown arrays that started life with nothing in them. Suppose we want to compile our program with specific values already fixed in the array? This is analogous to initializing a simple variable:

```
int george = 45;
```

Here's a program demonstrating the initializing of an array. The program makes change; you type in a price in cents, and the program tells you how many half-dollars, quarters, dimes, nickels, and pennies it takes to make up this amount.

```
/* change.c */
/* program to make change */
```

```
#define LIM 5
int table[LIM] = { 50, 25, 10, 5, 1 };

main()
{
    int dex, amount, quantity;
    printf("Enter amount in cents (form 367): ");
    scanf("%d", &amount);
    for (dex=0; dex<LIM; dex++)
        {
        quantity = amount / table[dex];
        printf("Value of coin=%2d, ", table[dex] );
        printf("number of coins=%2d\n", quantity );
        amount = amount % table[dex];
        }
}
```

Here's a sample run:

```
C>change
Enter amount in cents (form 367): 143
Value of coin=50, number of coins= 2
Value of coin=25, number of coins= 1
Value of coin=10, number of coins= 1
Value of coin= 5, number of coins= 1
Value of coin= 1, number of coins= 3
```

The program has figured out that $1.43 is two half-dollars, one quarter, one dime, one nickel, and three pennies. This is smarter than some checkout people are.

The program works by taking the value of the largest coin, 50, and dividing it into the amount typed in (the variable **amount**). It prints out the answer, which is the number of half-dollars necessary, and then it performs the same division but this time with the remainder operator ( % ). This remainder, in turn, is used as the new amount, which is divided by the next smallest size of coin, 25. The process is repeated five times, once for each coin.

The array is used to hold the values, expressed in cents, of the various coins. Here's the statement that initializes the array to these values:

```
int table[LIM] = { 50, 25, 10, 5, 1 };
```

The list of values is enclosed by braces, and the values are separated by commas. The values are assigned in turn to the elements of the array, so that table[0] is 50, table[1] is 25, and so on, up to table[4], which is 1.

### Storage Classes and Array Initialization
You may be wondering why we put the array declaration outside of the **main()** function, thus making it an external variable. The reason is that you can't initialize an array that is a local (automatic) variable. Why not? Because C

doesn't create such an array until the function containing it is called, and by then it's too late to put initial values in it.

> You can't initialize a local (automatic) array.

Thus if you want to initialize an array, it must use a variable that stays in existence for the life of the program. There are two classes of variables that do this. One is the **external** storage class, which we've used in the example above. The other is the **static** class. Unlike external variables, **static** variables are not visible outside the function in which they're declared, but like external variables, they don't disappear when the function terminates. As we noted in Chapter 5, how long a variable lasts is called its "lifetime." Lifetime, and the related idea of visibility, are characteristics of a variable's *storage class*. We'll discuss storage classes in more detail in Chapter 15.

Here's the change.c program rewritten to use a **static** variable class for the array **table[ ]**:

```
/* change2.c */
/* program to make change */
#define LIM 5

main()
{
    static int table[] = { 50, 25, 10, 5, 1 };
    int dex, amount, quantity;

    printf("Enter amount in cents (form 367): ");
    scanf("%d", &amount);
    for (dex=0; dex<LIM; dex++)
        {
        quantity = amount / table[dex];
        printf("Value of coin=%2d, ", table[dex] );
        printf("number of coins=%2d\n", quantity );
        amount = amount % table[dex];
        }
}
```

This is similar to the first version, but the array definition has been moved inside the function **main()** and the word "static" has been added to it. The two programs operate in exactly the same way, but if there were other functions in the program, they would be able to access the external array in change.c, while the static array in change2.c would be invisible to them.

## Array Size and Initialization

We've made another kind of change in the array declaration between change.c and change2.c.

The change.c program used the value LIM (which was #**defined** as 5) in the array declaration:

```
int table[LIM] = { 50, 25, 10, 5, 1 };
```

But in change2.c this number is simply left out, leaving an empty pair of brackets following "table":

```
static int table[] = { 50, 25, 10, 5, 1 };
```

How can we get away with this? The answer is that if no number is supplied for the size of the array, the compiler will very kindly count the number of items in the initialization list and fix that as the array size.

What happens if a number *is* supplied, but it does not agree with the actual number of items on the list? If the number is larger than the number of items, the extra spaces in the array will be filled in with zeros. If the number is too small, the compiler will complain (as well it might; where could it put the leftover values?).

## Array Contents and Initialization

You should also know what the initial values of array elements will be if they are not initialized explicitly. In other words, if we execute an array declaration inside the function, like this:

```
main()
{
    int array[10];
    - - - - -
```

and then, without putting anything into the array, we say

```
printf("Array element 3 has the value %d", array[3]);
```

what value will be printed out? Would you guess 0? That's close, but not right. In fact, what you'll get is a garbage number: whatever value was sitting in that particular part of memory before the function was called and the array declared. At least that's true in the case of the automatic variable declaration shown. However, if the array was declared as an external or static variable, it *will* be initialized to 0.

The lesson is that if you want your array initialized to all zeros, but don't want to do it yourself, make sure it's external or static.

## More than One Dimension

So far we've looked at arrays with only one dimension: that is, only one sub-script. It's also possible for arrays to have two or more dimensions. This permits them to emulate or "model" multidimensional objects, such as graph paper with rows and columns, or the computer display screen itself.

Here's a sample program that records, not one list of data as our previous programs have, but two lists side-by-side. This program stores the travel expenses for a number of secret agents who are known only by their code numbers.

```
/* travel.c */
/* stores list of secret agents' travel expenses */
#define ROWS 10        /* number of rows in array */
#define COLUMNS 2      /* number of columns in array */
main()
{
    float agents [ROWS] [COLUMNS];
    int index=0, outdex;

    printf("Enter 3-digit agent numbers,\n");
    printf("then travel expenses (007 1642.50)\n");
    printf("Enter 0 0 to quit.\n");

    do                        /* get list of agents and expenses */
        {
        printf("Agent's number and expenses: ");
        scanf( "%f %f", &agents[index][0], &agents[index][1] );
        }
    while ( agents[index++][0] != 0 );

    for (outdex=0; outdex<index-1; outdex++)   /* print list */
        {
        printf("Agent %3.0f ", agents[outdex][0] );
        printf("spent %7.2f.\n", agents[outdex][1] );
        }
}
```

There are two parts to the program: a **do-while** loop that gets the data from the user and stores it in the two-dimensional array **table[ ][ ]**, and a **for** loop that prints out the contents of the array. Here's a sample run:

```
C>travel
Enter 3-digit agent numbers,
then travel expense (007 1642.50)
Enter 0 0 to quit.
Agent's number and expenses: 101 2331.50
Agent's number and expenses: 007 8640
Agent's number and expenses: 901 123.25
Agent's number and expenses: 904 500.6
Agent's number and expenses: 0 0
Agent 101 spent 2331.50.
Agent   7 spent 8640.00.
Agent 901 spent  123.25.
Agent 904 spent  500.60.
```

The **do-while** loop is similar to that in the fltemp3.c program which obtained the temperature from the user. However, instead of getting only one piece of data each time through the loop, we get two placing them in the variables **agents[index][0]** and **agents[index][1]** with the **scanf()** statement:

```
scanf( "%f %f", &agents[index][0], &agents[index][1] );
```

The first subscript is the row number, which changes for each agent. The second subscript tells which of two columns we're talking about: the one on the left, which contains the agent numbers, or the one on the right, which lists expenses for a particular month. Each subscript goes in its own set of brackets following the variable name. The array arrangement is shown in Figure 6-4.

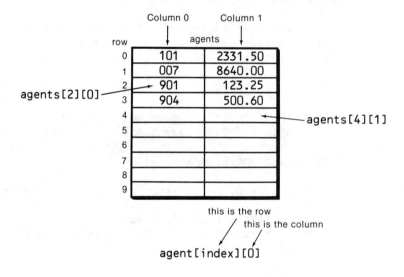

Figure 6-4. Array Used in travel.c Program

Notice that the entire array is of type **float**. We've tried to disguise this by not printing out decimal places with the agent numbers, but in reality the agent numbers are of type **float** just as the expenses are. We chose **float** because we wanted to use dollars and cents for the expenses. The ideal arrangement would be to have the agent numbers be of type **int** and the expenses of type **float**, but arrays must be of a single data type. This is an important limitation of arrays. In Chapter 9 we'll see how something called a "structure" will permit the use of multiple types in an array.

Here's a program that plots a two-dimensional grid on the screen. Initially, the grid is filled with dots (periods). But after the grid is drawn, the program then cycles through a loop asking the user for a pair of coordinates. When the user types the two coordinates (separated by a comma), the program draws a gray box at the corresponding location on the screen (or a light green or light amber box, depending on the color of your monitor).

Using this program provides a way to understand in a visual way how a two-dimensional coordinate system works. Try typing in pairs of numbers. Where will 0,0 be plotted? How about 5,0? Or 0,5? Remember that the horizontal, or x-coordinate, is typed in first, then the vertical, or y-coordinate. Here's the listing:

```c
/* plot.c */
/* plots coordinates on screen */
#define HEIGHT 5
#define WIDTH 10

main()
{
    char matrix [HEIGHT] [WIDTH];
    int x,y;

    for(y=0; y<HEIGHT; y++)              /* fill matrix with periods */
      for(x=0; x<WIDTH; x++)
        matrix[y][x] = '.';
    printf("Enter coordinates in form x,y (4,2).\n");
    printf("Use negative numbers to quit.\n");

    while ( x >= 0 )                     /* until neg coordinates */
      {
      for(y=0; y<HEIGHT; y++)        /* print matrix */
        {
        for(x=0; x<WIDTH; x++)
            printf("%c ", matrix[y][x] );
        printf("\n\n");
        }
      printf("Coordinates: ");
      scanf("%d,%d", &x, &y);        /* get coordinates */
      matrix[y][x]='\xB0';            /* put gray box there */
      }
}
```

Figure 6-5 shows a sample of interaction with the program. The user has previously entered the coordinates 2,1; on this turn, the coordinates are 5,2. The program has plotted both pairs on the screen.

Remember that the results of typing coordinates that exceed the bounds of the array can be disastrous. Don't type an x-coordinate greater than 9, nor a y-coordinate greater than 4. (You probably will anyway. The worst that can happen is a system crash.) Alternatively, you could modify the program to trap out-of-bounds entries, as we did earlier; for simplicity, we have not done this here.

## Initializing Two-Dimensional Arrays

We've learned how to initialize a one-dimensional array; what about two dimensions? As an example, we'll modify the plot.c program to play the game of battleship. In this game one player (the computer) has concealed a number of

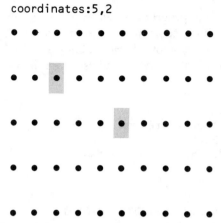
coordinates:5,2

Figure 6-5. Output of the plot.c Program

ships at different locations in a 10-by-5 grid. The other player (the human) tries to guess where the ships are by typing in coordinates. If the human guesses right, a hit is scored, and the coordinates on the grid are marked with a solid rectangle. If the human guesses wrong, the coordinates are marked with a light gray rectangle, making it easier to remember what areas have already been tested.

There are five ships concealed in the grid: one battleship 4 units long, two cruisers 3 units long, and two destroyers 2 units long. They are all placed either horizontally or vertically (not diagonally). In the program a ship will be represented by the number 1, and coordinates where there is no ship by the number 0.

We get the ships into the array by initializing the array when we write the program. Note that even though this is a character array (to save memory space), we use numbers as values:

```
/* bship.c */
/* plays battleship game */
#define HEIGHT 5
#define WIDTH 10

char enemy [HEIGHT] [WIDTH] =
    { { 0, 0, 0, 0, 0, 0, 0, 0, 0, 0 },
      { 0, 1, 1, 1, 1, 0, 0, 1, 0, 1 },
      { 0, 0, 0, 0, 0, 0, 0, 1, 0, 1 },
      { 1, 0, 0, 0, 0, 0, 0, 1, 0, 0 },
      { 1, 0, 1, 1, 1, 0, 0, 0, 0, 0 }   };

main()
{
    char friend [HEIGHT] [WIDTH];
    int x,y;

    for(y=0; y<HEIGHT; y++)              /* fill array with periods */
      for(x=0; x<WIDTH; x++)
        friend[y][x] = '.';
```

```
    printf("Enter coordinates in form x,y (4,2).\n");
    printf("Use negative numbers to quit.\n");

    while ( x >= 0 )                    /* until neg coordinates */
       {
       for(y=0; y<HEIGHT; y++)          /* print array */
          {
          for(x=0; x<WIDTH; x++)
             printf("%c ", friend[y][x] );
          printf("\n\n");
          }
       printf("Coordinates: ");
       scanf("%d,%d", &x, &y);          /* get coordinates */
       if ( enemy[y][x]==1 )            /* if it's a hit */
          friend[y][x]='\xDB';          /* put solid box there */
       else                             /* otherwise */
          friend[y][x]='\xB1';          /* gray box */
       }
}
```

The ships are located in the array initialization at the start of the program. You should be able to see the battleship on the left, oriented horizontally, in the second row down. A sample run is shown in Figure 6-6.

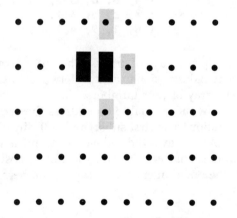

Figure 6-6. Output of the bship.c Program

In this figure the user tried 4,0, which was a miss, and then 4,1, which was a hit. Then, thinking the ship might be located vertically, the user tried 4,2 to no avail. Trying 5,1 proved that the ship didn't extend to the right. The next choice, 3,1, was a hit, so now the user will see how big a ship it is by going further left. The other ships still lurk in the darkness, waiting to be discovered.

(It would be fun to modify the program so that two people could compete, but that would take us too far afield.)

Notice the format used to initialize the array: an outer set of braces, and then 5 inner sets of braces, each with 10 members separated by commas. The inner sets of braces are separated from each other by commas as well.

We can conclude that lists go in braces, and that the elements of the list are separated by commas, whether the members of the list are composed of numbers or other lists.

> The list of values used to initialize an array are separated by commas and surrounded by braces.

## Initializing Three-Dimensional Arrays

We aren't going to show a programming example that uses a three-dimensional array. However, an example of initializing a three-dimensional array will consolidate your understanding of subscripts:

```
int threed[3][2][4] =
    {   {   { 1, 2, 3, 4 },
            { 5, 6, 7, 8 },  },
        {   { 7, 9, 3, 2 },
            { 4, 6, 8, 3 },  },
        {   { 7, 2, 6, 3 },
            { 0, 1, 9, 4 }   }    };
```

This is an array of arrays of arrays. The outer array has three elements, each of which is a two-dimensional array of two elements, each of which is a one-dimensional array of four numbers.

Quick now, how would you address the array element holding the only 0 in this declaration? The first subscript is [2], since it's in the third group of three two-dimensional arrays; the second subscript is [1], since it's in the second of two one-dimensional arrays; and the third subscript is [0], since it's the first element in the one-dimensional array of numbers. We could say, therefore, that the expression

```
threed[2][1][0] == 0
```

is true.

## Arrays as Arguments

We've seen examples of passing various kinds of variables as arguments to functions. Is it also possible to pass an *array* to a function? The answer is, sort of. Let's see what this means.

Here's a program that uses a function called **max()** to find the element in an array with the largest value:

```
/* maxnum.c */
/* tells largest number in array typed in */
#define MAXSIZE 20              /* size of array */
int max(int[], int);           /* prototype */
main()
{
    int list[MAXSIZE];
    int size = 0;              /* start at element [0] */
    int num;                   /* temp storage */
    do                         /* get list of numbers */
        {
        printf("Type number: ");
        scanf("%d", &list[size]);
        }
    while ( list[size++] != 0 );  /* exit loop on 0 */
    num = max(list,size-1);       /* get largest number */
    printf("Largest number is %d", num);    /* print it */
}

/* max() */
/* returns largest number in array */
int max(int list[], int size)
{
    int dex, max;
    max = list[0];                  /* assume 1st element largest */
    for (dex=1; dex<size; dex++) /* check remaining elements */
        if ( max < list[dex] )     /* if one bigger, */
            max = list[dex];       /*   make it the largest */
    return(max);
}
```

The user types in a set of numbers (no more than 20) and the program prints out the largest one. Here's a sample run:

```
C>maxnum
Type number: 42
Type number: 1
Type number: 64
Type number: 33
Type number: 27
Type number: 0
Largest number is 64
```

The first part of this program should look familiar: it's our usual **do-while** loop for reading in a list of numbers. The only new element here is the statement:

```
num = max(list,size);
```

This is the call to the function **max()**, which returns the largest number. There are two arguments to the function: the first is the array **list**, the second is the variable **size**.

The critical thing to notice here is how we pass the array to the function: we use the name of the array, all by itself. We've seen array elements, which look like **list[index]**, before, but what does the array name mean without any brackets? It turns out that the array name used alone is equivalent to the *address* of the array. Actually, it's equivalent to the address of the first element in the array, which is the same thing.

Thinking about addresses and values can become confusing, so let's recapitulate what we know about the addresses of simple variables. Let's imagine an integer variable **num** with a value of 27. Perhaps it has been initialized like this:

```
int num = 27;
```

Figure 6-7 shows how this variable looks in memory.

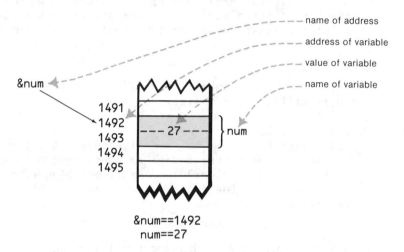

&num==1492
num==27

Figure 6-7. The Address and Value of a Simple Variable

There are four things to know about the variable: its name (**num**), its value (27), its address (which happens to be 1492, although this will vary from program to program and system to system), and—watch closely—the name of the address, which is **&num**.

Now let's see what a similar representation looks like for an array.

> An array is referred to by its address, which is represented by the name of the array, used without subscripts.

Figure 6-8 shows the array **list[ ]**, which in this instance is located in memory starting at address 1500. Again there are four important aspects to the figure: the values of the elements in the array (64), the names of these elements (**list[2]**), the address of the array (1500), and the name of this address (**list**). Why isn't the address of the array called something like **&list**? This would be consistent with the way the addresses of variables are named, but it would leave the word "list," which isn't used to name anything else about the variable, going begging. Thus **list** refers to an address if **list** is an array, but would refer to a value if **list** were a simple variable.

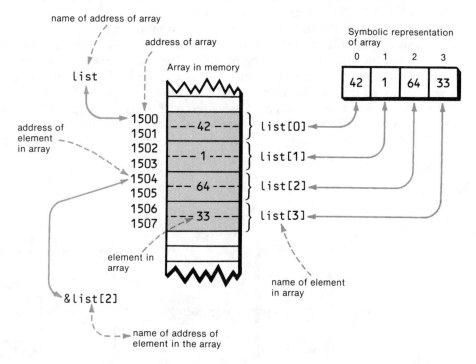

Figure 6-8. The Address and Elements of an Array

Incidentally, can you think of another way to represent the address **list**? How about this?

```
&list[0]
```

Since **list[0]** is the first element of the array, it will have the same address as the array itself. And since & is the address operator, **&list[0]** gives the address of the first element of the array. In other words,

```
list == &list[0]
```

An understanding of addresses will become increasingly important as we move on to the study of pointers in the next chapter, since addresses are closely related to pointers.

To summarize, to tell the compiler we want to talk about the address of an array, we use the name of the array, with no brackets following it. Thus (to return to the maxnum.c program), our call to the function **max()** passes the address of the array, represented by the word **list**, to the function.

### Addresses of Things versus Things

It's important to realize that passing the *address* of something is not the same thing as passing the something. When a simple variable name is used as an argument passed to a function, the function takes the *value* corresponding to this variable name and installs it as a new variable in a new memory location created by the function for that purpose.

But what happens when the address of an *array* is passed to a function as an argument? Does the function create another array and move the values into it from the array in the calling program? No. Since arrays can be very large, the designers of C determined that it would be better to have only *one* copy of an array no matter how many functions wanted to access it. So instead of passing the *values* in the array, only the *address* of the array is passed. The function then can use the address to access the *original* array. This process is shown in Figure 6-9. Thus, in the **max()** function, when we reference elements of the array, as in

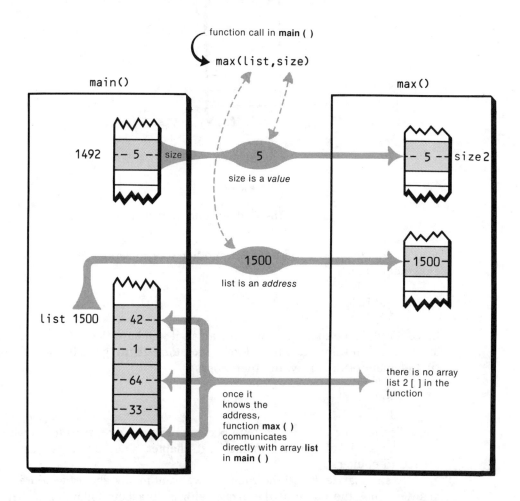

Figure 6-9. Passing a Value and an Array Address to a Function

the statement

```
max = list2[dex];
```

references to the array **list2[ ]** are actually references to the array **list[ ]**. We can give the array any name we want in the function, but all we are doing is telling the function where the original array, **list[ ]**, is. There *is* no array **list2[ ]**: this is simply the way the function refers to the array **list[ ]**.

> Passing an array name to a function does not create a new copy of the array.

## Sorting an Array

Before we go on to strings, let's look at a function that sorts the values in an array. Sorting is an important task in many applications, particularly database programs, in which a user wants to rearrange a list of items, in numerical or alphabetical order. Here's the listing:

```
/* sortnum.c */
/* sorts numbers typed in to array */
#define MAXSIZE 20              /* size of buffer */
void sort(int[], int);         /* prototype */

main()
{
    static int list[MAXSIZE];  /* buffer for numbers */
    int size = 0;              /* size 0 before input */
    int dex;                   /* index to array */

    do                         /* get list of numbers */
        {
        printf("Type number: ");
        scanf("%d", &list[size]);
        }
    while ( list[size++] != 0 ); /* exit loop on 0 */
    sort(list,--size);           /* sort numbers */
    for (dex=0; dex<size; dex++)  /* print sorted list */
        printf("%d\n", list[dex]);
}

/* sort() */
/* sorts array of integers */
void sort(int list[], int size)
{
    int out, in, temp;

    for (out=0; out<size-1; out++)     /* for each element */
        for (in=out+1; in<size; in++)  /* look at those lower */
```

```
        if (list[out] > list[in])    /* if element greater than */
        {                            /*   any lower down, */
        temp = list[in];             /* swap them */
        list[in] = list[out];
        list[out] = temp;
        }
}
```

And here's an example of the program at work:

```
C>sortnum
Type number: 46
Type number: 25
Type number: 73
Type number: 58
Type number: 33
Type number: 18
Type number: 0
18
25
33
46
58
73
```

The program first asks for a list of numbers (as you can see from the array declaration, you shouldn't type more than 20). As the user types in the numbers, they are placed in the array **list[ ]**. Once the user terminates the list by typing 0 (which is not placed on the list), the program then calls the **sort()** function, which sorts the values in the list.

The overall structure of the program is similar to that of maxnum.c. It first gets a series of numbers from the user and puts them in an array, **list[ ]**. Then it calls the **sort()** function, and finally it prints out the contents of the newly sorted array.

In this program we've used the same name, **list[ ]**, for the array in the function as in the calling program. A different name could be used to refer to the array; either way, it's the same array.

### The Bubble Sort

The sorting process used in the **sort()** function may require a word of explanation. The function starts off thinking about the first array variable, **list[0]**. The goal is to place the smallest item on the list in this variable. So the function goes through all the *remaining* items on the list, from list[1] to list[size-1], comparing each one with the first item. Whenever it finds one that is smaller than the first item, it swaps them. This will put the smallest item in **list[0]**.

Once the smallest item is dealt with, the function wants to put the next smallest item in **list[1]**. So it goes through all the remaining items, from **list[2]** on, comparing them with **list[1]**. Whenever it finds one that is smaller, it swaps them. This will end up with **list[1]** containing the second smallest item. This process is continued until the entire list is sorted. This approach is called the "bubble sort," because the smaller values bubble up through the list. Figure 6-10 shows how it works. (We should note that the bubble sort, while easy to program, is less efficient than many other sorting algorithms.)

The outer loop, with the variable **out**, determines which element of the array will be used as the basis of comparison (as **list[0]** is the first time through the loop). The inner loop, with the variable **out**, steps through the remaining items, comparing each one with the first (from **list[1]** to the end of the list, the first time through). When the comparision of two items shows they are out of order, they're swapped.

The swapping process requires us to put the value of the first variable, **list[in]**, in a temporary location; put the second value, **list(out)**, in the first variable; and finally return the temporary value (originally from **list[in]** to **list[out]**).

Remember that all this swapping and rearranging of values takes place in the original array, **list[ ]**, in the calling program. The **sort()** function finds out where the array is (from the address passed to it) and manipulates it by "remote control," without having to drag all the values from the array into the function.

## Two-Dimensional Arrays as Arguments

We've seen how to pass a one-dimensional array as an argument, but what about a two-dimensional array? As an example, we'll blend our travel.c program, which recorded the travel expenses for a list of secret agents, and our maxnum.c program, which figured out the largest element in an array. The resulting program will print out the agent number and the amount spent by the agent with the highest travel expenses.

Here's the program listing:

```
/* highex.c */
/* stores list of secret agents' travel expenses */
/* reports number of agent with highest expenses */
#define ROWS 10        /* number of rows in array */
#define COLUMNS 2      /* number of columns in array */
int maxex(float[][COLUMNS], int);   /* prototype */

main()
{
    float agents [ROWS] [COLUMNS];
    int index=0;

    printf("Enter 3-digit agent numbers,\n");
    printf("then travel expenses (007 1642.50)\n");
    printf("Enter 0 0 to quit.\n");

    do                      /* get list of agents and expenses */
        {
        printf("Agent's number and expenses: ");
```

```
                scanf( "%f %f", &agents[index][0], &agents[index][1] );
                }
        while ( agents[index++][0] != (float)0.0 );
        index--;                    /* restore to size of array */

        index = maxex(agents, index);     /* find agent's index */
        printf("Agent with highest expenses: %03.0f. ",
                                            agents[index][0] );
        printf("Amount: %.2f.", agents[index][1] );
}


/* maxex() */
/* returns array index to largest amount in column 1 */
int maxex(float list[][COLUMNS], int size)
{
    int dex, maxdex;
    float max;
    max = list[0][1];            /* assume 1st element largest */
    maxdex = 0;                  /* save its index */
    for (dex=1; dex<size; dex++) /* check remaining elements */
        if ( max < list[dex][1] ) /* if one bigger, */
            {
            max = list[dex][1];   /* make it the largest */
            maxdex = dex;         /* save its index */
            }
    return(maxdex);              /* return index */
}
```

Here's a sample run. Now we've typed in a list of agent numbers and expenses, and the program has figured out the agent with the highest expenses and printed out the number and the amount.

```
        C>highex
        Enter 3-digit agent numbers,
        then travel expenses (007 1642.50)
        Enter 0 0 to quit.
        Agent's number and expenses: 901 645.25
        Agent's number and expenses: 801 784.50
        Agent's number and expenses: 302 112.95
        Agent's number and expenses: 007 9456.99
        Agent's number and expenses: 405 298.60
        Agent's number and expenses: 006 5019.00
        Agent's number and expenses: 0 0
        Agent with highest expenses: 007. Amount: 9456.99.
```

In many ways, passing a two-dimensional array is similar to passing an array of one dimension, but there is at least one surprise.

The method of passing the address of the array to the function is identical

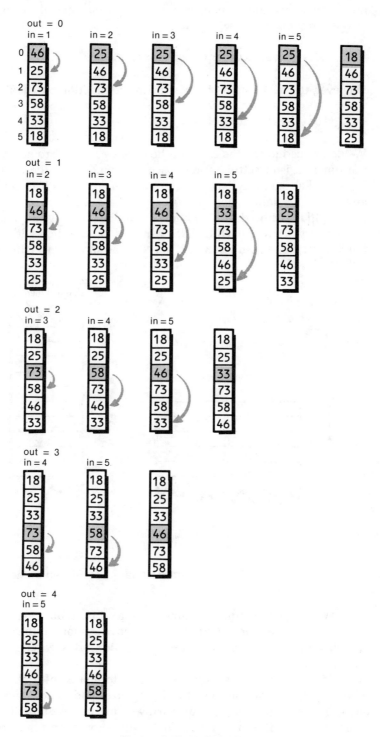

Figure 6-10. Bubble Sort

no matter how many dimensions the array has, since all we pass is the address of the array (in this case, **agents**):

```
index = maxex(agents, index);
```

However, the declaration of the array in the function may look a bit mysterious:

```
float list[][COLUMNS];
```

We don't need to tell the function how many *rows* there are. Why not? Because the function isn't setting aside space in memory for the array. All it needs to know is that the array has two columns; this permits it to reference accurately any array variable. For instance, to find the space in memory where **agents[3][1]** is stored, the function multiplies the row index (3) by the number of elements per row (COLUMNS, which is 2), and then adds the column index (which is 1). The result is 3 * 2 + 1 = 7, as shown in Figure 6-11.

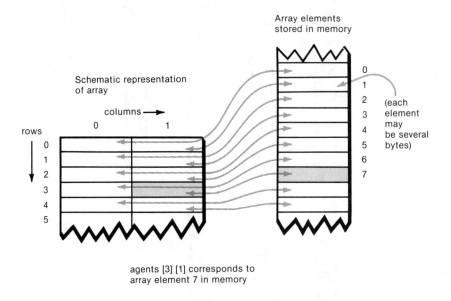

agents [3] [1] corresponds to
array element 7 in memory

Figure 6-11. Two-Dimensional Array Stored in Memory

We've had to modify the function **max()** from our earlier program in order to return the row index of the agent in question, rather than a numerical quantity as before. This involves saving the index whenever we save a new maximum.

At this point you should be starting to feel comfortable with arrays. You know how to declare arrays of differing sizes and dimensions, how to initialize arrays, how to refer to particular array elements, and how to pass an array to a function. With this under your belt, you should be ready to handle strings, which are simply a special kind of array.

# Strings

Strings are the form of data used in programming languages for storing and manipulating text, such as words, names, and sentences. In C, a string is not a formal data type as it is in some languages (e.g., Pascal and BASIC). Instead, it is an array of type **char**. When you think about it, this makes a good deal of sense; a string is a series of characters, and that's just what an array of type **char** is. Most languages actually treat strings as arrays of characters, but conceal this fact from the programmer to varying degrees. BASIC, for example, never lets on that strings are arrays, but Pascal, although treating strings as a separate data type, does permit you to reference individual string characters as array members.

## String Constants

We've already seen examples of strings, as in the statement:

```
printf("%s", "Greetings!");
```

"Greetings!" is a string constant. That means that the string itself is stored someplace in memory, but that it cannot be changed (just as your program cannot change the 3 in the expression **x = 3;**). Figure 6-12 shows what this string constant looks like stored in memory.

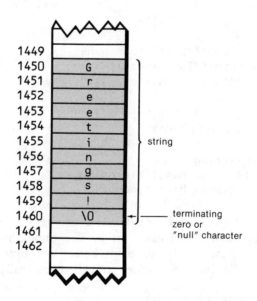

Figure 6-12. String Constant Stored in Memory

Each character occupies one byte of memory, and the last character of the string is the character '\0'. What character is that? It looks like two characters, but it's actually an escape sequence, like '\n'. It's called the "null character," and it stands for a character with a value of 0 (zero). Note that this is not the same as the character 0.

> All strings must end with a null character, '\0', which has a numerical value of 0.

The terminating null ('\0') is important, because it is the only way functions that work with the string can know where the end of the string is. In fact, a string not terminated by a '\0' character is not really a string at all, but merely a collection of characters.

## String Variables

We've looked at a string constant, now let's see what a string variable looks like. Here's an example program that reads in a string from the keyboard, using **scanf()**, and prints it out as part of a longer phrase:

```
/* ezstring.c */
/* reads string from keyboard and prints it */
main()
{
    char fname[15];

    printf("Enter your name: ");
    scanf("%s", fname);
    printf("Greetings, %s.", fname);
}
```

And here's a sample run:

```
C>ezstring
Enter your name: Hieronymous
Greetings, Hieronymous.
```

Before a string can be read into a program, some space in the computer's memory must be set aside for it. This shouldn't be too surprising; after all, memory must also be set aside before a simple variable can be stored in a program. For instance, before we can successfully execute the line

```
scanf("%d", &num);
```

we need to declare the variable **num**, causing the compiler to set aside an appropriately sized chunk of memory to store the value the user enters.

The situation is similar for strings, except that, since there is going to be a *series* of characters arriving, a series of bytes must be set aside for them. In ezstring.c, we've declared an array of 15 characters. This should be enough for names 15 characters long, right? Well, not quite. Don't forget the terminating null character '\0'. When **scanf()** gets the name from the keyboard, it automatically includes the '\0' when it stores the string in memory; thus, if your array is 15 characters long, you can only store strings of 14 characters.

The operation of ezstring.c is shown in Figure 6-13.

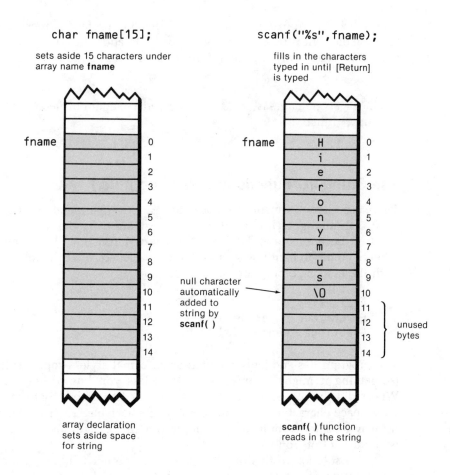

Figure 6-13. String Placed in Memory by *scanf()*

The warning applied to arrays in general applies to strings: don't overflow the array that holds the string. If the user of ezstring.c typed a name of more than 14 characters, the additional characters would be written over other data or the program itself. Perhaps a better choice for the array declaration would have been:

```
char fname[81]
```

This would permit a name to go all the way across the screen: 80 characters. Hardly anyone's name is that long!

You may have noticed something odd about the **scanf()** statement in the ezstring.c program. That's right; there's no address operator ( & ) preceding the name of the string we're going to print:

```
scanf("%s", fname);
```

This is because **fname** is an *address*. We need to preface numerical and character variables with the **&** to change values into addresses, but **fname** is already the name of an array, and therefore it's an address and does not need the **&**.

> Since a string name is an address, no address operator need precede it in a **scanf()** function.

## The String I/O Functions *gets()* and *puts()*

There are many C functions whose purpose is to manipulate strings. One of the most common (**gets()**) is used to input a string from the keyboard. Why is it needed? Because our old friend, the **scanf()** function, has some limitations when it comes to handling strings. For example, consider the following trial run with the ezstring.c program:

```
C>ezstring
Enter your name: Genghis Khan
Greetings, Genghis.
```

The program has suddenly adopted an informal style, dropping the last name (something it might be unwise to do unless you knew Genghis very well). Where did the second word of our string go? Remember that **scanf()** uses *any* whitespace character to terminate entry of a variable. The result is that there is no way to enter a multiword string into a single array using **scanf()** (at least without a lot of trouble).

The solution to this problem is to use another C library function: **gets()**. The purpose of **gets()** is, as you may have guessed, to GET a String from the keyboard. It is not as versatile an input function as **scanf()**; it specializes in doing one thing: reading strings. It is terminated *only* when the [Return] key is struck; so spaces and tabs are perfectly acceptable as part of the input string.

The **gets()** function is part of a matching pair; there is a function to *output* strings as well: **puts()** (for PUT String).

Here's a revised version of our ezstring.c program that makes use of both of these functions:

```
/* getput.c */
/* reads string and prints string using gets() and puts() */
```

```
main()
{
    char name[81];

    puts("Enter your name: ");
    gets(name);
    puts("Greetings, ");
    puts(name);
}
```

Let's see what happens when our favorite Mongol warrior tries this new version of the program:

```
C>getput
Enter your name:
Genghis Khan
Greetings,
Genghis Khan
```

Now the program remembers the entire name and there's less chance of Genghis being offended. The **gets()** function has done just what we wanted.

The **puts()** function is a special-purpose output function specializing in strings. Unlike **printf()**, it can only output one string at a time and, like **gets()**, it has no ability to format a string before printing it. The syntax of **puts()** is simpler than **printf()**, however, so it's the function to use when you want to output a single string.

## Initializing Strings

Just as arrays can be initialized, so can strings. Since a string is an array of characters, we can initialize one in exactly that way, as the following example demonstrates:

```
char feline[] = { 'c', 'a', 't', '\0' } ;
```

However, C concedes that strings are a special kind of character array by providing a shortcut:

```
char feline[] = "cat" ;
```

As you can see, this is considerably easier to write (and read); but it means the same thing to the compiler. Notice that while the individual characters were surrounded by single quotes, the string is surrounded by double quotes. Notice too that we don't need to insert the null character '\0'. Using the string format causes this to happen automatically.

Let's look at a variation on the last program, making use of an initialized string:

```
/* strinit.c */
/* reads string and prints string, shows string
initialization */
main()
{
    static char salute[] = "Greetings,";
    char name[81];

    puts("Enter your name: ");
    gets(name);
    puts(salute);
    puts(name);
}
```

The output will be exactly the same as before (assuming the same name is typed in). However, "Greetings," is no longer printed as a string constant in the **puts()** function; instead, it's included in the array declaration. The **puts()** function can then print it out using the array address as an argument.

We've had to give the array **name[]** in this program the storage class **static**. As you'll remember from our discussion of arrays, only external arrays or arrays given the class **static** can be initialized.

Here's a sample run with the program:

```
C>strinit
Enter your name:
Cato the Elder
Greetings,
Cato the Elder
```

So we see that our initialization process works just fine. However, the format of the output could be improved: it would have been nicer if the name was on the same line as the salutation:

```
Greetings, Cato the Elder
```

What's happened is that the **puts()** function automatically replaces the null character at the end of the string with a newline character as it prints the string, so that all strings printed by **puts()** end with a newline. So, sometimes **puts()** is not the ideal choice for outputting strings, and **printf()** must be used instead.

## Examining a String

We've told you how a string looks in memory, but you shouldn't take our word for it; you can write a program to investigate this for yourself. The following program examines each memory location occupied by a string and prints out what it finds there. In the process it demonstrates a new C library function, **strlen()**:

```
/* strexam.c */
/* looks at string in memory */
main()
{
    char name[81];
    int dex;

    puts("Enter your name: ");
    gets(name);
    for (dex=0; dex < strlen(name)+4; dex++)
        printf("Addr=%5u char='%c'=%3d\n",
                       &name[dex], name[dex], name[dex] );
}
```

Here's an example of the output:

```
C>strexam
Enter your name:
Plato
Addr= 3486 char='P'= 80
Addr= 3487 char='i'=108
Addr= 3488 char='a'= 97
Addr= 3489 char='t'=116
Addr= 3490 char='o'=111
Addr= 3491 char=' '=  0
Addr= 3492 char='<'= 60
Addr= 3493 char='#'= 35
Addr= 3494 char='u'=117
```

To show what happens after the end of the string, we've printed out four characters beyond the end of the string that was typed in. First there's the terminating null character, which doesn't print out but has the value 0. Then there are garbage characters, which have whatever values were in memory before this part of memory was declared to be an array. If we had declared a **static** or **external** array these spaces would all have been 0, instead of garbage characters.

We've used the address operator ( & ) to get the address of each of the characters that make up the string:

```
&name[dex]
```

We've also used our old trick of printing the characters in two different formats: once as a character and once as a number. The last new thing in this program is the use of the new string function, **strlen()**. We use the value returned by this function to tell us how many characters to print out from the **for** loop.

```
for (dex=0; dex < strlen(name)+4; dex++)
```

Let's examine the **strlen()** function and string-handling functions in general.

## String Functions

In keeping with its philosophy of using a small language kernel and adding library functions to achieve greater power, C has no special string-handling operators. In BASIC you can assign a value to a string with an equal sign, and in Pascal you can compare two strings with a less-than sign. But in C, which thinks of strings as arrays, there are no special operators for dealing with them.

However, C does have a large set of useful string-handling library functions. We've used one of the most common in the strexam.c program: the **strlen()** function. This function returns the length of the string whose address is given it as an argument. Thus in our program, the expression

```
strlen(name)
```

will return the value 5 if the string name has the value "Plato". (As you can see, **Strlen()** does not count the terminating null character.)

## An Array of Strings

Earlier in the chapter we saw several examples of two-dimensional arrays. Let's look now at a similar phenomenon, but one dealing with strings: an array of strings. Since a string is itself an array, an array of strings is really an array of arrays, or a two-dimensional array.

Our example program asks you to type in your name. When you do, it checks your name against a master list to see if you're worthy of entry to the palace (or perhaps it's only an "in" restaurant on the Upper East Side). Here's the listing:

```
/* compare.c */
/* compares word typed in with words in program */
#define MAX 5
#define LEN 40
main()
{
    int dex;
    int enter=0;
    char name[40];
    static char list[MAX][LEN] =
                      { "Katrina",
                        "Nigel",
                        "Alistair",
                        "Francesca",
                        "Gustav"     };
    printf("Enter your name: ");              /* get name */
    gets(name);
    for (dex=0; dex<MAX; dex++)               /* go thru list */
        if( strcmp(&list[dex][0],name)==0 )   /* if match */
            enter = 1;                        /* set flag */
    if ( enter == 1 )                         /* if flag set */
```

```
        printf("You may enter, oh honored one.");  /* one response */
    else                                            /* otherwise */
        printf("Guards! Remove this person!");      /* different one */
}
```

There are two possible outcomes when you interract with this program. Either your name is on the list:

```
C>compare
Enter your name: Gustav
You may enter, oh honored one.
```

or it isn't:

```
C>compare
Enter your name: Robert
Guards! Remove this person!
```

Notice how our array of strings is initialized. Because a phrase in quotes is already a one-dimensional array, we don't need to use braces around each name as we did for two-dimensional character arrays. We do need braces around all the strings, however, since this is an array of strings. As before, the individual elements of the array—strings in this case—are separated by commas.

The order of the subscripts in the array declaration is important. The first subscript, MAX, gives the number of items in the array, while the second subscript, LEN, gives the length of each string in the array. Having a fixed length array for each string, no matter how long it actually is, can lead to a considerable waste of space. (In Chapter 7, when we explore pointers, we'll show how to avoid this problem.)

We've used another string function, **strcmp()**, in this program, in the expression

```
strcmp( &list[dex][0], name ) == 0
```

The **strcmp()** function, compares two strings and returns an integer value based on the comparison. If we assume that **string1** is on the right side within the parentheses and **string2** is on the left

```
strcmp(string2,string1)
```

then the value returned will have the following meanings:

| Returned Value | Meaning |
| --- | --- |
| less than zero | string1 less than string2 |
| zero | string1 identical to string2 |
| greater than zero | string1 greater than string2 |

In this context, "less than" and "greater than" mean that if you put **string1** and **string2** in alphabetical order, the one that appeared first (closer to the A's) would be considered "less than" those following. However, we don't make use of the "less than" and "greater than" capabilities of the function in this program; here we only need to know when the the strings are identical, which is true when the function returns a value of 0.

A further wrinkle in this program is the use of a "flag" to remember whether there has been a match. The flag, a variable that remembers a condition for a short time, is called **enter**, and it is set to 1 (true) if any of the names match and remains 0 if there are no matches at the end of the loop. The **if-else** statement then queries the flag to find out what to print.

## Deleting Characters

It's often useful to be able to delete a character from the middle of a string (if you're writing a word processing program or text editor, for example). There are no library functions to do this with our C compiler, so we'll develop a routine to perform this function. (We'll leave as an exercise the complementary problem of *inserting* a character into a string.)

Here's a program that demonstrates **strdel()**, our homemade STRing DE-Lete function:

```
/* delete.c */
/* deletes a character from a string */
void strdel(char str[], int n);   /* prototype */
main()
{
    char string[81];               /* buffer for string */
    int position;                  /* position of character */

    printf("Type string [Return], position\n");
    gets(string);                  /* get string */
    scanf("%d", &position);        /* get character */
    strdel(string,position);       /* delete character */
    puts(string);                  /* print new string */
}

/* strdel() */
/* deletes character from string */
void strdel(char str[], int n)     /* buffer, size of buffer */
{
    strcpy(&str[n], &str[n+1] );   /* move 2nd part of string */
}                                  /* one space to left */
```

This program asks for a string and for the position in the string of the character to be deleted (remember that the first character is 0). Then the program calls the **strdel()** function to delete the character at that position. Here's a sample interaction:

```
C>delete
Type string [Return], position
cart
2
cat
```

The program has deleted character number 2, 'r', from the string "cart".

The **strdel()** function works by moving one space to the left all characters that are to the right of the character being deleted. This is shown in Figure 6-14.

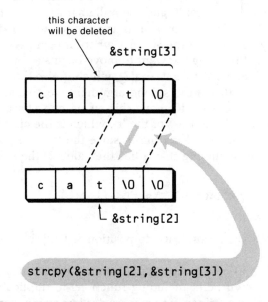

Figure 6-14. Operation of the *strdel()* Function

To move the characters, the function makes use of the **strcpy** library function. This function simply copies one string to another. For instance, if a program included the following statements:

```
char buffer[10];
- - - - -
strcpy(buffer, "Dante");
```

the string "Dante" would be placed in the array **buffer[ ]**. The string would include the terminating null, which means that six characters in all would be copied.

If you're a BASIC programmer, you may be wondering why we can't achieve the same effect more simply by saying:

```
buffer = "Dante";      /* illegal construction */
```

We can't do this because C treats strings far more like arrays than BASIC does. Since it is impossible to set one array equal to another one with an assignment statement, it is also impossible to set one string equal to another in this way. A function must be used instead.

Now let's look closely at which string is being copied and where it's being copied to. Two arguments are needed by the **strcpy()** function: the string to be copied is the second argument and the place it will be copied to is the first argument.

We want to move one space to the left the string following the character being deleted. In the "cart" to "cat" example, the string we want to copy has only two characters: 't' and the null character '\0'. But what is the name of this string? How do we represent it as an argument to **strcpy()**? Remember that we identify an array by the address where it begins. The same is true of strings. In this case, the string we want to move begins at the letter 't'. What's the address of this character? It's **&string[3]**, which is also the address of the string we want to move, so this is the second argument we give **strcpy()**.

Now we want to move this string one character to the left. That means putting it at the address of the 'r', which is the character we want to delete. The address of the 'r' is **&string[2]**, since the 'r' is in position 2 in the string.

Thus, assuming that n has the value 2, the statement

```
strcpy(&str[n], &str[n+1] );
```

will copy the string "t\0" to position &str[2], blotting out the character 'r' as it does so.

The Microsoft C compiler comes with many more string functions than we've shown here, including functions to duplicate a string, concatenate (put together) two strings, find a character in a string, convert a string to all lower- or all uppercase, and so on. Using some of these string operations requires an understanding of pointers, which will be our topic in Chapter 7.

## Summary

In this chapter we've learned how to handle arrays in a variety of forms. We've learned how to declare arrays, how to access their elements, and how to give them initial values when the program is compiled. We've covered one- and two-dimensional arrays and even taken a peek at initializing a three-dimensional array. We've learned that the addresses of arrays can be passed to functions, so that functions can access the elements of the array.

Next, we looked at strings, which are simply arrays of type **char**. We've seen how to initialize strings and how to use two new I/O functions: **gets()** and **puts()**. We've also examined a trio of string functions: **strlen()**, which returns the length of a string; **strcmp()**, which compares two strings; and **strcpy()**, which copies one string into the space occupied by another.

# Questions

1. An array is a collection of variables of

    a. different data types scattered throughout memory

    b. the same data type scattered throughout memory

    c. the same data type placed next to each other in memory

    d. different data types placed next to each other in memory

2. Why is a string like an array?

    a. They are both character arrays

    b. An array is a kind of string

    c. They both access functions the same way

    d. A string is a kind of array

3. An array declaration specifies the t_____,
   n_____, and s_____ of the array.

4. Is this a correct array declaration?

    ```
    int num(25);
    ```

5. Which element of the array does this expression reference?

    ```
    num[4]
    ```

6. What's the difference between the 3s in these two expressions?

    ```
    int num[3];
    num[3] = 5;
    ```

    a. first is particular element, second is type

    b. first is size, second is particular element

    c. first is particular element, second is array size

    d. both specify array elements

7. What does this combination of statements do?

    ```
    #define LIM 50
    char collect[LIM];
    ```

    a. makes LIM a subscript

    b. makes LIM a variable of type **float**

    c. makes **collect[ ]** an array of type LIM

    d. makes **collect[ ]** an array of size LIM

8. If an array has been declared this way:

```
float prices[MAX];
```

is the following a good way to read values into all the elements of the array?

```
for(j=0; j<=MAX; j++)
    scanf("%f", prices[j]);
```

9. Is this a correct way to initialize a one-dimensional array?

```
int array = { 1, 2, 3, 4 };
```

10. What will happen if you try to put so many variables into an array when you initialize it that the size of the array is exceded?

    a. nothing

    b. possible system malfunction

    c. error message from the compiler

    d. other data may be overwritten

11. What will happen if you put too few elements in an array when you initialize it?

    a. nothing

    b. possible system malfunction

    c. error message from the compiler

    d. unused elements will be filled with 0s or garbage

12. If you want to initialize an array it must be a _____ or a
    _____ array.

13. What will happen if you assign a value to an element of an array whose subscript exceeds the size of the array?

    a. the element will be set to 0

    b. nothing, it's done all the time

    c. other data may be overwritten

    d. possible system malfunction

14. Can you initialize a two-dimensisional array this way?

```
int array[3][3] = {  { 1, 2, 3 },
                     { 4, 5, 6 },
                     { 7, 8, 9 }  };
```

15. In the array in the question immediately above, what is the name of the array variable with the value 4?

16. If an array had been declared like this:

    ```
    int array[12];
    ```

    the word **array** represents the a _____ of the array

17. If you don't initialize a **static** array, what will the elements be set to?

    a. 0

    b. an undetermined value

    c. a floating point number

    d. the character constant '\0'

18. When you pass an array as an argument to a function, what is actually passed?

    a. the address of the array

    b. the values of the elements in the array

    c. the address of the first element in the array

    d. the number of elements in the array

19. True or false: a function operates on an integer array passed to it as an argument by placing the values of that array into a separate place in memory known only to the function.

20. A string is:

    a. a list of characters

    b. a collection of characters

    c. an array of characters

    d. an exaltation of characters

21. "A" is a _____ while 'A' is a _____ .

22. What is the following expression?

    ```
    "Mesopotamia\n"
    ```

    a. a string variable

b. a string array

c. a string constant

d. a string of characters

23. A string is terminated by a _____ character, which is written _____.

24. The function _____ is designed specifically to read in one string from the keyboard.

25. If you have declared a string like this:

```
char name[10];
```

and you type in a string to this array, the string can consist of a maximum of _____ characters.

26. True or false: the function **puts()** always adds a '\n' to the end of the string it is printing.

27. Which is more appropriate for reading in a multi-word string?

a. **gets()**

b. **printf()**

c. **scanf()**

d. **puts()**

28. Assuming the following initialization:

```
char string[] = "Blacksmith";
```

how would you refer to the string "smith" (the last five letters of the string)?

29. What subtle format problem does this statement exhibit?

```
name = "George";
```

30. What expression would you use to find the length of the string **name**?

## Exercises

1. Modify the temp.c program so that it not only accepts seven temperatures and calculates the average but also prints out the temperatures that have been read in.

2. Modify the fltemp2.c program to use a **while** loop instead of a **do-while** loop.

3. Write a function, and a program to test it, that will insert a character anywhere in a string. The call to the function should have the form

```
strins(string, character, position);
```

Before writing this function, ask yourself which end of the string **strcpy()** starts copying from.

4. Write a program that will print out all the rotations of a string typed into it. For example, the rotations of the word "space" are

```
space
paces
acesp
cespa
espac
```

Use a function that rotates the string one character position each time it is called.

# 7

# *Pointers*

- Pointers
- Returning multiple values from functions
- Pointers and arrays
- Pointer arithmetic
- Pointers and strings
- Double indirection
- Pointers to arrays

# 7

Pointers are regarded by most people as one of the most difficult topics in C. There are several reasons for this. First, the concept behind pointers—indirection—may be a new one for many programmers, since it isn't commonly used in such languages as BASIC or Pascal. And second, the symbols used for pointer notation in C are not as clear as they might be; for example, the same symbol is used for two different but related purposes, as we'll see.

Conceptually, however, pointers aren't really that obscure, and with a little practice the symbols start to make a sort of sense. In other words, pointers may be difficult, but they aren't *too* difficult. Our goal in this chapter is to demystify pointers, to explain as clearly as possible what they're for and how they work. To this end we start slowly, in an attempt to ensure that the groundwork is laid carefully before we go on to use pointers in more advanced situations.

## Pointer Overview

Before we show programming examples that demonstrate the use of pointers, we're going to examine generally what pointers are and why they're used.

### What Is a Pointer?

A pointer provides a way of accessing a variable (or a more complex kind of data, such as an array) without referring to the variable directly. The mechanism used for this is the *address* of the variable. In effect, the address acts as an intermediary between the variable and the program accessing it. There is a somewhat analogous mechanism in the spy business, in which an agent in the field might leave his or her reports in a special place (a post office box or a hollow tree) and have no direct contact with the other members of the network. Thus if captured, there is very little information the agent can be forced to reveal about the organization. We can say that the agent has only *indirect* access to those for whom the information is intended.

In a similar way, a program statement can refer to a variable *indirectly*, using the address of the variable as a sort of post office box or hollow tree for the passing of information.

## Why Are Pointers Used?

Pointers are used in situations when passing actual values is difficult or undesirable. (It's seldom the case that an enemy program will force a function to reveal the names of variables in the calling program!) Some reasons to use pointers are to:

1. return more than one value from a function
2. pass arrays and strings more conveniently from one function to another
3. manipulate arrays more easily by moving pointers to them (or to parts of them), instead of moving the arrays themselves
4. create complex data structures, such as linked lists and binary trees, where one data structure must contain references to other data structures
5. communicate information about memory, as in the function **malloc()**, which returns the location of free memory by using a pointer.

We'll explore some of these uses for pointers in this chapter. We'll save the use of pointers with structures, linked lists, and **malloc()** for Chapter 9.

Another reason sometimes given for using pointers is that pointer notation compiles into faster or more efficient code than, for example, array notation. It's not clear that this is actually a major factor for modern compilers; probably many programmers become enamored of pointer notation and grasp at any excuse to use it.

## You've Already Used Pointers

If you think that reason 2—passing arrays more conveniently from one function to another—sounds familiar, that's because it is; in Chapter 6 you used pointers to pass arrays and strings to functions. Instead of passing the array itself, you passed the *address* of the array. This address is an example of a pointer *constant*. There are also pointer variables; it's the interplay between pointer constants and pointer variables that gives pointers such power. We'll see further examples of pointers used with arrays later in this chapter.

A pointer constant is an address; a pointer variable is a place to store addresses.

# Returning Data from Functions

We're going to start our examination of pointers by finding out how functions can return multiple values to the program that called them. You've already seen that it's possible to pass many values to a function and return a single value from a function, but what happens when you want to return more than one value from a function to the calling program? Since there is no mechanism built into functions to do this, we must rely on pointers. Of the many ways pointers can be used, this is perhaps the simplest; at the same time, it is a technique that accomplishes an essential task. There are many situations in which a function must communicate more than one value to the calling program.

## Review: Passing Values to a Function

Before we show how this works, let's review what happens when we pass values *to* a function. (You've already seen examples of such functions in Chapter 5—the function that adds two numbers, for example.) Here's a very simple program that passes two values, the integers 4 and 7, to a function called **gets2()**:

```
/* values.c */
/* tests function which accepts two values */
void gets2(int, int);             /* prototype */
main()
{
    int x=4, y=7;                 /* initialize variables */

    gets2(x, y);                  /* pass vars to function */
}

/* gets2() */
/* prints out values of two arguments */
void gets2(int xx, int yy)
{
    printf("First is %d, second is %d", xx, yy);
}
```

This is not an enormously useful function: it simply prints out the two values passed to it. However, it demonstrates an important point: the function receives the two values from the calling program and stores them—or rather, stores duplicates of them—in its own private memory space. In fact, it can even give these values different names, known only to the function: in this case, **xx** and **yy** instead of **x** and **y**. Figure 7-1 shows how this looks. The function then can operate on the new variables, **xx** and **yy**, without affecting the original **x** and **y** in the calling program.

## Passing Addresses to a Function

Now let's look at the reverse situation: passing two values from the function back to the calling program. How do we do this? A two-step process is used. First, the

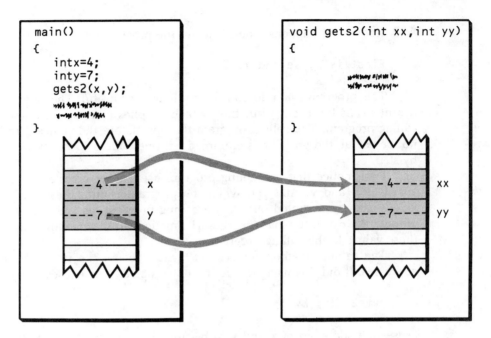

```
main()                                  void gets2(int xx,int yy)
{                                       {
    intx=4;
    inty=7;
    gets2(x,y);


}                                       }
```

Values are passed to function
and duplicated in the function's
memory space.

Figure 7-1. Values Duplicated in Function's Memory

calling program, instead of passing *values* to the function, passes it *addresses*. These addresses are where the calling program wants the function to place the data it generates; in other words, they are the addresses of the variables in the calling program where we want to store the returned values. Here's the program:

```
/* passback.c */
/* tests function that returns two values */
void rets2(int *, int *);   /* prototype */

main()
{
    int x, y;                   /* variables */

    rets2( &x, &y );            /* get values from function */
    printf("First is %d, second is %d", x, y);
}

/* rets2() */
/* returns two numbers */
void rets2(int *px, int *py)
{
    *px = 3;                    /* set contents of px to 3 */
    *py = 5;                    /* set contents of py to 5 */
}
```

And here's what happens when you run the program:

```
First is 3, second is 5.
```

This program again doesn't do anything very useful. The calling program, **main()**, calls the **rets2()** function, which supplies two values, 3 and 5, to the calling program. The calling program then prints out the values. While it may not be useful, the program is crammed with new ideas. Let's take it apart step-by-step.

First, notice that the calling program itself never gives any values to the variables **x** and **y**. And yet, when the program is run, these variables have values; they are printed out by the calling program, as we can see from the output. We can infer that the **rets2()** function must somehow have supplied these values to the calling program.

The calling program told **rets2()** where to put the values by passing it addresses. It did this using the address operator **&**. The expression

```
rets2( &x, &y );
```

causes the addresses of **x** and **y** to be passed to the function and stored in the function's private memory space. These addresses have been given names by the function: **px** and **py**. That's how the function can refer to them, just as if they were any other kind of variables (of course we could have used any names we wanted here, like the more descriptive but longer **ptr_to_x** and **ptr_to_y**).

## Declaring Pointer Variables

As with any variables, the places set aside for these addresses, **px** and **py**, must be *declared*, so the compiler will know how large a memory space to allot for them and what names we want to give them. Since we are storing addresses, or pointer constants, you might expect a whole new data type here, something along the lines of:

```
ptr px, py;      /* not exactly how pointers are declared */
```

where **ptr** might be the data type for pointers. After all, addresses are all the same size, and we want to set aside enough memory to hold an address. Ordinarily, two bytes will hold an address. (When memory models other than "small" are used, this may not be true; however, the small model is used for all programs in this book. We'll have more to say about memory models in Chapter 14.)

Declaring a pointer variable does in fact set aside two bytes of memory, but there is an added complexity. For reasons which we'll explain later, the compiler needs to know, not only that we're declaring a pointer, but also *to which kind of data item the pointer points*. In other words, every time we set aside space to store the address of a variable, we need to tell the compiler the data type of the variable. This information must be communicated to the compiler, along with the fact that we're declaring a pointer. Let's make a second guess at what such a declaration might look like:

```
int_ptr px, py;    /* still not how pointers are declared */
```

where **int_ptr** is the data type for pointers that point to integer variables. We're getting closer. However, C is a concise language, so instead of using the word "ptr", C uses the asterisk ( * ). The asterisk is used differently from the words representing simple data types (e.g., **int** and **float**); the asterisk is used immediately before *each* variable, rather than being used once at the beginning of the declaration. Thus, the real declaration for two integer pointers is:

```
int *px, *py;      /* correct declaration of two pointers */
```

The declaration sets aside two bytes in which to store the address of an integer variable and gives this storage space the name **px**. It also sets aside another two bytes in which to store the address of another integer variable and gives this space the name **py**. The asterisks tell the compiler that these variables will contain *addresses* (not values), and the **int** tells it that the addresses will point to integer variables. Note that the declaration itself doesn't say anything about what will be placed in these variables.

The format of this declaration is shown in Figure 7-2.

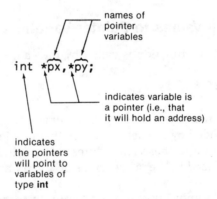

Figure 7-2. Format of Pointer Declaration

(Note that the asterisk as it's used here, as an indirection operator, is a *unary* operator: it operates on only one variable (such as **px** in **\*px**). Thus, the compiler cannot confuse it with the same symbol used for multiplication, which is a **binary** operator, operating on two variables.)

The concise nature of this declaration format is one of the causes of confusion about pointers, so we'll reiterate what's happening: for each variable name (**px** and **py** in this case) the declaration causes the compiler to set aside a two-byte space in memory into which an address can be placed, as shown in Figure 7-3.

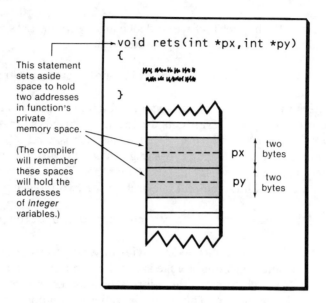

```
void rets(int *px,int *py)
{

}
```

This statement sets aside space to hold two addresses in function's private memory space.

(The compiler will remember these spaces will hold the addresses of *integer* variables.)

px — two bytes
py — two bytes

Figure 7-3. Operation of Pointer Declaration

In addition, the compiler is aware of the type of variable the address refers to; in this case, integers.

## Supplying Values to Pointer Variables

Now, when the function is called by the calling program with the statement

```
rets2( &x, &y );
```

the two addresses provided by the calling program, **&x** and **&y**, are placed in the spaces provided by the declaration in the function. Thus, control is passed to the function, but also these two addresses (which, in this case, might be 1310 and 1312) are placed in the space set aside for **px** and **py**. This process is shown in Figure 7-4.

Let's examine this process carefully to make sure we've got the terms straight. We can say that **px** and **py** are pointer *variables*, and that the addresses 1310 and 1312 are pointer *constants*. Figure 7-5 shows a closeup view of these variables being assigned these constant values.

## The Indirection Operator

The function now knows the addresses of the variables into which the calling program wants values placed. The big question is, how does the function *access* these variables? (To return to our spy analogy: how does the spy go about leaving a message in the hollow tree?)

Think about this question for a moment, because in the answer lies the key

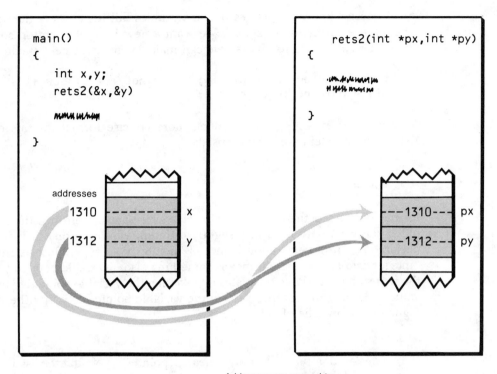

Addresses are passed to
function, and stored
in the function's memory
space.

Figure 7-4. Addresses Stored in Function's Memory

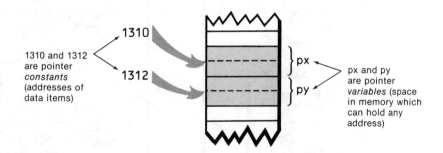

Figure 7-5. Pointer Constants Placed in Pointer Variables

to what pointers really are. If the function knew the names for **x** and **y** (if they were external variables, for example), it could simply say:

```
x = 3;
y = 5;
```

But it doesn't know the names of the variables; all it knows is the addresses where these variables are stored. We want a new kind of operator, something like **place_pointed_to_by**, so we can make such assignment statements as:

```
place_pointed_to_by_px = 3;    /* not really how it's done */
place_pointed_to_by_py = 5;
```

As you might expect, C uses a much more concise format for this operator. Here's how pointers are actually used:

```
*px = 3;
*py = 5;
```

It's our old friend the asterisk again. However—and herein lies the source of much confusion—it's used in a slightly different way here than it is in pointer declarations. In a declaration it means "pointer data type," just as **int** means "integer data type." Here it means something else: "variable pointed to by." So the first statement above translates into "assign the variable pointed to by **px** the value of 3," and the second, "assign the variable pointed to by **py** the value 5." Figure 7-6 shows the effect.

In a declaration the ( * ) symbol means "pointer type"; in other statements it means "variable pointed to by."

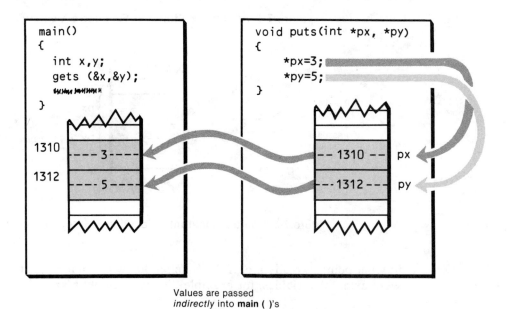

Values are passed
*indirectly* into **main ( )**'s
memory space.

Figure 7-6. Values Returned to Calling Program

The function has *indirectly* passed the values 3 and 5 to the variables **x** and **y**. It's indirect because the function didn't know the names of the variables, so it used their addresses (which were stored in the function, having been passed to it from the calling program), along with the indirection operator ( * ), to achieve the same effect. Figure 7-7 shows the structure of an assignment statement using the indirection operator.

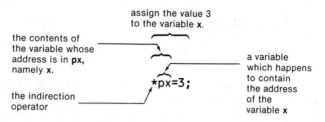

Figure 7-7. The Indirection Operator

We can conclude that the **main()** program has one way of accessing the variables **x** and **y**, while **rets2()** has another. **Main()** calls them **x** and **y**, while **rets2()** calls them **\*px** and **\*py**. This situation is depicted somewhat fancifully in Figure 7-8.

So now, finally, we know how a function can return values to the calling program.

## Going Both Ways

Once a function knows the addresses of variables in the calling program, it not only can place values in these variables, it can also take values out. That is, pointers can be used not only to pass values from a function to the calling program, but also to pass them from the program to the function. Of course, we've seen in earlier chapters that values can be passed directly to a function, but once pointers are being used to go one way, they can easily be used to go the other.

Consider the following function, which adds a constant to two values in the calling program. The function reads the value from the calling program's address space, adds the constant to it, and returns the result to the same spot.

```
/* addtotwo.c */
/* tests function that adds constant to two values */
void addcon(int *px, int *py);   /* prototype */

main()
{
    int x=4, y=7;                 /* initialize variables */

    addcon(&x, &y);              /* add 10 to both variables */
    printf("First is %d, second is %d", x, y);
}
```

```
/* addcon() */
/* adds constant to values in calling program */
void addcon(int *px, int *py)
{
    *px = *px + 10;                    /* add 10 to contents of px */
    *py = *py + 10;                    /* add 10 to contents of py */
}
```

When the program is run, it prints out:

Fi rst is 14, second is 17.

Here the values 4 and 7 are stored in the variables **x** and **y** in the calling program. The calling program passes the addresses of these variables to the function **addcon()**, which adds the constant 10 to them.

This program looks much like passback.c, except for the assignment statements in the function:

main()                             rets2()

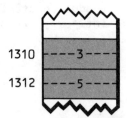

Figure 7-8. Different Perspectives

```
*px = *px + 10;
*py = *py + 10;
```

Here the indirection operator has been used on both sides of the equal sign. The first statement means that we get the contents of the variable pointed to by **px** (this is **x**, whose value is 4), add 10 to it, and return the result to the same place (the variable pointed to by **px**—which is still **x**, but whose value will now be 14). In a similar way the second statement will cause the variable **y** to end up being 17.

In other words, we can use the symbol **\*px**, where **px** is a variable containing the address of **x**, almost exactly as we could have used the variable **x** itself, had it been accessible to us.

## Pointers Without Functions

Our examples so far have dealt with pointers that store addresses passed to functions. This is a common use for pointers, and an easy one to implement, but it may tend to obscure some of the operation of pointers. The reason for this is that the function-call mechanism itself takes over the task of assigning an address to the pointer variable. That is, when we call a function with the statement

```
addcon(&x, &y);
```

then the function **addcon()**, which starts with the statements

```
addcon(px, py)
int *px, *py;
```

will *automatically* assign the addresses of **x** and **y** to the pointer variables **px** and **py**.

Let's look at an example in which we need to perform this assignment "by hand" in the program itself, rather than using a call to a function to do it for us.

The following program carries out the same task as did the addtotwo.c program. However, instead of calling a function to add a constant to the two variables, it does so directly in the program.

```
/* addin.c */
/* shows use of pointers within program */
main()
{
    int x=4, y=7;
    int *px, *py;                   /* pointer variables */

    printf("x is %d, y is %d.\n", x, y);
    px = &x;                        /* put addresses of numbers */
    py = &y;                        /*      in pointers */
    *px = *px + 10;                 /* add constant to contents */
    *py = *py + 10;                 /*      of pointers */
```

```
    printf("x is %d, y is %d.\n", x, y);
}
```

We use a **printf()** statement to print out the values of **x** and **y**, then add 10 to them, then use another **printf()** statement to print out the new values:

```
C>addin
x is 4, y is 7.
x is 14, y is 17.
```

Of course all this could have been handled much more easily with the statements

```
x = x + 10;
y = y + 10;
```

However, directly assigning values to the variables would not reveal nearly as much about pointers. (Actually, as battle-scarred C programmers, we should be using

```
x += 10;
y += 10;
```

but this tends to obscure the details of the operation for those not entirely comfortable with arithmetic assignment statements.)

The new elements in the program are the assignment statements

```
px = &x;
py = &y;
```

These statements take the addresses of the variables **x** and **y** and put them in the pointer variables **px** and **py**. This is what the function call **addcon( &x, &y )** did automatically in the addtotwo.c program. The statements

```
*px = *px + 10;
*py = *py + 10;
```

work just as they did in addtotwo.c; in fact, the output of the program is identical. The operation of the program is shown in Figure 7-9.

An important lesson can be learned by imagining what would happen if the statements **px** = **&x** and **py** = **&y** were left out of the program. Would it still work? No, because then there would be no address or at least not a correct address in the variables **px** and **py**. So the references to **\*px** and **\*py** would refer not to **x** and **y**, but to whatever was located in the addresses that happened to be in **px** and **py**. Since these addresses could point to the program itself, or to the operating system, disaster could swiftly follow.

The moral is, make sure you assign a pointer variable an appropriate address before you use it.

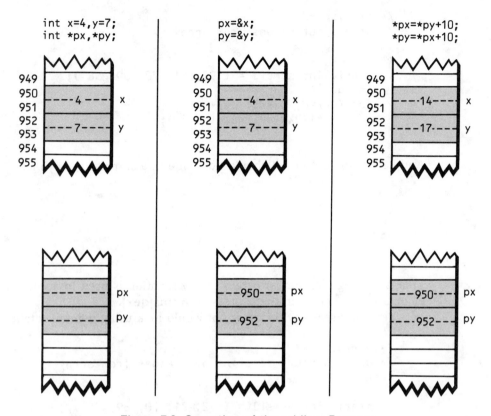

Figure 7-9. Operation of the addin.c Program

> **\*ptr**   is the contents of **ptr**
>
> **&var**   is the address of **var**

## Pointers and Arrays

In Chapter 6 we explored arrays and saw examples of array notation: how to reference array elements with such statements as **table[x][y]**. As it turns out, this array notation is really nothing more than a thinly disguised form of pointer notation. In fact, the compiler translates array notation into pointer notation when compiling, since the internal architecture of the microprocessor understands pointers but does not understand arrays.

To make clearer the relationship between pointers and arrays, let's look at a simple program, expressed first in array notation and then in pointer notation.

Here's the array version:

```
/* array.c */
/* prints out values from array */
main()
{
    static int nums[] = { 92, 81, 70, 69, 58 };
    int dex;
    for (dex=0; dex<5; dex++)
        printf("%d\n", nums[dex] );
}
```

And here is the output—it should not come as a surprise to anyone:

```
92
81
70
69
58
```

This is a straightforward program. Array notation is used to access individual elements of the array in the expression **nums[dex].**

Now let's see how this program would look using pointer notation:

```
/* parray.c */
/* uses pointers to print out values from array */
main()
{
    static int nums[] = { 92, 81, 70, 69, 58 };
    int dex;
    for (dex=0; dex<5; dex++)
        printf("%d\n", *(nums+dex) );
}
```

This version is identical to the first, except for the expression **\*(nums+dex)**. What does it mean? Its effect is exactly the same as that of **nums[dex]** in the earlier example; in other words, it accesses that element of the array **nums** whose subscript is contained in the variable **dex**. (Thus, if **dex** is 3, we'll get element **nums[3]**, which is 69.)

How do we interpret **\*(nums+dex)**? First, as we know, **nums** is the address of the array. Now if we add, say, the number 3 to this address, what will we get? In other words, if **dex** is 3, what is **nums+dex**? Would you guess the result would be an address three bytes from the start of the array? If so, you have not counted on the extreme cleverness of the designers of C.

After all, what we want is not an address three bytes from the start of the array, but the address of *element number 3* in the array. If each element of the array is an integer, it takes up two bytes, so we want to look at the address *six* bytes from the start of the array. As shown in Figure 7-10, if the array **nums** starts at 1400, then when **dex** is 3 we want **nums+dex** to have the value 1406—which is the address of **nums[3]**—not the value 1403 (which is the second half of **nums[1]** and meaningless).

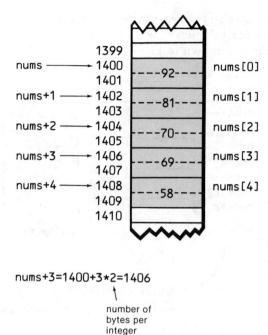

nums+3=1400+3*2=1406

number of
bytes per
integer

Figure 7-10. Pointer Addition

In other words, if we say **nums + 3**, we don't mean three *bytes*, we mean three *elements of the array*: three integers if it's an integer array, three floating point numbers if it's a floating point array, and so on.

And that's exactly what the C compiler delivers. It looks at the context of the plus sign, and if we're adding 3 to a pointer, it doesn't add 3, it adds 3 *times* however many bytes each element of the array occupies. How does it know how many bytes per element? In this case, since we're adding something to an address at the start of an array, **nums[ ]**, it looks at the array declaration, finds out it's an array of type **int**, and, since there are two bytes per integer, multiplies by 2.

Now that you know this, you should be able to figure out the meaning of the expression

```
*(nums+dex)
```

If **dex** is 3, then this expression means "the contents of element 3 of the array **nums[ ]**"; this value is 69. Thus, as we've noted, **\*(nums + dex)** is the same thing as **nums[dex]**. They are both ways of referring to the contents of an array element.

**\*(array + index)** is the same as **array[index]**

There are also two ways to refer to the *address* of an array element. We can say **nums + dex** in pointer notation, and **&nums[dex]** in array notation. These relationships are shown in Figure 7-11.

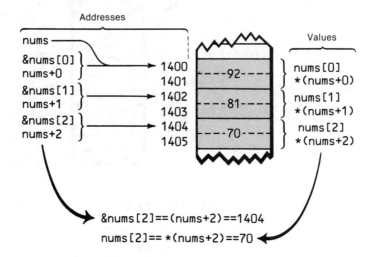

Figure 7-11. Addresses and Values

What do we gain by using pointer notation as opposed to array notation? Probably not very much in this context. However, pointer notation is commonly used with arrays in this way, so it's good to be familiar with it. More important, similar notation is used in many other instances where array notation would not work at all, as we'll see directly.

## Return of the Killer Averages

As another example of the equivalence of array and pointer notation, we're going to translate the temperature-averaging program fltemp2.c from Chapter 6 into pointer notation. We'll use this program, and a variant of it, to demonstrate some important aspects of pointer variables and constants. You might want to refer back to fltemp2.c before looking at this modified version:

```
/* ptrtemp.c */
/* averages arbitrary number of temperatures */
/* uses pointer notation */
main()
{
    float temper[40];              /* array declaration */
    float sum=0.0;
    int num, day=0;

    do                             /* put temps in array */
        {
```

```
        printf("Enter temperature for day %d: ", day);
        scanf("%f", temper+day);
        }
    while ( *(temper+day++) > 0 ); /* lacks elegance */

    num = day-1;                    /* number of temps entered */
    for (day=0; day<num; day++)     /* calculate average */
        sum += *(temper+day);
    printf("Average is %.1f", sum/num);
}
```

This works as it did in Chapter 5; you type in an arbitrary number of temperatures, and the program prints out the average.

We've modified three different expressions in this program, with the goal of changing the address **&temper[day]** into **temper + day** and the value stored there from **temper[day]** into **\*(temper + day)**. Here are the three lines affected:

```
    scanf("%f", temper+day);
    - - - -
    while ( *(temper+day++) > 0 );
    - - - -
    sum += *(temper+day);
```

What we've done here is perform almost a literal translation from array notation to pointer notation. However, such a literal translation does not yield the most efficient or elegant programming.

### Pointer Constants and Pointer Variables

Is there any way to simplify these three unwieldy expressions? In each, we're using the expression **temper + day** as a way to reference individual items of the array by varying the value of **day**. Could we get rid of **day** by using the increment operator on the address itself, instead of using the variable **day**? For example, can we use an expression like this?

```
    while ( *(temper++) > 0 );    /* can't do this */
```

The answer is no, and the reason is that **temper** is a pointer constant. It is not a variable. It is the address of the array **temper**, and this value will not change while the program is running. The linker has decided where this array will go—say address 810—and that's where it will stay. So trying to increment this address has no meaning; it's like saying

```
    x = 3++;    /* can't do this either */
```

Since you can't increment a constant, the compiler will flag this as an error.

You can't change the value of a pointer constant, only of a pointer variable.

So we've run into a problem. It would be nice to use a statement as clear as *(temper + +), but we can't increment a constant. However, we **can** increment *variables*. This is one of the real strengths of the C language: the ability to use pointer variables. So let's rewrite the program to make use of such variables.

```
/* ptrtemp2.c */
/* averages arbitrary number of temperatures */
/* uses pointer variables */
main()
{
    float temper[40];                    /* array declaration */
    float sum=0.0;
    int num, day=0;
    float *ptr;                          /* pointer variable */

    ptr = temper;                        /* set pointer to array */
    do                                   /* put temps in array */
        {
        printf("Enter temperature for day %d: ", day++);
        scanf("%f", ptr);
        }
    while ( *(ptr++) > 0 );

    ptr = temper;                        /* reset pointer to array */
    num = day-1;                         /* number of temps entered */
    for (day=0; day<num; day++)          /* calculate average */
        sum += *(ptr++);
    printf("Average is %.1f", sum/num);
}
```

The strategy here is to place the address **temper** (say it's 810) into a pointer variable called **ptr**. Now we can refer to **ptr** in much the same way we refer to **temper**. We can use **ptr** as an address that will point to an array element, and we can use **\*ptr** as the contents of that address. Moreover, since **ptr** is a variable, we don't need to add something to it to point to each element of the array in turn; all we need to do is increment it:

```
ptr++
```

We set **ptr** equal to the address **temper** before we enter the loop to read in the temperatures, and we reset it again before we enter the loop to average them. Then in both these loops we increment **ptr** with the ( + + ) operator so that it points to each array element in turn. (Because **ptr** points to an array of type **float**, the ( + + ) operator causes it to be incremented by four bytes.) The process is shown in Figure 7-12.

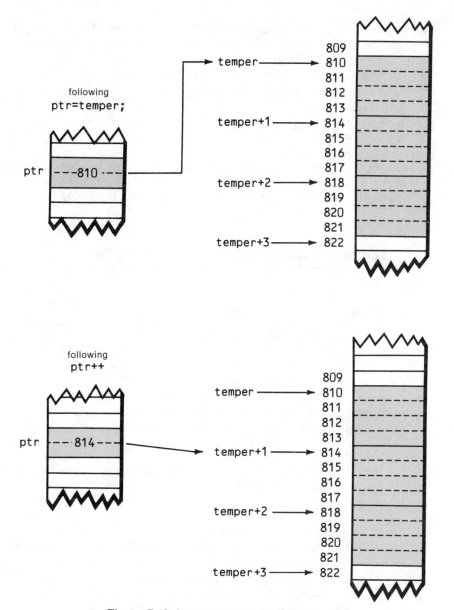

Figure 7-12. Incrementing a Pointer Variable

By using pointer variables we have simplified the program and made it run faster, since only one variable, **ptr**, must be referenced each time through the loop, instead of both **temper** and **dex**.

## Pointers to Arrays in Functions

We started this chapter by learning how pointers can be used for communication among functions, and then we examined how pointers can be used to reference array elements. Let's combine these two techniques to see how a function can use pointers to access elements of an array whose address is passed to the function as an argument.

As an example, we'll modify our program addtotwo.c, which adds a constant to two variables in the calling program, to add a constant to all the elements in an array. This is a function that might prove useful in a variety of circumstances. Here's the listing:

```
/* addarray.c */
/* tests function to add constant to array values */
#define SIZE 5                     /* size of array */
void addcon(int *, int, int);      /* prototype */

main()
{
    static int array[SIZE] = { 3, 5, 7, 9, 11 };
    int konst = 10;                /* constant to be added */
    int j;

    addcon(array, SIZE, konst);    /* call funct to add consts */
    for (j=0; j<SIZE; j++)         /* print out array */
        printf("%d ", *(array+j) );
}

/* addcon() */
/* adds constant to each element of array */
void addcon(int *ptr, int size, int con)
/* arguments: array, array size, constant */
{
    int k;
    for(k=0; k<size; k++)          /* add const to each element */
        *(ptr+k) = *(ptr+k) + con;
}
```

Here the calling program supplies the address of the array, **array**; the size of the array, SIZE (which is #**define**d to be 5); and the constant to be added to each element, **const** (which is assigned the value 10).

The function assigns the address of the array to the pointer **ptr**, the size to the variable **num**, and the constant to the variable **con**. Then a simple loop serves to add the constant to each element of the array.

The output of this program shows the new contents of the array to verify that the function has done its work. Here's what it looks like:

```
C>addarray
13  15  17  19  21
```

## Pointer to Whatever: Type *void* *

We'll mention here the use of the **void** type with pointers, although we won't see an example of its use until we explore **malloc()** in Chapter 9.

Sometimes a function returns a pointer that can point to variables of different data types. In other words, it might return a pointer to **char** one time, a pointer to **int** another time, and so on. Many library functions are of this type. The declaration of a pointer of this type looks like this:

```
void *vpointer;
```

This signifies that the type the pointer will be applied to is unknown.

# Pointers and Strings

Let's turn now to the relationship of pointers and strings. Since strings are arrays and arrays are closely connected with pointers, you might expect that strings and pointers are closely related, and this is correct.

## String Functions and Pointers

Many of the C library functions that work with strings do so by using pointers. As an example, let's look at an example of a string function that returns a pointer. The function is **strchr()**, which returns a pointer to the first occurrence of a particular character in a string. If we say

```
ptr = strchr(str, 'x');
```

then the pointer variable **ptr** will be assigned the address of the first occurrence of the character 'x' in the string **str**. Note that this isn't the *position* in the string, from 0 to the end of the string, but the *address*, from 2343—or wherever the string happens to start—to the end of the string.

Here is the function **strchr()** used in a simple program that allows the user to type in a sentence and a character to be searched for. The program then prints out the address of the start of the string, the address of the character, and the character's position relative to the start of the string (0 if it's the first character, 1 if it's the second, and so forth). This relative position is simply the difference between the two addresses.

```
/* search.c */
/* searches string for a given character */
main()
{
    char ch, line[81], *ptr, *strchr();

    puts("Enter the sentence to be searched: ");
    gets(line);
    printf("Enter character to search for: ");
    ch = getche();

    ptr = strchr(line,ch);      /* return pointer to char */
    printf("\nString starts at address %u.\n", line);
```

```
        printf("First occurrence of char is address %u.\n", ptr);
        printf("This is position %d (starting from 0)", ptr-line);
    }
```

Here's a sample run:

```
C>search
Enter the sentence to be searched:
The quick brown fox jumped over the lazy dog.
Enter character to search for: x
String starts at address 3610.
First occurrence of character is address 3628.
This is character position 18.
```

In the declaration statement, we've set aside a pointer variable, **ptr**, to hold the address returned by **strchr()**. Since this is the address of a character, **ptr** is of type **char**. Once the function has returned this address, we can print it out and use it to calculate the position of the character in the string: the value **ptr-line**.

Are you wondering what the expression **\*strchr()** is doing in the declaration statement? As we discussed in Chapter 5, any function that doesn't return an integer value must be declared. The **strchr()** function returns a pointer to a character, so it must be declared to be of this type. We could have left this declaration out if we'd included the preprocessor statement

```
#include <string.h>
```

at the beginning of the program. This would work just as well, since the header file STRING.H contains declarations for the string handling functions.

## Strings Initialized as Pointers

We showed an example of initializing a string as an array in the program strinit.c in Chapter 6. Our next example shows how this program can be modified so that the string is initialized as a pointer. Here's the listing:

```
/* strinitp.c */
/* shows string initialization */
/* uses pointers */
main()
{
    char *salute = "Greetings,";
    char name[81];

    puts("Enter your name: ");
    gets(name);
    puts(salute);
    puts(name);
}
```

Here, to initialize the string, we've used the statement

```
char *salute = "Greetings,";
```

instead of

```
static char salute[] = "Greetings,";
```

These two forms appear to have much the same effect in the program. Is there a difference? Yes, but it's quite a subtle one. The array version of this statement sets aside an array with enough bytes (in this case 10) to hold the word, plus one byte for the '\0' (null) character. The address of the first character of the array is given the name of the array, in this case, **salute**. In the pointer version, an array is set aside in the same way, but a *pointer variable* is also set aside; it is this pointer that is given the name **salute**. Figure 7-13 shows how this looks.

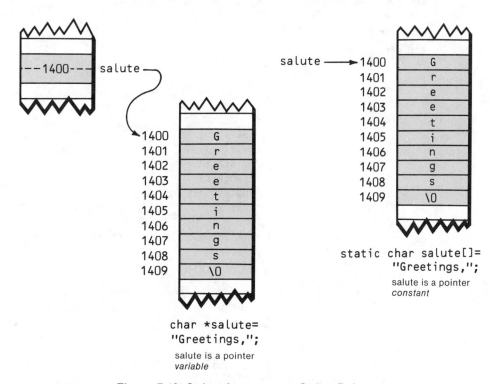

Figure 7-13. String Array versus String Pointer

In the array style of initialization, **salute** is a pointer constant, an address which cannot be changed. In the pointer style, **salute** is a pointer variable, which can be changed. For instance, the expression

```
puts(++salute);
```

would print the string starting with the second character in the string:

```
reetings,
```

The added flexibility of the pointer approach can often be used to advantage, as we'll see shortly.

## Initializing an Array of Pointers to Strings

There's another difference between initializing a string as an array or as a pointer. This difference is most easily seen when we talk about an array of strings (or if we use pointers, an array of pointers to strings).

In Chapter 6 we showed how to initialize an array of strings in the program compare.c. In the following example we'll modify this program so that the strings are initialized as pointers.

```
/* comparep.c */
/* compares word typed in with words in program */
/* uses pointers */
#define MAX 5
main()
{
    int dex;
    int enter=0;
    char name[40];
    static char *list[MAX] =
                    { "Katrina",
                      "Nigel",
                      "Alistair",
                      "Francesca",
                      "Gustav"     };
    printf("Enter your name: ");                /* get name */
    gets(name);
    for (dex=0; dex<MAX; dex++)                 /* go thru list */
        if( strcmp(list[dex],name)==0 )         /* if match */
            enter = 1;                          /* set flag */
    if ( enter == 1 )                           /* if flag set */
        printf("You may enter, oh honored one."); /* one response */
    else                                        /* otherwise */
        printf("Guards! Remove this person!");  /* different one */
}
```

What does the expression **char \*list[MAX]** mean? Such complex expressions are generally deciphered from right to left, so, as shown in Figure 7-14, this one means an array of pointers to characters.

In the array version of this program the strings were stored in a rectangular array with 5 rows and 10 columns. In the new version the strings are stored contiguously in memory; they don't form an array so there is no wasted space between them. However, an array of *pointers to* these strings has been created. Figure 7-15 shows the differences between these two approaches.

As you can see, the pointer version takes up less space in memory; it ends at 1038, while the array version ends at 1049. Thus, one reason to initialize strings as pointers is to use memory more efficiently. Another reason is to obtain greater flexibility in the manipulation of the strings in the array, as the next example will show.

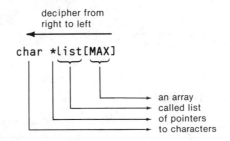

Figure 7-14. Declaration of Array of Pointers

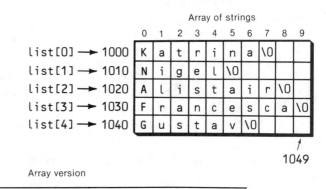

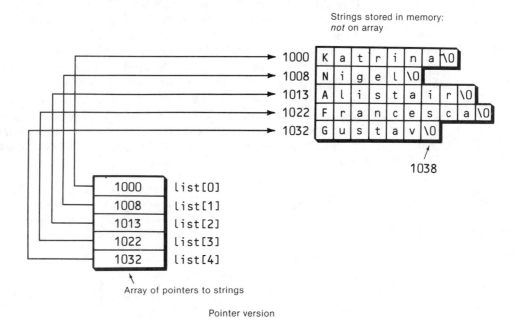

Figure 7-15. Array of Strings versus Array of Pointers

> Initializing a group of strings using pointer notation uses less memory than initializing them as a two-dimensional array.

## Lvalue and Rvalue

Occasionally, when experimenting with pointers and strings, you may receive error messages from the compiler that use the term *lvalue*, as in "expression must be lvalue." What does this mean?

Essentially, an lvalue is a variable, as opposed to an rvalue which is a constant. The terms arose from the left-right positions available in a typical assignment statement:

```
var = 3;
```

An expression that can appear on the left side of an assignment statement is a variable and is called an "lvalue." An expression that must remain on the right side of the equal sign because it is a constant is called an "rvalue." If you attempt to use a constant on the left side of the equal sign in the assignment statement, the compiler will flag it as an error.

## Manipulating Pointers to Strings

As you know, when an array is passed as an argument to a function, it is not actually the array that is passed, but only its address. The array itself does not move. The same is true of strings: when we pass a string to a function, we are passing only its address. This ability to reference strings by addresses can be very helpful when we want to manipulate a group of strings. In the following example we will sort an array of strings, using an approach similar to that of the sortnum.c program in Chapter 6. However, we won't move the strings themselves around in the array; instead, we'll sort an array of pointers to the strings.

This program accepts a series of names typed in by the user, places them in an array, and sorts the pointers to the array so that, in effect, the names are rearranged into alphabetical order. Then, the resulting sorted list is printed out. Here's the program:

```
/* sortstr.c */
/* sorts list of names typed in to array */
#define MAXNUM 30               /* maximum number of names */
#define MAXLEN 81               /* maximum length of names */
main()
{
    static char name[MAXNUM][MAXLEN];    /* array of strings */
    char *ptr[MAXNUM];              /* array of pntrs to strings */
    char *temp;                     /* extra pointer */
    int count = 0;                  /* how many names */
    int in, out;                    /* sorting indexes */
```

```
    while ( count < MAXNUM )        /* get names */
       {
       printf("Name %d: ", count+1);
       gets(name[count]);
       if ( strlen(name[count])==0 )
          break;                     /* quit if no name */
       ptr[count++] = name[count]; /* each ptr points to name */
       }

                                    /* sort the pointers */
    for (out=0; out<count-1; out++)   /* for each string */
       for (in=out+1; in<count; in++) /* look at those smaller */
          if ( strcmp(ptr[out],ptr[in]) > 0 )  /* compare */
             {                          /* if any smaller, */
             temp = ptr[in];           /* swap pointers */
             ptr[in] = ptr[out];
             ptr[out] = temp;
             }

    printf("\nSorted list: \n");
    for (out=0; out<count; out++) /* print sorted list */
       printf("Name %d: %s\n", out+1, ptr[out]);
}
```

And a sample run:

```
C>sortstr
Name 1: Thomas
Name 2: Cummings
Name 3: Sandburg
Name 4: Masefield
Name 5: Shelley
Name 6: Auden
Name 7:

Sorted list:
Name 1: Auden
Name 2: Cummings
Name 3: Masefield
Name 4: Sandburg
Name 5: Shelley
Name 6: Thomas
```

This program uses both an array of strings and an array of pointers. The pointers occupy the array declared by the expression:

```
char *ptr[MAXNUM];
```

The strings occupy a two-dimensional array:

```
static char name[MAXNUM][MAXKEN];
```

Because we don't know in advance how long they will be, we must use a rectangular array to hold the strings that are typed in (rather than initializing them as pointers to strings). We use rows 81 characters long; these will hold names extending across the entire screen.

As the strings are read in, the statement

```
ptr[count++] = name[count];
```

assigns the address of each string, which is stored in the array **name[ ][ ]**, to an element of the pointer array **ptr[ ]**. Then this array of pointers is sorted. Finally, the strings are printed out in alphabetical order, using the array of pointers as a reference. Figure 7-16 shows how the pointers look before and after sorting. The array **name[ ][ ]** itself remains unchanged; only the pointers to the elements of the array have been rearranged.

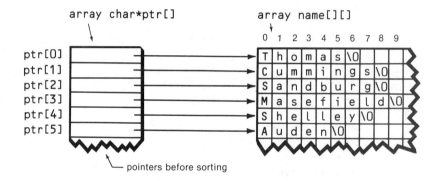

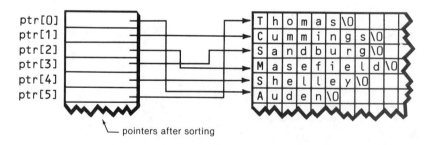

Figure 7-16. Sorting Pointers to Strings

There is a subtle aspect to this program that may have slipped your notice. Let's take a closer look.

## Parts of Arrays Are Arrays

The C language embodies an unusual but powerful capability: it can treat parts of arrays *as arrays*. More specifically, each *row* of a two-dimensional array can be thought of as a one-dimensional array. This can be very useful if one wishes to rearrange the rows of a two-dimensional array, as we just did in the sortstr.c example.

Do you see anything unusual about the following statement from sortstr.c?

```
ptr[count++] = name[count];
```

That's right: although the array **name[ ][ ]** is a two-dimensional array, we use only one subscript when we refer to it in this statement: **name[count]**. What does **name[count]** mean, if **name[ ][ ]** is a two-dimensional array?

Remember that we can think of a two-dimensional array as an array of arrays. In this case, the declaration

```
static char name[MAXNUM][MAXLEN];
```

can be thought of as setting up a one-dimensional array of MAXNUM elements, each of which is a one-dimensional array MAXLEN characters long. In other words, we have a one-dimensional array of MAXNUM strings. We refer to the elements of a one-dimensional array with a single subscript, as in **name[count]**, where **count** can range up to MAXNUM. More specifically, **name[0]** is the address of the first string in the array, **name[1]** is the address of the second string, and so forth. Thus the expression **name[count]** makes sense and simplifies the coding of the program.

# Double Indirection: Pointers to Pointers

The ability of the C language to treat part of an array as an array is actually a disguised version of another C topic, double indirection, or pointers that point to pointers. Being able to reference a pointer with a pointer gives C enormous power and flexibility in creating complex arrangements of data. As a hint of what's involved, let's look at an example of double indirection, derived from a two-dimensional array.

In the sortstr.c program above we dealt with parts of arrays as strings. This was in some ways easier than dealing with parts of arrays as arrays, which we will now look at in a two-dimensional array of numbers.

We'll start off with a simple program that takes an existing two-dimensional array, adds a constant to each element, and prints out the result. We'll use normal array notation for this program, so it should hold no surprises:

```
/* double.c */
/* shows use of 2-dimensional arrays */
#define ROWS 4
#define COLS 5
```

```
main()
{
   static int table[ROWS][COLS] =
                     { { 13, 15, 17, 19, 21 },
                       { 20, 22, 24, 26, 28 },
                       { 31, 33, 35, 37, 39 },
                       { 40, 42, 44, 46, 48 }  };

   int const = 10;                   /* constant to be added */
   int j, k;

   for(j=0; j<ROWS; j++)             /* add const to each element */
      for(k=0; k<COLS; k++)
         table[j][k] = table[j][k] + const;
   for(j=0; j<ROWS; j++)             /* print out array */
      {
      for (k=0; k<COLS; k++)
         printf("%d ", table[j][k] );
      printf("\n");
      }
}
```

Since the program adds a constant 10 to each element, the output looks like this:

```
C>double
23 25 27 29 31
30 32 34 36 38
41 43 45 47 49
50 52 54 56 58
```

Now, suppose we rewrite this program to use pointer notation instead of array notation. The question is, how do we write the expression **table[j][k]** in pointer notation? To do this, we make use of the fact that a two-dimensional array is an array of one-dimensional arrays as shown in Figure 7-17.

Let's figure out how to use pointers to refer to the fourth element in the third row of the array, or **table[2][3]**, which is 37 (before the 10 is added).

First, the address of the entire array is **table**. Let's assume the array starts at address 1000 in memory, so **table** == 1000. It's an integer array, so each element takes two bytes. There are five elements in each row, so each row takes 10 bytes. Thus each row starts 10 bytes further along than the last one. And, since each row is a one-dimensional array, each of these one-dimensional arrays starts 10 bytes further along than the last one, as shown in the top part of Figure 7-18.

The compiler knows how many columns there are in the array, since we specified this in the array declaration. So it knows how to interpret the expression **table + 1**; it takes the address of **table** (1000), and adds the number of bytes in a row (5 columns times 2 bytes per column, equaling 10 bytes). Thus **table + 1** is interpreted as the address 1010. This is the address of the second one-dimensional array in the array, **table + 2** is the address of the third such array, and so

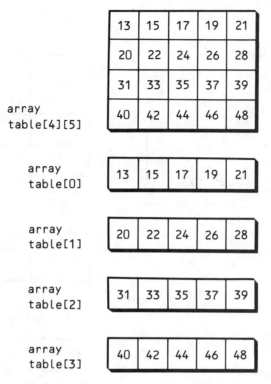

Figure 7-17. Each Row of an Array Is an Array

on. We're looking for an item in the third row, whose address is **table + 2**, or 1020.

Now, how do we refer to the individual elements of a row? We've mentioned before that the address of an array is the same as the address of the first element in the array. For example, in the one-dimensional array **list[SIZE]**, **list** is the same as **&list[0]**. Again referring to Figure 7-18, we've already determined that the address of the array formed by the third row of **table[ ][ ]** is **table[2]**, or **table + 2** in pointer notation. The address of the first element of this array is **&table[2][0]**, or **\*(table + 2)** in pointer notation. Both pointer expressions, **table + 2** and **\*(table + 2)**, refer to the contents of the same address, 1020. Why use two different expressions for the same thing? The difference between **\*(table + 2)** and **table + 2** is in the units of measurement. If you add 1 to **table + 2** you get **table + 3**, or the address of the fourth row of **table[ ][ ]**; you've added 10 bytes. But if you add 1 to **\*(table + 2)**, you get the address of the next element in the row; you've added 2 bytes.

An element of a two-dimensional array can be referenced with a pointer to a pointer.

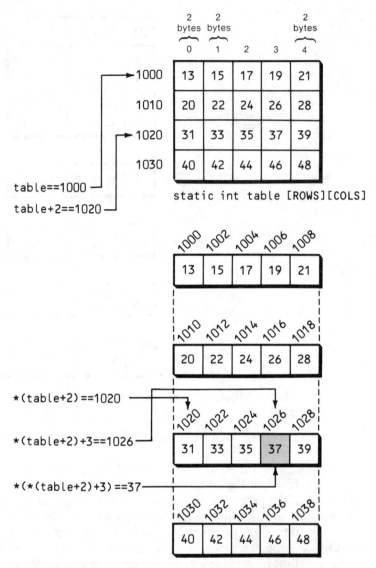

Figure 7-18. Pointing to Element in Two-Dimensional Array

So the address of the fourth element is **\*(table + 2) + 3**. And, finally, the *contents* of that element is **\*(\*(table + 2) + 3)**, which is 37. This expression is a pointer to a pointer.

In other words,

```
table[j][k] == *(*(table+j)+k)
```

We've figured out how to translate two-dimensional array notation into pointer notation. Now we can rewrite our program, incorporating this new notation:

```
/* double2.c */
/* shows use of pointers on 2-dimensional arrays */
#define ROWS 4
#define COLS 5
main()
{
    static int table[ROWS][COLS] =
                     { { 13, 15, 17, 19, 21 },
                       { 20, 22, 24, 26, 28 },
                       { 31, 33, 35, 37, 39 },
                       { 40, 42, 44, 46, 48 }  };

    int const = 10;                    /* constant to be added */
    int j, k;

    for(j=0; j<ROWS; j++)              /* add const to each element */
       for(k=0; k<COLS; k++)
         *(*(table+j)+k) = *(*(table+j)+k) + const;

    for(j=0; j<ROWS; j++)              /* print out array */
       {
       for (k=0; k<COLS; k++)
          printf("%d ", *(*(table+j)+k) );
       printf("\n");
       }
}
```

This version of the program will work just the same as the old one did.

## The Rocketship Program

Let's look at a slightly more ambitious example that incorporates double indirection. This program models a very crude rocketship taking off. As a spectacular graphics display, the program leaves something to be desired (especially since we haven't learned how to clear the screen between pictures), but it does demonstrate how to manipulate array elements using pointers.

The program consists of a large loop. Each time through the loop, the program draws a line, representing the ground, consisting of five double lines (graphics character '\xCD'). It then draws the rocketship, defined in the program as four elements of a character array—a main body ('\DB'), a nose cone, and two engines ('\x1E'). After drawing the rocket, the rows of the array that contain the rocket are, in effect, rotated; each row moves up one character, and the top row is placed on the bottom. (Actually we don't rotate the array itself, as we'll see in a moment.) Then the array is printed again. The effect is of the rocketship rising from the ground, as shown in Figure 7-19. Here's the listing for the program:

```
/* move.c */
/* moves image on screen */
```

```
#define ROWS 10
#define COLS 5

main()
{
   int count, j, k;
   char *ptr[ROWS];                    /* pointers to rows */
   char *temp;                         /* pointer storage */

   static char pict[ROWS][COLS] =      /* rocketship */
        {  { 0,       0,       0,       0,       0      },
           { 0,       0,       0,       0,       0      },
           { 0,       0,       0,       0,       0      },
           { 0,       0,       0,       0,       0      },
           { 0,       0,       0,       0,       0      },
           { 0,       0,       0,       0,       0      },
           { 0,       0,       0,       0,       0      },
           { 0,       0,       0,       0,       0      },
           { 0,       0,      '\x1E',   0,       0      },
           { 0,      '\x1E',  '\xDB',  '\x1E',   0      }  };

   static char gnd[] =                 /* ground line */
          { '\xCD', '\xCD', '\xCD', '\xCD', '\xCD' };

   for(count=0; count<ROWS; count++)    /* set up pointers */
      *(ptr+count) = *(pict+count);

   for(count=0; count<ROWS-1; count++)
      {
      for(j=0; j<ROWS; j++)             /* print rocket */
         {
         for(k=0; k<COLS; k++)
            printf("%c", *(*(ptr+j)+k) );
         printf("%c", '\n' );
         }
      printf("%s\n", gnd);             /* print ground */

      temp = *ptr;                     /* rotate pointers */
      for(j=0; j<ROWS-1; j++)
         *(ptr+j) = *(ptr+j+1);
      *(ptr+ROWS-1) = temp;
      }
}
```

Here's how the program works. We declare an array of pointers to characters.

```
   char *ptr[ROWS];
```

In each of the elements of this array, we place the address of one row of the array **pict[ ][ ]** using the loop:

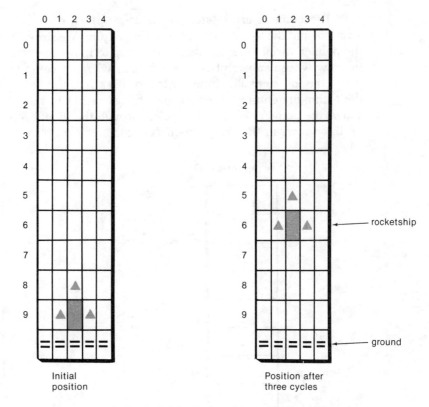

Figure 7-19. Rocketship Rising from the Ground

```
for(count=0; count<ROWS; count++)
   *(ptr+count) = *(pict+count);
```

We print out the elements of the array as individual characters using two nested loops, a process we used in Chapter 6. In this case, however, we use pointer notation to refer to individual elements of the array, in the expression

```
printf("%c", *(*(ptr+j)+k) );
```

Notice that we don't actually refer to the array **pict[ ][ ]** itself, but rather to the array of pointers, **ptr[ ]**, that point to it.

To make the rocket appear to rise off the ground line, we in effect move the elements in each row of the array **pict[ ][ ]**, upward one row at a time. If we actually moved all the array elements we would need to move all 50 characters in memory, and this would be time consuming. So instead of moving the rows of the array, we simply move the pointers that point to these rows. There are only 10 pointers, so this is a much faster operation than moving 50 characters. (If we were trying to move an object wider than five characters, the speed advantage would be greater still.)

The pointers are rotated in the array **ptr[ ]**: each element moves up one location, and the top element goes to the bottom. We store the top row, **ptr[0]**, in the pointer variable **temp**, then use a loop to move the contents of each row to the row whose subscript is one less than where it came from, and finally we insert the top element, stored in **temp**, back into the bottom row. (This is like the technique employed for sorting strings earlier in this chapter.) Figure 7-20 shows the pointers after three cycles through the loop; each pointer has moved up three rows in the array **\*pict[ROWS]**.

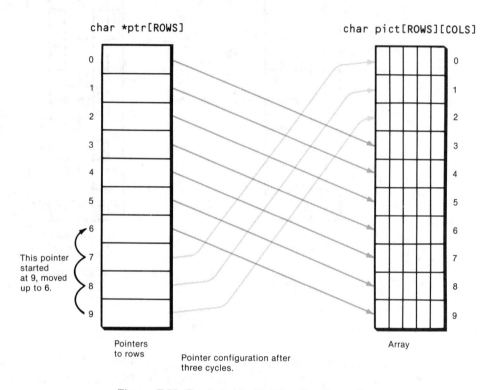

char *ptr[ROWS]

char pict[ROWS][COLS]

This pointer started at 9, moved up to 6.

Pointers to rows

Pointer configuration after three cycles.

Array

Figure 7-20. Rocketship Pointer Configuration

Now when we print out the array, we'll see that the rocket appears to have risen one character from the ground line each time through the loop. Actually, the array **pict[ ][ ]** remains unaltered, with the rocket still in the lowest position. However, by printing out the rows of the array in a different order, the rocket appears to move.

## Summary

This chapter has introduced the subject of pointers and has covered some of the less complex ways pointers can be used. We've seen how to declare pointer variables with such statements as **int \*ptr2** and how to refer to the values pointed to by pointers, using such expressions as **\*ptr2** (the asterisk having a different meaning in the two cases). We've used pointers to return multiple values from a function to the calling program and to permit a function to modify values contained in the calling program, with the use of expressions like **\*ptrx = \*ptfx + 10**.

The second major topic in the chapter was the relationship of pointers to arrays. We saw how to reference individual array elements using pointer notation and how to perform arithmetic on pointers. We've seen that pointer variables can be modified, but that pointer constants—the addresses of data structures—cannot.

We've investigated the use of pointers with strings, seeing how some string library functions return pointers and the uses that can be made of such functions. We've also learned how to initialize strings using pointers instead of arrays and the benefits of this approach.

Finally we've learned how to use pointer notation to refer to the elements of a two-dimensional array, and we've seen how this relates to the idea of a pointer to a pointer.

## Questions

1. Why are pointers sometimes found to be difficult to understand?

    a. They point to data beyond our control.

    b. They use the same symbol to refer to two different things.

    c. The idea of indirection is not used in some languages.

    d. They require a knowledge of quantum mechanics.

2. Which of these are reasons for using pointers?

    a. To manipulate parts of arrays

    b. To refer to key words such as **loop** and **if**

    c. To return more than one value from a function

    d. To refer to particular programs more conveniently

3. True or false: the address of an array is a pointer constant.

4. True or false: passing the addresses of arrays to functions is beyond the scope of this book.

5. True or false: passing a value to a function places the address of that value in the function's private memory space.

6. For a function to return more than one value, it must first be passed the addresses of the variables to be returned. This is because:

a. The function must always contain the same amount of numbers, whether addresses or values.

b. The addresses are actually a code that is deciphered into values by the function.

c. The function needs to know where to find library routines.

d. The function needs to know where to put the values it returns.

7. If we call a function with the statement **blotch(&white,&black)**, what purpose do **&white** and **&black** serve?

a. They are integer values we're passing to the function.

b. They are the addresses of the function and the calling program.

c. They are the addresses of the variables where we want values returned or modified in the calling program.

d. They are the addresses of library routines needed by the function.

8. To return more than one value from a function, we must pass the function the _____ of the values we want returned; then, in the function, we must first _____ pointers to hold these values, and finally we access the values using _____.

9. Which is the correct way to declare a pointer?

a. int_ptr x;

b. int *ptr;

c. *int ptr;

d. *x;

10. Which are correct ways to refer to the variable **ch**, assuming the address of **ch** has been assigned to the pointer **fingerch**?

a. *fingerch;

b. int *fingerch;

c. *finger;

d. ch

e. *ch

11. In the expression **float *fptr;** what has type float?

a. The variable **fptr**

b. The address of **fptr**

c. The variable pointed to by **fptr**

d. None of the above

12. Assuming that the address of the variable **var** has been assigned to the pointer variable **pointvar**, write an expression that does not use **var** and that will divide **var** by 10.

13. Assuming that the address of **vox** has been assigned to the pointer variable **invox**, which of the following expressions are correct?

    a. vox = = &invox

    b. vox = = *invox

    c. invox = = *vox

    d. invox = = &vox

14. When a function is called using **&x** as a parameter, where is the value of **&x** placed?

15. What statement must be added to the following program to make it work correctly?

```
main()
{
    int j, *ptrj;
    *ptrj = 3;
}
```

16. Assuming we want to read in a value for **x**, and the address of **x** has been assigned to **ptrx**, does this statement look all right?

```
scanf("%d", *ptrx);
```

17. Assuming that **spread[]** is a one-dimensional array of type int, which of the following refers to the value of the third element in the array?

    a. *(spread+2)

    b. *(spread+4)

    c. spread+4

    d. spread+2

18. Suppose an array has been declared as:

```
int arr[3];
```

Can you use the expression **arr++**?

19. What will the following program do when executed?

```
main()
{
```

```
      static int arr[] = { 4, 5, 6 };
      int j;
      for(j=0; j<3; j++)
         printf("%d  ", *(arr+j) );
}
```

20. In the program above, the plus sign in the expression **arr+j** means to add **j** times _____ bytes, to **arr**.

21. What will the following program do when executed?

```
main()
{
   static int arr[] = { 4, 5, 6 };
   int j;
   for(j=0; j<3; j++)
      printf("%d  ", arr+j );
}
```

22. What will the following program do when executed?

```
main()
{
   static int arr[] = { 4, 5, 6 };
   int j, *ptr;
   ptr = arr;
   for(j=0; j<3; j++)
      printf("%d  ", *ptr++ );
}
```

23. Are the following statements equivalent?

```
char errmsg[] = "Error!";
char *errmsg = "Error!";
```

24. One difference between using array notation to declare a group of strings and using pointer notation is that in array notation each string occupies _____ of memory, while using pointer notation each string occupies _____ of memory.

25. Given the declaration

```
static char s7[] = "I come not to bury Caesar";
```

what will the following statements cause to be printed?

```
printf("%s", s7 );
printf("%s", &s7[0] );
printf("%s", s7+11 );
```

26. When you declare a string using pointer notation, and the string is 10 characters long, _____ bytes are set aside in memory. (Note: this isn't as easy as it looks.)

27. True or false: every column of a two-dimensional array can be considered to be another two-dimensional array.

28. Given the following array declaration:

```
static int arr7[2][3] = {  { 10, 11, 12 },
                           { 13, 14, 15 }  };
```

refer to the element occupied by the number 14 in array notation and then in pointer notation.

29. If you want to exchange two rows in a two-dimensional array, the fastest way is to:

    a. exchange the elements of the two rows

    b. exchange the addresses of each element in the two rows

    c. set the address of one row equal to the address of the other, and vice versa

    d. store the addresses of the rows in an array of pointers and exchange the pointers

30. How do you refer to **arr7[x][y]** using pointer notation?

# Exercises

In the following exercises, use pointer notation wherever possible.

1. Write a function, and a program to test it, that will place a zero in each of three variables in the calling program.

2. Write a function, and a program to test it, that will place a zero in each element of an array passed to it from the calling program.

3. Write a function, and a program to test it, that will change a string to the null string. The string is defined in the calling program.

4. Write a program that contains two arrays and generates a third array in which each element is the sum of the corresponding elements from the other two arrays.

# Keyboard and Cursor

- Extended keyboard codes
- ANSI.SYS cursor control
- Key reassignment
- Command-line arguments
- Redirection of input and output

# 8

In this chapter we're going to change our focus from the C language itself to C's interaction with the IBM computer. This doesn't mean that we've covered everything there is to know about C; we'll take up other key aspects of the language in later chapters. You now know enough, however, to begin exploring some of the features of the IBM PC computer family in order to put C to work in real-world situations.

We'll cover two major topics in this chapter: first, the IBM extended character codes, which enable a program to read the function keys, cursor control keys, and special key combinations and second, the ANSI.SYS control functions, which give the programmer control over where the cursor is on the screen and permit other operations as well. Almost all applications programs—word processors, database programs, and even games—need to make use of these capabilities to provide a more sophisticated level of interaction with the user.

At the end of the chapter we'll explain command-line arguments: arguments typed in the command line when you call your program from DOS. We'll show an example that uses the ANSI.SYS routines and command-line arguments to redefine the IBM's function keys. We'll show how redirection can be used to give even simple programs the ability to read and write files. As we go along, we'll also discuss several new C library functions.

The material in this chapter, besides extending your capability to write interesting and powerful programs, also serves as an introduction to directly accessing the monochrome display memory, a topic we'll return to in Chapter 10.

## Extended Keyboard Codes

We've already seen that the keyboard generates the usual ASCII codes for letters, numbers, and punctuation, as well as various other codes for foreign language characters and graphic symbols. These codes are numbered from 1 to

255; each can be represented by just one byte. (See Appendix E for a table of these values.)

However, there are a great many keys and key combinations not represented by this one-byte character set. For instance, the function keys, F1 to F10, are not represented, nor are the cursor control keys on the numeric keypad. How does a program determine when these keys are being pressed?

The IBM provides a second set of 256 keys and key combinations by using an *extended code*. This code consists of *two* bytes; the first byte is 0 and the second byte is a number indicating the particular key or key combination. When a key that is not in the normal character set—the F1 key, for example—is pressed, it first sends a 0 to the keyboard buffer and then the specific code. (The keyboard buffer is a temporary storage area where characters typed at the keyboard are stored until they are read by a program.) Thus, when a nonstandard key is pressed, two characters are sent. A program that expects to read extended codes checks for a character with the value 0. If it finds one, it knows the next character will be an extended code, with a completely different interpretation than the normal code.

> Extended keyboard codes use two characters, the first of which has an ASCII value of 0.

Because no character is represented by 0 in the normal IBM character set, there is no confusion when this character is received; it always indicates an extended code will follow. Figure 8-1 shows the format of the extended code.

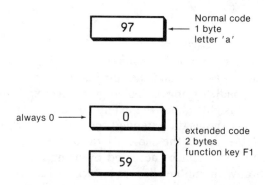

Figure 8-1. Normal and Extended Codes

## Exploring the Extended Codes

Here's a program that will permit us to explore these extended keyboard codes:

```
/* kbdtest.c */
/* prints code of keyboard key */
```

```
main()
{
char key, key2;

while ( (key=getch()) != 'X' )    /* read keyboard */
    if( key == 0 )                /* if extended code, */
       {
       key2 = getch();            /* read second code */
       printf("%3d %3d\n", key, key2);
       }
    else
       printf("%3d\n", key);      /* not extended code */
}
```

This program prints out the code for any key typed: either the normal one-byte IBM character code or the two-byte extended code. We don't want to echo the character typed, since there is no printable equivalent for the extended codes, so we use the function **getch()**, which works just like **getche()**, except that the character is not printed on the screen.

In the **while** test expression, the program reads the first code. If it's 0, the program knows it's dealing with an extended code, so it reads the second part of the code, using **getch()** again, and prints out the numerical value of both parts. If the first part is *not* 0, the program concludes it is simply a normal character, and prints out its value.

Here's a sample run:

```
C>kbdtest
  0  59
97
  0  75
```

The first code shown here results from pressing function key [F1], the second is simply a lowercase 'a', and the third is the left arrow (on the number 4 of the numeric keypad). Typing in this program and experimenting with it will provide a variety of insights about the extended codes available.

Table 8-1 shows the extended codes that can be obtained by typing a single key. The table shows the second byte of the code; the first byte is always 0. Many more codes can be accessed by using the [Alt], [Ctrl], or [Shift] keys in combination with another key, as shown in Table 8-2. These two-key codes are less often used than the single-key variety, but they do provide an amazing variety of choices for programs that need them. These two tables are found on page 264.

## Interpreting the Extended Codes

A common approach to writing C functions to interpret the extended codes is to use the **switch** statement, as we do in the following demonstration:

```
/* extend.c */
/* tests extended codes */
main()
{
int key, key2;
while ( (key=getch()) != 'X' )      /* read keyboard */
   if( key == 0 )                   /* if extended code, */
      {
      key2 = getch();               /* read second code */
      switch (key2)
         {
         case 59:
            printf("Function key 1\n"); break;
         case 60:
            printf("Function key 2\n"); break;
         case 75:
            printf("Left arrow\n"); break;
         case 77:
            printf("Right arrow\n"); break;
         default:
            printf("Some other extended code\n");
         }
      }
   else
      printf("Normal code: %3d=%c\n", key, key);
}
```

This program is similar to kbdtest.c, but it uses **switch** to analyze and print out interpretations of some of the codes. We'll be using this same format in a variety of programs later in this chapter.

Notice that we've placed more than one statement on the same line in this program:

```
printf("Function key 1\n"); break;
```

It is generally easier to read a C program when only one statement is used per line, but in the **switch** construct, statements are often doubled up this way to save space and provide a cleaner format.

Typing an uppercase 'X' causes an exit from the **while** loop and terminates the program.

Now that we've introduced the extended keyboard codes, let's see how they're used in a typical situation: for cursor control.

# ANSI.SYS

The IBM PC family of computers, and most MS-DOS compatibles, comes with a system for directly controlling the position of the cursor on the screen. However, this capability is not built into the IBM's read-only memory (ROM) as are the normal routines for accessing I/O devices. Rather it is contained in a separate file called the ANSI.SYS file.

### Table 8-1. One-Key Extended Codes

| Second Byte (Decimal) | Key that Generates Extended Code |
|:---:|:---:|
| 59 | F1 |
| 60 | F2 |
| 61 | F3 |
| 62 | F4 |
| 63 | F5 |
| 64 | F6 |
| 65 | F7 |
| 66 | F8 |
| 67 | F9 |
| 68 | F10 |
| 71 | Home |
| 72 | Up arrow |
| 73 | PgUp |
| 75 | Left arrow |
| 77 | Right arrow |
| 79 | End |
| 80 | Down arrow |
| 81 | PgDn |
| 82 | Ins |
| 83 | Del |

### Table 8-2. Two-Key Extended Codes

| Second Byte (Decimal) | Keys that Generate Extended Code |
|:---:|:---|
| 15 | Shift   Tab |
| 16 to 25 | Alt   Q, W, E, R, T, Y, U, I, O, P |
| 30 to 38 | Alt   A, S, D, F, G, H, J, K, L |
| 44 to 50 | Alt   Z, X, C, V, B, N, M |
| 84 to 93 | Shift   F1 to F10 |
| 94 to 103 | Ctrl   F1 to F10 |
| 104 to 113 | Alt   F1 to F10 |
| 114 | Ctrl   PrtSc (start and stop printer echo) |
| 115 | Ctrl   left arrow |
| 116 | Ctrl   right arrow |
| 117 | Ctrl   End |
| 118 | Ctrl   PgDn |
| 119 | Ctrl   Home |
| 120 to 131 | Alt   1, 2, 3, 4, 5, 6, 7, 8, 9, 0, -, = |
| 132 | Ctrl   PgUp |

ANSI stands for American National Standards Institute, and the ANSI.SYS file provides a standardized set of codes for cursor control. This file is actually an example of an *installable device driver*: a section of code written to control an I/O device, which is added to the operating system (DOS) after DOS is installed.

Once placed in DOS, ANSI.SYS intercepts all the numeric codes being sent to the screen for printing. If any of these codes contains a special *escape code* (a special sequence of characters), the ANSI.SYS file deals with the code itself, moving the cursor or performing other functions. If the code arriving is a normal character, it is simply passed to the regular video routines in ROM, which display it on the screen in the usual way.

As we'll see later, ANSI.SYS not only allows control of the cursor, it also lets us redefine keys on the keyboard; thus it also intercepts the code for any key typed and checks to see if any special action is necessary. We'll look at key redefinitions later in the chapter.

## Installing ANSI.SYS

Since ANSI.SYS is an optional part of DOS, it must be installed each time you power up your computer. Fortunately, using the CONFIG.SYS file, this job is automated, so that once you've got your system set up, you don't need to worry about it again. Here's how it's done.

> To use ANSI.SYS, the ANSI.SYS driver must be installed in the operating system.

### CONFIG.SYS File Must Be Present

You must have a CONFIG.SYS file in your main directory. The operating system examines this file when the system is first powered up and makes any changes or additions to the operating system this file requests. In fact, you should be using this file already (as we described in Chapter 1) to set the file and buffer parameters required by your C compiler.

### CONFIG.SYS File Must Refer to ANSI.SYS

To use ANSI.SYS, the CONFIG.SYS file must contain this line:

```
DEVICE=ANSI.SYS
```

This tells DOS to look for the ANSI.SYS file and incorporate it into the operating system.

The complete CONFIG.SYS file (as used in this book) looks like this:

```
C>type config.sys
files=15
buffers=10
DEVICE=ANSI.SYS
```

### ANSI.SYS File Must Be Present

ANSI.SYS is a file that comes with your operating system. It must be available somewhere in your disk system, so that the operating system can find it when it's told to do so by the CONFIG.SYS file, but it need not be in the main directory.

(Some compatible computers, such as the TI Professional, include the functions of ANSI.SYS as part of the operating system, and in these cases, the installation procedure described here is not necessary.)

Once it is installed, ANSI.SYS is actually incorporated into the operating system, so DOS will be increased by the size of ANSI.SYS: about 1,600 bytes.

# Cursor Control with ANSI.SYS

Cursor control is achieved with ANSI.SYS using escape sequences: a string of several special characters. ANSI.SYS looks for this escape sequence, which can be transmitted as part of a string in a **printf()** function, and interprets the commands that follow it. The escape sequence is always the same: the nonprinting character, '\x1B' (sometimes called the "escape character"), followed by a left bracket, '['. After the escape sequence comes either a single letter or a more complex set of characters. Using such sequences, the cursor can be moved up or down and left or right, or it can be positioned at a specific row or column.

Here's a simple program that demonstrates the use of a cursor control sequence. The sequence involved is **"\x1B[B"**. In other words, the normal escape sequence '\x1B' and '[', followed by a capital 'B', as shown in Figure 8-2.

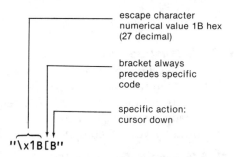

Figure 8-2. Format of ANSI.SYS Escape Sequence

The effect of this sequence is to move the cursor down one line, keeping its horizontal position unaltered. The example program will print whatever you type at the keyboard, but it will do so diagonally; that is, the letters will go down at the same time they're going across. Here's the program:

```
/* diag.c */
/* moves cursor diagonally */
main()
{
```

```
    while ( getche() != '.')        /* print character */
        printf("\x1B[B");           /* cursor down */
}
```

Since you can't move the cursor below the bottom of the screen, this program will only work if you clear the screen, using the DOS command **cls**, before you invoke the program. Then you type a short message, terminated by a period. Here's some sample output:

```
C>cls
C>diag
H
  a
    c
      k
        e
          r
            s
              .
C>
```

### Using #define with Escape Sequences

The escape sequence, "\x1B[B", is cryptic and difficult to read. As we get into more complicated programs it will be useful to use mnemonics to represent the sequences so our **printf()** statements won't look like an alchemist's equations. We can do this easily with the **#define** directive, as the following rewrite of diag.c shows:

```
/* diag2.c */
/* moves cursor diagonally */
#define C_DOWN "\x1B[B"                 /* move cursor down */
main()
{
    while ( getche() != '.')        /* print character */
        printf(C_DOWN);             /* cursor down */
}
```

Here **#define** permits us to substitute the easily understandable identifier C_DOWN for the obscure "\x1B[B". We'll make extensive use of **#define** in the rest of the programs in this chapter.

## Cursor Command Summary

Of course moving the cursor down is only one of the possible commands we can give. Table 8-3 lists the most common ones.

These commands are listed in the IBM *DOS Technical Reference* manual. We'll explore many of them in this chapter.

## Table 8-3. ANSI.SYS Cursor Control Codes

| Code | Effect |
|---|---|
| "[2J" | Erase screen and home cursor |
| "[K" | Erase to end of line |
| "[A" | Cursor up one row |
| "[B" | Cursor down one row |
| "[C" | Cursor right one column |
| "[D" | Cursor left one row |
| "[%d;%df | Cursor to row and column specified |
| "[s" | Save cursor position |
| "[u" | Restore position |
| "[%dA" | Cursor up number of rows specified |
| "[%dB" | Cursor down number of rows specified |
| "[%dC" | Cursor right number of columns specified |
| "[%dD" | Cursor left one row number of columns specified |

\* All codes must be preceded by the character '\x1B'. The symbol '%d' is a placeholder for a number, to be filled in by a **printf** argument.

## Cursor Control from the Keyboard

Now that we know about extended character codes and cursor control, we can put both ideas together to control the cursor with the arrow keys.

Here's a program that permits you to draw simple designs on the screen:

```
/* draw.c */
/* moves cursor on screen,leaves trail */
#define CLEAR  "\x1B[2J"
#define C_LEFT "\x1B[D"
#define C_RITE "\x1B[C"
#define C_UPUP "\x1B[A"
#define C_DOWN "\x1B[B"
#define L_ARRO 75
#define R_ARRO 77
#define U_ARRO 72
#define D_ARRO 80
#define ACROSS 205
#define UPDOWN 186
main()
{
int key;

printf(CLEAR);
while ( (key=getch() ) == 0 )
   {
   key=getch();
   switch (key)
      {
      case L_ARRO : printf(C_LEFT); putch(ACROSS);
```

```
            break;
        case R_ARRO : printf(C_RITE); putch(ACROSS);
            break;
        case U_ARRO : printf(C_UPUP); putch(UPDOWN);
            break;
        case D_ARRO : printf(C_DOWN); putch(UPDOWN);
            break;
        }
    printf(C_LEFT);
    }
}
```

This program waits for you to press any of the four arrow keys. (These keys share the number keys 8, 4, 6, and 2 on the numeric keypad, so the [NumLock] key must be toggled appropriately for the program to work.)

The program begins by clearing the screen, using the escape sequence "\x1B[2J". This also puts the cursor in the "home" position: the upper left corner of the screen.

All ANSI.SYS commands begin with the escape sequence, "\x1B[".

The **while** loop then waits for an extended code. If a normal key is pressed, the program exits, but pressing any of the cursor keys will cause the cursor to move in the appropriate direction (down if the down-arrow is pressed, etc.). If the direction is up or down, the vertical double-line character is printed; if left or right, the horizontal double-line character is printed. The result is a crude line-drawing capability that generates what looks like piping diagrams for nuclear reactors. Figure 8-3 shows a sample drawing session.

This program uses a **switch** statement to interpret the key being pressed. For each of the four cursor control keys, the cursor is first moved in the corresponding direction using a **printf()** statement; then the appropriate graphics character is printed using the **putch()** function. This function is analogous to the **getch()** function we've used before, except that it prints a character on the screen, rather than reading a character from the keyboard.

Notice that we've used #**define** directives not only for the cursor escape sequences, but also for the values of the cursor control keys and graphics characters. This not only clarifies the program, it provides a convenient way, using comments following the directives, to explain what the codes mean.

Printing a character causes an automatic right shift of the cursor. We must return the cursor to its position under the last character printed, so after any character is printed, we need to move the cursor back to the left.

## Moving the Cursor to an Arbitrary Position

Besides moving the cursor one row or column at a time, we can also move it directly to any location on the screen using a somewhat more complex escape

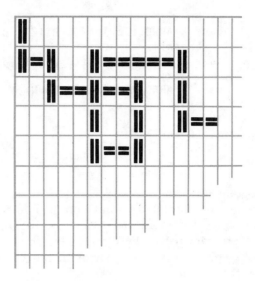

Figure 8-3. Session with draw.c

sequence. This sequence starts with the usual escape character, '\x1B', followed by the left bracket. Then there is a number representing the *row* we want the cursor to move to, then a semicolon, then another number representing the *column* we want to move to, and finally a lowercase 'f'. Figure 8-4 shows the format of this sequence.

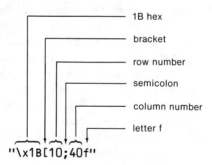

Figure 8-4. Format of Cursor-Positioning Sequence

The following program demonstrates this sequence in use:

```
/* position.c */
/* demonstrates cursor position command */
#define TRUE 1
#define CLEAR "\x1B[2J"              /* clear screen */
#define ERASE "\x1B[K"              /* erase line */
main()
{
```

```
     int row=1, col=1;
     printf(CLEAR);
     while ( TRUE )
        {
        printf("\x1B[23;1f");           /* cursor at row=23, col=1 */
        printf(ERASE);                  /* erase line */
        printf("Type row and column number (form 10,40): ");
        scanf("%d,%d", &row, &col);      /* get coordinates */
        printf("\x1B[%d;%df", row, col); /* position cursor */
        printf("*(%d,%d)", row, col);    /* print coordinates */
        }
}
```

This program clears the screen with the sequence "\x1B[2J" and cycles in the **while** loop, waiting for the user to type a pair of coordinates. The prompt to the user is always printed low on the screen, at row 23, so it won't interfere with the coordinates to be plotted; this is accomplished with the statement:

```
     printf("\x1B[23;1f");
```

Another escape sequence, "\x1B[K", then erases from the cursor position to the end of the line; finally the prompt itself is printed, inviting the user to type in the row and column numbers, separated by a comma. When the coordinates are typed in, the program moves the cursor to this location, prints an asterisk, and labels the location with the coordinates.

Here's a sample session:

```
                                      *(2,35)
                 *(3,15)
                                           *(4,40)
     *(5,5)
                              *(6,30)
                      *(7,20)
             *(9,10)
     *(10,1)
```

Lower down on the screen is the prompt:

```
     Type row and column number (form 10,40): 10,1
```

which will remain in the same place while the program is running.

## Writing Anywhere on the Screen

Here's another program that uses the cursor-positioning sequence. This one prints two menus, positioning them along the top of the screen. Menus are popular because they enable the user to make a selection from a list, rather than having to remember complex commands. Here's the listing:

```
/* putmenus.c */
/* demonstrates placing text on screen */
```

```
#define SIZE1 5                    /* # of items on menu1 */
#define SIZE2 4                    /* # of items on menu2 */
#define CLEAR "\x1B[2J"            /* clears screen */
void display(char **, int, int);   /* prototype */

main()
{
    static char *menu1[] =        /* first menu */
                { "Open",
                  "Close",
                  "Save",
                  "Print",
                  "Quit", };
    static char *menu2[] =        /* second menu */
                { "Cut",
                  "Copy",
                  "Paste",
                  "Reformat", };

    printf(CLEAR);                /* clear screen */
    display(menu1,SIZE1,20);      /* display first menu */
    display(menu2,SIZE2,40);      /* display second menu */
    getch();                      /* exit on any keystroke */
}

/* display() */
/* displays menu at given column number */
void display(char **arr, int size, int hpos)
/* arguments:      array, array size, column */
{
    int j;

    for(j=0; j<size; j++)        /* for each menu item */
        {
        printf("\x1B[%d;%df", j+1, hpos); /* position cursor */
        printf("%s\n", *(arr+j) );        /* print item */
        }
}
```

The items for each menu are stored as an array of pointers to strings. The program then uses a function to display the menus. The function positions the cursor using the ANSI.SYS cursor-positioning sequence, taking the row number from the number of the item on the menu and the column number passed from the main program. The menu item is then printed out at that location.

The output of the program looks like this:

```
            Open            Cut
            Close           Copy
            Save            Paste
            Print           Reformat
            Quit
```

In a larger program a similar function could be used to print as many menus as desired or to print text in columns.

We will soon show a more sophisticated version of this menu program, but first we need to explore another aspect of the ANSI.SYS file: the ability to change character *attributes*.

## Character Attributes

Every character displayed on the monochrome screen is stored in the computer's memory as two bytes. One byte contains the normal code for the character; while the other byte contains the character's attribute. The "attribute" of a character describes its appearance: blinking, printed in bold (intensified), underlined, or printed in reverse video—black on white instead of the normal white on black.

> Every character is stored in the monochrome display memory as two bytes: one for the ASCII code of the character and one for the attribute.

The attribute of a character or string can be set using an ANSI.SYS escape sequence. The sequence, following the usual escape character and bracket, consists of a number, followed by the letter 'm'. Here's a list of the numbers that produce effects in the monochrome display:

0   Turns off attributes: normal white on black
1   Bold (high intensity)
4   Underline
5   Blinking
7   Reverse video: black on white
8   Invisible: black on black

Figure 8-5 shows the format for the sequence to turn on blinking characters.

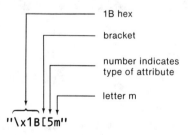

Figure 8-5. Format of Attribute Control Sequence

These sequences are sent during the printing process. Once a particular attribute has been turned on, all characters printed from then on will have this attribute. The attribute will remain in effect until turned off with another escape sequence.

Here's a program that demonstrates the character attributes:

```
/* attrib.c */
/* changes graphics attributes */
#define NORMAL  "\x1B[0m"
#define BOLD    "\x1B[1m"
#define UNDER   "\x1B[4m"
#define BLINK   "\x1B[5m"
#define REVERSE "\x1B[7m"
main()
{
    printf("Normal %s Blinking %s Normal \n\n", BLINK, NORMAL);
    printf("Normal %s Bold %s Normal\n\n", BOLD, NORMAL);
    printf("Normal %s Underlined %s Normal\n\n", UNDER, NORMAL);
    printf("Normal %s Reversed %s Normal\n\n", REVERSE, NORMAL);
    printf("%s %s Reversed and blinking %s", BLINK, REVERSE, NORMAL);
}
```

Figure 8-6 shows what the output looks like, although of course the blinking attribute cannot be effectively rendered on paper. (If you're using a color monitor, underlining may be shown by a different color.)

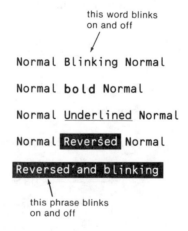

Figure 8-6. Output of the attrib.c Program

As you can see from the last line of the program, attributes can be combined: you can use any combination you like as long as it's logically consistent. You can't combine reverse video and invisible, or reverse video and underlining.

# Selectable Menu

Now that we know something about operating the ANSI.SYS file, we can put this knowledge to work in a more sophisticated program: a "selectable menu." By this we mean a menu on which different items will be "highlighted" (displayed in reverse video) as the user moves up and down the menu with the arrow keys.

When it is first started, the program displays a menu with five items: Open, Close, Save, Print, and Quit. By operating the up-arrow and down-arrow keys, the user can cause any of these items to be displayed in reverse video. If the user presses the [Enter] key while a particular item is highlighted, an action corresponding to that item will be performed. In this particular program the action on four of the items is the same: the name of the item selected is printed out. Of course in a real application program more substantive actions would follow from the menu selections. The fifth item, Quit, behaves just as it does in more serious programs; selecting it causes the program to terminate and control to return to the operating system.

For brevity, we have not made all program listings in this book completely ANSI-compatible, but this one is. It includes all appropriate header files, declares **main()**, and should compile with no warning messages, even at level 3.

Here's the listing:

```
/* menu.c */
/* demonstrates simple menu */
#include <stdio.h>               /* for printf() */
#include <conio.h>               /* for getch() */
#include <process.h>             /* for exit() */
#define TRUE 1
#define NUM 5                    /* number of menu items */
#define CLEAR "\x1B[2J"          /* clear screen */
#define ERASE "\x1B[K"           /* erase line */
#define NORMAL "\x1B[0m"         /* normal attribute */
#define REVERSE "\x1B[7m"        /* reverse video attribute */
#define HOME "\x1B[1;1f"         /* cursor to top left */
#define BOTTOM "\x1B[20;1f"      /* cursor to lower left */
#define U_ARRO 72                /* up-arrow key */
#define D_ARRO 80                /* down-arrow key */
#define ENTER 13                 /* [Enter] key */
void display(char **, int, int);  /* prototypes */
int getcode(void);
void action(int);

void main(void)                  /* real ANSI usage */
{
    static char *items[NUM] =    /* menu items */
             { "Open",
               "Close",
               "Save",
               "Print",
```

```
                     "Quit",  };
        int curpos;                  /* position of selected item */
        int code;
        printf(CLEAR);               /* clear screen */
        curpos=0;                    /* select top of menu */
        while (TRUE)
            {
            display(items,NUM,curpos); /* display menu */
            code = getcode();          /* check keyboard */
            switch (code)              /* act on key pressed */
                {
                case U_ARRO:              /* move selection up */
                    if( curpos>0 ) --curpos; break;
                case D_ARRO:              /* move selection down */
                    if( curpos<NUM-1 ) ++curpos; break;
                case ENTER:               /* take action */
                    action(curpos); break;
                default:                  /* wrong key: beep */
                    printf("\x7");
                }
            }
        }


/* display() */
/* displays menu */
void display(char **arr, int size, int pos)
/* arguments:     array, array size, column */
{
    int j;
    printf(HOME);                /* cursor to top left */
    for(j=0; j<size; j++)        /* for each menu item */
        {
        if(j==pos)               /* if selected, */
            printf(REVERSE);     /* print in reverse video */
        printf("%s\n", *(arr+j) );   /* print item */
        printf(NORMAL);          /* restore normal attribute */
        }
    printf(BOTTOM);              /* cursor to lower left */
}


/* getcode() */
/* gets keyboard code */
int getcode(void)
{
    int key;

    if( (key=getch()) != 0)    /* if not extended code, */
        return(key);           /* return key code */
    return( getch() );         /* otherwise, return next code */
}
```

```
/* action() */
/* performs action based on cursor position */
void action(int pos)                    /* pos is menu position */
{
    printf(ERASE);                      /* erase lower line */
    switch(pos)                         /* depending on position, */
        {
        case 0:
            printf("Open"); break;      /* calls to routines */
        case 1:                         /* could be inserted here */
            printf("Close"); break;
        case 2:
            printf("Save"); break;
        case 3:
            printf("Print"); break;
        case 4:
            exit(0);                    /* exit from program */
        }
}
```

This program consists of a **main()** function and three other functions: one to display the menu, one to get the extended code from the keyboard, and one to take action depending on the menu item selected.

The **main()** function consists of a simple loop. In the loop, the menu is first displayed by calling **display()**, then the keyboard is checked by using **getcode()** to see if the user has pressed an up- or down-arrow or the [Ins] key. Moving up or down the menu with the arrows causes a variable, called **curpos** (for CURsor POSition), to be incremented (cursor going down) or decremented (cursor going up). If the [Ins] key is pressed, control goes to the **action()** function, which either prints the name of the menu item or exits from the program if Quit has been selected.

### The exit() Function

Notice the use of the C library **exit()** function. This function immediately terminates the program and passes control back to the calling entity, in this case the PC-DOS or MS-DOS operating system. It doesn't matter how deeply you're nested within functions; **exit()** still terminates the entire program.

If an argument is placed in the parentheses of the **exit()** function, it is returned to the operating system, where it is available to the ERRORLEVEL subcommand in the batch file processor. That is, you can put such commands as

```
IF ERRORLEVEL 1 GOTO ERR1
```

in a batch file to sample the value placed in the **exit()** function by the program. This gives the batch file the chance to change its operation depending on the results of the program.

We won't pursue this matter further here. Ordinarily we'll leave the parentheses empty in **exit()**, but it's nice to know this facility exists if needed in more sophisticated systems.

### The display() and getcode() Functions

The **display()** function uses the identifier HOME to position the cursor at row 1, column 1. Then it displays the menu by looping through each menu item, incrementing the row number so that each item is printed directly below the last. If the number of the row is the same as **curpos**, it means the menu item is selected (**curpos** keeps track of what's selected), and that item is printed in reverse video.

The **getcode()** function is similar to the programs used before to read extended character codes, except that it waits for the first 0, ignoring ordinary one-byte codes. Once a 0 is detected it reads the second byte of the extended code and returns it to the calling program.

Figure 8-7 shows how the top part of the screen looks with the Save item selected. If an item is printed out, it is shown farther down the screen, on line 20.

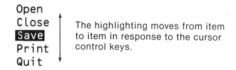

Figure 8-7. Operation of the menu.c Program

The menu.c program could be used as the basis for a more powerful menu-driven program. Menus could be added, and these could be made into "pull-down" menus; that is, their contents normally would be hidden, but a particular menu would be displayed when selected with the left or right arrow.

## Function Key Assignment Using ANSI.SYS

Let's turn our attention to another capability of the ANSI.SYS file: assigning different strings to the function keys.

Assigning strings to function keys enables you to configure your keyboard for the kind of work you usually do. For instance, if you write a lot of C programs, you might want to list the C source files in a particular directory:

```
C>dir *.c
```

If you could assign this string to a function key, you could save yourself a lot of time printing this phrase. The convenience would be even greater for longer commands:

```
type \accounts\1987\march\receive.dat
```

Here's a program that performs just this sort of function key reassignment.

```
/* assign.c */
/* assigns function key to string typed by user */
```

```
main()
{
    char string[81];
    int key;
    printf("Enter number of function key: ");
    gets(string);
    key = atoi(string);
    puts("Enter string to assign to that key:");
    gets(string);
    printf("\x1B[0;%d;\"%s\";13p", key+58, string);
}
```

Probably the most difficult part of this program to unravel is the escape sequence in the final **printf()** statement. The escape sequence for assigning a string to a function key is shown in Figure 8-8.

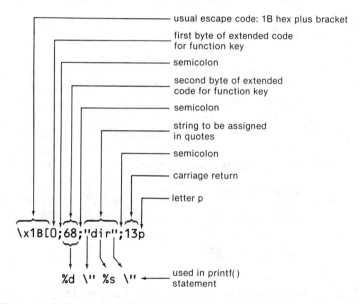

Figure 8-8. Format of Function Key Assignment Sequence

If this convoluted syntax isn't enough to make you abandon programming in favor of woodcarving, nothing will be.

Because quotes cannot be used in a string in C, they must be represented by backslash-quotes ( \" ). Since we want to use variables for the number of the function key and the string to be assigned to it, we represent these with the format specifiers %d and %s, which the function replaces with the variables **key + 58** and **string**. The function obtains these values from the user, plugs them into the string, executes the **printf()** statement, and voilà, the function key is reassigned.

### Avoiding scanf()

Perhaps you're wondering why the **gets()** and **atoi()** functions are used to read the function key number in the program, rather than a **scanf()**. The reason is that **scanf()** has a number of peculiarities, and one of them is that a newline character may be left, unread, in the keyboard buffer after **scanf()** has finished reading a number. For example, if we execute the statement

```
scanf("%d", &num);
```

the user will type a number, press [Return], and wait for **scanf()** to digest the number. The number will be read and removed from the buffer all right, but often (depending on the system) the newline character will be left in the buffer. If so, then the *next* input command (a **gets()**, for example) will read the newline. If the input command is looking for a string, it will see the newline and think the user has entered a string with no characters but the newline.

There are various ways around this problem. One that works on some systems is to include a newline in the format string of the **scanf()** function:

```
scanf("%d\n", num);
```

This should force **scanf()** to read the newline from the buffer, since any character in the format string matching one in the input string should be read and removed from the keyboard buffer. This doesn't work on all systems, however, including Microsoft C and MS-DOS. In any case, **scanf()** is a rather large function in terms of the number of bytes it adds to your compiled program, so it's nice to have an alternative approach to reading variables. The **gets()** function is preferable for strings, but what about numbers?

> The **scanf()** function is bulky and does not always behave as one would like.

In this program we use a combination of two functions to read the number representing the function key. The first function is **gets()**, which reads in the number *as a string*. The second function is **atoi()**, which stands for "ASCII to integer." This function takes a string as an argument and returns an integer with the same value. In other words, if the string was "21", the function would return the number 21. The resulting program, using **gets()** and **atoi()**, requires substantially less memory than if we had used **scanf()**.

Now, our assign.c program works just as it's supposed to, assigning any phrase we like to any function key we like. However, we'd like to improve it; we'd like to be able to assign the function keys by using this program in a *batch file*. This way, many keys could be automatically assigned when we power up our system. Unfortunately, the present version of assign.c requires that its input come from the user and not from the parameters of a batch file. What can we do? To solve this problem, we need to know about our next topic: command-line arguments.

# Command-Line Arguments

You've probably used applications programs in which, when you invoke the program from the operating system, you can type not only the name of the program, but various other items as well, such as the name of a file the application is to work on. A typical example might be

```
C>wordproc letter.txt
```

where wordproc is an application program and letter.txt is a file this application will open and process. Here the string "letter.txt" is used as a "command-line argument": an argument that appears on the command line following the C> or A> prompt.

Use of multiple arguments in the command line is clearly a useful feature. So how can we access these arguments from within the application?

Here's another question: will we ever find anything to put inside the parentheses of the **main()** function?

As you may have guessed, the answers to these seemingly unrelated questions are in fact two sides of a coin. By putting the right things inside the parentheses of **main()**, we can allow our program to read command line arguments to its heart's content. C automatically adds the capability to read these arguments to all C programs. As programmers, all we need to do is make use of it. The following program shows how:

```
/* comline.c */
/* demonstrates command line arguments */
main(argc,argv)
int argc;
char *argv[];
{
    int j;
    printf("Number of arguments is %d\n", argc);
    for(j=0; j<argc; j++)
        printf("Argument number %2d is %s\n", j, *(argv+j) );
}
```

If you're using QuickC, there are two ways to handle command-line arguments. You can select Set Runtime Options from the Run menu, and type the command-line arguments in the Command Line box that appears there. Or, you can create an .exe file, quit QuickC, and execute the .exe file from DOS, typing in the command-line arguments when you invoke it. We'll assume you're following this latter approach.

Here's a sample run with the program, in which we simply type the words "one", "two", and "three" as command-line arguments following the program name:

```
C>comline one two three
Number of arguments is 4
```

```
Argument number  0 is C:\MSOFT\PROGS\COMLINE.EXE
Argument number  1 is one
Argument number  2 is two
Argument number  3 is three
```

The two arguments used in the parentheses following **main()** are **argc** and **argv**. The variable **argc** is the total number of command-line arguments typed; in this case, 4 (the name of the program itself is counted as the first argument).

> The arguments in **main(argc,argv)** are the number of command-line arguments and an array of pointers to the individual arguments.

The variable **argv** represents an array of pointers to strings. The strings can be accessed by referring to them as **\*(argv + 1)**, **\*(argv + 2)**, and so on (or in array notation, **argv[1]**, **argv[2]**, etc.). The first string, **\*(argv + 0)**, returns the complete pathname of the program itself, as we can see in the program output.

The names **argc** (for ARGument Count) and **argv** (for ARGument Values) are traditionally used in these roles, but any other name could be used instead (although you might confuse tradition-bound C programmers).

## Assigning Function Keys with Command-Line Arguments

Now that we understand command-line arguments, we can incorporate them into the program described in the last section, which reassigns the function keys. We'll do this in two steps.

Here's the first version of the program:

```
/* funkey0.c */
/* assigns function key to string typed by user */
/* uses command-line arguments */
main(argc,argv)
int argc;
char *argv[];
{
    int key;
    if(argc != 3)
       {
       printf("example usage: C>funkey0 2 dir");
       exit();
       }
    key = atoi(argv[1]);
    printf("\x1B[0;%d;\"%s\";13p", key+58, argv[2]);
}
```

For simplicity, we've restricted this version of the program to one-word strings; in other words, you can assign the string "dir" to a function key, but you can't assign "dir *.c" because this string contains two words, and they will be treated as two separate command-line arguments. We'll first investigate this program and then expand it to handle multiword strings.

The funkey0.c program first checks to be sure the user has entered exactly three command-line arguments. The first is the program name itself, the second is the number of the function key to be assigned, and the third is the one-word string to be assigned to that key. Users who have entered the wrong number of arguments are shown an example of correct usage; then the program exits so they can try again. It is common practice in dealing with command-line arguments to perform some of this kind of checking to see if the user appears to know what to type in.

Assuming the number of arguments is correct, the program converts **argv[1]** (or **\*(argv + 1)** if you prefer) into a number, using the **atoi()** function. The **argv[2]** argument is the one-word string to be typed in. The number and the string are then incorporated into the escape sequence, which is transmitted to ANSI.SYS using the **printf()** statement.

## Assigning Function Keys with Multiple Arguments

Although what we type into the command line appears to be a string of characters, the operating system interprets it as a series of separate variables, with each space signaling the end of a variable. To make it possible for our program to assign a string with multiple words ("dir \*.c", for example) to a function key, we must combine the command-line arguments into a single string.

The following program does this, using the function **strcpy()** to place the first argument in the empty buffer **string**, and then using the function **strcat()**, which concatenates one string with another, to add a space, and then each argument in turn, to **string**. Here's the listing:

```
/* funkey.c */
/* assigns function key to string typed by user */
/* uses any number of command-line arguments */
main(argc,argv)
int argc;
char *argv[];
{
    int key, j;
    char string[80];
    if(argc < 3)                        /* if too few */
        {                               /* arguments, */
        printf("example usage: A>funkey 2 dir *.c");
        exit();                         /* then exit */
        }
    key = atoi(argv[1]);                /* funct key number */
    strcpy(string,argv[2]);             /* first word in line */
    for(j=3; j<argc; j++)               /* if more words, */
        {
        strcat(string," ");             /* add space */
        strcat(string,argv[j]);         /* add word */
        }
```

```
    if( strcmp(string, "null") == 0 )    /* if string is "null" */
        strcpy(string, "");               /* no string */
    printf("\x1B[0;%d;\"%s\";13p", key+58, string);
}
```

If we want to erase the string that has been assigned to a function key, we type "null" as our string; the null string will then be assigned to the function key.

Before we leave the subject of the ANSI.SYS file we should point out some of the pluses and minuses of using ANSI.SYS for cursor control. On the plus side, it's fairly easy to program the necessary escape sequences to move the cursor and perform the other functions of ANSI.SYS. However, it's not a particularly fast way to move the cursor, and it requires that the ANSI.SYS file be loaded into memory and that the CONFIG.SYS file be properly configured to reference it. For a commercial product this might present a problem, since some users would not want to go to the trouble of setting up these files. For less formal programs, and for exploring the capabilities of the system, ANSI.SYS provides a very convenient and powerful group of capabilties.

In later chapters we'll show how some of these capabilities can be handled in ways that are faster and more convenient for the user, although more difficult to program.

There is another programming technique that, like command-line arguments, lies in the gray area between C and MS-DOS. This is the process of *redirection*, which we'll examine now.

## Redirection

The PC-DOS (or MS-DOS) operating system incorporates (in versions 2.0 and later) a powerful feature that allows a program to read and write files, even when this capability has not been built into the program. This is done through a process called "redirection."

Redirection provides an easy way to save the results of a program; its use is similar to that of the [Ctrl] [PrtSc] key combination to save program output to the printer, except that the results can be sent to a disk file. This is often a more convenient and flexible approach than providing a separate function in the program to write to the disk. Similarly, redirection can be used to read information from a disk file directly into a program.

Ordinarily, a program derives its input from the "standard input device," which is assumed to be the keyboard, and sends its output to the "standard output device," which is assumed to be the display screen. In other words, DOS makes certain assumptions about where input should come from and output should go. Redirection permits us to change these assumptions.

Output can be redirected to go to a file instead of the screen; input can be redirected to come from a file instead of the keyboard.

If you're using QuickC, the most convenient way to use redirection is to compile an .exe file and execute it from the DOS prompt, inserting the redirection symbols as appropriate.

## Redirecting Output

Let's see how we might redirect the output of a program, from the screen to a file. We'll start by considering the simple program shown below:

```
/* mirror.c */
/* echoes typing to the screen */
main()
{
    while( getche() != 'X' )
        ;
}
```

Ordinarily, when we run this program, the **getche()** function will cause whatever we type to be printed on the screen, until the character 'X' is typed, at which point the program will terminate, as shown in this sample run:

```
C>mirror
All's well that ends well.X
C>
```

However, let's see what happens when we invoke the program from DOS in a different way, using redirection:

```
C>mirror >file.txt
C>
```

Now when we call the program and type the same phrase, "All's well that ends well," nothing appears on the screen! Where did our typing go? We've caused it to be redirected to the file called file.txt. Can we prove that this has actually happened? Yes, by using the DOS command TYPE:

```
C>type file.txt
All's well that ends well.X
```

There's the result of our typing, sitting in the file. The redirection operator, which is the "greater than" symbol ( > ), causes any output intended for the screen to be written to the file whose name follows the operator.

The data to be redirected to a file doesn't need to be typed by a user at the keyboard; the program itself can generate it. Any output normally sent to the screen can be redirected to a disk file. As an example, we could invoke the putmenus.c program, developed earlier in this chapter, and redirect its output to a file:

```
C>putmenus >file.txt
```

Then if we were to examine file.txt with TYPE, we'd see that the output of putmenus.c had been written to the file. Even the cursor control commands are saved, so that using TYPE clears the screen before the menus are displayed.

This can be a useful capability any time you want to capture the output of a program on a file, rather than displaying it on the screen.

DOS predefines a number of filenames for its own use. One of these names is PRN, which stands for the printer. Output can be redirected to the printer by using this filename. For example, if you invoke the mirror.c program this way:

```
C>mirror >PRN
```

anything you type will be printed on the printer.

## Indicating End of File

You may have noticed the unpleasant-looking 'X' used as the terminating character for the mirror program. When we use the TYPE command, this character is read back from the file and displayed on the screen.

It would be nice if there was a character which indicated to TYPE and other commands that the end of the file had been reached. Stored in a file, this command would then cause the command to stop reading the file, without itself being displayed. There is such a character: '\x1A', which can be obtained by typing the [Ctrl] [z] key combination, and that prints out as a small right-facing arrow.

Let's rewrite our program to terminate on this character:

```
/* transfer.c */
/* echoes typing */
/* to be used with redirection */
main()
{
    while( getche() != '\x1A' )
        ;
}
```

To use this program, we type in a message as before, but this time we terminate it with [Ctrl] [z]. This both terminates the program and places the '\x1A' character in the file. Now when we examine the file with TYPE there will be no visible terminating character, since the '\x1A' causes the reading of the file to be terminated.

The '\x1A' character represents an end-of-file.

## Redirecting Input

We can also redirect *input* to a program so that, instead of reading characters from the keyboard, the program reads them from a file. Happily, we can demonstrate this with the same program, transfer.c, we used to demonstrate redirection of output. This is because the program both accepts input from the keyboard and outputs it to the screen.

To redirect the input, we need to have a file containing something to be printed. We'll assume we've placed the message "The greatest of these is charity" in the file called file.txt using a word processor (or redirecting the output of transfer.c). Then we use the "less than" sign ( < ) before the file name:

```
C>transfer <file.txt
The greatest of these is charity.>
C>
```

The phrase is printed on the screen with no further effort on our part. Using redirection we've made our transfer.c program perform the work of the DOS TYPE command.

Figure 8-9 shows how redirected input and output look compared with normal input and output.

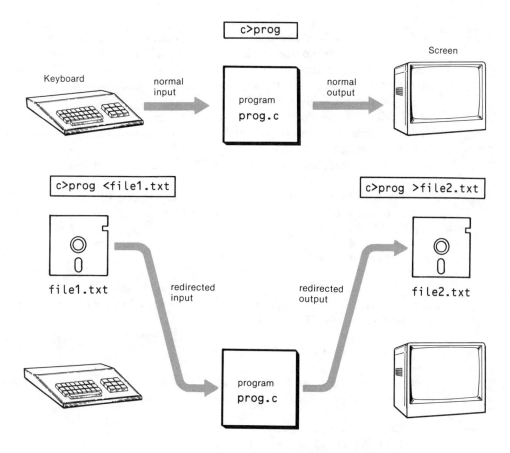

Figure 8-9. Normal and Redirected Input/Output

## Both Ways at Once

Redirection of input and output can be used together; a program's input can come *from* a file via redirection, while at the same time its output is being redirected *to* a file. In DOS nomenclature, we can say the program acts as a *filter*.

To demonstrate this process, we'll use a slightly fancier program than before. Instead of simply storing and retrieving files in their original form, we'll develop a pair of programs, one to code a message and another to decode it.

Here's the program that does the coding:

```
/* code.c */
/* encodes file */
/* to be used with redirection */
#define CTRL_Z '\x1A'
main()
{
    char ch;
    while( (ch=getch()) != CTRL_Z )
        putch(ch+1);
    putch(CTRL_Z);
}
```

This program reads a character, either from the keyboard or—using redirection—from a file, and outputs it in coded form, either to the screen or to another file. The code is rudimentary; it consists of adding 1 to the ASCII code for the character. Of course any 10-year-old could break this code, but if you're interested you can probably think of ways to make it tougher.

Notice that we don't encode the '\x1A' character: that's why we leave the writing of this character outside the loop. As you can see, we've also **#define**d this character as CTRL_Z.

Let's assume you've generated a file, called file1.txt, which contains the message you wish to code. You can create this file using either the transfer.c program with redirection (although it's hard to use because the characters aren't echoed to the screen) or by using your word processor. We can verify what's in the file this way:

```
C>type file1.txt
Meet me at the hollow tree.
```

To code this file, we redirect our input *from* file1.txt, to code.c, and also redirect it *to* a different file, file2.txt, like this:

```
C>code <file1.txt >file2.txt
```

Data will be read from file1.txt, coded, and written to file2.txt. Having done this, we can use TYPE to see what the coded file looks like.

```
C>type file2.txt
Nffu!nf!bu!uif!ipmmpx!usff/
```

To *decode* the file, we use a program that looks very much like code.c:

```
/* decode.c */
/* decodes file coded with code.c */
/* to be used with redirection */
#define CTRL_Z '\x1A'
main()
{
    char ch;
    while( (ch=getch()) != CTRL_Z )
        putch(ch-1);
    putch(CTRL_Z);
}
```

This program subtracts 1 from the value of each character, thus reversing the coding process. We'll write the decoded results to file3.txt. Here's how we apply the program, again using double redirection, to our coded file:

```
C>decode <file2.txt >file3.txt
```

Finally, to prove that both the coding and decoding have worked correctly, we print out the file containing the decoded message:

```
C>type file3.txt
Meet me at the hollow tree.
```

A point to note about redirection: the output file is erased before it's written to, so don't try to send output to the same file from which you're receiving input.

Redirection can be a powerful tool for developing utility programs to examine or alter data in files. As an example, see Exercise 3 at the end of this chapter.

Redirection is used to establish a relationship between a program and a file. Another DOS operator can be used to relate two programs directly, so that the output of one is fed directly into another, with no files involved. This is called "piping," and uses the bar character ( ¦ ). We won't pursue this topic, but you can read about it in the *Disk Operating System* manual.

## Summary

You now can read the codes of the extended character set, so that your program can tell when such keys as the function and cursor-control keys are pressed. You've also learned how to use the ANSI.SYS file for clearing the screen, controlling the cursor, and assigning strings to the function keys.

You know how your program can interpret command-line arguments (words typed following a program name at the C> prompt), and you've seen how the input and output of a program can be redirected to come from and be sent to disk files, using the DOS redirection operators ( < ) and ( > ).

Finally, you've learned a handful of new functions: **exit()**, which permits a quick return from your program to DOS, **putch()**, which writes a single character to the screen, **atoi()**, which converts from a string to a number, and **strcat()**, which attaches or concatenates two strings together.

In the next chapter we'll look into structures, an important topic in the C language, and we'll see how they and their cousin the union can help access other important features of the IBM.

## Questions

1. The purpose of the extended keyboard codes is to:

    a. read foreign language characters

    b. read letter keys typed with [Alt] and [Ctrl]

    c. read the function and cursor control keys

    d. read graphics characters

2. How many extended codes are there (including codes that are not used)?

3. How many bytes are used to represent an extended keyboard code?

4. True or false: extended keyboard codes represent only single keys such as F1.

5. Which of the following is the extended code for the F1 key?

    a. 97

    b. 1 78

    c. '\xDB'

    d. 0 59

6. ANSI.SYS is

    a. a rare nerve disease

    b. an installable device driver

    c. a file enabling expanded keyboard and cursor capability

    d. a file always searched for by DOS on startup

7. CONFIG.SYS is

    a. a file always searched for by DOS on startup

    b. a file containing instructions for modifying DOS

    c. a file that can tell DOS to install ANSI.SYS

    d. none of the above

8. Describe what needs to be in the system before ANSI.SYS can be used.

9. All ANSI.SYS "escape sequences" start with
    a. '\x['
    b. '['
    c. '\x1B'
    d. '\x1B['

10. Write the escape sequence to clear the screen: _____.

11. True or false: the cursor can be moved to any screen location, but only in increments of one row or column.

12. Write four character attributes:
    a. Bo _____
    b. Bl _____
    c. Un _____
    d. Re _____

13. Write the escape sequence to move the cursor right one column: _____.

14. True or false: the **exit()** function causes an exit from a function.

15. Write a statement that will transform the string **str** into a number **num**, assuming that **str** equals "122".

16. True or false: using ANSI.SYS escape sequences, an arbitrary string can be assigned to any function key.

17. Command-line arguments are:
    a. something that happens in the military
    b. additional items following the C> prompt and a program name
    c. the arguments **argc** and **argv**
    d. the arguments **argv[0]**, **argv[1]**, and so forth

18. Write two program statements which combine the word "steeple" with the word "chase" and leave the result in an array called **str[ ]**.

19. Redirection is
    a. sending the output of a program somewhere besides the screen
    b. getting a program from somewhere besides a .exe file

c. getting input to a program from somewhere besides the keyboard

d. changing the standard input and output devices

20. Write a DOS command that will cause a program called **prog1** to take its input from a file called **f1.c** and send its output to a file called **f2.c**.

## Exercises

1. Write a program that will enable the user to type in a phrase, echoing characters to the screen. If the user presses the left-arrow key (not the backspace), the program should erase the character to the left of the cursor, so that the whole phrase can be erased one character at a time. Use extended keyboard codes and ANSI.SYS cursor control.

2. Write a program that uses a command-line argument to perform decimal to hexadecimal conversion; that is, the decimal number will be typed on the command line, following the program name:

```
C>decihex 128
Hex=80
C>
```

Use long integers so the program can convert values between 0 and 65535.

3. Write a program that will read a C source code file using redirection, and determine if the file contains the same number of left and right braces. This program can then be used to check for mismatched braces before compiling. Its operation should look like this in the cases where there are unequal numbers of braces:

```
C>braces <prog.c
Mismatched braces
C>
```

4. Write a program that will enable a user to type in a phrase and then highlight individual letters in the phase in reverse video, as the user moves the cursor with the left- and right-arrow keys.

# 9

# Structures, Unions, and ROM BIOS

- Structures
- Nested structures
- Arrays of structures
- Linked lists
- Unions
- ROM BIOS routines

# 9

In this chapter we explore C's most versatile device for representing data: the structure. We'll also describe another data storage mechanism that is in some ways similar to a structure, but in other ways is completely different: the union. Finally we'll put our knowledge of structures and unions together to find out how to access the family of powerful routines built into the IBM's hardware: the Read-Only Memory Basic Input/Output System (ROM BIOS). Knowing how to use the ROM BIOS routines will be important when we investigate character and color graphics in following chapters.

## Structures

We have seen how simple variables can hold one piece of information at a time and how arrays can hold a number of pieces of information of the same data type. These two data storage mechanisms can handle a great variety of situations. But we often want to operate on data items of different types together as a unit. In this case, neither the variable nor the array is adequate.

For example, suppose you want a program to store data concerning an employee in an organization. You might want to store the employee's name (a character array), department number (an integer), salary (a floating point number), and so forth. Perhaps you also have other employees, and you want your program to deal with them as elements of an array.

Even a multidimensional array will not solve this problem, since all the elements of an array must be of the same data type. You could use several different arrays—a character array for names, a floating point array for salaries, and so on—but this is an unwieldy approach that obscures the fact that you're dealing with a group of characteristics relating to a single entity: the employee.

To solve this sort of problem, C provides a special data type: the *structure*. A structure consists of a number of data items—which need not be of the same type—grouped together. In our example, a structure would consist of the employee's name, department number, salary, and any other pertinent information. The structure could hold as many of these items as we wanted. Figure 9-1 shows the differences among simple variables, arrays, and structures.

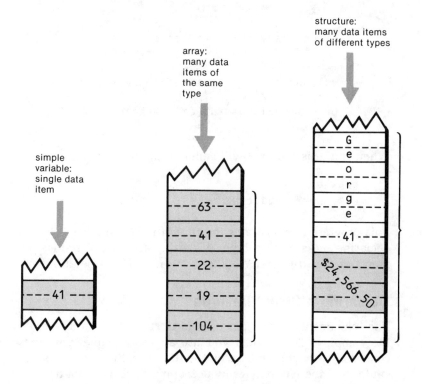

Figure 9-1. Simple Variables, Arrays, and Structures

Pascal programmers will recognize a C structure as similar to a *record*; there is no equivalent in BASIC.

Structures are useful, not only because they can hold different types of variables, but also because they can form the basis for more complex data constructions, such as linked lists. We'll provide an example of this later on.

## A Simple Structure

Here's a program that uses a simple structure containing two data items: an integer variable **num** and a character variable **ch**.

```
/* struct.c */
/* demonstrates structures */
main()
{
```

```
struct easy          /* defines data type 'struct easy' */
   {
   int num;          /* integer variable in structure */
   char ch;          /* character variable in structure */
   };

struct easy ez1;     /* declares 'ez1' to be */
                     /*   of type 'struct easy' */

ez1.num = 2;         /* reference elements of 'ez1' */
ez1.ch = 'Z';
printf("ez1.num=%d, ez1.ch=%c\n", ez1.num, ez1.ch );
}
```

When run, this program will generate the following output:

```
C>easy
ez1.num=2, ez1.ch=Z
```

This program demonstrates the three fundamental aspects of using structures: declaring the structure type, declaring structure variables, and accessing elements of the structure. We'll look at these three operations in turn.

## Declaring a Structure Type

The fundamental data types used in C, such as **int** and **float**, are predefined by the compiler. Thus, when you use an **int** variable, you know it will always consist of two bytes (at least on the IBM) and that the compiler will interpret the contents of these two bytes in a certain way. This is not true of structures. Since a structure may contain any number of elements of different types, the programmer must tell the compiler what a particular structure is going to look like before using variables of that type.

In the example program, the following statement declares the structure type:

```
struct easy
   {
   int num;
   char ch;
   };
```

This statement defines a new data type called **struct easy**. Each variable of this type will consist of two elements: an integer variable called **num**, and a character variable called **ch**. Note that this statement doesn't declare any variables, and so it isn't setting aside any storage in memory. It just tells the compiler what the data type **struct easy** looks like, conveying the *plan* for the structure. Figure 9-2 shows the format of a structure type declaration.

The keyword **struct** introduces the statement. The name **easy** is called the "tag." It names the kind of structure being defined. Note that the tag is not a

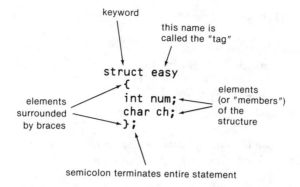

Figure 9-2. Format of a Structure Type Declaration

variable name, since we are not declaring a variable; it is a *type* name. The elements of the structure are surrounded by braces, and the entire statement is terminated by a semicolon.

A structure is a data type whose format is defined by the programmer.

## Declaring Structure Variables

Once we've defined our new data type, we can declare one or more variables to be of that type. In our program, we declare a variable **ez1** to be of type **struct easy**:

```
struct easy ez1;
```

This statement *does* set aside space in memory. It establishes enough space to hold all the items in the structure: in this case, three bytes: two for the integer, and one for the character. (In some situations the compiler may allocate more bytes, so that the next variable in memory will come out on an even address.) The variable declaration **struct easy ez1;** performs a function similar to such variable declarations as **float salary** and **int count**; it tells the compiler to set aside storage for a variable of a specfic type and gives a name to the variable. Figure 9-3 shows what the structure variable **ez1** looks like, first grouped together conceptually and then as the elements of the structure would look in memory.

## Accessing Structure Elements

Now how do we refer to individual elements of the structure? In arrays, we can access individual elements with a subscript: **array[7]**. Structures use a different approach: the "dot operator" ( . ), which is also called the "membership operator." Here's how we would refer to the **num** part of the **ez1** structure:

```
ez1.num
```

The variable name preceding the dot is the structure name; the name following it is the specific element in the structure. Thus the statements

```
ez1.num = 2;
ez1.ch = 'Z';
```

give a value of 2 to the **num** element of the structure **ez1** and a value of 'Z' to the **ch** element. Similarly, the statement

```
printf("ez1.num=%d, ez1.ch=%c\n", ez1.num, ez1.ch );
```

causes the values of these two variables to be printed out.

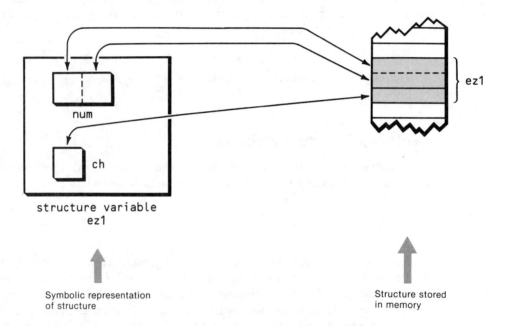

Figure 9-3. Structure **ez1** Stored in Memory

The dot operator ( . ) connects a structure variable name with a member of the structure.

The dot operator provides a powerful and clear way to specify members of a structure. An expression like **employee.salary** is more comprehensible than **employee[27]**.

## Multiple Structure Variables of the Same Type

Just as there can be more than one **int** or **float** variable in a program, there also can be any number of variables of a given structure type. In the following program, for example, there are two variables, **ez1** and **ez2**, both of type **struct easy**:

```
/* struct2.c */
/* uses two structure variables */
main()
{
    struct easy          /* defines data type 'struct easy' */
        {
        int num;
        char ch;
        };

    struct easy ez1;  /* declares 'ez1' and 'ez2' to be */
    struct easy ez2;  /*    of type 'struct easy' */

    ez1.num = 2;         /* reference elements of 'ez1' */
    ez1.ch = 'Z';
    ez2.num = 3;         /* reference elements of 'ez2' */
    ez2.ch = 'Y';
    printf("ez1.num=%d, ez1.ch=%c\n", ez1.num, ez1.ch );
    printf("ez2.num=%d, ez2.ch=%c\n", ez2.num, ez2.ch );
}
```

Notice how the elements of the two different structures are accessed: **ez1.num** gets **num** from the structure **ez1**, while **ez2.num** gets it from **ez2**.

## Combining Declarations

You can combine in one statement the declaration of the structure type and the structure variables. As an example, the struct2.c program can be rewritten like this:

```
/* struct2a.c */
/* combines declarations for structure type and variables */
main()
{
    struct easy          /* declares data type 'struct easy' */
        {
        int num;
        char ch;
        } ez1, ez2;   /* declares 'ez1' and 'ez2' to be */
                      /*    of type 'struct easy' */

    ez1.num = 2;         /* reference elements of 'ez1' */
    ez1.ch = 'Z';
```

```
      ez2.num = 3;          /* reference elements of 'ez2' */
      ez2.ch = 'Y';
      printf("ez1.num=%d, ez1.ch=%c\n", ez1.num, ez1.ch );
      printf("ez2.num=%d, ez2.ch=%c\n", ez2.num, ez2.ch );
   }
```

The effect is the same as that provided by the separate statements, but the format is more compact (though perhaps less clear).

## Entering Data into Structures

Let's examine a slightly more realistic programming example. This involves placing data into structures and reading it out again. This will be the first version of a program that will evolve throughout the chapter. Our goal, which will require several intermediate steps, is to develop a simple database program that will demonstrate one of the most useful ways data can be organized in C: as an array of structures.

In the following program we construct a database for a typical employee category: the secret agent. If you're setting up a clandestine operation in a foreign country, the program will be right up your dark alley. If your needs are more pedestrian, you'll find the program is easily adaptable to other sorts of personnel.

In this program the database stores two items of information about each secret agent: a name, represented by a character array, and a code number, represented by an integer. This information is entered into the program by the user and is then printed out again by the program. In this version of the program there is space to store the data for only two agents; in later versions we'll show how to store the data for more agents.

Here's the program:

```
/* twoagent.c */
/* stores and retrieves data for two secret agents */
#include "stdio.h"
main()
{
   struct personnel                  /* define data structure */
      {
      char name [30];                /* name */
      int agnumb;                    /* code number */
      };

   struct personnel agent1;          /* declares a struct variable */
   struct personnel agent2;          /* declares another one */

   printf("\nAgent 1.\nEnter name: ");    /* get first name */
   gets(agent1.name);
   printf("Enter agent number (3 digits): "); /* get number */
   scanf("%d", &agent1.agnumb);
   fflush(stdin);                         /* clear buffer */
```

```
      printf("\nAgent 2.\nEnter name: ");    /* get 2nd name */
      gets(agent2.name);
      printf("Enter agent number (3 digits): "); /* get number */
      scanf("%d", &agent2.agnumb);

      printf("\nList of agents:\n" );
      printf("   Name: %s\n", agent1.name);     /* first agent */
      printf("   Agent number: %03d\n", agent1.agnumb);
      printf("   Name: %s\n", agent2.name);     /* second agent */
      printf("   Agent number: %03d\n", agent2.agnumb);
}
```

We declared a structure type called **personnel**, which will be used as the model for the structure variables that hold the data for the two agents. The structure variables **agent1** and **agent2** are then declared to be of type **struct personnel**.

Data is then placed into the appropriate structure elements using the statements

```
      gets(agent1.name);
```

and

```
      scanf("%d", &agent1.agnumb);
```

These statements are similar to those that we would use for simple variables, but the dot operator indicates that we're dealing with structure elements.

Similarly, the four **printf()** statements print out the contents of our small database.

### The scanf() Problem: Round Two

Perhaps you noticed a new function in the program above: **fflush()**. What is its role in the program? In the last chapter we mentioned that **scanf()** left a newline character in the keyboard buffer, where it lay in wait to trick the next input statement into thinking that it had read nothing but the newline. Our earlier solution to this problem involved using a combination of the **gets()** and **atoi()** (or **atof()**) functions to eliminate **scanf()** altogether.

The twoagent.c program uses another approach: the **fflush()** function, which is designed to remove or "flush out" any data remaining in a buffer. The function, though, must be told which input/output device to act on. C recognizes several standard names for I/O devices; here we use "stdin", which means the "standard input" device: the keyboard. (We'll learn more about these standard names in the chapter on files.)

We need to define "stdin" so that the C compiler will understand it. This definition goes in the file STDIO.H, so we must compile that file along with our source code; hence the statement **#include "stdio.h"** at the beginning of the program.

Here's a sample run:

```
Agent 1.
Enter name: Harrison Tweedbury
Enter agent number (3 digits): 102

Agent 2.
Enter name: James Bond
Enter agent number (3 digits): 007

List of agents:
   Name: Harrison Tweedbury
   Agent number: 102
   Name: James Bond
   Agent number: 007
```

Notice that we can print out leading zeros: this is accomplished by preceding the field width in the **printf()** statement with a zero: **%03d**.

Figure 9-4 shows how the structure variable **agent1** looks symbolically and how it looks stored in memory.

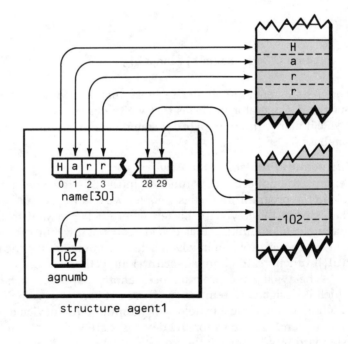

Symbolic representation
of structure

Structure
stored in
memory

Figure 9-4. Structure *agent1* Stored in Memory

Let's look at some other structure operations that will be useful later on: initializing structures, passing their values in assignment statements, and using them as arguments to functions.

## Initializing Structures

Like simple variables and arrays, structure variables can be initialized—given specific values—at the beginning of a program. The format used is quite similar to that used to initialize arrays.

Here's an example, using a modified version of our twoagent.c program. In this case the data on the two agents is contained in initialization statements within the program, rather than being input by the user:

```
/* initage.c */
/* demonstrates initialization of structures */

struct personnel                    /* defines data structure */
    {
    char name[30];                  /* name */
    int agnumb;                     /* code number */
    };

struct personnel agent1 =        /* initializes struct variable */
    { "Harrison Tweedbury", 012 };

struct personnel agent2 =        /* initializes another one */
    { "James Bond", 007 };

main()
{
    printf("\nList of agents:\n" );
    printf("   Name: %s\n", agent1.name);       /* first agent */
    printf("   Agent number: %03d\n", agent1.agnumb);
    printf("   Name: %s\n", agent2.name);       /* second agent */
    printf("   Agent number: %03d\n", agent2.agnumb);
}
```

Here, after the usual declaration of the structure type, the two structure variables are declared and initialized at the same time. As with array initialization, the equal sign is used, followed by braces enclosing a list of values, with the values separated by commas.

When this program is executed it will generate output similar to that of our previous version.

## Assignment Statements Used with Structures

In the original version of C defined by Kernighan and Ritchie, it was impossible to assign the values of one structure variable to another variable of the same type using a simple assignment statement. In modern versions of C, including the Microsoft C compiler, this is possible. That is, if **agent1** and **agent2** are structure variables, the following statement can be used: **agent2 = agent1;**.

> The value of one structure variable can be assigned to another structure variable of the same type.

This is an important capability, so let's look at an example of its use. In this modification of our secret agent program, information is obtained from the user about one agent and is then assigned to a second structure variable, using an assignment statement:

```
/* twins.c */
/* demonstrates assignment of structures */
main()
{
    struct personnel                /* define data structure */
        {
        char name [30];             /* name */
        int agnumb;                 /* code number */
        };

    struct personnel agent1;        /* declares a struct variable */
    struct personnel agent2;        /* declares another one */

    printf("\nAgent 1.\nEnter name: ");    /* get first name */
    gets(agent1.name);
    printf("Enter agent number (3 digits): "); /* get number */
    scanf("%d", &agent1.agnumb);

    agent2 = agent1;                /* assigns one structure */
                                    /* to another */
    printf("\nList of agents:\n" );
    printf("   Name: %s\n", agent1.name);     /* first agent */
    printf("   Agent number: %03d\n", agent1.agnumb);
    printf("   Name: %s\n", agent2.name);     /* second agent */
    printf("   Agent number: %03d\n", agent2.agnumb);
}
```

When we run this program, data on two agents will be printed out as before, but it will be exactly the same data for both agents.

This is a rather amazing capability when you think about it: when you assign one structure to another, all the values in the structure are actually being assigned, all at once, to the corresponding structure elements. Only two values are assigned in this example, but there could be far more. Simple assignment statements cannot be used this way for arrays, which must be moved element by element.

## Nested Structures

Just as there can be arrays of arrays, there can also be structures that contain other structures. This can be a powerful way to create complex data types.

As a simple example, imagine that our secret agents are sent out as a team, consisting of one "chief" and one "indian." The following program creates a structure with the tag **team**. This structure consists of two other structures of type **personnel**.

```c
/* team.c */
/* demonstrates nested structures */

struct personnel              /* defines structure type */
   {
   char name [30];            /* name */
   int agnumb;                /* code number */
   };

struct team                   /* defines structure type */
   {
   struct personnel chief;    /* structure within structure */
   struct personnel indian;   /* structure within structure */
   };

struct team team1 =                      /* declares and */
   { { "Harrison Tweedbury", 102 },      /* initializes struct */
     { "James Bond", 007         } };   /* variable 'team1' */

main()
{
   printf("\nChief:\n" );
   printf("   Name: %s\n", team1.chief.name);
   printf("   Agent number: %03d\n", team1.chief.agnumb);
   printf("Indian:\n" );
   printf("   Name: %s\n", team1.indian.name);
   printf("   Agent number: %03d\n", team1.indian.agnumb);
}
```

Figure 9-5 shows the arrangement of nested structures.

Let's look at some details in this program.

First, we've declared a structure variable **team1**, which is of type **team**, and initialized it to the values shown. As when multidimensional arrays are initialized, nested braces are used to initialize structures within structures.

Second, notice the method we used to access the elements of a structure that is part of another structure. Here the dot operator is used *twice*, as in the expression

```
team1.chief.name
```

This refers to element **name** in the structure **chief** in the structure **team1**.

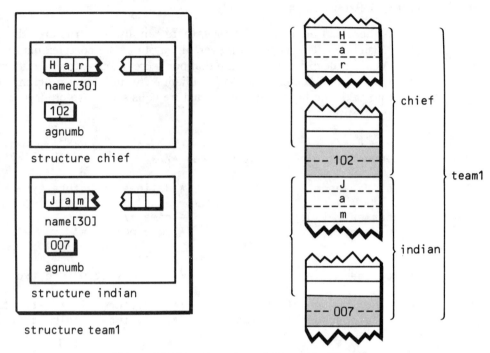

Figure 9-5. Structure **team1** Stored in Memory

Of course, the nesting process need not stop at this level; we can nest a structure within a structure within a structure. Such constructions give rise to variable names that can be surprisingly self-descriptive, for instance:

```
triumph.1962.engine.carb.bolt.large
```

## Passing Structures to Functions

In the same way that it can be passed in an assignment statement, the value of a structure variable can also be passed as a parameter to a function. This is a powerful feature that greatly simplifies the use of functions and thus the writing of well-constructed modular programs that use structures.

As an example, we'll rewrite our twoagent.c program to use functions to obtain the data about the agents from the user and to print it out. This is another step along the road to being able to access an array of structures, which is one of the most natural ways to model a database. Here's the program:

```
/* passtwo.c */
/* stores two agents */
/* demonstrates passing structures to functions */
#include <stdio.h>                /* for printf(), etc. */
struct personel newname(void); /* prototypes */
void list(struct personel);
```

```c
struct personel                      /* define data structure */
   {
   char name [30];                   /* agent name */
   int agnumb;                       /* agent number */
   };

void main(void)
{
   struct personel agent1;           /* declare structure variable */
   struct personel agent2;           /* declare another one */

   agent1 = newname();               /* get data for first agent */
   agent2 = newname();               /* get data for 2nd agent */
   list(agent1);                     /* print data for first agent */
   list(agent2);                     /* print data for 2nd agent */
}

/* newname() */
/* puts a new agent in the database */
struct personel newname(void)
{
   struct personel agent;                       /* new structure */

   printf("\nNew agent\nEnter name: ");       /* get name */
   gets(agent.name);
   printf("Enter agent number (3 digits): ");  /* get number */
   scanf("%d", &agent.agnumb);
   fflush(stdin);                               /* clear buffer */
   return(agent);                               /* return struct */
}

/* list() */
/* prints data on one agent */
void list(struct personel age)
{                                               /* from main */
   printf("\nAgent: \n");
   printf("   Name: %s\n", age.name);
   printf("   Agent number: %03d\n", age.agnumb);
}
```

Since both functions, as well as the main program, need to know how the structure type **personnel** is declared, this declaration is made global by placing it outside of all functions, before **main()**. The functions **main()**, **newname()**, and **list()** declare their own internal structure variables, called **agent1** and **agent2**, **agent**, and **age**; to be of this type.

The function **newname** is called from the main program to obtain information from the user about the two agents. This function places the information in the internally declared structure variable, **agent**, and returns the value of this variable to the main program using a **return** statement, just as if it were returning a simple variable. The function **newname()** must be declared to be of type **struct personnel** in **main()**, since it returns a value of this type.

The main program assigns the values returned from **newname()** to the structure variables **agent1** and **agent2**. Finally **main()** calls the function **list()** to print out the values in **agent1** and **agent2**, passing the values of these two structures to the function as variables. The **list()** function assigns these values to an internal structure variable **age** and accesses the individual elements of this structure to print out the values.

## Arrays of Structures

We now know enough to realize our goal of creating an array of structures, where each structure represents the data for one secret agent. This is a more ambitious program. We've provided a simple user interface, consisting of a choice of two single-letter selections. If the user types an 'e', the program will allow information on one agent to be entered. If the user types an 'l', the program will list all the agents in the database.

We've also added an additional item of information: the agent's height (a floating point variable), just to prove that structures can have more than two elements. Here's the listing:

```c
/* agent1.c */
/* maintains list of agents in memory */
#include <stdio.h>                /* for printf() */
#include <conio.h>               /* for getche() */
#define TRUE 1
void newname(void);              /* prototypes */
void listall(void);

struct personel                  /* define data structure */
   {
   char name [30];               /* name */
   int agnumb;                   /* code number */
   float height;                 /* height in inches */
   };
struct personel agent[50];       /* array of 50 structures */
int n = 0;                       /* number of agents listed */

void main(void)
{
   int ch;
   while (TRUE)
      {
      printf("\nType 'e' to enter new agent");    /* print */
      printf("\n   'l' to list all agents: ");     /* selections */
      ch = getche();                               /* get choice */
      switch (ch)
         {
         case 'e':                            /* enter new name */
            newname(); break;
         case 'l':                            /* list entire file */
            listall(); break;
         default:                             /* user mistake */
```

```
                puts("\nEnter only selections listed");
          } /* end switch */
      } /* end while */
} /* end main */


/* newname() */
/* puts a new agent in the database */
void newname(void)
{
   printf("\nRecord %d.\nEnter name: ", n+1); /* get name */
   gets(agentlb][n].name);
   printf("Enter agent number (3 digits): "); /* get number */
   scanf("%d", &agent[n].agnumb);
   printf("Enter height in inches: ");          /* get height */
   scanf("%f", &agent[n++].height);
   fflush(stdin);                               /* clear buffer */
}


/* listall() */
/* lists all agents and data */
void listall(void)
{
   int j;
   if (n < 1)                              /* check for empty list */
      printf("\nEmpty list.\n");
   for (j=0; j < n; j++)                    /* print list */
      {
      printf("\nRecord number %d\n", j+1);
      printf("   Name: %s\n", agent[j].name);
      printf("   Agent number: %03d\n", agent[j].agnumb);
      printf("   Height: %4.2f\n", agent[j].height);
      }
}
```

And here's a sample run:

```
   Type 'e' to enter new agent
     'l' to list all agents: e
   Record 1.
   Enter name: Harrison Tweedbury
   Enter agent number (3 digits): 102
   Enter height in inches: 70.5

   Type 'e' to enter new agent
     'l' to list all agents: e
   Record 2.
   Enter name: Ursula Zimbowski
   Enter agent number (3 digits): 303
   Enter height in inches: 63.25

   Type 'e' to enter new agent
     'l' to list all agents: e
```

```
Record 3.
Enter name: James Bond
Enter agent number (3 digits): 007
Enter height in inches: 74.3

Type 'e' to enter new agent
   'l' to list all agents: l

Record number 1
   Name: Harrison Tweedbury
   Agent number: 102
   Height: 70.50

Record number 2
   Name: Ursula Zimbowski
   Agent number: 303
   Height: 63.25

Record number 3
   Name: James Bond
   Agent number: 007
   Height: 74.30
```

Following this interaction we could then have continued by adding more agents, or listing the agents again, as the spirit moved us.

### Declaring an Array of Structures

Notice how the array of structures is declared:

```
struct personnel agent[50];
```

This statement provides space in memory for 50 structures of type **personnel**. This structure type is defined by the statement

```
struct personnel              /* define data structure */
   {
   char name [30];            /* name */
   int agnumb;                /* code number */
   float height;              /* height in inches */
   };
```

Figure 9-6 shows conceptually what this array of structures looks like.

For simplicity, we've declared the array of structures as a global variable, so that all the functions in the program can access it.

### Accessing Members of Array of Structures

Individual elements of a structure in our array of structures are accessed by referring to the structure variable name **agent**, followed by a subscript, followed by the dot operator, and ending with the structure element desired, as in this example:

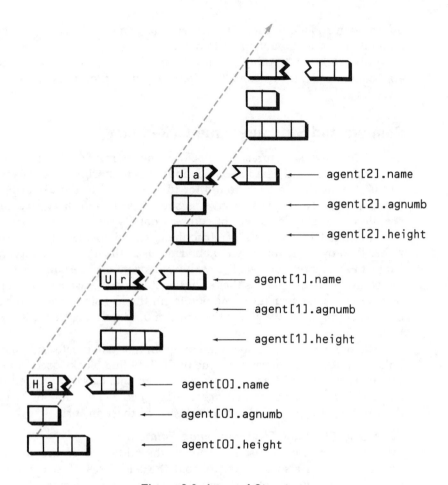

Figure 9-6. Array of Structures

```
agent[n].name
```

The balance of the program uses constructions we've discussed before.

The expression **agent[n].name** refers to element **name** of the **nth** structure in an array of structures of type **agent**.

The overall scheme of this program can be applied to a wide variety of situations for storing data about particular entities. It could, for example, be used for inventory control, where each structure variable contained data about a particular item, such as the stock number, price, and number of items available. Or it could be used for a budgeting program, where each structure contained information about a budget category, such as name of the category, the budgeted amount, and the amount spent to date.

About the only thing lacking to make this program a useful database application is a way to store the data as a disk file, a topic we'll explore in Chapter 12.

## Pointers and Structures: the Linked List

Before we leave structures, let's look at one more way that structures can be used: the linked list. The linked-list approach to storing data is useful in itself, and it also provides a background for further study of the use of pointers with functions. This example will give us some insight into how structures can be used to create a wide variety of complex data types.

A linked list consists of structures related to one another by pointers, rather than by being members of an array, as in the agent.c example. To demonstrate this construction, we'll rewrite our agent.c program to store data as a linked list. The basic idea is that each structure on the list contains a pointer that points to the next structure. The pointer in the last structure on the list doesn't point to anything, so we give it the value of 0, or null. Figure 9-7 shows how this looks.

Before we can understand the program that will create and manipulate our linked list, we need to explore some of the building blocks used in its operation. There are two new ideas: how structure elements can be accessed using pointers, and how an area of memory can be assigned to a variable using pointers and the **malloc()** function. Let's examine each of these in turn.

### Accessing Structure Elements Using Pointers

Just as pointers can be used to contain the addresses of simple variables and arrays, they can also be used to hold the addresses of structures. Here's an example that demonstrates a pointer pointing to a structure:

```
/* ptrstr.c */
/* demonstrates pointers to structures */
main()
{
    struct xx             /* declare structure type */
       {
       int num1;
       char ch1;
       };
    struct xx xx1;        /* declare structure variable */
    struct xx *ptr;       /* declare pointer to structure */

    ptr = &xx1;           /* assign address of struct to ptr */
    ptr->num1 = 303;      /* refer to structure members */
    ptr->ch1 = 'Q';
    printf("ptr->num1=%d\n", ptr->num1 );
    printf("ptr->ch1=%c\n", ptr->ch1 );
}
```

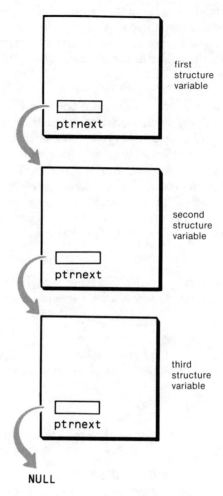

Figure 9-7. Linked List

Here we've declared a structure **xx** and a structure variable **xx1** of type **struct xx**. You've seen this before, but the next step is new: we declare a variable of type "pointer to structure xx" in the statement:

```
struct xx *ptr;
```

Next we assign the address of the structure variable **xx1** to **ptr** using the line

```
ptr = &xx1;
```

Thus, if the structure **xx1** happened to be located at address 1000, the number 1000 would be placed in the variable **ptr**.

Now, can we refer to the elements of the structure using the pointer instead of the structure name itself? As you've learned, if we know the name of a given structure variable, we can access its elements using this name and the dot operator. For instance, in the example above, the expression **xx.num1** refers to the element **num1** in the structure **xx**. Is there an analogous construction using **ptr** instead of **xx**? We can't use **ptr.num1** because **ptr** is not a structure but a pointer to a structure, and the dot operator requires a structure on the left side.

A literal approach would be to use the expression **(\*ptr).num1**. Since we know that **ptr** points to **xx1**, it follows that **\*ptr** is the contents of **xx1**. So substituting in the expression **xx1.num1** gives us **(\*ptr).num1**. The parentheses are needed around **\*ptr** because the dot operator has higher priority than the indirection operator. However, this is an unwieldy expression, so C provides a simpler approach: the two-part operator –> is used: a combination of the minus and less-than signs called the "arrow operator," as in the expression **ptr–>num1**. This has exactly the same effect as **(\*ptr).num1**.

> The ( . ) operator connects a *structure* with a member of the structure; the ( –> ) operator connects a *pointer* with a member of the structure.

In the ptrstr.c program example above, we've used this construction to assign values to the members of the structure, as in the expression

```
ptr->num1 = 303;
```

Similar constructions are used to read those values back out again with **printf()** statements.

### Allocating Memory: the malloc() Function

When we declare an array of structures, the compiler allocates enough memory to hold the entire array. This is not efficient if we don't come close to filling the entire array; in the agent.c example, for instance, we put 3 secret agents in an array that could hold 50, so the space for the 47 unused structure variables was wasted.

One of the advantages of using the linked-list approach (which we really will demonstrate soon) is that we use only as much memory as is needed to hold the data actually entered. Each time we decide to add an agent to the list, the program will acquire just enough memory to do the job. The mechanism for acquiring this memory is the C library function **malloc()**. A program can tell **malloc()** how much memory it needs, and **malloc()** will return a pointer to a space in memory just that large.

Let's look at a short example of the **malloc()** function at work:

```
/* maltest.c */
/* tests malloc() */
main()
```

```
{
    struct xx
        {
        int num1;
        char ch1;
        };
    struct xx *ptr;
    int j;

    printf("sizeof(struct xx)=%d\n", sizeof(struct xx) );
    for(j=0; j<4; j++)
        {
        ptr = (struct xx *) malloc( sizeof(struct xx) );
        printf("ptr=%x\n", ptr );
        }
}
```

This program declares a structure type called **xx**. It calls **malloc()** four times. Each time, **malloc()** returns a pointer to an area of memory large enough to hold a new version of the structure. Note that we don't use a variable definition to set aside memory for the structure variables. In effect, the structure variables are *created* by the function **malloc()**; the program does not know the *names* of these structure variables, but it knows where they are in memory because **malloc()** has returned pointers to them. These structure variables can therefore be accessed, using pointers, just as if they had been declared at the beginning of the program.

Here's the program's output:

```
C>maltest
sizeof(struct xx)=4
ptr=e66
ptr=e6c
ptr=e72
ptr=e78
```

Each time we call **malloc()** we need to tell it the size of the structure we want to store. We could do this by adding up the bytes used by each of the elements in our structure, or we can turn the task over to a C library function called **sizeof()**. This function takes a *data type* as an argument and returns the size in bytes that the data type occupies. For instance, the expression

```
sizeof(float)
```

would return the value 4, since type **float** occupies four bytes in memory.

In our program we've used **sizeof()** in a **printf()** statement so we can see what value it returns for the size of the structure **xx**. The surprise is that it returns 4, when we would expect it to return 3 (two bytes for the integer **num1** and one byte for the character **ch1**). It does this because the C compiler likes to start variables on even-numbered addresses; thus structure sizes are always even numbers.

Another surprise is that even though **malloc()** is told to return a memory area of four bytes, it spaces the starting addresses of these areas six bytes apart. (We've used hexadecimal notation for the addresses, a common practice in C programming. If hexadecimal is unfamiliar to you, consult Appendix C.) The reason for this is less clear, but it doesn't matter too much if **malloc()** wastes a few bytes here and there, as long as it sets aside enough space for each structure variable.

The key statement in maltest.c is:

```
ptr = (struct xx *) malloc( sizeof(struct xx) );
```

This statement assigns the pointer value (the address) returned by **malloc()** to the pointer variable **ptr**. The argument taken by **malloc()**, **sizeof(struct xx)**, is the size of the structure. What is the expression **(struct xx \*)** that *precedes* **malloc()**? To understand the use of this expression, we need to know about a C feature called *typecasting*, so let's digress briefly to see what this means.

### Typecasting

Sometimes we need to force the compiler to return the value of an expression as a particular data type. For example, suppose we've been using a floating point variable **flovar** in a program, and at some point we want to calculate the square root of its value. Microsoft C contains a library routine **sqrt()**, which will return a square root, but the argument sent to this function must be of type **double**. If we send the function a variable of type **float**, it will return a nonsense result. So we need to convert our variable **flovar** to type **double**. To do this, we use the *cast* operator, which consists of putting parentheses around the name of the data type. In this example we would say:

```
answer = sqrt( (double)flovar );
```

The expression **(double)** causes **flovar** to be converted from type **float** to type **double** before it is used.

We need to perform a similar data conversion on the pointer returned by **malloc()**, although for a different reason. Remember that the compiler needs to know two pieces of information about every pointer: the address of the item pointed to and its data type. The **malloc()** function returns the address, but it conveys no information about the data type. In fact, **malloc()** returns a pointer of type **void\***, meaning a pointer to an undetermined data type. In order to avoid confusing the compiler, we must ensure that the value returned by **malloc()** is of type **pointer to struct xx**. We do this by using a typecast: the name of the data type enclosed in parentheses, preceding the value being assigned. This forces the value to be of that type, and ensures that the compiler will assign a pointer of the correct size to the variable **ptr**.

When **malloc()** returns a pointer to a structure, the compiler must be told the type of the structure pointed to.

### Using malloc()

As a simple example of **malloc()** at work, we'll rewrite our ptrstr.c example, this time using a pointer value obtained from **malloc()**, rather than using the address operator on a declared structure variable as we did in ptrstr.c.

```
/* ptrstr2.c */
/* demonstrates pointers to structures, uses malloc() */
main()
{
    struct xx            /* declare structure type */
        {
        int num1;
        char ch1;
        };
    struct xx *ptr;    /* declare pointer to structure */

                       /* get memory to hold structure */
    ptr = (struct xx *) malloc( sizeof(struct xx) );

    ptr->num1 = 303;   /* refer to members of structure */
    ptr->ch1 = 'Q';
    printf("ptr->num1=%d\n", ptr->num1 );
    printf("ptr->ch1=%c\n", ptr->ch1 );
}
```

Notice the similarities to the earlier version of ptrstr.c. Everything is the same, except that the structure variable is not declared in the listing, it is created by **malloc()** at run time.

With this background under our belts, it's time (finally) to take a look at the linked-list version of agent.c.

### The Agent Program Using Linked Lists

Here's the listing for the program. In many ways it is similar to the earlier agent.c program that used an array of structures, but the differences are significant and will require some explanation.

```
/* agent2.c */
/* maintains list of agents */
/* uses linked list */
#include <stdio.h>              /* for printf(), 'stdin' */
#include <conio.h>              /* for getche() */
#include <stdlib.h>             /* for malloc() */

#define TRUE 1
void newname(void);            /* prototypes */
void listall(void);

struct prs                     /* define data structure */
    {
    char name [30];            /* agent's name */
    int agnumb;                /* agent's number */
```

```
      float height;                    /* height in inches */
      struct prs *ptrnext;             /* ptr to next structure */
      };
   struct prs *ptrfirst, *ptrthis, *ptrnew;

   void main(void)
   {
      int ch;
      ptrfirst = (struct prs *)NULL;              /* no input yet */
      while (TRUE)
         {
         printf("\nType 'e' to enter new agent"); /* print */
         printf("\n    'l' to list all agents: "); /* selections */
         ch = getche();                           /* get choice */
         switch (ch)
            {
            case 'e':                        /* enter new name */
               newname(); break;
            case 'l':                        /* list entire file */
               listall(); break;
            default:                         /* user mistake */
               puts("\nEnter only selections listed");
            }  /* end switch */
         }  /* end while */
   }  /* end main */

   /* newname() */
   /* puts a new agent in the database */
   void newname(void)
   {                                        /* get space */
      ptrnew = (struct prs *) malloc( sizeof(struct prs) );
      if(ptrfirst == (struct prs *)NULL )  /* if none already */
         ptrfirst = ptrthis = ptrnew;      /* save addr */
      else                                 /* not first item */
         {                                 /* go to end of list */
         ptrthis = ptrfirst;               /* (start at begin) */
         while( ptrthis->ptrnext != (struct prs *)NULL )
            ptrthis = ptrthis->ptrnext;    /* find next item */
         ptrthis->ptrnext = ptrnew;        /* pt to new item */
         ptrthis = ptrnew;                 /* go to new item */
         }
      printf("\nEnter name: ");            /* get name */
      gets(ptrthis->name);
      printf("Enter number: ");            /* get number */
      scanf("%d", &ptrthis->agnumb);
      printf("Enter height: ");            /* get height */
      scanf("%f", &ptrthis->height);
      fflush(stdin);                       /* clear buffer */
      ptrthis->ptrnext = (struct prs *) NULL;    /* this is end */
   }
```

```
/* listall() */
/* lists all agents and data */
void listall(void)
{
   if (ptrfirst == (struct prs *)NULL )        /* if empty list */
      { printf("\nEmpty list.\n"); return; }  /*    return */
   ptrthis = ptrfirst;                         /* start at first item */
   do
      {                                        /* print contents */
      printf("\nName: %s\n", ptrthis->name );
      printf("Number: %03d\n", ptrthis->agnumb );
      printf("Height: %4.2f\n", ptrthis->height );
      ptrthis = ptrthis->ptrnext;          /* move to next item */
      }
   while (ptrthis != (struct prs *)NULL ); /* quit on null ptr */
}
```

In operation, this program is much like agent.c, except that it no longer prints record numbers; since we do not have an array subscript to work with, it complicates the program to keep track of the record numbers (although this capability could be easily added to the program if desired). Here's the sample interaction with the program:

```
C>agent2
Type 'e' to enter new agent
   'l' to list all agents: e
Enter name: George Smiley
Enter number: 999
Enter height: 64.3

Type 'e' to enter new agent
   'l' to list all agents: e
Enter name: James Bond
Enter number: 007
Enter height: 74.25

Type 'e' to enter new agent
   'l' to list all agents: e
Enter name: Mata Hari
Enter number: 121
Enter height: 58.75

Type 'e' to enter new agent
   'l' to list all agents: l
Name: George Smiley
Number: 999
Height: 64.30

Name: James Bond
Number: 007
Height: 74.25
```

```
Name: Mata Hari
Number: 121
Height: 58.75
```

The challenging part of understanding this program is following what happens to the pointers. As we've noted, the basic idea is that each structure variable contains a pointer to the next structure on the list; the pointer in the last structure contains the null pointer. These pointers are called **ptrnext**, since they point to the next structure. Figure 9-8 shows how this looks, assuming that the first structure is assigned the address 3000.

In addition to the **ptrnext** variable contained in each structure, the program also keeps track of three other pointers declared at the beginning of the program.

One of these pointers, called **ptrfirst**, will be used to hold the address of the first structure in the list. This is a key address, since it's how the program finds the list. The pointer is set to null at the beginning of the program by the statement:

```
ptrfirst = (struct prs *)NULL;
```

Let's look at this statement. First, NULL is #**defin**ed to be 0 in the file stdio.h; this is a standard definition used by C programmers, and since we had included the file anyway, to define "stdin," it's easy to use NULL instead of 0. Since this value is going to be assigned to a pointer, it must be typecast to the same type as the other pointers, namely (**struct prs \***).

The **main()** function is otherwise much the same as in agent.c; it consists mostly of a **switch** statement to route control to different functions. It's in the functions **newname()** and **listall()** that most of the pointer manipulation takes place.

### Adding an Agent to the Database

If the user wants to add an agent to the database, the program calls on the function **newname()**. This function uses **malloc()** to get a pointer to a space big enough for the structure (40 bytes, as it turns out). This address is assigned temporarily to a pointer called **ptrnew**. If this is the first item to be placed on the list, the **ptrfirst** variable will still be set to null, as the program will discover with the statement

```
if(ptrfirst == (struct prs *)NULL )
```

The program then sets both **ptrfirst** and **ptrthis** to the new address in **ptrnew**. The individual items in the structure are then filled in by the user's replies, which are assigned to the variables **ptrthis->name**, **ptrthis->agnumb**, and so forth.

However, if this isn't the first item on the list, the program must work its way to the end of the list, so it can change the pointer **ptrnext** (the last element of the structure) from null to the address in **ptrnew**, thus linking the new item. The **while** loop in **newname()** is used to move to the end of the list. It starts by assigning **ptrfirst** to **ptrthis**. Then it looks to see if the expression

```
ptrthis->ptrnext
```

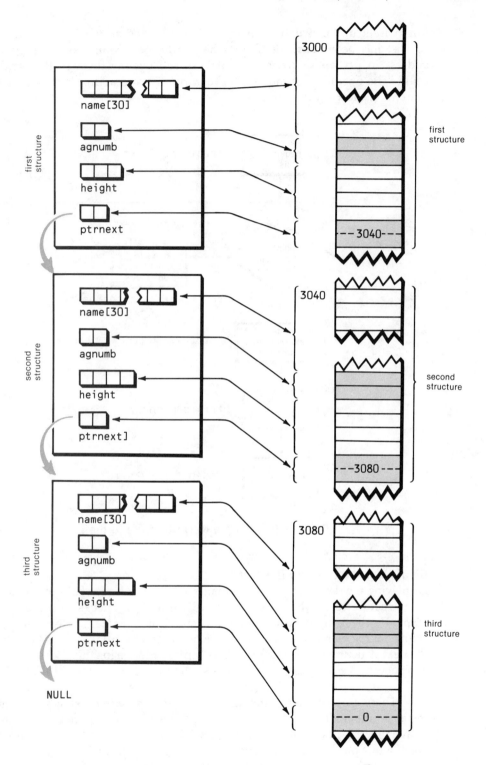

Figure 9-8. Structures in the agent2.c Program

(the pointer in the structure currently being looked at) is null. If so, the end of the list has been reached. If not, the **while** loop continues by assigning the address in **ptrthis->ptrnext** to **ptrthis** and cycling through the **while** loop again. The operation of moving through the list and adding a new structure to the end is shown in Figure 9-9.

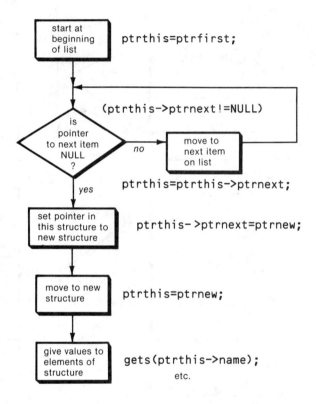

Figure 9-9. Adding a New Structure to the List

### Displaying the Data on the List

Displaying the data on the list is a matter of following the chain of pointers from one structure to another. The function **listall()** first checks to see if the list is empty by checking **ptrfirst** to see if it is null. If not, it enters a **do while** loop that prints out the elements of the structure pointed to by **ptrthis**, gets the address of the next structure in line from **ptrthis->ptrnext**, assigns this address to **ptrthis**, and repeats the process. The loop ends when **ptrthis->ptrnext** turns out to be null.

There are many refinements that can be made when using linked lists. For instance, the address of the last item on the list is often stored (sometimes as a pointer in the first item of the list, which is then treated as a dummy item). Having this pointer available avoids having to read through the entire list to add a new item to the end; the program can go directly to the last item. This is a timesaver when the list becomes long. Also, lists can be linked in the backwards as well as the forward direction, as we've shown, or they can be circular.

Deleting an item from a linked list is fairly easy. Say the structure to be deleted is B. Then the pointer in the preceding structure, A, is changed to point to C rather than B. If it is desired to free the memory used by the deleted structure, a library function **free()** can be used. This function takes as an argument a pointer to the structure to be deleted. This technique can result in significant memory savings when many items are being added and deleted.

It is easy to search through linked lists for a particular name or other data item. The search program follows the chain of pointers, as in our example, and checks each structure to see if it contains the desired item. An exercise at the end of the chapter deals with this operation.

> Very complex data organizations can be built on the idea of a structure containing a pointer.

Pointers to structures can be used for many other configurations besides the simple linked list we've shown here. For example, there is the tree, where each element points to two or more elements, each of which points to other elements, and so on. We'll leave these topics to other books.

# Unions

Unions have the same relationship to structures that you might have to a distant cousin who resembled you but turned out to be smuggling contraband in a third-world country; they may look the same, but they are engaged in different enterprises.

Both structures and unions are used to group a number of different variables together. But while a structure enables us to treat as a unit a number of different variables stored at different places in memory, a union enables us to treat the same space in memory as a number of different variables. That is, a union is a way for a section of memory to be treated as a variable of one type on one occasion, and as a different variable, of a different type, on another occasion.

You might wonder why it would ever be necessary to do such a thing, but we'll be seeing a very practical application soon. First, let's look at a simple example:

```
/* union.c */
/* demonstrates unions */
main()
{
    union intflo        /* define union of type 'intflo' */
        {
        int intnum;
```

```
        float fltnum;
        } unex;              /* declare 'unex' to be type intflo */

    printf("sizeof(union intflo)=%d\n", sizeof(union intflo) );
    unex.intnum = 734;
    printf("unex.intnum=%d\n", unex.intnum );
    unex.fltnum = 867.43;
    printf("unex.fltnum=%.2f\n", unex.fltnum );
}
```

As you can see, we declare a union type (**intflo**) and a union variable (**unex**) in much the same way we declare structure types and variables. However, the similarity ends there, as we can see from the output of the program:

```
C>union
sizeof(union inflo)=4
unex.intnum=734
unex.fltnum=867.43
```

Although the union holds a floating point number (**fltnum**) and an integer (**intnum**) its size is only four bytes. Thus, it is big enough to hold one element or the other but not both at the same time. In the program we first give a value to the variable **unex.intnum** and read it out. Then we give a value to **unex.fltnum** and read it out. We can't give values to these two variables at the same time, because they occupy the same space in memory; if we assigned **unex.intnum** a value, and then tried to read out a value of **unex.fltnum**, we'd get nonsense because the program would try to interpret an integer as a floating point number. Figure 9-10 shows a conceptual view of the union **intflo** and its relationship to memory.

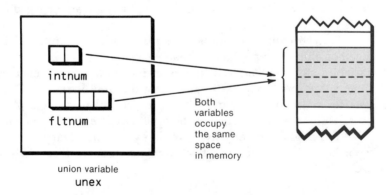

Figure 9-10. Union Variable *unex* Stored in Memory

Why use unions? One reason is to use a single variable name to pass data of different types. We could rewrite the C library function **sqrt()**, for example, so that instead of requiring an argument of type **double**, it would accept any data type. A union could be used in the function to store the incoming data: any data type would be acceptable. The union might look like this:

```
union number
    {
    double dnum;
    float fnum;
    long lnum;
    int inum;
    char cnum;
    };
```

In this way the same function would serve for all data types. (The function would need to examine the data in the union to determine which type it was or it would need to be told the type via a second parameter.)

Another use for unions is to give the *same* data different names and treat it as different types, depending on the needs of the function using it. We'll see an example of this in the next section. But before we go on to that topic we need to be familiar with one more C construction.

A union provides a way to look at the same data in several different ways.

## Unions of Structures

Just as structures can be nested within each other, so too can unions be nested in unions, unions in structures, and structures in unions. Here's an example of a structure nested in a union:

```
/* unistruc.c */
/* demonstrates union of structures */

main()
{
struct twoints             /* define structure 'twoints' */
    {
    int intnum1;
    int intnum2;
    } stex;                /* 'stex' is of type struct twoints */

union intflo               /* define union 'intflo' */
    {
    struct twoints stex;   /* union contains a structure */
    float fltnum;          /*    and also a number of type float */
    } unex;                /* 'unex' is of type union intflo */

printf("sizeof(union intflo)=%d\n", sizeof(union intflo) );
```

```
unex.stex.intnum1 = 734;
unex.stex.intnum2 = -333;
printf("unex.stex.intnum1=%d\n", unex.stex.intnum1 );
printf("unex.stex.intnum2=%d\n", unex.stex.intnum2 );
unex.fltnum = 867.43;
printf("unex.fltnum=%f\n", unex.fltnum );
}
```

Here's the output of unistruc.c:

```
c>unistruc
sizeof(union intflo)=4
unex.stex.intnum1=734
unex.stex.intnum2=-333
unex.fltnum=867.429993
```

In this program we declare a structure type **twoints** and a structure variable **stex** of that type. The elements of the structure are two integers, **intnum1** and **intnum2**. We also declare a union type **intflo** and a union variable **unex** of that type. The elements of the union are the structure **stex** and a floating point variable **fltnum**.

As we do with nested structures, we access members of this union of structures using the dot operator twice. Thus,

```
unex.stex.intnum1
```

is the element **intnum1** in the structure **stex** in the union **unex**.

This configuration, the union of structures, will be important when we explore the ROM BIOS.

# The ROM BIOS

As we noted at the beginning of this chapter, the computers in the IBM family come with a set of built-in routines collectively called the ROM BIOS. These routines are a permanent part of the machine; in this sense, they are more hardware than software. Our C programs can make use of these routines to perform a variety of input/output activities. In the remainder of this chapter we'll explore the ROM BIOS and see how it can be accessed from C.

## Advantages of Using ROM BIOS

As the name implies, the BIOS routines mostly handle input/output operations. Some of the routines duplicate C library functions. For example, there is a ROM BIOS routine to put a character on the screen, similar in operation to **putch()**, and another routine similar to **getche()**. For many of the routines built into ROM, however, there is no equivalent in C. The most important capability lacking in the C library is in graphics. For instance, to change graphics modes or to put a dot on the graphics screen requires a call to a ROM BIOS routine. As a consequence, if you want to exercise control over various graphics operations, it is important to know how to access the ROM BIOS.

Because the routines in ROM BIOS are so closely related to the hardware, they often operate faster than the corresponding routine in C. In fact, C functions often work by calling a ROM BIOS routine, so calling the routine directly from your program cuts out the intermediary and speeds execution.

## ROM BIOS and Non-IBM Compatibles

IBM clones also contain ROM BIOS routines. In a compatible clone these routines exactly duplicate the operation of those in the corresponding IBM machine. However, in some MS-DOS computers that are not accurate duplicates of the IBM, the operation of the ROM BIOS is different. Thus there can be a disadvantage to using the ROM BIOS: you may make it harder to transport your program to different computers.

## Overview of the ROM BIOS Library

There are dozens of ROM BIOS routines. The exact number depends on which computer in the IBM family you're using.

The largest category of routines deals with the video display. There are routines to set the video mode, control the cursor size and position, read and write characters, and place dots on the color screen, among others. There are also ROM routines for other input/output devices, including the diskette drives, the serial port, the cassette reader (does anyone ever use this device?), joysticks, user-defined devices, the keyboard, and the printer.

We cannot cover all the ROM BIOS routines in this book; there are far too many. For a complete explanation of all the ROM BIOS routines, you have two choices. The most fundamental source is the actual assembly language source code listing of the routines, which can be found in the IBM *Technical Reference* manual. Comments in these listings explain the workings of the routines. A more readable analysis may be found in popular computer books. See the bibliography for suggestions.

In this section we'll explore several ROM BIOS routines; we'll cover more graphics-oriented ROM routines in Chapters 10 and 11.

## Accessing the ROM BIOS

The ROM BIOS routines are written in assembly language and were designed to be called by assembly language programs. As a consequence, calling them from C is not as simple as calling C library functions. C compilers working on the IBM generally provide a method to access these routines, but using this method requires at least some understanding of the architecture of the microprocessor chip that powers the computer. This chip can be the 8088, 8086, 80286, or 80386, depending on the particular machine. For our discussion we will assume that all these chips operate in the same way.

## Microprocessor Architecture for C Programmers

When we call a C function from a C program, we can pass values using arguments placed in the parentheses following the function name, as in the expression **strcat(s1,s2)**. These values (in this example the addresses of strings) are placed in an area of memory called the stack, where the function can find and operate on them.

When we use C to call a BIOS routine, the process is somewhat different. Instead of values being placed in an area of memory, they are placed in hardware devices called "registers." These are somewhat like memory locations, but they have far more capabilities. Registers are the heart of the microprocessor; they are used to perform arithmetic and many other operations, but here we are concerned only with using them as locations for passing arguments to the BIOS.

There are a number of registers in the microprocessor; the ones we will be most concerned with are shown in Figure 9-11. As you can see, each of these four registers, AX, BX, CX, and DX, consists of two bytes. (Either upper- or lowercase may be used for register names, so they can be called ax, bx, cx, and dx as well.) In some ways the registers are like integer variables in C. They can hold two bytes of data, and we can put whatever values we like into them, just as we can assign whatever value we want to a variable. Unlike C variables, however, the registers are fixed; they are always there, and they always have the same names. They can be thought of as special-purpose permanent variables.

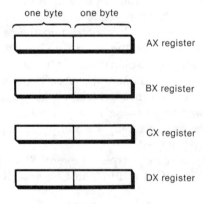

Figure 9-11. The Main 8086 Registers

## The Dual Role of the Registers

Another difference between C variables and registers is that registers can be accessed in two different ways: either as four two-byte registers, or as eight one-byte registers, as shown in Figure 9-12.

In the one-byte interpretation each register is split into a high half (AH, BH, CH, and DH) and a low half (AL, BL, CL, DL). Although the register itself is the

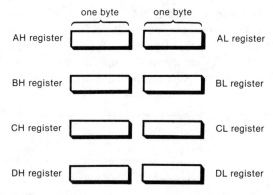

Figure 9-12. Registers as One-Byte Storage

same physical object whether used as one two-byte device or two one-byte devices, the rest of the hardware in the chip interprets each differently, and so, each must be accessed differently by the software.

The idea of using the same variable storage in two different ways should sound familiar; it is similar to our description of a union in the last section. In fact, a union is the mechanism used to communicate with the registers. But before we show an example of this we need to explore one other idea.

## Interrupt Numbers

The ROM BIOS routines are accessed through *interrupts*. We need not concern outselves with exactly how interrupts work; for our purposes an interrupt can be thought of as *a group of functions*. Each of these groups has its own *interrupt number*. For instance, all the routines that deal with the video display use interrupt number 10 (hex), and all those that deal with the disk drive use number 13 (hex). Thus, in order to call a ROM BIOS routine, we must first know its *interrupt number*.

An interrupt provides access to a group of ROM BIOS routines.

To specify a routine within one of these groups, we place a value in the one-byte AH register. Various other registers may also hold values, depending on the specific function called.

## The *int86()* Function

The mechanism used to access a ROM BIOS routine is a C library function called **int86()**. The "int" stands for "interrupt" and the "86" refers to the 8088/8086/80286/80386 family of chips. This function takes the interrupt number and two union variables as arguments. The first union represents the values in the registers being sent *to* the ROM routine, and the second represents the values in the registers being returned *from* the ROM routine to the C program. Figure 9-13 shows the format of this function. Notice that the function actually requires the *addresses* of the unions, not the unions themselves (in the same way **scanf()** requires the addresses of numerical variables).

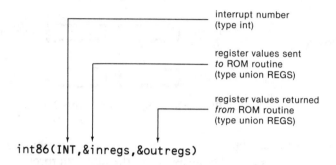

interrupt number
(type int)

register values sent
*to* ROM routine
(type union REGS)

register values returned
*from* ROM routine
(type union REGS)

```
int86(INT,&inregs,&outregs)
```

Figure 9-13. Format of the *int86()* Function

Now, we're ready for an actual example of a program that accesses the ROM BIOS.

## Finding the Memory Size

One of the routines built into the ROM BIOS will return the size of the RAM memory installed in the machine. This can be an interesting capability when used in a stand-alone program, if you don't happen to know how much memory there is in the machine you're using. It can be even more useful to a program that uses large amounts of memory, runs on various computers that may have a variety of memory sizes, and needs a way to find out just how much memory is available.

The data required for this ROM BIOS routine is summarized in the box. We'll use similar boxes for other ROM BIOS routines as we go along.

| | |
|---|---|
| ROM BIOS routine: | Memory size |
| Interrupt 12 hex: | Memory size |
| Input registers: | none. |
| Output registers: | AX = memory size in Kbytes. |

Here there are only two pertinent items of data about the routine; we invoke it by calling interrupt 12 hex and the memory size is read from the AX register. (Other ROM BIOS routines will use additional input and output parameters.)

Here's the program.

```
/* memsize0.c */
/* prints memory size */
#define MEM 0x12                    /* BIOS interrupt number */
main()
{
    struct WORDREGS                 /* registers as 16-bit words */
        {
        unsigned int ax;
        unsigned int bx;
        unsigned int cx;
        unsigned int dx;
        unsigned int si;
        unsigned int di;
        unsigned int flags;
        };

    struct BYTEREGS                 /* registers as 8-bit bytes */
        {
        unsigned char al, ah;
        unsigned char bl, bh;
        unsigned char cl, ch;
        unsigned char dl, dh;
        };

    union REGS                      /* either bytes or words */
        {
        struct WORDREGS x;
        struct BYTEREGS h;
        };

    union REGS regs;                /* regs to be type union REGS */
    unsigned int size;
    int86(MEM, &regs, &regs);       /* call memory interrupt */
    size = regs.x.ax;               /* get value from AX register */
    printf("Memory size is %d Kbytes", size );
}
```

And here's the output generated on a particular machine:

```
C>memsize0
Memory size is 256 Kbytes
```

## A Union of Structures

As you can see, the program uses two structures and a union. The first structure, whose tag is WORDREGS, consists of all the registers in their two-byte interpretation. (In assembly language a two-byte piece of data is called a "word," hence the name WORDREGS, for "word registers.") The data type used is

**unsigned int**, since the numbers stored in the registers are not considered to be signed.

The structure declares the four two-byte registers we discussed: the AX, BX, CX, and DX registers. It also declares several registers we didn't mention: the SI, DI, and FLAGS registers. We don't need these registers in the ROM calls we use, but they must appear in the structure, since the **int86** function is expecting them.

The second structure, whose tag is BYTEREGS, consists of the same registers interpreted as eight one-byte registers.

The union consists of these two structures (a construction described in the last section). This union creates a set of variables that can be looked at either as four two-byte registers or as eight one-byte registers. The WORDREGS structure is given the variable name **x** (since all the two-byte registers end in this letter), while the BYTEREGS structure is given the name **h** (since the high half of the registers end in this letter). The union variable declared to be of type REGS is called **regs**.

Thus to access a register we use the dot operator twice:

```
regs.x.bx
```

means the BX register, while

```
regs.h.cl
```

refers to the CL register.

In our program, we don't need to send any values to the routine, so nothing is placed in any of the registers before we call **int86()**. Interrupt number 12 (hex) is unusual in this respect; most interrupt numbers require more information, as we'll see. Since one argument is not used, we can use the same union variable, **regs**, for both the outgoing and incoming values:

```
int86(MEM, &regs, &regs);
```

On the return from **int86()** the memory size has been placed in the AX register, which we access in the expression

```
size = regs.x.ax
```

The data type of **size** agrees with that of **regs.x.ax** since they are both unsigned integers.

## Using the Declarations in DOS.H

Actually, in Microsoft C the structures WORDREGS and BYTEREGS and the union REGS are already declared in a file called DOS.H. Thus, if we **#include** this file in our program, we can dispense with the explicit declarations, as this version of the program shows:

```
/* memsize.c */
/* prints memory size */
#include "dos.h"              /* declares REGS */
#define MEM 0x12              /* BIOS interrupt number */
main()
{
    union REGS regs;          /* regs to be type union REGS */
    unsigned int size;
    int86(MEM, &regs, &regs);  /* call video interrupt */
    size = regs.x.ax;          /* get value from AX register */
    printf("Memory size is %d Kbytes", size );
}
```

This is certainly a much handier format, although it does not reveal as much about what is going on.

## Setting the Cursor Size

Let's look at an example that requires us to send values *to* a ROM routine. This program will call a ROM routine that changes the size of the cursor, so let's first examine how the cursor is created.

On the monochrome screen the cursor consists of 14 short horizontal lines, numbered from 0 to 13 (reading from top to bottom), as shown in Figure 9-14. If you're using an EGA color display, there are only nine lines, numbered from 0 to 8.

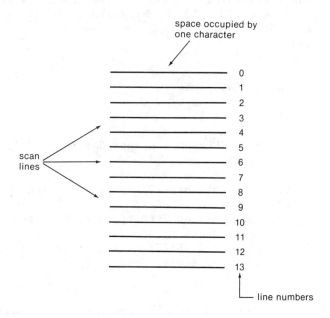

Figure 9-14. The Monochrome Cursor

The default cursor, the one you are most used to seeing, uses only two of these lines, 12 and 13, at the bottom of the character position (7 and 8 in EGA). To redefine the size of the cursor, we call the BIOS routine at interrupt 10 (hex), with the AH register containing 1.

| | |
|---|---|
| ROM BIOS routine: | Set cursor size |
| Interrupt 10 hex: | video |
| Input registers: | AH = 01 |
| | CH = starting scan line (0 to 13 dec) |
| | CL = ending scan line (0 to 13 dec) |
| Output registers: | none |

We also place the starting cursor line number in the CH register, and the ending line number in the CL register.

Here's the program:

```
/* setcur.c */
/* sets cursor size */
#include "dos.h"          /* declares REGS */
#define CURSIZE 1         /* "set cursor size" service */
#define VIDEO 0x10        /* video BIOS interrupt number */
main(argc,argv)
int argc;
char *argv[];
{
    union REGS regs;
    int start, end;
    if (argc != 3)
        {
        printf("Example usage: C>setcur 12 13");
        exit();
        }
    start = atoi( argv[1] );    /* string to integer */
    end = atoi( argv[2] );
    regs.h.ch = (char)start;    /* starting line number */
    regs.h.cl = (char)end;      /* ending line number */
    regs.h.ah = CURSIZE;        /* service number */
    int86(VIDEO, &regs, &regs); /* call video interrupt */
}
```

In this example we make use of command-line arguments (described in Chapter 8) to get the starting and ending cursor lines numbers from the user. To cause the cursor to fill the entire character block, we would type:

```
C>setcur 0 13
```

To return to the normal cursor, we would type:

```
C>setcur 12 13
```

Specifying a starting number greater than the ending number causes a two-part cursor, as you'll see if you try this:

```
C>setcur 12 1
```

## Making the Cursor Disappear

You can make the cursor vanish if you set bit 5, in the byte placed in the CH register, to 1. What do we mean by bit 5? The bits in every byte are numbered from 0 to 7, with the least significant bit being 0, as shown in Figure 9-15. To set bit 5 on, we can place the hex number 20 in the CH register. Hex 20 is 00100000 in binary, which is just the bit configuration we need.

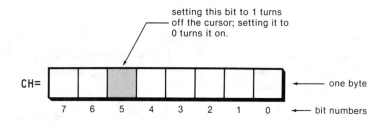

Figure 9-15. The Cursor On/Off Bit

The following program accomplishes the task:

```
/* curoff.c */
/* turns cursor off */
#include "dos.h"            /* declares REGS */
#define CURSIZE 1           /* "set cursor size" service */
#define VIDEO 0x10          /* video BIOS interrupt number */
#define STOPBIT 0x20        /* this bit turns cursor off */
main()
{
    union REGS regs;
    regs.h.ch = STOPBIT;       /* turns cursor off */
    regs.h.ah = CURSIZE;       /* service number */
    int86(VIDEO, &regs, &regs); /* call video interrupt */
}
```

This program is similar to setcur.c, except that we don't need to put anything into the CL register. When you run it, the cursor will vanish (which can be unnerving).

To turn the cursor back on, use the setcur.c program. Since it sends a value in CH that includes a 0 value for bit 5, the cursor will reappear no matter which values you use for the starting and stopping lines (provided they're between 0 and 13).

There are many other ways to use ROM BIOS; we've only scratched the surface here. We'll return to the topic in Chapter 10.

### Using Interrupts to Call DOS

In addition to the routines built into the ROM BIOS, there are also a number of routines in the PC-DOS (or MS-DOS) operating system that can be called by a C program. In general, these "DOS call" routines are less useful for the C programmer. Many of them deal with disk input/output, which is already handled very well by normal C library functions, and we will not explore them in this book. However, the method of accessing these interrupt routines is very similar to that for accessing the ROM BIOS routines.

## Summary

In this chapter we've covered the use of structures, which allow us to combine several variables of different types into a single entity, and unions, which allow one area of memory to be treated in several different ways. We've also explored the use of structures and unions in accessing the routines built into the ROM BIOS of the IBM computer.

## Questions

1. Array elements must all be of the _____ _____, whereas structure members can be of _____ _____.

2. True or false: an appropriate use for a structure is to store a list of prices.

3. The purpose of declaring a structure type is to:

    a. set aside the appropriate amount of memory

    b. define the format of the structure

    c. specify a list of structure elements

    d. define a new data type

4. Write a statement that declares a structure type consisting of two elements: a string of 10 characters and an integer.

5. How many structure variables of a given type can you use in a program?

    a. one

    b. none

c. as many as you like

d. as many as there are elements in the structure

6. Before you can access an element of a structure you must

(a) declare the structure _____,

(b) declare a structure _____,

(c) give the item in step b a _____.

7. Write a statement that will declare a structure variable **car** to be of structure type **vehicle**.

8. Assume the following declarations have been made:

```
struct body
    {
    int arms;
    int legs;
    };
struct body jim;
```

write an assignment statement that will set the number of arms in jim's body equal to 2.

9. Is it possible to declare a structure type and a structure variable in the same statement? If so, rewrite the example in question 8 to use this approach.

10. Assuming that **struct1** and **struct2** are structure variables of the same type, is the following statement possible?

```
struct1 = struct2;
```

11. Given the statement

```
xxx.yyy.zzz = 5;
```

which of the following are true?

a. Structure **zzz** is nested within structure **yyy**.

b. Structure **yyy** is nested within structure **xxx**.

c. Structure **xxx** is nested within structure **yyy**.

d. Structure **xxx** is nested within structure **zzz**.

12. Write a statement that declares a structure of type **partners** containing two structures of type **body**.

13. True or false: it is possible to pass a structure to a function in the same way a simple variable is passed.

14. Write a statement that declares a pointer to type **struct book**.

15. If **temp** is a member of the structure **weather**, and the statement

    addweath = &weather;

    has been executed, then which of the following represents **temp**?

    a. weather.temp
    b. (*weather).temp
    c. addweath.temp
    d. addweath->temp

16. The function **malloc()** returns a pointer to _____.

17. One advantage a linked list has over an array is that the linked list can use less _____.

18. In a linked list, each structure on the list contains a pointer to the _____ _____.

19. True or false: the **sizeof()** function returns the size of a variable.

20. A union consists of a number of elements that

    a. all have the same type
    b. must be structures
    c. are grouped next to each other in memory
    d. all occupy the same space in memory

21. Write a statement that declares a union type with two elements: a string 10 characters long and an integer.

22. What does ROM BIOS stand for?

23. The routines in the ROM BIOS are located

    a. in the operating system
    b. in the C compiler
    c. in the C library
    d. in the hardware of the computer

24. True or false: the ROM BIOS consists mostly of routines that perform input/output operations.

25. The registers used in microprocessors

    a. are used to hold floating point numbers

    b. are used to hold addresses of I/O devices

    c. act somewhat like C functions

    d. act somewhat like C variables

26. Name the four main registers in the microprocessor of IBM computers.

27. List eight other names that can be used for these four registers.

28. A union is used to represent the registers because:

    a. there are so many registers

    b. the registers can hold either characters or integers

    c. the registers all have two names

    d. no one is sure what to call the registers

29. If one wants to put the value 3 in the DL register, which of the following statements is appropriate?

    a. regs.l.dl = 3;

    b. regs.x.dx = 3;

    c. regs.h.dx = 3;

    d. regs.h.dl = 3;

30. True or false: there is no way for a program to determine how large a memory it is running in.

# Exercises

1. Write a short program that will: (a) set up a structure to hold a date. The structure will consist of three integer values, for the month, day, and year. (b) Assign values to the members of the structure and (c) print out the values in the format 12/31/88.

2. Modify the program of exercise 1 so that the date is printed out by a function. Pass the structure to the function.

3. Modify the program of exercise 2 so that the date is part of a larger structure, representing books lent by a library. The structure should consist of the title of the book and an inner structure representing the due date. Assign

values to the members of the structure. Have a function print out the values from the structure passed to it.

4. There is a ROM BIOS routine that will set the position of the cursor. It uses interrupt number 0x10, with AH = 2, DH = row number, and DL = column number (both of which start at 0, unlike the numbering for the ANSI.SYS command, in which numbering starts at 1). BH must contain 0. Modify the position.c program in Chapter 8 so that it performs in the same way, placing coordinates on the screen, but uses this ROM routine to position the cursor instead of the ANSI.SYS sequence.

5. Extra credit: modify the agent.c program to include a new element in the structure **personnel**: a string that can contain a list of special skills an agent might possess (such as Spanish, explosives, skiing, scuba diving, first aid, and so forth). Add a function that will ask the user what skill to look for, and then search through the array of structures and print out the information on only those agents who possess the required skill. It may be easier to combine the functions of this new search function and the **listall()** function, taking advantage of the fact that *every* string contains the null character '\0'. You'll need to develop a routine that will search for one string in another one.

# 10

# Memory and
# the Character Display

- Bitwise operators
- Memory-mapped displays
- The IBM character display
- The attribute byte
- Segment/offset addressing
- **Far** pointers
- Equipment list word

# 10

This chapter focuses on manipulating the character display using *direct memory access*. The character display places characters on the screen, as opposed to graphics. It operates whether you have a monochrome or a color graphics display adaptor (CGA, EGA, etc.) In past chapters we've explored a variety of techniques to place characters on the screen, but all these techniques have made use of C library functions. Now we'll show how to access the screen directly, an approach that provides a much faster way to place characters on the screen and has other advantages as well. This chapter is a prerequisite for the next chapter, on CGA, EGA, and VGA Color Graphics, since an understanding of the techniques of direct memory access is important to working with the color graphics modes.

Getting the maximum utility out of direct memory access requires an understanding of the C *bitwise operators*, which permit individual bits in memory to be accessed and manipulated. Accordingly, we'll start this chapter with a discussion of the bitwise operators. Then we'll explore the concept of memory-mapped displays, and show how direct memory access can be used for a very simple word processing program. This will involve the use of *far pointers*, a kind of pointer that can point to anyplace in memory. We'll also see how the attribute byte can be manipulated using the bitwise operators and look at a different way of operating on the bit level, using a construction called a "bit field." Finally, we'll explore a special area of the IBM's memory where various kinds of data about the system are stored, and see how, using this area, a program can find out what sorts of equipment are connected to the computer.

This chapter requires some understanding of the hexadecimal and binary numbering systems. If these topics are unfamiliar to you, you should study Appendix C before continuing.

## The Bitwise Operators

So far we've dealt with fixed types of data: characters, integers, and so forth. We haven't attempted to look *within* these data types to see how they are constructed out of individual bits and how these bits can be manipulated. Being able to operate on the bit level, however, can be very important in programming, especially when a program must interact directly with hardware. While programming languages are data oriented, hardware tends to be bit oriented; that is, a hardware device often requires input and output in the form of individual bits rather than in the form of byte-oriented data types such as characters and integers.

One of C's unusual features is a powerful set of bit-manipulation operators. These make it possible for the programmer to perform any desired manipulation of individual bits within a piece of data. In this section we'll explore these operators.

## The Bitwise AND ( & ) Operator

C uses six bitwise operators, summarized in the following table:

| Operation | Symbol |
|---|---|
| AND | & |
| Inclusive OR | ¦ |
| Exclusive OR (XOR) | ^ |
| Right shift | >> |
| Left shift | << |
| Complement | ~ |

These operators can be applied to characters and integers (signed and unsigned) but not to floating point numbers. Since the operators affect individual bits, it's important to know how to refer to the bits in a character or integer. The bits are numbered from right to left, as shown in Figure 10-1.

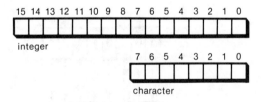

Figure 10-1. Bit Numbering

We'll start off by looking at just one of these operators in action, the bitwise AND operator. This operator is represented by the ampersand ( & ). Don't confuse this operator with the logical AND operator, represented by two ampersands ( && ).

The AND operator takes two operands, which must be of the same type. The idea is that the two operands are compared on a bit-by-bit basis. If bit 0 of the first operand is a one *and* bit 0 of the second operand is also a one, then bit 0 of the answer is a one; otherwise bit 0 is a zero. This rule can be summarized as shown in Figure 10-2.

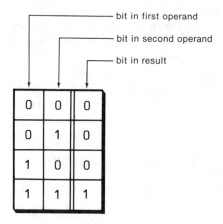

Figure 10-2. Rules for Combining Bits Using AND ( & ) Operator

The bitwise operators AND, OR, and XOR operate on a pair of bits to yield a third bit. The process is applied to each bit position of the operands in turn.

The rule is applied to all the bits of a data item in turn. Unlike operations involving normal arithmetic, each pair of corresponding bits is completely independent; there is no carry from one column to another. Figure 10-3 shows an example of two variables of type **char** being bitwise ANDed together:

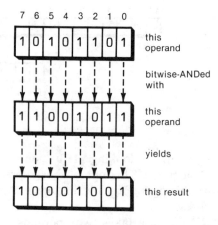

Figure 10-3. Example of Bitwise AND

A good way to become familiar with the logical operators is to write a program that allows experimentation with different inputs to see what results are produced by particular operators. The most convenient format for input and output is hexadecimal, since each hex digit corresponds to exactly four bits. Here's a simple program that permits testing of the AND operator, using hexadecimal character variables:

```
/* andtest.c */
/* demonstrates bitwise AND operator */
#define TRUE 1
main()
{
    unsigned char x1, x2;
    while(TRUE)
        {
        printf("\nEnter two hex numbers (ff or less): ");
        scanf("%x %x", &x1, &x2);
        printf("%02x & %02x = %02x\n", x1, x2, x1 & x2 );
        }
}
```

This program uses the ( & ) operator in the expression

```
x1 & x2
```

to find the appropriate answer, which is then printed out by the **printf()** statement.

Here are some examples of the AND operator at work using the program. The first four examples summarize the four ways two bits can be ANDed:

```
Enter two hex numbers (ff or less): 0 0
00 & 00 = 00
```

and (with the prompt line and user input not shown):

```
01 & 00 = 00

00 & 01 = 00

01 & 01 = 01
```

For a more advanced example, here are the two hex digits c and 7 ANDed together:

```
0c & 07 = 04
```

The expansion of these hex digits into bits is shown in Figure 10-4.

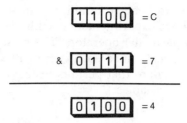

Figure 10-4. Two Hex Digits ANDed Together

The bitwise AND operator is often used to test whether a particular bit in a data item is set to 0 or 1. The testing process works because 0 ANDed with either 0 or 1 is still 0, while 1 ANDed with a bit is whatever the bit is. For example, to test if bit 3 of a character variable **ch** is 0 or 1, the following statement can be used:

```
bit3 = ch & 0x08;
```

Figure 10-5 shows this process in operation. Here if bit 3 of **ch** is 1, then the variable **bit3** will be assigned the value 1, otherwise 0 will be assigned.

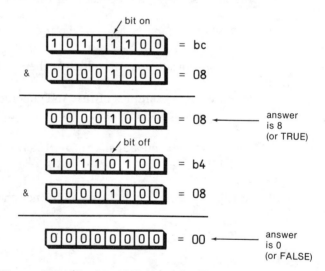

Figure 10-5. Bitwise AND Used for Test

We'll see an example of the bitwise AND used for testing bits in the program hextobin.c, coming up soon.

## The Bitwise OR ( ¦ ) Operator

Another important bitwise operator is OR, represented by the vertical bar ( ¦ ). When two bits are ORed together, the resulting bit is 1 if either or both of the two operand bits is one. If neither of the two bits is 1, the result is 0. This rule is shown in Figure 10-6.

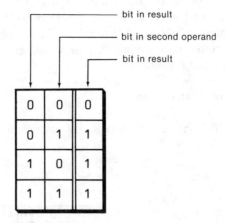

Figure 10-6. Rules for Combining Bits Using OR ( ¦ ) Operator

Here's a program that demonstrates the OR operator:

```
/* ortest.c */
/* demonstrates bitwise OR operator */
#define TRUE 1
main()
{
    unsigned char x1, x2;
    while(TRUE)
        {
        printf("\nEnter two hex numbers (ff or less): ");
        scanf("%x %x", &x1, &x2);
        printf("%02x ¦ %02x = %02x\n", x1, x2, x1 ¦ x2 );
        }
}
```

And here's some sample output (without the prompt lines):

```
00 ¦ 00 = 00
00 ¦ 01 = 01
01 ¦ 00 = 01
01 ¦ 01 = 01
0c ¦ 07 = 0f
ad ¦ cb = ef
```

If you're hazy about these results—or those in the last section on AND—you should verify that they're correct by expanding them into their binary form, performing the OR operation on each pair of corresponding bits, and translating them back into hexadecimal.

The bitwise OR operator is often used to combine bits from different variables into a single variable. For example, suppose we had two character variables, **ch1** and **ch2**, and suppose bits 0 through 3 of **ch1** contained a value we wanted, while bits 4 through 7 of **ch2** were the ones we wanted. Assuming the unwanted part of both variables was set to all 0s, we could then combine the two with the statement:

```
ans = ch1 | ch2;
```

Figure 10-7 shows how this works, assuming that **ch1** is 0x07 and **ch2** is 0xd0.

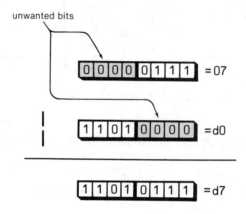

Figure 10-7. Bitwise OR Operator Used to Combine Values

## The Bitwise Right-Shift ( >> ) Operator

Besides bitwise operators that operate on two variables, there are several bitwise operators that operate on a single variable. An example is the right-shift operator, represented by two "greater than" symbols ( >> ). This operator moves each bit in the operand to the right. The number of places the bits are moved is determined by the number following the operand. Thus, the expression

```
ch >> 3
```

causes all the bits in **ch** to be shifted right three places. Figure 10-8 shows an example of the hex value 72 being shifted right two places. Note that shifting right one bit is the same as dividing the operand by 2.

Here's a program that demonstrates the right-shift operator:

```
/* shiftest.c */
/* demonstrates bitwise right shift operator */
#define TRUE 1
main()
```

```
{
    unsigned char x1, x2;
    while(TRUE)
        {
        printf("\nEnter hex number (ff or less) and number of bits ");
        printf("\nto shift (8 or less; example 'cc 3'): ");
        scanf("%x %d", &x1, &x2);
        printf("%02x >> %d = %02x\n", x1, x2, x1 >> x2 );
        }
}
```

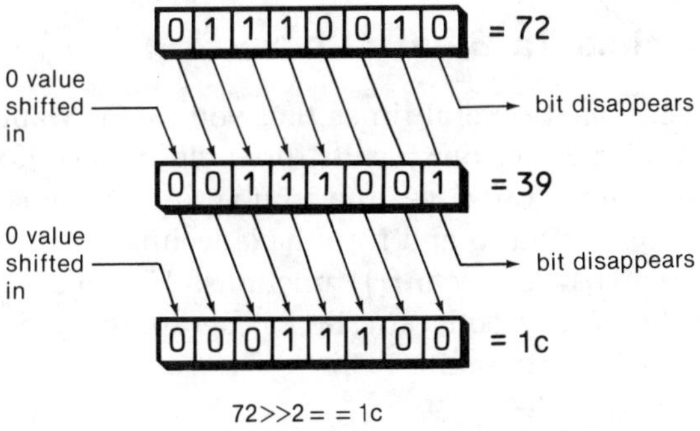

Figure 10-8. Example of Right-Shift Operator

Here's some sample output:

```
Enter hex number (ff or less) and number of bits
to shift (8 or less; example 'cc 3'): 80 1
80 >> 1 = 40
```

Here are some other examples:

```
80 >> 2 = 20
80 >> 7 = 01
f0 >> 4 = 0f
```

Again, if this isn't clear, translate the hex numbers into binary, shift them by hand, and translate back into hex to verify that the results are correct.

In the examples so far zeros are inserted into the left-most bit. This is because the data type being shifted is **unsigned char**. However, this may not be the case if the data type is **char**, which is assumed to be signed, with the left-most bit being the sign bit. If the left-most bit of a type **char** variable starts out equal to 1, the number is considered negative. To maintain the sign of the number when it is right-shifted, 1s are inserted in the left-most bit. Thus the following statement will be true:

```
80 >> 2 == e0
```

If unsigned types are used, zero is always shifted in on the left, and if a signed number is positive, 0s are also shifted in. The same is true also of signed and unsigned integer types.

> If the sign bit is set in a signed operand, right shifts will cause 1s to be shifted in from the left.

## Hexadecimal to Binary Conversion

We've mentioned several times that you might want to perform hex to binary conversions to verify our results. It would be nice if we could get the computer to do this, saving ourselves the trouble. As we've seen in the past, it's easy to perform conversion to and from hexadecimal in C by using the %x type specifier in **printf()** and **scanf()** functions. However, there is no corresponding specifier for binary, so let's write a program to carry out this conversion for us.

Here's the program:

```
/* hextobin.c */
/* converts hex number to binary */
#define TRUE 1
main()
{
    int j, num, bit;
    unsigned int mask;
    char string[10];
    while(TRUE)
       {
       mask = 0x8000;                       /* 1000000000000000 binary */
       printf("\nEnter number: ");
       scanf("%x", &num);
       printf("Binary of %04x is:  ", num);
       for(j=0; j<16; j++)                  /* for each bit */
          {
          bit = (mask & num) ? 1 : 0;  /* bit is 1 or 0 */
          printf("%d ", bit);          /* print bit */
          if(j==7)                     /* print dash between */
             printf("-- ");            /*      bytes */
          mask >>= 1;                  /* shift mask to right */
          }
       }
}
```

This program operates on integers rather than characters as in previous examples. Here's some sample interaction:

```
C>hextobin
```

```
Enter number: 1
Binary of 0001 is:   0 0 0 0 0 0 0 0--0 0 0 0 0 0 0 1
Enter number: 80
Binary of 0080 is:   0 0 0 0 0 0 0 0--1 0 0 0 0 0 0 0
Enter number: 100
Binary of 0100 is:   0 0 0 0 0 0 0 1--0 0 0 0 0 0 0 0
Enter number: f00
Binary of 0f00 is:   0 0 0 0 1 1 1 1--0 0 0 0 0 0 0 0
Enter number: f0f0
Binary of f0f0 is:   1 1 1 1 0 0 0 0--1 1 1 1 0 0 0 0
```

This program uses a **for** loop to go through all 16 bits of an integer variable, from left to right. The heart of the operation is contained in two statements that use bitwise operators:

```
bit = (mask & num) ? 1 : 0;
```

and

```
mask >>= 1;
```

In the first statement we make use of a mask. This is a variable that starts out with a single bit in the left-most position. The mask is then ANDed with the number that we want to express in binary, the variable **num**. If the result is nonzero (true), then we know the corresponding bit in **num** is 1; otherwise it's 0. The conditional statement assigns the value 1 to the variable **bit** if the bit being tested in **num** is 1, and 0 otherwise.

The left-shift statement then shifts the mask to the left, and the process is repeated for the next bit. The first time through the loop the mask will be 1000000000000000 binary, while the second time through it will be 0100000000000000, and so forth. Eventually all 16 bits will be printed out.

## Other Logical Operators

There are six bitwise operators in all, of which we've now looked at three. We'll briefly review the remaining three and then show a six-function bitwise calculator which, if you type it in and compile it, will enable you to experiment with and learn more about the bitwise operators.

### The Bitwise XOR ( ^ ) Operator

The ordinary bitwise OR operator ( ¦ ), discussed earlier, returns a value of 1 when either bit, or both bits, in the operand is 1. The bitwise *exclusive OR*, or XOR operator, by contrast, returns a value of 1 when either bit, but *not both* bits, is 1. This operator is represented by the caret ( ^ ). Figure 10-9 shows the rules for this operator.

The XOR operator can be useful for "toggling" a bit: that is, switching it back and forth between 0 and 1. This is true because a 1 XORed with 1 is 0, while a 1 XORed with a 0 is 1.

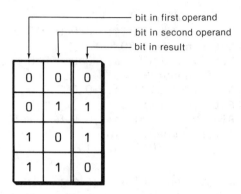

Figure 10-9. Rules for Combining Bits Using XOR Operator

An XOR operation applied twice to particular bits in an operand yields the original operand.

For instance, to toggle bit 3 in a variable **ch** of type **char**, we could use the statement:

```
ch = ch ^ 0x08;
```

Figure 10-10 shows how repeated application of this operation toggles bit 3 back and forth, while leaving the other bits unchanged. The variable **ch** is assumed to start out with the value 0xBC. We'll see an example of a bit being toggled to produce a useful result later on in the chapter.

### The Bitwise Left-Shift Operator ( << )
The left-shift operator is, as you might guess, similar to the right-shift operator, except that bits are shifted left instead of right. The value of the bits inserted on the right is always 0, regardless of the sign or data type of the operand.

### The Bitwise Complement Operator ( ~ )
The bitwise complement operator ( ~ ) acts on a single operand; it takes every bit in the operand and makes it 1 if it was a 0 and 0 if it was a 1. For example, the following equalities are true:

```
~03 == fc
~ffff == 0
~cc == 33
~88 == 77
```

Complementing a number twice always returns the original number.

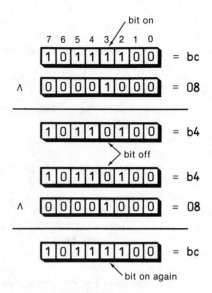

Figure 10-10. Bitwise XOR Operator Used as Toggle

## The Bitwise Calculator

Let's put all the bitwise operators together into one program. This program acts as a bitwise calculator, into which we type any suitable operand and a bitwise operator; it then displays the result. It is a useful program for exploring and learning about all the bitwise operations.

```
/* bitcalc.c */
/* performs bitwise calculations */
#define TRUE 1
#include <stdio.h>
void pbin(int);          /* prototypes */
void pline(void);

void main(void)
{
    char op[10];
    int x1, x2;
    while(TRUE)
        {
        printf("\n\nEnter expression (example 'ff00 & 1111'): ");
        scanf("%x %s %x", &x1, op, &x2);
        printf("\n");
        switch( op[0] )
            {
            case '&':
                pbin(x1); printf("& (and)\n"); pbin(x2);
                pline(); pbin(x1 & x2);
```

```
                                break;
                    case '|':
                        pbin(x1); printf("| (incl or)\n"); pbin(x2);
                        pline(); pbin(x1 | x2);
                        break;
                    case '^':
                        pbin(x1); printf("^ (excl or)\n"); pbin(x2);
                        pline(); pbin(x1 ^ x2);
                        break;
                    case '>':
                        pbin(x1); printf(">> "); printf("%d\n", x2);
                        pline(); pbin(x1 >> x2);
                        break;
                    case '<':
                        pbin(x1); printf("<< "); printf("%d\n", x2);
                        pline(); pbin(x1 << x2);
                        break;
                    case '~':
                        pbin(x1); printf("~ (complement)\n");
                        pline(); pbin(~x1);
                        break;
                    default: printf("Not valid operator.\n");
                    }
            }
    }

/* pbin */
/* prints number in hex and binary */
void pbin(int num)                      /* num = number to print */
{
    unsigned int mask;
    int j, bit;
    mask = 0x8000;                      /* one-bit mask */
    printf("%04x  ", num);              /* print in hex */
    for(j=0; j<16; j++)                 /* for each bit in num */
        {
        bit = (mask & num) ? 1 : 0;     /* bit is 1 or 0 */
        printf("%d ", bit);             /* print bit */
        if(j==7)                        /* print dash between */
            printf("-- ");              /*    bytes */
        mask >>= 1;                     /* shift mask to right */
        }
    printf("\n");
}

/* pline() */
void pline(void)
{
    printf("----------------------------------------\n");
}
```

As you can see, this program consists mostly of a large **switch** statement containing all the bitwise operations. The user types in an operand, a bitwise operator, and another operand. The program displays the result. The only anomaly is in the complement operator, which takes only one operand but requires a second operand to be typed after the operator ( ~ ) to satisfy the variable list in the **scanf()** statement (any number will do).

Here are some examples of interaction with the program. For brevity, the initial prompt is only shown on the first example:

```
Enter expression (example 'ff00 & 1111'): f0f0 ¦ 3333
f0f0  1 1 1 1 0 0 0 0--1 1 1 1 0 0 0 0
¦ (incl or)
3333  0 0 1 1 0 0 1 1--0 0 1 1 0 0 1 1
-------------------------------------------
f3f3  1 1 1 1 0 0 1 1--1 1 1 1 0 0 1 1

f0f0  1 1 1 1 0 0 0 0--1 1 1 1 0 0 0 0
<< 2
-------------------------------------------
c3c0  1 1 0 0 0 0 1 1--1 1 0 0 0 0 0 0

f0f0  1 1 1 1 0 0 0 0--1 1 1 1 0 0 0 0
^ (excl or)
3333  0 0 1 1 0 0 1 1--0 0 1 1 0 0 1 1
-------------------------------------------
c3c3  1 1 0 0 0 0 1 1--1 1 0 0 0 0 1 1

f0f0  1 1 1 1 0 0 0 0--1 1 1 1 0 0 0 0
~ (complement)
-------------------------------------------
0f0f  0 0 0 0 1 1 1 1--0 0 0 0 1 1 1 1
```

This program makes use of the routine from the hextobin.c program, transformed into the function **pbin()**, to print out binary versions of the operands and results.

Now that you know how to manipulate bits, we're ready to explore memory-mapped graphics and see what role bit manipulation plays in influencing the display.

## The Character Display Memory

When you attach a video monitor to your IBM computer you must also install in the computer a printed circuit board called the Graphics Adaptor. This board has on it the circuitry necessary to convey information from the computer to the display. What does this hardware consist of, and how can we access it from our programs?

Communication between the Graphics Adaptor and the computer takes place using a special section of memory as a sort of common ground. This section of memory is physically located on the Graphics Adaptor board and can be accessed both by the microprocessor and by the display screen. The microprocessor can insert values into this memory and read them out just as it can with ordinary random-access memory (RAM). The display hardware continuously takes the values from this memory and places the corresponding character on the screen.

The normal character display consists of 25 lines of 80 characters each, for a total of 2,000 characters. Each of these characters is associated with a particular address in the display memory. Two bytes in the memory are used for each character: one to hold the extended ASCII character code, a value from 0 to 255 (0 to ff in hex), and one to hold the attribute. (We'll investigate the details of the attribute byte later in this chapter.) Thus 4,000 bytes of memory are needed to represent the 2,000 characters on the screen.

The monochrome memory starts at address B0000 (hex) and goes up to B0F9F (F9F hex is 3999 decimal). Figure 10-11 shows the relationship between this memory and the display.

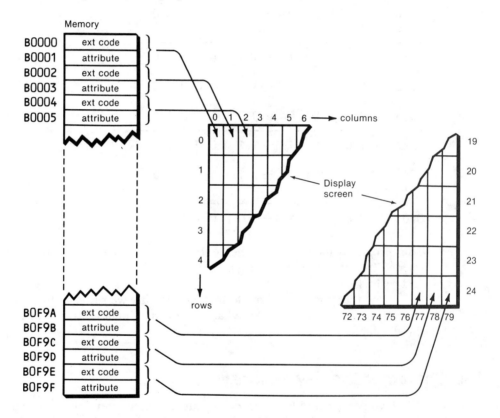

Figure 10-11. The Monochrome Display and MA Memory

If you have a color monitor attached to your computer and are using it for your text display, the text display memory occupies a different set of addresses. It starts at B8000 and runs up to B8F9F. Thus you should translate references to address B0000 in the text to address B8000.

When we call a C library routine to display a character on the screen it calls a routine in ROM BIOS. The ROM BIOS routine puts the character on the screen by placing the values for the character's extended code and attribute byte in the appropriate address in the adaptor's memory. But we can take a shortcut. If our program inserts values for these bytes directly into memory, we can save a lot of time, because (among other reasons) we eliminate the overhead of calling one routine which calls another routine.

## *Far* Pointers

When we know the address, the usual way we insert values into memory is to make use of pointers. Thus, you might expect that to place a character in the first location of the screen memory we might use statements such as the following:

```
int *ptr;            /* looks plausible */
- - - -
ptr = 0xB0000;       /* but */
- - - -
*(ptr) = ch;         /* won't work */
```

We first declare a pointer-to-int. We want to point to integers so we can treat the two-byte combination of extended character code and attribute together. We then set this pointer equal to the address of screen memory. Finally, we access this location using the indirection operator.

Unfortunately, we've made a mistake: the normal pointer variable type (no matter what data type it points to) consists of a *two*-byte quantity, while the address B0000 hex is a *two and one-half* byte (5-digit) number. No matter how hard we try, we can't cram this number into two bytes.

### Segments

The reason for this embarrassing situation is that normal pointers are used to contain addresses in only one *segment.* In the 8086 family of microprocessors (the 8088, 8086, 80286, and 80386) a segment is a section of memory containing 10000 (hex), or 65,536 (decimal) bytes. Within the segment, addresses run from 0 to FFFF hex. Ordinarily (at least in the small memory model, which we are using in this book) all the data in a C program is located in one segment. Thus, the normal two-byte pointer works perfectly in most situations. To access addresses outside the segment, however, a different scheme must be used.

Internally, the 8086 handles this situation with a special set of registers called "segment registers." Addresses outside a segment are formed by combining the starting address of a segment, called the "segment address," with the address within the segment, called the "offset address." The starting address of the segment is placed in a segment register.

As an example, let's take an address half-way through the monochrome memory. This is the 1,000th character, which is 2,000 decimal bytes or 7d0 hex. The segment containing the monochrome memory can be assumed to start at the same place the memory starts: at address B0000. The segment register holds only the top four of these digits, or B000. This arrangement is shown in Figure 10-12.

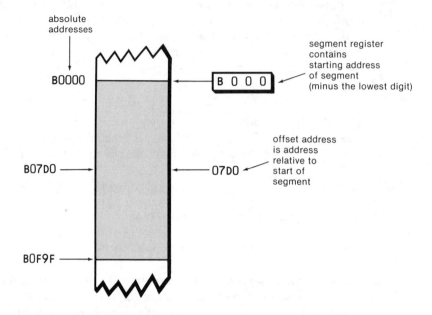

Figure 10-12. Segment Register and Video Memory

To obtain the absolute address, the address in the segment register is combined with the offset address. This combination takes place in a strange way; in effect, the contents of the segment register are shifted left four bits and then added to the offset address. Figure 10-13 shows how this looks in the case of the address in the middle of the display memory.

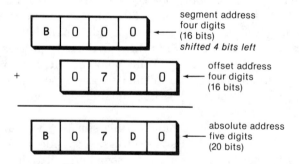

Figure 10-13. Combining Segment and Offset Addresses

In Figure 10-13 the segment address, B000, is shifted left four bits and then added to the offset address, 07D0. The result is the real—or absolute—memory address, B07D0.

In the microprocessor the absolute address is obtained by shifting the segment address left four bits and then adding the offset address.

### Using Segment-Offset Addresses in C

In C, an address that is outside of the program's normal data segment also makes use of this segment-plus-offset combination. However, the address is represented slightly differently. Instead of using the absolute address, C requires a 32-bit (four-byte, 8-hex digits) representation consisting of the four digits of the segment address followed by the four digits of the offset address. Thus, in C, the absolute address B07D0 is rendered as 0xB00007D0 (B000 followed by 07D0).

In C, 32-bit pointers are calculated by shifting the segment address left 16 bits and then adding the offset address.

Since a normal pointer can't hold these 32-bit addresses, how do we make use of them? There are several approaches. One is to use the large memory model. This approach, which is intended to accommodate programs that use more data than can fit in a single segment, automatically makes all data references using the segment-offset combination. (We'll have more to say about memory models in Chapter 14). In this model all pointers become four-byte quantities, rather than two-byte. The disadvantage of the large memory model is that references to *all* data now will be made with four-byte pointers. This is inefficient, since it takes the computer longer to access memory using a four-byte pointer.

A better approach is to use the small memory model but to declare a **far** pointer specifically in those cases when we need to point outside the normal data segment. A **far** pointer is one that holds a four-byte address, rather than the usual two-byte address. Thus it can hold the segment-offset combination. We declare a far pointer by inserting the **far** keyword just before the variable name. Our skeleton program can thus be rewritten like this:

```
int far *ptr;          /* declares far pointer */
- - - -
ptr = 0xB0000000;      /* segment B000 plus offset 0000 */
- - - -
*(ptr) = ch;           /* now this will work */
```

### Compiler Option: the far Keyword

If you're using version 4.0 of the Microsoft compiler you can skip this section. However, if you're using version 3.0, you'll need to give special instructions to the compiler so it will recognize the **far** keyword used in the declaration above. For the compiler to recognize **far**, an "option" must be used in the command line typed to invoke the compiler. An option adds a new capability to the compiler. The capability to recognize the **far** keyword (and several other keywords as well) is invoked with the characters "/Ze". Normally the compiler command line reads

```
msc prog;
```

With the option, the command line becomes

```
msc /Ze prog;
```

Or, if you're using a batch file to automate the compile-link cycle (see Chapter 1):

```
msc /Ze %1;
link %1;
```

Don't forget to use this option when using version 3.0 to compile any program that uses a far pointer. It's easy to forget to type the option, but if you do, the compiler will flood you with error messages.

### QuickC and the Video Memory

Because QuickC maintains a copy of the output screen, rather than using the real thing, it sometimes produces unexpected results when direct memory access and normal output using **printf()** and other library functions are mixed in the same program. For instance, if you clear the screen using direct access, then write to it with a library function; you may find the screen you're writing to hasn't been cleared after all.

The simplest way to avoid such problems is to compile all programs to .exe files before running them. Choose Exe from the Output Options list in the Compile option in the Run menu. Another ploy is to make sure all programs begin with a call to a library function such as **printf()** or **getch()**, even if it doesn't do much, *before* the video memory is accessed directly.

We suggest compiling the examples in this chapter to .exe files before running them.

### Filling the Screen with a Character

Let's use the far-pointer approach to fill the screen with 2,000 copies of a single character. To show how rapid this approach is, compared with using such C library routines as **putch**, we'll make it possible to change the character by pressing a key. Each time the user presses a new key, the entire screen is filled, almost instantaneously, with the new character. The program terminates when the user types an 'X'. Here's the listing:

```
/* dfill.c */
/* uses direct memory access to fill screen */
#define LENGTH 2000
main()
{
    int far *farptr;
```

```
    int addr;
    char ch;
    printf("Type character to start, type again to change");
    farptr = (int far *) 0xB0000000;
    while( (ch=getche()) != 'X' )
        for(addr=0; addr<LENGTH; addr++)
            *(farptr + addr) = ch | 0x0700;
}
```

Remember that if you are using a color monitor (either EGA or CGA) for text display, you should use the constant 0xB8000000 instead of 0xB0000000 in dfill.c, since the text memory of the color display occupies a different space in memory. This is true of all programs in this chapter that directly address the display memory; if you're using color, change the address.

This program uses a simple **for** loop, running from 0 to 2,000, to fill in all the memory addresses in the monochrome memory. The statement that does the job is

```
    *(farptr + addr) = ch | 0x0700;
```

This statement references each address in turn by adding the number **addr**, which runs from 0 to 1999, to the starting address of video memory, which we set **farptr** to before the loop.

On the right side of this assignment statement the variable **ch** is the character we want to place in memory; it was obtained from the keyboard. The constant 0x0700 is the attribute byte, shifted left one byte to place it on the left side of the two-byte (integer) quantity. This constant, 0x07, is the "normal" attribute; that is, the one that creates nonblinking, nonbold, white-on-black text. We'll see why soon.

Cycling through the loop 2,000 times inserts 2,000 integers in memory; the high byte of the integer being the extended character code and the low byte being the attribute.

Another statement that requires explanation is

```
    farptr = (int far *) 0xB0000000;
```

What is the expression in parentheses, and why is it necessary? The problem here is that the constant 0xB0000000 and the variable **farptr** are of different types: the constant looks like a long integer, while **farptr** is a far pointer to *int*. To avoid a warning from the compiler, we force the constant to be a far pointer to **int**, by preceding it with the name of the type in parentheses. This is another example of "typecasting," mentioned in Chapter 9.

The attribute byte also requires more explanation; we'll further investigate its format later in this chapter. First, however, let's make a small change to the program.

```
/* dfill2.c */
/* uses direct memory access to fill screen */
#define ROMAX 25
```

```
#define COMAX 80
main()
{
    int far *farptr;
    int col, row;
    char ch;
    printf("Type character to start, type again to change");
    farptr = (int far *) 0xB0000000;
    while( (ch=getche()) != 'X' )
        for(row=0; row<ROMAX; row++)
            for(col=0; col<COMAX; col++)
                *(farptr + row*COMAX + col) = ch | 0x0700;
}
```

In future programs we'll make use of functions that accept as input the row and column number of a character and then display the character on the screen at the appropriate place using direct memory access. This program shows how it's done. In the last line, the variables **row** and **col** represent the row and column number of the character to be inserted. The corresponding memory address is found by multiplying the row number by the number of columns in a row, then adding the result and the column number to the starting address of the monochrome memory in **farptr**. Since we are now imagining the screen as a two-dimensional entity of rows and columns (rather than a one-dimensional group of memory addresses), we use two nested loops to insert the characters.

### Speed Comparison

To get an idea of the speed advantage provided by direct memory access using **far** pointers, we'll rewrite dfill2.c to use the **putch()** library function. Here's the listing:

```
/* cfill.c */
/* uses putch() to fill screen */
#define ROMAX 25
#define COMAX 80
#define CLEAR "\x1B[2J"
main()
{
    int col, row;
    char ch;
    printf("Type character to start, type again to change");
    while( (ch=getche()) != 'X' )
        {
        printf(CLEAR);
        for(row=0; row<ROMAX; row++)
            for(col=0; col<COMAX; col++)
                putch(ch);
        }
}
```

This program also fills the screen with a single character, but, at least on our system, it takes about *20 times longer* than dfill2.c.

In Chapter 15 we'll see another way to speed up this program: the use of register variables.

## One-Line Word Processor

To see how **far** pointers might be used in a somewhat more useful situation than filling the screen with a single character, let's create a very simple word processing program—one that is so simple it operates on only a single line of text. We'll do this in two steps. First we'll show a program which allows the user to type in a line of characters and to move the cursor back and forth along the line. Any character can be erased by moving the cursor to it and typing over it. Later, when we've learned more about attributes, we'll show an improved model of the program that permits insertion, deletion, and underlining. (Again, remember that if you're using a color display you should use the address 0xB8000000; for the monochrome display, use 0xB0000000.)

Here's the first version:

```
/* wpro1.c */
/* rudimentary word-processing program */
/* with delete, insert and underlining */
#include <stdio.h>              /* for printf() */
#include <conio.h>             /* for getch() */
#include <dos.h>               /* for int86(), REGS definition */

#define VIDEO_ADDR 0xB8000000  /* start of video memory */
#define TRUE 1
#define COMAX 80               /* max number of columns */
#define R_ARRO 77              /* right arrow */
#define L_ARRO 75              /* left arrow */
#define VIDEO 0x10             /* video ROM BIOS service */
char col=0;                    /* cursor position */
int far *farptr;               /* pointer to video memory */
union REGS regs;               /* for ROM BIOS calls */
void cursor(void);             /* prototypes */
void insert(int);
void clear(void);

void main(void)
{
    int ch;                          /* keyboard key */

    farptr = (int far *)VIDEO_ADDR;  /* start of screen mem */
    clear();                         /* clear screen */
    cursor();                        /* position cursor */
    while(TRUE)
        {
        if( (ch=getch()) == 0 )      /* if char is 0 */
            {
            ch = getch();            /* read extended code */
```

```
        switch(ch)
          {
          case R_ARRO: if(col<COMAX) ++col; break;
          case L_ARRO: if(col>0)     --col; break;
          }
        }
    else                              /* not extended code */
        if(col<COMAX) insert(ch);     /* print char at col */
    cursor();                         /* reset cursor */
    }
}

/* cursor() */
/* move cursor to row=0, col */
void cursor(void)
{
    regs.h.ah = 2;                    /* 'set cursor pos' service */
    regs.h.dl = col;                  /* column varies */
    regs.h.dh = 0;                    /* always top row */
    regs.h.bh = 0;                    /* page zero */
    int86(VIDEO, &regs, &regs);       /* call video interrupt */
}

/* insert() */
/* inserts character at cursor position */
void insert(int ch)
{
    int j;

    *(farptr + col) = ch | 0x0700;    /* insert char */
    ++col;                            /* move cursor right */
}

/* clear() */
/* clears screen using direct memory access */
void clear(void)
{
    int j;

    for(j=0; j<2000; j++)             /* fill screen memory */
        *(farptr + j) = 0x0720;       /* with spaces (attr=07) */
}
```

Almost everything in this program should already be familiar to you. The program first clears the screen, using a routine that fills the screen memory with 0s; this is the same approach we used to fill the screen with a character in dfill.c. Then the cursor is moved to the beginning of the single line (the top line of the screen) using the "Set cursor position" video ROM BIOS service, which we described in Exercise 4 in Chapter 9.

| | |
|---|---|
| ROM BIOS routine: | Position cursor |
| Interrupt 10 hex: | Video |
| Input registers: | AH = 02 |
| | DH = row number |
| | DL = column number |
| | BH = page number (usually 0) |
| Output registers: | none |

The **switch** statement approach to deciphering the cursor keys was used in Chapter 8. Pressing the appropriate cursor key increments or decrements the variable **col**, which indicates the column the cursor is on. A call to the **cursor()** function moves the cursor to this column.

If the character typed is not an extended character (namely a cursor key) it is inserted into the display at column **col** using the insert() subroutine, which should be familiar from the discussion of far pointers above. The **col** variable is incremented when a character is inserted so that the next character will be typed just to its right.

Now it's time to explore the oft-postponed subject of the attribute byte.

## The Attribute Byte

As we've noted before, the location in the monochrome memory corresponding to a single character position on the screen consists of two bytes: one to hold the extended code of the character, the other to hold its attribute. In Chapter 8 we discussed the attributes: underline, intensified, blinking, and reverse video. How do these relate to the attribute byte?

Figure 10-14 shows how the attribute byte is divided into sections. Two of these sections consist of a single bit. Bit 3 controls intensity, and bit 7 controls blinking. If one of these bits is set to 1, the corresponding attribute (blinking or intensified) is turned on; when the bit is set to 0, the attribute is off.

The two other sections of the attribute byte consist of three bits each. Bits 0, 1, and 2 make up the "foreground color," while bits 4, 5, and 6 make up the "background color." (Of course in the monochrome display there is no color, but the same attribute byte format is used in the color display.) There are three choices for the monochrome display foreground color: black, white (really green or amber, depending on your display), and underline. The underline attribute is treated as a color, for some reason. For the background there are only two color choices: black or white. Figure 10-14 shows the four meaningful ways these "colors" can be combined, yielding nondisplay (invisible), underline, normal video (white on black), and reverse video (black on white).

Here's a revision of our dfill2.c program that fills the screen with charac-

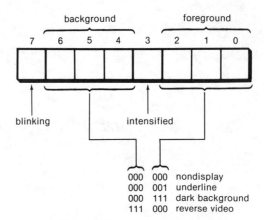

Figure 10-14. The Attribute Byte

ters all having the blinking attribute. The operating system won't reset the attribute bytes to normal when the program is done, so to make the screen stop blinking you'll need to use the DOS command CLS, which does reset the attribute bytes.

```
/* dfill3.c */
/* fills screen using blinking attribute */
#define ROMAX 25
#define COMAX 80
main()
{
    int far *farptr;
    int col, row;
    char ch;
    printf("Type character to start, type again to change");
    farptr = (int far *) 0xB0000000;
    while( (ch=getche()) != 'X' )
        {
        for(row=0; row<ROMAX; row++)
            for(col=0; col<COMAX; col++)
                *(farptr + row*COMAX + col) = ch | 0x8700;
        }
}
```

In the last program we used the attribute 07, which is 00000111 in binary. That is, the three bits of the foreground color are set to 1s, while everything else is a 0. To turn on blinking, we want to set bit 7 to 1, so we use the hex number 87, which is 10000111 in binary. This byte then is in effect shifted left eight bits, as described earlier, so it's on the left side of the integer which will be placed in memory.

## The Attribute Fill Program

To get a better idea of the attributes and how they interact, type in and compile the following program. This is a variation of dfill.c, but it includes a **switch** statement that permits different attributes to be selected when the screen is filled. Besides demonstrating the attribute byte, this program also provides a good example of the bitwise operators at work.

```
/* attrfill.c */
/* uses direct memory access to fill screen */
#define VIDEO_ADDR 0xB8000000    /* start of video memory */
#define ROMAX 25                 /* rows in display */
#define COMAX 80                 /* columns in display */
#define TRUE 1
void fill(char, char);           /* prototype */

main()
{
    char ch, attr;

    printf("Type 'n' for normal,\n");
    printf("     'u' for underlined,\n");
    printf("     'i' for intensified,\n");
    printf("     'b' for blinking,\n");
    printf("     'r' for reverse video,\n");
    while( (ch=getch()) != 'x')
       {
       switch (ch)
          {
          case 'n':
             attr = 0x07;         /* set to normal */
             break;               /* 0000 0111 */
          case 'u':
             attr = attr & 0x88;  /* set to underline */
             attr = attr | 0x01;  /* x000 x001 */
             break;
          case 'i':
             attr = attr ^ 0x08;  /* toggle intensified */
             break;               /* xxxx Txxx */
          case 'b':
             attr = attr ^ 0x80;  /* toggle blinking */
             break;               /* Txxx xxxx */
          case 'r':
             attr = attr & 0x88;  /* set to reverse */
             attr = attr | 0x70;  /* x111 x000 */
             break;
          }
       fill(ch,attr);
       }
}

/* fill() */
```

---

```
/* fills screen with character 'ch', attribute 'attr' */
void fill(char ch, char attr)
{
    int far *farptr;
    int col, row;

    farptr = (int far *)VIDEO_ADDR ;
    for(row=0; row<ROMAX; row++)
        for(col=0; col<COMAX; col++)
            *(farptr + row*COMAX + col) = ch | attr<<8;
}
```

When the screen is filled, using the **fill()** function, the variable **attr** is used for the attribute byte, rather than a constant as before. This value of **attr** is set by the various options in the **switch** statement.

Different options are handled in differing ways. Typing 'n' for normal always resets **attr** to 07 hex, which provides the standard attribute. The two one-bit attributes, blinking and intensified, can be toggled on and off, using the bitwise XOR operator on the appropriate bit. Reverse video and underline are set by masking off only the "color" attributes and resetting them without disturbing the one-bit attributes.

In previous programs we placed the attribute in an integer: 0x0700. Here we use a character for the attribute, so we need to shift it left one byte before combining it with the character **ch**. We do this using the left-shift ( << ) operator in the last statement in **fill()**.

A style note: for clarity we've written the bitwise operations as separate statements. To achieve compactness, however, they could have been combined, so that, for example, these lines

```
attr = attr & 0x88;   /* set to underline */
attr = attr | 0x01;   /* x000 x001 */
```

would become

```
attr = (attr & 0x88) | 0x01;
```

## Bit Fields

In the attrfill.c program we accessed individual bits and groups of bits using the bitwise operators. We can take an entirely different approach to accessing bits: the use of "bit fields." A bit field is a special kind of structure. Each of the members of such a structure occupies a certain number of bits. The number of bits each occupies is specified following a colon in the structure declaration. The members of the structure then are packed into an integer. The members must all be of type **unsigned int**. Here's an example of a bit-field declaration:

```
struct
    {
```

```
unsigned int twobits  : 2;   /* bits 0 and 1 */
unsigned int sixbits  : 6;   /* bits 2 through 7 */
unsigned int againsix : 6;   /* bits 8 through 13
unsigned int onebit   : 1;   /* bit 14 */
unsigned int extrabit : 1;   /* bit 15 */
} sample;
```

Figure 10-15 shows how the integer represented by this structure looks.

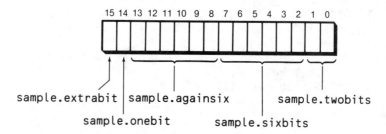

Figure 10-15. Bit Fields

Accessing the members of a field requires the same format as accessing members of other structures: the dot operator is used to connect the name of the structure variable with the name of the member, as in these examples:

```
sample.twobits = 3;
sample.sixbits = 63;
sample.onebit = 1;
```

Note that you can't give a field element a value that exceeds its capacity; a one-bit field can have only two values, 0 and 1, while a six-bit field can have values from 0 up to 63. Thus the values assigned above are all maximums.

The version of the attrfill.c program shown below uses bit fields to access the various parts of the attribute byte.

```
/* attrf2.c */
/* uses direct memory access to fill screen */
#define VIDEO_ADDR 0xB8000000    /* start of video memory */
#define ROMAX 25                 /* screen rows */
#define COMAX 80                 /* screen columns */
#define TRUE 1
void fill(char, unsigned int);   /* prototype */

main()
{
    struct
        {
        unsigned int foregnd : 3;   /* bits 0, 1, 2 */
        unsigned int intense : 1;   /* bit 3 */
```

```
              unsigned int backgnd : 3;    /* bits 4, 5, 6 */
              unsigned int blinker : 1;    /* bit 7 */
              } attr;

          char ch;
          unsigned int *ptrattr;  /* pointer to attr */

          printf("Type 'n' for normal,\n");
          printf("     'u' for underlined,\n");
          printf("     'i' for intensified,\n");
          printf("     'b' for blinking,\n");
          printf("     'r' for reverse video,\n");

          attr.intense = 0;                 /* initialize intensity */
          attr.blinker = 0;                 /*    and blinking */
          while( (ch=getch()) != 'x')
             {
             switch (ch)
                {
                case 'n':                /* set to normal */
                   attr.foregnd = 7;
                   attr.backgnd = 0;
                   break;
                case 'u':                /* set to underline */
                   attr.foregnd = 1;
                   break;
                case 'i':                /* toggle intensity */
                   attr.intense = (attr.intense==1) ? 0 : 1;
                   break;
                case 'b':                /* toggle blinking */
                   attr.blinker = (attr.blinker==1) ? 0 : 1;
                   break;
                case 'r':                /* set to reverse */
                   attr.foregnd = 0;
                   attr.backgnd = 7;
                   break;
                }
             ptrattr = (unsigned int *)&attr;  /* pointer to attr */
             fill(ch, *ptrattr);               /* contents is attr */
             }
       }

/* fill() */
/* fills screen with character 'ch', attribute 'attr' */
void fill(char ch, unsigned int attr)
{
   int far *farptr;
   int col, row;

   farptr = (int far *) VIDEO_ADDR;    /* point to video mem */
   for(row=0; row<ROMAX; row++)        /* down rows */
```

```
        for(col=0; col<COMAX; col++)      /* across columns */
          *(farptr + row*COMAX + col) = ch | attr<<8;
}
```

To set foreground and background colors, the appropriate fields are assigned the desired values. To toggle the blinking and intensity attributes, the conditional operator is used to assign values to the appropriate bits.

> Bit fields provide an organized approach to accessing individual bits and groups of bits.

Using fields probably gives a cleaner-looking approach, while the bitwise operators, which closely mirror the underlying assembly language instructions, are faster.

## Word Processing Revisited

Now that we know about attributes we can expand our rudimentary word processing program. We'll give it the capability to underline words. To start underlining, the user types the [Alt] [u] key combination; to stop underlining, the user repeats the combination.

In addition to adding underlining, we'll also give the program the capability to insert and delete characters. To insert a character, the user simply moves the cursor to the desired spot and starts typing. The characters to the right will be shifted further right to make room. To delete, the user hits the backspace key; this deletes the character to the left of the cursor. Any characters to the right will be shifted left to fill in the space.

Here's the listing:

```
/* wpro2.c */
/* rudimentary word-processing program */
/* with delete, insert and underlining */
#include <dos.h>          /* for int86() and REGS definition */
#include <conio.h>        /* for getch() */
#define VIDEO_ADDR 0xB8000000  /* start of video memory */
#define TRUE 1
#define COMAX 80          /* max number of columns */
#define R_ARRO 77         /* right arrow */
#define L_ARRO 75         /* left arrow */
#define BK_SPC 8          /* backspace */
#define ALT_U 22          /* [Alt] and [u] keys */
#define VIDEO 0x10        /* video ROM BIOS service */
#define NORM 0x07         /* normal attribute */
#define UNDR 0x01         /* underline attribute */
int col=0;                /* cursor position */
int length=0;             /* length of phrase */
```

```
int far *farptr;          /* pointer to video memory */
union REGS regs;          /* for ROM BIOS calls */
void cursor(void);        /* prototypes */
void insert(char, char);
void delete(void);
void clear(void);

void main(void)
{
    char ch, attr=NORM;
    farptr = (int far *)VIDEO_ADDR;   /* start of screen mem */
    clear();                          /* clear screen */
    cursor();                         /* position cursor */
    while(TRUE)
        {
        if ( (ch=getch()) == 0 )      /* if char is 0 */
            {
            ch = getch();             /* read extended code */
            switch(ch)
                {
                case R_ARRO: if(col<length) ++col; break;
                case L_ARRO: if(col>0)      --col; break;
                case ALT_U:
                    attr = (attr==NORM) ? UNDR : NORM;
                }
            }
        else
            switch(ch)
                {
                case BK_SPC: if(length>0) delete(); break;
                default: if(length<COMAX) insert(ch,attr);
                }
        cursor();
        }
}

/* cursor() */
/* move cursor to row=0, col */
void cursor(void)
{
    regs.h.ah = 2;                /* 'set cursor pos' service */
    regs.h.dl = col;              /* column varies */
    regs.h.dh = 0;                /* always top row */
    regs.h.bh = 0;                /* page zero */
    int86(VIDEO, &regs, &regs);  /* call video interrupt */
}

/* insert() */
/* inserts character at cursor position */
void insert(char ch, char attr)
{
```

```
    int j;
    for(j=length; j>col; j--)                /* shift chars left */
        *(farptr + j) = *(farptr + j - 1); /*    to make room */
    *(farptr + col) = ch | attr<<8 ;         /* insert char */
    ++length;                                /* increment count */
    ++col;                                   /* move cursor right */

}


/* delete() */
/* deletes character at position one left of cursor */
void delete(void)
{
    int j;
    for(j=col; j<=length; j++)               /* shift chars right */
        *(farptr + j - 1) = *(farptr + j);
    --length;                                /* decrement count */
    --col;                                   /* move cursor left */
}


/* clear() */
/* clears screen by inserting 0 at every location */
void clear(void)
{
    int j;
    for(j=0; j<2000; j++)                    /* fill screen memory */
        *(farptr + j) = 0x0700;              /* with 0's (attr=07) */
}
```

When the [Alt] [u] key combination is typed, the conditional expression at the end of the **switch** construct,

```
attr = (attr==NORM) ? UNDR : NORM;
```

toggles the **attr** variable back and forth between UNDR and NORM, which are the 07 (normal) and 01 (underline) attribute bytes.

The **insert()** function now sports a new **for** loop. This loop uses direct memory access and a **far** pointer to shift all the characters that are right of the cursor, one space to the right. This shifting process must start at the right-hand end of the existing phrase; if the shifting were to start on the left, the left-most character would overwrite the character next to it before it could be shifted. When all the characters have been shifted out of the way, the character typed by the user is inserted at the cursor position. Figure 10-16 shows this process.

Deletion is carried out in a similar way; all the characters to the right of the cursor are shifted left one space; the left-most character writes over the character to be deleted. In this case the shifting starts on the left-hand end.

This word processing program should give at least some idea of the possibilities of direct memory access.

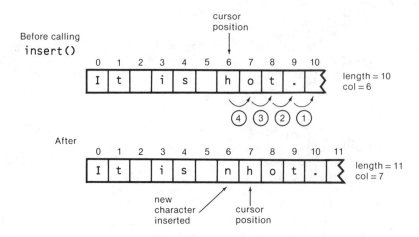

Figure 10-16. The *insert()* Function

# The Equipment List Word

Before we leave this chapter we should examine one other feature of the IBM computer: the equipment list word. This is a two-byte area in low memory—absolute address 410 hex—that contains information about the equipment connected to the computer. When the IBM is first turned on, the ROM BIOS startup routine examines the computer's various connectors to see what peripherals are in use and then sets the bits in this word accordingly.

This word can be useful in two ways. First, a program often needs to know if a certain piece of equipment is present. There's no use trying to print on the serial printer, for instance, if one isn't hooked up to the system. Second, as we'll see in Chapter 11, it's sometimes necessary to alter the settings in the equipment list word.

Figure 10-17 shows the layout of the equipment list word. To access the word, we use a **far** pointer, as we did with video memory. In this case, however, the pointer will point to segment 0000, offset address 0410 (hex), which is represented in C as 00000410 hex, or simply 0x410. (This same address could also be represented as segment 0040, offset 10, which is how it's shown in the ROM BIOS listings in the IBM *Technical Reference* manual.)

To examine the individual bits and groups of bits in the word, we'll use the bitwise operators (we could also have used fields). In general, we'll shift the equipment list word to the right, to put the bits we want on the right of the word, and then we'll mask any unwanted bits on the left with the bitwise AND operator.

In addition to the equipment list word, we also read a word that contains the size of installed memory in Kbytes. We showed earlier how to check the memory size using a ROM BIOS routine; accessing this word directly is another, probably slightly faster method.

The memory size word is located at absolute address 413 hex, so to access it we need to reset the variable **farptr** to point to this new address.

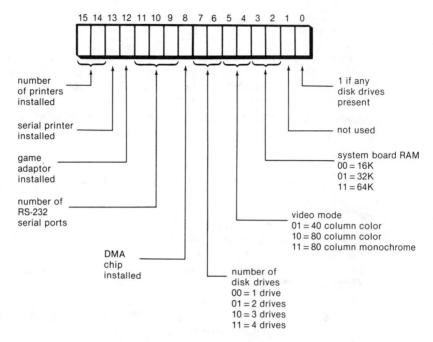

Figure 10-17. The Equipment List Word

Here's the listing:

```
/* eqlist.c */
/* lists equipment attached to computer */
#define EQLIST 0x410      /* location of equipment list word */
#define MEMSIZ 0x413      /* location of memory size word */
main()
{
    int far *farptr;
    unsigned int eq, data;
    farptr = (int far *) EQLIST;
    eq = *(farptr);
    data = eq >> 14;                  /* printers */
    printf("Number of printers is %d.\n", data);
    if(eq & 0x2000)                   /* serial printer */
        printf("Serial printer is present.\n");
    data = (eq >> 9) & 7;             /* serial ports */
    printf("Number of serial ports is %d.\n", data);
    if(eq & 1)                        /* diskette drives */
        {
        data = (eq >> 6) & 3;
        printf("Number of diskette drives is %d.\n", data+1);
        }
    else
        printf("No diskette drives attached.\n");
```

```
          data = (eq >> 4) & 3;                    /* video mode */
          switch (data)
             {
             case 1: printf("Video is 40 column color.\n"); break;
             case 2: printf("Video is 80 column color.\n"); break;
             case 3: printf("Video is 80 column monochrome.\n");
             }
          farptr = (int far *) MEMSIZ;  /* reset to mem size word */
          printf("Memory is %d Kbytes.\n", *(farptr) );
       }
```

And here's a sample run for a particular installation:

```
C>eqlist
Number of printers is 1.
Number of serial ports is 1.
Number of diskette drives is 2.
Video is 80 column monochrome.
Memory is 256 Kbytes.
```

There's a variety of useful words and bytes stored in the data area from 400 to 600 hex. To learn more about this area, you can consult the IBM *Technical Reference* manual or one of the books referred to in Appendix D.

## Summary

This chapter has focused on the character display and its relation to a special area of memory. We've learned that, for each character on the screen, there corresponds a two-byte area of memory: one byte to hold the extended ASCII character code, the other byte to hold the attribute. To help manipulate such hardware-oriented data as attribute bytes, we learned about the bitwise operators: AND, OR, XOR, left shift, right shift, and complement. We explored a simple one-line word processing program, and finally we saw how to access various areas in low memory, specifically the equipment list word, which tells what equipment is connected to the computer.

In the next chapter we'll put what we've learned here to use in investigating color graphics on the IBM.

## Questions

1. Express the following hexadecimal values in binary:

   a. 0x01

   b. 0xf8

   c. 0x1234

   d. 0xfc0a

2. Numbers are represented internally in the computer as

   a. decimal

   b. binary

   c. hexadecimal

   d. none of the above

3. True or false: the bitwise operators treat all variables as true or false values.

4. Which of the following will be true if bit 5 of the character variable **ch** is a 1?

   a. (ch & 8)

   b. (ch & 10)

   c. (ch & 20)

   d. (ch & 40)

5. The bitwise AND operator is often used to _____ off unwanted bits.

6. What does the expression (0xff ¦ 0x32) evaluate to?

   a. 0x32

   b. 0x00

   c. 0xff

   d. 0xcd

7. If **num** is of type **int**, what does (num >> 8) evaluate to when **num** has the value 0xf000?

   a. 0x000f

   b. 0x00f0

   c. 0xff00

   d. 0xfff0

8. The bitwise OR operator is often used to _____ different bits in different variables.

9. The 8086 family of chips uses a combination of two addresses to access data outside the normal segment. These addresses are called the _____ address and the _____ address.

10. A normal two-byte pointer cannot hold addresses outside a given segment because:

    a. it can't get through the segment barrier

    b. it isn't large enough

    c. it doesn't know where other segments are

    d. it's not a segment register

11. Before being added to the offset address, the value in the segment register is:

    a. shifted left four bits

    b. multiplied by 0x10

    c. converted to decimal

    d. complemented

12. When the segment address is combined with the offset address, the result is the _____ address.

13. A **far** pointer is a variable that can hold addresses _____ bytes long.

14. Suppose the segment address is A100 (hex) and the offset address is 1234 (hex). The resulting absolute address, expressed as a C **far** pointer constant, is

    a. 0xA1234

    b. 0xA234

    c. 0xA2234

    d. 0xA1001234

15. True or false: the following is a valid way to declare a **far** pointer:

```
char far *farptr;
```

16. One reason to use direct memory access to put characters on the screen, rather than going through C library routines, is to make the process _____.

17. The phrase "memory-mapped video" means that:

    a. the program must remember what it drew on the display.

    b. for each location on the screen there corresponds a location in memory.

    c. the display is usually used for drawing maps.

    d. display characters are mapped from ROM.

18. True or false: the following is a valid way to assign a value to a **far** pointer:

    ```
    farptr = 0xA1001234;
    ```

19. To use **far** pointers in a program it is necessary to
    a. know the address of the segment to be used
    b. use a compiler option (in 3.0) that permits the **far** keyword
    c. know the offset address of the data
    d. use the indirection operator

20. True or false: the following is a valid way to access the memory location pointed to by a **far** pointer:

    ```
    value = *(farptr);
    ```

21. The attribute byte is located
    a. in low memory
    b. at the beginning of each segment
    c. after each character
    d. in the display memory

22. The intensity and blinking attributes are controlled by individual _____ in the attribute byte, while the foreground and background "colors" are controlled by _____.

23. Bit fields provide a way to
    a. access individual bits
    b. simplify access to arrays of data
    c. access groups of bits
    d. modify bits

24. The monochrome screen memory starts at absolute memory address _____ (hex) and ends at _____ (hex).

25. The equipment list word provides information about
    a. the video display
    b. the diskette drive
    c. serial and parallel printers
    d. serial ports

## Exercises

1. Write a program that resembles ortest.c but which allows the user to play with the XOR bitwise operator rather than the OR bitwise operator.

2. Write a program that will allow the user to type a binary number (up to 16 1s and 0s) and that will then convert this number into both hexadecimal and decimal.

3. Write a program that in operation resembles the draw.c program from Chapter 8, which draws lines on the screen in response to the user pressing the cursor keys. But instead of using the ANSI.SYS codes to place each character, use direct access to the display memory (a **far** pointer). Note: when the character being placed on the screen is one of the extended character set (such as the cursor keys), a problem may arise because the character will be interpreted as being negative. Use bitwise operators to remove the offending bits.

4. Add a function to the wpro2.c word processing program that will permit the user to erase an entire word at once, using the [Ctrl] and backspace keys pressed together (127 decimal). All characters to the left of the cursor, up to the first space character, should be deleted. If the first word in the line is to be deleted, the cursor should end up in column 0.

# Direct-Access Color Graphics

- Graphics modes
- ROM BIOS graphics routines
- Direct access to graphics memory
- CGA graphics modes
- EGA bit-plane graphics
- VGA 256 color mode

# 11

The ability to draw pictures—in color, in a few seconds—is one of the most fascinating capabilities of modern computers. Graphics can be used in almost any computer program; graphs can help the user make sense of the numbers produced in spreadsheet or database programs, most games rely heavily on graphics, and entire operating systems are now using graphics-oriented user interfaces. The chances are that the program you're writing could profit from graphics too.

In this and the next chapter we'll show how a C programmer can produce graphics images on the IBM family of computers. This chapter explores the direct approach: using ROM BIOS routines and direct access to the video memory. These techniques are the fastest and most flexible. They will also work (with some variations) with C compilers other than Microsoft C, and they teach you the most about using C and about the computer itself. In the next chapter we'll look at the special-purpose functions Microsoft C makes available for graphics.

The first part of this chapter is applicable to the Color Graphics Adaptor (CGA), the Enhanced Graphics Adaptor (EGA), and the Video Graphics Array (VGA), so no matter which board you have you'll be able to follow what we're doing. In the second part of the chapter we'll explore some capabilities of EGA and VGA systems that are not shared by the CGA.

## Modes

Just as an artist can choose from a variety of media when creating a picture (oils, etching, watercolors, collage, and so forth), so an IBM graphics programmer can choose from a variety of modes, or formats. Each mode provides a different combination of graphics characteristics. These characteristics include the resolution, the number of possible colors, whether text or graphics are to be displayed, and other elements. Each mode requires certain hardware (monitors and adaptor boards) and programming approaches. This can be confusing for some-one new to graphics, so in this section we'll briefly discuss the various graphics elements and how they come together to make up each of the modes.

In the following section we'll show how to change to the desired mode, and then we'll get down to the business at hand: putting pixels on the screen.

Table 11-1 summarizes the available modes and the graphics characteristics of each one. We'll explain the elements of this table in the following sections.

### Table 11-1. IBM Color Graphics Modes

| Mode (dec) | Colors | Resolution | Adaptor | Monitor | Minimum Memory | Pages | Starting Address |
|---|---|---|---|---|---|---|---|
| 0 text | 16 grey | 40x25* | CGA | CD | 2K | 8 (16K) | B8000 |
| 1 text | 16 | 40x25* | CGA | CD | 2K | 8 (16K) | B8000 |
| 2 text | 16 grey | 80x25* | CGA | CD | 4K | 4 (16K) | B8000 |
| 3 text | 16 | 80x25* | CGA | CD | 4K | 4 (16K) | B8000 |
| 4 grph | 4 | 320x200 | CGA | CD | 16K | 1 (16K) | B8000 |
| 5 grph | 4 grey | 320x200 | CGA | CD | 16K | 1 (16K) | B8000 |
| 6 grph | 2 (B&W) | 640x200 | CGA | CD | 16K | 1 (16K) | B8000 |
| 7 text | 2 (B&W) | 80x25* | MA | MD | 4K | 1 (4K) | B0000 |

Modes 8, 9, and 10 are for the PC jr.
Modes 11 and 12 are used internally by the EGA board.

| Mode (dec) | Colors | Resolution | Adaptor | Monitor | Minimum Memory | Pages | Starting Address |
|---|---|---|---|---|---|---|---|
| 13 grph | 16 | 320x200 | EGA | ECD | 32K | 2 (64K) | A0000 |
| 14 grph | 16 | 640x200 | EGA | ECD | 64K | 1 (64K) | A0000 |
| 15 grph | 2 (B&W) | 640x350 | EGA | ECD | 64K | 1 (64K) | A0000 |
| 16 grph | 16 | 640x350 | EGA | ECD | 128K | 1(128K) | A0000 |
| 17 grph | 2 (B&W) | 640x480 | VGA | VD | 64K | 4(256K) | A0000 |
| 18 grph | 16 | 640x480 | VGA | VD | 256K | 1(256K) | A0000 |
| 19 grph | 256 | 320x200 | VGA | VD | 64K | 4(256K) | A0000 |

*Characters. Other resolutions in pixels

grph = graphics
MD = Monochrome Display
CD = Color Display
ECD = Enhanced Color Display
VD = VGA Display
MA = Monochrome Adaptor
CGA = Color Graphics Adaptor
EGA = Enhanced Graphics Adaptor
VGA = Video Graphics Array

## Resolution

Graphics images on a computer screen are composed of tiny dots called pixels, for "picture elements." (For some reason, IBM calls them "pels," but we'll stick with the more common term.) Pixels are arranged on the screen in horizontal rows;

there are a fixed number of rows and each row contains a certain number of pixels. The number of pixels used on the screen is called the "resolution." Each graphics mode uses a particular resolution: for example, mode 4 uses a resolution of 200 rows, each 350 pixels across. This is abbreviated 350 by 200, or 350x200.

In general, the higher the resolution, the more pleasing the picture. Higher resolution means a sharper, clearer picture, with less pronounced "jaggies" (the stairstep effect on diagonal lines). On the other hand, higher resolution also requires more memory for the display.

Each pixel can appear in a variety of colors (assuming the correct mode is set and the correct hardware is available). The arrangement of pixels on the screen is shown in Figure 11-1.

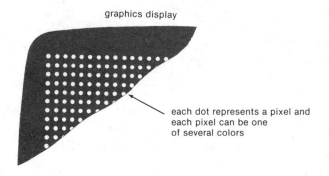

Figure 11-1. Graphic Images Are Made from Pixels

## Text or Graphics

Some modes exist only to place text on the color screen, others are made for graphics.

In the graphics modes, each bit, or each group of bits, corresponds to a particular pixel on the screen. In the text modes, as we saw in Chapter 9, a group of bits (actually two bytes) corresponds to a character. In this chapter we'll be concentrating on the graphics modes; we covered many of the basic aspects of the text modes in Chapters 9 and 10.

## Color

Some graphics modes permit more colors than others. Several modes permit only 2 colors: black and white (or perhaps black and green or amber, depending on your monitor). Other modes permit 4 colors, 16 colors, or 256 colors.

The situation is actually slightly more complicated than this. For example, a particular mode may allow only four colors, but it may be possible to switch to a second group of four colors (although the second group cannot appear on the screen at the same time as the first). These groups of colors are called "palettes."

## Display Monitors

IBM currently makes available several different types of monitors or display devices. (Don't confuse these with graphics adaptors, which we'll cover in the next section.) You're probably already familiar with the monochrome display (MD), the standard monitor used to output text on the majority of IBMs sold. A color monitor was also introduced along with the IBM PC. It was called, appropriately, the Color Display (CD). This display provided a maximum resolution of 640x200 pixels (that is, 640 pixels across and 200 rows). Later IBM introduced a third monitor, the Enhanced Color Display (ECD). This monitor allows for an increased resolution of 640x350 pixels. More recently several new monitors were introduced with the PS/2 series to display VGA graphics. A multisync monitor will display all the modes, from CGA to VGA.

Not all monitors can be used in all modes. The older CD cannot be used with modes 15 and 16, for example, since it lacks the ability to display 350 lines; and the MD can only be used in mode 7, since it is normally a text-only display.

Of course, other vendors besides IBM make monitors that can be used with the IBM family of computers. Any suitable monitor can be connected to the IBM and may work just as well (or in some cases, better) than the IBM products.

## The Display Adaptor

Except for the PS/2 series, IBM computers and clones do not come with the ability to send the signals necessary to produce images on a display screen. To do this, a printed circuit board called a "graphics adaptor" must be plugged into one of the slots inside the computer. A monitor is usually matched with the appropriate display adaptor. The MD display goes with the MA (Monochrome Adaptor), the CD monitor requires a CGA (Color Graphics Adaptor), the ECD display matches the EGA (Enhanced Graphics Adaptor), and VGA monitors require the VGA (Video Graphics Array) adaptor.

Each graphics adaptor can emulate the features of the less powerful adaptors. That is, the VGA can create all the CGA and EGA modes, and the EGA can create all the CGA modes.

VGA capability is built into PS/2 machines, but a VGA adaptor can be purchased as a separate item for PC and AT class computers.

## Display Memory

As we saw in Chapter 10, one of the key elements on any of the graphics adaptors is *memory*. This random-access memory is similar to that in the computer, except that data placed in it causes an immediate change in the picture on the monitor.

The different display adaptors come with differing amounts of memory. The monochrome adaptor has only 4K, enough for two bytes for each of 2,000 characters (80 columns times 25 rows). The CGA has more memory: 16K. This is enough for 640x200 pixels if only two colors are used. In this case, each bit in memory corresponds to one pixel. We get the figure 16K by finding the total number of pixels: 640 times 200 is 128,000 pixels. Then, since each pixel corresponds to one bit, we divide by 8 bits per byte to arrive at 16,000 bytes (this is actually slightly less that 16K, which is 16,384 bytes).

If the resolution is cut in half, to 320x200, we can now use two bits for each pixel, and two bits can represent four colors. This is another mode available on the CGA.

The EGA by contrast comes standard with 64K of memory. This allows 16 colors with a resolution of 640x200. (We can verify this by doing the arithmetic as shown above, remembering that 16 colors requires four bits per pixel.)

Additional memory can also be added to the EGA to provide a total of either 128K or 256K. If 128K is available, another mode becomes possible: 640x350 with 16 colors. (Extending the memory to 256K makes possible additional *pages*, a feature we describe below.)

The following table summarizes the amount of memory necessary to support different numbers of colors at different resolutions:

| Resolution | Colors | | | |
|---|---|---|---|---|
| | 2 | 4 | 16 | 256 |
| 320x200 | 8K | 16K | 32K | 64K |
| 640x200 | 16K | 32K | 64K | 128K |
| 640x350 | 32K | 64K | 128K | 256K |
| 640x480 | 64K | 128K | 256K | 512K |

## Pages

When enough graphics memory is available in the adaptor, it's possible to keep several screensfull of data in the memory at the same time. Thus, on the EGA board, mode 13 (320x200, 16 colors) requires only 32K, but 64K is available. The extra memory can be used to hold a second screen image (page). By switching from one page to another, very rapid changes can be made to the image on the screen.

## Starting Address

As with other parts of RAM, a memory location in a graphics adaptor card is identified by its address. We've already learned that the monochrome memory starts at absolute address B0000. The memory in the color adaptors starts at different addresses, depending on the mode. In the CGA modes (modes 0 to 6) it starts at B8000, and in the EGA- and VGA-only modes (13 to 19) it starts at A0000. These addresses are important if we want to access the display memory directly from our program.

## Summarizing the Modes

Mode 7 is the normal monochrome mode, used with the monochrome display and the monochrome adaptor.

Modes 0, 2, and 5 are called "color suppressed" modes; they generate images in shades of grey for use on monitors that display graphics but not colors. We won't be concerned with these modes.

Modes 1 and 3 are the normal text modes for the color monitors, providing 25 lines of 40 characters or 25 lines of 80 characters, respectively. If you have only a color display, the operating system will automatically use one of these modes.

Modes 13 through 16 were added with the EGA, and provide increased resolution, additional colors, or both. Modes 15 and 16 require the ECD (or its equivalent from another vendor, such as a multisync monitor), which has special circuitry permitting 350 rows to be displayed. Mode 16 also requires 128K of memory on the EGA board, rather than the standard 64K.

Modes 17 through 19 were introduced with the VGA. Again they provide increased resolution and more colors. The VGA modes require a special display that uses analogue circuitry. You can also use many of the multisync monitors with these modes. The 640 by 480 modes are noteworthy in that they permit square pixels; we'll have more to say about this in the next chapter.

In this chapter we'll concentrate on mode 4, which is a four-color 320x200 mode available for the CGA, EGA, and VGA adaptors, and mode 13, which is available only on the EGA and VGA adaptors. These modes can be used regardless of the type of color monitor you have, and both can be used with a VGA graphics system. First, we need to know how to switch from one mode to another.

# Setting Modes

If you're using the monochrome monitor and the monochrome adaptor, when you first turn on your computer, it will boot up in mode 7. If you're using a color display with the CGA or EGA, you'll probably boot up in mode 3, a text-only mode. Neither of these modes permits you to do graphics. Even if you have both a color display and the monochrome display connected at the same time, it's likely you'll end up in mode 7; if you don't switch modes, your color screen will remain blank.

To draw graphics on the color screen, you'll need to know how to switch from mode 7 (or mode 3) to a graphics mode. Depending on the kind of equipment you're using, this either involves one or two steps.

## The Equipment Word

If you're already using a color monitor, with the CGA, EGA, or VGA adaptor as your primary display, then you don't have to worry too much about the equipment word (although you should read this section anyway, to understand the program that follows).

However, if you have both a monochrome display and a color display attached to your system, each with its own adaptor card, and the monochrome display is the primary display (the one that starts displaying operating system messages when you boot up your system), then you'll need to know about the equipment word and its role in changing modes.

Actually, we discussed the equipment word at the end of Chapter 10, where we took it apart to see what equipment was connected to the computer. Now we need to do more; we need to *modify* this word. Why? When the computer is first turned on, the operating system investigates its environment to see what equipment is connected. If it finds the monochrome adaptor plugged in (and if its switch settings show that this is the primary adaptor), it will route all display output to this adaptor, ignoring the color adaptor.

> Changing modes may involve telling the operating system which of several monitors to use.

There are several ways to convince the operating system that we want to send output to the color monitor. One way is for the user to type the command MODE from DOS. There are a number of graphics options for the MODE command: BW40, BW80, CO40, CO80, and MONO. Except for MONO, any of these options will cause the computer to switch to the color adaptor, but the BW commands will not allow a color display. (MONO will cause it to switch back to the monochrome adaptor.) Switching to a color graphics mode can be accomplished with either CO40 or CO80.

To use the MODE command, though, means that we must be human, not a program; and we must be in DOS. Usually, it is more convenient to have our program switch automatically to the desired display device, but to do this, we need a method other than the MODE command. The alternative is to modify the equipment word, and the program we're about to examine will do that for us. Before we look at the program, however, we need to examine the second step necessary for changing graphics modes.

## The ROM BIOS Set Mode Command

Once the operating system knows to which display device we want our output sent, we're in a position to select the mode. To do this we make use of a ROM BIOS routine called "Set Video Mode." This involves putting 0 in the AH register, the desired mode number in the AL register, and executing an interrupt number 10 (hex).

| | |
|---|---|
| ROM BIOS routine: | Set video mode |
| Interrupt 10 hex: | video |
| Input registers: | AH = 0 |
| | AL = mode number |
| Output registers: | none |

## The setmode.c Program

Here's the program that lets us switch graphics modes. It reads the command-line argument to know which mode we want. Thus, to switch to mode 4 from DOS, we would type

```
C>setmode 4
```

Here's the program:

```c
/* setmode.c */
/* sets graphics mode to value supplied */
#include "dos.h"              /* declares REGS */
#define SETMODE 0             /* "set video mode" service */
#define VIDEO 0x10            /* video BIOS interrupt number */
#define MASK 0xCF             /* mask for video bits in equip word */
main(argc,argv)
int argc;
char *argv[];
{
    union REGS regs;
    int mode;
    unsigned char far *farptr;   /* pointer to equip flag */
    unsigned char ch;
    unsigned char vidbits;        /* code for video card */
    if (argc != 2)
        {
        printf("Example usage: C>setmode 7");
        exit();
        }
    mode = atoi( argv[1] );      /* string to integer */
    if (mode == 7)               /* if mono display */
        vidbits = 0x30;          /* 00110000 mono card */
    else
        vidbits = 0x10;          /* 00010000 color, 40 columns */
    farptr = (int far *) 0x410; /* set pointer to address */
    ch = *(farptr);             /* get byte at address */
    ch = ch & MASK;             /* mask off video bits 11001111 */
    *(farptr) = ch | vidbits;   /* OR vidbits to eq flag */
    regs.h.al = (char)mode;     /* mode number in AL register */
    regs.h.ah = SETMODE;        /* service # in AH register */
    int86(VIDEO, &regs, &regs); /* call video interrupt */
}
```

There are two parts to this program. The first changes the appropriate bits in the equipment word to the value necessary to choose between the monochrome adaptor and the color adaptor. The bits that must be modified occupy positions 4 and 5 in the byte at absolute address 410 hex. To switch to mode 7 (the monochrome display), we turn both these bits on (put 1s in them). To use any of the other modes, all of which require the color adaptor, we turn the left bit off and the right bit on.

If you use a color monitor as your primary display device, you won't need to modify the equipment word, so you can simply delete this whole first part of the program.

In the second part of the program we call ROM BIOS interrupt 10 (hex) with the appropriate values in the AH and AL registers. This switches us into the mode specified in the command line.

Assuming you've got your color board (CGA or EGA) plugged in, and your color monitor connected, try out the program. Switch to mode 4 by typing

```
C>setmode 4
```

The A> or C> prompt should appear on the color display, but you won't see the flashing cursor: that's because the graphics modes don't support the cursor. Want to see the cursor? Switch to a text mode, say mode 3. There's the prompt with the cursor. Now switch back to mode 7; the monochrome screen will clear, and you'll see the prompt and the cursor. Notice that switching modes clears the screen. This can be a useful (though slow) way to clear the screen, either by using setmode.c or by calling the Set Mode ROM routine from within a program.

If you're using QuickC, you should compile all the example programs in this chapter to .exe files before running them. (Select Exe from the Output Options list in the Compile option in the Run menu.) You can't execute the examples from the QuickC environment because you need to set the mode immediately before running the program. So compile an .exe file, exit to DOS, change the mode with setmode.c, execute the example program, and then set the mode back to the appropriate text mode (probably mode 3).

## Displaying Pixels with ROM Routines

Now that we know something about graphics, and have a way to change to a graphics mode, we're finally ready to put some pixels on the screen.

The simplest way to display graphics images is to use a ROM routine called "Write Dot." The ROM routines for video displays are not especially fast, but they are easy to program. (We'll see how to speed things up later.)

The following program, cstripes.c, is designed for use with mode 4, which is available whether you're using the CGA or EGA adaptor. Before you execute this program you must use the setmode.c program developed in the last section to switch to mode 4.

The cstripes.c program draws four vertical stripes on the screen, each in a different color, as shown in Figure 11-2.

This program shows all the colors that can be displayed at one time in this mode. (Later we'll see how to double the number of colors by changing palettes.) Here's the listing:

```
/* cstripes.c */
/* fills CGA screen with 4 color bars. Use mode 4 (320x200) */
```

```
#include "dos.h"                        /* to declare REGS */
#define MAXR 200                        /* rows */
#define MAXC 320                        /* columns */
#define VIDEO 0x10                      /* video interrupt # */
#define WDOT 0x0C                       /* 'write dot' ROM BIOS */
main()
{
   union REGS regs;
   int row, col;
   for(row=0; row<MAXR; row++)
      for(col=0; col<MAXC; col++)
         {
         regs.h.ah = WDOT;              /* 'write dot' service */
         regs.x.dx = row;               /* row in DX */
         regs.x.cx = col;               /* column in CX */
         regs.h.al = col/80;            /* colr chng evry 80 rows */
         regs.h.bh = 0;                 /* page number */
         int86(VIDEO, &regs, &regs);    /* call video services */
         }
}
```

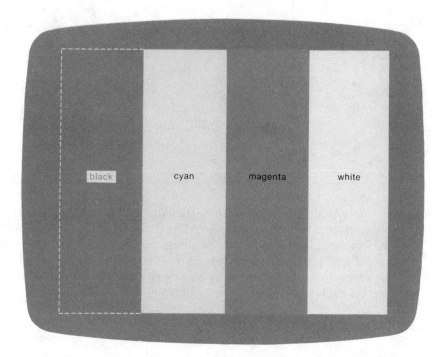

Figure 11-2. Output of the cstripes.c Program

This program consists of an inner **for** loop to draw each row (in this mode each row has 320 pixels) and an outer loop to step through the 200 rows. For each pixel the program calls interrupt 10, the video services interrupt. The AH register contains 12 (dec) to specify the ROM BIOS Write Dot service; DX and CX contain the row and column; BH contains the page number, which must be 0 in this mode; and AL contains the color. Set the graphics mode to 4 before running the program.

| | |
|---|---|
| ROM BIOS routine: | Write dot |
| Interrupt 10 hex: | video |
| Input registers: | AH = 0C hex |
| | CX = column number |
| | DX = row number |
| | AL = color |
| | BH = page number |
| Output registers: | none |

The normal or "default" set of colors in this mode is as follows:

| Palette 1 | |
|---|---|
| Number | Color |
| 0 | black |
| 1 | cyan |
| 2 | magenta |
| 3 | white |

To specify the color for a particular pixel we simply put the appropriate color number, from 0 to 3, in the AL register when calling the Write Dot ROM BIOS routine. In the cstripes.c program we want to create four vertical stripes, each of a different color. The column numbers (the variable **col**) run from 0 to 319, so we divide this number by 80 to arrive at color numbers that run from 0 to 3 across each row, using the statement:

```
regs.h.al = col/80;
```

This results in four vertical stripes being drawn. Since the first stripe is black, it will look as if nothing is being drawn in the left quarter of the screen.

We noted earlier that the Write Dot ROM BIOS routine is not too fast. How slow it is depends on which member of the IBM computer family you're using. On the slowest machine, a PC or XT running at 4.77 megahertz, it takes 40 seconds to generate the display in cstripes.c. We'll soon see how to speed this up.

## Drawing Rectangles

Now that we know how to put a dot on the screen we can create patterns other than stripes. The next program draws a series of concentric rectangles on the screen, as shown in Figure 11-3.

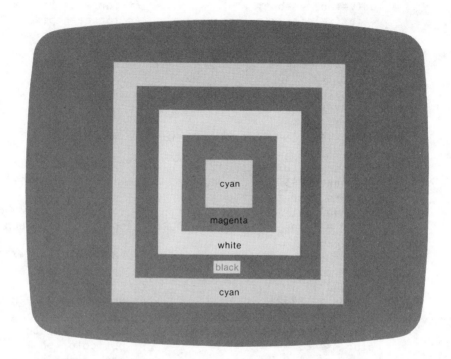

Figure 11-3. Output of the conrect.c Program

Here's the listing:

```
/* conrect.c */
/* draws concentric rectangle of different colors */
#define VIDEO_ADDR  0xB8000000    /* address of video memory */
void rect(int, int, int, int, unsigned char);  /* prototypes */
void putpt(int, int, unsigned char);

void main(void)
{
    int z;

    for(z=50; z>=10; z-=10)            /* do each rectangle */
        rect(100-z, 100+z, 160-z, 160+z, (z/10)%4);
}

/* rect() */
```

```
/* draws rectangle on screen using putpt() */
void rect(int top, int bot, int left, int rite,
                                       unsigned char color)
{
   int x, y;

   for(y=top; y<=bot; y++)              /* for each line */
      for(x=left; x<=rite; x++)         /* for each pixel */
         putpt(x,y,color);              /* color the pixel */
}

/* putpt() */
/* displays point at location col, row */
#define BYTES 40                        /* (bytes per row) / 2 */
#define PIX   4                         /* pixels per byte */
void putpt(int col, int row, unsigned char color)
{
   int addr, j, bitpos;
   int mask=0xFF3F;                     /* 11111111 00111111 */
   unsigned char temp;
   unsigned char far *farptr;           /* to hold screen address */
   farptr = (char far *)VIDEO_ADDR;     /* set ptr to screen addr */

   /* calculate offset address of byte to be altered */
   addr = row*BYTES + col/PIX;          /* calculate address */
   if(row & 1)                          /* if odd row number */
      addr += 8152;                     /* use 2nd memory bank */

   /* shift two-bit color & mask to appropriate place in byte */
   color <<= 6;                         /* put color on left */
   bitpos = col & 0x03;                 /* get lower 2 bits */
   for(j=0; j<bitpos; j++)              /* shift mask & color */
      {                                 /*    to right */
      mask >>= 2;                       /*    bitpos times */
      color >>= 2;
      }

   /* put two color bits in screen memory location */
   temp = *(farptr+addr) & (char)mask;  /* and off color bits */
   *(farptr+addr) = temp | color;       /* or on new color */
}
```

We've broken the program into three parts: a function **putpt()**, which uses the ROM BIOS routine to put a point on the screen; a function **rect()**, which draws a rectangle, given the column numbers of the left and right sides of the rectangle and the row numbers of the top and bottom; and the **main()** program, which calls the **rect()** routine five times, asking for a smaller rectangle each time. The variable **color** cycles repeatedly through the series 0, 1, 2, 3, as each new rectangle is drawn.

# Setting Color Palette and Background

As we've noted, we can choose a different set of four colors if we wish. Let's see how this is done.

In mode 4 there are two possible sets of colors or palettes. We've already seen the first one: black, cyan, magenta, and white. How do we switch to the second set? Once again, a ROM BIOS routine, this one called "Set Color Palette," does the job.

| | |
|---|---|
| ROM BIOS routine: | Set color palette |
| Interrupt 10 hex: | video |
| Input registers: | AH = 0B (hex) |
| | BH = 1 (to change palette) |
| | BL = palette number |
| Output registers: | none |

Here's a program that allows you to switch to any desired palette. Like setmode.c, it uses a command-line argument to specify the palette. Here's the listing:

```
/* setpal.c */
/* sets color palette to one of two values */
#include "dos.h"              /* declares REGS */
#define SETPAL 0x0B           /* "set color palette" service */
#define VIDEO 0x10            /* video BIOS interrupt number */
main(argc,argv)
int argc;
char *argv[];
{
   union REGS regs;
   int pal;                        /* palette number */
   if (argc != 2)
      {
      printf("Example usage: C>setpal 0");
      exit();
      }
   pal = atoi( argv[1] );       /* string to integer */
   regs.h.bh = 1;               /* BH=1 to set palette */
   regs.h.bl = pal;             /* palette # from user */
   regs.h.ah = SETPAL;          /* service # in AH register */
   int86(VIDEO, &regs, &regs);  /* call video interrupt */
}
```

To try out this program, first switch to mode 4, then run the conrect.c program.

This will give you a picture of concentric rectangles on the screen, in the default palette, which is number 1. Then switch to the second palette, type

```
C>setmode 4
C>conrect
C>setpal 0
```

Now you'll see the same pattern, but this time in the colors of the second palette.

|  | Palette 0 |
|---|---|
| *Number* | *Color* |
| 0 | black |
| 1 | green |
| 2 | red |
| 3 | brown |

The color black remains the same for both palettes; this is the background color—the color on the screen where nothing has been written.

## Changing the Background

Both the CGA and EGA adaptors are capable of generating 16 colors (in other modes the EGA can generate even more). Even in mode 4, which allows only 8 colors (two palettes of four colors each), we can see all 16 colors by changing the *background* color from black.

| | |
|---|---|
| ROM BIOS routine: | Set background |
| Interrupt 10 hex: | video |
| Input registers: | AH = 0B (hex) |
| | BH = 0 (to change background) |
| | BL = palette number |
| Output registers: | none |

Here's a program that uses a variation of the Set Color Palette ROM routine to change the background. We specify that we want to change the background by placing a 0 in the BH register instead of a 1, as we do for changing the palette.

```
/* setback.c */
/* sets color of background to one of 16 values */
#include "dos.h"        /* declares REGS */
```

```
#define SETPAL 0x0B        /* "set color palette" service */
#define VIDEO 0x10         /* video BIOS interrupt number */
main(argc,argv)
int argc;
char *argv[];
{
    union REGS regs;
    int pal;                     /* palette number */
    if (argc != 2)
        {
        printf("Example usage: C>setback 15");
        exit();
        }
    pal = atoi( argv[1] );       /* string to integer */
    regs.h.bh = 0;               /* BH=0 to set background */
    regs.h.bl = pal;             /* palette # from user */
    regs.h.ah = SETPAL;          /* service # in AH register */
    int86(VIDEO, &regs, &regs);  /* call video interrupt */
}
```

Now when you invoke this program in mode 4, you have a choice of 16 possible colors. Table 11-2 lists them.

### Table 11-2. Available Colors

| Num | Color | Num | Color |
|-----|-------|-----|-------|
| 0 | Black | 8 | Grey |
| 1 | Blue | 9 | Light blue |
| 2 | Green | 10 | Light green |
| 3 | Cyan | 11 | Light cyan |
| 4 | Red | 12 | Light red |
| 5 | Magenta | 13 | Light magenta |
| 6 | Brown | 14 | Yellow |
| 7 | White | 15 | Intense white |

You can use setback.c to experiment with colors. In graphics modes the background and the border both change to the color specified. In the text modes only the border (the area of the screen outside where printing can appear) changes. By changing the background color you can alter the effective color of the pixels you put on the screen, making all 16 colors available in mode 4, although not at the same time.

## Color Generation

Where do these 16 colors come from? The CGA, and the EGA in this mode, generate four signals that are sent to the display for each pixel. These signals are blue, green, red, and intensity.

These four signals can be combined in specific ways to produce the 16 colors shown in Table 11-2. First, any combination of blue, green, and red signals can be made to yield one of 8 colors. Then, if the intensity signal is added, 8 more colors (lighter versions of the first eight) are generated. Table 11-3 shows how the signals are combined to produce the colors. A 1 indicates that the signal is present and a 0 indicates it's not. Later we'll see how these combinations of signals can be represented as combinations of bits in the EGA-specific graphics modes.

### Table 11-3. Signal Combinations

| Num | Color | Components | | | |
|---|---|---|---|---|---|
| | | Intensity | Red | Green | Blue |
| 0 | Black | 0 | 0 | 0 | 0 |
| 1 | Blue | 0 | 0 | 0 | 1 |
| 2 | Green | 0 | 0 | 1 | 0 |
| 3 | Cyan | 0 | 0 | 1 | 1 |
| 4 | Red | 0 | 1 | 0 | 0 |
| 5 | Magenta | 0 | 1 | 0 | 1 |
| 6 | Brown | 0 | 1 | 1 | 0 |
| 7 | White | 0 | 1 | 1 | 1 |
| 8 | Grey | 1 | 0 | 0 | 0 |
| 9 | Light blue | 1 | 0 | 0 | 1 |
| 10 | Light green | 1 | 0 | 1 | 0 |
| 11 | Light cyan | 1 | 0 | 1 | 1 |
| 12 | Light red | 1 | 1 | 0 | 0 |
| 13 | Light magenta | 1 | 1 | 0 | 1 |
| 14 | Yellow | 1 | 1 | 1 | 0 |
| 15 | Intense white | 1 | 1 | 1 | 1 |

## Direct Memory Access and the Graphics Display

So far we've used ROM routines to put pixels on the screen. As we've noted, this is easy but slow. Now let's look at an alternative method that is harder to program, but that can have a significant speed advantage: direct memory access to the display memory. We've already explored this topic as it relates to the memory in the character display (see Chapter 10), so you should understand the fundamentals of the process. The difference is that we will be accessing bits representing pixels, rather than bytes representing characters.

### Memory Usage in Mode 4

Before we can manipulate the bits in the display adaptor's memory, we need to understand how these bits relate to the pixels on the screen.

In mode 4, two bits are used to represent each pixel, since there are four possible colors associated with the pixel. Figure 11-4 shows how these combinations look. Four of these two-bit combinations are placed in each byte of the screen memory, so that, for example, the top row of 320 pixels requires 320 divided by 4, or 80 bytes of memory.

| color | two-bit combination |
|---|---|
| 0 | 00 |
| 1 | 01 |
| 2 | 10 |
| 3 | 11 |

Figure 11-4. Two-Bit Combinations Used for Colors

There is an added complexity in the way the memory relates to the screen. The *even* rows of pixels go in one part of memory, while *odd* rows go in another. This scheme was designed to make the hardware more efficient, but it complicates life for the programmer. The part of the memory holding the even rows starts at B8000, while that for the odd rows starts at BA000. BA000 is B8000 plus 2000 hex; 2000 hex is 8192 decimal, and we need 8,000 decimal bytes to hold the information for all the even lines, since we have 80 bytes per row times 100 rows. We need another 8,000 bytes for odd lines.

> In CGA memory, the even scan lines occupy a different area of memory than the odd lines.

Figure 11-5 shows how pixels on the screen relate to the display memory. A two-bit combination represents each pixel, so each byte represents four pixels.

## Putting Bytes in Memory

For filling large patterns on the screen with color, it's more efficient to place whole bytes—each of which represents four pixels—in memory at once, rather than placing individual pixels. The following program imitates the behavior of the earlier cstripes.c program but operates more briskly: about 15 times faster. This speed increase is made possible by using direct memory access rather than a ROM routine and by putting four pixels on the screen at once, rather than one.

Here's the listing:

```
/* fstripes.c */
/* fills CGA screen with 4 color bars. Use mode 4 (320x200) */
/* uses direct memory access */
#define MAXR 200                    /* rows */
```

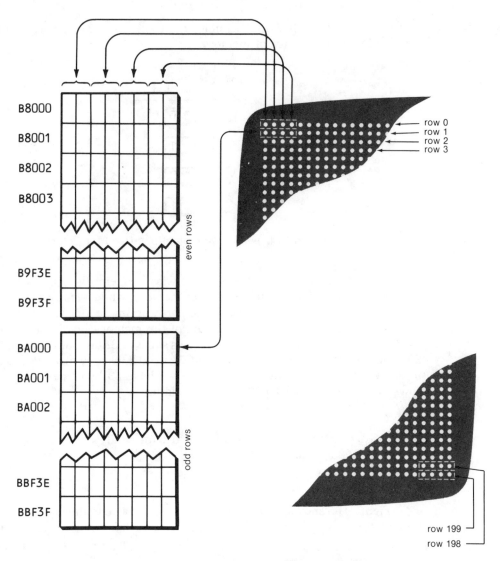

Figure 11-5. Memory Organization for Mode 4

```
#define MAXC 320                       /* columns */
#define MAXB (MAXC/4)                  /* bytes in a row (80) */
#define BPC (MAXB/4)                   /* bytes per color (20) */
char table[4] =
      { 0x00, 0x55, 0xAA, 0xFF };      /* color byte table */
main()
{
   char color, far *farptr;
   int addr, index, row, col;
   farptr = (int far *) 0xB8000000; /* set ptr to EGA mem */
   for(row=0; row<MAXR; row++)
```

```
     for (col=0; col<MAXB; col++)
        {
        index = (col/BPC) & 0x03;   /* colr chng evry 20 bytes */
        color = table[index];       /* get color pattern */
        addr = (row/2)*MAXB + col;  /* address of byte */
        if(row & 1)                 /* if odd row number */
            addr += (8192-40);      /* use second bank */
        *(farptr + addr) = color;   /* set 4 pixels */
        }
}
```

As in the cstripes.c, this program is built around two nested **for** loops; the inner loop moves across a row, while the outer loop steps down from row to row. There are several complexities in this program, though, that weren't present in cstripes.c.

First, because there are four pixels per byte, and we want to address each byte in turn rather than each pixel, the variable **col** actually counts across the 80 bytes in a row, rather than the 320 pixels. Thus, the limit in this loop is MAXB, the number of pixels in a row divided by the number of pixels in a byte.

The second complexity is that the program must calculate the memory address that corresponds to a particular group of four pixels. For even rows, this address will be the row number (the variable **row**) divided by 2 (since we're only counting the even rows) times the number of bytes per row, which is MAXB, all added to the column number (the number of bytes across). This is calculated in the line:

```
addr = (row/2)*MAXB + col;
```

For odd rows we must add a constant to this address. The constant is the number of bytes between B8000, where the section of memory for the even rows begins, and BA000, where the section of memory for the odd rows begins. This is 2000 hex, or 8,192 decimal. From this must be subtracted MAXB/2, because, although we're on row 1, for example, this is really row 0 in the second memory bank; the effect is the same as using row − 1.

The third complexity is to figure out what color information to place in each byte before inserting it in memory.

In the fstripes.c program all four pixels in each byte will be the same color, since the wide stripes we're drawing don't require fine detail. Thus, a byte can be configured in any of four possible ways, depending on the color being used. Each of these configurations can be represented by a hex number, as shown in Figure 11-6.

In fstripes.c these four bytes are stored in the array called **table**. The program selects which of these four representations to use by dividing the column number by the number of bytes to be devoted to each color stripe: in this case, MAXB divided by 4, or 20 bytes per stripe.

Finally, using a **far** pointer, the program inserts the correct byte into memory.

Try this program. You'll be amazed at the speed increase over cstripes.c.

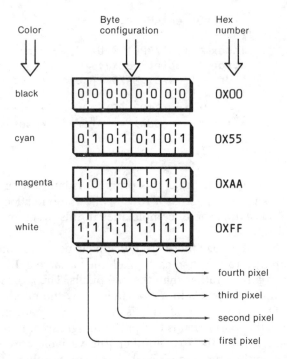

Figure 11-6. Hex Representations of Solid-Color Bytes

## Putting Single Pixels in Memory

Now that we know how to access a particular byte in the display memory, there is nothing to stop us getting at the individual bit-pairs that represent an individual pixel. This will give us the power to imitate the Write Dot ROM BIOS routine, using direct memory access. This is not only educational, in that it shows what Write Dot has to do to access a given pixel, it also provides us with a faster routine than Write Dot.

The following program uses a function called **putpt()** (for "put point") to emulate the operation of the Write Dot routine. To test this function, the main part of the program draws four lines, two diagonal—colored cyan and magenta—and one vertical and one horizontal—colored white—as shown in Figure 11-7.

Here's the listing:

```
/* diagline.c */
/* draws diagonal lines on screen using putpt() */
#define CYAN 0x01                    /* 2-bit patterns */
#define MAGENTA 0x02                 /* for CGA colors */
#define WHITE 0x03
void putpt(int, int, unsigned char);  /* prototype */
main()
{
    int x;
```

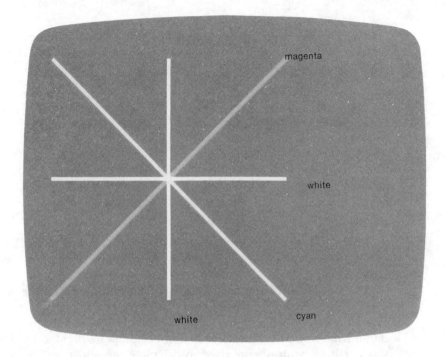

Figure 11-7. Output of the diagline.c Program

```
    for(x=0; x<200; x++)
        {
        putpt(x,x,CYAN);                    /* diagonal line */
        putpt(x,199-x,MAGENTA);             /* diagonal line */
        putpt(x,100,WHITE);                 /* horizontal line */
        putpt(100,x,WHITE);                 /* vertical line */
        }
}

/* putpt() */
/* displays point at location col, row */
#define BYTES 40                            /* (bytes per row) / 2 */
void putpt(int col, int row, unsigned char color)
{
    int addr, j, bitpos;
    int mask=0xFF3F;                        /* 11111111 00111111 */
    unsigned char temp;
    unsigned char far *farptr;              /* to hold screen address */
    farptr = (char far *) 0xB8000000;/* set ptr to screen addr */

    /* calculate offset address of byte to be altered */
    addr = row*BYTES + (col >> 2);   /* calculate address */
    if(row & 1)                             /* if odd row number */
        addr += 8152;                       /* use 2nd memory bank */
```

```
/* shift two-bit color & mask to appropriate place in byte */
color <<= 6;                      /* put color on left */
bitpos = col & 0x03;             /* get lower 2 bits */
for(j=0; j<bitpos; j++)          /* shift mask & color */
   {                             /*     to right */
   mask >>= 2;                   /*     bitpos times */
   color >>= 2;
   }

/* put two color bits in screen memory location */
temp = *(farptr+addr) & (char)mask; /* and off color bits */
*(farptr+addr) = temp | color;      /* or on new color */
}
```

In the following discussion we make extensive use of the bitwise operators. If you're hazy on these, you may want to review the appropriate section of
Chapter 10.

The **putpt()** function has three parts. First it must find the address of the
memory byte to be modified. This is handled in a way similar to that in the
fstripes.c program, except that the variable **col** now actually represents a pixel
location from 0 to 319. This column number must be divided by the number of
pixels per byte before being used to calculate the address. For example, if we
want to access a location on the screen 102 pixels from the left edge of the
screen, this is 102/4 or the 25th byte from the start of the row.

Actually, instead of dividing by 4, we shift the column number to the right
two bits, which has the same effect but is faster (since the shift instructions in
the microprocessor are faster than the division instructions). This approach also
emphasizes that the lower two bits of the column number have no effect on
which byte we're addressing.

The bitwise left-shift and right-shift operators have the same effect and are
faster than multiplying and dividing by powers of 2.

The second part of **putpt()** positions the two color bits correctly so that
they can be placed in the appropriate location within the byte whose address
we've just calculated. This is done by starting with these two color bits (which
are passed to **putpt()** from the calling program) on the left side of the byte, and
then shifting them right, as many times as is necessary to put them in the
appropriate place in the byte. The number of times to shift is determined by the
lower two bits of the column number: a value from 0 to 3, which is the position
of the two color bits in the byte. This is found in the statement

```
bitpos = col & 0x03;
```

Thus, if our column number is 102, by masking off all but the lower two bits, we retain only the 2, which is assigned to **bitpos**. Now we know not only the address of the byte being accessed, but the position in the byte of the two bits representing the pixel.

There may be a color other than black already on the screen when we want to put our pixel there. If this is true, it's important that we don't change the six other bits in the byte we're addressing, otherwise we'd erase the underlying color. For this reason, we must first read the byte, then AND off (remove) the two bits we want to change, leaving the other six unaltered; then OR on (insert) the two color bits. We use a mask to AND off the appropriate bits. To create the mask, we start with the constant 0xFF3F, which is 11111111-00111111 binary. We then shift this constant to the right the same number of times we shift the two color bits. (We use an integer so we can guarantee 1s will be shifted in on the left.)

The shifting of the color bits and the mask can take place in the same loop, since they're shifted the same number of times. Figure 11-8 shows this process where the color bits are 01 (cyan) and the last two bits of the column number are the number 2, meaning that we must shift the color bits and the mask to the right twice (shifting two bits each time).

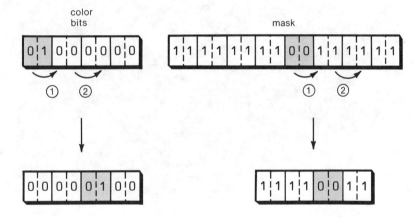

Figure 11-8. Shifting the Color Bits and Mask

Once we've got the color bits and the mask in the right place, we read the value of the byte from the video memory, AND it with the mask, OR on the color bits, and put it back into memory. This is the function of the statements in the third and final part of the program:

```
temp = *(farptr+addr) & (char)mask; /* AND off color bits */
*(farptr+addr) = temp | color;      /* OR on new color */
```

To prove that the **putpt()** function can write over other colors without disturbing them, run fstripes.c to put colored stripes on the screen, then run diagline.c to draw lines over it. You'll see that the colors in the background stripes remain undisturbed.

## The Bouncing Ball

Besides drawing rectangles and lines on the screen, we can also draw other shapes. And we can make these shapes appear to move, by drawing and redrawing them in different positions. In the following program we create a ball and set it in motion on the screen, at a 45-degree angle. Every time it hits the edge of the screen it reflects or "bounces," like a ball on a pool table, so it ends up traversing a complicated pattern, as shown in Figure 11-9.

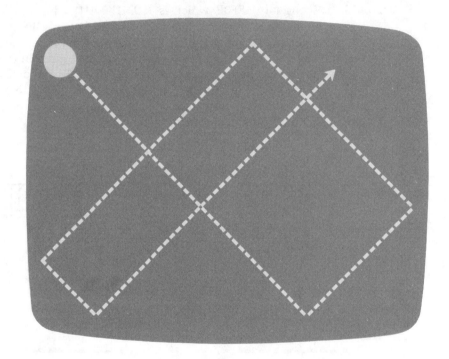

Figure 11-9. Bouncing Ball

```
/* bounce.c */
/* draws bouncing ball */
#define MAXC 320                        /* pixels per line */
#define MAXR 200                        /* lines */
#define RED 2                           /* 2-bit color value */
#define BLACK 0                         /* 2-bit color value */
void drawball(int, int, unsigned char); /* prototypes */
void putpt(int, int, unsigned char);

main()
{
    int x=10, y=10, dx=4, dy=4;

    while( kbhit()==0 )                 /* bounce until key */
```

```
            {
            drawball(x, y, BLACK);                /* erase old ball */
            x+=dx; y+=dy;                         /* move coordinates */
            if(x<10 || x>MAXC-20)  dx *= -1;      /* if at edge, */
            if(y<10 || y>MAXR-20)  dy *= -1;      /* change direction */
            drawball(x,y,RED);                    /* draw ball */
            }
   }

/* drawball() */
/* draws ball, radius 16 pixels. Upper-left corner at col, row */
void drawball(int col, int row, unsigned char color)
{
    unsigned int mask;
    int x, y, dotpat;
    static unsigned int ball[16] =              /* picture of ball */
                  { 0x07E0, 0x1FF8, 0x3FFC, 0x7FFE,
                    0x7FFE, 0xFFFF, 0xFFFF, 0xFFFF,
                    0xFFFF, 0xFFFF, 0xFFFF, 0x7FFE,
                    0x7FFE, 0x3FFC, 0x1FF8, 0x07E0 };
    for(y=0; y<16; y++)                     /* each of 16 rows */
        {
        dotpat = ball[y];                   /* pattern for this row */
        mask = 0x8000;                      /* one-bit mask on left */
        for(x=0; x<16; x++)                 /* each of 16 columns */
            {
            if(mask & dotpat)               /* if part of pattern */
                putpt(col+x, row+y, color); /* draw dot */
            mask >>= 1;                     /* move mask right */
            }
        }
}

/* putpt() */
/* displays point at location col, row */
#define BYTES 40                    /* (bytes per row) / 2 */
#define BANK 8192-BYTES             /* 2nd bank - one row */
void putpt(int col, int row, unsigned char color)
{
    int addr, j, bitpos;
    unsigned int mask=0xFF3F;              /* 11111111 00111111 */
    unsigned char temp;
    unsigned char far *farptr;            /* to hold screen address */
    farptr = (char far *) 0xB8000000;/* set ptr to screen addr */

    /* calculate offset address of byte to be altered */
    addr = row*BYTES + (col >> 2);   /* calculate address */
    if(row & 1)                      /* if odd row number */
        addr += BANK;                /* use 2nd memory bank */
    /* shift two-bit color & mask to appropriate place in byte */
    color <<= 6;                     /* put color on left */
```

```
    bitpos = col & 0x03;              /* get lower 2 bits */
    for(j=0; j<bitpos; j++)           /* shift mask & color */
       {                              /*    2 bits right */
       mask >>= 2;                    /*    bitpos times */
       color >>= 2;
       }
    /* put two color bits in screen memory location */
    temp = *(farptr+addr) & (char)mask;  /* AND off color bits */
    *(farptr+addr) = temp | color;       /* OR on new color */
}
```

This program uses the **putpt()** function from the last example. It also introduces a new function, **drawball()**. This function uses a pattern, consisting of an array of integers, to represent the ball. Each integer has 16 bits, and there are 16 integers, so this array can define a rectangular object of 16 by 16 pixels. The relationship between the hex numbers and the pattern is shown in Figure 11-10.

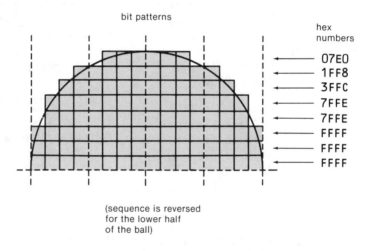

bit patterns

hex numbers

07E0
1FF8
3FFC
7FFE
7FFE
FFFF
FFFF
FFFF

(sequence is reversed
for the lower half
of the ball)

Figure 11-10. Hex Numbers Representing Ball

The **drawball()** function uses a **for** loop to go through each of the 16 integers in turn. For each number, an inner **for** loop uses a one-bit mask to test each bit of the pattern word. If the bit is on, a dot is written to the screen using **putpt()**. If it's not on, no bit is drawn. The result is a drawing of a ball, reproduced on the screen.

To move the ball, the main program draws it, then erases it, then calculates the new location and draws it again. When the ball comes too close to the edge of the screen, which is checked for by the **if** statements, the signs of **dy** and **dx**—the increments by which the x and y coordinates of the ball are increased—are reversed, thus reversing the ball's direction of motion.

Of course other patterns could be used here as well— spaceships, running men, icons representing disks or files, or whatever. The size of the pattern could also be changed: an array of type **char**, with 64 pixels, could be drawn faster than the present 256-pixel pattern.

The C library function **kbbit()** returns a 0 if no key was struck, and 1 when the user hits any key.

# EGA-Specific Modes

The EGA adaptor makes available several modes that don't exist on the CGA board. These modes use a different conceptual approach to putting colors on the screen than do the CGA modes, so in this section we'll explore a representative EGA-specific mode, number 13. Mode 13 provides a resolution of 320x200, with 16 colors (instead of the 4 colors provided by CGA mode 4). Mode 13 doesn't require the ECD, but it can be used with this display, and the principles involved are the same for the higher-resolution modes 15 and 16, which do require the ECD.

## ROM Routines and the EGA

As with the CGA modes, the simplest approach to putting color on the screen with the EGA modes is to use the Write Dot ROM BIOS routine. Here's an example that draws 16 differently colored vertical bars. The effect is shown in Figure 11-11. (Don't forget to switch to mode 13.)

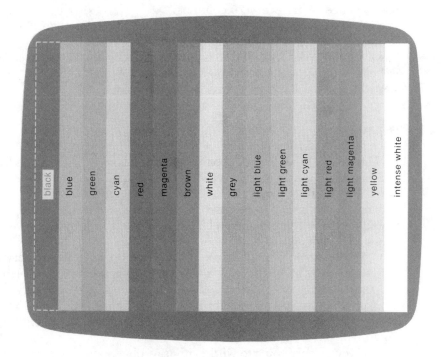

Figure 11-11. Output of the estripes.c Program

```
/* estripes.c */
/* fills EGA screen with 16 color bars. Use mode 13 (320x200) */
#include "dos.h"                          /* to declare REGS */
#define MAXR 200                          /* rows */
#define MAXC 320                          /* columns */
#define VIDEO 0x10                        /* video interrupt # */
#define WDOT 0x0C                         /* 'write dot' ROM BIOS */
main()
{
    union REGS regs;
    int row, col;
    for(row=0; row<MAXR; row++)
        for(col=0; col<MAXC; col++)
            {
            regs.h.ah = WDOT;             /* 'write dot' service */
            regs.x.dx = row;              /* row in DX */
            regs.x.cx = col;              /* column in CX */
            regs.h.al = col/20;           /* colr chng evry 20 rows */
            regs.h.bh = 0;                /* page number */
            int86(VIDEO, &regs, &regs);   /* call video services */
            }
}
```

This program is similar to the cstripes.c program used for mode 4, except that we can now display 16 colors (15 not counting black) instead of four. Thus we must change colors every 20 columns.

With the Write Dot routine we can do anything in mode 13 we did in mode 4: draw rectangles, lines, bouncing balls, and so forth. As with the CGA modes, however, the Write Dot routine is easy to program but slow. To speed things up we can access the EGA memory directly, but to do that we need to know something about how the EGA works with colors.

## Bit Planes

Earlier we saw how the CGA board forms pixels of varying colors by combining two bits in all possible ways, yielding four colors. Each pixel is represented by two adjacent bits in a byte; so each byte can hold the information for four pixels. You might think that to achieve 16 colors we would use more bits; four bits would do the job, and we could pack two pixels in a byte. However, the EGA uses a different approach.

The EGA thinks of each color as occupying a separate area of memory. The 64K standard EGA memory is divided into four sections, or "planes," one for red, one for blue, one for green, and one for intensified. In any given plane, each bit represents one pixel, so eight blue pixels are packed into a byte in the blue plane, eight red pixels into a byte in the red plane, and so on. Figure 11-12 shows how this looks.

If you're only going to work with, say, blue pixels, then you can do all your work in bit plane 0. However, to combine colors, you'll need to work in several

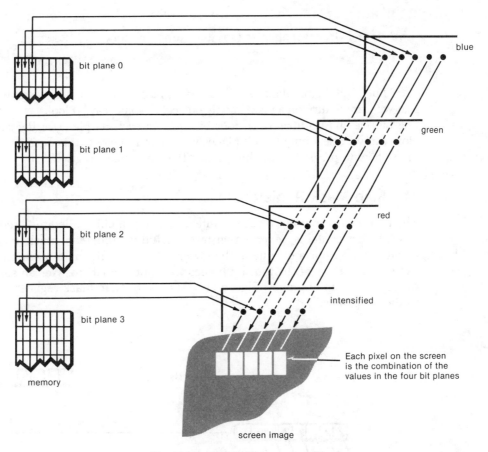

**Figure 11-12. Bit Planes and Pixels**

bit planes at the same time. For instance, to set a pixel to light cyan, you'll need to set the appropriate bit to 1 in plane 0 (blue), in plane 1 (green), and in plane 3 (intensified).

Now you might suppose that each of the four bit planes would occupy a different address space (range of addresses) in memory, so that accessing a particular byte in a particular bit plane would simply be a matter of figuring out the appropriate address. However, the designers of the EGA were more devious than that. Why? Suppose the bit planes were in separate address spaces (perhaps A000, A2000, A4000, and A6000). Then, to put a light cyan pixel on the screen, we'd need to put a bit in three different places in memory; this would require three separate write operations (using **far** pointers). Not very efficient.

Instead, the EGA is designed so that—hold onto your hat—*all four bit planes occupy the same address space*. They all start at address A0000 hex. In the case of mode 13, with 320 times 200 or 64,000 pixels, the amount of memory needed is 64,000 divided by 8 pixels per byte, which is 8,000 (dec) or 1F40 (hex) bytes. So all four bit planes start at A0000 and run up to A1F3F.

All four EGA bit planes occupy the same memory address space.

But, if all the bit planes are in the same place in memory, how can we specify that we want to turn on a pixel in only one color—blue, say? It looks as if, to turn on one bit, we end up turning on four bits, one in each bit plane, at the same time. How can we select only the bit planes we want? To answer this question, we must know how to program something called the "map mask register."

## The Map Mask Register

The EGA board contains a custom integrated circuit chip called the "sequencer." This device contains several registers, including the map mask register. By placing an appropriate value in the lower four bits of the map mask register, we can specify which of the four bit planes we want to write to. We can specify one plane or a group of planes. Figure 11-13 shows the map mask register in relation to the bit planes.

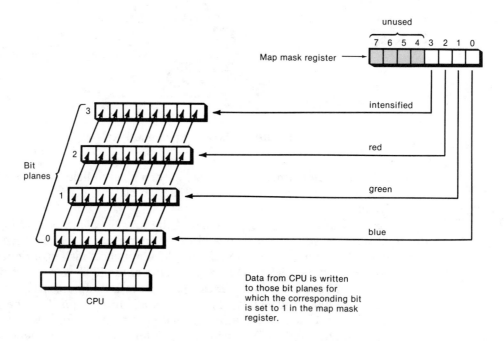

Figure 11-13. The Map Mask Register

For a pixel to be set to a particular color, the bits in the correct bit planes must be turned on. For this to happen, the bit must be set to 1 in the byte sent from the CPU, *and* the bit in the map mask register at the position corresponding to the desired color must also be set to 1. Figure 11-14 shows a single bit being set to the color red. We could turn on several different bits at once and several different bit planes could be activated as well, so that the pixels could be colored with composite colors.

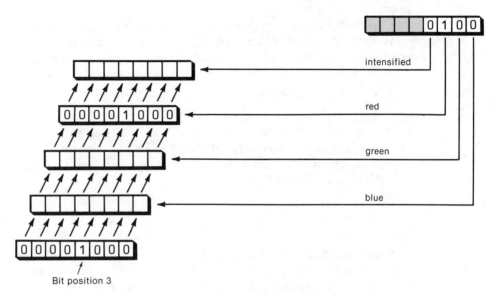

Figure 11-14. Turning on Red Bit at Bit Position 3

But how do we go about putting values into the map mask register? To answer this question, we need to know how to use C to communicate with a generalized set of I/O devices called "ports."

## Input/Output Ports

So far in this book we've learned to communicate with a variety of I/O devices: the character display, the keyboard, the printer, and, in this chapter, the color graphics display. Most of this communication has been performed by calling a C library routine, as when we print something on the screen using **printf( )**, or a ROM BIOS routine, as when we put a dot on the screen using the Write Dot routine. Using ROM BIOS gets us closer to the hardware than do the routines in the C library, but sometimes we need an even closer connection between our program and the hardware. At the most fundamental level, hardware on the IBM is accessed through the medium of *input/output ports*.

A port is an eight-bit register. It can be accessed by software, but it is also physically connected to a hardware device; in fact, it is usually part of a hardware device. The IBM can have 65,536 ports connected to it; they are numbered from 0 to FFFF hex. However, only a small number of these addresses are actually used.

The ROM BIOS communicates with almost all I/O devices using ports.

Usually we can use a ROM BIOS routine to access a device, so we don't need to know how the program accesses the ports. For some devices, though, there are no ROM BIOS routines available to our program. One example of this is the IBM's speaker; if we want our computer to make noise (other than a simple beep), we must use ports. Another instance where we can directly access ports is in programming the EGA.

How do we access a port using the C language? C provides two functions for this purpose: **outp()**, which writes a byte to a port, and **inp()**, which reads a byte from a port. Here's an example of the **inp()** function. The statement

```
result = inp(portno);
```

reads the byte from the port with the address **portno**. The variable **portno** must be an unsigned integer between 0 and FFFF hex, and the function returns an integer value (although only the lower byte contains information).

Similarly, the C statement

```
outp(portno,value);
```

causes the information in **value** to be written to the port with the address **portno**. Here **portno** is an unsigned integer as before and **value** is also an integer, though it cannot have a value greater than FF (hex).

Thus, to output a value to an I/O port, all we need to know is the address of the port and the value to be sent to it; then we use **outp()**.

## Writing to the Map Mask Register

At this point we know almost everything necessary to put the appropriate bit plane value in the map mask register. However, there is one added complexity. There are several registers associated with the sequencer (a clocking mode register, a character map select register, a memory mode register, and so on) in addition to the one we want, the map mask register. To simplify the hardware, all these registers use the same port address: 3C5 hex. Therefore, we need to be able to specify which of these registers we want to access through the port. This is done with yet another register in the sequencer; this one is called the "address register," and its address is 3C4 hex. First we put an index number in the address register to tell it which register we want to refer to; for the map mask register, the index is 2. Then we put a number, representing the bit plane we want to reference, into 3C5.

Accessing a register in the EGA generally requires writing to two ports: one to select the register, one to send it a value.

## Writing Bytes to the EGA Memory

Now, finally, we're ready to write colors to the screen using EGA mode 13. The following program places 16 horizontal stripes on the screen, each one with a different color.

```
/* hstripes.c */
/* horizontal stripes. Use mode 13 (320x200) */
/* use EGA write mode 0 */
#define MAXR 200                    /* rows */
#define MAXC 320                    /* columns */
#define MAXB (MAXC/8)               /* bytes in a row */
main()
{
    char far *farptr;
    int row, col;
    unsigned char color;
    farptr = (char far *) 0xA0000000;  /* set ptr to EGA mem */
    for(row=0; row<MAXR; row++)     /* draw rows of pixels */
        {
        color = (row/12) & 0x0f;    /* colr chng evry 12 rows */
        outp(0x3C4,2);              /* set color to write */
        outp(0x3C5,color);          /*    in map mask register */
        for (col=0; col<MAXB; col++)
            *(farptr + row*MAXB + col ) = 0xff; /* set 8 pixels */
        }
}
```

While similar to the fstripes.c program for mode 4, in this program changing colors involves the two **outp()** functions and the stripes are drawn horizontally instead of vertically. Figure 11-15 shows how this looks.

Because eight pixels are set with each memory access, it's a fast program, as you can see by comparing it with estripes.c.

## Writing Bits to the EGA Memory

It's not necessary to display whole bytes at a time; we can also turn on individual bits. The following program draws 20 vertical lines on the screen. Each line is two pixels wide, so in the appropriate bytes, two bits are set to 1, while the remaining six are set to 0. Here's the listing:

```
/* vlines.c */
/* draws vertical lines. Use mode 13 (320x200) */
/* use EGA write mode 0 */
#define MAXR 200                    /* rows */
#define MAXC 320                    /* columns */
#define PIX  8                      /* pixels per byte */
#define MAXB (MAXC/PIX)             /* bytes in a row */
main()
```

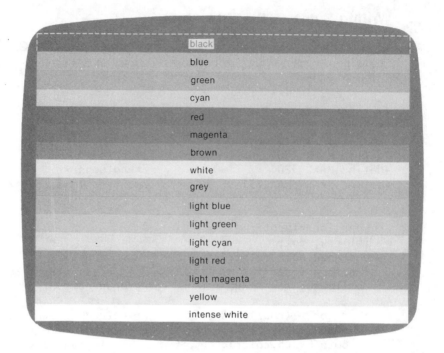

Figure 11-15. Output of the hstripes.c Program

```
{
    char far *farptr;
    int row, col, addr;
    unsigned char color, temp;
    farptr = (char far *) 0xA0000000;   /* set ptr to EGA mem */

    /* vertical lines, each two pixels wide */
    for(col=0; col<MAXC; col+=16)   /* space vertical lines */
        {                           /*    every 16 pixels */
        color = col/16;             /* change color every line */
        outp(0x3C4,2);              /* set color to write */
        outp(0x3C5,color);          /*    in map.mask register */
        for(row=0; row<MAXR; row++)  /* draw one vertical line */
            {
            addr = row*MAXB + col/PIX;   /* calculate address */
            *(farptr+addr) = 0xC0;   /* turn on bits 7, 6 only */
            }
        }
}
```

The output of this program is shown in Figure 11-16.

For simplicity, the lines are separated by 16 pixels, or two bytes. Thus, the left-most two bits (numbers 7 and 6) of every other byte are set to the appropriate color, using the statement

```
*(farptr+addr) = 0xC0;
```

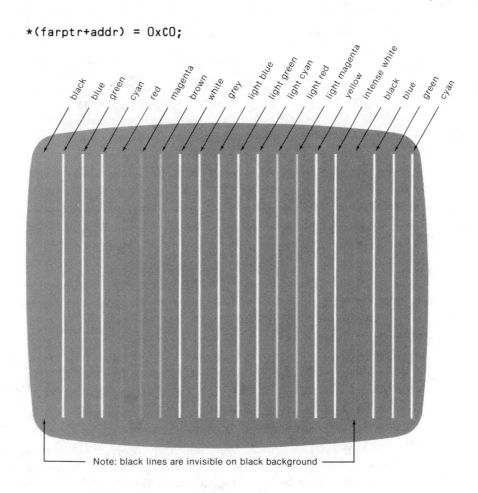

Figure 11-16. Output of the vlines.c Program

As before, the color is selected with the map mask register.

For some simple operations, the technique used in hstripes.c and vlines.c will suffice. However, when we try to use this technique in a more complicated situation, such as drawing one color on top of another, we run into trouble. To see the problem, clear the graphics screen (using the setmode.c program), run hstripes.c and then, without clearing the screen, run vlines.c:

```
C>setmode 13
C>hstripes
C>vlines
```

The vertical stripes will be drawn over the horizontal stripes. This is a rigorous test of a graphics system; if there is any inadequacy in the approach used, it will show up when one color is written on top of another. And, as it turns out, there is a problem; where a line crosses a stripe, in most cases there is an area to the right of the line where the stripe's color is changed or set to black, as shown in Figure 11-17.

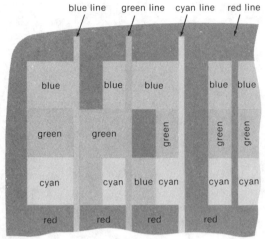

Figure 11-17. Incorrect Interaction of Stripes and Lines

The problem is that when a byte is written to a certain address on a given bit plane, those bits that are set to 1 are turned on, while those that are set to 0 are turned off. So, when we run vstripes.c, the two left-most bits in the byte being written to are set to the appropriate color, but the remaining six bits are turned off, causing a loss of that color in the six pixels to the right of each line.

In the CGA modes the solution to this problem was to *read* the contents of the existing byte from the CGA memory, OR on the appropriate bits, and rewrite the entire byte. This technique cannot be applied so simply in the EGA because there are four separate bit planes to read; doing four reads to achieve one write would not be very efficient. So the designers of the EGA provided another solution: a way to protect some bits from being changed.

> Changing selected bits in a byte in the EGA bit planes requires protecting those bits that will not be changed.

## The Bit Mask Register

We know that the map mask register can specify which bit planes are to be accessed when a byte is written to the EGA memory. In this case, those bit planes for which a bit is set to 1 in the map mask register can be written to, while those for which the bit is set to 0 will be unaffected by a write.

In a similar way it is possible to specify which bits in a byte (in all four bit planes) can be written to and which will be immune to change. The mechanism for this is the *bit mask register*. Figure 11-18 shows the relation of this register to the bit planes. To write to a certain bit in a particular bit plane, the corresponding bits in *both* the map mask register and the bit mask register must be set to 1.

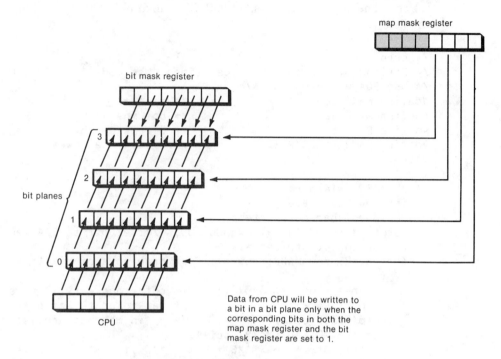

Figure 11-18. The Map Mask Register

When the EGA is first powered up, the bit mask register is set to all 1s, so all the bits can be written to. To protect a bit from being written to, we change this bit to 0. Like the map mask register, the bit mask register is accessed using I/O ports. And, again like the map mask register, it requires that an index number be sent to a different port before the register itself can be accessed. Here's what the necessary program statements look like:

```
outp(0x3CE,8);      /* select the bit mask register */
outp(0x3CF,0xC0);   /* specify bits to be changed */
```

The bit mask register is part of a chip called the graphics controller register. To select the bit mask register, an 8 is sent to port 0x3CE. Then the desired bit configuration is sent to port 0x3CF.

### The ecross.c Program

Now that we know how to prevent certain bits from being altered when we write to a byte in the EGA memory, we can solve the problem uncovered when we attempted to write vertical lines on top of horizontal stripes. The following program combines the earlier hstripes.c and vlines.c programs. The stripes part of the program is the same, but the line-drawing routine has been altered so that all but the left-most two bits of each byte being written to are rendered immune to change. This is done by setting the right-most six bits to 0 in the bit mask register. The appropriate constant is 0xC0, which is 11000000 in binary. Here's the listing:

```
/* ecross.c */
/* horizontal stripes, vertical lines. Use mode 13 (320x200) */
/* use EGA write mode 0 */
#define MAXR 200                    /* rows */
#define MAXC 320                    /* columns */
#define PIX  8                      /* pixels per byte */
#define MAXB (MAXC/PIX)             /* bytes in a row */
main()
{
    char far *farptr;
    int row, col, addr;
    unsigned char color, temp;
    farptr = (char far *) 0xA0000000;  /* set ptr to EGA mem */
    /* horizontal stripes */
    for(row=0; row<MAXR; row++)      /* draw rows of pixels */
        {
        color = (row/12) & 0x0f;        /* colr chng evry 12 rows */
        outp(0x3C4,2);                  /* set color to write */
        outp(0x3C5,color);              /*    in map mask register */
        for (col=0; col<MAXB; col++)
            *(farptr + row*MAXB + col ) = 0xff; /* set 8 pixels */
        }
    /* vertical lines, each two pixels wide */
    outp(0x3CE,8);                   /* select bit mask reg */
    outp(0x3CF,0xC0);                /* change bits 7 and 6 only */
    for(col=0; col<MAXC; col+=16)    /* space vertical lines */
        {                            /*    every 16 pixels */
        color = col/16;                 /* change color every line */
        outp(0x3C4,2);                  /* set color to write */
        outp(0x3C5,color);              /*    in map mask register */
        for(row=0; row<200; row++)      /* draw one vertical line */
            {
            addr = row*MAXB + col/PIX;     /* calculate address */
            temp = *(farptr+addr);    /* read byte into latches */
            *(farptr+addr) = 0xFF;    /* send all bits */
            }
        }                            /* restore settings */
    outp(0x3CE,8);                   /* select bit mask reg */
    outp(0x3CF,0xFF);                /* restore 'all bits' mode */
}
```

There's another important addition to the ecrosss.c program, one that demonstrates how the bit mask register is used. Before writing the 0xC0 byte, the program *reads* the contents of the existing byte from EGA memory. However, the contents of this read, placed in **temp**, are never used. What then is the purpose of the read? To understand why reading is necessary before writing you need to know about another set of EGA registers called the "latch registers."

## The Latch Registers

Our earlier diagrams of the bit planes simplified the situation; they showed data from the CPU going directly into the bit planes in EGA memory. Actually, there is another element in the data path between the CPU and the EGA memory: the latch registers. There is one latch register for each bit plane. When a byte is written by the CPU to the EGA, it actually goes to the latch registers first, then into memory. When it's read from memory, it goes to the latch registers on it's way to the CPU. This arrangement is shown in Figure 11-19.

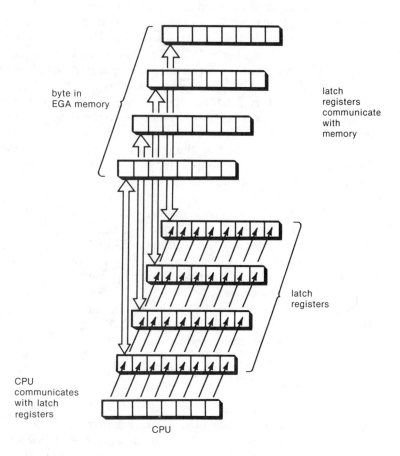

byte in
EGA memory

latch
registers
communicate
with
memory

latch
registers

CPU
communicates
with latch
registers

CPU

Figure 11-19. The Latch Registers

The latch registers are important in the functioning of the bit mask register. Here's the sequence of events when a byte is written by the CPU to EGA memory. First, the byte arrives at the latch registers. (If some of the bit positions have been made immune to change by the bit mask register, though, the bits from the CPU will be blocked at these positions before they can get to the latch registers.) Finally, the contents of the latch registers are written into the EGA memory.

The latch registers are an intermediate storage area between the CPU and the EGA memory.

The bits in the latch registers that did *not* receive CPU data are sent to memory as well. To ensure that these bits do not alter the data in memory, we read the data from memory into the latch registers before doing a write. Then when the write is performed, the new bits from the CPU are placed in the latches, the old bits remain as they were read from memory, and finally the complete contents of the latch registers are written back into memory. This process is shown in Figure 11-20. The figure shows only one of the four bit planes. However, a read or write operation transfers data between all four latch registers and all four bit planes simultaneously.

There is another detail to notice about the ecross.c program; it is necessary to restore the bit mask register to all 1s when the program is finished. If this is not done, only two bits in each byte can be written to by other programs accessing the EGA (including the operating system). This produces strange effects on the screen, so it's important for every program that uses the bit mask register to restore it before exiting.

The ecross.c program generates a much more pleasing picture on the screen than did the execution of hstripes.c followed by vlines.c. The lines no longer cause the unwritten pixels on their right to be destroyed. In fact, using the map mask register and the bit mask register as we've shown is a good way to handle a variety of situations, especially those involving complicated shapes. This system is, however, only one of three possible *write modes* available on the EGA; it is write mode 0.

In the following sections we'll examine the other two write modes. We'll start with write mode 2, which is more closely related to mode 0, and then we'll examine mode 1, which is used in special situations.

## EGA Write Mode 2

The EGA write mode 0 provides good control of individual pixels, since a write operation can turn each one of eight pixels either on or off. It is thus suitable for operating on complex shapes. Write mode 2, on the other hand, puts its emphasis on fine control of color, at the expense of detailed shape manipulation. Let's look at the difference in operation of these two modes.

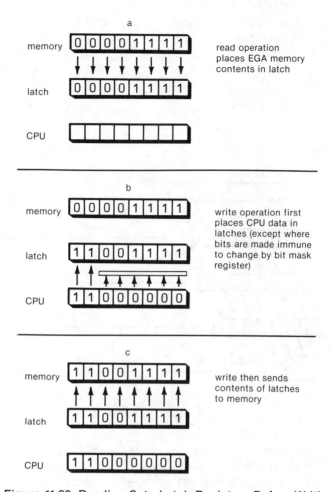

a

memory · read operation places EGA memory contents in latch

latch

CPU

b

memory · write operation first places CPU data in latches (except where bits are made immune to change by bit mask register)

latch

CPU

c

memory · write then sends contents of latches to memory

latch

CPU

Figure 11-20. Reading Sets Latch Registers Before Writing

In EGA write mode 0, CPU data forms a pattern of bits; in write mode 2 it forms a color.

In write mode 0 the map mask register determined which bit planes could be changed, the bit mask register determined which bits could be changed, and the data from the CPU specified which bits in the bit planes would be set to 0 and which to 1 (the bit configuration). Write mode 2 uses a different approach. In mode 2, the data from the CPU determines the color instead of the bit configuration. This is effected by sending the CPU data directly to the map mask register rather than to the latches. The write operation, in addition to specifying the color, then automatically sets all the bits in the byte addressed, to the color specified, unless they are protected by the bit mask register. Figure 11-21 shows how this looks.

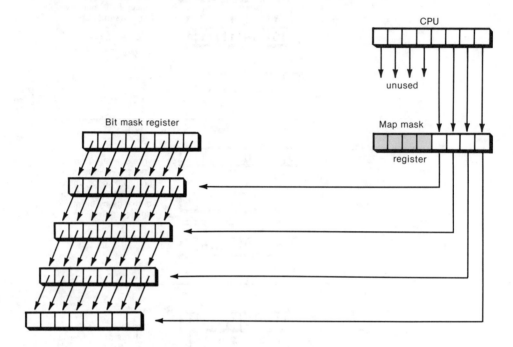

Figure 11-21. EGA Write Mode 2

The various write modes are selected by placing values in the *mode* register. This is another register in the graphics controller register. It's index number is 5, so the following **outp()** statements change to write mode 2:

```
outp(0x3CE,5);    /* select mode register */
outp(0x3CF,2);    /* set to write mode 2 */
```

Here's a modification of the earlier ecross.c program, rewritten to work in write mode 2:

```
/* ecross2.c */
/* horizontal stripes, vertical lines. Use mode 13 (320x200) */
/* uses EGA write mode 2 */
#define MAXR 200                    /* rows */
#define MAXC 320                    /* columns */
#define PIX  8                      /* pixels per byte */
#define MAXB (MAXC/PIX)             /* bytes in a row */
main()
{
    char far *farptr;
    int row, col, addr;
```

```
          unsigned char color, temp;
          farptr = (char far *) 0xA0000000; /* set ptr to EGA mem */
          outp(0x3CE,5);                     /* select mode register */
          outp(0x3CF,2);                     /*    set to mode 2 */
          outp(0x3C4,2);                     /* select map mask register */
          outp(0x3C5,0xF);                   /* activate all bit planes */

          /* horizontal stripes */
          outp(0x3CE,8);                     /* select bit mask reg */
          outp(0x3CF,0xFF);                  /* make all bits writeable */
          for(row=0; row<MAXR; row++)
             {
             color = (row/12) & 0x0f;        /* colr chng evry 12 rows */
             for (col=0; col<MAXB; col++)
                *(farptr + row*MAXB + col ) = color; /* set 8 pixels */
             }
          /* vertical lines, each two pixels wide */
          outp(0x3CE,8);                     /* select bit mask reg */
          outp(0x3CF,0xC0);                  /* change bits 7 and 6 only */
          for(col=0; col<MAXC; col+=16)      /* vertical lines */
             {                               /*    every 16 pixels */
             color = col/16;                 /* change color every line */
             for(row=0; row<200; row++)      /* draw vertical line */
                {
                addr = row*MAXB + col/PIX;   /* calculate address */
                temp = *(farptr+addr);       /* read byte into latches */
                *(farptr+addr) = color;      /* send color to address */
                }
             }                               /* restore settings: */
          outp(0x3CE,8);                     /* select bit mask reg */
          outp(0x3CF,0xFF);                  /* make all bits writeable */
          outp(0x3CE,5);                     /* select mode register */
          outp(0x3CF,0);                     /* set write mode 0 */
       }
```

There are a number of things to note about this program. First, it's necessary to select the correct mode, as described earlier. Then, using the map mask register, all the bit planes must be made active so that subsequent writes will be accepted. This is accomplished with the statements

```
          outp(0x3C4,2);    /* select map mask register */
          outp(0x3C5,0xF);  /* activate all bit planes */
```

For the horizontal stripes, all eight bit positions in each byte must be writeable; the following statements do that:

```
          outp(0x3CE,8);    /* select bit mask register */
          outp(0x3CF,0xFF); /* make all bits writeable */
```

The loops for writing both the stripes and the lines look much the same as in ecross.c, except that instead of being set to the bit configuration, the address pointed to is set to the *color* in the statements

```
*(farptr + row*MAXB + col ) = color;
```

and

```
*(farptr+addr) = color;
```

At the end of the program it's important to reset the write mode to 0 and make all bits writeable in the bit mask register, so other programs can use the EGA.

The screen image created by the ecross2.c program is much the same as that created by ecross.c. There is a difference, however, in the way colors interact when written over each other, which points up a difference in the operation of EGA write modes 0 and 2. The distinction is shown in Figures 11-22 and 11-23.

In write mode 0 (shown in Figure 11-22), when a color is written over another color, only those bit planes that are being turned on are affected. If other bit planes are already on, they remain on. This is because a single write operation will affect all four bit planes at a particular bit position the same way, turning them all either on or off (provided they are selected by the map mask register). Thus, where the blue line crosses the green stripe, the line appears cyan because the blue and the green are combined. Similar color mixtures appear at the other intersections.

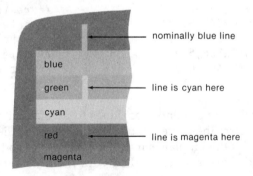

Figure 11-22. Section of Output of ecross.c Program

The background could be set to black in write mode 0 by sending a 0 to all the bit planes and then, in a second write operation, sending the bit of the desired color. Write mode 2 is more efficient. In write mode 2 (shown in Figure 11-23), the values sent to the map mask register can turn bit planes off as well as on. Thus there is no mixing of colors at the intersections. This also means that it's possible to draw black images on a colored background, since all four bit planes can be turned off where black is desired.

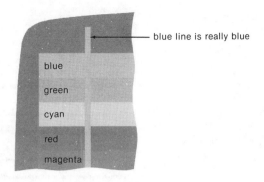

blue line is really blue

blue

green

cyan

red

magenta

Figure 11-23. Section of Output of ecross2.c Program

## EGA Write Mode 1

EGA write mode 1 is a special write mode intended for rapidly copying an image from one part of the screen to another. This is useful in operations such as scrolling the screen, or scrolling parts of the screen. A read operation in mode 1 reads all four bit planes at a particular address into the latch registers. A write operation then writes all four bit planes into a different address. Thus a single read followed by a single write can transfer a byte in all four bit planes at the same time, allowing a far more efficient operation than if four separate reads and writes had to be made. Figure 11-24 shows the operation of write mode 1.

The program following uses write mode 1 to scroll the entire screen downward.

```
/* escroll.c */
/* scrolls entire screen downward. Use mode 13 (320x200) */
/* uses EGA write mode 1 */
#define MAXR 200                    /* rows */
#define MAXC 320                    /* columns */
#define MAXB (MAXC/8)               /* bytes in a row */
main()
{
    char far *farptr;
    register int addr;              /* make it faster */
    farptr = (int far *) 0xA0000000; /* set ptr to EGA mem */
    outp(0x3C4,2);                  /* select map mask register */
    outp(0x3C5,0xF);                /*     activate all planes */
    for(addr=0; addr<MAXB; addr++) /* erase top row by */
        *(farptr+addr) = 0;         /*     setting all bits to 0 */
    outp(0x3CE,5);                  /* select mode register */
    outp(0x3CF,1);                  /*     set write mode 1 */
    while ( !kbhit() )              /* until key pressed, */
        for(addr=MAXR*MAXB; addr>MAXB; addr--)   /* move all bytes */
            *(farptr+addr) = *(farptr+addr-MAXB); /* down one row */
    outp(0x3CE,5);                  /* select mode register */
    outp(0x3CF,0);                  /*     set write mode 0 */
}
```

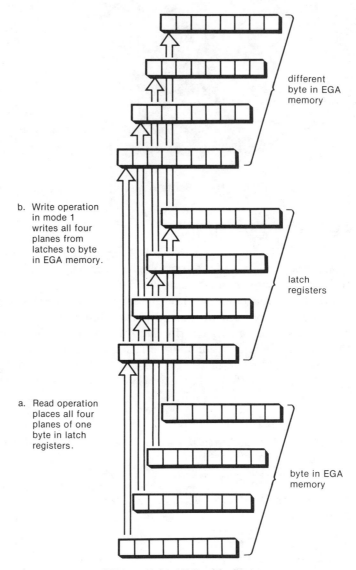

b. Write operation in mode 1 writes all four planes from latches to byte in EGA memory.

different byte in EGA memory

latch registers

a. Read operation places all four planes of one byte in latch registers.

byte in EGA memory

Figure 11-24. Write Mode 1

This program first erases the top row to avoid duplicating the line at the top of the screen. Then, using write mode 1, it shifts all the bytes in the EGA memory one row downward. The shifting process starts with the last address on the screen, which is MAXR*MAXB, and writes into it the contents of the address one row up, which is the same address minus MAXB (the number of bytes in a row). The shifting process then works its way up to the top of the screen.

Similar uses of write mode 1 can quickly copy any area of memory to any other area, making possible a variety of scrolling and animation effects.

# VGA-Specific Modes

The Video Graphics Array is built into most of the models in IBM's PS/2 series, and it is also available from IBM and other vendors as a board to plug into PC and AT class computers. VGA provides all the modes of CGA and EGA graphics, as well as three new modes: 17, 18, and 19. Mode 17 is a black and white mode; we won't cover it here. Mode 18 provides the same 16 colors as EGA, but with higher resolution. Mode 19 permits the simultaneous display of 256 colors. We'll examine these two modes in turn.

## VGA High Resolution

VGA mode 18 provides 640x480 resolution, using 16 colors. This mode operates almost exactly the same as EGA mode 13. It uses bit planes and registers (such as the map mask register and the bit mask register) in the same way the EGA does. Thus programming mode 18 is almost identical to programming for EGA mode 13, except that the vertical resolution must be changed to accommodate 480 lines instead of 350.

For example, here's the earlier hstripes.c program rewritten to run in VGA mode 18:

```
/* vgastrip.c */
/* horizontal stripes. Use mode 18 (640x480) */
/* uses VGA write mode 0 */
#define MAXR 480                    /* rows */
#define MAXC 640                    /* columns */
#define MAXB (MAXC/8)               /* bytes in a row */
main()
{
    char far *farptr;
    int row, col;
    unsigned char color;

    farptr = (char far *) 0xA0000000;   /* set ptr to VGA mem */
    for(row=0; row<MAXR; row++)          /* draw rows of pixels */
    {
    color = (row/30) & 0x0f;    /* color chng evry 30 rows */
    outp(0x3C4,2);              /* set color to write */
    outp(0x3C5,color);         /*    in map mask register */
    for (col=0; col<MAXB; col++)
        *(farptr + row*MAXB + col ) = 0xff;  /* set 8 pixels */
    }
}
```

The effect is similar to that shown in Figure 11-15. This program uses write mode 0 to put the same 16 horizontal color bars on the screen as did hstripes, but does it with the higher resolution of mode 18. The other write modes can also be used in VGA mode 18.

## VGA 256 Colors

VGA mode 19 can display 256 colors simultaneously, with a resolution of 320x200. (If you change palettes, you can access up to 262,144 colors, as we'll see in the next chapter.)

Conceptually, mode 19 is the simplest of the graphics modes. There are 64,000 pixels on the screen (320x200). Each pixel is represented by one byte in memory, so each pixel can have up to $2^8$, or 256 colors. The pixels are mapped onto the bytes in memory in the most straightforward way, starting with the upper-right pixel and scanning line by line down the screen. You don't need to set any registers or worry about memory banks or bit planes.

This example program draws 256 boxes on the screen, each in a different color.

```
/* vga256.c */
/* draws 256 different colored squares. Use VGA mode 19 */
#define MAXX 320          /* horizontal pixels */
#define MAXY 192          /* vert pixels (divisible by 16) */
#define PPBX (MAXX/16)    /* pixels per color box, horizontal */
#define PPBY (MAXY/16)    /* pixels per color box, vertical */

main()
{
    char far *farptr;     /* pointer to video memory */
    int x, y;             /* pixel coordinates (0-319, 0-191) */
    int row, col;         /* color box coordinates (0-15) */
    unsigned char color;  /* color of box (0-255) */

    farptr = (char far *) 0xA0000000;    /* set ptr to VGA */
    for(y=0; y<MAXY; y++)                 /* cycle down */
       for(x=0; x<MAXX; x++)             /* cycle across */
          {
          col = x/PPBX;                   /* find box coords */
          row = y/PPBY;
          color = col + row*16;           /* calculate color */
          *(farptr + y*MAXX + x) = color; /* set the pixel */
          }
}
```

Each box is 20 pixels wide and 12 pixels high, and there are 256 boxes on the screen, in a 16 by 16 matrix, as shown in Figure 11-25. Each box has a different color, starting with color 0 at the upper-left corner and continuing to color 255 at the lower right.

The program keeps track of two sets of coordinates: **x** and **y** specify the pixel location, and **col** and **row** specify the color-box location. For each pixel location the program calculates the box location and colors the pixel accordingly. (There are faster ways to do this, but they complicate the program.) The first row of boxes displays the 16 EGA colors, the second row is a gray scale, and subsequent rows contain a variety of color blends.

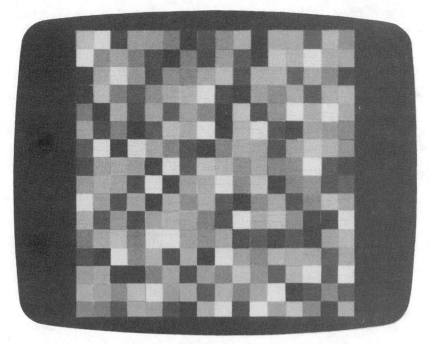

Figure 11-25. Output of the vga256.c Program

## Summary

Graphics is a complex topic, with an almost infinite number of possibilities. There is much more to know about the CGA, EGA, and VGA adaptors than we have presented here. The EGA and VGA especially are complicated pieces of hardware, and a complete discusssion of their features and the way they can be put to use would require a book in itself. However, we have at least had an introduction to graphics programming in C on the IBM.

We've discussed the IBM's graphics modes and the various characteristics that distinguish one mode from another: resolution, number of colors, text or graphics, type of display adaptor and monitor necessary, amount of graphics memory needed and its starting address, and number of pages. We've presented a program for switching from one mode to another, altering the equipment word in low memory and calling a ROM BIOS routine.

We've looked at mode 4, which is common to the CGA, EGA, and VGA displays, in some detail. We've shown how to use a ROM BIOS routine to write a pixel on the screen in this mode and used other ROM BIOS routines to change the color palette and background color. We've also seen how to address the graphics memory directly in this mode and developed programs to draw lines and bouncing balls.

As an example of an EGA-specific mode, we've looked at mode 13. We've seen that the Write Dot ROM BIOS routine works well for this mode, but that, as in other modes, direct memory access is faster. We've seen how direct memory access for the EGA modes differs from that for the CGA and how bit planes are used to store color data. Finally, we've looked at the three EGA write modes and their specialized uses and at the VGA modes.

## Questions

1. List eight characteristics of a graphics mode.

2. In computer graphics, resolution is
   a. the clarity of the displayed image
   b. the number of bits per byte
   c. the number of colors per pixel
   d. the number of pixels in the display

3. Without counting palette changes, how many colors are there in mode 4? How many, if you count palette changes?

4. In mode 4, a pixel gets its color value from a combination of
   a. bit planes
   b. bits in a byte
   c. rows and columns
   d. text and graphics

5. From a programmer's viewpoint, the easiest way to put a pixel on the screen is to use a _____ _____. The fastest way to fill an area with color is to use _____ _____.

6. What four signals are combined to form background colors in the display monitor?

7. Which of the following is necessary for direct memory access?
   a. setting a pointer to the start of display memory
   b. calculating how far into the memory a pixel is
   c. using the indirection operator to access a byte
   d. modifying only those bits corresponding to the pixel

8. How many pixels per byte are there in mode 4?

9. The second memory bank in mode 4 is used for
   a. attributes

b. unused in this mode

c. the cyan and magenta pixels

d. the odd-numbered rows

10. Mode 6 has a resolution of 640x200, with two colors: black and white. Which expression will find the address of the byte containing the pixel at **row** and **col**? (Ignore the memory bank correction.)

a. addr = row*40 + col/16

b. addr = row*80 + col/8

c. addr = row*40 + col/4

d. addr = row*60 + col/4

11. In mode 13 there are _____ colors.

12. One bit plane holds

a. the information about a single color

b. the even-numbered rows

c. the color values for certain pixels

d. the bits in certain positions in a byte

13. True or false: writing can take place to only one bit plane at a time.

14. To send information to a register in the EGA, one must use

a. direct memory access

b. the **outp()** function

c. a port

d. a ROM BIOS routine

15. The map mask register is used to tell the EGA what _____ pixels we want to write.

16. Which of the following statements is appropriate for sending a value to a port?

a. outp(portno, value);

b. value = inp(portno);

c. *(portno) = value;

d. port(number, value);

17. In mode 13 how many pixels are there per byte?

18. What is the correct bit plane number for the color cyan?

a. 0

    b. 1

    c. 2

    d. 3

19. The bit mask register is used to select which _____ will be written to.

20. The latch registers serve as an intermediate storage area between

    a. EGA memory and the bit map register

    b. the CPU and the map mask register

    c. the map mask register and the CPU

    d. EGA memory and the CPU

21. After the bit mask register has been set, a byte must be _____ to set the latch registers.

22. The mode register of the EGA board is used to

    a. switch the EGA to different graphics modes

    b. make sure certain bit planes are not used

    c. select an EGA write mode

    d. make sure certain bits are not used

23. True or false: in EGA write mode 0, any pixel in any bit plane can be turned either on or off by a single write operation.

24. In EGA write mode 2, the data from the CPU goes to

    a. the bit planes at the memory address specified

    b. the map mask register

    c. the bit mask register

    d. the latch registers

25. EGA write mode 1 is used to rapidly _____ a group of pixels.

## Exercises

1. Write a program for mode 4 that will fill the screen with a color of the user's choice from palette 1.

2. Modify the conrect.c program to write concentric rectangles using direct memory access, rather than the ROM BIOS Write Dot routine. Speed it up

by writing one byte at a time. Don't worry if the rectangles are not completely concentric.

3. Write a program for mode 4 that puts a small northeast-pointing arrow in the center of the screen and then moves the arrow around the screen in response to the cursor keys. Use the pattern method from bounce.c to generate a 16-by-16 pixel arrow.

4. Write a program that creates a bar chart with 16 bars. For variety, do the program in mode 14: 640x200, 16 colors. Have the color of each bar reflect its height: blue for the lowest bars, then green, yellow, red, and finally intense white for the highest bars. Use direct memory access and EGA write mode 0.

5. Write a program that duplicates the action of the diagline.c program (drawing four lines of different colors that cross at the center of the screen) but uses graphics mode 13, direct memory access, and EGA write mode 2. Develop a **putpte()** function for this program that can be called with the arguments **row**, **column**, and **color**, and that puts the appropriate pixel on the screen.

# 12

# Microsoft Graphics Functions

- Rectangles, Ellipses, and Polygons
- Filling and Patterns
- Bar and Pie Charts
- Color and Palettes
- Text and Windows
- Viewports and Pages
- Fractals and Mandelbrot

# 12

With the introduction of QuickC and version 5.0 of the Optimizing C Compiler, Microsoft has made available a library of rich and powerful graphics functions. Using a single call to a function, you can now draw a circle or rectangle, fill a shape with a solid color or pattern, draw lines in different styles, combine text with graphics, and much more.

These graphics library functions can be used for many of the effects described in the preceding chapters, where we used ROM BIOS routines or direct access to video memory. The Microsoft C library functions are often more convenient than those earlier techniques. They may not be as fast, and there are some effects they cannot achieve. But to quickly put together a prototype program, or to create a program where the highest performance is not necessary, the Microsoft graphics functions are a great convenience. They are also fun to play with. There are only a few new C concepts in this chapter, so you can relax, enjoy making pictures, and consolidate your knowledge of C.

There are more than 40 graphics functions. We describe most of them in this chapter and give examples of their use. As each function is introduced, its arguments are summarized in a box. Appendix J lists all the graphics functions, along with their arguments and the various structures and constants needed for their use. You'll find that this appendix is a convenient reference when you are writing graphics-oriented programs.

In general, we'll show a short easy-to-follow example program that demonstrates each function as it's introduced. Toward the end of the chapter there are a few more ambitious examples that demonstrate some of the effects possible with graphics functions. These include a hypnotic kinetic painting, a fractal generator, and a program that explores the extraordinary images of the Mandelbrot set.

Most of the example programs use CGA graphics. These examples can be used without modification on CGA, EGA, and VGA systems. In a few cases CGA is inadequate to a particular task, so the example uses EGA graphics. Text-oriented graphics functions, such as **_settextwindow()** and **_outtext()**, can be used on a monochrome text-only display.

# The Graphics Environment

Writing programs that use the Microsoft graphics functions requires a little more preparation than do normal C programs. In this section we'll discuss how to set up your development environment to write graphics programs and how the program itself must be structured to operate in the desired graphics mode.

Two additional files are necessary for graphics programs: the library file GRAPHICS.LIB and the include file GRAPH.H. The first contains the code for the graphics functions that will be linked to your program. We'll return to this file in a moment.

The GRAPH.H header file contains prototypes for the graphics functions and various constant and structure definitions. You combine it with the source code of your program by using an **#include** statement:

```
#include <graph.h>
```

This header file is not an option; you must include it in your source file when using the graphics functions.

How you combine the library file GRAPHICS.LIB with your program depends on whether you're using the Optimizing Compiler or QuickC. We'll look at these cases in turn.

## The Graphics System for the Optimizing Compiler

The simplest way to make the graphics functions available under the Optimizing Compiler is to include the file GRAPHICS.LIB in your combined library when you install your system. We recommended this course of action in Chapter 1: all you need to do is answer "yes" when the installation program asks if you want the graphics package included in your combined libraries.

If you've done this, then you can compile and link your program in the usual way; no further action is necessary. Including the graphics library adds about 60K to the size of SLIBCE.LIB (or whatever combined library you're using). If you have not added the graphics library to your combined library, then you'll need to invoke the file GRAPHICS.LIB explicitly when you compile and link your program. If you're using the CL utility, you type:

```
cl progname.c graphics.lib
```

It's most convenient to install this command in a batch file, as described in Chapter 1.

## The Graphics System in QuickC

The built-in QuickC core library does not include the graphics functions, so a library that contains them must be invoked explicitly whenever a program calls these functions. This can be done in two ways: from the command line or from a .mak file.

### The Command Line

The simplest approach is from the command line. When you installed your system, the installation program automatically created a file called GRAPHICS.QLB. This is a QuickC version of GRAPHICS.LIB. To combine this library file with the other built-in library functions, call up QuickC like this:

```
C>qc /l graphics.qlb progname.c
```

The slash is followed by a lowercase letter 'l' and the name of the library. This causes the graphics routines to be made available to QuickC at link time. Now you can write or edit your program and compile it in the usual way, using the Start option from the Run menu or creating a stand-alone .exe file.

Most of the examples in this chapter can be compiled using this approach. A few, however, use math functions such as **sin()** and **cos()**. These functions are not included in the built-in QuickC core library, so you must link the complete combined MLIBCE.LIB to your program. Because this is not a special QuickC .QLB library, you can't use the /l command-line option. So you create a .mak file with the Program List option in QuickC.

### Using a .mak File and a Program List

We'll assume that you specified that the graphics library be included in MLIBCE.LIB when you set up your system. If MLIBCE.LIB includes the graphics functions, once you've created the program list and the .mak file that cause MLIBCE.LIB to be linked to your file, you no longer need to worry about the graphics routines. Chapter 1 describes how to use program lists to create .mak files.

## Graphics Modes

As we discussed in Chapter 11, you must switch the hardware of your computer to a suitable mode if your graphics program is to generate appropriate images on the screen. In that chapter we used a program, setmode.c, to perform this operation. A Microsoft C graphics function accomplishes the same task: **_setvideomode()**.

---

### Select Display Mode

```
_setvideomode(mode)
short mode;    /* mode: number or constant */
```

---

This function can use a manifest constant to select the mode. These constants are defined in GRAPH.H and listed in Table 12-1. The mode number can be used in place of the constant.

## Table 12-1. Graphics Modes

| Constant | Value | Resolution | Adaptor | Mode Type |
|---|---|---|---|---|
| _DEFAULTMODE | −1 | (restore screen to previous mode) | | |
| _TEXTBW40 | 0 | 40x25 | CGA | text |
| _TEXTC40 | 1 | 40x25 | CGA | text, color |
| _TEXTBW80 | 2 | 80x25 | CGA | text |
| _TEXTC80 | 3 | 80x25 | CGA | text, color |
| _MRES4COLOR | 4 | 320x200 | CGA | graphics, 4 color |
| _MRESNOCOLOR | 5 | 320x200 | CGA | graphics, 4 gray |
| _HRESBW | 6 | 640x200 | CGA | graphics, B&W |
| _TEXTMONO | 7 | 80x25 | MGA | text, B&W |
| _MRES16COLOR | 13 | 320x200 | EGA | graphics, 16 color |
| _HRES16COLOR | 14 | 640x200 | EGA | graphics, 16 color |
| _ERESNOCOLOR | 15 | 640x350 | EGA | graphics, B&W |
| _ERESCOLOR | 16 | 640x350 | EGA | graphics, 16 color |
| _VRES2COLOR | 17 | 640x480 | VGA | graphics, 2 color |
| _VRES16COLOR | 18 | 640x480 | VGA | graphics, 16 color |
| _MRES256COLOR | 19 | 320x200 | VGA | graphics, 256 color |

In this chapter we'll largely be concerned with mode 4, the four-color CGA mode, and with mode 16, a 16-color EGA mode.

### Setting the Mode

Here's a short program that sets your system to any desired mode. Note that it leaves the system in the mode you've specified; to return to text mode you'll need to run the program again, usually specifying mode 3. (If you have a monochrome text monitor as well as a color monitor, you can return to mode 7.)

```
/* setgmode.c */
/* sets graphics mode specified on command line */
#include <graph.h>            /* needed for graphics functions */

main(argc,argv)
int argc;
char *argv[];
{
   if( argc != 2 )
      { printf("Syntax: C>chmode mode#"); exit(); }

   if( _setvideomode( atoi(argv[1]) )==0 )   /* set mode */
      printf("Can't set mode %s", argv[1] );
   else
      printf("Mode %s sucessfully set", argv[1] );
}
```

The program checks that the command line has the correct number of arguments: the user should type the mode number following the program name. The **_setvideomode()** function then attempts to set the mode specified. If it can't set it, the function returns the value 0, and the program prints an error message. This happens if, for instance, you attempt to set a VGA mode (like 19) on an EGA or CGA system. The program also informs you if the mode was sucessfully set.

Note that the program starts by including the GRAPH.H file. As noted, this is necessary in all programs using graphics functions.

### Finding Mode Information

Once you've set a particular mode, you can discover its characteristics using the **_getvideoconfig()** function. Here's a program that does just that:

```
/* getgmode.c */
/* displays information on current graphics mode */
#include <graph.h>
main()
{
    struct videoconfig vc;

    _getvideoconfig( &vc );
    printf("X pixels:   %d\n", vc.numxpixels);
    printf("Y pixels:   %d\n", vc.numypixels);
    printf("Cols:       %d\n", vc.numtextcols);
    printf("Rows:       %d\n", vc.numtextrows);
    printf("Colors:     %d\n", vc.numcolors);
    printf("Bits/pixel: %d\n", vc.bitsperpixel);
    printf("Pages:      %d\n", vc.numvideopages);
}
```

Use this program in conjunction with setgmode.c. Set a mode with setgmode.c, and then use getgmode.c to discover the details about it.

---

### Get Current Video Mode Information

```
_getvideoconfig( &config )
struct videoconfig config;      /* structure for video info */
```

---

The **_getvideoconfig()** function returns its mode information in a structure called **videoconfig**, which is defined in GRAPH.H. The structure looks like this:

```
struct videoconfig {
    short numxpixels;     /* horiz pixels */
    short numypixels;     /* vert pixels */
    short numtextcols;    /* text columns */
    short numtextrows;    /* text rows */
    short numcolors;      /* actual colors */
    short bitsperpixel;   /* bits per pixel */
```

```
    short numvideopages; /* video memory pages */
};
```

The program simply prints out the information found in the members of the structure. Here's the output if the program is executed while the system is in mode 4:

```
X pixels:    320
Y pixels:    200
Cols:        40
Rows:        25
Colors:      4
Bits/pixel:  2
Pages:       1
```

The pixel resolution is given; in this case, the display has 320 horizontal pixels by 200 vertical. There are 40 text columns by 25 rows and four possible colors. The system uses two bits to represent each pixel (see Chapter 11 for a discussion of CGA graphics formats). There is enough memory for only one page at this resolution. (If you have a multimode board it may actually have more memory than this, but CGA can only access 16K of it.)

The mode information can be useful for graphics programs that operate in several different modes, as we'll see in the next example.

# Graphics Shapes

One of the most useful features of the Microsoft graphics package is the ability to draw complete graphics shapes using only one call to a library function. Such shapes include rectangles, ellipses (and the circle, a special case of the ellipse), arcs, and polygons. Also, shapes of any complexity can be drawn using single pixels.

In this section we'll see how such shapes are created.

## Rectangles

A library function appropriately called _**rectangle()** creates rectangles of any size or shape. The example program uses this function to draw a border around the edge of the screen. The user selects the mode on the command line when the program is invoked, so the program does not know in advance what mode it will find itself in. It needs to know the size of the screen (in pixels) to compute the dimensions of the rectangle, so it invokes _**getvideoconfig()**.

```
/* border.c */
/* draws border around screen */
/* works in all graphics modes */
#include <graph.h>               /* needed for graphics */

main(argc,argv)
```

```
int argc;
char *argv[];
{
   struct videoconfig vc;

   if( argc != 2 )                 /* check number of arguments */
      { printf("Syntax: C>border mode#"); exit(); }
                                    /* set mode */
   if( _setvideomode( atoi(argv[1]) )==0 )
      { printf("Can't set mode %s", argv[1] ); exit(1); }

   _getvideoconfig( &vc );         /* get mode information */
                                   /* draw border around screen */
   _rectangle(_GBORDER, 0, 0, vc.numxpixels-1, vc.numypixels-1);

   getch();                        /* keep image until keypress */
   _setvideomode(_DEFAULTMODE); /* restore previous mode */
}
```

### Common Graphics Program Elements

This program demonstrates several features that will be common to most of the graphics examples in this chapter.

First, it begins by setting the mode, using **_setvideomode()**, and returns an error message if the mode cannot be set.

Second, the last line of the program again uses **_setvideomode()** to *reset* the mode to its original value; this is accomplished with the constant _DEFAULTMODE. The system does not take care of this, so you must include this instruction at the end of every program (unless you don't mind the system remaining in the new mode).

Third, the next-to-last line in the program uses **getch()** so the program will wait for a keypress before returning to the operating system. This instruction keeps the image on the screen long enough to see; without it, the image would vanish immediately when the program returned to the operating system or QuickC.

### The _rectangle() Function

The **_rectangle()** function needs to know whether the rectangle will be filled or not and the coordinates of the top left corner and the bottom right corner of the rectangle.

---

**Draw a Rectangle**

```
_rectangle(fill, left, top, right, bot)
short fill;         /* _GFILLINTERIOR or _GBORDER */
short left, top;    /* top left corner */
short right, bot;   /* bottom right corner */
```

The _GBORDER and _GFILLINTERIOR constants are defined in GRAPH.H. The first causes only the outline of the rectangle to be drawn, while the second causes the rectangle to be filled with the current color and pattern. The present example draws the rectangle's outline; we'll see how to use the fill option later.

The pixel coordinate system assumes that the upper-left corner of the screen is at 0,0. The program places the upper-right corner of the rectangle here. The coordinates of the lower-right corner are obtained from the appropriate members of the **videoconfig** structure. The result is a border around the entire screen display area.

## Circles and Ellipses

Ellipses are specified in Microsoft C by a *bounding rectangle*. This is a rectangle into which the ellipse will exactly fit. There are other ways to describe an ellipse, such as specifying the center and x and y radii. The Microsoft approach is advantageous in some but not all circumstances, as we'll see.

The next program draws both a circle (an ellipse with the same width and height) and a rectangle. The rectangle happens to be drawn in the same place as the bounding rectangle for the circle.

```
/* circbox.c */
/* draws circle and box */
#include <graph.h>                    /* needed for graphics */
#define LEFT   0                      /* rectangle */
#define TOP    0
#define RIGHT 199
#define BOT   199
main()
{
                                      /* initialize graphics */
   if( _setvideomode(_MRES4COLOR)==0 )
      { printf("Can't set mode"); exit(1); }

   _rectangle(_GBORDER, LEFT, TOP, RIGHT, BOT); /* draw box */
   _ellipse(_GBORDER, LEFT, TOP, RIGHT, BOT); /* draw circle */

   getch();                           /* keep image until keypress */
   _setvideomode(_DEFAULTMODE); /* restore old mode */
}
```

The result is a circle exactly circumscribed by a box, as shown in Figure 12-1. The function that draws the circle is _**ellipse()**.

You may notice that, although the _**ellipse()** function is given the same height and width for the bounding rectangle, the circle does not appear exactly circular. It is somewhat squashed in at the middle. The rectangle is also a bit higher than it is wide. This results from the fact that the pixels in CGA mode 4 are not "square." We'll see what this means and how to correct it when we discuss the aspect-ratio problem at the end of this section.

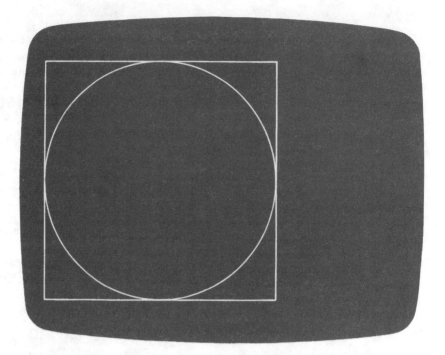

Figure 12-1. Output of circbox.c

**Draw an Ellipse**

```
_ellipse(fill, left, top, right, bot)
short fill;       /* _GFILLINTERIOR or _GBORDER */
short left, top;  /* boundary rectangle top left corner */
short right, bot; /* boundary rectangle bottom right corner */
```

If you change the RIGHT constant in circbox.c you can see how ellipses look, as opposed to circles. Giving it a value of 300 will make the ellipse considerably wider than it is high.

## Lines and Polygons

A function called _**lineto**() is used for drawing a line to a specified point. Thus _**lineto**(100,200) draws a line to x = 100 and y = 200. Where does the line start? Wherever the *current position* (or CP) was. Think of the CP as the position of an imaginary pen used to draw graphics figures. If you draw a line, the CP remains at the end of the line when you're done, so the next line starts from that point.

You can also move the CP without drawing a line by using the _**moveto**() function. This is the usual way to position the pen at the start of a drawing.

The **_moveto()** and **_lineto()** functions can be used to construct *polygons*. A polygon is simply a closed figure formed from straight lines. Our next example program forms a three-dimensional representation of a box from a rectangle and two polygons, as shown in Figure 12-2.

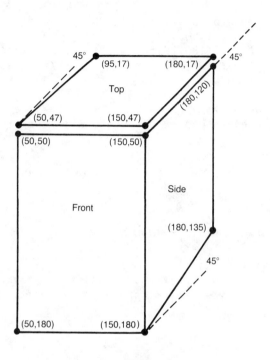

Figure 12-2. Box in poly.c Program

The front rectangle is drawn using the **_rectangle()** function. The top and side of the box are constructed from polygons: a series of lines generated with the **_lineto()** function. Both polygons use four lines, but the side polygon uses only three line segments; the fourth line is the edge of the original rectangle. The top polygon is raised 3 pixels up from the rest of the box, so it needs all four edges. For both polygons the **_moveto()** function is used to position the pen before starting to draw the lines.

```
/* poly.c */
/* draws polygons */
#include <graph.h>                  /* needed for graphics */
main()
{
                            /* initialize graphics */
    if( _setvideomode(_MRES4COLOR)==0 )
        { printf("Can't set mode"); exit(1); }
                            /* draw front rectangle */
    _rectangle(_GBORDER, 50, 50, 150, 180);
```

```
        _moveto(150,50);              /* draw right polygon */
        _lineto(180,20);              /*    top */
        _lineto(180,135);             /*    right */
        _lineto(150,180);             /*    bottom */

        _moveto(50,47);               /* draw top polygon */
        _lineto(150,47);              /*    front */
        _lineto(180,17);              /*    right */
        _lineto(95,17);               /*    back */
        _lineto(50,47);               /*    left */

        getch();                      /* keep image until keypress */
        _setvideomode(_DEFAULTMODE);  /* restore previous mode */
}
```

Both **_moveto()** and **_lineto()** take only two parameters.

***Move Current Position to x, y***

```
_moveto(x, y)
short x;   /* x-coordinate to position CP */
short y;   /* y-coordinate to position CP */
```

***Draw Line from Current Position to x, y***

```
_lineto(x, y)
short x;   /* x-coordinate of end of line */
short y;   /* y-coordinate of end of line */
```

Note in the program that, as is shown in the figure, not all the diagonal lines are drawn at exactly 45 degrees. To achieve correct perspective, the diagonal lines must appear to converge on an imaginary "vanishing point" behind the figure. On the screen the figure looks as if all the diagonal lines are parallel, but measurement will confirm that they actually converge.

## Arcs

An arc is a section of an ellipse or circle. Our next example uses four arcs to join four straight lines, thus creating a box with rounded corners, as shown in Figure 12-3. A new function, called **_arc()**, is used to draw the four arcs. The _moveto() and _lineto() functions are used to draw the line segments on the edges of the box.

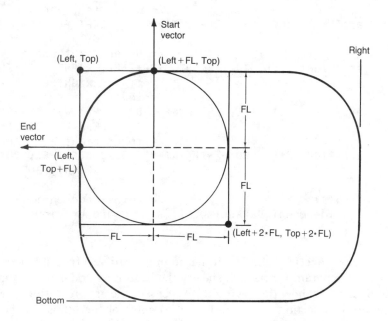

Figure 12-3. Rounded Corners in arc.c Program

```
/* arc.c */
/* draws rounded corners, using _arc() */
#include <graph.h>                 /* needed for graphics */
#define LEFT     120               /* coordinates of box */
#define TOP       10
#define RIGHT    200
#define BOT       80
#define FL        10               /* size of fillet */

main()
{
   double dataSum, startAngle, endAngle, relAngle;
   double startVecX, startVecY, endVecX, endVecY;
   int j;

   if( _setvideomode(_MRES4COLOR)==0 )
     { printf("Can't set mode"); exit(1); }
                                   /* draw four line segments */
   _moveto(LEFT+FL, TOP);          /*    top line */
   _lineto(RIGHT-FL, TOP);
   _moveto(LEFT,    TOP+FL);       /*    left line */
   _lineto(LEFT,    BOT-FL);
   _moveto(LEFT+FL, BOT);          /*    bottom line */
```

```
        _lineto(RIGHT-FL, BOT);
        _moveto(RIGHT,    TOP+FL);   /*     right line */
        _lineto(RIGHT,    BOT-FL);
                                     /* upper left arc */
        _arc(LEFT, TOP, LEFT+2*FL, TOP+2*FL, LEFT+FL, TOP,
                                        LEFT,    TOP+FL );
                                     /* upper right arc */
        _arc(RIGHT-2*FL, TOP, RIGHT, TOP+2*FL, RIGHT, TOP+FL,
                                        RIGHT-FL, TOP );
                                     /* lower left arc */
        _arc(LEFT, BOT-2*FL, LEFT+2*FL, BOT, LEFT,    BOT-FL,
                                        LEFT+FL, BOT ); .
                                     /* lower right arc */
        _arc(RIGHT-2*FL, BOT-2*FL, RIGHT, BOT, RIGHT-FL, BOT,
                                        RIGHT, BOT-FL );

        getch();                     /* hold image until keypress */
        _setvideomode(_DEFAULTMODE); /* restore previous mode */
}
```

The _**arc**() function is similar to the _**ellipse**() function, except that it has four more parameters which specify the beginning and ending points of the arc. To understand how the beginning and end of the arc are defined, remember that the arc is a section of an ellipse. The center of the ellipse is the same as the center of the box that defines the ellipse. Draw a line from the center of this box outward past the edge of the rectangle, as shown in Figure 12-4.

Where this line crosses the ellipse defines the start of the arc. Draw another line from the center in a different direction to define the end of the arc. These start and end lines can be specified using any pair of coordinates that lie on them; not just the coordinates where the line crosses the ellipse.

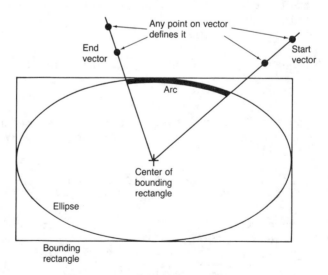

Figure 12-4. Specifying an Arc

### Draw Arc (Section of Ellipse)

```
_arc(left, top, right, bot, xStart, yStart, xEnd, yEnd)
short left, top;        /* boundary rectangle upper left corner */
short right, bot;       /* boundary rectangle bottom right corner */
short xStart, yStart;   /* start vector coordinates */
short xEnd, yEnd;       /* end vector coordinates */
```

## Pixels

If you wish to draw a shape for which there is no appropriate function, you can always construct it from individual pixels. The function that does this is _setpixel().

### Put One Pixel on the Screen

```
_setpixel(x, y)
short x;    /* x coordinate of pixel */
short y;    /* y coordinate of pixel */
```

This function requires only the coordinates of the pixel. The next example shows the _setpixel() function used to plot the sine of an angle from 0 to 360 degrees.

```
/* plot.c */
/* plots sin function, demonstrates _setpixel() */
#include <graph.h>                   /* needed for graphics */
#include <math.h>                    /* for sin() */
#define LEFT    0
#define RIGHT 200
#define VCTR  100
main()
{
    double angle, sinofA;       /* angle and sine of angle */
    int x, y;                   /* screen coordinates */
                                /* initialize cga graphics */
    if( _setvideomode(_MRES4COLOR)==0 )
        { printf("Can't set mode"); exit(1); }

    _moveto( LEFT, VCTR );      /* draw line along x-axis */
    _lineto( RIGHT, VCTR );
    for( x=LEFT; x<RIGHT; x++ )
        {
```

```
        angle = ((double)x / (RIGHT-LEFT)) * (2 * 3.14159265);
        sinofA = sin( angle );
        y = VCTR - VCTR*sinofA;
        _setpixel( x, y );
        }
    getche();                       /* keep figure until keypress */
    _setvideomode(_DEFAULTMODE); /* restore old video mode */
}
```

QuickC programmers will need to construct a program list to use this program, because the **sin()** library function is not built into the QuickC core library. See Chapter 1 for a description of program lists.

At the beginning of the program the horizontal axis is drawn. The sine curve is controlled by a loop variable **x**, which starts at the left edge of the screen and moves pixel by pixel to the right. Pixels are plotted at each point, with the **y** variable determining their vertical position.

The **sin()** library function operates on angles measured in radians. There are 2∗pi radians in 360 degrees, so the angle to be plotted goes from 0 to 2∗pi radians (about 6.2) as **x** goes from left to right. The sine of the angle starts at 0 at 0 radians, increases to 1 at 1.6 radians, decreases to 0 again at 3.1 radians, continues falling to −1 at 4.7 radians, and finally returns to 0 at 6.2 radians. The **y** variable is actually at 100 when the sine of the angle is 0. This offset permits the angle to go both above and below the origin. Figure 12-5 shows the effect.

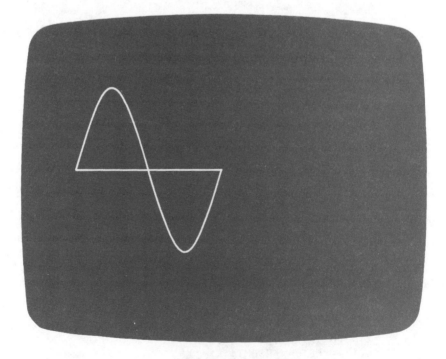

Figure 12-5. Output of plot.c

## The Aspect-Ratio Problem

As we noted earlier, in some graphics modes, including the one we've been using (CGA mode 4), a circle may appear a bit higher than it is wide: it looks elliptical, rather than truly round. This happens because the pixels used to create graphics images in this mode are not square; that is, they are not quite as wide as they are high. A video screen typically has a width-to-height ratio of 4 to 3; it might be 12 inches wide by 9 inches high. In mode 4 there are 320 pixels across by 200 pixels down, so for a 12x9 screen size there would be 320/12 or 26.67 pixels per inch horizontally, and 200/9 or 22.22 pixels per inch vertically. Or, to turn the fractions upside down, a pixel is 0.038 inch wide and 0.045 inch high. This is not a square pixel, since it does not have the same width and height. (We might note that even a square pixel might not look square on the screen; the little blob of light may actually be round.)

On this screen, if you draw a circle that is 100 pixels wide and 100 pixels high, it will be narrower than it is high by a ratio of 0.038/0.045. To make a circle look round, its width must be made somewhat larger to compensate for this disparity.

The area of the screen actually used for the display varies not only from one monitor to another, but from one display adaptor board to another and from one mode to another. The most accurate way to determine the ratio of width to height on a particular system is to run a program like border.c that shows the edges of the display, and measure them.

The following program draws our circle-in-a-box design, but takes into account the aspect ratio of the particular system and graphics mode. The actual dimensions of the screen as measured using the border.c program are 9.5 inches wide by 6.4 inches high. You can modify the WIDTH and HEIGHT constants to reflect your particular display. The program uses the __getvideoconfig()__ function to obtain the number of horizontal and vertical pixels. This makes it easier to modify the program to work in different graphics modes.

```
/* aspect.c */
/* draws circle and box with correct proportions */
#include <graph.h>
#define LEFT      0           /* boundary of rectangle */
#define TOP       0
#define BOT       199
#define WIDTH     9.5         /* actual screen dimensions */
#define HEIGHT    6.4         /*   (inches or cm) */
main()
{
    int right;               /* right boundary */
    float xPPU, yPPU;        /* pixels per unit */
    float ratio;             /* aspect ratio */
    struct videoconfig config;
                             /* initialize graphics */
    if( _setvideomode(_MRES4COLOR)==0 )
        { printf("Can't set mode"); exit(1); }
```

```
        _getvideoconfig(&config);        /* get pixel info */
        xPPU = (float)config.numxpixels / WIDTH;
        yPPU = (float)config.numypixels / HEIGHT;
        ratio = xPPU / yPPU;             /* calculate aspect ratio */
        right = ratio * BOT;             /* calculate right boundary */

        _rectangle(_GBORDER, LEFT, TOP, right, BOT); /* draw box */
        _ellipse(_GBORDER, LEFT, TOP, right, BOT); /* draw circle */

        getch();
        printf("ratio=%f", ratio);
        getch();                         /* keep image until keypress */
        _setvideomode(_DEFAULTMODE);     /* restore old mode */
}
```

When you run this program you'll see that the circle appears round and the box square. The program also prints out the aspect ratio: 1.0778 in this case. You can apply this technique in any program where correctly proportioned figures are important.

# Filling

Any graphics shape that is completely surrounded by solid lines or curves can be filled with a solid color or with a pattern. Three functions let you fill a shape at the same time you draw it: **_rectangle()**, **_ellipse()**, and **_pie()**. Other shapes can be filled with the function **_floodfill()**. If a pattern is set prior to filling, shapes can be filled with different patterns. In this section we'll see how filling is handled.

## Filling with Solid Colors

The next example is a variation on the poly.c program. It draws the same view of a three-dimensional box, but it fills the front, side, and top of the box with different colors.

```
/* fillpoly.c */
/* draws and fills polygons */
#include <graph.h>                   /* needed for graphics */

main()
{
                                     /* initialize graphics */
    if( _setvideomode(_MRES4COLOR)==0 )
        { printf("Can't set mode"); exit(1); }
                                     /* draw front rectangle */
    _setcolor( 1 );                  /* solid light cyan */
    _rectangle(_GFILLINTERIOR, 50, 50, 150, 180);
```

```
_moveto(150,50);              /* draw right polygon */
_lineto(180,20);              /*    top */
_lineto(180,135);             /*    right */
_lineto(150,180);             /*    bottom */
_setcolor( 2 );               /*    fill with light magenta */
_floodfill(165, 100, 1);      /*    fill polygon */

_setcolor( 1 );               /* reset outline light cyan */
_moveto(50,47);               /* draw top polygon */
_lineto(150,47);              /*    front */
_lineto(180,17);              /*    right */
_lineto(95,17);               /*    back */
_lineto(50,47);               /*    left */
_setcolor( 3 );               /*    fill with white */
_floodfill(125, 35, 1);       /*    fill polygon */

getche();                     /* keep image until keypress */
_setvideomode(_DEFAULTMODE);  /* restore previous mode */
}
```

The front rectangle of the box is filled using the _GFILLINTERIOR option to the _**rectangle()** function. This causes the shape being drawn to be filled with the current color. This color is set using the _**setcolor()** function. The default palette in CGA mode 4 is the following:

| Number | Color |
| --- | --- |
| 0 | Black (background color) |
| 1 | Light cyan |
| 2 | Light magenta |
| 3 | White |

The default color is the highest numbered one available in a particular palette, in this case white. The numbers used as arguments to _**setcolor()** are called *pixel values*, rather than colors, since they don't always refer to the same colors. We'll see in the section on color how different palettes of colors can be selected in CGA mode.

### Set Current Pixel Value (Color)

```
_setcolor(pixelValue)
short pixelValue;        /* pixel value (0, 1, 2, 3) */
```

The appropriate number is supplied as a parameter to _**setcolor()** to select the color. Once a color is set, all subsequent drawing activity—lines, rectangles, ellipses, and so on—will take place in this color until it is changed.

The **_rectangle()** function both outlines the rectangle and fills it, using the same color. We have more flexibility with the polygons that form the top and side of the box, since they are filled with a separate function, **_floodfill()**. In fillpoly.c the current color is set to one value to create the outline, and then to another color before filling.

---

**Fill Area with Color or Pattern**

```
_floodfill(x, y, boundaryColor)
short x;               /* x coordinate of seed point */
short y;               /* y coordinate of seed point */
short boundaryColor; /* color bounding shape to be filled */
```

---

The **_floodfill()** function is given the coordinates of the point where filling should begin: the "seed point." This point must be inside the shape to be filled (unless you want to fill everything *but* the shape). You must also specify the color of the line that forms the boundary of the shape. The fill process will fill up to this color, but not beyond. Figure 12-6 shows the result of filling the surfaces of the box with solid colors.

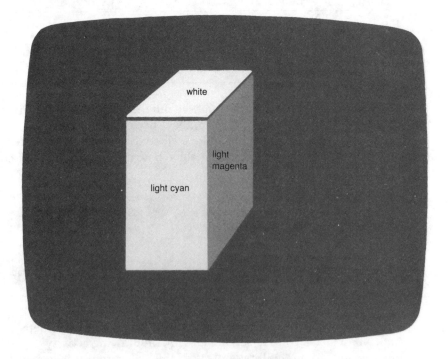

Figure 12-6. Output of fillpoly.c

## Filling with Patterns

Any shape that can be filled with a solid color can also be filled with a pattern. To do this, the *current pattern* is set using the function **_setfillmask()**.

### Creating a Fill Pattern

In some graphics packages the programmer can choose from a handful of preset patterns. Microsoft C takes a different approach. The good news is that you can create any pattern you want. The bad news is that it takes a little extra trouble to specify the pattern.

Patterns are specified using an 8x8 grid. Any pixel in the grid can be either on or off. To construct a pattern, begin by drawing the grid and darkening in the pattern, as shown in Figure 12-7.

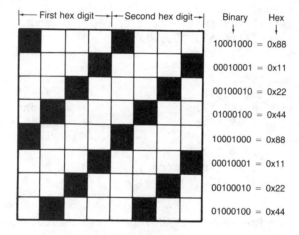

Figure 12-7. Creating a Fill Pattern

This pattern consists of diagonal lines. Now, assume that the darkened squares are 1s and the open squares are 0s. Write the hexadecimal equivalent of each line of the pattern. There will be eight of these hex numbers. Create an array of type **char** or **unsigned char** that is initialized to these eight values. The pattern.c program shows three such arrays: one makes a pattern of squares, one makes vertical lines, and one makes horizontal lines.

```
/* pattern.c */
/* draws and fills polygons with pattern */
#include <graph.h>                /* needed for graphics */

char pattern1[] = { 0x00, 0x00, 0x3C, 0x3C,    /* square */
                    0x3C, 0x3C, 0x00, 0x00 };

char pattern2[] = { 0x88, 0x88, 0x88, 0x88,    /* vert lines */
                    0x88, 0x88, 0x88, 0x88 };

char pattern3[] = { 0xFF, 0x00, 0x00, 0x00,    /* horiz lines */
                    0xFF, 0x00, 0x00, 0x00 };
```

```
main()
{                                    /* initialize graphics */
    if( _setvideomode(_MRES4COLOR)==0 )
        { printf("Can't set mode"); exit(1); }
                                     /* draw front rectangle */
    _setcolor( 1 );                  /*     fill with light green */
    _setfillmask(pattern1);          /*     fill with squares */
    _rectangle(_GBORDER,        50, 50, 150, 180);  /* border */
    _rectangle(_GFILLINTERIOR, 50, 50, 150, 180);  /* fill */

    _moveto(150,50);                 /* draw right polygon */
    _lineto(180,20);                 /*     top */
    _lineto(180,135);                /*     right */
    _lineto(150,180);                /*     bottom */
    _setcolor( 2 );                  /*     use light red, */
    _setfillmask(pattern2);          /*     and vertical lines, */
    _floodfill(165, 100, 1);         /*     to fill polygon */
    _setcolor( 1 );                  /* reset outline color */

    _moveto(50,47);                  /* draw top polygon */
    _lineto(150,47);                 /*     front */
    _lineto(180,17);                 /*     right */
    _lineto(95,17);                  /*     back */
    _lineto(50,47);                  /*     left */
    _setcolor( 3 );                  /*     use yellow, */
    _setfillmask(pattern3);          /*     and horizontal lines, */
    _floodfill(125, 35, 1);          /*     to fill polygon */

    getch();                         /* keep image until keypress */
    _setvideomode(_DEFAULTMODE);     /* restore previous mode */
}
```

This program is an extension of poly.c and fillpoly.c. Here the three shapes
are filled, but with different patterns instead of a solid color. The result is shown
in Figure 12-8.

The **_setfillmask()** function takes as its only argument the address of the
array containing the pattern to be set.

---

**Set Fill Pattern**

```
_setfillmask(array)
unsigned char far *array;  /* array specifying pattern */
```

---

## Patterns in Lines

Lines can also be given a pattern, although the pattern is one-dimensional. The
pattern for a line is specified by a single variable of type **unsigned short**. This
provides 16 bits, which correspond into a line segment 16 pixels long.

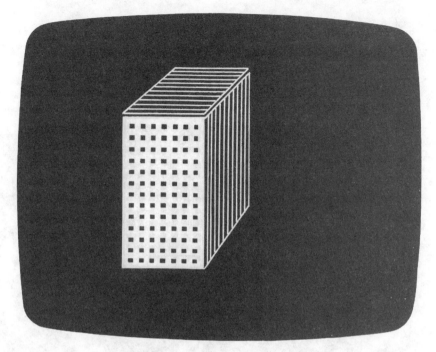

Figure 12-8. Output of pattern.c

The next example draws three lines, each with a different line style. The first is a dashed line with long dashes, the second has dashes only half as long, and in the third the dashes are shorter still.

```
/* linetype.c */
/* draws lines with different styles */
#include <graph.h>
main()
{
    unsigned short mask;
                                    /* initialize graphics */
    if( _setvideomode(_MRES4COLOR)==0 )
        { printf("Can't set mode"); exit(1); }
    mask = 0xFF00;                  /* 1111111100000000 */
    _setlinestyle(mask);
    _moveto(0, 10);
    _lineto(200, 10);
    mask = 0xF0F0;                  /* 1111000011110000 */
    _setlinestyle(mask);
    _moveto(0, 20);
    _lineto(200, 20);
    mask = 0xCCCC;                  /* 1100110011001100 */
    _setlinestyle(mask);
    _moveto(0, 30);
    _lineto(200, 30);
```

```
        getch();                        /* keep picture until keypress */
        _setvideomode(_DEFAULTMODE); /* restore old mode */
}
```

Figure 12-9 shows the output of this program.

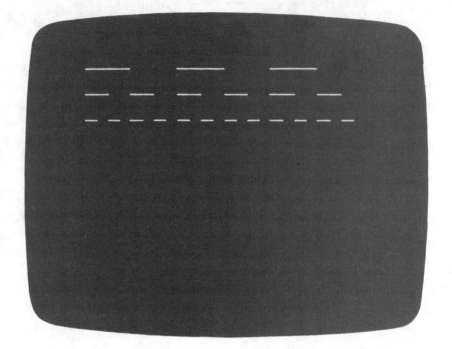

Figure 12-9. Output of linetype.c

Even shorter dashes can be created if you wish. Or you can alternate long and short dashes with a constant such as 0xFCFC.

## Bar and Pie Charts

One important application for filling graphics shapes is in the creation of bar and pie charts. In this section we'll see how to create both kinds.

The bar chart consists of a series of rectangles usually filled with solid colors or patterns. Our next example graphs 10 data values, as shown in Figure 12-10.

The program is written so that the number of data values can be easily changed: simply insert an appropriate value for N and put the new data values in the array **data[N]**. It's easy to change other characteristics of the graph by changing **define#** statements. The width of the bars, the spacing between them, and the vertical range of the graph (pixels per data unit) can all be varied to accommodate different amounts and types of data.

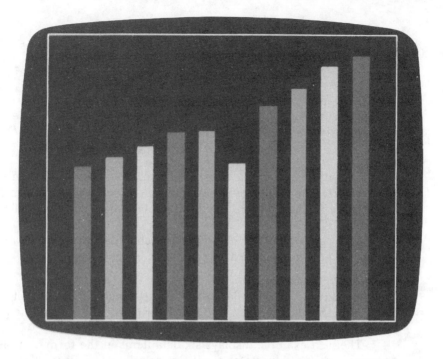

Figure 12-10. Output of bargraph.c

```c
/* bargraph.c */
/* generates bar graph */
#include <graph.h>               /* needed for graphics */
#define N        10              /* number of values to graph */
#define BWIDTH   10              /* width of each bar */
#define SEP      12              /* separation between bars */
#define DI      (BWIDTH+SEP)     /* distance from bar to bar */
#define SHFT     15              /* between border and 1st bar */
#define WIDTH  ( (N+1) * DI )    /* width of chart */
#define LEFT     5               /* left side of graph */
#define BOT      170             /* bottom of graph */
#define TOP      5               /* top of graph */
#define PPD (float)(BOT-TOP)/100   /* pixels per data unit */
                                 /* data to display */
int data[N] = { 41, 47, 54, 62, 63, 59, 75, 83, 89, 96  };

main()
{
    int j;
                                 /* set cga mode 4 */
    if( _setvideomode(_MRES4COLOR)==0 )
      { printf("Can't set mode"); exit(1); }
                                 /* draw border */
    _rectangle( _GBORDER, LEFT, TOP, LEFT+WIDTH, BOT );

    for( j=0; j<N; j++ )         /* draw bars */
```

```
         {
         _setcolor( 1+j%3 );              /* alternate 3 colors */
         _rectangle( _GFILLINTERIOR,
                     LEFT+SHFT+j*DI,          BOT-data[j]*PPD,
                     LEFT+SHFT+j*DI+BWIDTH, BOT );
         }
      getche();                           /* keep image until keypress */
      _setvideomode(_DEFAULTMODE); /* restore old mode */
}
```

The program draws a rectangle around the chart and then, in a loop, it repeatedly sets the color of the bar with **_setcolor()** and draws the bar with **_rectangle()**. The bars are filled with solid colors since the fill flag is set to _GFILLINTERIOR.

We'll see a more sophisticated bar chart later in this chapter when we investigate how to place text in a graphics image.

### The _pie() Function

The **_pie()** function is similar to the **_arc()** function, except that it draws lines connecting the ends of the arc to its center and fills the resulting pie slice. It is commonly used to create pie charts.

The next example displays six data items in the form of a pie chart. The program first finds the total of all the data items. A particular data item is a certain percent of the total, and the pie slice representing that data item occupies the same percentage of the circle. The first slice begins at the 3 o'clock position and grows counter-clockwise. Each succeeding slice begins where the last one ended. The slices are filled with color by cycling through the three CGA color values: 1, 2, and 3. The output of the program is shown in Figure 12-11.

```
/* pie.c */
/* generates pie chart */
#include <graph.h>               /* needed for graphics */
#include <math.h>                /* for sin() and cos() */
#define N        6               /* number of data items */
#define XCTR    100              /* x-coordinate of pie center */
#define YCTR    100              /* y-coordinate of pie center */
#define XRAD     75              /* x-radius of pie */
#define YRAD     70              /* y-radius of pie */
#define LEFT    (XCTR-XRAD)      /* rectangle holding pie */
#define TOP     (YCTR-YRAD)
#define RIGHT   (XCTR+XRAD)
#define BOT     (YCTR+YRAD)
#define RAD     500              /* large for accuracy */

int data[N] = { 11, 19, 41, 32, 15, 7, };  /* data items */
main()
{
    double dataSum, startAngle, endAngle, relAngle;
    double startVecX, startVecY, endVecX, endVecY;
    int j;
```

```
if( _setvideomode(_MRES4COLOR)==0 )
   { printf("Can't set mode"); exit(1); }
                            /* sum the data values */
for(j=0, dataSum=0; j<N; j++)
   dataSum += data[j];
endAngle = 0;                   /* start at 3 o'clock angle */
for( j=0; j<N; j++ )            /* draw slices */
   {
   startAngle = endAngle;    /* start at end of last slice */
                             /* find angle for this data */
   relAngle = 2 * 3.1415927 * data[j] / dataSum;
   endAngle = startAngle + relAngle;   /* find end angle */
   _setcolor( 1 + j % 3);             /* cycle 3 colors */
   startVecX = XCTR + RAD*cos(startAngle);  /* translate */
   startVecY = YCTR - RAD*sin(startAngle);  /*    angles */
   endVecX =   XCTR + RAD*cos(endAngle);    /*    to */
   endVecY =   YCTR - RAD*sin(endAngle);    /*    vectors */
                                    /* draw one slice */
   _pie(_GFILLINTERIOR, LEFT, TOP, RIGHT, BOT,
                            startVecX, startVecY,
                            endVecX, endVecY );

   }  /* end for */
getch();                       /* hold image until keypress */
_setvideomode(_DEFAULTMODE); /* restore previous mode */
}
```

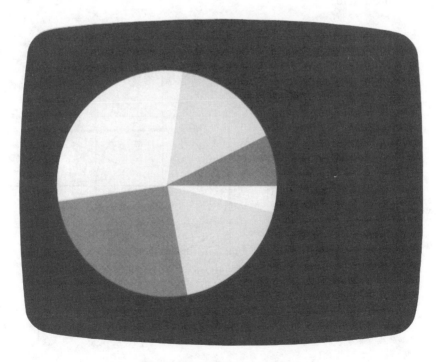

Figure 12-11. Output of pie.c

The _**pie()** function takes nine arguments. These are the fill control flag, the coordinates of a rectangle bounding the ellipse of which the pie slice is a part, and the coordinates of the start and stop vectors that determine where the ellipse starts and ends.

### Draw Pie Slice

```
_pie(fill, left, top, right, bot, xStart, yStart, xEnd, yEnd)
short fill;              /* _GFILLINTERIOR or _GBORDER */
short left, top;         /* boundary rectangle upper left corner */
short right, bot;        /* boundary rectangle bottom right corner */
short xStart, yStart;    /* start vector coordinates */
short xEnd, yEnd;        /* end vector coordinates */
```

If the _**pie()** function specified the start and end points of the pie slice using angles instead of the coordinates of vectors, this program would have been simpler. As it is, we need to translate the angle for each slice into an appropriate set of vector coordinates; essentially a polar-to-rectangular coordinates transformation. This requires calculating the sine and cosine of the angles. Figure 12-12 shows the relationship of the angle and the vector coordinates.

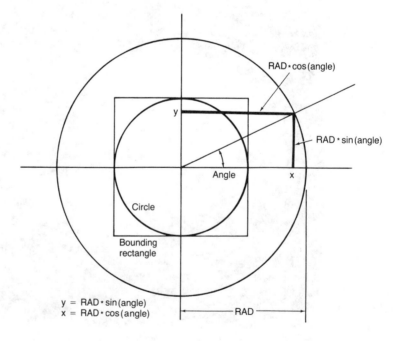

Figure 12-12. Transformation of Angles to Vectors

As we noted earlier, the point specifying the vector does not need to lie on the ellipse. In fact, the farther away it is, the more accurately the angles of the pie slices will be drawn. Accuracy is important so the end of the last pie slice will coincide with the same 3 o'clock position where the first slice started. In the program we use a radius of 500.

To use the **sin()** and **cos()** library functions in QuickC, the program must be compiled using a program list, since these functions are not part of the core library.

Ordinarily pie charts should be as round as possible, so it's important to compensate for the aspect ratio of your particular graphics mode and screen. We've taken a quick-and-dirty approach to the problem by making the horizontal radius of the pie slice 75 and the vertical radius 70. In other graphics modes this ratio would be different, and a similar approach to that described in the aspect.c program should be used.

# Colors

So far we've used only the three colors available from the default CGA color palette. Other colors can be displayed in CGA, and the EGA and VGA adaptors provide an even richer assortment of colors. Let's see how to generate the colors that each of these adaptors makes available.

## Colors in CGA

In _MRES4COLOR—the normal CGA graphics mode—there are four different palettes. A palette can be thought of as a mapping of the CGA pixel values (0, 1, 2, and 3) into actual colors. The default palette, which we've used until now, causes these four pixel values to be mapped into the colors black (or whatever the background color is), light cyan, light magenta, and white. Three other palettes are available, as shown in Table 12-2.

### Table 12-2. CGA Palettes

| Palette | Pixel Value 0 | 1 | 2 | 3 |
|---------|---------|------------|---------------|------------|
| CGA 0 | Backgrnd | Green | Red | Brown |
| CGA 1 | Backgrnd | Cyan | Magenta | Light gray |
| CGA 2 | Backgrnd | Light green | Light red | Yellow |
| CGA 3 | Backgrnd | Light cyan | Light magenta | White |

The palette in use is changed with the _**selectpalette()** function. Changing the palette changes all the colors on the screen at once. If an image has been drawn using one palette, changing the current palette causes every color in the image to be transformed into a different color without the image being redrawn.

**Select CGA Palette**

```
_selectpalette(palette)
short palette;     /* number of palette: 0 to 3 */
```

The next example program demonstrates palette changes. It draws four color bars on the screen, using the default colors. Then, each time a keyboard key is pressed, it changes the palette. All four colors change simultaneously. (Press the [Esc] key to quit the program.)

```c
/* cgacolor.c */
/* demonstrates cga colors */
#include <graph.h>
#define XMAX     320            /* x pixels from 0 to 319 */
#define YMAX     200            /* y pixels from 0 to 199 */
#define COLORS   4              /* four colors at once */
#define PALETTES 4              /* four possible palettes */
#define INC      (XMAX/COLORS)  /* column width for 1 color */
#define ESC      27             /* [Esc] key ASCII code */
main()
{
    int pal, color, x;
                                /* initialize graphics */
    if( _setvideomode(_MRES4COLOR)==0 )
        { printf("Can't set mode"); exit(1); }
    _setbkcolor( _GREEN );      /* set background color */

    printf("Default");          /* default palette */
                                /* draw four color bars */
    for(color=0, x=0; color<COLORS; color++, x+=INC)
        {                       /* colors from 0 to 3 */
        _setcolor(color);       /* bars from left to right */
        _rectangle(_GFILLINTERIOR, x, 10, x+INC, YMAX-10);
        }
    pal = 0;                    /* cycle thru palettes */
    while( getch() != ESC )             /* exit on [Esc] */
        {
        _selectpalette(pal);            /* change palette */
        _settextposition(0, 0);         /* print at top left */
        printf("Palette %d", pal);      /* print palette # */
        pal = ++pal<COLORS ? pal : 0;   /* increment pal */
        }
    _setvideomode(_DEFAULTMODE); /* restore old mode */
}
```

The palette number is displayed in the upper-left corner of the screen, as shown in Figure 12-13.

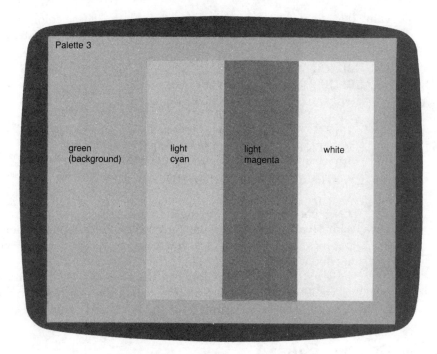

Figure 12-13. Output of cgacolor.c

The **_settextposition()** function positions the cursor at the upper-left corner of the screen before writing takes place. We'll examine this function in the section on text.

### The Background Color

The background color remains unchanged when the palette changes. That is, color 0 always produces the background color, no matter which palette is used. In cgacolor.c we set the background color to green, using the **_setbkcolor()** function.

---

***Set Background Color***

```
_setbkcolor(color)
long color;    /* background color constant (_BLUE, etc.) */
```

---

The argument for this function is not the same as that for **_setcolor()**. We've seen how the **_setcolor()** function takes a short integer value as its argument. Depending on the palette used, this integer pixel value is then mapped into one of several different screen colors.

The argument to **_setbkcolor()**, on the other hand, is an actual color value that is not changed by changing the palette. These color values require the **long int** data type. The following list shows these color constants.

| | |
|---|---|
| _BLACK | _GRAY |
| _BLUE | _LIGHTBLLUE |
| _GREEN | _LIGHTGREEN |
| _CYAN | _LIGHTCYAN |
| _RED | _LIGHTRED |
| _MAGENTA | _LIGHTMAGENTA |
| _BROWN | _LIGHTYELLOW |
| _WHITE | _BRIGHTWHITE |

These constants are **#defined** in GRAPH.H to have rather complex hexadecimal values. We'll see the purpose of these values when we examine VGA graphics. In CGA graphics you can use these constant names without worrying about the numerical values they represent.

The **_setbkcolor()** function can also set the background color in text mode, as we'll see in the section on text. When used with text, numerical values from 0L to 15L can be substituted for the **#defined** constants.

## Colors in EGA

An EGA graphics adaptor provides higher resolution than CGA graphics and more colors. There are normally 16 colors available. These are the same 16 colors used as background colors in the CGA mode. The following example program displays all 16 colors, using the **_setcolor()** function with arguments from 0 to 15. It draws 16 vertical color bars, surrounded by a white border, as shown in Figure 12-14.

```
/* egacolor.c */
/* demonstrates ega colors */
#include <graph.h>
#define TOP    10              /* tops of bars */
#define BOT    340             /* bottoms of bars */
#define LEFT   0               /* left edge of screen */
#define RIGHT  639             /* right edge of screen */
#define COLORS 16              /* 16 colors */
#define INC ((RIGHT-LEFT)/COLORS) /* column width per color */

main()
{
   int color, x;
                                /* initialize graphics */
   if( _setvideomode(_ERESCOLOR)==0 )
     { printf("Can't set mode"); exit(1); }
                                /* draw 16 color bars */
   for(color=0, x=LEFT; color<COLORS; color++, x+=INC)
     {                          /* colors from 0 to 15 */
```

```
      _setcolor(15);              /* draw white border */
      _rectangle(_GBORDER, x, TOP, x+INC, BOT);
      _setcolor(color);          /* fill interior with color */
      _rectangle(_GFILLINTERIOR, x+1, TOP+1, x+INC-1, BOT-1);
      }
   getch();                      /* keep image until keypress */
   _setvideomode(_DEFAULTMODE); /* restore old mode */
}
```

Figure 12-14. Output of egacolor.c

Pixel value 0 produces the background color, as it does in CGA modes. Here we don't set the background color, so pixel value 0, the bar on the right, is a white outline filled with black, the default background. Values 1 through 15 produce different colors, as you can see by trying out the program.

Notice that pixel values from 0 to 15 are used as arguments to _**setcolor**(); the **long int** color constants needed by _**setbkcolor**() are not appropriate for this function. Table 12-3 shows the colors and the corresponding pixel values.

### Remapping Colors

The _**setpalette**() function does not work in EGA graphics. It is possible, however, to remap the 16 EGA pixel values so that each refers to a different color. This produces an effect similar to _**setpalette**(), in that a single function can immediately change every color on the screen. The function that accomplishes this is _**remapallpalette**().

## Table 12-3. Pixel Values for EGA Colors

| Color | Pixel Value |
|---|---|
| Black | 0 |
| Blue | 1 |
| Green | 2 |
| Cyan | 3 |
| Red | 4 |
| Magenta | 5 |
| Brown | 6 |
| White | 7 |
| Gray | 8 |
| Light blue | 9 |
| Light green | 10 |
| Light cyan | 11 |
| Light red | 12 |
| Light magenta | 13 |
| Light yellow | 14 |
| Bright white | 15 |

### Remaps All Pixel Values to Different Colors

```
_remapallpalette(array)
long far *array;  /* array of color values */
```

To use this function, you first set up an array. Each element in the array contains one of the **long int** color constants, such as _BLUE. The constant placed in array element 0 specifies the color that pixel value 0 will generate, the constant placed in element 1 specifies the color that pixel value 1 will generate, and so on for all 16 array elements. Thus if array element 5 contains _GREEN, **_setpixel(5)** will produce a green dot (even though the default color for 5 is magenta).

The following example shows this remapping in action. The first part of the program is similar to egacolor.c in that 16 color bars are drawn. After drawing the bars, however, the program goes into a loop in which each tap of a keyboard key remaps the colors in a different way.

```
/* remap.c */
/* demonstrates  remapping */
#include <graph.h>
#define TOP    10              /* tops of bars */
#define BOT    340             /* bottoms of bars */
#define LEFT    0              /* left edge of screen */
```

```
#define RIGHT   639             /* right edge of screen */
#define COLORS  16              /* 16 colors */
#define INC ((RIGHT-LEFT)/COLORS) /* column width per color */
#define ESC     27              /* [Esc] key ASCII value */

long palette[16] =              /* normal color palette */
      { _BLACK, _BLUE, _GREEN, _CYAN, _RED, _MAGENTA, _BROWN,
       _WHITE, _GRAY, _LIGHTBLUE, _LIGHTGREEN, _LIGHTCYAN,
       _LIGHTRED, _LIGHTMAGENTA, _LIGHTYELLOW, _BRIGHTWHITE };

main()
{
   int color, x, j;
   long temp;
                                /* initialize graphics */
   if( _setvideomode(_ERESCOLOR)==0 )
     { printf("Can't set mode"); exit(1); }
                                /* draw 16 color bars */
   for(color=0, x=LEFT; color<COLORS; color++, x+=INC)
      {                         /* colors from 0 to 15 */
      _setcolor(15);            /* draw white border */
      _rectangle(_GBORDER, x, TOP, x+INC, BOT);
      _setcolor(color);         /* fill bars with colors */
      _rectangle(_GFILLINTERIOR, x+1, TOP+1, x+INC-1, BOT-1);
      }
   while( getch() != ESC )      /* change palette on keypress */
      {                         /* exit on [Esc] */
      temp = palette[0];            /* save color 1 */
      for(j=0; j<COLORS-1; j++)     /* move each color left */
         palette[j] = palette[j+1];  /*    in palette */
      palette[15] = temp;           /* color 0 to color 15 */
      _remapallpalette(palette);    /* remap all colors */
      }
   _setvideomode(_DEFAULTMODE); /* restore old mode */
}
```

The array is initialized with the colors in their normal order. The remapping is done by rotating the color constants around the array. Each time through the loop the program shifts the constants one array element to the left, and moves element 0 to element 15. It then remaps this new arrangement of colors to the hardware, using **_remapallpalette()**. The effect is of the colors shifting across the screen. No redrawing of the image is necessary to achieve this effect, so a complex display can be recolored very quickly.

If you modify the program so that it cycles through the palette changes rapidly, rather than waiting for a keypress, you'll see that the pattern appears to move from right to left across the screen. In this way complex images can be given the appearance of motion.

Another function, **_remappalette()**, can be used to remap a single color rather than the entire palette. We'll see an example of its use in the next section.

## Colors in VGA

VGA graphics can put 256 colors on the screen at the same time, using mode _MRES256COLOR. These colors can be obtained by supplying pixel values from 0 to 255 to the _**setcolor()** function. The following example draws 256 rectangles to the screen, each with a different color. These rectangles form a 16x16 matrix.

```
/* vgacolor.c */
/* demonstrates 256 VGA colors */
#include <graph.h>                /* needed for graphics */
#define XMAX    320               /* x pixels from 0 to 319 */
#define YMAX    200               /* y pixels from 0 to 199 */
#define COLORS 256                /* 256 colors (16*16) */
#define XINC   (XMAX/16)          /* width of 1 column */
#define YINC   (YMAX/16)          /* width of 1 row */
main()
{
    int color, x, y;
                                  /* initialize graphics */
    if( _setvideomode(_MRES256COLOR)==0 )
       { printf("Can't set mode"); exit(1); }

    color = 0;                    /* start colors at 0 */
    for(y=0; y<YMAX-1; y+=YINC)   /* go down rows */
       for(x=0; x<XMAX-1; x+=XINC)  /* go across columns */
          {
          _setcolor(color++);     /* set and incr color */
                                  /* draw box at x, y */
          _rectangle(_GFILLINTERIOR, x, y, x+XINC, y+YINC);
          }
    getch();                      /* save until keypress */
    _setvideomode(_DEFAULTMODE);  /* restore old mode */
}
```

The first 16 colors (the top row of rectangles) produced by the vgacolor.c program are the same as those available with EGA graphics and listed in Table 12-3. The second row contains 16 shades of gray, and the remaining rows contain a large spectrum of colors.

### Remapping VGA Colors

The 256 colors demonstrated by vgacolor.c may seem like a lot, especially compared with the 16 available under EGA. By remapping, however, you can create 262,144 colors, although only 256 can be on the screen at one time. That is, there are 256 pixel values, but 262,144 colors. The VGA hardware maps the pixel values into a palette of 256 colors, but you can select these colors from a 262,144-color palette, using the _**remappalette()** and _**remapallpalette()** functions.

How are the VGA color values defined? Each of the primary colors—blue, green, and red—is represented by six bits which determine the intensity of the primary color. Actually, each primary color requires one byte, but the topmost two bits are not used, leaving values from 0 to 3F hex or from 0 to 63 decimal. Each of the three colors can have one of 64 intensities. The total number of colors that can be represented in this scheme is 64x64x64, or 262,144.

The constant denoting a particular color can be readily created using a six-digit hexadecimal value. The first two digits specify the blue intensity, the second two specify the green intensity, and the last two (the low-order byte) represent the red intensity. For instance, the number 0x3f0000 produces a bright blue. The first two digits are set to their maximum value of 3F hex, and the pairs of digits representing green and red are set to 00. The number 0x2a002a produces magenta, since moderate amounts of blue and red, but not green, are specified. Gray is 0x1f1f1f. Here each color is exactly in the middle of its range. Bright white is 0x3f3f3f, the maximum for each primary. The color constants in GRAPH.H are defined to be equal to the hex values shown in Table 12-4.

### Table 12-4. Color Constants in GRAPH.H

| Constant | Hex Value |
| --- | --- |
| _BLACK | 0x000000L |
| _BLUE | 0x2a0000L |
| _GREEN | 0x002a00L |
| _CYAN | 0x2a2a00L |
| _RED | 0x00002aL |
| _MAGENTA | 0x2a002aL |
| _BROWN | 0x00152aL |
| _WHITE | 0x2a2a2aL |
| _GRAY | 0x151515L |
| _LIGHTBLUE | 0x3F1515L |
| _LIGHTGREEN | 0x153f15L |
| _LIGHTCYAN | 0x3f3f15L |
| _LIGHTRED | 0x15153fL |
| _LIGHTMAGENTA | 0x3f153fL |
| _LIGHTYELLOW | 0x153f3fL |
| _BRIGHTWHITE | 0x3f3f3fL |

To see how these values produce colors, run the following program. It will generate any of the 262,144 colors, filling a rectangle on the screen with the color. The values of the three primary colors are selected from the keyboard, so you can easily mix a color to your specification. It's as if you had a book with almost three hundred thousand color samples, making the program a natural for interior decorators—or anyone thinking of repainting the kitchen.

```
/* allcolor.c */
/* displays all 262,144 VGA colors */
#include <graph.h>              /* needed for graphics */
#define LEFT    20              /* dimensions of color box */
#define TOP     20
```

```
#define RIGHT  300
#define BOT    180
#define ESC     27              /* [Esc] key ASCII value */
#define MAX    0x3f             /* maximum 6-bit color value */
main()
{
    char ch;
    long color, red, green, blue;   /* color values */
                                    /* initialize graphics */
    if( _setvideomode(_MRES256COLOR)==0 )
      { printf("Can't set mode"); exit(1); }

    _setbkcolor( 0x1f1f1fL );        /* set background to gray */
    red =   0x1fL;                   /* set color box to gray */
    green = 0x1fL;
    blue  = 0x1fL;

    while( (ch=getch()) != ESC )     /* quit on [Esc] key */
      {
      switch(ch)                     /* change color value */
         {
         case 'r': if(red>0)      --red;   break;
         case 'R': if(red<MAX)    ++red;   break;
         case 'g': if(green>0)    --green; break;
         case 'G': if(green<MAX)  ++green; break;
         case 'b': if(blue>0)     --blue;  break;
         case 'B': if(blue<MAX)   ++blue;  break;
         }
      color = blue<<16 | green<<8 | red;  /* construct color */
      _remappalette(1, color);            /* remap color 1 */
      _setcolor(1);                       /* set color 1 */
                                          /* fill rectangle */
      _rectangle(_GFILLINTERIOR, LEFT, TOP, RIGHT, BOT );
                                          /* print values */
      _settextposition(0,0);              /* in upper-left */
      printf("blue=%02lx green=%02lx red=%02lx",
                                    blue, green, red);
      }  /* end while */
    _setvideomode(_DEFAULTMODE);          /* restore old mode */
}
```

When you first start the program you'll see a completely gray screen. This is actually a gray rectangle on a gray background. Press the 'B' key to increase the amount of blue, and the 'b' key to decrease it. Green and red are adjusted similarly with 'G' and 'g' or 'R' and 'r' keys. The program displays the current hex values of the three colors, so you can see the color, and the values used to create it, at the same time. Figure 12-15 shows how this looks.

The program uses the **_remappalette()** function to map the desired color onto the pixel value 1. This pixel value is then set with **_setcolor()**, and a rectangle is drawn and filled with the color using **_rectangle()**.

Figure 12-15. Output of allcolor.c

### Remap a Single Pixel Value

```
_remappalette()
short pixel;    /* pixel value to be reassigned (0, 1, etc.) */
long color;     /* new color for pixel value (0x1f1f1f, etc.) */
```

The color value is created from three separate values for the primary colors, represented by the variables **blue**, **green**, and **red**. The value for blue is shifted left 16 bits, the value for green is shifted left 8 bits, and then all three variables are bitwise ORed together to produce the complete color value.

It's fun to experiment with this program. Increasing blue and red together creates purple, just as when you mix paint. Decreasing the amount of red, while leaving blue and green at a medium value, produces cyan. Similarly, any shade of any color can be displayed. A change of only one unit is usually not perceptible; one color blends smoothly into another as you hold down a key.

# Text

Many Microsoft C graphics functions exist to manipulate text, rather than pixel images. These text-oriented functions can be used for text alone or to combine text with graphics. In this section we'll examine these functions.

One aspect of the text functions that's different from the graphics functions we've used so far is that you don't usually need to change modes when using them. They operate perfectly well in text modes such as _TEXTC80 and _TEXTMONO. For this reason, the next few programs don't invoke the **_setvideomode()** function. Only if text and graphics are combined does a graphics mode need to be selected.

Text-oriented functions do require that the library file GRAPHIC.LIB (or GRAPHICS.QLB) be linked with the program and that the header file GRAPH.H be included in the source file.

## Text Windows

One of the most important features provided by the text-oriented graphics functions is the ability to create windows. A window is a rectangular area of the screen used to constrain text output. When text is written into a window, it starts at the left edge of the window instead of the left edge of the screen and it wraps down to the next line at the right edge of the window. The entire window full of text scrolls upward when additional text is written at the bottom of the window. In other words, the window acts like a small version of the screen.

Windows are useful in constructing a variety of applications. QuickC uses several windows in its display. There's one window to hold the text of your program. As you scroll your program listing you'll see that it is bounded by the top and bottom of the window, not the entire screen. You may also see an error window at the bottom of the screen and another window at the top to hold watch expressions. The use of text windows to separate different functional screen areas is becoming increasingly popular in today's applications.

Our example program creates a text window and then writes the word "Greetings" to it one hundred times. You'll see that the text is all written inside the window, wrapping at the right edge and scrolling upward when the window is filled. Before exiting, the program prints "THE END" in the middle of the window. The result is shown in Figure 12-16.

```
/* window.c */
/* tests character graphics functions */
#include <graph.h>                    /* needed for graphics */
#define TOP     8                     /* define window */
#define LEFT    10                    /*     rows and columns */
#define BOT     21
#define RIGHT   52
#define HEIGHT  (BOT-TOP+1)           /* screen height */
#define DELAY 12000                   /* delay loop constant */

main()
{
```

```
      int j, k;

      _clearscreen(_GCLEARSCREEN);          /* clear entire screen */
      _settextwindow(TOP,LEFT,BOT,RIGHT);   /* specify window */
      _settextcolor(1);                     /* set text color */
      _setbkcolor(2L);                      /* set text background */

      for( j=0; j<100; j++ )                /* 100 words */
         {
         _outtext( "Greetings " );          /* print word */
         for(k=0; k<DELAY; k++ );           /* slow down the loop */
         }
      _settextposition( 8, 15 );            /* go to window center */
      _outtext( "   THE   END   " );        /* print phrase */
      _settextposition( HEIGHT,1 );         /* cursor to bottom line */
}
```

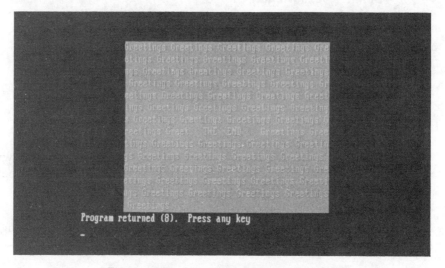

Figure 12-16. Output of window.c Program

### Clearing the Screen

Because we don't change modes at the beginning of the program, it's necessary to clear the screen so our image will not compete with existing text. The _clearscreen() function is used for this purpose.

---

#### Clear Screen, Viewport, or Window

```
_clearscreen(areaType)
short areaType;  /* _GCLEARSCREEN = screen,
                    _GVIEWPORT    = viewport,
                    _GWINDOW      = text window */
```

---

Three possible values can be given to this function's single argument. The one we want clears the entire screen. Other options clear a viewport (which we'll explore later) and the text window.

### Defining the Window

The window is defined using the _**settextwindow**() function. This function takes as arguments the row and column numbers defining the window. Annoyingly, these arguments are in a different order than those used in such pixel-oriented functions as _**rectangle**(). Instead of a left, top, right, bottom order, _**settextwindow**() uses a top, left, bottom, right order. In other words, for each row-column pair, the row comes first. Rows and columns start at 1,1 at the upper-left corner, rather than at 0,0 as do the pixel-oriented functions.

---

**Define a Text Window**

```
_settextwindow(topRow, leftCol, botRow, rightCol)
short topRow;      /* top row of window */
short leftCol;     /* left column of window */
short botRow;      /* bottom row of window */
showrt rightCol;   /* right column of window */
```

---

You can only define one window at a time, but that doesn't mean you can't have more than one window on the screen. To display multiple windows, use the _**window**() function to define one of several windows just before writing to it.

### Specifying Text and Background Colors

The color of the text to be written into the window can be changed with the _**settextcolor**() function.

---

**Set Text Color**

```
_settextcolor(pixelValue)
short pixelValue;           /* pixel value (0, 1, 2, etc.) */
```

---

The possible pixel values used as arguments to this function run from 0 to 15. They produce the same colors as those used by _**setcolor**() in EGA mode. In window.c we set the text color to 1, which corresponds to blue.

If you use pixel values from 16 to 32 with _**settextcolor**(), you'll get the same range of values, but with the blinking attribute. In other words, add 16 to the pixel value to turn on blinking.

We also set the background to 2, or green, using _**setbkcolor**(). Because we are setting a text background rather than graphics, we set the color using a number from 0 to 15, rather than a constant like _BLUE. However, it is still of type **long int**.

### Writing Text to a Window

Normal text output functions such as **printf()** can't be used to write to a window because they don't recognize the window's boundaries. If you want text to wrap at the right edge of the window and scroll the window upward when it reaches the bottom, you must use the _**outtext()** function.

### Write Text to Window

```
_outtext(textString)
char far *textString;    /* string to be written */
```

This function's only argument is the address of the text string to be written. It writes to the window at the current text position (TP). When the window is first opened, this position is the upper-left corner, at 1,1. Thus in our window.c program, writing starts at this point and continues down the window, each write starting at the end of the previous one. The cursor ordinarily follows the TP.

### Positioning Text

To write at an arbitrary point in the window it's necessary to reposition the TP. This is handled by the _**settextposition()** function, which requires the row and column number to which the text position will be reset. This function works with such normal text output functions as **printf()**, as well as with _**outtext()**.

### Set Text Position

```
_settextposition(row, col)
short row;    /* text position row */
short col;    /* text position column */
```

In window.c we use this function to reposition the TP before writing "THE END" in the middle of the window. We also use it to set the TP to the bottom of the window at the end of the program. This prevents the DOS prompt from overwriting the window when the program terminates.

Notice that _**settextposition()** operates on *window* coordinates (if a window is defined), rather than screen coordinates. Thus the coordinates (8,15) given this function in the window.c program specify the center of the window, rather than the center of the screen, and (HEIGHT,1) is the bottom of the window.

## A Simple Text Editor

Let's put what we've learned about text functions together in a simple editor program. This example is derived from the wpro1.c and wpro2.c programs in Chapter 10, but it edits text in a window, rather than the entire screen. You can use all four cursor keys to move around in the window, so you can insert text anywhere, as shown in Figure 12-17. You can also change the color of the text by pressing the [Alt] [c] key combination and then typing a digit from 1 to 9. Press [Esc] to leave the program.

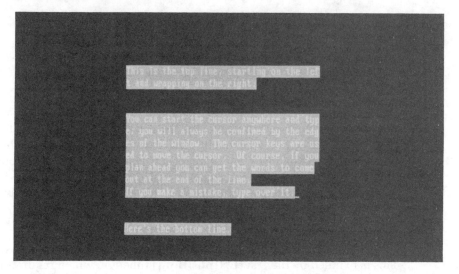

Figure 12-17. Using the ezedit.c Program

```
/* ezedit.c */
/* mini editor works in text window */
#include <graph.h>              /* needed for graphics */
#define LEFT    10              /* left side of window */
#define TOP      8              /* top of window */
#define RIGHT   50              /* right side of window */
#define BOT     21              /* bottom of window */
#define WIDTH   (RIGHT-LEFT+1)  /* width of window */
#define HEIGHT  (BOT-TOP+1)     /* height of window */
#define ESC     27              /* escape key */
#define L_ARRO  75              /* cursor control keys */
#define R_ARRO  77
#define U_ARRO  72
#define D_ARRO  80
#define ALT_C   46              /* keys for color change */


main()
{
    char key;                           /* keyboard char */
```

```
    int row, col;                        /* cursor row & column */
    char string[2];                      /* 1-char string */
    struct rccoord rc;                   /* for text position */

    _clearscreen(_GCLEARSCREEN);         /* clear entire screen */
    _settextwindow(TOP, LEFT, BOT, RIGHT);  /* define window */
    row = HEIGHT/2; col = WIDTH/2;       /* cursor to middle */
    _settextposition(row, col);
    _setbkcolor(1L);                     /* set background color */

    while( (key=getch()) != ESC )        /* if [Esc], exit loop */
       {
      if( key == 0 )                     /* if extended code, */
         {
         switch( getch() )               /* read second character */
            {
            case L_ARRO:                 /* move cursor left */
               if(col > 1)
                  _settextposition(row, --col);
               break;
            case R_ARRO:                 /* move cursor right */
               if(col < WIDTH)
                  _settextposition(row, ++col);
               break;
            case U_ARRO:                 /* move cursor up */
               if(row > 1)
                  _settextposition(--row, col);
               break;
            case D_ARRO:                 /* move cursor down */
               if(row < HEIGHT)
                  _settextposition(++row, col);
               break;
            case ALT_C:                  /* change text color */
               _settextcolor(getch()-'0');
               break;
            }  /* end switch */
         }  /* end if */
      else                               /* not extended code */
         {
         *string = key;                  /* make 1-char string */
         *(string+1) = 0;                /* terminate string */
         _outtext(string);               /* print character */
         rc = _gettextposition();        /* get new cursor pos */
         row = rc.row;
         col = rc.col;
         }
      }  /* end while */
    }
```

If the user presses a key with an extended code, the program checks if it is
a cursor key or the color-change key combination and takes appropriate action.

The variables **row** and **col** always indicate the current cursor position. Pressing a cursor key changes one of these variables and then uses **_settextposition()** to update the cursor position.

If it is not an extended code, the character must be printed on the screen. Since only one function, **_outtext()**, exists to place text in a window, the process of echoing a character to the screen is somewhat complicated. The single character is first made into a string by placing it in a buffer called **string[2]** and appending a '\0' to terminate it. Then this one-character string is written to the window with **_outtext()**.

More complex strings can be written to a window using **sprintf()**. This library function works the same as **printf()**, except that its output is written to a buffer rather than to the screen. From the buffer, the string can be displayed in the window using **_outtext()**.

The text position must be reset after every use of **_outtext**, because this function may have wrapped the cursor to the next line. The function **_gettextposition()** is used to discover the text position (where the cursor is).

---

### Get Current Text Position

```
_gettextposition()
/* coordinates returned in struct rccoord */
```

---

The function returns the row and column information in a structure called **rccoords**, defined in GRAPH.H like this:

```
struct rccoord {
    short row;      /* row text position */
    short col;      /* column text position */
};
```

The program uses the variable **rc**, of type **struct rccoords**, to hold this information.

The backspace key does not work in this program. We'll add a working backspace in an exercise at the end of the chapter. We'll see another example of a text window in the section on viewports, later in this chapter.

## Combining Text and Graphics

Our next example combines text and graphics in one display. This is a somewhat more complicated program—an extension of the bargraph.c example earlier in this chapter. In addition to drawing vertical bars as that program did, barega.c also adds a title to the graph, draws tick marks on the vertical edges, numbers the tick marks, and labels each bar with the name of a month. Figure 12-18 shows the output of the program.

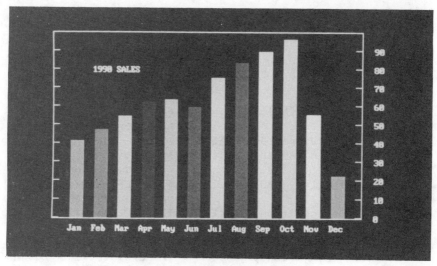

Figure 12-18. Output of barega.c

Because it is difficult to create satisfactory text in CGA graphics modes, this program uses EGA mode __ERESCOLOR (640x350 resolution, 16 colors).

```
/* barega.c */
/* generates bar graph, uses EGA 640x350 graphics */
#include <graph.h>                 /* needed for graphics */
#define N          12              /* number of values to graph */
#define BWIDTH     22              /* width of each bar */
#define SEP        18              /* separation between bars */
#define SHFT       30              /* between border and 1st bar */
#define LEFT        5              /* left side of graph */
#define BOT       285              /* bottom of graph */
#define TOP         5              /* top of graph */
#define TICKS      10              /* number of tick marks */
#define TWIDTH     10              /* width of tick marks */
#define UNDER      28              /* from bottom to months */
#define BESIDE     28              /* from right edge to numbers */
#define MAXDATA   100              /* maximum data units */
#define TITLEROW    5              /* location of title */
#define TITLECOL   10
#define PPCOL ( 640/80 )           /* pixels per text column */
#define PPROW ( 350/25 )           /* pixels per text row */

#define DI      (BWIDTH+SEP)       /* distance from bar to bar */
#define WIDTH   ( (N+1) * DI )     /* width of chart */
                                   /* pixels between ticks */
#define PBT ( (float)(BOT-TOP ) / TICKS )
                                   /* pixels per data unit */
#define PPD ( (float)(BOT-TOP) / MAXDATA )
                                   /* data to display */
int data[N] = { 41, 47, 54, 62, 63, 59, 75, 83, 89, 96, 55, 22 };
```

```
                                        /* names of months */
     char months[12][4]={ "Jan", "Feb", "Mar", "Apr", "May", "Jun",
                          "Jul", "Aug", "Sep", "Oct", "Nov", "Dec"  };
     main()
     {
        int j;
        char string[40];
                                        /* set ega mode 16 */
        if( _setvideomode(_ERESCOLOR)==0 )
           { printf("Can't set mode"); exit(1); }
                                        /* draw border */
        _rectangle( _GBORDER, LEFT, TOP, LEFT+WIDTH, BOT+1 );
                                        /* draw title */
        _settextposition( TITLEROW, TITLECOL );
        _outtext("1990 SALES");

        for(j=0; j<TICKS; j++)          /* draw ticks and numbers */
           {
           _moveto(LEFT,             BOT-j*PBT);    /* left tick */
           _lineto(LEFT+TWIDTH,      BOT-j*PBT);
           _moveto(LEFT+WIDTH-TWIDTH, BOT-j*PBT);   /* right tick */
           _lineto(LEFT+WIDTH,       BOT-j*PBT);
                                                    /* y axis */
           _settextposition( (BOT-j*PBT+14)/PPROW,  /* positions */
                          (LEFT+WIDTH+BESIDE)/PPCOL );
           itoa(j*(MAXDATA/TICKS), string, 10);     /* get number */
           _outtext( string );                      /* display it */
           }
        for(j=0; j<N; j++)              /* draw bars and months */
           {
           _setcolor( 1+j );                        /* set bar color */
           _rectangle(_GFILLINTERIOR,               /* draw bar */
                   LEFT+SHFT+j*DI,          BOT-data[j]*PPD,
                   LEFT+SHFT+j*DI+BWIDTH, BOT );
           _settextposition( (BOT+UNDER)/PPROW, /* print month */
                          (LEFT+SHFT+j*DI)/PPCOL+1 );
           _outtext(months[j]);
           }
        getche();                       /* keep image until keypress */
        _setvideomode(_DEFAULTMODE); /* restore old mode */
     }
```

As in bargraph.c, this program uses **#defined** constants to specify the dimensions of the graph elements. By changing these constants, the program can be adapted to work in different graphics modes and to display different numbers of bars and different magnitudes of data.

### Placing Text

This program demonstrates one of the problems of combining text with graphics: you can't place a text character anywhere you want; it can only be written at the standard row and column coordinates. In the present mode there are 640 pixel positions horizontally, but only 80 columns. 640 divided by 80 gives 8 pixels per column. Thus a character must go at pixel position 0, or 8, or 16, and so on.

This inflexibility on the part of the text dictates the dimensions of the graph. Each bar must be separated from the next by an integral number of columns, so the months will line up with the bars. In the program the width of each bar is set at 22 and the separation at 18, so the bar-to-bar distance is 40, a multiple of 8. Likewise, the tick marks on the vertical axis must correspond with text rows, so the numbers will line up with the marks. There are 350/25 or 14 pixels per row. The graph is made 280 pixels high, with 10 divisions. As 28 is a multiple of 14, each of the numbers on the vertical axis is adjacent to a tick mark.

Another potential disappointment with Microsoft's approach to text is that only one character size and font is available. This limits the effects possible for presentation graphics. However, multiple fonts impose considerable overhead and complexity on a graphics system.

# Advanced Graphics

In this section we'll explore several more complex graphics topics: logical coordinates, storage of graphics images in memory, video memory pages, and viewports.

## Logical Coordinates

We've learned that the screen coordinates—those used as arguments for such graphics functions as **_rectangle()** and **_setpixel()**—start with (0,0) in the upper-left corner. Actually, the coordinates used for these functions are *logical coordinates*; they are not necessarily the same as the physical coordinates of the screen. It is possible to redefine the logical coordinate system so that (0,0) no longer corresponds to the upper-left corner.

In the following example a function draws our circle-in-a-box image over and over using the same logical coordinates, but the image appears at different places on the screen. The location where the image is actually drawn is specified by changing the logical origin. The program creates a matrix of these images, as shown in Figure 12-19.

A function, **boxcirc()**, is used to draw the design. It always draws it at the same place: with the top left corner at (0,0). Using two nested loops, the program moves the logical origin down from row to row and across from column to column, calling **boxcirc()** each time.

```
/* logico.c */
/* uses logical coordinates to */
/*    draw many circle-and-box figures */
#include <graph.h>
#define LEFT    0               /* boundary rectangle */
#define TOP     0               /*    coordinates */
#define RIGHT   33
```

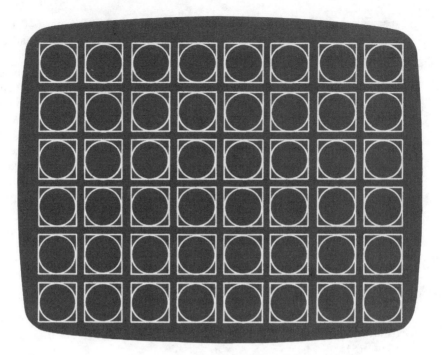

Figure 12-19. Output of logico.c

```
#define BOT     30
#define WIDTH  (RIGHT-LEFT+3)        /* width of rectangle */
#define HEIGHT (BOT-TOP+3)           /* height of rectangle */
void boxcirc(void);                  /* function prototype */

main()
{
   int x, y;                         /* logical origin */
                                     /* initialize graphics */
   if( _setvideomode(_MRES4COLOR)==0 )
     { printf("Can't set mode"); exit(1); }

   for(y=0; y<200-HEIGHT; y+=HEIGHT)    /* move down */
     for(x=0; x<320-WIDTH; x+=WIDTH)   /* move across  */
       {
       _setlogorg(x,y);              /* move logical origin */
       boxcirc();                    /* design at logical origin */
       }
   getche();                         /* keep image until keypress */
   _setvideomode(_DEFAULTMODE); /* restore old mode */
}

/* boxcirc() function */
/* draws box and circle at logical origin */
void boxcirc(void)
```

```
{
    _rectangle(_GBORDER, LEFT, TOP, RIGHT, BOT);   /* box */
    _ellipse(_GBORDER, LEFT, TOP, RIGHT, BOT);     /* circle */
}
```

The logical origin is changed with the **_setlogorg()** function, which takes as its two arguments the physical x and y coordinates where the logical origin will be placed.

---

### Set Logical Origin

```
_setlogorg(x, y)
short x;  /* physical x coordinate to place logical origin */
short y;  /* physical y coordinate to place logical origin */
```

---

Changing the logical origin is also useful in plots of negative numbers. For example, in our plot.c program, the sin function was plotted above and below the x axis: it took on both positive and negative values. We had to add a constant so the entire curve would be plotted on the screen, since there are no negative physical coordinates. We could have set the logical y coordinate at the center of the screen, thereby simplifying the equation used for the plot. The logical origin is frequently set to the center of the screen so the screen can emulate the coordinate system used in geometry or complex number calculations.

## Storing Graphics Images

A graphics image can be taken from the screen and saved in memory. Later, it can be written back to the screen at the same place or a different one. There are several reasons why this might be useful. It is usually faster to copy a completed image from memory to the screen than it is to draw the image in the first place—especially if the image is complex or makes extensive use of curves and filled areas.

One application in which the rapid drawing of images is important is in animation, where an image gives the illusion of motion by being drawn and rapidly redrawn at successive locations on the screen.

Our next example shows an animated bouncing ball. A rectangle forms a border around the screen, and a ball appears to bounce endlessly inside this border, reflected from the sides of the rectangle like a ball on a pool table.

```
/* image.c */
/* bouncing ball created from bit image */
#include <graph.h>                       /* needed for graphics */
#define LEFT     0                       /* screen border */
#define TOP      0
#define RIGHT    319
#define BOTTOM   199
```

```
#define RAD    8                          /* radius of ball */

main()
{
    int x, y, dx, dy, oldx, oldy;    /* ball coordinates */
    char *ballbuff;                  /* pointer to buffer */
    long size;                       /* size of buffer */

    if( _setvideomode(_MRES4COLOR)==0 ) /* set cga mode */
        { printf("Can't set mode"); exit(1); }
                                     /* draw boundary */
    _rectangle(_GBORDER, LEFT, TOP, RIGHT, BOTTOM);
                                     /* set center of ball */
    x = y = RAD+10;                  /* create image of ball */
    _setcolor( 1 );                  /* light green in cga 0 */
                                     /* draw circle at x,y  */
    _ellipse(_GFILLINTERIOR, x+RAD, y+RAD, x-RAD, y-RAD);
                                     /* get size of image */
    size = _imagesize(0, 0, 2*RAD, 2*RAD);
    ballbuff = (char *)malloc(size); /* get memory for image */
                                     /* place image in memory */
    _getimage( x-RAD, y-RAD, x+RAD, y+RAD, ballbuff );
    dx = 2;                          /* set speed of ball */
    dy = 1;
    while ( !kbhit() )               /* exit on keypress */
        {                            /* memory image to screen */
        _putimage( x-RAD, y-RAD, ballbuff, _GPSET );
        oldx = x; oldy = y;          /* remember where it was */
        x += dx;  y += dy;           /* move its coordinates */
                                     /* reflect it at edges */
        if( x<=LEFT+RAD+2 || x>=RIGHT-RAD-2 )
            dx = -dx;
        if( y<=TOP+RAD+2 || y>=BOTTOM-RAD-2 )
            dy = -dy;                /* erase old image */
        _putimage( oldx-RAD, oldy-RAD, ballbuff, _GXOR );
        }
    _setvideomode(_DEFAULTMODE);     /* restore previous mode */
}
```

There are two parts to this program. In the first part the image of the ball is created, using _ellipse() and the _GFILLINTERIOR option. The result is shown in Figure 12-20. The image of the ball is then stored in a memory buffer using the _getimage() function. It's usually best to determine the size of this buffer at run-time and allocate memory with **malloc()**. Use the function _imagesize() to find how large the buffer should be.

This function returns the number of bytes needed for the image in a variable of type **long int**. Once the size needed to store the image is known, the **malloc()** function is used to obtain a pointer to the storage area. This pointer, and the coordinates of the image, are then used as arguments to _getimage() to store the image in the buffer.

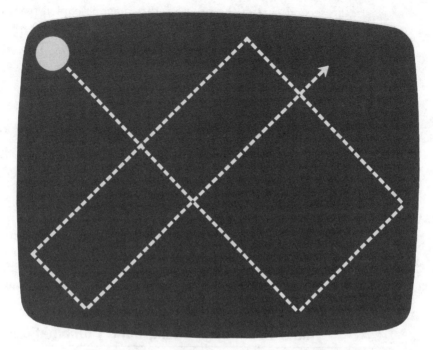

Figure 12-20. Initial Position of Ball in image.c

### Determine Size of Screen Image

```
long _imagesize(left, top, right, bot)
short left;    /* coordinates of image */
short top;
short right;
short bot;
```

### Store Screen Image in Memory

```
_getimage(left, top, right, bot, buffer)
short left;          /* coordinates of image */
short top;
short right;
short bot;
char far *buffer;  /* memory storage for screen image */
```

In the second part of the program the image is copied from the buffer to the screen, using the function _**putimage()**.

---

**Transfer Image from Memory to Screen**

```
_putimage(left, top, buffer, action)
short left;        /* coordinate for left edge of image */
short top;         /* coordinate for top edge of image */
char far *buffer;  /* buffer where image is stored */
short action;      /* way to combining image with background */
```

---

The first two arguments are the x and y coordinates where the top left corner of the image will be placed. Next is the address of the buffer where the image is stored. The last argument, **action**, specifies which of several techniques will be used to combine the image with the background. These are shown in Table 12-5.

### Table 12-5. Image-Background Combinations

| Constant | Purpose |
|----------|---------|
| _GPSET | Erases background, inserts image |
| _GPRESET | Erases background, inserts inverted image (black becomes white, green becomes magenta, etc.) |
| _GAND | ANDs color values of image and background (image unchanged on white, disappears on black) |
| _GOR | ORs color values of image and background (image unchanged on black, disappears on white) |
| _GXOR | XORs color values of image and background (image unchanged on black, inverted on white) |

The image is placed on the screen using the _GPSET option. This simply obliterates anything already on the screen, and copies the image from memory.

The image is repeatedly copied to the screen in a loop, and the coordinates where the ball is placed vary continuously, producing the effect of the moving ball. If the coordinates of the ball reach the border, the ball's direction in the appropriate coordinate is reversed, so the ball seems to bounce off the walls.

Before a new image of the ball is drawn, the old image must be erased. This is done by writing the image over top of the old one with the **action** parameter set to _GXOR. This has the effect of erasing the image, since two 1 bits XORed with each other produce a 0 bit, and two 0 bits also produce a 0 bit.

## Video Pages

In some video modes there is more graphics memory available than is actually used. This extra memory can be put to use holding alternate images of the screen. For example, EGA graphics mode _MRES16COLOR requires 32K of memory (320x200/2, since each byte holds two pixels). However, many EGA graphics boards have 256K of memory installed. This is eight times as much as is necessary for a screen image, so eight screen images can be stored at one time, each in a separate page of memory. Ordinarily only the lowest page of memory is mapped to the screen, but a graphics function can be used to switch pages. If each page has a different image, these images can be displayed almost instantly by selecting the appropriate page.

To run the example program you need an EGA (or VGA) system with 256K of memory. The program first creates a series of eight ellipses and stores one in each page of memory. The ellipses are all the same height. They start out narrow (in fact the first one is actually a tall thin rectangle), and grow progressively larger. The eighth ellipse is a circle. The program then cycles through a loop, switching pages each time. First it displays the pages in ascending order, so the ellipses get bigger. Then it displays them in reverse order, so the images get smaller. The effect is that of a coin spinning about a vertical axis, as shown in Figure 12-21.

Figure 12-21. Output of coin.c

```
/* coin.c */
/* uses pages to display coin rotating about vertical axis */
```

```
/* must have 256K of graphics memory */
#include <graph.h>
#define XC      160             /* center of ellipse */
#define YC      100
#define RAD      90             /* vertical radius */
#define N         8             /* number of views (256/32) */
#define DELAY 10000             /* delay between views */

main()
{
    int xRad;
    int j, k;
                                        /* 320x200, 16 colors */
    if(_setvideomode(_MRES16COLOR)==0 )  /* uses 32K of memory */
        { printf("Can't set mode"); exit(1); }

    for( j=0; j<N; j++ )            /* make and store */
        {                          /*     images of ellipses */
        if(_setactivepage(j) < 0 )  /* set page to write image */
            { printf("Can't set page"); exit(1); }
        if( j == 0 )               /* rectangle edge-on */
            _rectangle(_GBORDER, XC-2, YC-RAD, XC+2, YC+RAD );
        else
            {
            xRad = j * RAD / (N-1) ; /* find x radius */
                                     /* draw ellipse */
            _ellipse(_GBORDER, XC-xRad, YC-RAD, XC+xRad, YC+RAD );
            }
        } /* end for */
    while( !kbhit() )              /* display ellipses */
        {                          /*      until keypress */
        for( j=0; j<N; j++)        /* increasing width */
            {
            _setvisualpage( j );   /* select page to display */
            for(k=0; k<DELAY; k++); /* delay */
            }
        for( j=N-2; j>0; j--)      /* decreasing width */
            {
            _setvisualpage( j );   /* select page */
            for(k=0; k<DELAY; k++); /* delay */
            }
        } /* end while */
    _setvideomode(_DEFAULTMODE);   /* restore previous mode */
}
```

Pages can be switched very rapidly. In the program, a delay loop slows down the page switching, otherwise the images would blur together rather than appearing to rotate.

The __setactivepage()__ function is used before drawing a graphics image. This function causes all subsequent drawing activities to be written to the page specified. This is usually not the page being displayed, so the images created will be invisible.

---

### Specify Page Where Graphics Output Is Written

```
short _setactivepage(pageNumber)
short pageNumber;     /* page number (0, 1, etc.) */
```

---

This function returns a negative number if the page specified is not available. Such a return may be an indication of insufficient graphics memory.

A particular page is called up for display using the **_setvisualpage()** function.

---

### Specify Page to Be Displayed

```
short _setvisualpage(pageNumber)
short pageNumber;     /* page number (0, 1, etc.) */
```

---

This function also returns a negative value if the page specified is unavailable.

## Viewports

A viewport does for graphics images what a window does for text: it restricts an image to a rectangular area of the screen. Any pixels drawn outside an active viewport are simply not displayed; they are "clipped" at the edges of the viewport. This is useful when a display contains several graphics images that should not overwrite one another or when it contains graphics and text windows that should remain separate.

The example program uses both a viewport to hold graphics output and a window to hold text-based interaction with the user. The program prompts the user to enter the coordinates of the center of a circle and prompts again for the diameter of the circle. The circle specified, or that part of it that will fit, is then drawn in the viewport. A sample interaction is shown in Figure 12-22.

The user can enter data for as many circles as desired. The text scrolls off the top of the window, without interfering with the graphics. The graphics output is confined by the viewport and doesn't conflict with the text window.

```
/* viewport.c */
/* tests character graphics functions */
#include <graph.h>                          /* needed for graphics */
```

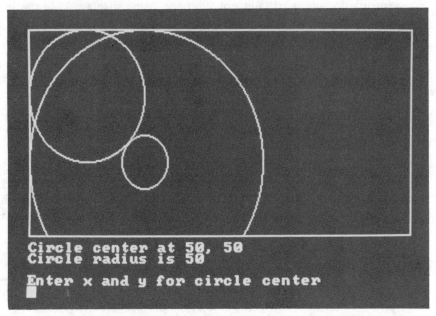

Figure 12-22. Sample Interaction with viewport.c

```
#define GLEFT    0                        /* define viewport */
#define GTOP     0
#define GRIGHT 319
#define GBOT   155
#define TLEFT    1                        /* define text window */
#define TTOP    21
#define TRIGHT  80
#define TBOT    25
void getsnoe(char *ptr);          /* function prototype */

main()
{
    char string[80];                      /* user input buffer */
    int x, y, rad=1;                      /* circle specs */

    if(_setvideomode(_MRES4COLOR)==0 )       /* set mode */
      { printf("setvideomode error\n"); exit(1); }
                                          /* viewport */
    _setviewport(GLEFT, GTOP, GRIGHT, GBOT);
    _rectangle(_GBORDER, GLEFT, GTOP, GRIGHT, GBOT);

    _settextwindow(TTOP,TLEFT,TBOT,TRIGHT); /* text window */
    _displaycursor(_GCURSORON);             /* cursor on */

    while( rad != 0 )
      {                              /* get circle center */
```

```
        _outtext("\nEnter x and y for circle center\n");
        getsnoe(string);
        sscanf(string, "%d %d", &x, &y);
                                    /* get circle radius */
        _outtext("\nEnter circle radius");
        _outtext("\n   (Enter 0 to quit)\n");
        getsnoe(string);
        sscanf(string, "%d", &rad);
                                    /* repeat the input */
        sprintf(string,"\nCircle center at %d, %d\n", x, y);
        _outtext(string);
        sprintf(string,"Circle radius is %d\n", rad);
        _outtext(string);
                                    /* construct circle */
        _ellipse(_GBORDER, x-rad, y-rad, x+rad, y+rad);
        }
    _setvideomode(_DEFAULTMODE);
}

/* getsnoe() function */
/* reads string from keyboard with _outtext() echo */
void getsnoe(char *ptr)             /* arg is pntr to buffer */
{
    char ch;                        /* character read */
    char stringchar[2];             /* 1-character string */

    while( (ch=getch()) != '\r' )   /* quit on [Enter] */
        {
        *ptr++ = ch;                /* put char in buffer */
        stringchar[0] = ch;         /* save char for echo */
        stringchar[1] = '\0';       /* terminate 1-char string */
        _outtext(stringchar);       /* echo 1-char string */
        }
    *ptr = '\0';                    /* terminate buffer */
}
```

The viewport is defined using the __setviewport()__ function.

## Define a Viewport

```
_setviewport(left, top, right, bot)
short left;        /* viewport coordinates */
short top;
short right;
short bot;
```

Note that once the viewport is defined, the origin of the graphics coordinate system is changed to the upper-left corner of the viewport. Another function, _**setcliprgn()**, works the same way but does not change the logical origin.

Ordinarily, a function like **scanf()** would be used to accept the coordinates of the circle and its diameter when the user typed them. However, this function, and possible substitutes like **gets()** and **getche()**, doesn't recognize the text window boundaries. Any text output—even if it's only the echo of input—must be written with _**outtext()** if it is to remain within the window.

To work around this problem, the program uses a "homemade" function called **getsnoe()**. It reads a string from the keyboard, like **gets()**, but each character is echoed with _**outtext**. The technique used is similar to that used to echo characters in the ezedit.c program. The string typed by the user is placed in a buffer. Once the string (presumably consisting of several digits) has been read, the **sscanf()** function takes the string from the buffer and assigns the numbers entered to the appropriate variables. (The **sscanf()** function works like **scanf()**, except that its input comes from a buffer rather than the keyboard.)

The cursor is ordinarily turned off in graphics mode. When using graphics and text at the same time, however, it may be necessary to turn the cursor back on. A function called _**displaycursor()** is used for this purpose.

---

*Turn Cursor On and Off*

```
short far _displaycursor(mode)
short mode;  /* _GCURSORON or _GCURSOROFF */
```

---

This function takes one argument, which can have one of two values, as shown in the box.

# Just for Fun

This section contains several longer programs. These don't introduce any new graphics functions, but they do demonstrate how the functions we've learned so far can be used to create some fascinating and even educational effects.

## Bouncing Lines

This example works on a simple principle. Two points bounce (at different speeds) around the screen, as the ball did in the image.c program. At each position a line is drawn between the two points. The resulting series of lines is displayed as the two points follow their separate trajectories around the screen. The line color changes every few hundred lines, with the result that colored shapes are drawn on top of each other in an ever-changing kaleidoscopic pattern. Surprisingly, curved and wave-like shapes are produced.

The effect is much more dazzling in EGA graphics, with its higher resolution and 16 colors, than it is in CGA, so the example is written in _ERESCOLOR mode. It can easily be converted to other modes. Because the effect of this program depends so much on color and the rapid changing of the design, a figure cannot do it justice, but a rough idea can be gained from Figure 12-23.

Figure 12-23. Output of linerega.c

```
/* linerega.c */
/* bouncing line creates abstract patterns */
#include <graph.h>              /* needed for graphics */
#define LEFT       0            /* screen borders */
#define TOP        0
#define RIGHT    639
#define BOTTOM   349
#define LINES    200            /* lines per color change */
#define MAXCOLOR 15             /* maximum color value */
main()
{
    int x1, y1;                 /* one end of line */
    int x2, y2;                 /* the other end of line */
    int dx1, dy1, dx2, dy2;     /* increments to move points */
    int count=0;                /* how many lines drawn */
    int color=0;                /* color being used */

    if( _setvideomode(_ERESCOLOR)==0 )
        { printf("Can't set mode"); exit(1); }
    x1 = x2 = y1 = y2 = 10;     /* start points */
    dx1 = 1;                    /* point 1: pixels per cycle */
```

```
      dy1 = 2;
      dx2 = 3;                          /* point 2: pixels per cycle */
      dy2 = 4;
      while ( !kbhit() )                /* terminate on keypress */
         {
         _moveto( x1, y1 );             /* go to start of line */
         _lineto( x2, y2 );             /* draw line */
         x1 += dx1;  y1 += dy1;         /* move points */
         x2 += dx2;  y2 += dy2;
         if( x1<=LEFT || x1>=RIGHT )    /* if points are */
            dx1 = -dx1;                 /*    off the screen, */
         if( y1<=TOP || y1>=BOTTOM )    /*    reverse direction */
            dy1 = -dy1;
         if( x2<=LEFT || x2>=RIGHT )
            dx2 = -dx2;
         if( y2<=TOP || y2>=BOTTOM )
            dy2 = -dy2;
         if( ++count > LINES )          /* every LINES lines, */
            {                           /*     change color */
            _setcolor( color );         /* MAXCOLOR colors */
            color = (color >= MAXCOLOR)  ?  0  :  ++color;
            count = 0;
            }
         }
      _setvideomode(_DEFAULTMODE);      /* restore old mode */
   }
```

This program will run until a key pressed.

## Fractals

Fractals are complex and fascinating mathematical entities. They are the subject of much research and are used to create mountain ranges, trees, and other lifelike natural forms in computer graphics.

A fractal begins with a pattern. Each element of the original pattern—which consists of a simple graphics element such as a straight line—is then transformed to the same pattern on a smaller scale. Then each element of the smaller pattern is transformed to the same pattern on an even smaller scale.

To put this in more concrete terms, let's say you're watching an ant walking on a tabletop. The ant is trying to go from point A to point B, which is 3 inches to the right. The ant can walk only in straight line segments 1 inch long, and it can only make right-angle turns.

The shortest route is R, R, R: three segments 1 inch long, heading to the right, straight at the destination, as shown in Figure 12-24a. (R stands for Right, U for Up, L for Left, and D for down.)

There are other routes, however. Let's assume the ant follows the route R, D, R, U, R. It will cover 5 inches instead of 3, but it will still reach the same destination. This is shown in Figure 12-24b.

Now let's put the ant back at its starting point and set it off again to the same

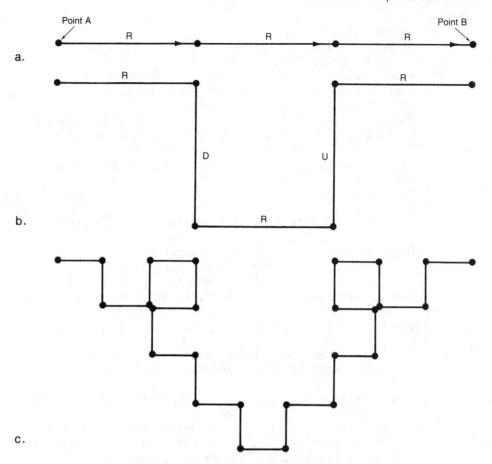

Figure 12-24. Fractal Development

destination. The basic outline of the path it takes is the same as before: R, D, R, U, R. This time, however, the line segments it follows will be only ⅓ inch long. On each of the five 1-inch segments, it will follow the same pattern in miniature, making five ⅓-inch straight lines. The result is shown in Figure 12-24c. The ant will now cover 5x5, or 25, line segments, each ⅓ inch long (8⅓ inches).

When it accomplishes this task, we'll start it over again, with ⅑-inch line segments, dividing each ⅓-inch segment into the same pattern. Then we'll divide these into ¹⁄₂₇-inch segments, and so on. If we keep doing this, the resulting route will become more and more complex. It will also grow longer and longer and cover the surface of the table more and more densely. The result is a representation of a fractal.

The program fractal.c is designed to construct fractals, using a pattern of the programmer's choice. To create a pleasing and symmetrical effect, the design begins as four straight-line segments in the shape of a square. The pattern is then applied to each of these four sides. This process is then repeated on each of the resulting line segments as often as desired; by the time the segments have been divided four or five times they are usually too small to see.

```
/* fractal.c */
/* makes fractal designs */
#include <graph.h>
#define DEPTH    4      /* depth of recursion */
#define LEN      4      /* length of pattern (in segments) */
#define SEGS     8      /* number of segments in pattern */
#define PIXELS 192.0    /* pixels per original segment */
#define LEFT   150.0    /* upper left hand corner */
#define TOP     65.0    /*    of original box */
#define R        0      /* values for directions */
#define D        1
#define L        2
#define U        3
void frac(int direction, float pixels);  /* prototype */

float x, y;             /* current pen position */
int level;              /* current recursion level */
                        /* pattern */
char pattern[SEGS] =    { R, U, R, D, D, R, U, R };

main()
{
   if(_setvideomode(_ERESCOLOR)==0 )          /* set mode */
     { printf("Can't set mode"); exit(1); }

   x = LEFT;                  /* set initial position */
   y = TOP;
   _moveto(x,y);             /* start drawing there */
   level = DEPTH;            /* set initial recursion level */
   frac(R, PIXELS);         /* top of box */
   frac(D, PIXELS);         /* right side of box */
   frac(L, PIXELS);         /* bottom of box */
   frac(U, PIXELS);         /* left side of box */
   getch();                 /* keep image until keypress */
   _setvideomode(_DEFAULTMODE);  /* restore old mode */
}

void frac(int dir, float pix)     /* function draws pattern */
/* dir=orientation to start drawing, pix=pixels per segment */
{
   int j, newdir;            /* counter and new direction */

   --level;                  /* drop down one level */
   if(level==0)              /* if bottom level, */
     {                       /*    draw straight line */
     switch(dir)            /*    instead of pattern */
       {
       case R:  x += pix;  break;      /* move coordinates */
       case L:  x -= pix;  break;      /*    to end of line */
       case D:  y += pix;  break;
       case U:  y -= pix;  break;
```

```
        }
    _lineto(x, y);                          /* draw line */
    }
    else                      /* not at bottom level, so call */
        {                     /* frac() again to draw segment */
        pix /= LEN;                          /* length of new seg */
        for(j = 0; j<SEGS; j++)              /* for each segment */
            {                                /*     in the pattern */
            newdir = (pattern[j]+dir) % 4;   /* get new direction */
            frac( newdir, pix );             /* draw segment */
            }
        }
    ++level;                 /* pop back up one level */
}
```

The pattern used in fractal.c is shown in the array pattern[SEGS], where SEGS is the number of line segments used in the pattern. This is a somewhat more complicated pattern than that shown in the previous figure.

DEPTH is the number of times to repeat the process of redrawing the pattern with smaller line segments, in this case 4. The result at this depth is shown in Figure 12-25.

Figure 12-25. Output of fractal.c

You can experiment with this program by changing the pattern, the number of segments in the pattern, and the depth. A depth of 1 draws the square. A depth of 2 draws the original version of the pattern on each side of the square. A depth of 3 imposes the pattern on each segment of the pattern in level 2, and so on. All sorts of patterns are possible. Try R, U, U, R, D, D, D, D, R, U, U, U, U,

R, D, D, R. It makes a sort of oriental snowflake. You may need to adjust the number of pixels per segment for different patterns, so you have an integral number of pixels for the smallest line segment.

This program makes use of recursion: a function that calls itself. The main part of the program draws the square. To draw each of the four line segments of the square, it calls the function **frac()**. This function reproduces the pattern specified, so it goes through a loop SEGS times, drawing SEGS line segments, each in the appropriate direction. However, until the lowest level each line segment is made up of the original pattern in smaller form, so it calls itself to draw this smaller pattern of segments.

Each of these smaller segments may require another call to **frac()**, and so on. Only when segments have reached the smallest size (that is, when the variable **level** is equal to DEPTH) does **frac()** actually draw any straight lines.

Notice how the directions are calculated. The pattern R, U, D, etc., can be drawn moving to the right, in which case R really means to go right. But if it's drawn moving down, then R means down, D means left, and so on. To calculate the true direction, we add the direction from the pattern **pattern[j]**, to the overall direction given **frac()** when it was called: **dir**. The result is the true direction.

## The Mandelbrot Program

In the past few years a mathematical construct called "the Mandelbrot set" has emerged as one of the most fascinating— and beautiful—objects in mathematics. The set consists of those points on a two-dimensional plane that satisfy certain characteristics. The boundary of the set, which occupies the area between about –2 and 0.5 on the x axis, and 1.25 and –1.25 on the y axis, is astonishingly complex. Looked at in its entirety, the boundary consists of several rounded shapes with other rounded shapes attached to them, and strange lightninglike filaments radiating from them. If we "zoom in" on small areas of this boundary, details are visible: more rounded shapes, fernlike curlicues, spirals. It turns out that the boundary is a fractal. Each time you zoom in to a smaller area, more details and more astonishing shapes are revealed. There is no end to how far you can zoom in. It is easy to zoom down to a detail never before seen by human eyes.

The mandel.c program shown here permits you to explore the Mandelbrot set. You can view the complete set or, by changing parameters in the program, zoom in for more detailed views.

The program contains two nested loops. The outer loop steps down from line to line, and the inner one steps across from pixel to pixel on each line. At each pixel location the program calculates whether the corresponding point is a member of the Mandelbrot set. If it is, the pixel is drawn as black. If not, the pixel is colored. How are the colors chosen? This has to do with how the set is defined. Before we get into that, here's the listing:

```
/* mandel.c */
/* generates the mandelbrot set */
```

```c
#include <graph.h>              /* needed for graphics */
#define XMAX 100                /* change these to change size */
#define YMAX 100                /*    of picture */
#define MAXCOUNT 16             /* number of iterations */
main()
{
    int x, y;                   /* location of pixel on screen */
    float xscale, yscale;       /* distance between pixels */
    float left, top;            /* location of top left corner */
    float xside, yside;         /* length of sides */
    float zx, zy;               /* real and imag parts of z */
    float cx, cy;               /* real and imag parts of c */
    float tempx;                /* briefly holds zx */
    int count;                  /* number of iterations */

    left = -2.0;                /* coordinates for entire */
    top = 1.25;                 /*    mandelbrot set */
    xside = 2.5;                /*    change to see details */
    yside = -2.5;               /*    of set */
    xscale = xside / XMAX;       /* set scale factors */
    yscale = yside / YMAX;
    if( _setvideomode(_ERESCOLOR)==0 )
        { printf("Can't set mode"); exit(1); }
    _rectangle(_GBORDER, 0, 0, XMAX+1, YMAX+1);

    for(y=1; y<=YMAX; y++)      /* for each pixel column */
        {
        for(x=1; x<=XMAX; x++)   /* for each pixel row */
            {
            cx = x*xscale+left;  /* set c to pixel location */
            cy = y*yscale+top;
            zx = zy = 0;         /* set z = 0 */
            count = 0;           /* reset count */
                                 /* size of z < 2 */
            while( zx*zx+zy*zy<4 && count<MAXCOUNT )
                {
                tempx = zx*zx - zy*zy + cx;  /* set z = z*z + c */
                zy = 2*zx*zy + cy;
                zx = tempx;
                count++;         /* another iteration */
                }
            if( count < MAXCOUNT )  /* if count not max */
                {
                _setcolor(count);   /* set color to count */
                _setpixel(x, y);    /* draw pixel (don't */
                }                   /*    draw black pixels) */
        if( kbhit() )            /* to abort program */
            break;               /* before image completed */
        }  /* end for(x) */
    }  /* end for(y) */
    getche();                   /* keep image until keypress */
```

```
    _setvideomode(_DEFAULTMODE); /* restore old mode */
}
```

The program runs in EGA graphics, which provides a far more satisfactory picture than in CGA. As shown, the program generates a picture 100 pixels high and 100 pixels wide. This is a small part of the EGA screen. The reason for using a small picture is that it takes the program a considerable time to generate its output. The 100x100 pixel picture takes several minutes. (It will be much faster if you have a math coprocessor in your system.) A good way to use the program is to generate a small picture to preview what you want to see. When you like the image, expand the picture size by changing XMAX and YMAX to, say, 400x300, and let the program run all night. The effect is shown in Figure 12-26. (Unfortunately, the figure cannot do justice to the intricate colored image produced by the program.)

Figure 12-26. Output of mandel.c

A description of the algorithm used to generate the Mandelbrot set is beyond the scope of this book. Very roughly, a point is in the set if a certain iterated calculation performed on it does not escape to infinity. If the calculation does escape to infinity, the point is outside the set, and the speed with which it escapes determines the color of the pixel at that point. Refer to the Mathematical Recreations column in *Scientific American* for August 1985 and November 1987 for a very lucid presentation. (These articles are reprinted in *The Armchair Universe* by A. K. Dewdney, W. H. Freeman Company, 1988.)

Almost any spot on the boundary provides an interesting place to start exploring the details of the Mandelbrot set. For instance, try the following settings:

```
left = -1.5;
top = -0.2;
```

```
xside = 0.25;
yside = 0.4;
```

## Summary

This chapter has focused on the graphics functions provided in Microsoft C. We've seen how to organize the system to use the graphics library. The GRAPH-ICS.LIB file must be available to the linker, and the GRAPH.H file must be **#included** with the source file. In the program, a graphics mode must be set with **_setvideomode()**.

Graphics functions are used to draw rectangles, ellipses, lines, arcs, and pixels. These shapes may need to have their aspect ratio adjusted to compensate for unsquare pixels. Shapes can be filled with a color and pattern. We saw some applications of these techniques in the creation of bar and pie charts.

The number of colors available depends on the graphics mode. Different palettes can be used, or colors can be remapped, to change the colors already on the screen.

Some graphics functions exist to handle text. A text window can be created and text written to it will be confined by the borders of the window. Text can also be combined with graphics.

The logical coordinate system can be moved around on the screen. Graphics images can be stored in memory, a technique valuable for animation. In some modes, more than one page of video memory is available; pages can also be used for animated effects. A viewport can be used to restrict the screen area in which graphics appear.

## Questions

1. What are the advantages of the Microsoft C graphics functions over ROM BIOS or direct memory access?

2. What are the advantages of direct memory access over the Microsoft C graphics functions?

3. The library file needed with most graphics functions is

   _____.

4. A viewport is a screen area in which
   a. colors can be confined
   b. text can be confined
   c. graphics can be confined
   d. both text and graphics can be confined

5. To use the **_ellipse()** function, the file _____ must be **#included** in your program.

6. The function _**settextposition()** positions the following item(s):

    a. the text position (TP)

    b. the text about to be written

    c. the next line to be drawn

    d. the cursor

7. The number of bytes required to store an image when using _**getimage()** depends on:

    a. the graphics mode in use

    b. the size of the image

    c. the color of the image

    d. the amount of detail in the image

8. True or false: a Microsoft C graphics function can be used to determine if a particular program requires text or graphics mode.

9. The data type **void \*** indicates

    a. nothing is returned by a function

    b. a null pointer

    c. a function takes no arguments

    d. a pointer to any data type

10. Which library file must be available to your program if you want to write text in a window?

11. True or false: the origin of the logical coordinate system is always at the upper-left corner of the screen.

12. Graphics pages hold

    a. different parts of a manuscript

    b. different screen images

    c. different parts of the same screen image

    d. the same screen image in different colors

13. A graphics mode is initialized with the _____ function.

14. True or false: all graphics functions return a negative value if they cannot perform their task.

15. The purpose of the _**remappalette()** function is to assign

    a. a different palette to a color

b. a different color to a pixel value

c. a different pixel value to a palette

d. a different palette to the display

16. The pattern in a dashed line is created by the function

_____.

17. In Microsoft C the angles for arcs and pie slices are measured starting at

a. the coordinates 0,0

b. the straight up direction

c. the 3 o'clock position

d. 180 degrees

18. A window is a screen area in which

a. graphics can be confined

b. text can be confined

c. colors can be confined

d. both text and graphics can be confined

19. Functions that perform relative line drawing do so relative to

a. the cursor position

b. the last text written

c. the last relative line drawn

d. the last pixel drawn

20. Square pixels

a. have an aspect ratio of 1.0

b. have the same height and width

c. cause no distortion of images

d. are often really round

## Exercises

1. Write a program that allows the user to draw on the screen, using the cursor keys. Each time a cursor key is pressed, the program should place a dot, so that patterns of vertical and horizontal lines can be created. Use only Microsoft C graphics functions—no ROM BIOS calls or direct memory access for these exercises.

2. Revise the coin.c program (which created the animated image of a coin

rotating about its vertical axis) so that it uses the _**getimage**() and _**putimage**() functions instead of paging to create the animation.

3. Revise the ezedit.c program so that a backspace will delete the character to the left of the cursor, leaving the cursor in that position. (Don't worry about deleting the character in the right-most column.)

# 13

## Files

- Standard file I/O
- Character, string, and formatted I/O
- Block I/O
- Binary and text modes
- System-level I/O
- Standard files and redirection

# 13

Most programs need to read and write data to disk-based storage systems. Word processors need to store text files, spreadsheets need to store the contents of cells, and databases need to store records. In this chapter we explore the facilities that C makes available for input and output (I/O) to a disk system.

Disk I/O operations are performed on entities called "files." A file is a collection of bytes that is given a name. In most microcomputer systems, files are used as a unit of storage primarily on floppy-disk and fixed-disk data storage systems (although they can be used with other devices as well, such as CD-ROM players, RAM-disk storage, tape backup systems, and other computers). The major use of the MS-DOS or PC-DOS operating system is to handle files: to manage their storage on the disk, load them into memory, list them, delete them, and so forth.

A C-language program can read and write files in a variety of different ways. In fact, there are so many options that sorting them all out can prove rather confusing. So in the first section of this chapter we'll discuss the various categories of disk I/O. Then we'll examine the individual techniques.

## Types of Disk I/O

A group of objects can be divided into categories in more than one way. For instance, automobiles can be categorized as foreign or domestic; cheap or expensive; four, six, or eight cylinders; and so on. A car will fit into more than one category at the same time; it might be a cheap foreign car with four cylinders, for example. Similarly, the various ways file I/O can be performed in C form a number of overlapping categories. In this section we'll give a brief overview of the most important of these categories: a view of the forest before we enter the trees.

## Standard I/O versus System I/O

Probably the broadest division in C file I/O is between *standard I/O* (often called *stream I/O*), and *system-level* (or *low-level I/O*). Each of these is a more or less complete system for performing disk I/O. Each has functions for reading and writing files and performing other necessary tasks, and each provides variations in the way reading and writing can be performed. In many ways these two systems are similar, and in fact, most I/O tasks can be handled by either system. But there are also important differences between the two.

Standard I/O, as the name implies, is the most common way of performing I/O in C programs. It has a wider range of commands, and in many respects is easier to use than system I/O. Standard I/O conceals from the user some of the details of file I/O operations, such as buffering, and it automatically performs data conversion (we'll see what this means later). If there were only one system available for disk I/O in C, standard I/O probably would be it.

System I/O provides fewer ways to handle data than standard I/O, and it can be considered a more primitive system. The techniques it employs are very much like those used by the operating system. The programmer must set up, and keep track of, the buffer used to transfer data, and the system does not perform any format translations. Thus, in some ways, system I/O is harder to program than standard I/O. Since it is more closely related to the operating system, however, it is often more efficient, both in terms of speed of operation and the amount of memory used by the program.

## Character, String, Formatted, and Record I/O

The standard I/O package makes available four different ways of reading and writing data. (System-level I/O, by contrast, only uses one of these ways.) Happily, three of these four ways of transferring data correspond closely to methods you've already learned for reading data from the keyboard and writing it to the display.

First, data can be read or written one character at a time. This is analogous to how such functions as **putchar()** and **getche()** read data from the keyboard and write it to the screen.

Second, data can be read or written as strings, as such functions as **gets()** and **puts()** do with the keyboard and display.

Third, data can be read or written in a format analogous to that generated by **printf()** and **scanf()** functions: as a collection of values that may be mixed characters, strings, floating point, and integer numbers.

And fourth, data may be read or written in a new format called a "record," or "block." This is a fixed-length group of data, and is commonly used to store a succession of similar data items, such as array elements or structures.

We'll look at each of these ways to transfer data in the section on standard I/O. Figure 13-1 shows the relationship of standard and system I/O to these four categories and the functions used to read and write data for each one.

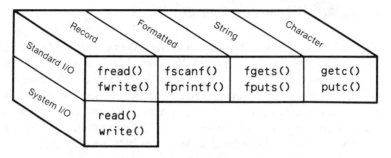

Figure 13-1. Categories of Disk I/O

## Text versus Binary

Another way to categorize file I/O operations is whether files are opened in *text mode* or *binary mode*. Which of these two modes is used to open the file determines how various details of file management are handled: how newlines are stored, for example, and how end-of-file is indicated. The reason that these two modes exist is historical: Unix systems (on which C was first developed) do things one way, while MS-DOS does them another. The two modes are, as we'll see, an attempt to reconcile the standards of the two operating systems.

Just to confuse matters, there is a second distinction between text and binary: the *format* used for storing numbers on the disk. In text format, numbers are stored as strings of characters, while in binary format they are stored as they are in memory: two bytes for an integer, four for floating point, and so on, as we learned in Chapter 2. Some file I/O functions store numbers as text, while others store them as binary.

> Text versus binary *mode* is concerned with newline and EOF translation; text versus binary *format* is concerned with number representation.

These two formats arise not from different operating system standards (as with text versus binary modes), but because different formats work more conveniently in different situations.

We'll have more to say about both these text-versus-binary distinctions later on. At this point we'll narrow our focus from an overview of I/O categories to the details of the various techniques.

## Standard Input/Output

Standard I/O is probably the easier to program and understand, so we'll start with it, leaving system-level I/O for later in the chapter.

Of the four kinds of standard I/O, we'll explore the first three in this section: character I/O, string I/O, and formatted I/O. (We'll save record I/O for a later section.) We'll initially look at these three approaches using text mode; later we'll see what differences occur when binary mode is used.

## Character Input/Output

Our first example program will take characters typed at the keyboard and, one at a time, write them to a disk file. We'll list the program and show what it does, then dissect it line by line. Here's the listing:

```
/* writec.c */
/* writes one character at a time to a file */
#include "stdio.h"                   /* defines FILE */
main()
{
    FILE *fptr;                      /* ptr to FILE */
    char ch;
    fptr = fopen("textfile.txt","w"); /* open file, set fptr */
    while( (ch=getche()) != '\r' )   /* get char from kbd */
        putc(ch,fptr);               /* write it fo file */
    fclose(fptr);                    /* close file */
}
```

In operation the program sits there and waits for you to type a line of text. When you've finished, you hit the [Return] key to terminate the program. Here's a sample run (with a phrase from the nineteenth-century poet William Blake):

```
C>writec
Tiger, tiger, burning bright / In the forests of the night
C>
```

What you've typed will be written to a file called textfile.txt. To see that the file has in fact been created, you can use the MS-DOS TYPE function, which will read the contents of the file:

```
C>type textfile.txt
Tiger, tiger, burning bright / In the forests of the night
C>
```

Now that we know what the program does, let's look at how it does it.

### Opening a File

Before we can write a file to a disk, or read it, we must *open* it. Opening a file establishes an understanding between our program and the operating system about which file we're going to access and how we're going to do it. We provide the operating system with the name of the file and other information, such as whether we plan to read or write to it. Communication areas are then set up between the file and our program. One of these areas is a C structure that holds information about the file.

This structure, which is defined to be of type **struct FILE**, is our contact point. When we make a request to open a file, what we receive back (if the request is indeed granted) is a pointer to a particular FILE structure. Each file we open will have its own FILE structure, with a pointer to it. Figure 13-2 shows this process.

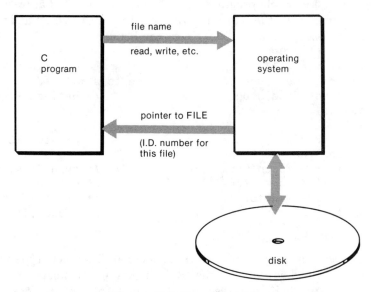

Figure 13-2. Opening a File

The FILE structure contains information about the file being used, such as its current size and the location of its data buffers. The FILE structure is declared in the header file STDIO.H (for "standard I/O"). It is necessary to **#include** this file with your program whenever you use standard I/O (although not system-level I/O). In addition to defining the FILE structure, STDIO.H also defines a variety of other identifiers and variables that are useful in file-oriented programs; we'll come across some of them later.

In the writec.c program we first declare a variable of type **pointer-to-FILE**, in the statement:

```
FILE *fptr;
```

Then, we open the file with the statement

```
fptr = fopen("textfile.txt","w");
```

This tells the operating system to open a file called "textfile.txt". (We could also have specified a complete MS-DOS pathname here, such as \samples\jan \textfile.txt.) This statement also indicates, via the "w", that we'll be writing to the file. The **fopen()** function returns a pointer to the FILE structure for our file, which we store in the variable **fptr**.

The one-letter string "w" (note that it is a string and not a character; hence the double- and not single-quotes) is called a "type." The "w" is but one of several types we can specify when we open a file. Here are the other possibilities:

"r"    Open for reading. The file must already exist.

"w"    Open for writing. If the file exists its contents will be written over. If it does not exist it will be created.

"a"    Open for append. Material will be added to the end of an existing file, or a new file will be created.

"r+"   Open for both reading and writing. The file must already exist.

"w+"   Open for both reading and writing. If the file exists its contents are written over.

"a+"   Open for both reading and appending. If the file does not exist it will be created.

In this section we'll be concerned mostly with the "r" and "w" types.

### Writing to a File
Once we've established a line of communication with a particular file by opening it, we can write to it. In the writec.c program we do this one character at a time, using the statement:

```
putc(ch,fptr);
```

The **putc()** function is similar to the **putch()** and **putchar()** functions. However, these functions always write to the console (unless redirection is employed), while **putc()** writes to a file. What file? The file whose FILE structure is pointed to by the variable **fptr**, which we obtained when we opened the file. This pointer has become our key to the file; we no longer refer to the file by name, but by the address stored in **fptr**.

The writing process continues in the **while** loop; each time the **putc()** function is executed another character is written to the file. When the user types [Return], the loop terminates.

### Closing the File
When we've finished writing to the file we need to close it. This is carried out with the statement

```
fclose(fptr);
```

Again we tell the system what file we mean by referring to the address stored in **fptr**.

Closing the file has several effects. First, any characters remaining in the buffer are written out to the disk. What buffer? We haven't said much about a buffer before, because it is invisible to the programmer when using standard

I/O. However, a buffer is necessary even if it is invisible. Consider, for example, how inefficient it would be to actually access the disk just to write one character. It takes a while for the disk system to position the head correctly and wait for the right sector of the track to come around. On a floppy disk system the motor actually has to start the disk from a standstill every time the disk is accessed. If you typed several characters rapidly, and each one required a completely separate disk access, some of the characters would probably be lost. This is where the buffer comes in.

When you send a character off to a file with **putc()**, it is actually stored in a buffer—an area of memory—rather than being written immediately to the disk. When the buffer is full, its contents are written to the disk all at once. Or, if the program knows the last character has been received, it forces the buffer to be written to the disk by closing the file. A major advantage of using standard I/O (as opposed to system I/O) is that these activities take place automatically; the programmer doesn't need to worry about them. Figure 13-3 shows this "invisible" buffer.

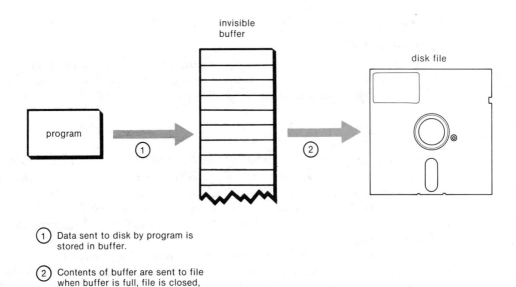

(1) Data sent to disk by program is stored in buffer.

(2) Contents of buffer are sent to file when buffer is full, file is closed, or program terminates.

Figure 13-3. Invisible Buffer

Another reason to close the file is to free the communications areas used by that particular file so they are available for other files. These areas include the FILE structure and the buffer itself.

### Reading from a File
If we can write to a file, we should be able to read from one. Here's a program that does just that, using the function **getc()**:

```
/* readc.c */
/* reads one character at a time from a file */
#include <stdio.h>                   /* defines FILE */
main()
{
    FILE *fptr;                      /* ptr to FILE */
    int ch;                          /* character of type int */
    fptr = fopen("textfile.txt","r"); /* open file, set fptr */
    while( (ch=getc(fptr)) != EOF )  /* get char from file */
        printf("%c", ch);            /* print it */
    fclose(fptr);                    /* close file */
}
```

As you can see, this program is quite similar to writec.c. The pointer FILE is declared the same way, and the file is opened and closed in the same way. The **getc()** function reads one character from the file "textfile.txt"; this function is the complement of the **putc()** function. (When you try this program, make sure that the file has already been created by writec.c.)

### End-of-File

A major difference between this program and writec.c is that readc.c must be concerned with knowing when it has read the last character in the file. It does this by looking for an end-of-file (EOF) signal from the operating system. If it tries to read a character, and reads the EOF signal instead, it knows it's come to the end of the file.

What does EOF consist of? It's important to understand that it is *not a character*. It is actually an integer value, sent to the program by the operating system and defined in the STDIO.H file to have a value of − 1. No character with this value is stored in the file on the disk; rather, when the operating system realizes that the last character in a file has been sent, it transmits the EOF signal. (We'll have more to say about how the operating system knows where the file ends when we look at binary mode files later on.)

> The EOF signal sent by the operating system to a C program is not a character, but an integer with a value of − 1.

So our program goes along reading characters and printing them, looking for a value of − 1, or EOF. When it finds this value, the program terminates. We use an *integer* variable to hold the character being read so we can interpret the EOF signal as the integer − 1. What difference does it make? If we used a variable of type **char**, the character with the ASCII code 255 decimal (FF hex) would be interpreted as an EOF. We want to be able to use all the character codes from 0 to 255—all possible 8-bit combinations, that is; so by using an integer variable we ensure that only a 16-bit value of − 1, which is not the same as any of our character codes, will signal EOF.

## Trouble Opening the File

The two programs we've presented so far have a potential flaw; if the file specified in the **fopen()** function cannot be opened, the programs will not run. Why couldn't a file be opened? If you're trying to open a file for writing, it's probably because there's no more space on the disk. If for reading, it's much more common that a file can't be opened; you can't read it if it hasn't been created yet.

Thus it's important for any program that accesses disk files to check whether a file has been opened successfully before trying to read or write to the file. If the file cannot be opened, the **fopen()** function returns a value of 0 (defined as NULL in STDIO.H). Since in C this is not considered a valid address, the program infers that the file could not be opened.

Here's a variation of readc.c that handles this situation:

```
/* readc2.c */
/* reads one character at a time from a file */
#include <stdio.h>                    /* defines FILE */
main()
{
    FILE *fptr;                        /* ptr to FILE */
    int ch;
    if( (fptr=fopen("textfile.txt","r"))==NULL )  /* open file */
        {
        printf("Can't open file textfile.txt.");
        exit();
        }
    while( (ch=getc(fptr)) != EOF )    /* get char from file */
        printf("%c", ch);              /* print it */
    fclose(fptr);                      /* close file */
}
```

Here the **fopen()** function is enclosed in an **if** statement. If the function returns NULL, then an explanatory message is printed and the **exit()** is executed, causing the program to terminate immediately, and avoiding the embarrassment of trying to read from a nonexistent file.

## Counting Characters

The ability to read and write to files on a character-by-character basis has many useful applications. For example, here's a variation on our readc.c program that counts the characters in a file:

```
/* charcnt.c */
/* counts characters in a file */
#include <stdio.h>
main(argc,argv)
int argc;
char *argv[];
{
    FILE *fptr;
    char string[81];
```

```
    int count=0;
    if(argc != 2)                           /* check # of args */
       { printf("Format: C>type2 filename"); exit(); }
    if( (fptr=fopen(argv[1], "r")) == NULL)  /* open file */
       { printf("Can't open file %s.", argv[1]); exit(); }
    while( getc(fptr) != EOF )            /* get char from file */
       count++;                          /* count it */
    fclose(fptr);                        /* close file */
    printf("File %s contains %d characters.", argv[1], count);
}
```

In this program we've used a command-line argument to obtain the name of the file to be examined, rather than writing it into the **fopen()** statement. We start by checking the number of arguments; if there are two, then the second one, **argv[1]**, is the name of the file. For compactness, we've also placed the two statements following the **if** on one line.

The program opens the file, checking to make sure it can be opened, and cycles through a loop, reading one character at a time and incrementing the variable **count** each time a character is read.

If you try out the charcnt.c program on files whose length you've checked with a different program—say the DOS DIR command—you may find that the results don't quite agree. The reason for this has to do with the difference between text and binary mode files; we'll explore this further in the section on string I/O.

### Counting Words

It's easy to modify our character-counting program to count words. This can be a useful utility for writers or anyone else who needs to know how many words an article, chapter, or composition comprises. Here's the program:

```
/* wordcnt.c */
/* counts words in a text file */
#include <stdio.h>
main(argc,argv)
int argc;
char *argv[];
{
   FILE *fptr;
   int ch, string[81];
   int white=1;                          /* whitespace flag */
   int count=0;                          /* word count */
   if(argc != 2)                         /* check # of args */
      { printf("Format: C>type2 filename"); exit(); }
   if( (fptr=fopen(argv[1], "r")) == NULL)  /* open file */
      { printf("Can't open file %s.", argv[1]); exit(); }

   while( (ch=getc(fptr)) != EOF )    /* get char from file */
      switch(ch)
         {
         case ' ':                      /* if space, tab, or */
```

```
        case '\t':                        /* newline, set flag */
        case '\n': white++; break;
        default: if(white) { white=0; count++; }
        }
   fclose(fptr);                          /* close file */
   printf("File %s contains %d words.", argv[1], count);
}
```

What we really count in this program is the *change* from whitespace characters (spaces, newlines, and tabs) to actual (nonwhitespace) characters. In other words, if there's a string of spaces or carriage returns, the program reads them, waiting patiently for the first actual character. It counts this transition as a word. Then it reads actual characters until another whitespace character appears. A "flag" variable keeps track of whether the program is in the middle of a word or in the middle of whitespace; the variable **white** is 1 in the middle of whitespace, 0 in the middle of a word. Figure 13-4 shows the operation of the program.

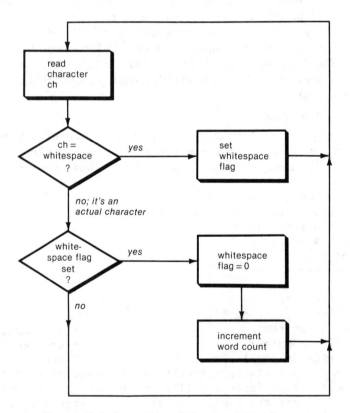

Figure 13-4. Operation of the wordcnt.c Program

This program may not work accurately with files produced by some word processing programs, such as WordStar in document mode, which use nonstandard characters for spaces and carriage returns. However, it will work with standard ASCII files.

The wordcnt.c program shows the versatility of character I/O in C. For many purposes, character I/O is just what's needed. However, in other situations, different functions may be more efficient: for instance, in reading and writing whole strings of characters at a time, which is our next topic.

## String (line) Input/Output

Reading and writing strings of characters from and to files is almost as easy as reading and writing individual characters. Here's a program that writes strings to a file, using the string I/O function **fputs()**.

```
/* writes.c */
/* writes strings typed at keyboard, to file */
#include <stdio.h>
main()
{
    FILE *fptr;                            /* declare ptr to FILE */
    char string[81];                       /* storage for strings */
    fptr = fopen("textfile.txt", "w"); /* open file */
    while(strlen(gets(string)) > 0)        /* get string from keybd */
        {
        fputs(string,fptr);                /* write string to file */
        fputs("\n",fptr);                  /* write newline to file */
        }
    fclose(fptr);                          /* close file */
}
```

The user types a series of strings, terminating each by hitting [Return]. To terminate the entire program, the user hits [Return] at the beginning of a line. This creates a string of zero length, which the program recognizes as the signal to close the file and exit.

We've set up a character array to store the string; the **fputs()** function then writes the contents of the array to the disk. Since **fputs()** does not automatically add a newline character to the end of the line, we must do this explicitly to make it easier to read the string back from the file.

Note that—for simplicity—in this and the next program we have not included a test for an error condition on opening the file, as we did in previous examples. In any serious program this test should be included.

Here's a program that reads strings from a disk file:

```
/* reads.c */
/* reads strings from file, displays them on screen */
#include <stdio.h>
main()
{
    FILE *fptr;                               /* ptr to FILE */
    char string[81];                          /* stores strings */
```

```
    fptr = fopen("textfile.txt", "r");      /* open file */
    while( fgets(string,80,fptr) != NULL )  /* read string */
       printf("%s",string);                 /* print string */
    fclose(fptr);                           /* close file */
}
```

The function **fgets()** takes three parameters. The first is the address where the string is stored, and the second is the maximum length of the string. This parameter keeps the **fgets()** function from reading in too long a string and overflowing the array. The third parameter, as usual, is the pointer to the FILE structure for the file.

Here's a sample run (again courtesy of William Blake), showing the operation of both writes.c and reads.c:

```
C>writes
I told my love, I told my love,
I told her all my heart,
Trembling, cold, in ghastly fears,
Ah! she did depart!

C>reads
I told my love, I told my love,
I told her all my heart,
Trembling, cold, in ghastly fears,
Ah! she did depart!
```

### The Newline Problem

Earlier we mentioned that our charcnt.c program might not always return the same results as other character-counting programs, such as the DOS DIR command. Now that we can write a file containing several strings, let's investigate this further.

Here's what happens when we try to verify the length of the four-line William Blake excerpt shown above:

```
C>dir textfile.txt
TEXTFILE TXT        116  10-27-87    2:36a
        1 File(s)   1568768 bytes free

C>charcnt textfile.txt
File textfile.txt contains 112 characters.
```

Using DIR we find 116 characters in the textfile.txt file, whereas using our homemade charcnt.c program we find 112.

This discrepancy occurs because of the difference in the way C and MS-DOS represent the end of a line. In C the end of a line is signalled by a single character: the *newline* character, '\n' (ASCII value 10 decimal). In DOS, on the other hand, the end of a line is marked by *two* characters, the carriage return (ASCII 13 decimal), and the linefeed (which is the same as the C newline: ASCII 10 decimal).

The end of a line of text is represented by a single character in C (the newline), but by two characters in MS-DOS files (carriage return and linefeed).

When your program writes a C text file to disk, the operating system causes all the newlines to be translated into the carriage return plus linefeed (CR/LF) combination. When your program reads in a text file, the CR/LF combination is translated back into a single newline character. Thus, DOS-oriented programs such as DIR will count two characters at each end of line, while C-oriented programs, such as charcnt.c, will count one. In our example there are four lines, so there is a discrepancy of four characters.

As we'll see later, binary mode files handle this translation differently from text files.

### Reproducing the DOS TYPE Command

As a practical use for string I/O, we can reproduce the DOS TYPE command, as demonstrated in this example:

```
/* type2.c */
/* reads strings from file */
#include <stdio.h>
main(argc,argv)
int argc;
char *argv[];
{
   FILE *fptr;
   char string[81];
   if(argc != 2)                              /* check args */
      { printf("C>type2 filename"); exit(); }
   if( (fptr=fopen(argv[1], "r")) == NULL)  /* open file */
      { printf("Can't open file %s.", argv[1]); exit(); }
   while( fgets(string,80,fptr) != NULL )   /* read string */
      printf("%s",string);                   /* print string */
   fclose(fptr);                             /* close file */
}
```

This program takes the content of a text file and displays it on the screen, just as the DOS TYPE command does. The advantage of using a homemade command is that you can customize it; you could, for example, add line numbers to your printout or interpret certain characters differently.

### Standard Files and the Printer

We've seen how, by using the **fopen()** function, we can obtain a pointer that refers to a particular file. MS-DOS also predefines the pointers for five *standard files*. These pointers are available without using the **fopen()** function. They are:

| Name | Device |
|------|--------|
| stdin | standard input device (keyboard) |
| stdout | standard output device (display) |
| stderr | standard error device (display) |
| stdaux | standard auxiliary device (serial port) |
| stdprn | standard printing device (parallel printer) |

Thus, the statement **fgets(string,80,stdin)** would read a string from the keyboard rather than from a file. We could use this statement without any **fopen()** or **fclose()** statements.

We can make use of this technique to access the printer. Here's a program that uses **fgets()** and **fputs()** to print the contents of a disk file on the printer:

```
/* print.c */
/* prints file on printer */
#include "stdio.h"
main(argc,argv)
int argc;
char *argv[];
{
   FILE *fptr;
   char string[81];
   if(argc != 2)                            /* check args */
      { printf("Format: C>type2 filename"); exit(); }
   if( (fptr=fopen(argv[1], "r")) == NULL)  /* open file */
      { printf("Can't open file %s.", argv[1]); exit(); }
   while( fgets(string,80,fptr) != NULL )   /* read string */
      fputs(string,stdprn);                 /* send to prntr */
   fclose(fptr);                            /* close file */
}
```

The statement

```
   fputs(string,stdprn);
```

writes a string to the printer. Although we opened the file on the disk, **argv[1]**, we didn't need to open **stdprn**, the printer.

We'll have more to say about standard files and their use with redirection in the section on system-level I/O.

## Formatted Input/Output

So far we have dealt with reading and writing only characters and text. How about numbers? To see how we can handle numerical data, let's take a leaf from our secret agent dossier in Chapter 9: we'll use the same three items we used there to record the data for an agent: name (a string), code number (an integer), and height (a floating point number). Then, we'll write these items to a disk file.

This program reads the data from the keyboard, then writes it to our "textfile.txt" file. Here's the listing:

```
/* writef.c */
/* writes formatted data to file */
#include <stdio.h>
main()
{
    FILE *fptr;                         /* declare ptr to FILE */
    char name[40];                      /* agent's name */
    int code;                           /* code number */
    float height;                       /* agent's height */
    fptr = fopen("textfile.txt", "w"); /* open file */
    do {
        printf("Type name, code number, and height: ");
        scanf("%s %d %f", name, &code, &height);
        fprintf(fptr, "%s %d %f", name, code, height);
        }
    while(strlen(name) > 1);            /* no name given? */
    fclose(fptr);                       /* close file */
}
```

The key to this program is the **fprintf()** function, which writes the values of the three variables to the file. This function is similar to **printf()**, except that a FILE pointer is included as the first argument. As in **printf()**, we can format the data in a variety of ways; in fact, all the format conventions of **printf()** operate with **fprintf()** as well.

For simplicity this program requires the user to indicate that input is complete by typing a one-letter agent name followed by dummy numbers; this avoids using extra program statements to check if the user is done, but it's not very user-friendly. Here's some sample input:

```
C>writef
Type name, code number, and height: Bond 007 74.5
Type name, code number, and height: Salsbury 009 72.25
Type name, code number, and height: Fleming 999 69.75
Type name, code number, and height: x 0 0
```

This information is now in the "textfile.txt" file. We can look at it there with the DOS TYPE command—or with type2.c—although when we use these programs all the output will be on the same line, since there are no newlines in the data. To format the output more conveniently, we can write a program specifically to read textfile.txt:

```
/* readf.c */
/* reads formatted data from file */
#include <stdio.h>
```

```
main()
{
    FILE *fptr;                       /* declare ptr to FILE */
    char name[40];                    /* agent's name */
    int code;                         /* code number */
    float height;                     /* agent's height */
    fptr = fopen("textfile.txt", "r"); /* open file */
    while( fscanf(fptr, "%s %d %f", name, &code, &height) != EOF )
        printf("%s %03d %.2f\n", name, code, height);
    fclose(fptr);                     /* close file */
}
```

This program uses the **fscanf()** function to read the data from the disk. This function is similar to **scanf()**, except that, as with **fprintf()**, a pointer to FILE is included as the first argument.

We can now print out the data in a more readable format, using **printf()**:

```
C>readf
Bond 007 74.50
Salsbury 009 72.25
Fleming 999 69.75
x 000 0.00
```

Of course, we can use similar techniques with **fprintf()** and **fscanf()** for other sorts of formatted data: any combination of characters, strings, integers, and floating point numbers.

### Number Storage in Text Format

It's important to understand how numerical data is stored on the disk by **fprintf()**. Text and characters are stored one character per byte, as we would expect. Are numbers stored as they are in memory, two bytes for an integer, four bytes for floating point, and so on? No. They are stored as strings of characters. Thus, the integer 999 is stored in two bytes of memory, but requires three bytes in a disk file, one for each '9' character. The floating point number 69.75 requires four bytes when stored in memory, but five when stored on the disk: one for each digit and one for the decimal point. Numbers with more digits require even more disk space. Figure 13-5 shows how this looks.

Numbers with more than a few significant digits require substantially more space on the disk using formatted I/O than they do in memory. Thus, if a large amount of numerical data is to be stored on a disk file, using text format can be inefficient. The solution is to use a function that stores numbers in binary format. We'll explore this option in the section on record I/O.

We've now described three methods in standard I/O for reading and writing data. These three methods write data in text format. The fourth method, record I/O, writes data in binary format. When writing data in binary format it is often desirable to use binary mode, so we'll investigate the differences between binary and text modes before discussing record I/O.

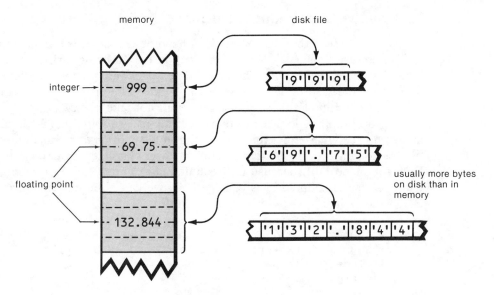

Figure 13-5. Storage of Numbers in Text Format

## Binary Mode and Text Mode

As we noted at the beginning of this chapter, the distinction between text and binary can be applied to two different areas of disk I/O. On the one hand, there is the question of how numbers are stored; this is the distinction between text versus binary *format*. On the other hand, we can talk about how files are opened and the format interpretations this leads to; this can be called text versus binary *mode*. It's this second distinction we want to examine in this section.

The need for two different modes arose from incompatibilities between C and the MS-DOS (or PC-DOS) operating system. C originated on UNIX systems and used UNIX file conventions. MS-DOS, which evolved separately from UNIX, has its own, somewhat different, conventions. When C was ported over to the MS-DOS operating system, compiler-writers had to resolve these incompatibilities. The solution decided on by Microsoft (but not by all C compiler-writers on the IBM) was to have two modes. One, the text mode, made files look to C programs as if they were UNIX files. The other, binary mode, made files look more like MS-DOS files.

Text mode imitates UNIX files, while binary mode imitates MS-DOS files.

There are two main areas where text and binary mode files are different: the handling of newlines and the representation of end-of-file. We'll explore these two areas here.

## Text versus Binary Mode: Newlines

We've already seen that, in text mode, a newline character is translated into the carriage return-linefeed (CR/LF) combination before being written to the disk. Likewise, the CR/LF on the disk is translated back into a newline when the file is read by the C program. However, if a file is opened in binary mode, as opposed to text mode, these translations will not take place.

As an example, let's revise our charcnt.c program to open a file in binary mode and see what effect this has on the number of characters counted in the file. As you may recall, charcnt.c counted fewer characters in a file than did the DOS command DIR, because DIR counted each end-of-line as two characters, while charcnt.c counted it as one. Perhaps we can eliminate this discrepancy. Here's the listing:

```
/* charcnt2.c */
/* counts characters in a file opened as binary */
#include <stdio.h>
main(argc,argv)
int argc;
char *argv[];
{
   FILE *fptr;
   char string[81];
   int count=0;
   if(argc != 2)                           /* check # of args */
      { printf("Format: C>charcnt2 filename"); exit(); }
   if( (fptr=fopen(argv[1], "rb")) == NULL)  /* open file */
      { printf("Can't open file %s.", argv[1]); exit(); }
   while( getc(fptr) != EOF )        /* get char from file */
      count++;                       /* count it */
   fclose(fptr);                     /* close file */
   printf("File %s contains %d characters.", argv[1], count);
}
```

There is only one difference between this program and the original charcnt.c; we have introduced the letter "b" as part of the type string, following the "r":

```
fptr=fopen(argv[1], "rb")
```

The "b" means that the file should be opened in binary mode. (We could also use a "t" to specify text mode, but since this is the default for character I/O, this is not normally necessary.)

Now if we apply charcnt2.c to our earlier example of the William Blake poem, we'll get the same character count we got using the DOS DIR command—116 characters; while with the text mode charcnt.c we get 112 characters:

```
C>charcnt2 textfile.txt
File textfile.txt contains 116 characters.
```

```
C>charcnt textfile.txt
File textfile.txt contains 112 characters.
```

There are four carriage return-linefeed combinations in the file. Each counts as one character in the text mode program charcnt.c, but as two characters in the binary mode program charcnt2.c; hence the difference of four characters. In binary mode the translation of the CR/LF pair into a newline does not take place: the binary charcnt2.c program reads each CR/LF as two characters, just as it's stored on the file.

## Text versus Binary: End-of-File

The second difference between text and binary modes is in the way end-of-file is detected. Both systems actually keep track of the total length of the file and will signal an EOF when this length has been reached. In text mode, however, a special character, 1A hex (26 decimal), inserted after the last character in the file, is also used to indicate EOF. (This character can be generated from the keyboard by typing [Ctrl] [z] and is often written ^Z.) If this character is encountered at any point in the file, the read function will return the EOF signal ( – 1) to the program.

This convention arose in the days of CP/M, when all files consisted of blocks of a certain minimum length. To indicate that a file ended in the middle of a block, the ^Z character was used, and its use has carried over into MS-DOS.

There is a moral to be derived from the text-mode conversion of 1A hex to EOF. If a file stores numbers in binary format, it's important that binary mode be used in reading the file back, since one of the numbers we store might well be the number 1A hex (26 decimal). If this number were detected while we were reading a file in text mode, reading would be terminated (prematurely) at that point.

Also, when writing in binary format, we don't want numbers that happen to have the value 10 decimal to be interpreted as newlines and expanded into CR/LFs. Thus, both in reading and writing binary format numbers, we should use binary mode when accessing the file.

Figure 13-6 shows the differences between text and binary mode.

## Binary Dump Program

Before leaving the subject of binary versus text modes, let's look at a program that uses binary mode to investigate files. This program looks at a file byte-by-byte, in binary mode, and displays what it finds there. The display consists of two parts: the hexadecimal code for each character and—if the character is displayable—the character itself. This program provides a sort of x-ray of a disk file. It is modelled after the "dump" function in the DEBUG utility in MS-DOS.

*Text mode*

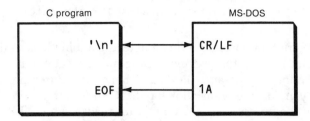

*Binary mode*

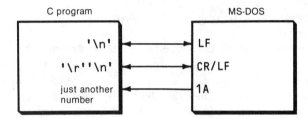

Figure 13-6. Text and Binary Modes

Here's the listing:

```
/* bindump.c */
/* does binary dump of disk file */
/* each line is ten ASCII codes followed by ten characters */
#include <stdio.h>
#define LENGTH 10
#define TRUE 0
#define FALSE -1

main(argc,argv)
int argc;
char *argv[];
{
    FILE *fileptr;                     /* pointer to file */
    unsigned int ch;
    int j, not_eof;
    unsigned char string[LENGTH+1];    /* buffer for chars */
    if(argc != 2)
        { printf("Format: C> bindump file.xxx"); exit(); }
    if( (fileptr = fopen(argv[1],"rb"))==NULL) /* binary read */
        { printf("Can't open file %s.", argv[1]); exit(); }
    not_eof = TRUE;                    /* not EOF flag */
    do
        {
        for (j=0; j < LENGTH; j++)      /* chars in one line */
            {
```

```
        if ( (ch=getc(fileptr)) == EOF ) /* read character */
            not_eof = FALSE;                /* clear flag on EOF */
        printf( "%3x ", ch );               /* print ASCII code */
        if (ch > 31)
            *(string+j) = ch;               /* save printable char */
        else                                /* use period for */
            *(string+j) = '.';              /* nonprintable char */
        }
    *(string+j) = '\0';                     /* end string */
    printf("   %s\n", string);              /* print string */
    }
while ( not_eof == TRUE );                  /* quit on EOF */
fclose(fileptr);                            /* close file */
}
```

To use this program, you type the name of the program followed by the name of the file to be investigated. If the file is too big to fit on one screen, scrolling can be paused with the [Ctrl] [s] key combination.

Earlier we wrote a William Blake poem to the file textfile.txt. Let's see what happens when we apply bindump.c to that file.

```
C>bindump textfile.txt
 49   20   74   6f   6c   64   20   6d   79   20      I told my
 6c   6f   76   65   2c   20   49   20   74   6f      love, I to
 6c   64   20   6d   79   20   6c   6f   76   65      ld my love
 2c    d    a   49   20   74   6f   6c   64   20      ,..I told
 68   65   72   20   61   6c   6c   20   6d   79      her all my
 20   68   65   61   72   74   2c    d    a   54       heart,..T
 72   65   6d   62   6c   69   6e   67   2c   20      rembling,
 63   6f   6c   64   2c   20   69   6e   20   67      cold, in g
 68   61   73   74   6c   79   20   66   65   61      hastly fea
 72   73   2c    d    a   41   68   21   20   73      rs,..Ah! s
 68   65   20   64   69   64   20   64   65   70      he did dep
 61   72   74   21    d    a ffff ffff ffff ffff      art!..~~~~
```

In each row the numbers correspond to the characters printed on the right: 49 hex is 'I', 20 is a space, 74 is 't', and so on. Notice that the CR/LF combination is represented as D hex followed by A hex. If we had opened the file in text mode, we would have seen only the a's. Also, if the program encounters the number 1A hex, it will print it out just like any other number; it will not be interpreted as EOF, as it would have been in text mode.

At the end of the file the program starts to read real EOFs, which are printed as ffff hex. The program reads until the end of a line, even if it has found an EOF, so the rest of the line is filled out with ffff. With a modest increase in complexity, the program could be rewritten to terminate on the first EOF. Also, if you prefer decimal to hexadecimal output, changing the format specifier in the **printf()** statement will do the trick.

Binary mode is ordinarily used for binary format data and text mode for text format data, although there are exceptions.

Now that we know something about binary mode, let's investigate the fourth method of performing standard I/O: record I/O.

# Record Input/Output

Earlier we saw how numbers can be stored using the formatted I/O functions **fscanf()** and **fprintf()**. However, we also saw that storing numbers in the format provided by these functions can take up a lot of disk space, because each digit is stored as a character. Formatted I/O presents another problem; there is no direct way to read and write complex data types such as arrays and structures. Arrays can be handled, but inefficiently, by writing each array element one at a time. Structures must also be written piecemeal.

In standard I/O one answer to these problems is record I/O, sometimes called "block I/O." Record I/O writes numbers to disk files in binary (or "untranslated") format, so that integers are stored in two bytes, floating point numbers in four bytes, and so on for the other numerical types—the same format used to store numbers in memory. Record I/O also permits writing any amount of data at once; the process is not limited to a single character or string or to the few values that can be placed in a **fprintf()** or **fscanf()** function. Arrays, structures, structures of arrays, and other data constructions can be written with a single statement.

## Writing Structures with *fwrite()*

Taking the structure used for secret agent data in Chapter 9, we'll devise a pair of programs to read and write such structures directly. The first one, listed here, will write a file consisting of a number of agent records, each one consisting of the structure **agent** defined in the program.

```
/* writer.c */
/* writes agent's records to file */
#include "stdio.h"
main()
{
    struct                          /* define structure */
       {
       char name[40];               /* name */
       int agnumb;                  /* code number */
       float height;                /* height */
       } agent;
    float dummy=0.0;                /* see text */
```

```
FILE *fptr;                          /* file pointer */
if( (fptr=fopen("agents.rec","wb"))==NULL )   /* open file */
   { printf("Can't open file agents.rec"); exit(); }
do
   {
   printf("\nEnter name: ");         /* get name */
   gets(agent.name);
   printf("Enter number: ");         /* get number */
   scanf("%d", &agent.agnumb);
   printf("Enter height: ");         /* get height */
   scanf("%f", &agent.height);
   fflush(stdin);                    /* flush kbd buffer */
                                     /* write struct to file */
   fwrite(&agent, sizeof(agent), 1, fptr);
   printf("Add another agent (y/n)? ");
   }
while(getche()=='y');
fclose(fptr);                        /* close file */
}
```

This program will accept input concerning name, number, and height of each agent, and will then write the data to a disk file called "agents.rec". Any number of agents can be entered. Here's a sample interaction:

```
C>writer
Enter name: Holmes, Sherlock
Enter number: 010
Enter height: 73.75
Add another agent (y/n)? y
Enter name: Bond, James
Enter number: 007
Enter height: 74.5
Add another agent (y/n)? n
```

Most of this program should be familiar to you from Chapter 9 and from earlier examples in this chapter. Note, however, that the agents.rec file is opened in binary mode.

The information obtained from the user at the keyboard is placed in the structure **agent**. Then the following statement writes the structure to the file:

```
fwrite(&agent, sizeof(agent), 1, fptr);
```

The first argument of this function is the address of the structure to be written. The second argument is the size of the structure. Instead of counting bytes, we let the program do it for us by using the **sizeof()** function. The third argument is the number of such structures we want to write at one time. If we had an array of structures, for example, we might want to write the entire array all at once. This number could then be adjusted accordingly, as we'll see shortly. In this case, however, we want to write only one structure at a time. The last argument is the pointer to the file we want to write to.

Finally, we should note the statement:

```
float dummy=0.0;
```

This circumvents a peculiarity of at least some versions of the Microsoft C compiler. When the program is executed without this statement, the message

```
Floating point not loaded
```

appears. The reason for this is that the floating point package is not linked with the program file unless the compiler decides it is needed. The statement

```
scanf("%f", &agent.height);
```

requires the floating point package at run time, but it doesn't alert the compiler to this fact at compile time. So the compiler doesn't tell the linker to provide the package, and the fact that the package is needed but not available isn't discovered until the program is running. Initializing a dummy floating point number causes the compiler to include the floating point package and solves the problem.

If your version of the compiler doesn't need this statement, then by all means remove it.

## Writing Arrays with *fwrite()*

The **fwrite()** function need not be restricted to writing structures to the disk. We can use it (and its complementary function, **fread()**, which we'll examine next) to work with other data as well. For example, suppose we wanted to store an integer array of 10 elements in a disk file. We could write the 10 items one at a time using **fprintf()**, but it is far more efficient to take the following approach:

```
/* warray.c */
/* writes array to file */
#include "stdio.h"
int table[10] = { 1, 2, 3, 4, 5, 6, 7, 8, 9, 10 };
main()
{
    FILE *fptr;                                    /* file pointer */
    if( (fptr=fopen("table.rec","wb"))==NULL )   /* open file */
        { printf("Can't open file agents.rec"); exit(); }
    fwrite(table, sizeof(table), 1, fptr);       /* write array */
    fclose(fptr);                                  /* close file */
}
```

This program doesn't accomplish anything useful, but it does demonstrate that the writing of an array to the disk is similar to the writing of a structure. (We'll soon see an example of writing an array of structures.)

## Reading Structures with *fread()*

To read the structure written by writer.c, we can concoct another program, similar to writer.c:

```
/* readr.c */
/* reads agent's records from file */
#include "stdio.h"
main()
{
    struct
      {
      char name[40];                        /* name */
      int agnumb;                           /* code number */
      float height;                         /* height */
      } agent;
    FILE *fptr;
    if( (fptr=fopen("agents.rec","rb"))==NULL )
      { printf("Can't open file agents.rec"); exit(); }
    while( fread(&agent,sizeof(agent),1,fptr)==1 )
      {                                     /* read file */
      printf("\nName: %s\n", agent.name);      /* print name */
      printf("Number: %03d\n", agent.agnumb); /* print number */
      printf("Height: %.2f\n", agent.height); /* print height */
      }
    fclose(fptr);                           /* close file */
}
```

The heart of this program is the expression

```
fread(&agent,sizeof(agent),1,fptr)
```

This causes data read from the disk to be placed in the structure **agent**; the format is the same as **fwrite()**. The **fread()** function returns the number of items read. Ordinarily this should correspond to the third argument, the number of items we asked for—in this case, 1. If we've reached the end of the file, however, the number will be smaller—in this case, 0. By testing for this situation, we know when to stop reading.

The **fread()** function places the data from the file into the structure; to display it, we access the structure members with **printf()** in the usual way. Here's how it looks:

```
C>readr

Holmes, Sherlock
010
73.75
```

```
Bond, James
007
74.50
```

In record I/O, numerical data is stored in binary mode. This means that an integer always occupies two bytes, a floating point number always occupies four bytes, and so on. Figure 13-7 shows the relationship of data stored in memory and on the disk in binary format. As you can see, record I/O, because it makes use of binary format, is more efficient for the storage of numerical data than functions that use text format, such as **fprintf()**.

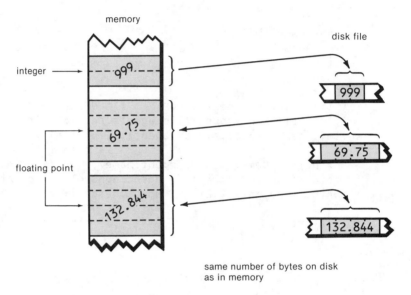

Figure 13-7. Storage of Numbers in Binary Format

Since data is stored in binary format, it's important to open the file in binary mode. If it were opened in text mode, and should the number 26 decimal be used in the file (as an agent number, for instance), the program would interpret it as an EOF and stop reading the file at that point. We also want to suppress the conversion of newlines to CR/LFs.

### A Database Example

As a more ambitious example of record I/O at work, we'll add disk reading and writing capability to our agent.c program from Chapter 9. The resulting program will allow data for up to 50 agents to be entered into an array of structures in memory. Then a single command will write the entire array to disk, thus saving the database for future access. Another command reads the array back in again.

Here's the listing:

```
/* agentr.c */
/* maintains list of agents in file */
#include <stdio.h>              /* for FILE, etc. */
```

```c
#include <conio.h>                /* for getch() */
#define TRUE 1
void newname(void);              /* prototypes */
void listall(void);
void wfile(void);
void rfile(void);

struct personel                  /* define data structure */
   {
   char name [40];               /* name */
   int agnumb;                   /* code number */
   float height;                 /* height in inches */
   };
struct personel agent[50];       /* array of 50 structures */
int n = 0;                       /* number of agents listed */

void main(void)
{
   int ch;

   while (TRUE)
      {
      printf("\n'e' enter new agent\n'l' list all agents");
      printf("\n'w' write file\n'r' read file: ");
      ch = getche();
      switch (ch)
         {
         case 'e': newname(); break;
         case 'l': listall(); break;
         case 'w': wfile(); break;
         case 'r': rfile(); break;
         default:                         /* user mistake */
            puts("\nEnter only selections listed");
         }  /* end switch */
      }  /* end while */
}  /* end main */

/* newname() */
/* puts a new agent in the database */
void newname(void)
{
   printf("\nRecord %d.\nEnter name: ", n+1); /* get name */
   gets(agent[n].name);
   printf("Enter agent number (3 digits): "); /* get number */
   scanf("%d", &agent[n].agnumb);
   printf("Enter height in inches: ");        /* get height */
   scanf("%f", &agent[n++].height);
   fflush(stdin);                             /* clear buffer */
}

/* listall() */
/* lists all agents and data */
void listall(void)
{
```

```
      int j;
      if (n < 1)                              /* check for empty list */
         printf("\nEmpty list.\n");
      for (j=0; j < n; j++)                   /* print list */
         {
         printf("\nRecord number %d\n", j+1);
         printf("   Name: %s\n", agent[j].name);
         printf("   Agent number: %03d\n", agent[j].agnumb);
         printf("   Height: %4.2f\n", agent[j].height);
         }
}

/* wfile() */
/* writes array of structures to file */
void wfile(void)
{
   FILE *fptr;
   if(n < 1)
      { printf("\nCan't write empty list.\n"); return; }
   if( (fptr=fopen("agents.rec","wb"))==NULL )
      printf("\nCan't open file agents.rec\n");
   else
      {
      fwrite(agent, sizeof(agent[0]), n, fptr);
      fclose(fptr);
      printf("\nFile of %d records written.\n", n);
      }
}

/* rfile() */
/* reads records from file into array */
void rfile(void)
{
   FILE *fptr;
   if( (fptr=fopen("agents.rec","rb"))==NULL )
      printf("\nCan't open file agents.rec\n");
   else
      {
      while( fread(&agent[n],sizeof(agent[n]),1,fptr)==1 )
         n++;                        /* count records */
      fclose(fptr);
      printf("\nFile read. Total agents is now %d.\n", n);
      }
}
```

In use, we can enter a number of secret agents, using the 'e' option:

```
C>agentr

'e' enter new agent
'l' list all agents
```

```
'w' write file
'r' read file: e
Record 1.
Enter name: Mike Hammer
Enter agent number (3 digits): 004
Enter height in inches: 74.25
```

We can continue this process for as many names as we want. Once we've entered the names as we write them to disk with the 'w' option. Then we can quit the program, turn off the computer, whatever; it doesn't matter if the array in memory is destroyed. When we run the program again, we can read the list back in from the disk. The following sequence shows that there is nothing in the list until we read the file; then we can list the contents:

```
C>agentr5

'e' enter new agent
'l' list all agents
'w' write file
'r' read file: l
Empty list.

'e' enter new agent
'l' list all agents
'w' write file
'r' read file: r
File read. Total agents is now 3.

'e' enter new agent
'l' list all agents
'w' write file
'r' read file: l

Record number 1
   Name: Mike Hammer
   Agent number: 004
   Height: 74.25

Record number 2
   Name: Lew Archer
   Agent number: 026
   Height: 71.50

Record number 3
   Name: Sam Spade
   Agent number: 492
   Height: 71.75
```

The new capabilities of this program are in the functions **wfile()** and **rfile()**. In the **wfile()** function the statement

```
fwrite(agent, sizeof(agent[0]), n, fptr);
```

causes the entire array of n structures to be written to disk all at once. The address of the data is at **agent**; the size of one record is **sizeof(agent[0])**, which is the size of the first record; the number of such records is **n**; and the file pointer is **fptr**.

When the function **rfile()** reads the data back in, it must do so one record—that is, one structure—at a time, since it doesn't know in advance how many agents are in the database. Thus, the expression

```
fread(&agent[n],sizeof(agent[n]),1,fptr)
```

is embedded in a **while** loop, which waits for the **fread()** function to report that no bytes were read, indicating end-of-file. This expression causes the data in the structure to be stored at address **&agent[n]**, and to have the size of **agent[n]**. It causes one such structure to be read at a time, from the file pointed to by **fptr**.

> The **fread()** and **fwrite()** functions work with any kind of data, including arrays and structures, and store numbers in binary format.

This program, although it deals with secret agents, could serve as a skeleton for all sorts of database applications, from recipes and stamp collecting to employee records and inventory control.

## Random Access

So far all our file reading and writing has been sequential. That is, when writing a file we've taken a group of items—whether characters, strings, or more complex structures—and placed them on the disk one at a time. Likewise, when reading, we've started at the beginning of the file and gone on until we came to the end.

It's also possible to access files "randomly." This means directly accessing a particular data item, even though it may be in the middle of the file.

The following program allows random access of the file agents.rec, created with the agentr.c program above.

```
/* randr.c */
/* reads one agent's record, selected by user, from file */
#include "stdio.h"
main()
{
    struct
        {
        char name[40];                    /* name */
        int agnumb;                       /* code number */
        float height;                     /* height */
        } agent;
```

```
FILE *fptr;
int recno;                              /* record number */
long int offset;                        /* must be long */
                                        /* open file */
if( (fptr=fopen("agents.rec","r"))==NULL )
   { printf("Can't open file agents.rec"); exit(); }
printf("Enter record number: ");        /* get record num */
scanf("%d", &recno);
offset = recno * sizeof(agent);         /* find offset */
if(fseek(fptr, offset, 0) != 0)         /* go there */
   { printf("Can't move pointer there."); exit(); }
fread(&agent,sizeof(agent),1,fptr);     /* read record */
printf("\nName: %s\n", agent.name);     /* print name */
printf("Number: %03d\n", agent.agnumb); /* print number */
printf("Height: %.2f\n", agent.height); /* print height */
fclose(fptr);                           /* close file */
}
```

And here—assuming the same database exists that we created with the agentr.c program earlier—is what it looks like if we use randr.c to ask for the second record in the file:

```
C>randr
Enter record number: 2

Name: Lew Archer
Number: 026
Height: 71.50
```

## File Pointers

To understand how this program works, you need to be familiar with the concept of *file pointers*. A file pointer is a pointer to a particular byte in a file. The functions we've examined in this chapter all made use of the file pointer: each time we wrote something to a file, the file pointer moved to the end of that something—whether character, string, structure, or whatever—so that writing would continue at that point with the next write function.

When we closed a file and then reopened it, the file pointer was set back to the beginning of the file, so that if we then read from the file, we would start at the beginning. If we had opened a file for append (using the "a" type option), then the file pointer would have been placed at the end of an existing file before we began writing.

> The file pointer points to the byte in the file where the next access will take place. The **fseek()** function lets us move this pointer.

The function **fseek()** gives us control over the file pointer. Thus, to access a record in the middle of a file, we use this function to move the file pointer to that record. In the program above the file pointer is set to the desired value in the expression:

```
if(fseek(fptr, offset, 0) != 0)
```

The first argument of the **fseek()** function is the pointer to the FILE structure for this file. (As you know, this is also referred to as a "file pointer," but it means something quite different from the file pointer that indicates where we are in the file. We have to trust to context to indicate which file pointer we mean.)

The second argument in **fseek()** is called the "offset." This is the number of bytes from a particular place to start reading. Often this place is the beginning of the file; that's the case here. (We'll see other possibilities in a moment.) In our program the offset is calculated by multiplying the size of one record—the structure **agent**—by the number of the record we want to access. In the example we access the second record, but the program thinks of this as record number 1 (since the first record is 0) so the multiplication will be by 1. It is essential that the offset be a *long* integer.

The last argument of the **fseek()** function is called the mode. There are three possible mode numbers, and they determine where the offset will be measured from.

| Mode | Offset is measured from |
| --- | --- |
| 0 | beginning of file |
| 1 | current position of file pointer |
| 2 | end of file |

Once the file pointer has been set, we read the contents of the record at that point into the structure **agent** and print out its contents.

For simplicity we've demonstrated random access to the agents.rec file as a separate program, but it could easily be incorporated into agentr.c as a function, becoming another option for the user.

Another function, **ftell()**, returns the position of the file pointer. We examine this function in an exercise at the end of the chapter.

## Error Conditions

In most cases, if a file can be opened, it can be read from or written to. There are situations, however, when this is not the case. A hardware problem might occur while either reading or writing is taking place, a write operation might run out of disk space, or some other problem might occur.

In our programs so far, we have assumed that no such read or write errors occur. But in some situations, such as programs where data integrity is critical, it may be desirable to check explicitly for errors.

Most standard I/O functions do not have an explicit error return. For example, if **putc()** returns an EOF, this might indicate either a true end-of-file or an error; if **fgets()** returns a NULL value, this might indicate either an EOF or an error, and so forth.

To determine whether an error has occurred we can use the function **ferror()**. This function takes one argument: the file pointer (to FILE). It returns a value of 0 if *no* error has occurred, and a nonzero (TRUE) value if there is an error. This function should be reset by closing the file after it has been used.

Another function is also useful in conjunction with **ferror()**. This one is called **perror()**. It takes a string supplied by the program as an argument; this string is usually an error message indicating where in the program the error occurred. The function prints out the program's error message and then goes on to print out a system-error message.

Here's how we could rewrite the earlier writef.c program to incorporate these two error-handling functions:

```c
/* writef2.c */
/* writes formatted data to file */
/* includes error-handling functions */
#include <stdio.h>
main()
{
    FILE *fptr;                         /* declare ptr to FILE */
    char name[40];                      /* agent's name */
    int code;                           /* code number */
    float height;                       /* agent's height */
                                        /* open file */
    if( (fptr=fopen("textfile.txt","w"))==NULL )
        { printf("Can't open textfile.txt"); exit(); }
    do {
        printf("Type name, code number, and height: ");
        scanf("%s %d %f", name, &code, &height);
        fprintf(fptr, "%s %d %f", name, code, height);
        if( ferror(fptr) )              /* check for error */
            {
            perror("Write error");      /* write message */
            fclose(fptr);               /* close file */
            exit();
            }
        }
    while(strlen(name) > 1);            /* no name given? */
    fclose(fptr);                       /* close file */
}
```

In the event that, for example, the disk becomes full during a write operation, **ferror()** will return a nonzero value and **perror()** will print out the following message:

```
Write error: No space left on device.
```

The first part of this message is supplied by the program and the second part, from the colon on, is supplied by the system.

Explicit error messages of this type can be informative both for the user and for the programmer during development.

We've completed our exploration of standard I/O so we're ready to move into the second type of C-language input/output: system-level I/O.

## System-Level Input/Output

System-level (sometimes called low-level) I/O parallels the methods used by MS-DOS for reading and writing files. In system-level I/O, data cannot be written as individual characters, or as strings, or as formatted data, as is possible using standard I/O. There is only one way data can be written: as a buffer full of bytes.

Writing a buffer full of data resembles record I/O in the standard I/O package. However, unlike standard I/O, the programmer must set up the buffer for the data, place the appropriate values in it before writing, and take them out after reading. Figure 13-8 shows that the buffer in system I/O is part of the program, rather than being invisible as in standard I/O.

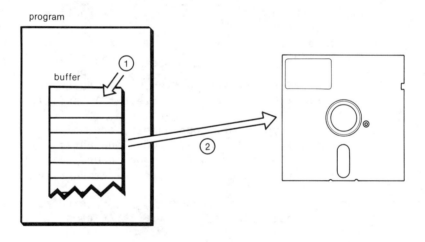

① data is placed in the buffer by the program

② **write( )** function sends contents of buffer to disk file

Figure 13-8. Visible Buffer

There are advantages to system-level I/O. Because it parallels the methods that MS-DOS uses to write to the disk, system-level I/O is more efficient than standard I/O. The amount of code used by the C library routines is less than with standard I/O, so programs can be smaller. Finally, because there are fewer layers of routines to go through, system I/O can also operate faster. Actually, because it is the more basic system, system I/O routines are used by many compiler writers to create the standard I/O package.

## Reading Files in System I/O

Our first example is a program that reads a file from the disk and displays it on the screen. We've seen several examples of how this operation is carried out in standard I/O, so this program will point up the differences between the two approaches.

As an example of the program's operation, we'll use it to display its own source file:

```
C>sysread sysread.c
/* sysread.c */
/* reads and displays file */
#include "fcntl.h"                        /* needed for oflags */
#define BUFFSIZE 512                      /* buffer size */
char buff[BUFFSIZE];                      /* buffer */
main(argc,argv)
int argc;
char *argv[];
{
    int inhandle, bytes, j;
    if(argc != 2)                         /* check arguments */
       { printf("Format: C>sysread file.xxx"); exit(); }
                                          /* open file */
    if( (inhandle = open(argv[1], O_RDONLY | O_BINARY)) < 0)
       {printf("Can't open file %s.", argv[1]); exit(); }
                                          /* read one buffer */
    while( (bytes = read(inhandle,buff,BUFFSIZE)) > 0)
       for(j=0; j<bytes; j++)             /* print buffer */
          putch(buff[j]);
    close(inhandle);                      /* close file */
}
```

### *Setting Up the Buffer*

The first difference you'll notice in this program is that we declare a character buffer with the statements:

```
#define BUFFSIZE 512
char buff[BUFFSIZE];
```

This is the buffer in which the data read from the disk will be placed. The size of this buffer is important for efficient operation. Depending on the operating system, buffers of certain sizes are handled more efficiently than others. In MS-DOS, the optimum buffer size is a multiple of 512 bytes. As we'll see later, the absolute size of the buffer is also important. In some cases a large buffer is more efficient, so multiples of 512, such as 2048 or 4096, should be used.

### Opening the File

As in standard I/O, we must open the file before we can access it. This is done in the expression

```
if( (inhandle = open(argv[1], O_RDONLY | O_BINARY)) < 0)
```

We open the file for the same reason we did in standard I/O: to establish communications with the operating system about the file. We tell the system the name of the file we want to open—in this case, the name placed in the command-line array **argv[1]** by the user. We also indicate whether we want to read or write to the file and whether we want the file opened in binary or text mode. However, the method used to indicate this information is different in system I/O. Each characteristic is indicated by a constant called an "oflag." A list of oflags is shown in Table 13-1.

### Table 13-1. System-Level Oflags

| Oflag | Meaning |
|---|---|
| O_APPEND | Place file pointer at end of file |
| O_CREAT | Create a new file for writing (has no effect if file already exists) |
| O_EXCEL | Return error value if file already exists (used only with O_CREAT) |
| O_RDONLY | Open a new file for reading only |
| O_RDWR | Open file for both reading and writing |
| O_TRUNC | Open and truncate existing file to 0 length |
| O_WRONLY | Open file for writing only |
| O_BINARY | Open file in binary mode |
| O_TEXT | Open file in text mode |

Some of the possibilities listed in Table 13-1 are mutually exclusive: you can't open a file for read-only and read-write at the same time, for example.

In our sysread.c program we open a file using the oflags O_RDONLY and O_BINARY. We'll see examples of other oflags in use as we go along. The oflags are defined in the file FCNTL.H, so this file must be **#include**d in programs using system I/O. (Note, though, that the STDIO.H file, which was necessary in standard I/O, is not necessary here.)

When two or more oflags are used together, they are combined using the bitwise OR operator ( | ).

### File Handles

Instead of returning a pointer, as **fopen()** did in standard I/O, **open()** returns an integer value called a "file handle." This is a number assigned to a particular file, which is used thereafter to refer to the file.

If **open()** returns a value of – 1 rather than a valid file handle (which must be greater than 0), an error has occurred. (We can find out more about the error by using another function, as we'll see in the next example.)

> The system-level function **open()** returns a file handle, which is not a pointer, but simply a reference number to identify a file.

### Reading the File into the Buffer

The following statement reads the file—or as much of it as will fit—into the buffer:

```
bytes = read(inhandle,buff,BUFFSIZE)
```

The **read()** function takes three arguments. The first is the file handle. The second is the address of the buffer—in this case, the variable **buff**. The third argument is the maximum number of bytes we want to read. In this case we'll allow the function to fill the entire buffer, but in some situations reading fewer bytes might be desirable. Reading more bytes than the buffer can hold is not, of course, recommended.

The **read()** function returns the number of bytes actually read. This is an important number, since it may very well be less than the buffer size, and we'll need to know just how full the buffer is before we can do anything with its contents. We assign this number to the variable **bytes**.

Once the buffer is full we can print it out. We do this with a **for** loop running from 0 to **bytes**, printing one character at a time.

### Closing the File

No surprises here: we use the **close()** function to close the file. This releases the communications areas and the file handle for use by other files.

## Error Messages

As with standard I/O, it is possible in system I/O to query the system about what went wrong in the event that an error condition is encountered when an **open()** or other file operation is attemped. A return value of – 1 indicates an error, and the type of error can be determined with the function **perror()**. This function, as we saw earlier, uses as its argument an error message from the program and, when executed, prints not only the program's message, but also the system-error message.

Here's a modification of sysread.c that incorporates this function to check for errors on opening the file:

```
/* sysread2.c */
/* reads and displays file, uses perror()  */
#include "fcntl.h"                          /* needed for oflags */
```

```
#define BUFFSIZE 512                    /* buffer size */
char buff[BUFFSIZE];                    /* buffer */
main(argc,argv)
int argc;
char *argv[];
{
   int inhandle, bytes, j;
   if(argc != 2)                        /* check arguments */
      { printf("Format: C>search file.xxx"); exit(); }
                                         /* open file */
   if( (inhandle = open(argv[1], O_RDONLY | O_BINARY)) < 0)
      perror("Can't open input file");
                                         /* read one buffer */
   while( (bytes = read(inhandle,buff,BUFFSIZE)) > 0)
      for(j=0; j<bytes; j++)            /* print buffer */
         putch(buff[j]);
   close(inhandle);                     /* close file */
}
```

Here's a sample of the program's operation when the user attempts to operate on a nonexistent file:

```
C>sysread2 nofile.xxx
Can't open input file: No such file or directory
```

The first part of the message is the program's, the second comes from the system.

This technique can be used to provide information about read and write errors as well as errors in opening a file.

## Buffer Operations

Putting the contents of a file in a buffer has certain advantages; we can perform various operations on the contents of the buffer without having to access the file again. There are several functions that can speed up operations on buffered data, as our next example demonstrates. This program searches a text file for a word or phrase typed by the user.

```
/* fsearch.c */
/* searches file for phrase */
#include <fcntl.h>                      /* needed for oflags */
#include <io.h>                         /* for open(), etc. */
#include <stdio.h>                      /* needed for NULL etc */
#include <memory.h>                     /* needed for memchr() */
#include <process.h>                    /* for exit() */
#include <string.h>                     /* for strlen() */
#define BUFFSIZE 1024                   /* buffer size */
char buff[BUFFSIZE];                    /* buffer */
void search(char *, int);              /* prototype */
```

```
void main(argc, argv)
int argc;
char *argv[];
{
    int inhandle, bytes;

    if(argc != 3)                         /* check arguments */
       { printf("Format: C>search source.xxx phrase"); exit(0); }
                                          /* open file */
    if( (inhandle = open(argv[1], O_RDONLY )) < 0)
       { printf("Can't open file %s.", argv[1]); exit(0); }
                                          /* read file */
    while( (bytes = read(inhandle,buff,BUFFSIZE)) > 0)
       search(argv[2],bytes);             /* search for phrase */
    close(inhandle);                      /* close file */
    printf("Phrase not found");
}


/* search() */
/* searches buffer for phrase */
void search(char *phrase, int buflen)
{
    char *ptr, *p;                    /* pointers into file */

    ptr = buff;                       /* beginning of buffer */
                                      /* look for first char */
    while( (ptr=memchr(ptr,phrase[0],buflen)) != NULL)
                                      /* look for phrase */
       if( memcmp(ptr,phrase,strlen(phrase)) == 0)
          {
          printf("First occurrance of phrase:\n.");
          for(p=ptr-100; p<ptr+100; p++)
             putchar(*p);
          exit(0);
          }
       else ptr++;
}
```

This program requires the user to type two arguments on the command line (in addition to the program name): the name of the file to be searched and the phrase to be searched for. The program then finds the first occurrence of this phrase. To show where the phrase is in the file, the characters on each side of the phrase are printed out so that it can be seen in context.

Here's an example of the program searching the manuscript version of Chapter 9 of this book for the word "aside":

```
C>fsearch chp9.ms aside
First occurrence of phrase:
```

list of prices.
3. The purpose of declaring a structure type is to
   a. set aside the appropriate amount of memory
   b. define the format of the structure
   c. specify

The main part of this program is similar to sysread.c. One difference is that the file has been opened in text mode. This is the default when no mode is specified, and we did not include the O_BINARY oflag. This means that CR/LFs will be translated into newlines when we read the file.

### Buffer Manipulation Functions

The function **search()**, called by the main program, makes use of several buffer manipulation functions. The first such function is **memchr()**. This function searches a buffer for a specific character. In our example, the expression

```
ptr=memchr(ptr,phrase[0],buflen)
```

shows the three arguments necessary for **memchr()**. The first is the address of the buffer. Here we've assigned the address to the pointer variable **ptr**. The second argument is the character to be searched for—in this case, the first character of the phrase typed by the user, argv[2]. This is passed to the function **search()** and stored in the variable **phrase**. The third parameter is the length of the buffer to be searched.

The **memchr()** function returns a NULL if the character is not found, otherwise it returns a pointer to the character in the buffer. Here it assigns the pointer to the variable **ptr**.

The **search()** function then enters an **if** statement to see if the character actually marks the beginning of the sought-after phrase. This comparison is handled by the function **memcmp()**, in the expression

```
if( memcmp(ptr,phrase,strlen(phrase)) == 0)
```

This function also takes three arguments: a pointer to the place in the buffer where the comparison should begin, the address of the phrase to be compared, and the length of the phrase. The function then compares the phrase with the characters in the buffer; if they match, it returns 0.

If a match is found, the **search()** function prints the characters on both sides of the match and exits. Otherwise, the process is repeated until **memchr()** can no longer find the character in the file.

The buffer manipulation functions require that the memory.h file be **#include**d with the program.

## Writing Files in System I/O

Writing a file in system I/O is somewhat more complicated than reading a file. As an example, let's look at a program that copies one file to another; that is, it imitates the DOS COPY command.

To use this function, the user types the name of the source file (which should already exist) and the destination file (which will be created) on the command line.

```
C>copy2 source.txt dest.txt
```

Since the files are opened in binary, any file can be copied, whether a text file or a binary file such as an executable program.

Here's the listing:

```
/* copy2.c */
/* copies one file to another */
#include "fcntl.h"                    /* needed for oflags */
#include "sys\types.h"                /* needed for sys\stat.h */
#include "sys\stat.h"                 /* needed for pmode */
#define BUFSIZ 4096                   /* buffer size */
char buff[BUFSIZ];                    /* buffer */
main(argc,argv)
int argc;
char *argv[];
{
    int inhandle, outhandle, bytes;
    if(argc != 3)                     /* check arguments */
    { printf("Format: C>copy2 source.xxx dest.xxx"); exit(); }
                                      /* open files */
    if( (inhandle = open(argv[1], O_RDONLY | O_BINARY)) < 0)
       {printf("Can't open file %s.", argv[1]); exit(); }
    if( (outhandle = open(argv[2],
         O_CREAT | O_WRONLY | O_BINARY, S_IWRITE)) < 0)
       { printf("Can't open file %s.", argv[2]); exit(); }
                                      /* copy file */
    while( (bytes = read(inhandle,buff,BUFSIZ)) > 0)
       write(outhandle,buff,bytes);
    close(inhandle);                  /* close files */
    close(outhandle);
}
```

Two files are opened. One is the source file, whose handle is assigned to the variable **inhandle**. The other is the destination file, whose handle will be in **outhandle**. The expression that opens the source file should look familiar from previous examples. The one that opens the destination file, though, has some unfamiliar features:

```
if( (outhandle = open(argv[2],
     O_CREAT | O_WRONLY | O_BINARY, S_IWRITE)) < 0)
```

This expression is so large it must be written on two lines. To create a nonexistent file, we use the O_CREAT oflag. We want to write and not read to this file, so we also use O_WRONLY. And we want to use binary mode, so we use O_BINARY.

Whenever the O_CREAT oflag is used, another variable must be added to the **open()** function to indicate the read/write status of the file to be created. These options are called the "pmode" (for "permission") arguments. There are three possibilities:

| Pmode | Meaning |
|-------|---------|
| S_IWRITE | Writing permitted |
| S_IREAD | Reading permitted |
| S_IREAD ¦ S_IWRITE | Reading and writing permitted |

Actually, all files are readable in MS-DOS, so some of these possibilities are not relevant and are included only for compatibility with other systems. The only one necessary is S_IWRITE.

Inconveniently, if the pmode flags are to be recognized, both the files sys \types.h and sys\stat.h must be **#include**d with the source file for this program, along with fcntl.h.

The **write()** function is similar in format to **read()**. Like **read()**, it takes three arguments: the handle of the file to be written to, the address of the buffer, and the number of bytes to be written.

To copy the file, we use both the **read()** and **write()** functions in a **while** loop. The **read()** function returns the number of bytes actually read; this is assigned to the variable **bytes**. This value will be equal to the buffer size until the end of the file, when the buffer probably will be only partially full. The variable **bytes** therefore is used to tell the **write()** function how many bytes to write from the buffer to the destination file.

Notice that we've used a larger buffer size in this program than in previous examples. The larger the buffer, the fewer disk accesses the program must make, so increasing the size of the buffer significantly speeds up the operation of the program; it copies an 80K file twice as fast with a buffer size of 4096 as it does with 512. You can experiment with buffer size to see which works best in your particular application.

When large buffers are used they must be made global variables, otherwise stack overflow occurs.

## Redirection

In Chapter 8 we discussed redirection: the capability built into DOS and the C runtime system to redirect output to a disk file that would normally go to the screen and to take input from a disk file that would normally come from the keyboard.

It is also possible to modify disk-oriented programs, such as those in this chapter, so that they make use of redirection. This can be helpful if the programs are to be used, Unix-style, in such a way that they act as *filters*, taking input from one program via indirection, modifying it, and passing it on to another program, again via indirection. (For more on filters and the related subject of pipes, see your DOS manual, or the other books listed in the bibliography.)

Let's see how we would modify the copy2.c program to use indirection. Essentially we rewrite the program so that its input, instead of coming from a file, comes from the keyboard, and its output, instead of going to a file, goes to the display. Then, when the program is used, indirection can be employed to specify that input should again come from a file and that output should also go to a file (or be piped to another program).

The simplest way to invoke this new version of the program would be:

```
C>copy3 <source.ext >dest.ext
```

where source.ext is the file we want to copy and dest.ext is the destination file. However, if we wanted to copy the output of another program, say prog1, and send the copied file to a third program, say prog2, we could write:

```
C>prog1 ¦ copy3 ¦ prog2
```

A fringe benefit of using redirection is that the programming is somewhat simplified. Here's the modified version of copy2.c:

```
/* copy3.c */
/* copies one file to another */
/* uses redirection; format is C>copy3 <source.xxx >dest.xxx */
#include "fcntl.h"                   /* needed for oflags */
#define inhandle 0                   /* stdin file */
#define outhandle 1                  /* stdout file */
#define BUFSIZ 4096                  /* buffer size */
char buff[BUFSIZ];                   /* buffer */
main()
{
   int bytes;
   setmode(inhandle, O_BINARY);      /* set file mode */
   setmode(outhandle, O_BINARY);     /*    to binary */
                                     /* copy file */
   while( (bytes = read(inhandle,buff,BUFSIZ)) > 0)
      write(outhandle,buff,bytes);
}
```

The numbers 0 and 1 are predefined by DOS to be file handles for the keyboard and the display, respectively. These numbers correspond to the standard input and output devices stdin and stdout described earlier. Here's a complete list:

We can use these numbers as file handles without having to open any files.

| Device | Number |
|--------|--------|
| stdin | 0 |
| stdout | 1 |
| stderr | 2 |
| stdaux | 3 |
| stdprn | 4 |

Since we don't need to open files, we can't use the **open()** function to specify which mode—text or binary—we want the file to be in. However, there is another way to do this: the **setmode()** function. **Setmode()** can take one of two arguments: O_TEXT and O_BINARY. You'll recognize these from our discussion of the **open()** function; they're defined in the file FCNTL.H.

The actual reading and writing of the files is done the same way in this program as in the earlier copy2.c.

## When to Use What

With the multiplicity of functions available for file access in C it's sometimes hard to know which method to use.

Standard I/O is probably most valuable where it's natural to handle data as characters, strings, or formatted **printf()** style form. System I/O is more natural in situations where blocks of data, such as arrays, are to be handled. In many cases, standard I/O is simpler to program, while system I/O usually generates more efficient code, both in terms of speed and the size of the executable file.

It's important not to mix standard and system-level I/O. If a file has been opened with **fopen()**, don't try to use **read()** or **write()** with it, and vice versa. Thus, while system-level I/O would usually be used for reading blocks of data, for compatibility, **fread()** and **fwrite()** might be used if the file is already being used by other standard I/O functions.

Text mode is usually used with files containing text, and binary mode is used for files that may contain numbers other than ASCII codes. This avoids translation problems that would corrupt numerical data. However, as in the bindump.c program, it is occasionally useful to use binary mode on text files.

## Summary

The subject of file input/output in Microsoft C is a rich and complex one. In this chapter we've only covered the highlights. But you probably have enough of a head start to finish the exploration of files on your own.

We've shown that there are two main families of file-handling functions: standard I/O and system-level I/O. Standard I/O can deal with data in a larger variety of ways, but system I/O is generally the more efficient. In standard I/O we showed examples of the four ways to handle data: as characters, as strings, as formatted data in the style of **printf()**, and as fixed-length records or blocks.

We saw that the first three of these ways store data—whether text or numbers—as ASCII characters, while the fourth way, record I/O, causes numerical data to be stored in binary format.

We also explored the difference between text and binary modes (not to be confused with text and binary formats). In text modes C newlines are translated into the MS-DOS CR/LF pair, and the character 1A indicates an EOF; in binary mode neither of these is true.

We finished the chapter with a look at system-level I/O. This family of commands requires that the programmer set up a buffer for the data and use only one system for reading and writing; data is always considered to consist of a block of bytes. Buffer manipulation functions can help with operations on the data in the buffer.

## Questions

1. The two main systems of I/O available in C are _____ I/O and _____ I/O.

2. A file must be opened so that
   a. the program knows how to access the file
   b. the operating system knows what file to access
   c. the operating system knows if the file should be read from or written to
   d. communications areas are established for communicating with the file

3. A file opened with **fopen()** will thereafter be referred to by its

   _____ .

4. The function **fopen()** can specify which of the following?
   a. The file may be opened for appending.
   b. The file may be opened in binary mode.
   c. The file may be given read-only status.
   d. Numbers in the file will be written in binary format.

5. In standard I/O the function used to close a file is _____ .

6. When reading one character at a time, which of the following functions is appropriate?
   a. **fread()**
   b. **read()**
   c. **fgets()**
   d. **getc()**

7. True or false: closing a file after writing to it is optional.

8. Text and binary mode have to do with

   a. the way numbers are stored on the disk

   b. the way numbers are stored in memory

   c. the way newlines are handled

   d. the way EOF's are handled

9. To examine every single byte of a file, is text or binary mode more suitable?

10. Which of the following are valid parts of standard input/output?

    a. record I/O

    b. structure I/O

    c. character I/O

    d. array I/O

    e. string I/O

    f. formatted I/O

11. When writing numbers to disk, the file should usually be opened in _____ mode.

12. To write a small number of mixed string and integer variables to a file, the appropriate function is

    a. **fputs()**

    b. **fgets()**

    c. **fprintf()**

    d. **fwrite()**

13. True or false: since files must be read sequentially, there is no way to read data from the middle of a file without starting at the beginning.

14. Whenever a file is open, a number indicates at what position in the file the next access will be made. This number is called the

    a. read/write status (type int)

    b. file handle (type int)

    c. file pointer (type pointer to char)

    d. file pointer (type long int)

    e. file handle (type long int)

15. To write a block of data to a file in standard I/O, the appropriate function is _____.

16. The offset is the number of _____ from a certain point in a file.

17. The function **fseek()**
    a. finds a given word or phrase in a file
    b. finds the correct file
    c. helps access records in the middle of a file
    d. moves the file pointer to the desired location

18. A file opened by **open()** will thereafter be referred to by its file _____.

19. Which of the following describes system I/O?
    a. closer to DOS methods
    b. slower
    c. more data formats
    d. smaller executable programs

20. In system-level I/O, the function used to read from a file is _____.

21. When a predefined file handle is used, text or binary mode may be specified using the _____ function.

22. Which of the following functions will search a block of data for a specific character?
    a. **search()**
    b. **strchr()**
    c. **memchr()**
    d. **buffcmp()**

23. True or false: a system-level file can be opened for reading and writing at the same time.

24. An oflag can
    a. signal when a file is unreadable
    b. specify if a file should be read or written
    c. signal when EOF is detected
    d. specify binary mode

25. If O_CREAT is used, the _____ argument must be added to indicate the read/write protection mode for the file.

26. If data is to be treated in large blocks, the _____ I/O system is usually more appropriate.

27. The advantage of using redirection is that the input to a program may then come from
    a. the keyboard
    b. pipes
    c. filters
    d. other programs

28. Write a DOS command to use indirection to read input data from the file file1.txt to the program encrypt, and then write the output of this program to the file file2.txt.

29. If a system-level program employs redirection, it should
    a. use standard file handles for keyboard and display
    b. open files in binary mode
    c. set binary mode using the **setmode()** function
    d. use the **redir()** function

30. True or false: there is only one right way to do things in the world of C files.

## Exercises

1. Write a program that will read a C source file and verify that the number of right and left braces in the file are equal. Use a command-line argument for the name of the file and the **getc()** function to read in the file.

2. It is sometimes desirable to store a group of strings of different lengths in the same file. It is also sometimes desirable to access these strings randomly—that is, to read only the desired one, without starting at the beginning of a file. To do this, the offset of each string can be placed in a table. To compile the table of offsets, one can use the function **ftell()**, which returns the current offset, taking only the file pointer (**fptr**) as an argument.

    Write a program that uses string I/O, permitting the user to type a group of phrases, and that tells the user the offset of each phrase typed in, like this:

```
C>writedex
Open the pod bay doors, Hal.
Offset=0
```

```
Klingons attacking!
Offset=29

Your fuel is dangerously low.
Offset=49

Unknown craft approaching at warp factor 7.
Offset=79
```

3. Write a program that will read any given string from the file created in the previous exercise and display it on the screen. The program should use a table of offsets and random access to locate the string. Sample interaction with the program should look like this:

```
C>readdex
Enter index number (0 to 3) of string: 0
Open the pod bay doors, Hal.

Enter index number (0 to 3) of string: 3
Unknown craft approaching at warp factor 7.
```

4. Write a function that can be added to the agentr.c program, so that an agent's record can be deleted from the database. The file is first read in, the deletion is made in memory, then the revised list of agents is written out to the file.

5. Write a program that will concatenate two files: that is, add the contents of one file to another and write the result into a third file. Use system-level I/O, and command-line arguments that look like this:

```
C>concat source1.ext source2.ext dest.ext
```

# Larger Programs

- Separate compilation
- External variables and separately compiled files
- Modular programming and separate compilation
- Conditional compilation using **#ifdef**
- Memory models

# 14

The C language is particularly rich in tools for creating large, sophisticated programs. However, in this book our program examples have, of necessity, been comparatively small. In this chapter we'll examine some of the techniques used when programs become larger and more complex.

In particular, we'll discuss how sections of larger programs can be compiled separately and linked together, and we'll explore the related issue of how data can be shared by such separately compiled modules. We'll show how parts of a source file can be compiled under some circumstances but not others, and finally we'll discuss memory models, which permit programs and data to occupy very large amounts of memory.

## Separate Compilation

So far in this book we have always written, compiled, and linked one program at a time. The program might have had several functions in it, but they were all treated as a single entity for the purpose of compilation. However, it is possible to break a program apart into separate *files*, each file consisting of one or more functions. These files can be compiled separately and then linked together to form the final executable program.

Let's examine some simple examples of this process; then we'll discuss why we might want to use separate compilation.

Here's a complete C source file, called mainprog.c.

```
/* mainprog.c */
/* main program to test separate compilation */
int sumsqr(int, int);                    /* prototype */
main()
{
    int a, b, ans;
```

```
    printf("Type two integers: ");
    scanf("%d %d", &a, &b);              /* get two integers */
    ans = sumsqr(a,b);                   /* find sum of squares */
    printf("Sum of squares of %d and % d is %d", a, b, ans);
}
```

This is a variation of a program from Chapter 5, multifun.c, which calculates the sum of the squares of two numbers. However, part of the multifun.c program is missing here. We'll see where it went in a moment.

Type in this source file, but don't try to compile or link it. Why not? Because the linker would produce the error message "unresolved external" when it encountered the reference to the function **sumsqr()**:

```
    ans = sumsqr(a, b);
```

Save mainprog.c to disk. Now type in a completely separate file called sumsqr.c and save it to disk in the same way.

```
/* sumsqr.c */
/* function returns sum of squares of arguments */
int sumsqr(int x, int y)
{
    return( x*x + y*y );
}
```

We have now produced two separate source files, mainprog.c and sumsqr.c. Our goal is to compile these files separately and then link the resulting .obj files into a single executable .exe file. This .exe file, called MAIN-PROG.EXE, will contain the function **main()** and the function **sumsqr()**, connected properly so they work together. Figure 14-1 shows this process.

How do we compile the files separately, and link them? That depends on whether you're using the Optimizing Compiler or QuickC.

## Separate Compilation with the Optimizing Compiler

Only one step is required both to compile and link the two files with the Optimizing Compiler. From DOS, type the following:

```
C>cl mainprog.c sumsqr.c
```

CL will first generate two .obj files: MAINPROG.OBJ and SUMSQR.OBJ. It will then link these together to produce MAINPROG.EXE. (The name of the first file on the command line is given to the .exe file.) You can see all three new files if you examine your directory with DIR.

Versions of the Optimizing Compiler prior to 5.0 required several steps to perform the same operation. Two commands compiled the .C files into .obj files, and a final invocation of LINK.EXE linked them into mainprog.c. The sequence was:

```
C>msc mainprog;
C>msc sumsqr;
C>link mainprog+sumsqr;
```

The new one-step process is more convenient, but it tends to obscure what's happening.

## Separate Compilation with QuickC

To compile and link separate files in QuickC you must create a program list in the following manner.

Bring up QuickC with the mainprog.c file. Select Set Program List from the File menu. Enter "mainprog.mak" in the File Name box. Answer "yes" to the "does not exist, create?" question. When the new window appears, enter "mainprog.c"; it will appear in the File List. Then enter "sumsqr.c." It will also appear in the File List. Select Save List. This writes the program list MAINPROG.MAK to disk and returns you to the view window.

Now that the program list is created, you can select Start from the Run menu in the usual way. QuickC will automatically compile mainprog.c, see from the program list that it needs to compile sumsqr.c, compile that, and finally link the two .obj files together and run the program.

If you compile in memory, no .obj or .exe files will be generated. However, if you select Compile from the Run menu and request an .exe file, then both the .obj and the .exe files will be created; you can see them with DIR when you exit QuickC.

Does this actually work? Of course. Here's some sample output from the program:

```
C>mainprog
Type two integers: 3 4
The sum of the squares is 25
```

## Advantages of Separate Compilation

Now that we've shown how to generate a single .exe file from two source files, what have we accomplished? With a program this small, not much. But when programs start to get larger, with many functions and hundreds or thousands of lines of code, then separate compilation starts to have some real advantages. Why?

One reason is that compile time is proportional to the size of the file being compiled. And, usually, a programmer is only working on one part of a program at a time. So to minimize compile time, a programmer compiles only those parts of a program that have been changed since the last compilation. The parts of the program that are already working and debugged are not recompiled; they form a

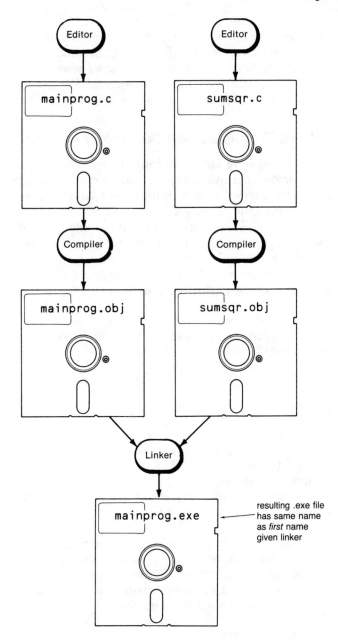

Figure 14-1. Separate Compilation of Functions

group of permanent object files. Each time a new version of the current file—the part of the program that is being written and debugged—is compiled, it can be linked with the previously compiled files. Using this approach, only a small part of the program need be compiled at any one time; the rest already exists in the form of .obj files. If several programmers are working on a project they can share previously developed object files. Since a module need not be recompiled after it is developed and debugged, there is less chance that it will be inadvertently modified or that two programmers will be using different versions of one function.

A more important reason for using separate compilation is that it enables you to write well-structured, modular programs. We'll say more about this in the next section. Now let's look at how functions in separately compiled files share data.

## External Variables and Separately Compiled Files

In our example, in which **mainprog()** and **sumsqr()** were linked, two numbers were passed from **mainprog()** to **sumsqr()** using arguments, and the result from **sumsqr()** was returned to **mainprog()** with a **return** statement. This kind of data communication between separately compiled functions is easy to implement; it requires no special statement in either function. But suppose we wanted functions in separately compiled files to have access to the same *external* variable?

A function in one file can access an external variable located in another file if it declares the variable using the keyword **extern**. To show how this works, we'll rewrite the **mainprog()** and **sumsqr()** functions this way:

```
/* mainpro2.c */
/* main program to test global variables */
int sumsqr(void);    /* prototype */

int a, b;            /* global variables */

main()
{
    int ans;
    printf("Type two integers: ");
    scanf("%d %d", &a, &b);
    ans = sumsqr();
    printf("Sum of squares of %d and %d is %d", a, b, ans);
}
```

This is similar to the mainprog.c file shown earlier, except that we've moved the variables **a** and **b**, which hold the two integers the user types in, to a position outside the function. They are now external variables. Now when mainpro2.c calls **sumsqr2()**, it no longer needs to pass any arguments.

Here's the revised sumsqr.c file:

```
/* sumsqr2.c */
/* function returns sum of squares of external variables */
int sumsqr(void)
{
    extern int a, b;      /* declaration of external variables */

    return(a*a + b*b);    /* return sum of squares */
}
```

Here you can see that we no longer need to declare any variables as formal arguments to the function, but that we do declare the two variables **a** and **b** to be of type **extern int**. What does this mean?

The word **extern** is an example of a *storage class*, which we'll discuss in detail in Chapter 15. For the moment, what we need to know is that, for an external variable to be visible in a file other than the one in which it's defined, it must be declared using the **extern** keyword. This keyword tells the compiler: "Somewhere in another file we've defined these variables. Don't worry that they aren't defined in this file, but let the linker know about them." When the linker gets the message from the compiler that these variables are external, it looks for them in different files. When it finds them, it makes the appropriate connections. From then on, references in **sumsqr2()** to **a** and **b** will be correctly linked to the **a** and **b** defined in the mainpro2.c file. Figure 14-2 shows an external variable declared in two different files.

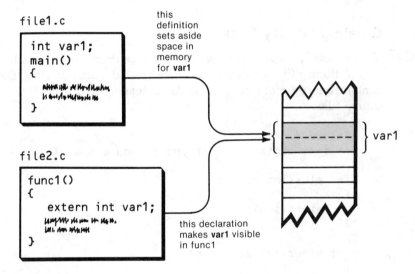

Figure 14-2. External Variable Declared in Different Files

There is more to be said about the use of external variables in different files. We'll look into this in Chapter 15.

## Library Files

We've seen how a number of functions constituting a program can either be kept together in a single file or divided among several files that are compiled separately and linked together. There is a third possibility we should mention here. Functions can also be included in a special kind of file called a "library." A library is a file consisting of a number of functions. The functions are combined into groups called modules, which have a special characteristic; when you link a program with the library, only those modules containing functions that are actually referenced by the program will be included in the resulting .exe file.

You've already used library files, perhaps without thinking much about it. Every time you use a C library function, such as **printf()**, it is a library file that supplies the actual code for the function. The object files of whatever C functions you referenced are linked with your program to generate the final .exe file. But not all the functions in the library file are added to your program; this would make every C program huge. The linker extracts only those functions you need and links them with your object file. This is an important characteristic of C, since it helps to minimize the size of the final program.

Most C programmers will purchase specialized libraries of functions not available in the standard C library. Commercially available libraries include those for window and menu creation, statistical functions, database handling, specialized I/O, and many others. Also programmers will develop their own libraries, which will include families of functions they use frequently. For a working programmer such libraries can significantly increase speed and productivity.

## Creating Library Files

You can easily create your own library files. Here, briefly, is how it's done.

A library file consists of modules created from .obj files. Each .obj file can contain one or more functions. As an example, consider the following two source files:

```
/* add.c */
/* file contains functions to add and subtract */

int plus(int a, int b)
{
    return(a+b);
}

int minus(int a, int b)
{
    return(a-b);
}

/* mult.c */
/* file contains functions to multiply and divide */

int times(int a, int b)
{
    return(a*b);
}

int divby(int a, int b)
{
    return(a/b);
}
```

Each of these files contains two functions for performing arithmetic. (Of course C has its own arithmetic operators; presumably a real library would be constructed of more useful functions.)

Before they can be made into a library, the source files must be compiled into .obj files. In QuickC, select Compile . . . from the Run menu, and choose Obj from the Output Options list. In the Optimizing Compiler, use the switch /c in the CL command line; this suppresses linking, leaving only the .obj file.

Use the LIB utility to combine the two .obj files into a single library file. Make sure the .obj files are in the current directory and then type

```
C>lib arith +add +mult
```

This produces a library file called ARITH.LIB, which contains all four functions, divided into two modules. To use these functions, you must link the library to your program. Suppose your program looks like this:

```
/* artest.c */
/* tests arith.lib library functions */
main()
{
    int x=20, y=10;

    printf("x plus y = %d\n",    plus(x, y) );
    printf("x minus y = %d\n",   minus(x, y) );
    printf("x times y = %d\n",   times(x, y) );
    printf("x divby y = %d\n",   divby(x, y) );
}
```

If you're using the Optimizing Compiler, invoke CL like this:

```
C>cl artest.c arith.lib
```

In QuickC, put artest.c and ARITH.LIB on a program list before compiling.

Both modules in ARITH.LIB will be linked with artest.c, since it calls functions from both. However, if you had used only the **plus()** function, for example, the ADD module (derived from add.c) would have been linked, but the MULT module would not have. By placing related functions together in the same module, the creator of a library can optimize the efficiency of function linking.

Prototypes should be added to the program calling the functions in the library (we've left them out for clarity). These can be placed directly into the program, but it's more common to bundle them into a header file, where they can all be added to the source file with a single **#include** directive, as they are in the Microsoft library.

## Modular Programming and Separate Compilation

Perhaps the most important reason for using separate compilation is that it is an important aid in writing well-structured, modular programs. Let's examine the relation of C to modular programming.

Dividing a program into separately compiled files can help make it modular.

You probably know that it isn't considered good programming practice to write a large program as a single unit. Instead, the program should be broken down into smaller, easily understood parts. A C program usually consists of a **main()** function which calls several other functions to carry out the important tasks of the program. Each of these functions in turn calls other functions, and so on, until the functions being called are so simple that they need make no further calls.

Each function should carry out a single clearly defined task. At the upper level a function might calculate a payroll, for example. This function might call another function to calculate withholding tax. This function might call still another function to look up tax rates in a table. The important points are these: first, the role of a function should be clearly defined, and second, the function should not be too large. Some programmers use a rule of thumb that no function should exceed one page in length, but of course many functions should be smaller.

How does separate compilation fit into modular programming? Using separate files gives us a different size building block to use when constructing programs. A program can be broken down into files and each file can be broken down into functions, as shown in Figure 14-3.

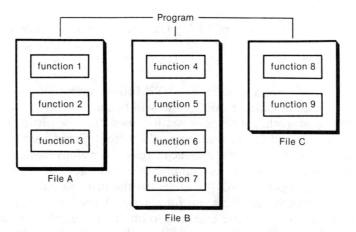

Figure 14-3. Separate Compilation and Modular Programming

As we'll see in Chapter 15, it's possible to restrict variables, not only to one function (as we've seen earlier with automatic variables), but to only one *file* as well. This ability to *hide* data from parts of the program is another aid to modular programming, since it is important that the variables in one part of a program not have access to variables in another part unless it is absolutely necessary.

## Program Design

C provides the tools for designing well-structured programs, but it's up to the programmer to use them effectively.

Any large program should be planned in considerable detail before a single line of code is written. Each function should be specified. The specification should include the purpose of the function, the arguments to be passed to it and returned by it, and the functions it will call. Most programmers recommend a "top down" approach. This means specifying the most general functions—probably starting with **main()**—first, and working down to the specific functions that perform low-level tasks, such as putting a character on the screen. In some situations, however, low-level functions must be planned concurrently with the higher-level ones.

Data storage should also be thoroughly specified before code is written. Special care must be paid to large data items such as arrays and structures. External variables should be used only when absolutely necessary. As we have noted, external variables are vulnerable to being altered inadvertently by functions that shouldn't be accessing them. Special care should be paid to the naming of external variables, so that their names do not conflict with other variables. Long, descriptive names are better than short ones. For instance, the variable names **a** and **b**, used earlier in this chapter, would not be appropriate in a large program; it would be too easy to confuse them with other variables. Names like **SystemTemperature** and **GlobalErrorStatus** would be better. Automatic variables should be given meaningful names as well, but it's less critical.

The programmer must decide how to divide the program into different files. Major sections of the program, or those to be worked on by different programmers, might be placed in different files. A group of routines that can be used with other programs as well as the one under development might be placed in a library file to facilitate its use in different situations.

If a program is thoroughly specified before the code is written, it is possible to write almost any individual function before those functions that it calls, and that call it, are written. Dummy functions can supply it with data, so it can be tested and debugged independently from the other parts of the program. Once all the functions have been tested and shown to work independently, it's far more likely that they will work together in the final program.

# Conditional Compilation Using #*ifdef*

In certain situations it may be useful to compile parts of a source file under some circumstances but not others. This capability is often used in larger programs, but let's first look at an application that can be used in programs of any size.

Suppose you want to measure the speed of a section in your program. You insert statements that will print "start" and "stop" messages at the beginning and end of the crucial section of code. This way, you can time the execution of the code with a stopwatch (assuming the program is slow enough). However, you only want these messages to be printed when you're testing the program, not when it's running normally.

> The directive **if**, along with other directives, permits sections of a program to be compiled in some circumstances but not others.

You could simply insert statements to print the "start" and "stop" messages each time you wanted to test the program and then remove them and recompile the program when testing was over. However, if there are a lot of such messages in a program, or they are complex, this could be inconvenient. A better way is to use a combination of preprocessor directives: **#define**, **#if**, and **#endif**. Using this system, you can keep your test statements in the listing at all times, but activate them only when you wish—by changing one **#define** statement at the beginning of the program. You will still need to recompile your program to activate or deactivate the test mode, but the rewriting of code is minimized.

Here's an example:

```
/* define.c */
/* demonstrates #if, #else, #endif */
#define TIMER                       /* remove if no test */
main()
{
   int j, k;

   #if defined(TIMER)              /* executed only if */
      printf("Starting test\n");  /* TIMER is defined */
   #endif

   for(j=0; j<3000; j++)           /* main part of program */
      for(k=0; k<100; k++)         /*     lengthy loop */
         ;

   #if defined(TIMER)              /* executed only if */
      printf("Ending test\n");    /*     timer is defined */
   #else                           /* executed only if */
      printf("Done\n");           /*     timer is not defined */
   #endif
}
```

In this program we want to test how long a timing loop, consisting of two nested **for** loops, takes to execute. We insert a statement to print "Starting test" at the beginning of the loop and another, to print "Ending test" at the end of the loop. By enclosing these statements in the **#if-#endif** combination, we ensure that they will be executed only if the directive **#define TIMER** is executed. If the program is compiled and executed as shown above, it will print

```
C>define
Starting test
Ending test
```

with a delay of several seconds between the two messages. If we remove the **#define TIMER** directive, or make it into a comment like this,

```
/* #define TIMER */
```

our "test" statements will not be executed. The program will run, printing out "Done" but not the test messages.

## The *#if* and *#endif* Directives

The first **#if** tells the compiler to compile the statements that follow it, only if TIMER is **#defined**. The **#endif** indicates that this conditional part of the compilation is over, and the compiler can go back to the normal mode of compiling all statements. Thus, **#define** acts as a switch, while **#if** and **#endif** act as delimiters for the section of code switched by **#define**.

## The *#else* Directive

In the program above, if TIMER is *not* **defined**, another message ("Done") will be printed out when the loop is over. This is arranged with the **#else** directive. It fulfills a role analogous to the **else** in a normal C **if . . . else** statement: whatever follows it is compiled only when the matching **#define** directive has *not* been executed.

## Other Uses for Conditional Compilation

There are many other circumstances in which conditional compilation might prove useful. For instance, you might need two versions of a program: one to run on the IBM AT, for example, and one to run on the PS/2 series. Instead of creating two complete source files, you could group those statements in the program that varied from one version to another and enclose them by appropriate **#if**, **#else**, and **#endif** statements. Then, inserting a single statement at the beginning of the program, such as

```
#define AT
```

would convert the program from the PS/2 version to the AT version.

There are additional possibilities with conditional compilation. Another directive, **#elif**, can be used the same way the **else-if** construction is used in programs: to create a ladder of possibilities, depending on the value of a constant. Also, **#if**-**#endif** pairs can be nested. We won't explore these complexities here.

(A previous construction for **#if defined()** was **#ifdef**, but this does not conform to the ANSI standard and should no longer be used.)

## The *#undef* Directive

Another related preprocessor directive is the **#undef** directive, which cancels the action of a previous **#define** directive. For example, if at some point in your program you insert the directive

```
#define TEST
```

and later in the program you insert

```
#undef TEST
```

then at this point TEST will no longer be defined. You can use this directive to make conditional compilation specific to certain sections of the program.

Another use for **#undef** is to "turn off" macros that you have previously defined with a **#define** directive. This might be useful in a large and complex program where the same name is used for different macros in different parts of the program, and you want to avoid the possibility of conflict. Turning off a macro with **#undef** makes your macro a "local" macro, known only in a limited section of the program.

# Memory Models

In Microsoft C a *memory model* is the specification for how much memory different parts of the program can occupy. Microsoft C version 4.0 specifies five possible options: small, compact, medium, large, and huge. So far we have used only the small memory model (or the medium model in QuickC). This is the default model—what you get if you don't specify otherwise. What are memory models, and why might you want to use one besides small?

To appreciate the necessity for different memory models it's important to understand the way the microprocessor used in the IBM computer family addresses memory. We discussed the topic of segments and segment/offset addressing in Chapter 10. Let's review the situation to see how it applies to memory models.

## Segment/Offset Addressing

The microprocessor uses 16-bit registers for addresses. A register this size can hold an address up to FFFF hex, which is 65,536 decimal, or 64K. This amount of memory is called a segment. To access addresses outside of this segment, the processor must use two registers. One, called the segment register, holds a number that is the starting address of a 64K segment. The other holds the offset address, which is the number of bytes from the start of the segment. To find the "real" or absolute address, the number in the segment register is multiplied by 16 (shifted left four bits) and added to the offset address. (See Chapter 10 if any of this is unclear.) This permits addressing FFFFF hex (1,048,576 decimal) bytes (although, with MS-DOS versions 2.x or 3.x, only 640K bytes are available for the user's program).

### Two Kinds of Microprocessor Instructions

The microprocessor uses two different techniques for referring to memory locations: if the location is *within* the 64K segment already specified in a segment register, the processor can use a single instruction to access data or change program flow. This approach, which corresponds to using **near** pointers in C, executes quickly. On the other hand, if the microprocessor needs to refer to an address in a segment *outside* the segment register, it must first alter the segment register, then perform the appropriate action using the offset address, and, finally, restore the segment register to its former value. This corresponds to using **far** pointers in C and is comparatively slow to execute.

We can categorize microprocessor instructions in a different way. There are instructions that deal with addresses in the *program code* itself, such as jumps and calls to subroutines, and there are instructions that reference *data*, such as fetching a data item from memory and placing it in a register. Instructions that refer to program code can be either **near** or **far**, and instructions that refer to data can also be either **near** or **far**. So we can think of four different types of microprocessor instructions: **near** instructions for program control and for data and **far** instructions for program control and data.

> References to memory can accomplish program control or data access, and can refer to addresses inside the current segment or outside it.

These four possibilities for microprocessor instructions correspond to four of the five memory models available in Microsoft C, as shown in Figure 14-4.

| Model | References to code | References to data |
|---|---|---|
| small | near | near |
| medium | far | near |
| compact | near | far |
| large | far | far |

Figure 14-4. Four Memory Models

If the code for your program fits inside one 64K segment and the data fits inside another 64K segment, you can use the small memory model. Most programs don't require more program or data space than this. If the code for your program is larger than 64K but the data fits inside 64K, you should use the medium model. If the code is less than 64K but the data is larger, the compact model is appropriate. If both code and data require more than 64K, the large model is necessary.

Note that these models all involve a trade-off; **far** instructions take longer to execute than **near** instructions, so programs written in memory models other than **small** will take longer to execute. The moral is, don't use a larger model than you need.

### Huge Arrays

What about the fifth model? This is provided for the case of a single data item, usually an array, that by itself is larger than 64K. (If you think this is unlikely, imagine an array of structures used for storing a database; for many applications, such an array could profitably use all available memory.)

A compiled program refers to an array in two ways: it specifies the base or starting address of the array and it refers to individual items within the array. The base address may be specified with a **far** instruction and references to individual elements in the array made with **near** instructions. This is the system used for the compact and large memory models. However, if the array is larger than one 64K segment, references to individual elements, as well as to the base, must be made using **far** instructions; this is what the huge memory model provides.

## Compiler Options

In the Optimizing Compiler the choice of memory model is specified with a compiler option (characters typed in the command line when invoking the compiler). These options are shown in Figure 14-5.

| Model | Compiler option | Code segments | Data segments | Segments for one data item |
|-------|-----------------|---------------|---------------|----------------------------|
| small | /AS* | 1 | 1 | 1 |
| medium | /AM | many | 1 | 1 |
| compact | /AC | 1 | many | 1 |
| large | /AL | many | many | 1 |
| huge | /AH | many | many | many |

*default option; need not be given explicitly

Figure 14-5. Memory Models and Compiler Options

For example, to specify the medium memory model using the Optimizing Compiler, you would type the following when invoking CL:

```
C>cl /AM filename.c
```

Memory models can't be used from the QuickC environment. However, QuickC owners can use the QCL compiler with the same options as the Optimizing Compiler.

Since the library routines must be accessed with the same kind of instructions as the rest of the program, a complete set of C library functions is provided for each of the memory models (except huge, which uses the large model's routines). The compiler ensures that the correct set of routines is linked to the program.

### Fine Tuning

We've already seen that, when using the small memory model, it is possible to use the **far** keyword when a variable is outside the normal data segment. Similarly, if we use the compact or large models, we can declare a **near** data type to refer to variables that we know are in the normal 64K data segment. This can reduce the time needed to access these variables.

By combining memory models and **near** and **far** data references in different ways, it's possible to achieve a good compromise between execution speed and program size.

## Optimization

Both QuickC and the Optimizing Compiler give you some control over the amount of optimization performed by the compiler. Optimization is the process of altering the code generated by the compiler so the resulting program will run faster or take up less space.

### Optimization in QuickC

There are several optimization choices in QuickC. They're all selected by checking the appropriate box in the Miscellaneous list in the Compile . . . window of the Run menu.

First, you can select Optimization. This performs a number of changes in your source code that will make your code run faster, but it might generate slightly larger code. Second, you can select Pointer Check, which inserts code in your program that makes sure you don't use pointers to reference data outside your program's data area. Third, you can select Stack Check, which inserts in your program code that ensures, each time a function is called, that there is enough room on the stack for the function's local variables.

These last two options are useful during program development to catch programming mistakes, but should probably not be enabled when you compile the final version of your program, since they make it run more slowly.

If you use the QCL compiler that comes with QuickC you can use command-line switches to achieve these same effects—and a few more besides.

## Optimization and the Optimizing Compiler

The Optimizing Compiler, as its name implies, offers more optimization options than does QuickC. The desired optimization is set using a command-line switch. The options are shown in the following table:

| Switch | Effect |
| --- | --- |
| /Od | Disable optimization |
| /Os | Smaller code size at the expense of speed |
| /Ot | Speed at the expense of code size |
| /Ol | Loop optimization |
| /Oa | No alias checking |
| /Oi | Enable intrinsic functions |
| /Op | Improve floating point consistency |
| /Ox | Maximize optimization |
| /Gs | Disable stack checking |

Disabling optimization is desirable when using CodeView, since optimized code may be in a different order than the source code. A complete description of these options can be found in the Optimizing Compiler user's guide.

## Summary

In this chapter we've reviewed some of the techniques that can be used when programs become large and complex. We've covered separate compilation of program files and discussed how external variables can be shared between such files using the **extern** keyword. We also mentioned library files and explored the advantages of separate compilation to speed up the compiling process and contribute to modular programming.

We examined conditional compilation, which uses the **#define**, **#if**, **#else**, and **#endif** preprocessor directives to permit selective compiling of various parts of a source file under different circumstances. And finally we discussed the use of different memory models, which permit a program to expand beyond the normal bounds of two 64K segments.

With these techniques you should be able to construct programs of almost any size, up to the limit of the memory in your computer.

# Questions

1. One advantage of separate compilation of program modules is

   a. the resulting program will be more modular.

   b. compilation time can be faster.

   c. program modules can be protected from inadvertent alteration during program development.

   d. the program will run faster.

2. Separately compiled modules are combined using the

   _____ .

3. For a variable to be visible in a file other than that where it was defined, it must be _____ using the _____ keyword.

4. Which of the following are ways to pass information from one function to another function in a separately compiled file?

   a. as arguments

   b. as static variables

   c. as external variables

   d. as automatic variables

5. True or false: when a library file is linked to a program, all the functions in the library file are used in the final program.

6. Separate compilation is an aid to modular programming because

   a. functions cannot access variables in other files

   b. only functions relating to the same program can be combined in one file

   c. external variables can be restricted to one file

   d. related functions can be combined in a file

7. Conditional compilation is used to

   a. compile only those programs that are error free

   b. compile some sections of programs and not others

   c. remove comments and compress the source file

   d. none of the above

8. The _____ preprocessor directive is used as a switch to turn compilation on and off.

9. The preprocessor directive **#ifdefine (ADV)** causes the code that follows it to be compiled only when

    a. ADV is an integer

    b. ADV is equal to a predefined constant

    c. ADV is TRUE

    d. ADV is **#defin**ed

10. Using different memory models is useful when a program or data becomes too _____.

11. The *medium* memory model permits

    a. more than one code segment

    b. more than one data segment

    c. only one code segment

    d. only one data segment

12. True or false: selecting the correct memory model determines the size of the stack segment.

13. Memory models are necessary because of the

    a. stack-based architecture of the microprocessor

    b. segmentation of memory

    c. large size of the data or code in some programs

    d. need to keep programmers guessing

14. The compiler option used to create the *large* memory model is

    _____.

15. The disadvantage of using a memory model that is larger than necessary is

    a. memory is wasted

    b. simple data type cannot be used

    c. program files are harder to link

    d. program instructions take longer to execute

# 15

# Advanced Variables

- Storage classes
- Lifetime and visibility
- Enumerated data types
- Typedef
- Identifiers and naming classes
- Type conversion and casting

# 15

Although we have been using variables all along in this book, we have, to avoid complicating the explanations of other topics, made certain assumptions about variables and their usage. We have also alluded to various properties of variables without explaining these properties in detail. In this chapter we'll take a more careful look at variables and investigate some of the advanced features the C language makes available for variable usage.

## Storage Classes

Every C variable possesses a characteristic called its "storage class." The storage class defines two characteristics of the variable: its *lifetime*, and its *visibility* (or *scope*). We've mentioned these characteristics before; now let's take a closer look.

First, why are storage classes necessary? The answer is that by using variables with the appropriate lifetime and visibility we can write programs that use memory more efficiently, run faster, and are less prone to programming errors. Correct use of storage class is especially important in large programs.

### Lifetime

The lifetime of a variable is the length of time it retains a particular value. In terms of their lifetime, variables can be divided into two categories: *automatic* variables have shorter lifetimes than do *static* and *external* variables. We'll look at these cases in turn.

#### Lifetime of Automatic Variables
Automatic variables are the most commonly used in C; the majority of the variables we've used so far have been of this class. In a program's source file automatic variables are written inside the braces that serve as delimiters for a

function. They are created (that is, memory space is allocated to them) when the function containing them is called, and destroyed (their memory space is "deallocated") when the function terminates. In the following function,

```
func()
{
    int alpha;
    auto int beta;
    register int gamma;
}
```

all three variables are created when the function **func()** is called and disappear when it has finished and control returns to the calling function. Such variables are called "automatic" because they are created and destroyed automatically.

> Variables of type **auto** and **register** are created when the function containing them is called and destroyed when control returns to the calling program.

The variable **alpha** is automatic by default, while **beta** has been made automatic explicitly, using the **auto** keyword. The effect is exactly the same, but the keyword **auto** is sometimes used to avoid confusion. The **gamma** variable is a special kind of automatic variable called a **register** variable; the compiler will assign it to one of the CPU registers—leading to faster operation—provided a register is available. We'll show an example of register variables later in this chapter.

### Lifetime of Static and External Variables

If we want a variable to retain its value after the function that defines it is terminated, we have several choices. First, the variable can be declared to be of type **static**, as shown in this example.

```
func()
{
    static int delta;
}
```

A static variable is known only to the function in which it is defined, but, unlike automatic variables, it does not disappear when the function terminates. Instead it keeps its place in memory and therefore its value. In the example above, even after the function **func()** has terminated, **delta** will retain the value it was given in the function. If program control returns to the function again, the value of **delta** will be there for the function to use.

Another way to ensure that a variable retains its value throughout the course of a program is to make it *external*, as we've mentioned in earlier chapters. This is done by placing the variable outside of any function, as **zeta** is in this example:

```
int zeta;
main()
{
}

func()
{
}
```

Like static variables, external variables exist for the life of the program. The difference between them has to do with their visibility, which we'll examine in the next section.

> Variables of type **external**, **static**, and **external static** exist for the life of a program.

### Reasons for Different Lifetimes

Why do some variables have longer lifetimes than others? The advantage of eliminating a variable when the function containing it terminates is that the memory space used for the variable can be freed and made available for other variables. Depending on the program, this can result in a considerable saving in memory. This is a good reason for using automatic variables whenever possible.

Static variables can be used in those situations when a variable in a function must retain its value between calls to the function.

## Visibility

The visibility (or scope) of a variable refers to which parts of a program will be able to recognize it. There are more distinctions involved in visibility than there are in lifetime: a variable may be visible in a block, a function, a file, a group of files, or an entire program. In this section we'll examine these possibilities in more detail.

### Visibility of Automatic and Static Variables

An automatic variable is only recognized within the function in which it is defined; therefore, it is sometimes called a "local" variable. For instance, in this example:

```
main()
{
}

func()
{
```

```
        int eta;
}
```

the variable **eta** is recognized only in the function **func()**, not in **main()**. In fact, we could have another variable called **eta** in **main()**; the two would be completely different.

The same is true of static variables (unless they're external, a possibility we'll examine later). They are visible only in the function where they are defined.

### Blocks

The visibility of automatic and static variables can be restricted even further; they can be defined inside a *block*. A block is a section of code set off by braces. Here's an example of a block within a function:

```
main()
{
    int epsilon;
    {
        int pi;
    }
}
```

In this example the variable **pi** is visible only within the inner set of braces, while **epsilon** is visible throughout the function **main()**. The braces used to group statements in an **if** or **while** construction form blocks; variables defined within such blocks won't be visible outside of the block.

It is not common practice to define variables within blocks, but in some complicated functions it can provide increased flexibility. Two variables with the same name could be used in the same function, for example.

### Visibility of External Variables

To create a variable that is visible to more than one function, we must make it external. As noted above in the discussion of lifetime, this means defining the variable outside of any function. Thus, in the example

```
int theta;
main()
{
}
func()
{
}
```

the variable **theta** will be visible to both **main()** and **func()**, or to any functions placed after the definition of **theta** in this file.

An external variable (unless it is declared elsewhere) is visible only to those functions that *follow* it in the file. If we rearranged our example like this:

```
main()
{
}
```

```
int theta;

func()
{
}
```

the variable **theta** will be visible only to the function **func()**; it will be invisible to **main()**.

In Chapter 14 we discussed how separate files, each containing part of a program, can be compiled separately and linked together to create a final program. As we saw there, it is possible for an external variable to be visible in files other than the one in which it is defined, provided it is declared in the other files with the keyword **extern**. We'll pursue this topic in a moment, but first let's clarify some definitions.

## Defining and Declaring

We've been using the terms "define" and "declare" often in this chapter, in ways that may be confusing. Let's backtrack for a moment and see how these terms are properly used in C.

According to Kernighan and Ritchie (see the bibliography), a variable is "defined" when it is named, its type is selected, and—most important—memory space is actually set aside to hold it. Such common expressions as

```
int num;
char ch;
```

are actually examples of definitions. On the other hand, a variable is *declared* when it is named and given a data type, but not necessarily any storage.

A declaration is an announcement that a variable with a particular name and type exists. The variable is defined, meaning that memory is set aside for it, elsewhere. Typically, a variable is defined in one file and then declared in every other file in which it will be used. In the multifile program example in Chapter 14, two variables **a** and **b** were defined (in the file containing mainpro2.c) with the statement

```
int a, b;          /* external variables defined in one file */
```

and declared (in the file containing sumsqr2.c) with the statement

```
extern int a, b;   /* and declared in another file */
```

A variable can be defined only once (since it can only exist in one place in memory), but it must be declared in any file that wishes to access it.

The distinction between declarations and definitions made above is reasonably clear. Unfortunately, due to historical usage, many texts—including this one—often use "declaration" to describe what is actually a definition. Microsoft explains this away by making a distinction between "defining" declarations (that set aside memory) and "referencing" declarations (such as those using **extern**).

Whatever terms are used, the point is that some declarations set aside memory, while others merely reference previously defined variables.

In any case, external variables are visible only in the file in which they are defined, unless they are declared in other files. Figure 15-1 shows the visibility of a variety of different variables.

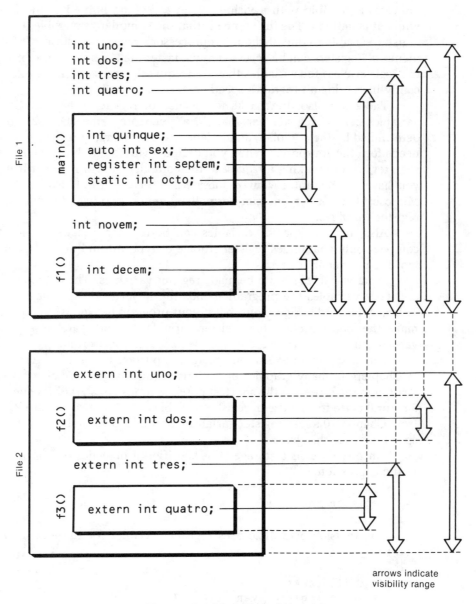

arrows indicate
visibility range

Figure 15-1. Visibility of Variables

The declaration of variables using the **extern** keyword follows the same visibility rules as the definition of variables. In Figure 15-1, the variables **uno**, **dos**, **tres**, and **quatro** are all defined at the same place in File 1, but they all have different visibilities in File 2, depending on where they are declared.

## Register Variables

Another storage class specifier is **register**. This specifier is like **auto** in that it indicates a variable with a visibility and a lifetime limited to the function in which it is defined. The difference is that the compiler, if possible, will assign a register variable to one of the microprocessor's registers instead of storing it in memory. Registers can be accessed much faster than memory locations, so using the register class for variables that are frequently accessed can result in significantly increasing a program's speed.

There are also drawbacks to the use of register variables. Only a few variables can be register variables in a given program. The exact number is determined by the compiler, and it depends on how many registers the program needs for other purposes. When you define a variable to have the storage class **register**, you're making a *request* to the compiler; it will honor it if it can, but you have no guarantee your request will be carried out. However, with the Microsoft C compiler, you can normally count on two registers being free from register variables.

Also, not all types of variables can be register variables. The Microsoft compiler only guarantees register storage of type **int** and normal pointer types (not **far** pointers).

What variables should be made register variables? The obvious candidates are those variables the program spends the majority of its time operating on. This may be hard to figure out, but if your program has loops, a good guess is to make the loop variables the register variables. If there are nested loops, the variables in the innermost loop will be executed most often.

One area where execution speed is important is graphics. As you learned in Chapter 10, many graphics operations require large numbers of pixels to be written to the screen in the shortest possible time. Thus graphics operations are a natural place for the use of register variables. We'll revise our dfill2.c program from Chapter 10 to use register variables for the loop variables and and see what speed increase this gives.

Since **register** is a storage class specifier, it precedes the variable type, as in the expression:

```
register int x, y;
```

The revision of dfill2.c uses register variables for the loop variables **col** and **row**.

```
/* dfill3.c */
/* tests register variables */
#define ROMAX 25
```

```
#define COMAX 80
main()
{
    int far *farptr;
    register int col, row;          /* register variables */
    char ch;
    printf("Type character to start, type again to change");
    farptr = (int far *) 0xB0000000;
    while( (ch=getche()) != 'X' )
        for(row=0; row<ROMAX; row++)
            for(col=0; col<COMAX; col++)
                *(farptr + row*COMAX + col) = (int)ch | 0x0700;
}
```

This change results in a 20 percent speed increase over the old version. While not as dramatic as the improvement provided by using direct memory access instead of the C library function **putch()**, it's not bad considering that only one word needed to be added to the program.

Learning how much speed increase you can expect from register variables is largely a matter of experimentation. Try giving different variables the **register** class and then time the resulting program. You may need to time several iterations, enclosing the active part of your program in a **for** loop, to slow the program's operation enough to measure.

## Summary of Storage Classes

Table 15-1 summarizes the lifetime and visibility of various types of variables.

### Table 15-1. Storage Classes

| Where Declared | Keyword | Lifetime | Visibility (scope) |
| --- | --- | --- | --- |
| function | auto (default) | function | function |
| function | register | function | function |
| function | static | program | function |
| external | static | program | one file only |
| external (not decl) | — | program | one file |
| external (declared) | extern | program | multifile |

The first three variable types shown in the table are local variables: those defined within a function. Their visibility is confined to that function, and their lifetime—except for static variables—is also the same as that of the function. These first three variable types can also be defined within a block (a pair of braces); in that case, they will only be visible within the block.

The second group of three variable types are defined external to any function.

The first case, that of an external static variable, is confined to a single file; the **extern** keyword cannot be used to reference it from other files. We use this storage class when we wish to hide the variables in one file—a library file, for instance—from other files.

The second case of external variables is probably the most common; the variable is defined externally but is not declared in any other files. The visibility of such a variable is confined to a single file. In this case (and in the case of external static variables) the variable is visible only from the place in the file where it's defined to the end of the file. It is invisible to functions occurring before it in the file.

In the third case, a variable is defined in one file, but also declared in other files. In this case, its visibility will extend to the appropriate parts of all the files in which it is declared.

By using the correct storage class for a variable, the programmer can economize on memory requirements by restricting the lifetime of the variables, and help maintain a modular, well-structured program by allowing access to variables only to those files and functions that need it. The number of ways to vary the visibility and lifetime of variables is an important reason for C's popularity with developers of large programs and systems.

## Enumerated Data Type

Let's examine another data type, one we haven't seen before. The enumerated (**enum**) type gives you the opportunity to invent your own data type and define what values it can take on. This can help to make listings more readable, which can be an advantage when a program gets complicated or when more than one programmer will be working on it. Using enumerated types can also help you reduce programming errors.

As an example, one could invent a data type called **birds** which had as its possible values **sparrow**, **robin**, **eagle**, and **egret**. Don't confuse these values with variable names; **sparrow**, for instance, has the same relationship to the variable **birds** that the number 12 has to an integer variable.

The format of the **enum** definition is similar to that of a structure. Here's how the preceding example would be implemented:

```
enum birds {                      /* define data type */
     sparrow,                     /* specify values */
     robin,
     eagle,
     egret };
enum birds thisbird, thatbird;    /* declare variables */
```

Like structures, the declaration has two parts. The first declares the data type itself—type **enum birds**—and specifies its possible values, which are called "enumerators." The second declares one or more variables— **thisbird** and **thatbird**—to be of this type. Now we can give values to these variables:

```
thisbird = sparrow;
thatbird = egret;
```

We can't use values that aren't in the original declaration. The expression

```
thisbird = magpie;
```

would cause an error.

Internally, the compiler treats enumerated variables as integers. Each value on the list of permissible values corresponds to an integer, starting with 0. Thus, in the **birds** example, sparrow is stored as 0, robin as 1, eagle as 2, and egret as 3.

This way of assigning numbers can be overridden by the programmer by initializing the enumerators to different integer values, as shown in this example:

```
enum birds {                      /* define data type */
       sparrow = 10,              /* specify and */
       robin = 20,                /* initialize values */
       eagle = 30,
       egret = 40 };
enum birds thisbird, thatbird;    /* declare variables */
```

Just because the enumerators are compiled into integers doesn't mean the compiler will let you treat them that way in the source file. The following expressions are illegal:

```
thisbird = 1;   /* illegal */
num = eagle;    /* illegal if num is not type enum birds */
```

Also, most numerical operations are illegal when applied to enumerated variables, and only two of the comparison operators can be used: = = and != . These restrictions usually make sense. What meaning could be reasonably imagined for the following illegal expressions?

```
eagle = 2*sparrow;    /* can't do arithmetic */
if(wren<sparrow)      /* or comparisons */
   magpie++;          /* with enum variables */
```

## Using the Enumerated Data Type

Enumerated variables are usually used to clarify the operation of a program. For instance, if we need to use a group of employee categories in a payroll program, it makes the listing easier to read if we use values like **management** and **clerical** rather than integer values like 0 and 2.

Here's a short example that makes use of enumerated variables, and also points out one of their weaknesses. (This approach would ordinarily be part of a larger program.)

```
/* enums.c */
/* uses enumerated variables */
main()
```

```
{
    enum empcats {management, research, clerical, sales};
    struct {
        char name[30];
        float salary;
        enum empcats category;
    } employee;

    strcpy(employee.name, "Benjamin Franklin");
    employee.salary = 118.50;
    employee.category = research;

    printf("Name = %s\n", employee.name);
    printf("Salary = %6.2f\n", employee.salary);
    printf("Category = %d\n", employee.category);

    if(employee.category==clerical)
        printf("Employee category is clerical.\n");
    else
        printf("Employee category is not clerical.\n");
}
```

We first define the type **enum empcats** (for "employee categories") and specify four possible values: management, research, clerical, and sales. A variable of type **enum empcats**, called **category**, is then defined in a structure. The structure, **employee**, has three variables containing employee information.

The program first assigns values to the variables in the structure. The expression

```
employee.category = research;
```

assigns the value research to the **employee.category** variable. This is much more informative to anyone reading the listing than a statement like

```
employee.category = 1;
```

The next part of the program shows the weakness of using enum variables: there is no way to use the enum values directly in input and output functions such as **printf()** and **scanf()**. Here's the output of the program:

```
C>enums
Name = Benjamin Franklin
Salary = 118.50
Category = 1
Employee category is not clerical.
```

The **printf()** function is not sophisticated enough to perform the translation; the category is printed out as "1", not as "research". Of course we could write a routine to print out the correct enumerated values, using a table or a **switch** statement, but that would decrease the clarity of the program.

Even with this limitation, however, there are many situations in which enumerated variables are a useful addition to the C language.

# Renaming Data Types with *typedef*

Let's look at another technique which in some situations can help to clarify the source code for a C program. This is the use of the **typedef** declaration, whose purpose is to redefine the name of an existing variable type. Its use can result in clearer programs because the name of a type can be shortened and made more meaningful.

As an example, consider the following statement in which the type **unsigned char** is redefined to be of type BYTE:

```
typedef unsigned char BYTE;
```

Now we can declare variables of type **unsigned char** by writing

```
BYTE var1, var2;
```

instead of

```
unsigned char var1, var2;
```

Our assumption here is that **var1** and **var2** will be used in a context in which declaring them to be of type BYTE is more meaningful than declaring them to be of type **unsigned char** (for example, they might be values to be placed in a one-byte register during a ROM BIOS call). Using the name BYTE suggests to anyone reading the program that the variables are used in one-byte registers. Uppercase letters are often used to make it clear that we're dealing with a renamed data type.

> The **typedef** declaration causes the compiler to recognize a different name for a variable type.

While the increase in readability is probably not great in this example, it can be significant when the name of a particular type is long and unwieldy, as it often is with structure declarations.

For example, the passtwo2.c program in Chapter 14 contained the declaration:

```
typedef struct personnel {      /* define data structure */
   char name [30];              /* agent name */
   int agnumb;                  /* agent number */
};
```

Using **typedef**, we could rewrite this:

```
typedef struct personnel AGENT;  /* new name for this type */
AGENT  {                         /* define data structure */
   char name [30];               /* agent name */
   int agnumb;                   /* agent number */
};
```

Subsequent references to **struct personnel** can now be replaced with AGENT throughout the program, for example:

```
AGENT agent1;            /* declare structure variable */
AGENT agent2;            /* declare another one */
```

**Typedef** looks something like the **#define** directive, but it actually works in a different way. Using **#define** causes the preprocessor to perform a simple substitution of one phrase for another throughout the program. Using **typedef**, on the other hand, causes the compiler to actually recognize a new name for a specific type. This can make a difference when pointers are concerned, as the following statement demonstrates:

```
typedef struct personnel *PTRAGENT;
```

This statement defines PTRAGENT to be a synonym for the data type "pointer to **struct personnel**." Now we can use the declaration

```
PTRAGENT agent1, agent2;
```

which is equivalent to

```
struct personnel *agent1, *agent2;
```

A **#define** directive could not have been used in this situation, since the asterisks are repeated for each variable.

By reducing the length and apparent complexity of data types, **typedef** can help to clarify source listings.

## Other Data Type Specifiers

The ANSI standard has introduced several data types that did not exist in the original K and R specification of C. We've already looked at the **void** type, which can specify three kinds of variables: a function with no return value, a function that takes no arguments, and a pointer to any data type. There are two other new type-specifiers as well.

### The const Specifier

Variables of type **const** may not be modified during the course of the program. This type is commonly used to declare variables stored in read-only portions of memory. An attempt to modify such a variable later in the program generates a compiler error. The format is

```
const int alpha;
```

We show an **int** here, but **const** can modify any data type, including structures and pointers.

The **const** specifier can also be used for any variable that does not change in the course of a program. For instance, a string constant can be defined like this:

```
const char *StringCon = "This is a string constant";
```

This usage makes it clear that **StringCon** will not be changed during the course of a program. Any attempt to write into it will elicit a compiler error.

### The volatile Specifier

Variables of type **volatile** may be modified by actions external to the program while the program is running. An example is a memory address that is modified by hardware during program execution. If the compiler does not know such a variable can change unexpectedly, it may be tempted to perform optimizations that will fail when the variable is altered. The **volatile** keyword alerts the compiler to this situation. The format is

```
volatile long beta;
```

## Identifiers and Naming Classes

So far we've named variables and functions without saying too much about what the restrictions are on such names. In this section we'll mention these restrictions, and then go on to show how the same name can be used, under some circumstances, for different elements in a program.

The names given to variables and functions (and various other programming elements) are called "identifiers." Allowable characters in identifiers are the letters from A to Z (in both upper- and lowercase), the digits from 0 to 9, and the underscore character ( _ ). The identifier must begin with a letter or an underscore. C distinguishes between upper- and lowercase, so the compiler will treat

```
BigVar
```

as a different variable from

```
bigvar
```

Identifiers can have any number of characters, but only the first 31 will be recognized by the compiler. It's not clear why anyone would want to use more than 31 characters anyway. For those of us who wrote programs in early versions of BASIC, which only recognized variable names of 2 characters, 31 is the ultimate in luxury.

As in most other computer languages, identifiers in C cannot be the same as certain keywords used in the language itself. Fortunately, there are fewer keywords in C than in many languages. These keywords fall into two classes. Those used for defining data are **auto, char, double, enum, extern, float, int, long, register, short, static, typedef,** and **void**. Those used for program control are **break, const, continue, default, do, else, for, goto, if, return, sizeof, struct, switch, union,** and **while**. The **const** keyword is not implemented in current versions of Microsoft C, but is reserved for future use.

## Naming Classes

The various program elements that are named with identifiers, such as functions and variables, are divided into *naming classes*. Within a naming class, each item must have a distinct identifier (in other words, you can't have two variables with the same name). However, you can use the same name for different elements if the elements are in different naming classes. The five naming classes are described next.

### 1. Variables and Functions

A variable cannot have the same name as a function in which it is visible. A function's formal parameters also fall into this naming class, so they cannot have the same name as any of the variables used in the function. (However, as we discussed in the section on storage classes, several variables within a function can have the same name if they are in separate blocks.) Enumeration constants are also part of this naming class; you can't use the same name for an enumeration constant as for a variable (unless they have different visibilities).

### 2. Tags

As you may recall, structures, unions, and classes of enumeration variables are named with a tag. For instance, in the structure definition

```
struct ex1 {
    int intnum;
    float fltnum;
    } svar1;
```

the identifier **ex1** is the tag, while **svar1** is a variable name. Tags form their own naming class, so it would be legal, for instance, to change the variable name **svar1** to **ex1** in this example, since the same identifier can be used for two elements if they are in different naming classes.

### 3. Members

Members of structures and unions, such as **intnum** and **fltnum** in our example, form a separate naming class. They must be distinct from other members of the same structure or union, but they can be the same as other identifiers in the program.

In the following example the identifier **apple** is used in three different places. Since each use is a different naming class, the compiler will find this perfectly acceptable.

```
struct apple {        /* 'apple' names a tag */
    int apple;        /* 'apple' names a member */
    float pear;       /* could not be 'apple' here */
    } apple;          /* 'apple' names a variable */
```

### 4. Statement Labels

Statement labels form a distinct naming class. Within a function, statement labels must all have distinct names, but these can be the same as those of variables or members of other naming classes. We'll discuss labels further at the end of this chapter.

### 5. Typedef Names

The names of types defined with **typedef** are treated by the compiler as if they were keywords. Thus, once a name has been defined in a **typedef** statement, no other program elements, no matter what naming class they are in, can use the same identifer.

Of course, none of the rules about naming classes alter the rules about visibility. If the visibility of two program elements is different, then they can have the same identifier, even if they are in the same naming class (for example, two automatic variables in different functions).

# Type Conversion and Casting

You have probably noticed by this time that it's possible to mix data types in C expressions. Thus the following program will elicit no error message from the compiler (as a similar construction would in Pascal, for instance):

```
main()
{
    int intnum = 2;           /* integer type */
    float fltnum = 3.3;       /* floating point type */
    double ans;               /* double precision type */
    ans = intnum + fltnum;    /* mixed expression is legal */
}
```

There are dangers involved in mixing types; that's why some languages make such mixing illegal. But the philosophy in C is that it's better to give the programmer the freedom to mix types, which often leads to simpler code, than to try to keep the programmer out of trouble by flagging type mismatches as an error. Of course, with the freedom to mix data types comes the responsibility to make sure that such mixing is not the result of a mistake, such as assuming a variable is of one type when it really is of another.

When data types are mixed in an expression, the compiler converts the variables to compatible types before carrying out the intended operation. In these conversions, variables of lower rank are converted to the rank of the higher-ranking operand. The ranking corresponds roughly to how many bytes each type occupies in memory. This is shown in Figure 15-2.

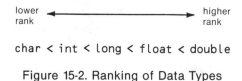

char < int < long < float < double

Figure 15-2. Ranking of Data Types

As an example, consider the following program:

```
main()
{
    char ch;
    int intnum;
    long longnum;
    float fltnum;
    double doubnum;
    int answer;
    answer = (ch * intnum) +  (ch * longnum) + (fltnum * doubnum);
}
```

Before each operator is applied to the appropriate pair of variables, the variable with the lower rank is converted to the rank of the higher-ranking variable. This process is shown in Figure 15-3.

Promotion, or moving from a lower rank to a higher rank, usually doesn't cause problems. Demotion, however, can easily result in a loss of precision or even yield a completely incorrect result. Table 15-2 details what happens when demotion occurs.

Roughly speaking, we can say that if a number is too large to fit into the type to which it is being demoted, its value will be corrupted. Some loss of precision can even occur in the *promotion* of **long** to **float**, since these two types both use four bytes.

The moral is, avoid type conversions unless there's a good reason for them, and be especially careful when demoting a variable, since you may lose data.

## Functions as Addresses

Sooner or later in your study of C you'll run into a situation in which you use a pointer to a function to refer to the function. For example, you might want to place the addresses of a group of related functions in a table and jump to the appropriate function. Or you might encounter a library function that returns a function address. How do you execute a function whose name you don't know, but whose address you do?

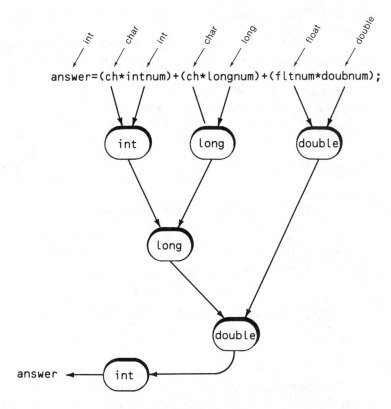

Figure 15-3. Data Type Conversion

## Table 15-2. Data Type Demotion

| Demotion | Result |
|---|---|
| int to char | low-order byte is used |
| long to char | low-order byte is used |
| float to char | float converted to long and low-order byte used |
| double to char | double converted to float, float to long, and low-order byte used |
| long to int | low-order word (two bytes) used |
| float to int | float converted to long and low-order word used |
| double to int | double converted to float, float to long, and low-order word used |
| float to long | truncate at decimal point; if result is too large for long, it is undefined |
| double to long | truncate at decimal point; if result is too large for long, it is undefined |

It turns out that the address of a function is the function name itself, without the parentheses. This is similar to using an array name without the brackets to denote the address of the array.

Here's a short example program that demonstrates assigning a function address to a pointer and executing the function by referring to the pointer.

```
/* funcaddr.c */
/* shows use of function addresses */
#include <stdio.h>          /* for printf() */
int func(int, int);         /* prototype for function */

void main(void)
{
    int ans;
    int (*fptr)(int, int); /* declare pointer to function */

    fptr = func;            /* put function address in pointer */
    ans = (*fptr)(3, 5);    /* call function using pointer */
    printf("ans=%d\n", ans);
}

int func(int a1, int a2)   /* function definition */
{
    return(a1 + a2);        /* returns sum of arguments */
}
```

The function is very simple: it returns the sum of the two arguments passed to it. However, the declaration of the pointer to the function is not so simple. This declaration is read "**fptr** is a pointer to a function taking two arguments of type **int** and returning type **int**." (We'll discuss how such declarations are unraveled in the next section.) Also note the statement that assigns the address of the function **func** to the pointer.

When we call the function we refer to the contents of the pointer, **\*(fptr)()**; we don't need to use the name of the function itself.

## Unraveling Complex C Declarations

The declaration of the pointer **fptr** in the funcaddr.c program above may not be immediately obvious. Earlier we said that C declarations can be unraveled by working from right to left. It's true that the data type (and possibly storage class and other modifiers) on the left are the last elements to be translated, but that's only part of the story. Let's see how complex C declarations can be understood.

Suppose you have a declaration like this:

```
int *aptr[];
```

How do you know whether this is a pointer to an array or an array of pointers? It turns out C declarations use strict precedence rules, in fact the same precedence rules as those used for C operators. Here's what you need to know: brackets [], denoting arrays, and parentheses (), denoting functions, have a higher priority than the indirection operator *.

So the expression above is interpreted "**aptr** is an array of pointers to **int**." You translate "array" first because it has a higher priority than *, meaning "pointer to."

As with other C operators, parentheses can be used to override the normal precedence. Thus the declaration

```
int (*aptr)[];
```

means "**aptr** is (1) a pointer to (2) an array of **int**." You translate what's inside the parentheses first.

The situation is similar for pointers to functions. The declaration

```
void *func();
```

means "**func** is (1) a function (2) returning a pointer to **void**." Again, the parentheses denoting a function have higher priority than the indirection operator. While

```
void (*func)();
```

means "**func** is (1) a pointer to (2) a function returning type **void**." This is the usage in the funcaddr.c program above.

Things can get more complicated, but the same rules apply. Start with the variable name, look to the right to see if it's a function or array, then look to the left to see if it's a pointer. Interpret things inside parentheses first.

How about

```
int **arr[];
```

Here, **arr** is (1) an array (2) of pointers (3) to pointers to **int**. On the other hand, in

```
int *(*func)();
```

**func** is (1) a pointer to (2) a function returning (3) a pointer to **int**.

One more:

```
float *(*arr[])();
```

means **arr** is (1) an array of (2) pointers to (3) functions returning (4) pointers to **float**.

With these rules you should be able to decipher most C declarations.

# Labels and the *goto* Statement

We have deliberately put off a discussion of the **goto** statement until the end of the book. There is seldom a legitimate reason for **goto**, and its use is one of the leading reasons that programs become unreliable, unreadable, and hard to debug. And yet many programmers (especially those using BASIC) find **goto** seductive. In a difficult programming situation it seems so easy to throw in a **goto** to get where you want to go. Almost always, however, there is a more elegant construction using an **if** or **switch** statement or a loop. Such constructions are far easier to understand than **goto** statements. A **goto** statement can cause program control to end up almost anywhere in the program, for reasons that are often hard to unravel.

We trust that, by getting this far in the book without using a **goto**, we have provided proof that, at least in most cases, its use can be avoided. If you turned to this page from the index, desperate to use a **goto**, try very hard to employ another approach.

For completeness, however, here's how **goto** is used. Consider the following program fragment:

```
- - -
if(temp>max)
   goto scramble;             /*goto label*/
- - -
scramble:                     /*note colon after label */
   printf("Emergency!");
- - -
```

The **goto** statement transfers control to the label **scramble**, causing the **printf()** statement to be executed immediately after the **goto**. The **goto** must specify a label, and the label must exist or a compiler error will result. Since the compiler doesn't care about whitespace, the label can be on a separate line or on the same line as another statement.

```
scramble: printf("Emergency!");
```

Labels are used only with **goto** statements. Other statements on the same line as a label will operate as if the label didn't exist. As we noted earlier in this chapter, labels form a naming class and are formed in the same way as other identifiers.

## Summary

This chapter has covered some of the less common aspects of variables. We've examined storage classes, which permit control of the lifetime and visibility of a variable; enumerated data types, which permit the programmer to define a data type and its values; and **typedef**, which lets the programmer give a new name to an existing data type. We've also examined the conventions used for naming variables and other elements in C programs, and we've seen how these names or identifiers apply to different categories of program elements called naming classes. We've seen how variables are converted automatically from one type to another and how this conversion can be overridden with typecasting. Finally we looked at labels and their use with the **goto** statement.

## Questions

1. The storage class of a variable is related to

    a. the amount of memory space the variable occupies

    b. the quality of the memory space occupied

    c. how long the variable will occupy a space in memory

    d. what parts of the program can "see" the function

2. For a variable to be visible in a file other than the one where it is defined, it must be _____ using the _____ keyword.

3. A variable definition differs from a declaration in that

    a. the declaration sets aside storage space

    b. the declaration specifies the name and type of the variable

    c. the definition sets aside storage space

    d. the definition specifies the name and type of the variable

4. An *automatic* variable is one that is automatically c_____ and d_____.

5. A *static* (nonexternal) variable can be seen only within

    a. a block

    b. a function

    c. a file

    d. many files

6. True or false: an external variable is always visible throughout the file in which it is defined.

7. To restrict the visibility of an external variable to one file, it must be of type _____ _____.

8. In an enumerated data type, the programmer can define

    a. whether the new type will be integer or floating point

    b. the number of bytes used by variables of the new type

    c. the values of the new type

d. many types of the same storage class

9. If **fish** has already been defined to an enumerated data type, what statement will define the variable **gamefish** to be of this type?

10. The **typedef** declaration is used to

a. declare a new data type

b. perform a #**define**-style substitution of one identifier for another

c. define a new data type

d. give a new name to a data type

11. Identifiers are the _____ given to variables and other elements in a program.

12. A naming class is

a. a category of variables of the same type

b. a place to learn how to name variables

c. a category in which identifiers must be distinct

d. the category of functions and variables

13. True or false: the same identifier can be used for a structure and a member of that structure.

14. The rank of a variable in data conversions is roughly indicated by the number of _____ _____ _____ used by the character.

15. A typecast is used to

a. force a value to be of a particular variable type

b. define a new data type

c. rename an old data type

d. provide harder than usual data

# *Appendices*

# A

---

# *Reference*

This appendix provides a reference for some of the more fundamental constructions in the C programming language. Our goal is not to cover the entire language; the manuals that accompany your compiler perform that task. Rather, we want to present, in an easily accessible format, those aspects of the language that will be most useful for readers of this book.

Wherever possible we've used examples, as this is the quickest and most easily grasped way to communicate particular formats. For more detailed explanations, see the relevant sections of the book. Note that the examples only demonstrate format; they are not intended as working programs. Also, they are not intended to cover all possible situations, only the most general ones.

## A. Control Constructions

In the following examples, the word "statement" represents any suitable program statement.

### 1. Structure of Simple C Program

```
main()
{
    statement;
    statement;
}
```

### 2. The for Loop

```
for(j=0; j<10; j++)        /* single-statement loop */
    statement;

for(j=0; j<10; j++)        /* multistatement loop */
    {
    statement;
    statement;
    }
```

```
/* multiple initialization and increments */
for(j=0, other=0; j<20; j++, other++)
    statement;
```

## 3. The while Loop

```
while (ch != 'X')           /* single-statement loop */
    statement;

while (y < 10)              /* multistatement loop */
    {
    statement;
    statement;
    }

while (getche() != 'X')             /* function used as variable */
    statement;

while ((ch=getche()) != 'X')        /* assignment statement used */
    statement;                      /* as variable */
```

## 4. The do while Loop

```
    do                  /* single-statement loop */
        statememt;
    while (ch != 'X');

    do                  /* multistatement loop */
        {
        statememt;
        statement;
        }
    while (x <= 42);
```

## 5. The if and if . . . else Statements

```
    if(x==42)           /* single statement if */
        statememnt;

    if(x < 19)          /* multistatement if */
        {
        statement;
        statement;
        }

    if(ch=='a')         /* if-else */
        statement;
```

```
      else
         statement;

      if(x < 10)          /* nested ifs */
         if(y > 5)
            statement;

      if(ch=='a')         /* "else-if" construct */
         statement;
      else if(ch=='b')
         statement;
      else if(ch=='c')
         statement;

      if(x > 5)           /* else paired with second of two ifs */
         if(y < 10)
            statement;
         else
            statement;

      if(x > 5)           /* else paired with first of two ifs */
         {                /* (braces are necessary) */
         if(y < 10)
            statement;
         }
      else
         statement;
```

## 6. The break Statement

```
      while(ch != "X")
         {
         statement;
         if( count>MAX )
            break;          /* causes exit from loop */
         statement;
         }
```

## 7. The continue Statement

```
      while(ch != 'X')
         {
         if(ch==SPACE)
            continue;     /* skip other loop statements, */
         statement;       /*    go to start of loop */
         statement;
         }
```

### 8. The switch Statement

```
switch (j)          /* integer switch */
    {
    case 1:
        printf("j is 1");
        break;
    case 2:
        printf("j is 2");
        statement;
        break;
    default;
        printf("j is anything else");
    }

switch (ch)         /* character switch */
    {
    case 'a':
    case 'b':
        printf("ch is 'a' or 'b'.");
        break;
    case 'c':
        printf("ch is 'c'.");
    }
```

# B. Function Formats

## 1. Function with No Return, No Arguments

```
void fun1(void);              /* function prototype */
main()
{
    puts("Main program");
    fun1();                   /* function call */
}

/* function definition */
void fun1(void)               /* function declarator */
{
    puts("Function fun1()");  /* function body */
}
```

## 2. Function Returns a Value

```
int return7(void);                /* function prototype */
main()
```

```
      {
          printf("Value returned is %d", return7() );
      }

      /* function definition */
      int return7(void)                    /* function declarator */
      {
          return(7);                       /* function body */
      }
```

## 3. Send Values to a Function

```
void sends2(int, int);          /* function prototype */
main()
{
    int x=4, y=7;               /* values to pass to function */

    sends2(x, y);               /* function call */
}

/* function definition */
void sends2(int arg1, int arg2)             /* declarator */
{
    printf("arg1=%d, arg2=%d", arg1, arg2);  /* function body */
}
```

## 4. Return Values from a Function Using Pointers

```
void rets2(int *, int *);              /* function prototype */
main()
{
    int x, y;                          /* variables */
    int *ptrx, *ptry;                  /* pointers */

    ptrx = &x;                         /* initialize pointers */
    ptry = &y;                         /*    to variables */
    rets2(ptrx, ptry);                 /* function call */
    printf("x=%d, y=%d", x, y);        /* values returned */
}

/* function definition */
void rets2(int *ptr1, int *ptr2)       /* declarator */
{
    *ptr1 = 4;                         /* function body */
    *ptr2 = 7;                         /* returns values */
}
```

# C. Data Constructions

## 1. Arrays

```
main()                   /* declaring arrays */
{
   int list[3];          /* one-dimensional array; 3 items */
   char table[4][3];     /* 2-dimen array, 4 rows, 3 columns */
   list[2] = 333;        /* referring to array elements */
   table[1][3] = 'c';
}

/* initializing arrays */
int lista[3] = { 23, 34, 45 };   /* initialize as external var */
main()
{
   static int listb[2][3] =      /* initialize as static var */
             { { 2, 4, 6 },
               { 3, 5, 7 }  };
}
```

## 2. Strings

```
char name[30];                          /* string is char array */
static char salute[] = "Greetings!";    /* initialize string */
static char *salute = "Greetings!";     /* initialize string */
puts(salute);                           /* refer to string */
salute[2]=='e'                          /* character in string */
static char names[3][30] =              /* array of strings */
                { "Katrina", "Sam", "Rodney" };
static char *names[30] =                /* array of strings */
                { "Nancy", "Robert", "Laurie" };
puts(&names[2][0]);                     /* ref to string in array */
```

## 3. Pointers

```
/* initializing pointers */
int *ptr;                      /* pointer to int (or int array) */
char *charptr;                 /* pntr to char (or char array) */
/* other variables used in example below */
int numb;                      /* integer variable */
int table[3] = {5, 6, 7};      /* array */

/* using pointers */
ptr = &numb;                   /* assign address to pointer */
*ptr = 8;                      /* assign 8 to numb */
prt=table;                     /* assign array address to pointer */
```

```
printf("%d", *ptr );          /* print first element of array */
printf("%d", *(ptr+1) );      /* print second element of array */
```

## 4. Structures

```
struct employee               /* declare structure of type employee */
   {
   int empno;                 /* three items in this structure */
   float  salary;
   char name[40];
   };
struct employee clerks;       /* declare clerk to be variable of */
                              /*     type struct employee */
struct employee staff;        /* declare other variables */
                              /* reference elements of structure */
printf("Clerk's employee number is %d", clerks.empno );
printf("Clerk's salary is %f", clerks.salary );

/* shorthand way to declare a structure variable */
struct                        /* no need to name structure type */
   {
   int empno;
   float  salary;
   char name[40];
   } clerks;                  /* declare clerk var of type struct */
```

## 5. Unions

```
union intflo                  /* declare union */
   {                          /* memory location can be referred to */
   int intnum;                /* as either float or int */
   float fltnum;
   } unionex;
unionex.intnum;               /* reference to two-byte int */
unionex.fltnum;               /* reference to four-byte float */
```

# D. Operators

## 1. Arithmetic Operators

| Symbol | Operator | Example |
|--------|----------|---------|
| + | addition | a+b |
| – | subtraction | a-b |
| * | multiplication | a*b |
| / | division | a/b |
| % | remainder | a%b |

## 2. Increment and Decrement Operators

| | | |
|---|---|---|
| ++ | increment | a++ or ++a |
| — | decrement | a— or —a |

## 3. Relational Operators

| Symbol | Operator | Example |
|---|---|---|
| < | less than | a<b |
| > | greater than | a>b |
| < = | less than or equal | a< =b |
| > = | greater than or equal | a> =b |
| = = | equal | a= =b |
| != | not equal | a!=b |

## 4. Logical Operators

| | | |
|---|---|---|
| && | AND | a<b && c>d |
| ¦¦ | OR | a<b ¦¦ c>d |
| ! | NOT | !(a<b) |

## 5. Bitwise Operators

| | | |
|---|---|---|
| & | AND | a & b |
| ¦ | inclusive OR | a ¦ b |
| ^ | exclusive OR | a ^ b |
| ~ | complement | ~a |
| >> | right shift | a >> 2 |
| << | left shift | b << 3 |

## 6. Assignment Operators

| | | |
|---|---|---|
| = | equal | a = b |
| += | addition | a += b (same as a=a+b) |
| — = | subtraction | a — = b (same as a=a-b) |
| *= | multiplication | a *= b (same as a=a*b) |
| \= | division | a /= b (same as a=a/b) |
| %= | remainder | a %= b (same as a=a%b) |
| &= | bitwise AND | a &= b (same as a=a&b) |
| ¦= | bitwise inclusive OR | a ¦= b (same as a=a¦b) |

| | | |
|---|---|---|
| ^= | bitwise exclusive OR | a ^= b (same as a=a^b) |
| <<= | left shift | a <<= 2 (same as a=a<<2) |
| >>= | right shift | a >>= 3 (same as a=a>>3) |

## 7. Conditional Operator

```
result = (expression) ? value1 : value2;      max = (a>b) ? a : b;
```

## 8. Address and Indirection Operators

| Symbol | Operator | Example |
|---|---|---|
| & | address | addr = &var |
| * | indirection | value = *addr |

## 9. Sizeof Operator

```
sizeof()                          sizeof(int), sizeof(struct emp)
```

## 10. Precedence and Associativity of Operators

| Operators | Type | Associativity |
|---|---|---|
| () [] . -> | groups, membership | left to right |
| - ~ ! * & | unary | right to left |
| ++ -- sizeof casts | unary | right to left |
| * / % | multiplicative | left to right |
| + - | additive | left to right |
| << >> | shift | left to right |
| < > <= >= | relational | left to right |
| == != | equality | left to right |
| & | bitwise AND | left to right |
| ^ | bitwise excl OR | left to right |
| ¦ | bitwise incl OR | left to right |
| && | logical AND | left to right |
| ¦¦ | logical OR | left to right |
| ?: | conditional | right to left |
| = *= /= %= += -= | | |
| <<= >>= &= ^= ¦= | assignment | right to left |
| , | comma (series) | left to right |

# E. Data Types

## 1. Character (char)

Characters occupy one byte, and have a range from −128 to 127 (−80 to 7F hex). Unsigned characters have a range from 0 to 255 (0 to FF hex).

```
char ch;                /* declare character variable */
unsigned char k;        /* declare unsigned character variable */
char c1 = 'a';          /* initialize character variable */
char c2 = 97;           /* initialize using decimal value */
char c3 = 0x61;         /* initialize using hexadecimal value */

/* special character constants */
'\n'    /* newline (linefeed); 0x0A */
'\b'    /* backspace; 0x08 */
'\r'    /* carriage return; 0x0D */
'\f'    /* formfeed; (0x0C) */
'\t'    /* tab; 0x09 */
'\v'    /* vertical tab; 0x0B */
'\\'    /* backslash; 0x5C */
'\''    /* single quote; 0x27 */
'\"'    /* double quote; 0x22 */
'\0'    /* null; 0x00 */
```

## 2. Short Integer (short)

Short integers occupy two bytes and have a range from −32,768 to 32,767 (−8,000 to 7FFF hex). Unsigned short integers have a range from 0 to 65,535 (0 to FFFF hex).

```
short x;                /* declare short integer */
short y = 12;           /* initialize short integer */
unsigned short c;       /* declare unsigned short integer */
12                      /* decimal const (no initial 0) */
0x0c                    /* hex constant (initial 0x) */
014                     /* octal constant (initial 0) */
```

## 3. Integer (int)

Integers are the same as type **short** or type **long**, depending on the machine used by the Microsoft compiler. For 8088, 8086, and 80286 machines, they're two bytes, similar to type **short**. On 80386 machines they're four bytes, as is type **long**.

```
int x;                  /* declare integer */
int y = 12;             /* initialize integer */
unsigned int c;         /* declare unsigned integer */
                        /* constants same as for short int */
```

### 4. Long Integer ( long )

Long integers occupy four bytes in memory and have a range from −2,147,483,648 to 2,147,483,647 (−80000000 to 7FFFFFFF hex). Unsigned long integers have a range from 0 to 4,294,967,295 (0 to FFFFFFFF hex).

```
long int bignum;        /* declare long integer */
long bignum;            /* alternative form */
long bn1 = 12L;         /* initialize long integer */
10L                     /* decimal constant */
0x0AL                   /* hexadecimal constant */
012L                    /* octal constant */
```

### 5. Floating Point (float)

Floating point numbers occupy four bytes of memory. The exponent has a range of $10^{-38}$ to $10^{38}$. The mantissa has up to six digits of precision.

```
float flnumb;           /* declaring floating point number */
float fnb = 37.42;      /* initializing floating point number */
99.99                   /* constant in decimal notation */
9999E-2                 /* constant in exponential notation */
/* floating point constants always have type double */
```

### 6. Double-Precision Floating Point (double)

Double-precision floating point numbers occupy eight bytes of memory. The exponent has a range of $10^{-308}$ to $10^{308}$. The mantissa has up to 15 digits of precision.

```
double verybig;       /* declaring double precision fp number */
long float verybig;   /* alternative form for declaration */
double vb = 7.1416;   /* initializing double precision number */
320000                /* constant in decimal notation */
3.2E5                 /* constant in exponential notation */
```

### 7. Strings (Array of Type char)

Strings are arrays of characters, terminated with the null character ('\0'). They occupy as many bytes as there are characters in the string, plus one for the null.

```
char name[30];      /* declaring character array for string */
char phrase[] = "Error.";  /* initializing string as array */
char *phrase = "Error.";   /* initializing string as pointer */
"Greetings!\n"             /* string constant */
```

## 8. Void

The **void** type has three uses. The first indicates that a function does not return a value.

```
void func()
```

The second indicates that a function takes no arguments.

```
func(void)
```

The third declares a pointer to any data type (rather than to a specific type).

```
void *ptr;
```

## 9. Enumeration Types

Creates a new type with a limited, user-defined set of values. (Actual values are stored as integers.)

```
enum change              /* creates new type */
   { penny, nickel,      /* specifies allowable values */
     dime, quarter };
enum change ch1;         /* declare variable of type change */
ch1 = penny;             /* give value to variable */
```

## 10. Typecasts

Changes the type of a variable.

```
long num = 12L;            /* num starts off as type long */
printf("%d", (int)num );   /* is cast as type int before use */
```

## 11. Typedef

Defines a new name for a data type.

```
typedef long big;    /* renames type long to be type big */
big num;             /* declares num to be of type big (long) */
```

## 12. Logical Types

There is no specific logical or binary type in C. An integer with a value of 0 represents false, and an integer with a value of 1 (or any other nonzero value) represents true.

# F. Storage Classes

The storage class of a variable determines the lifetime and scope of the variable. Lifetime refers to how long a variable will retain its value. Visibility (or scope) refers to where the variable will be recognized. The storage class is determined by the placement of the variable in the source file and by the use of the keywords auto, extern, static, and register.

## Table of Storage Classes

| Where Declared | Keyword | Lifetime | Visibility (Scope) |
|---|---|---|---|
| function | auto (default) | function | function (1) |
| function | register | function | function (1) |
| function | static | program | function (1) |
| external | static | program | one file only (2) |
| external (not decl) | — | program | one file (2) |
| external (declared) | extern (3) | program | multifile (4) |

(1) if defined in block, only visible in block
(2) visible from variable definition to end-of-file
(3) keyword extern used to declare variable in one or more files
(4) when variable is declared in file using extern, visibility is entire file (or multiple files, if declared in each one)

## Examples of Storage Classes

```
/* file 1 */
/* ("vis" means visibility) */
int ex1;                /* external; vis=file 1 */
int ex2;                /* external; vis=files 1 and 2 */
static int ex3;         /* static external; vis=this file only */
main()
{
    int loc1;           /* automatic; vis=this function */
    auto int loc2;      /* automatic; vis=this function */
    register int loc3;  /* register; vis=this function */
    static int loc4;    /* static; vis=this function */
    {
        int loc5;       /* automatic; vis=this block only */
    }
}
int ex4;                /* external; vis=from here to eof */
func()
{
}

/* file 2 */
extern int ex2;         /* declaration; extends vis to file 2 */
int ex5;                /* external; vis=file 2 */
func2()
{
}
```

# G. Library Functions

This section lists the C library functions used in this book. For more complete
explanations, use the index to find the description of the function in the text.
(The functions shown are only a fraction of the total available library functions.)

## 1. Screen and Keyboard I/O

### Character I/O

```
getchar()        /* returns kbd char ([Return] key needed) */
getch()          /* returns kbd char (no [Return] needed, no echo) */
getche()         /* returns kbd char (echo, no [Return] needed) */
putchar(ch)      /* displays char */
putch(ch)        /* displays char */
```

### String I/O

```
gets(str)        /* inputs string */
puts(str)        /* outputs string */
```

### Formatted I/O

```
scanf()          /* formatted input */
printf()         /* formatted output */
```

## 2. File I/O

### Standard I/O

```
fopen(name,type)        /* open file, return pointer */
fclose(ptr)             /* close file */
fseek(ptr,offset,type)  /* position file pointer */
fflush(ptr)             /* flush buffer */
ferror(ptr)             /* returns nonzero on error */
perror(str)             /* prints str and system error */
```

### Standard Character I/O

```
getc(ptr)               /* returns char */
putc(ch,ptr)            /* writes char */
```

### Standard String I/O

```
fgets(str,n,ptr)        /* reads string */
fputs(str,ptr)          /* writes string */
```

### Standard Formatted I/O

```
    fscanf()                  /* reads formatted data */
    fprintf()                 /* writes formatted data */
```

### Standard Block I/O

```
fread(buff,size,cnt,ptr)      /* read from file into buffer */
fwrite(buff,size,cnt,ptr)     /* write from buffer onto file */
```

### System Level I/O

```
    open(name,oflag,pmode)    /* open file, return handle */
    close(hndl)               /* close file */
    read(hndl,buff,cnt)       /* read cnt bytes into buff */
    write(hndl,buff,cnt)      /* write cnt bytes from buff */
    setmode(hndl,mode)        /* set mode to text or binary */
```

## 3. String Manipulation

```
    strcpy(s2,s1)      /* copies string1 to string2 */
    strcmp(s1,s2)      /* compares two strings */
    strlen(s)          /* returns length of string */
    strcat(s1,s2)      /* appends string2 to string1 */
```

## 4. Buffer Manipulation

```
    memcmp(buf1,buf2,cnt)   /* compares two buffers */
    memchr(buff,ch,cnt)     /* searches for ch in buff */
```

## 5. Miscellaneous Functions

```
    sizeof(type)       /* returns size of given data type */
    int86(FILE,&inregs,&outregs)   /* interrupt */
    inp(port)          /* read char from port */
    outp(port,ch)      /* write char to port */
    ftime(&timebuff)   /* get time, place in structure */
    atoi(str)          /* converts string to integer */
```

# H. printf() and scanf() Formats

Note that letter 'l' is used as a prefix to denote a long integer or double-precision floating point; "h" denotes a short integer. Examples: %ld, %lf.

| Type | printf() | scanf() |
|---|---|---|
| signed decimal integer | %d | %d |
| signed decimal integer | %i | |
| decimal, hex, or octal integer | | %i |
| unsigned dec integer | %u | %u |
| unsigned octal integer | %o | %o |
| unsigned hex integer (abcdef) | %x | %x |
| unsigned hex integer (ABCDEF) | %X | %x |
| floating point (decimal) | %f | %f, %e |
| floating point (exp, e) | %e | %f, %e |
| floating point (exp, E) | %E | %f, %e |
| f or e, whichever shorter | %g | |
| f or E, whichever shorter | %G | |
| character | %c | %c |
| string | %s | %s |

## Examples of printf() Format Specifiers

```
/* colons show margins of field */
printf("%d", num);      /* :25:        decimal */
printf("%7d", num);     /* :     25:   specify field width */
printf("%-7d", num);    /* :25     :   left-justify */
printf("%07d", num);    /* :0000025:   leading zeros */
printf("%f", fnum);     /* :7.333333:  floating point */
printf("%7.2f", fnum);  /* :   7.33:   decimal places */
```

# I. IBM Specific

## 1. Common Extended Character Codes

| Second Code | Key |
|---|---|
| 59–68 | Function keys [F1] to [F10] |
| 71 | [Home] |
| 72 | Up arrow |
| 73 | [PgUp] |
| 75 | Left arrow |
| 77 | Right arrow |
| 79 | [End] |
| 80 | Down arrow |
| 81 | [PgDn] |
| 82 | [Ins] |
| 83 | [Del] |
| 84–93 | Uppercase function keys |

(See the IBM *Technical Reference* manual for a complete list of extended codes.)

## 2. ANSI.SYS Cursor Control

| Escape Sequence | Action |
|---|---|
| "\x1B[2J" | Clear screen, home cursor |
| "\x1B[A" | Cursor up one line |
| "\x1B[B" | Cursor down one line |
| "\x1B[C" | Cursor right one character |
| "\x1B[D" | Cursor left one character |
| "\x1B[#;#H" | Cursor to position: first "#" is row (1 to 25), second "#" is column (1 to 80) |
| "\x1B[K" | Erase from cursor to end of line |
| "\x1B[s" | Save current cursor position |
| "\x1B[u" | Restore cursor position |

(See the IBM *Technical Reference* manual for a complete list of escape sequences.)

# J. Miscellaneous

## 1. Command-Line Arguments

```
main(argv,argc)
char *argv[];      /* array of pointers to argument strings */
int argc;          /* number of arguments */
{
    for(j=0, j<argc; j++)            /* print all command line */
        printf("%s\n", argv[j] );    /* arguments in order */
}
```

## 2. Redirection

```
C> prog <source.xxx >dest.xxx   /* input from file source.xxx, */
                                /* output to file dest.xxx */
```

## 3. Preprocessor Directives

```
#include <stdio.h>    /* includes file stdio.h in source file */
                      /*    start search in standard directory */
#include "user.h"     /* includes file user.h in source file */
                      /*    start search in current directory */
#define MAX 10        /* replace MAX by 10 in source file */
#define SUM(X,Y) X+Y  /* replace SUM(x,y) with x+y, */
                      /*    for all values of x and y */
#define TEST          /* makes TEST true (remove to make false) */
#if define(TEST)      /* if it's true, */
    statement;        /*    this will be done */
```

```
#else TEST            /* otherwise, */
  statement;          /*    this will be done */
#endif TEST           /* delimiter for #ifdef and #else */
#undef TEST           /* undefines TEST
```

# B

# Supplementary Programs

In this appendix we present several C programs that were either too large or too far removed from the main discussion for inclusion earlier. These programs show some additional programming techniques, and they also provide examples of how larger programs can be constructed from simple functions.

Space limitations preclude a detailed discussion of the operation of these programs. In general it is not too hard to figure out how they work by following the comments; this should constitute an interesting series of exercises for the motivated reader.

All the examples work on the monochrome display. In some examples (life.c, saveimag.c, maze.c) you may need to change the address of the video memory to correspond to your monitor. Usually 0xB8000000 works on color monitors and 0xB0000000 on the monochrome display. See Chapter 10 for more details.

## Conway's Life

Conway's game of Life is an old standby, and has been implemented on almost every computer with even a rudimentary graphics capability. It involves the birth, growth, and death of cells according to these rules: if a cell has three neighbors, it will be born. If it has two or three neighbors, it will live if it already exists. If it has more or fewer neighbors it will die. The application of these rules leads to a fascinating display of evolving patterns (provided an appropriate initial configuration of cells is specified). We can't explain Life in detail here; if you've seen it, you know what a hypnotic game it can be.

When the program is started, screen prompts will tell you to use the cursor keys to create the starting configuration—a pattern of squares. Press the [Ins] key wherever you want a square; when you're done, press [End]. The pattern will start to change and perhaps to grow. A good first pattern is a "U" shape, three squares wide and three high.

This program makes use of a novel graphics mode: 80x50 resolution on a normal monochrome display. Since the monochrome screen ordinarily shows 80 columns of 25 rows, how do we double the resolution? The extended character set includes two useful graphics characters; one is a box in the upper half of the character and the other is a box in the lower half of the character. By printing the appropriate box, we in effect double the resolution of the display. These half-height boxes have another advantage; they are square, instead of being twice as tall as they are wide, as a full-character box is. The square boxes make for a far more pleasing display in the Life program.

This program uses two graphics routines. One, putscr(), puts a half-height box on the screen at a particular location, and the other, getscr(), reads a particular screen location to see if there is a half-height box already there. These routines operate on the 80x50 coordinate system. The putscr() routine must read the full-size character at a particular location and combine the half-height character accordingly. For instance, if a box is to be placed in the bottom half, and the top half is already full, then the full-height box must be written into the character position.

The program first erases the screen and gets the initial pattern from the user. Then, in a loop that is repeated once for each "generation," it transfers the contents of the screen to an array, erases the screen, reconstructs on the screen the new generation of cells based on the old generation in the array, and erases the array.

The program uses the ANSI.SYS escape code to erase the screen, so you must load the ANSI.SYS driver in the operating system. Since it uses **far** pointers, it must be compiled with the \Ze option if you're using version 3.0 of the Microsoft compiler.

```
/* life2.c */
/* Conways's game of 'life' */
#include <stdio.h>              /* for printf() */
#include <conio.h>             /* for kbhit() */
#define MAXCOL 80              /* screen width */
#define MAXROW 50              /* screen height */
#define ERASE "\x1B[2J"        /* code to erase scr */
#define VIDEO_ADDR 0xB8000000  /* video address */
                               /* (use 0xB0000000 for mono) */
void getinit(void);           /* function prototypes */
void putscr(int col, int row);
char getscr(int col, int row);

void main(void)
{
    static char array[MAXCOL][MAXROW];   /* array echoes screen */
    char neigh;                          /* how many neighbors */
    int col, row;                        /* cell coordinates */
    int count=0;                         /* generation counter */

    getinit();                           /* get initial cells */
    while ( !kbhit() )                   /* cycle generations */
        {                                /*     until keypress */
        for(col=1; col<MAXCOL-1; col++)  /* transfer screen */
            for(row=1; row<MAXROW-1; row++)  /*   to array */
                array[col][row] = getscr(col,row);
        printf(ERASE);                   /* erase screen */
```

```
            printf("\x1B[24;1H");              /* position cursor */
            printf("Generation %d", ++count); /* print generation */
            for(col=1; col<MAXCOL-1; col++)   /* for every cell */
                for(row=1; row<MAXROW-1; row++)
                    {
                    neigh = array[col-1][row-1] +  /* find number */
                            array[col  ][row-1] +  /*  of neighbors */
                            array[col+1][row-1] +
                            array[col-1][row  ] +
                            array[col+1][row  ] +
                            array[col-1][row+1] +
                            array[col  ][row+1] +
                            array[col+1][row+1];
                    if (array[col][row]==0)    /* if no cell */
                        {
                        if (neigh==3)              /* and 3 neighbors */
                            putscr(col,row);       /*   a cell is born */
                        }
                    else                       /* cell already alive */
                        if ( neigh==2 || neigh==3) /* if 2 or 3 nbors */
                            putscr(col,row);       /*   cell lives */
                    }                          /* done one cell */
                for(col=0; col<MAXCOL; col++)     /* clear array */
                    for(row=0; row<MAXROW; row++)
                        array[col][row] = 0;
            }  /* end while */                 /* done generation */
    }  /* end main */                          /* end program */

/* getinit() */
/* gets initial elements, puts them on screen */
#define END 79            /* key codes */
#define INSERT 82
#define C_UPUP 72
#define C_DOWN 80
#define C_LEFT 75
#define C_RITE 77
void getinit(void)
{
    int col, row;                       /* cell coordinates */
    char keycode;                       /* from keyboard */

    printf(ERASE);                      /* erase screen */
    printf("\x1B[22;1H");               /* position cursor */
    printf("Move cursor with arrow keys.\n");
    printf("Place cell with [Ins] key, [End] when done.");
    col=40; row=25;
    while ( keycode != END )            /* return on [End] */
        {
        if( kbhit() )                   /* true if key struck */
            if( getch() == 0 )          /* extended code */
                {
```

```
                switch ( (keycode=getch()) )  /* read code */
                   {
                   case C_UPUP: --row; break;
                   case C_DOWN: ++row; break;
                   case C_RITE: ++col; break;
                   case C_LEFT: --col; break;
                   case INSERT: putscr(col,row); break;
                   }  /* end switch */
                }  /* end if(getch) */
          }  /* end if(kbhit) */
}  /* end getinit */

/* putscr() */
/* puts small square in screen memory at col, row */
/* cols from 0 to 79, rows from 0 to 49 */
#define TOP  '\xDF'      /* upper half of character */
#define BOT  '\xDC'      /* lower half of character */
#define BOTH '\xDB'      /* full character rectangle */
void putscr(int col, int row)
{
   char newch, ch;
   int far *farptr;                   /* ptr to screen mem */
   int actrow;                        /* actual row number */
   int topbot;                        /* top or bottom of row */

   farptr = (int far *) VIDEO_ADDR;  /* pointer to video mem */
   actrow = row >> 1;                 /* row divided by 2 */
   topbot = row & 0x0001;             /* odd or even row */
   ch = *(farptr + actrow*80 + col); /* get actual char */
   if (topbot)                        /* if we're placing bot */
      if ( ch==TOP || ch==BOTH )
            newch = BOTH;
      else
            newch = BOT;
   else                               /* if we're placing top */
      if ( ch==BOT || ch==BOTH )
         newch = BOTH;
      else
         newch = TOP;
                                      /* insert character */
   *( farptr + actrow*80 + col ) = (newch & 0x00ff) | 0x0700;
}

/* getscr() */
/* returns 1 or 0 from screen location col, row */
/* cols from 0 to 79, rows from 0 to 49 */
#define TOP  '\xDF'      /* upper half of character */
#define BOT  '\xDC'      /* lower half of character */
#define BOTH '\xDB'      /* full character rectangle */
#define TRUE 1
#define FALSE 0
```

```
char getscr(int col, int row)
{
    char ch;
    int far *farptr;                    /* ptr to screen mem */
    int actrow;                         /* actual row number */
    int bottom;                         /* top or bottom of row */

    farptr = (int far *) VIDEO_ADDR;    /* point to video mem */
    actrow = row >> 1;                  /* row divided by 2 */
    bottom = row & 0x0001;              /* odd or even row */
    ch = *( farptr + actrow*80 + col ) ;    /* get actual char */
    if (ch==BOTH)
        return(TRUE);
    else
        if ( (bottom && ch==BOT) || (!bottom && ch==TOP) )
            return(TRUE);
        else
            return(FALSE);
}
```

## Checking Comments in C Source Files

It's easy to forget either the opening or the closing comment symbol in a C source file. The result of doing this (or of mistyping a comment symbol) can result in program bugs that are difficult to figure out.

The following program searches through a C source file and makes sure that each opening comment symbol ( /* ) is matched with a closing comment symbol ( */ ).

```
/* comcheck.c */
/* verifies that all comment symbols in C listing are paired */
/* (signals first mis-pairing) */
#include "stdio.h"
#define TRUE 1
#define FALSE 0
main(argc,argv)
int argc;
char *argv[];
{
    FILE *fptr;
    char ch;
    int slash=FALSE, star=FALSE, comments=0;
    int line = 1;
    void chcount(), finalcnt();

    if ( argc != 2 )
        { printf("Type \"comcheck filename\"."); exit(); }
    if ( ( fptr=fopen(argv[1],"r") ) == NULL )
        { printf("Can't open file %s", argv[1]); exit(); }
```

```
    while ( (ch=getc(fptr)) != EOF )  {
       switch (ch)  {
          case '*':
             star = TRUE;
             if (slash == TRUE)  {       /* found start comment? */
                comments++;              /* toggle 'comments' */
                if ( comments > 1 )  { /* unmatched start comm */
                   printf("Unexpected start comment, line %d",
                                                           line);
                   exit();
                }
                slash = star = FALSE;  /* reset flags */
             }
             break;
          case '/':
             slash = TRUE;
             if (star == TRUE)  {       /* found end comment? */
                comments--;              /* toggle 'comments' */
                if ( comments < 0 )  { /* unmatched end comment */
                   printf("Unexpected end comment, line %d", line);
                   exit();
                }
                slash = star = FALSE;  /* reset flags */
             }
             break;
          case '\n':                      /* count lines */
             line++;
          default:                        /* not '/' or '*' */
             slash = star = FALSE;        /* reset flags */
       }  /* end switch */
    }  /* end while */
    fclose(fptr);
    if (comments > 0)                    /* open comment at EOF */
       printf("Unmatched open comment.");
}  /* end main */
```

## Saving the Screen to a File

It's easy to print out an image of the screen on the printer: the [Shift] and [PrtSc] key combination can be used for this purpose. This can be a useful way to record what the screen looks like in situations where a program doesn't save its own output in a file. (For instance, you might want to record the interaction between the user and the compiler's question-and-answer format.) But suppose you want to save what's on the screen to a disk file instead of to the printer? The saveimag.c program, shown here, does the trick.

To record the screen image, you type the name of the program, followed by the name of the file you want the screen image saved to. The program does the rest.

The program looks at each line of the display in turn. As it reads the characters from a line, it stores them in **buff[ ]**. The buffer is used so that only the number of characters actually used in a given line are stored in the disk file, instead of all 80 characters from the display. Most text lines don't contain 80 characters and it's wasteful to store sequences of spaces. As the program examines each character in turn from a single screen line, it places the character in a buffer. As it does so, it remembers the last nonspace character. When all 80 characters have been read, it inserts a newline and a null into the buffer immediately following the last nonspace character. The resulting string, which can be from 0 to 80 characters long, is then written from the buffer to the file. The process is repeated for all 25 lines.

```c
/* saveimag.c */
/* writes a screen image to a file */
#include <stdio.h>                    /* for printf() */
#include <process.h>                  /* for exit */
#define SPACE '\x20'                  /* ASCII char */
#define VIDEO_ADDR 0xB8000000         /* start of video mem */
                                      /* 0xB0000000 for mono */
char whatchar(int col, int row);     /* function prototype */

void main(argc, argv)
int argc;
char *argv[];
{
    FILE *fptr;                       /* file pointer */
    int col, row, lastchar;          /* screen coordinates */
    char ch;                          /* char from screen */
    char buff[80];                    /* buffer to hold one row */

    if (argc != 2)
        { printf("Type \"saveimag filename\"."); exit(1); }
    if ( ( fptr=fopen(argv[1],"w") ) == NULL )
        { printf("Can't open file %s.", argv[1]); exit(1); }
    for (row=1; row<25; row++)
        {                             /* to store last */
        lastchar = 0;                 /*    non-space char */
        for (col=1; col<80; col++)
            {
            ch = whatchar(col,row);   /* get character */
            buff[col-1] = ch;         /* store in buffer */
            if (ch != SPACE)          /* remember pos of last */
                lastchar = col;       /*        non-space char */
            }
        buff[++lastchar-1] = '\n';    /* insert \n and \0 after */
        buff[++lastchar-1] = '\0';    /* last non-space char */
        fputs(buff, fptr);            /* write row to file */
        }
    fclose(fptr);
}
```

```
/* returns character at screen location col, row */
/* cols from 1 to 80, rows from 1 to 25 */
char whatchar(int col, int row)
{
    int far *farptr;                    /* far pointer to int */
    char ch;                            /* screen character */

    farptr = (int far *) VIDEO_ADDR;    /* point to screen mem */
    ch = *( farptr + (row-1)*80 + col-1 ) ;  /* get character */
    return(ch);                         /* return char */
}
```

## Anagrams

This program generates all possible arrangements of letters in a given word. For instance, if you give it the word "post," it will print out pots, stop, spot, opts, and tops, as well as many four-letter combinations that aren't words: 24 permutations in all. If the word has n letters, there will be n factorial permutations. Thus, a four-letter word will have 24 permutations (4*3*2*1=24), and a five-letter word will have 120.

This probably isn't very useful, except for people who like word games; but the program does make use of an interesting programming technique: recursion. A recursive function is one that calls itself. Recursive functions are possible in C because all the variables for a particular function are kept on the stack. When the function calls itself, a new set of variables is created and placed on the stack; the new variables don't interfere with the variables created by a previous call to the same function.

An exception to this is when a function calls itself so many times that the stack overflows. The normal stack in Microsoft C contains about 2,048 bytes; if you get the error message "stack overflow" you know you've exceeded this capacity.

The recursive function in this program is called **permute()**. **Permute()** prints out all the permutations of whatever word is given it. It does this by printing out all the permutations of the word that is one letter shorter than the word passed to it. It then rotates the entire word, printing out all the permutations for the resulting word that again is one shorter than the original, and so on. For example, if the word is cat, **permute()** will permute the last two letters of the word, printing out cat and cta. Then it will rotate cat, getting atc. Then it will permute the last two letters of atc, printing atc and act. And so on. (Actually, for simplicity, the entire word is not passed to **permute()**, but only the initial position in the original word, starting with 0 for the left-most letter; this position is conveyed in the argument **startperm**.) The function **rotate()** simply rotates all the characters in the string **word**, starting at position **startrot**.

How does **permute()** permute all but one of the letters in a word? It calls itself, using the starting position of the shortened word as the argument. No matter how long a word it starts with, **permute()** keeps calling itself with shorter and shorter words, until finally it is left with a two-letter word. Since **permute()** rotates the word it is working on, it rotates these two letters, which is the same as permuting them. Then, instead of calling itself again, it returns—back up through all the calls to itself.

By using recursion, the function sidesteps the problem of how to permute the word; it just keeps rotating smaller and smaller parts of the word, and the result is to permute the word by a series of rotations.

If recursion is new to you, this process may require some thought. Here's the listing:

```c
/* anagram.c */
/* prints all possible permutations of a word */
#include <stdio.h>              /* for printf() */
#include <string.h>            /* for strlen() */

void permute(int position);    /* function prototypes */
void rotate(int position);

char word[40];
int length;
void main(void)
{
    printf("Type word: ");
    gets(word);               /* get word */
    length = strlen(word);
    permute(0);               /* call permute */
}

/* permute() */
/* prints all permutations of word2 */
void permute(int startperm)
{
    int j;
    if ( length-startperm < 2 )        /* exit if one char */
        return;
    for(j=startperm; j<length-1; j++) {   /* # chars in word -1 */
        permute(startperm+1);              /* permute all but first */
        rotate(startperm);                 /* rotate all chars */
        printf("%s\n", word);              /* print result */
    }
    permute(startperm+1);                 /* restore word to */
    rotate(startperm);                    /*    form at entry */
}

/* rotate() */
/* rotates word one character left */
/* word begins at character position startrot */
void rotate(int startrot)
{
    int j;
    char ch;
    ch = word[startrot];                  /* save first char */
```

```
    for (j=startrot; j<length-1; j++) /* move other chars left */
        word[j] = word[j+1];          /*    one position */
    word[length-1] = ch;              /* first char to last */
}
```

# WordStar Control Code Checker

Although this program applies specifically to the (original) WordStar word processing program, it can be modified to work with many other word processing programs as well, provided the programmer knows a little about the internal operation of the specific program.

In WordStar, special characters are used to signal the beginning and end of such text attributes as underlining and boldface. These characters show up on the screen as ^S (for underlining) and ^B (for bold). They are stored using the ASCII numbers for unused control codes: 13 hex for ^S and 2 hex for ^B. Usually the writer wants a pair of ^S symbols or a pair of ^B symbols, because if one member of a pair is left out, or the wrong symbol is typed, the entire text from that point on will be underlined or printed in bold. This sort of mistake is very common on large files.

The program shown here eliminates the problem by reading through a file and signalling instances of missing or unmatched control codes, giving the page and line number. The user can then edit the file to correct the mistakes.

A message is printed if matching codes are not found on the same line. This is a most conservative approach; messages will be printed, for example, in the case where an underlined phrase flows from one line to the next. This is easy to identify however; messages for two consecutive line numbers will be printed out.

This program not only checks for bold and underlining, but also for superscript codes: ^T. It assumes pages will be 55 lines long.

```
/* ccc.c */
/* control character check */
/* verifies that WordStar control codes are paired */
#include <stdio.h>
#define SS '\x13'    /* underline control code */
#define BB '\x02'    /* boldface control code */
#define TT '\x14'    /* superscript control code */
#define LPP 55       /* lines per page */
main(argc,argv)
int argc;
char *argv[];
{
    FILE *fptr;
    char ch, oldch;
    int linecnt = 0;
    int charcnt = 0;
    if ( argc != 2 )
        { printf("Type \"comcheck filename\"."); exit(); }
```

```
        if ( ( fptr=fopen(argv[1],"r") ) == NULL )
            { printf("Can't open file %s", argv[1]); exit(); }
        while ( (ch=getc(fptr)) != EOF )  {
            ch = ch & '\x7F';                 /* mask off high bit */
            if ( ch==SS || ch==BB || ch==TT ) {  /* control code? */
                charcnt++;                    /* count cc's */
                if ( charcnt % 2 == 0 )       /* even number of cc's? */
                    if (ch != oldch)  {       /* matches last cc? */
                        printf("Mismatched control codes");
                        printf(" on line %d", linecnt % LPP + 1 );
                        printf(" page %d\n",  linecnt / LPP + 1 );
                    }
                oldch = ch;                   /* new one becomes old */
            }
            else
                if ( ch == '\n' )  {          /* end of line? */
                    if (charcnt % 2 != 0) {   /* even number of cc's? */
                        printf("Odd no of control codes");
                        printf(" on line %d", linecnt % LPP + 1 );
                        printf(" page %d\n",  linecnt / LPP + 1 );
                    }
                    linecnt++;                /* count lines */
                    charcnt = 0;              /* reset cc count */
                }
        }  /* end while */
        fclose(fptr);
        if ( charcnt % 2 != 0)                /* check at EOF */
            printf("Odd no of control codes in last line.");
    }  /* end main */
```

## "Plumber's Nightmare" Maze

The IBM extended character set contains a family of characters that consist of double lines. There's a character with two vertical lines close together, one with two horizontal lines, and characters with bends to connect vertical to horizontal—both L and T bends are supplied.

With this assortment of parts it's possible to create, on the monochrome display, mazes that look like they were made from sections of pipe. That's what the program maze.c is designed to do.

This program starts by drawing a random line, using straight pipe sections and L bends. The line starts at the middle of the left side of the screen, and heads generally to the right, although it will take many random bends and twists—up, down, and back on itself. Eventually the line will make so many twists and turns that it will trap itself and be unable to continue (since lines can't cross each other). At this point, the program looks for anyplace in the maze having a vertical or horizontal line (not a bend). Finding a straight stretch, it installs a T intersection and starts another random line coming off the T. This process continues until the entire screen is filled with lines. The result looks like the proverbial plumber's nightmare.

When the maze is complete, you can either attempt to solve it right on the screen, or you can print it out, if you have a printer that supports the extended character set. Solving the maze is amusing, but the real fun comes from watching the program create the maze. The random lines hurry across the screen like maniacal worms; no one can tell what they'll do next.

The heart of the program is the **randline()** routine, which draws the random lines. A random number function, **random()** provides a random number between 1 and 7. (This routine uses the system clock as a starting point to generate the random number, so there's no need to "seed" the number before starting the program, as there is with many random-number generators.) A switch statement then selects the direction to go based on the random number. Four of the seven choices are to go right. This division of choice is done for two reasons. First, the initial line—or its descendants—eventually needs to reach the right side of the screen so there will be a complete path from left to right. Thus going too much to the left is a bad idea. Second, characters on the IBM are twice as high as they are wide, so it's important to minimize the amount of up and down motion in relation to the amount of left and right motion. Four moves to the right for each move in the other directions seems to provide about the right proportion.

Another important part of the program is the function **turn()**, which inserts the correct pipe connection for a particular kind of bend. For instance, if the random line finds itself going toward the right and is forced to turn upward by obstructions, then a right-to-up L-shaped connector must be inserted in the line at that point. Each such combination of initial direction and final direction requires a connection. The connections are placed in the array **table[4][4]**; and **turn()** uses this table to insert the correct fitting into the maze. Another function, **tee()**, selects the correct T-shaped fitting when a new random line is to start in the middle of an existing line.

After 200 random lines have been drawn, the program calls the **drawexit()** function to draw the exit. The exit consists of a T and a horizontal line; these are plugged into any straight section of pipe that lies on the right-hand border of the maze.

Maze.c requires the ANSI.SYS driver, since it clears the screen and positions the cursor using an escape sequence. Also, for version 3.0, it must be compiled with the \Ze option, since it uses **far** pointers to directly access the screen.

```
/* maze.c */
/* draws maze on screen */
/* uses direct screen memory access */
#include <stdio.h>               /* for printf() etc. */
#include <conio.h>               /* for kbhit() */
#include <time.h>                /* for time() */
#include <process.h>             /* for exit() */
#define VIDEO_ADDR 0xB8000000    /* video address */
                                 /*    use B0000000 for mono */
#define MAXROWS 23               /* dimensions within border */
```

```
#define MAXCOLS 78
#define FALSE 0                 /* logic values */
#define TRUE 1
#define RIGHT 0                 /* directions */
#define LEFT  1
#define UP    2
#define DOWN  3
#define BLANK 32                /* ASCII blank */
#define HORZ 205                /* horizontal double line */
#define VERT 186                /* vertical double line */
#define NONE   7
#define L_UP 188                /* L connections */
#define L_DN 187                /*    made from */
#define R_UP 200                /* double lines */
#define R_DN 201
#define T_DN 203
#define T_UP 202
#define T_RT 204
#define T_LF 185
#define BORDER 178              /* gray block */

int lastd;
char table[4][4]={ {HORZ, NONE, L_UP, L_DN},
                   {NONE, HORZ, R_UP, R_DN},
                   {R_DN, L_DN, VERT, NONE},
                   {R_UP, L_UP, NONE, VERT} } ;

void randline(int x, int y);    /* function prototypes */
int random(int rmax);
void turn(int direction, int x, int y);
void border(void);
void tee(char spot, int col, int row);
void drawexit(void);
void goexit(void);
void putscr(char ch, int col, int row);
char getscr(int col, int row);

void main(void)
{
   int col, row, j;
   char spot;
   int k;

   printf("\x1B[2J");                   /* clear screen */
   border();                            /* draw border */
   col=0; row=12; lastd=RIGHT;
   randline(col, row);                  /* draw first line */

   for (j=1; kbhit() == 0; j++ )        /* draw more lines */
      {
      do
```

```
                   {
                   col = random(MAXCOLS-1);      /* choose random spot */
                   row = random(MAXROWS-1);
                   spot = getscr(col, row);
                   }                             /* find spot with line */
             while ( spot != '\xCD' && spot != '\xBA' );
             tee(spot, col, row);   /* insert T in line, draw new line */
             if (j == 200)              /* after 200 lines */
                drawexit();             /* draw exit */
             } /* end of for */
        goexit();                       /* all over */
} /* end of main */

/* randline */
/* draws random line on screen, starting at x, y */
void randline(int x, int y)
{
    char trapped = FALSE;

    while (trapped == FALSE)
        {
        switch ( random(7) )
            {
            case 1 : /* Draw line to the right */
            case 2 :
            case 3 :
            case 4 :
               if ( getscr(x+1, y) == BLANK )
                  turn (RIGHT, x++, y);
               break;
            case 5 : /* Draw line to the left */
               if ( getscr(x-1, y) == BLANK )
                  turn (LEFT, x--, y);
               break;
            case 6 : /* Draw line up (decrease y) */
               if ( getscr(x, y-1) == BLANK )
                  turn (UP, x, y--);
               break;
            case 7 : /* Draw line down (increase y) */
               if ( getscr(x, y+1) == BLANK )
                  turn (DOWN, x, y++);
               break;
            } /* end of switch */
        if ( (getscr(x+1,y)!=BLANK) && (getscr(x-1, y)!=BLANK) &&
             (getscr(x,y+1)!=BLANK) && (getscr(x, y-1)!=BLANK) )
           trapped=TRUE;
        if (kbhit() != 0)
           goexit();
        } /* end of while */
} /* end of randline */
```

```
/* random */
/* returns random number between 1 and rmax */
int random(int rmax)
{
    long seconds;
    static int rand;
    time(&seconds);
    rand = 0x7fff & ( (int)seconds + rand*273 ) >> 4;
    return( (rand % rmax) + 1 );
}



/* turn */
/* function to print correct character to make turn */
/* direction is where we're going */
/* lastd is where we're coming from */
/* turn characters are in array table */
void turn(int direction, int x, int y)
{
    putscr( table [lastd] [direction], x, y );
    lastd=direction;
}

/* border */
/* draws border around screen */
void border(void)
{
    int j;
    for (j=0; j < MAXCOLS+2; j++)
        {
        putscr(BORDER, j, 0);              /* draw top */
        putscr(BORDER, j, MAXROWS+1);      /* draw bottom */
        }
    for (j=0; j < MAXROWS+2; j++)
        {
        putscr(BORDER, 0, j);              /* draw right */
        putscr(BORDER, MAXCOLS+1, j);      /* draw left */
        }
}

/* tee */
/* inserts T in existing horiz or vert line at col, row */
void tee(char spot, int col, int row)
{
    if (spot=='\xCD')                              /* horiz line */
        {
        if (getscr(col, row+1)==BLANK)             /* go down */
            {
            putscr(T_DN,col,row); lastd=DOWN;
            randline(col,++row);
            }
```

```
        else
           if (getscr(col, row-1)==BLANK)          /* go up */
              {
              putscr(T_UP,col,row); lastd=UP;
              randline(col,--row);
              }
        }
     else                                          /* vert line */
        {
        if (getscr(col+1, row)==BLANK)             /* go right */
           {
           putscr(T_RT,col,row); lastd=RIGHT;
           randline(++col,row);
           }
        else
           if (getscr(col-1, row)==BLANK)          /* go left */
              {
              putscr(T_LF,col,row); lastd=LEFT;
              randline(--col,row);
              }
        } /* end of else */
} /* end of tee */


/* drawexit */
/* draws exit line on right edge of maze */
/* looks for vertical line (\xBA) to start on */
void drawexit(void)
{
   int j;

   for ( j=8; getscr(MAXCOLS, j) != '\xBA'; j++ )
      ;
      putscr(T_RT, MAXCOLS,j);     /* right tee */
      putscr(HORZ, MAXCOLS+1,j);   /* horiz line */
}

/* goexit */
/* puts cursor in lower right corner and exits */
void goexit(void)
{
   printf("\x1B[%d;%dH", 24, 1); /* move cursor */
   getch();                        /* digest keystroke */
   getch();                        /* wait for another key */
   exit(0);
}

/* putscr */
/* puts character ch on screen */
/* at location col, row */
void putscr(char ch, int col, int row)
```

```
    {
        int far *farptr;
        int attr=0x0700;   /* attribute for normal text */

        farptr = (int far *) VIDEO_ADDR; /* screen memory */
        *( farptr + row*80 + col ) = ( (int)ch & 0x00ff) | attr;
    }


/* getscr */
/* returns character stored in screen memory */
/* at location col, row */
char getscr(int col, int row)
    {
        int far *farptr;
        char ch;
        farptr = (int far *) VIDEO_ADDR;
        ch = *( farptr + row*80 + col );
        return(ch);
```

## Sieve of Eratosthenes

The sieve of Eratosthenes is a way of calculating prime numbers. (A prime is an integer with no divisors but itself and 1.) The method works like this. We start with a list of integers. First, all the even numbers (except 2) are crossed off the list, since no number that is divisible by 2 can be a prime. Then all the numbers divisible by 3 (except 3) are crossed off, since they can't be primes. Then all the numbers divisible by 4 (except 4) are crossed off, and so on, until nothing but primes are left.

Using this method to calculate the primes up to 16,381 is widely used as a test for comparing the computational speed of different languages.

Here's a version of the Sieve of Eratosthenes written in Microsoft C version 4.0:

```
/* prime10.c */
/* calculates primes using sieve of Eratosthenes */
/* does 10 iterations */
/* #define PRINT   */                /* define to print primes */
char mark[16382];                    /* character array */
main()
    {
        int count, n;
        register int j, k;           /* register variables */
        printf("Starting\n");        /* start timing */
        for(n=0; n<10; n++)          /* ten iterations */
            {
            count = 0;               /* count number of primes */
            for(j=3; j<16382; j+=2)  /* set all even numbers */
                mark[j] = 0;         /*    in array to 0 */
```

```
        for(j=3; j<16382; j+=2)        /* examine even mumbers */
            if( !mark[j] )             /* if not crossed off list, */
                {                      /*    it's a prime */
                #ifdef PRINT           /* if in print mode, */
                printf("%8d", j);      /*    print it */
                #endif PRINT
                count++;               /* count it */
                for(k=j+j; k<16382; k+=j)  /* cross it, and all */
                    mark[k] = 1;       /* multiples, off list */
                }
        #ifdef PRINT                   /* if in print mode, */
        printf("\nCounted %d primes.\n", count); /* print total */
        #endif PRINT
        }
    printf("\nDone.\n");               /* stop timing */
}
```

When a timing test is run, the primes are not actually printed out, since the printing process would slow down the program and make comparison with other languages difficult. When the program is not used for timing, the PRINT identifier and #ifdef directives are used to activate printf() statements to print out the primes.

To improve timing accuracy, the program uses 10 iterations of the process.

In interpreted Microsoft BASIC, on a standard IBM XT, the process takes 1,830 seconds to complete the 10 iterations. In assembly language it takes 8 seconds. In Microsoft C 4.0 it also takes 8 seconds, which shows that, at least in this instance, the C compiler generates code that is about as good as assembly language.

To achieve this speed, the array must be of type **char** (not **int**), and **j** and **k** must be made register variables. Without this fine-tuning, the program takes 18 seconds.

# C

---

# *Hexadecimal Numbering*

When dealing with the internal operations of the IBM family of computers it is generally more convenient to use the hexadecimal numbering system than the decimal numbering system. This is because computers themselves actually use a third numbering system: binary.

If you're not familiar with numbering systems as they apply to computers, these statements may sound cryptic. You'll find, though, that there's a perfectly reasonable explanation for hexadecimal. In this appendix we'll discuss what numbering systems are, why computers use binary, how this relates to hexadecimal, and how to use hexadecimal in everyday life.

## Numbering Systems

When we talk about different numbering systems we're really talking about the *base* of the numbering systems. The decimal system is *base 10*, the hexadecimal system is *base 16*, and so forth. What is the base of a numbering system? Simply put, it's how many digits you use before you run out and have to start using a different column (sometimes called a "place-holder") instead of different digits.

For instance, in the decimal system, we count from 0 to 9; then we've run out of digits, so we put a 1 in the column to the left—the ten's column—and start out again in the one's column with 0:

```
 0
 1
 2
 3
 4
 5
 6
 7
 8
 9    ← last available digit
10    ← start using a new column
11
12
...
```

(The three dots indicate that the numbers go on and on—to infinity, if we want.) The 0 means there's nothing in a particular column, and each column represents numbers that are 10 times bigger than those in the column to the right.

This all seems perfectly natural to those of us who have graduated from third grade. However, the choice of 10 as a base is actually quite arbitrary, having its origins in the fact that we have 10 fingers. It's perfectly possible to use other bases as well. For instance, if we wanted to use a base 8 or *octal* system, which uses only eight digits (0 to 7), here's how counting would look:

```
0
1
2
3
4
5
6
7    ← last available digit
10   ← start using a new column
11
12
...
```

Many other numbering systems can be imagined. The Mesopotamians used a base 60 system, which survives in our era for measuring minutes and seconds, both for time and for angles. The number 12 has also been used as a base. From this system we retain our 12-hour system for time, the number of inches in a foot, and so on. The moral is that any base can be used in a numbering system, although some bases are more convenient than others.

## Computers and Binary

As it turns out, computers are most comfortable with a *binary* numbering system. In a binary system, instead of ten digits as in decimal, there are only two digits: 0 and 1. This means you can't count very far before you need to start using the next column:

```
0
1    ← last available digit
10   ← start using a new column
11
...
```

Binary is a natural system for computers because each of the thousands of electronic circuits in the computer can be in one of two states: on or off. These circuits are like the switches that turn on the lights in your house (unless you use dimmer switches): they can be either on or off, with nothing in between. Thus, the binary system corresponds nicely with the circuits in the computer: 0 means *off*, and 1 means *on*.

A unit of information that can have one of two possible values like this is called a "bit," a synonym for a binary digit.

These binary circuits are generally arranged in groups. Let's look at a very small group: two circuits. We'll list all the combinations of *on* and *off* the two circuits can represent:

| First Circuit | Second Circuit |
|---|---|
| off | off |
| off | on |
| on | off |
| on | on |

Thus the two circuits can be placed in four different states. Another way of saying this is that they can represent four different binary numbers:

| First Circuit | Second Circuit | Binary Number |
|---|---|---|
| off | off | 00 |
| off | on | 01 |
| on | off | 10 |
| on | on | 11 |

Suppose we used three circuits instead of two? We could represent twice as many binary numbers.

| First Circuit | Second Circuit | Third Circuit | Binary Number | Decimal Number |
|---|---|---|---|---|
| off | off | off | 000 | 0 |
| off | off | on | 001 | 1 |
| off | on | off | 010 | 2 |
| off | on | on | 011 | 3 |
| on | off | off | 100 | 4 |
| on | off | on | 101 | 5 |
| on | on | off | 110 | 6 |
| on | on | on | 111 | 7 |

Note that each time another circuit is added, the number of numbers that can be represented is doubled.

Using a group of three circuits like this to represent eight numbers corresponds to the octal system. In some computer systems, the octal system is a natural one because the number of circuits, or bits, grouped together is divisible by 3. A 12-bit number, for instance, could be represented by four octal (3-bit) numbers.

# Bytes and Four-Bit Combinations

However, on the IBM, groups of *eight* bits are typically placed together. This forms a *byte*. The eight-bit byte is useful because it provides a convenient way to represent *characters*. Actually, a seven-bit byte would be big enough to represent a character, since seven bits holds numbers up to 128 decimal, enough for upper- and lowercase letters, punctuation, digits, and some control characters. However, seven is an awkward number, being odd, so an eight-bit byte became the standard.

The eight-bit byte, however, is not divisible by 3, so octal is not so convenient for representing eight-bit bytes. However, the eight-bit byte is divisible by 4. Four bits can represent numbers from 0 to 15:

| Binary | Decimal | Binary | Decimal |
|--------|---------|--------|---------|
| 0000 | 0 | 1000 | 8 |
| 0001 | 1 | 1001 | 9 |
| 0010 | 2 | 1010 | 10 |
| 0011 | 3 | 1011 | 11 |
| 0100 | 4 | 1100 | 12 |
| 0101 | 5 | 1101 | 13 |
| 0110 | 6 | 1110 | 14 |
| 0111 | 7 | 1111 | 15 |

Placing two such four-bit groups together then forms an eight-bit byte:

| Left Side | | Right Side | | Eight-Bit Byte |
|-----------|-----|------------|------|----------------|
| 0000 | and | 0001 | make | 00000001 |
| 0001 | and | 0010 | make | 00010010 |
| 1110 | and | 0101 | make | 11100101 |
| and so on. | | | | |

From the table of correspondences between binary and decimal numbers, shown above, we can figure out the decimal equivalent of each four-bit combination, and from this we can calculate the value of the eight-bit byte.

```
0000 and 0001 make 00000001   ← binary
   0 and    1 make        1   ← decimal
```

This seems reasonable: 1 binary is 1 decimal. What about

```
0001 and 0010 make 00010010   ← binary
   1 and    2 make       18   ← decimal
```

Here 00010010 binary is 18 decimal. How do we know that 1 on the left and 2 on the right combine to make 18? The four-bit combination on the left is worth 16 times more than the four bits on the right, so we multiply it by 16: 1 times 16 is 16. We multiply the combination on the right by one, which gives us 2. Adding 16 and 2 gives us 18.

Similarly,

```
1110 and 0101 form 11100101   ← binary
  14 and    5 form       229  ← decimal
```

Here, 14 times 16 is 224. Adding 5 gives us 229.

## Hexadecimal

So we can figure out what binary numbers mean, by translating them into decimal. But the process is difficult. We need to look up the decimal values of the numbers in the table, and remember to multiply the 4-bit combination on the left by 16 before adding the 4-bit combination on the right. If we wanted to talk about numbers twice as big—2 bytes, or 16 bits—things would be harder still.

Worst of all, the decimal number doesn't immediately tell us anything about the bit configuration of the binary number it represents. You can't look at 229 decimal, for instance, and immediately see that the last four bits are 0101.

The problem is that one decimal digit does not represent an integral number of binary digits. A one-digit decimal number covers binary numbers up to 1001; the binary number after that, 1010, still uses four digits, while the decimal number shifts from one digit to two. When the binary number shifts from four digits (1111) to five digits (10000), the decimal representation remains at two digits, going from 15 to 16. This relationship between binary and decimal is complex; translating from one system to another is time-consuming and nonintuitive.

Using the hexadecimal numbering system solves these problems. Hexadecimal is base 16; there are 16 digits in the system. Since one hex digit can represent 16 numbers, it corresponds to exactly four binary digits. This makes for a very clean correspondence between binary and hexadecimal.

But representing 16 distinct digits poses a typographical problem. Which symbols should be used to represent the digits greater than 9? The ordinary decimal digits 0 to 9 are fine for the first 10 digits, but there are still 6 to go. An obvious solution is to use letters of the alphabet for the remaining digits. So the sixteen hex digits are commonly represented as 0, 1, 2, 3, 4, 5, 6, 7, 8, 9, A, B, C, D, E, and F. (Lowercase versions of the letters may also be used.)

## Correspondence Between Hex and Binary

Now each four bits is represented by exactly one hex digit. When the binary number changes from four to five digits, the hex number changes from 1 to two digits, as you can see in the table.

| Binary | Hex | Decimal | Binary | Hex | Decimal |
|--------|-----|---------|--------|-----|---------|
| 0000 | 0 | 0 | 1011 | B | 11 |
| 0001 | 1 | 1 | 1100 | C | 12 |
| 0010 | 2 | 2 | 1101 | D | 13 |
| 0011 | 3 | 3 | 1110 | E | 14 |
| 0100 | 4 | 4 | 1111 | F | 15 |
| 0101 | 5 | 5 | 10000 | 10 | 16 |
| 0110 | 6 | 6 | 10001 | 11 | 17 |
| 0111 | 7 | 7 | 10010 | 12 | 18 |
| 1000 | 8 | 8 | . . . | | |
| 1001 | 9 | 9 | . . . | | |
| 1010 | A | 10 | | | |

Now let's see how much more easily the translations of the binary numbers, shown above as binary to decimal, can be carried out from binary to hexadecimal:

```
0001 and 0010 make 00010010   ← binary
   1 and    2 make       12   ← hexadecimal
1110 and 0101 form 11100101   ← binary
   E and    5 form       E5   ← hexadecimal
```

Multiplication is not needed, nor is addition. All we need to do is look up the correspondence between binary and hex: 1 binary is 1 hex, 10 binary is 2 hex, 1110 binary is E hex, 0101 binary is 5 hex. Then we write down the hex digits side by side.

In fact, since there are only 16 hex digits, it's fairly easy to memorize the binary equivalent for each one. Quick now, what's binary 1101 in hex? That's right, D. You're already getting the hang of it. With a little practice it's easy to translate even long numbers into hex: 0100 1111 0110 1101 binary is 4F6D hex. This is how the two-byte quantities used to indicate integers in C are represented.

A useful thing to do until you've memorized the binary equivalents of the hex numbers is to write them on a card and paste it on the front of your computer.

## Using Hexadecimal

Hexadecimal numbers are used for a variety of purposes in the IBM computer system. One common use is to represent memory addresses. Assembly language programmers like this system because the hex numbers correspond so well with the binary pattern used in the microprocessor's registers to represent the address. Address registers on the IBM typically are 16-bit registers; they can hold four hex bits. Addresses run from 0 to FFFF hex (65,535 decimal).

Hex numbers are also used to indicate particular bit patterns in the microprocessor's registers and ports. Bits are numbered starting with 0 on the right; so for one byte the bits are numbered from 0 to 7. If bit 0 is to be set in a particular byte, this corresponds to the bit pattern 00000001, which is 01 hexadecimal. If bit 7 and bit 1 are to be set, this is 10000001 binary, which is 81 hex. In a program, rather than writing all those 0s and 1s, we can write 01 hex or 81 hex; it's much simpler and more compact than using binary (and, in any case, there is no binary representation of numbers in C).

As with most unfamiliar subjects, learning hexadecimal requires a little practice. Try writing down binary numbers and translating them into hex; then try going the other way. Then try going from decimal to hex and back again. Before long you'll be speaking hexadecimal as if you'd known it all your life.

# D

# *Bibliography*

There are hundreds of books on various aspects of C available. This bibliography covers only a very few of them—those we like and find especially useful for programming in C on the IBM.

Because C was originally developed on UNIX systems, many books on it assume a Unix environment. This assumption is not ideal for those working in MS-DOS on the IBM (or clones), but it is not fatal either. Here are some Unix-oriented C books that are nevertheless very helpful for the IBM C programmer.

Bolski, M. I., *The C Programmer's Handbook*, Prentice Hall, 1985. A well-organized small reference book, packed full of brief examples and explanations. A useful place to look something up in a hurry.

Feuer, Alan, *The C Puzzle Book*, Prentice Hall, 1982. Using this book will hone your programming ability to a fine edge. If you can answer all the questions it poses you're ready for anything.

Gehani, Narain, *Advanced C: Food for the Educated Palate*, Computer Science Press, 1985. A literate exploration of some of the finer points of C. This book is fun to read after you've digested the fundamentals.

Kernighan, Brian and Dennis Ritchie, *The C Programming Language*, Prentice Hall, 1978. This book defined the C language, at least for the UNIX-based systems on which C was originally developed. In C, the watchword still is: when in doubt, follow Kernighan and Ritchie. This is not a beginner's book, but it is useful and interesting and it covers C thoroughly. Serious C programmers will want to own a copy.

Kernighan, Brian and Dennis Ritchie, *The C Programming Language, The Second Edition*, Prentice Hall, 1988. Latest edition of this work.

Waite, Mitchell, Stephen Prata, and Donald Martin, *C Primer Plus*, Howard W. Sams & Co., 1987. A classic generic C tutorial, clearly written and easy to learn from, full of valuable insights about C.

Many recent books deal specifically with C on the IBM. We've listed some of these here. We've also included several books which, although they don't deal with C specifically, may be of interest to the C programmer working in the IBM environment.

Chesley, Harry and Mitchell Waite, *Supercharging C with Assembly Language*, Addison Wesley, 1987. This book explores ways to squeeze the last ounce of speed and capability from your C program. A principal method is the use of assembly language routines in critical places in the program.

Jordain, Robert, *Programmer's Problem Solver*, A Brady book (Prentice Hall Press), 1986. This book is crammed full of examples of how to get the IBM to do what you want.

Examples are in BASIC and assembly, and explanations are sometimes cryptic, but it's an extremely useful book for serious IBM programmers.

Lafore, Robert, *Assembly Language Primer for the IBM PC and XT*, New American Library, 1984. People tell us that this is still one of the best books for learning assembly language from scratch, should you want to incorporate AL routines into your C programs. It works on the AT as well as the PC and XT.

Norton, Peter, *The Peter Norton Programmer's Guide to the IBM PC*, Microsoft Press, 1985. This is essentially a guide to the ROM BIOS routines built into the IBM, although other topics are covered as well. It's a lot more fun trying to figure out the ROM BIOS from this book than it is from the cryptic program comments in IBM's *Technical Reference* manual.

Prata, Stephen, *Advanced C Primer+ +*, Howard W. Sams & Co., 1986. Dr. Prata provides an in-depth exploration of C on the IBM, including a very readable description of using assembly language routines with C programs.

# E

## ASCII Chart

**Table E-1. IBM Character Codes**

| DEC | HEX | Symbol | Key | Use in C |
|---|---|---|---|---|
| 0 | 00 | (NULL) | Ctrl 2 | |
| 1 | 01 | ☺ | Ctr-A | |
| 2 | 02 | ☻ | Ctrl B | |
| 3 | 03 | ♥ | Ctrl C | |
| 4 | 04 | ♦ | Ctrl D | |
| 5 | 05 | ♣ | Ctrl E | |
| 6 | 06 | ♠ | Ctrl F | |
| 7 | 07 | ● | Ctrl G | Beep |
| 8 | 08 | ◘ | Backspace | Backspace |
| 9 | 09 | ○ | Tab | Tab |
| 10 | 0A | ◙ | Ctrl J | Linefeed (newline) |
| 11 | 0B | ♂ | Ctrl K | Vertical Tab |
| 12 | 0C | ♀ | Ctrl L | Form feed |
| 13 | 0D | ♪ | Enter | Carriage Return |
| 14 | 0E | ♫ | Ctrl N | |
| 15 | 0F | ☼ | Ctrl O | |
| 16 | 10 | ► | Ctrl P | |
| 17 | 11 | ◄ | Ctrl Q | |
| 18 | 12 | ↕ | Ctrl R | |
| 19 | 13 | ‼ | Ctrl S | |
| 20 | 14 | ¶ | Ctrl T | |
| 21 | 15 | § | Ctrl U | |
| 22 | 16 | ▬ | Ctrl V | |
| 23 | 17 | | Ctrl W | |
| 24 | 18 | ↑ | Ctrl X | |
| 25 | 19 | ↓ | Ctrl Y | |
| 26 | 1A | → | Ctrl Z | |
| 27 | 1B | ← | Esc | Escape |
| 28 | 1C | | Ctrl \ | |
| 29 | 1D | ↔ | Ctrl ] | |
| 30 | 1E | ▲ | Ctrl 6 | |

## Table E-1 (cont)

| DEC | HEX | Symbol | Key |
|-----|-----|--------|-----|
| 31 | 1F | ▼ | Ctrl - |
| 32 | 20 | | SPACE BAR |
| 33 | 21 | ! | ! |
| 34 | 22 | " | " |
| 35 | 23 | # | # |
| 36 | 24 | $ | $ |
| 37 | 25 | % | % |
| 38 | 26 | & | & |
| 39 | 27 | ' | ' |
| 40 | 28 | ( | ( |
| 41 | 29 | ) | ) |
| 42 | 2A | * | * |
| 43 | 2B | + | + |
| 44 | 2C | , | , |
| 45 | 2D | – | – |
| 46 | 2E | . | . |
| 47 | 2F | / | / |
| 48 | 30 | 0 | 0 |
| 49 | 31 | 1 | 1 |
| 50 | 32 | 2 | 2 |
| 51 | 33 | 3 | 3 |
| 52 | 34 | 4 | 4 |
| 53 | 35 | 5 | 5 |
| 54 | 36 | 6 | 6 |
| 55 | 37 | 7 | 7 |
| 56 | 38 | 8 | 8 |
| 57 | 39 | 9 | 9 |
| 58 | 3A | : | : |
| 59 | 3B | ; | ; |
| 60 | 3C | < | < |
| 61 | 3D | = | = |
| 62 | 3E | > | > |
| 63 | 3F | ? | ? |
| 64 | 40 | @ | @ |
| 65 | 41 | A | A |
| 66 | 42 | B | B |
| 67 | 43 | C | C |
| 68 | 44 | D | D |
| 69 | 45 | E | E |
| 70 | 46 | F | F |
| 71 | 47 | G | G |
| 72 | 48 | H | H |
| 73 | 49 | I | I |

## Table E-1 (cont)

| DEC | HEX | Symbol | Key |
|-----|-----|--------|-----|
| 74 | 4A | J | J |
| 75 | 4B | K | K |
| 76 | 4C | L | L |
| 77 | 4D | M | M |
| 78 | 4E | N | N |
| 79 | 4F | O | O |
| 80 | 50 | P | P |
| 81 | 51 | Q | Q |
| 82 | 52 | R | R |
| 83 | 53 | S | S |
| 84 | 54 | T | T |
| 85 | 55 | U | U |
| 86 | 56 | V | V |
| 87 | 57 | W | W |
| 88 | 58 | X | X |
| 89 | 59 | Y | Y |
| 90 | 5A | Z | Z |
| 91 | 5B | [ | [ |
| 92 | 5C | \ | \ |
| 93 | 5D | ] | ] |
| 94 | 5E | ^ | ^ |
| 95 | 5F | _ | _ |
| 96 | 60 | ` | ` |
| 97 | 61 | a | a |
| 98 | 62 | b | b |
| 99 | 63 | c | c |
| 100 | 64 | d | d |
| 101 | 65 | e | e |
| 102 | 66 | f | f |
| 103 | 67 | g | g |
| 104 | 68 | h | h |
| 105 | 69 | i | i |
| 106 | 6A | j | j |
| 107 | 6B | k | k |
| 108 | 6C | l | l |
| 109 | 6D | m | m |
| 110 | 6E | n | n |
| 111 | 6F | o | o |
| 112 | 70 | p | p |
| 113 | 71 | q | q |
| 114 | 72 | r | r |
| 115 | 73 | s | s |
| 116 | 74 | t | t |

## Table E-1 (cont)

| DEC | HEX | Symbol | Key |
|-----|-----|--------|-----|
| 117 | 75 | u | u |
| 118 | 76 | v | v |
| 119 | 77 | w | w |
| 120 | 78 | x | x |
| 121 | 79 | y | y |
| 122 | 7A | z | z |
| 123 | 7B | { | { |
| 124 | 7C | ¦ | ¦ |
| 125 | 7D | } | } |
| 126 | 7E | ~ | ~ |
| 127 | 7F | Δ | Ctrl ← |
| 128 | 80 | Ç | Alt 128 |
| 129 | 81 | ü | Alt 129 |
| 130 | 82 | é | Alt 130 |
| 131 | 83 | â | Alt 131 |
| 132 | 84 | ä | Alt 132 |
| 133 | 85 | à | Alt 133 |
| 134 | 86 | å | Alt 134 |
| 135 | 87 | ç | Alt 135 |
| 136 | 88 | ê | Alt 136 |
| 137 | 89 | ë | Alt 137 |
| 138 | 8A | è | Alt 138 |
| 139 | 8B | ï | Alt 139 |
| 140 | 8C | î | Alt 140 |
| 141 | 8D | ì | Alt 141 |
| 142 | 8E | Ä | Alt 142 |
| 143 | 8F | Å | Alt 143 |
| 144 | 90 | É | Alt 144 |
| 145 | 91 | æ | Alt 145 |
| 146 | 92 | Æ | Alt 146 |
| 147 | 93 | ô | Alt 147 |
| 148 | 94 | ö | Alt 148 |
| 149 | 95 | ò | Alt 149 |
| 150 | 96 | û | Alt 150 |
| 151 | 97 | ù | Alt 151 |
| 152 | 98 | ÿ | Alt 152 |
| 153 | 99 | Ö | Alt 153 |
| 154 | 9A | Ü | Alt 154 |
| 155 | 9B | ¢ | Alt 155 |
| 156 | 9C | £ | Alt 156 |
| 157 | 9D | ¥ | Alt 157 |
| 158 | 9E | $P_t$ | Alt 158 |
| 159 | 9F | $f$ | Alt 159 |

## Table E-1 (cont)

| DEC | HEX | Symbol | Key |
|-----|-----|--------|-----|
| 160 | A0 | á | Alt 160 |
| 161 | A1 | í | Alt 161 |
| 162 | A2 | ó | Alt 162 |
| 163 | A3 | ú | Alt 163 |
| 164 | A4 | ñ | Alt 164 |
| 165 | A5 | Ñ | Alt 165 |
| 166 | A6 | a̲ | Alt 166 |
| 167 | A7 | o̲ | Alt 167 |
| 168 | A8 | ¿ | Alt 168 |
| 169 | A9 | ⌐ | Alt 169 |
| 170 | AA | ¬ | Alt 170 |
| 171 | AB | ½ | Alt 171 |
| 172 | AC | ¼ | Alt 172 |
| 173 | AD | ¡ | Alt 173 |
| 174 | AE | « | Alt 174 |
| 175 | AF | » | Alt 175 |
| 176 | B0 | ░ | Alt 176 |
| 177 | B1 | ▒ | Alt 177 |
| 178 | B2 | ▓ | Alt 178 |
| 179 | B3 | │ | Alt 179 |
| 180 | B4 | ┤ | Alt 180 |
| 181 | B5 | ╡ | Alt 181 |
| 182 | B6 | ╢ | Alt 182 |
| 183 | B7 | ╖ | Alt 183 |
| 184 | B8 | ╕ | Alt 184 |
| 185 | B9 | ╣ | Alt 185 |
| 186 | BA | ║ | Alt 186 |
| 187 | BB | ╗ | Alt 187 |
| 188 | BC | ╝ | Alt 188 |
| 189 | BD | ╜ | Alt 189 |
| 190 | BE | ╛ | Alt 190 |
| 191 | BF | ┐ | Alt 191 |
| 192 | C0 | └ | Alt 192 |
| 193 | C1 | ┴ | Alt 193 |
| 194 | C2 | ┬ | Alt 194 |
| 195 | C3 | ├ | Alt 195 |
| 196 | C4 | ─ | Alt 196 |
| 197 | C5 | ┼ | Alt 197 |
| 198 | C6 | ╞ | Alt 198 |
| 199 | C7 | ╟ | Alt 199 |
| 200 | C8 | ╚ | Alt 200 |
| 201 | C9 | ╔ | Alt 201 |
| 202 | CA | ╩ | Alt 202 |

## Table E-1 (cont)

| DEC | HEX | Symbol | Key |
|-----|-----|--------|-----|
| 203 | CB | $\overline{\top}$ | Alt 203 |
| 204 | CC | $\Vdash$ | Alt 204 |
| 205 | CD | = | Alt 205 |
| 206 | CE | $\#$ | Alt 206 |
| 207 | CF | $\perp$ | Alt 207 |
| 208 | D0 | $\parallel$ | Alt 208 |
| 209 | D1 | $\overline{\top}$ | Alt 209 |
| 210 | D2 | $\top$ | Alt 210 |
| 211 | D3 | $\parallel$ | Alt 211 |
| 212 | D4 | L | Alt 212 |
| 213 | D5 | F | Alt 213 |
| 214 | D6 | $\top$ | Alt 214 |
| 215 | D7 | $\#$ | Alt 215 |
| 216 | D8 | $\dagger$ | Alt 216 |
| 217 | D9 | $\lrcorner$ | Alt 217 |
| 218 | DA | $\ulcorner$ | Alt 218 |
| 219 | DB | █ | Alt 219 |
| 220 | DC | ▪ | Alt 220 |
| 221 | DD | ▌ | Alt 221 |
| 222 | DE | ▐ | Alt 222 |
| 223 | DF | ▪ | Alt 223 |
| 224 | E0 | $\alpha$ | Alt 224 |
| 225 | E1 | $\beta$ | Alt 225 |
| 226 | E2 | $\Gamma$ | Alt 226 |
| 227 | E3 | $\pi$ | Alt 227 |
| 228 | E4 | $\Sigma$ | Alt 228 |
| 229 | E5 | $\sigma$ | Alt 229 |
| 230 | E6 | $\mu$ | Alt 230 |
| 231 | E7 | $\tau$ | Alt 231 |
| 232 | E8 | $\Phi$ | Alt 232 |
| 233 | E9 | $\Theta$ | Alt 233 |
| 234 | EA | $\Omega$ | Alt 234 |
| 235 | EB | $\delta$ | Alt 235 |
| 236 | EC | $\infty$ | Alt 236 |
| 237 | ED | $\varphi$ | Alt 237 |
| 238 | EE | $\epsilon$ | Alt 238 |
| 239 | EF | $\cap$ | Alt 240 |
| 240 | F0 | $\equiv$ | Alt 241 |
| 241 | F1 | $\pm$ | Alt 242 |
| 242 | F2 | $\geq$ | Alt 243 |
| 243 | F3 | $\leq$ | Alt 244 |
| 244 | F4 | $\lceil$ | Alt 245 |
| 245 | F5 | $\rfloor$ | Alt 246 |

## Table E-1 (cont)

| DEC | HEX | Symbol | Key |
|-----|-----|--------|-----|
| 246 | F6 | ÷ | Alt 246 |
| 247 | F7 | ≈ | Alt 247 |
| 248 | F8 | ° | Alt 248 |
| 249 | F9 | • | Alt 249 |
| 250 | FA | • | Alt 250 |
| 251 | FB | $\sqrt{\ }$ | Alt 251 |
| 252 | FC | $\eta$ | Alt 252 |
| 253 | FD | $^2$ | Alt 253 |
| 254 | FE | ■ | Alt 254 |
| 255 | FF | (blank) | Alt 255 |

Those key sequences consisting of "Ctrl" are typed in by pressing the CTRL key, and while it is being held down, pressing the key indicated. These sequences are based on those defined for the IBM Personal Computer series keyboards. The key sequences may be defined differently on other keyboards.

IBM Extended ASCII characters can be displayed by pressing the Alt key and then typing the decimal code of the character on the keypad.

# F

# *The CodeView Debugger*

Debugging is a difficult process to describe. By their nature, program bugs are unexpected and irrational, so it is hard to develop a way of finding them that will work in all programming situations.

Staring hard at the program listing will uncover a fair number of bugs. Look for typos that have slipped by the compiler and for simple logic errors. Are the loop limits what they should be? Have you confused the ( = ) and ( == ) operators? Have you used the correct format specifiers in **printf()** and **scanf()** statements? Mentally step through the program, line-by-line. Does it really do what you intended?

If you've done all this and still can't see what's wrong, further steps are in order.

For short programs such as those in this book, the simple strategem of inserting **printf()** statements at appropriate places in the code may uncover most bugs. Such diagnostic statements print out the values of relevant variables at particular points in the program, so that the error eventually becomes clear. Many programmers use this system exclusively, but it has its disadvantages. One disadvantage is that each time the diagnostic **printf()** statements are changed, the program must be recompiled. This is time-consuming. Also, **printf()** statements are a cumbersome way to follow the path a program is taking from place to place in the listing, unless you put **printf()** statements almost everywhere. And in long loops, where trouble may not show up until after hundreds of iterations, a great deal of useless output may be generated before the error shows up.

It would be nice if we could step through a program, line-by-line, at whatever speed we wanted, checking the values of variables and expressions as we went along, without having to modify the program itself. Happily, the CodeView debugging program, included with the Microsoft C compiler 4.0, does just that. CodeView is so good and so versatile that it provides a reason, all by itself, for buying the Microsoft compiler.

Unlike most earlier debuggers (such as the DEBUG program included with MS-DOS), CodeView operates directly on the C source code of your program, rather than the machine language executable code (although you can use CodeView to debug that too, if you want). With CodeView, you see the listing of your C program on the screen. You can single-step through the program lines, examine variables, execute particular parts of the program, and watch both the program listing and the output it generates. In general, it will do almost anything you've ever dreamed of a debugger doing.

In this appendix we'll touch on some of the highlights of the CodeView debugger. This is by no means a comprehensive explanation of CodeView; the Microsoft manual and software tutorials do an excellent job of explaining its operations in detail. But we'll show the sorts of things the program can do, and we'll demonstrate a simple but useful way to set it up.

# The Operating Environment

CodeView comes with a great many files, most of which are for instructional purposes. The only ones you actually need to operate CodeView are cv.exe and cv.hlp. You'll probably want to put these in the same directory as your word processing program, so you can quickly create or modify the source file, compile and link it, and then debug the resulting executable file.

## Preparing a Program for CodeView

Before you can use CodeView on a program, the program must be compiled and linked. CodeView needs both the source file (prog.c) and the executable file (prog.exe) in order to operate. You must start with an error-free compilation; CodeView can't deal with errors of syntax in the source file. It's strength is in finding logical errors in your program's operation.

You must use several command-line options when using CL to compile and link your program. This is because CodeView requires a symbol table in order to operate, and this symbol table is not generated by the normal compile-link process.

The first option is /Zi. This causes an object file with a symbol table and line numbers to be created. The second option (which may not be necessary) is /Od. This disables optimization, which might rearrange the order in which statements are executed.

Let's consider a real program with a real bug. The program is called badloop.c. Its purpose is to calculate the sum of the squares of the integers from 1 to 10. (We want the program to add 1, which is 1 squared, to 4, which is 2 squared, add that to 9, which is 3 squared, and so on up to 100, which is 10 squared.) Here's the listing:

```
/* badloop.c */
/* sums the squares of the numbers from 1 to 10 */
main()
{
    int count, countsq, total;
    for(count=1; count<=10; count++)
        {
        countsq = count * count;
        total += countsq;
        }
```

```
        printf("Sum of squares is %d", total);
    }
```

Type in this program exactly as shown. If you spot the error, resist the urge to correct it.

Compile and link badloop.c by typing:

```
C>cl /Zi /Od badloop..c
```

Now you can run the program in the usual way, by typing

```
C>badloop
```

You'll get this output:

```
Sum of squares is 18444
```

This seems a little high. After all, 10 squared is 100, so the sum of the squares of the integers from 1 to 10 can't be more than 1,000, and is probably considerably less. What's wrong with the program? Let's use CodeView to find out.

## Invoking CodeView

Once you've used the appropriate options to compile and link a version of your program that is acceptable to CodeView, you can invoke CodeView and your program at the same time by typing "cv" followed by the program's name.

```
C>cv badloop
```

At this point, the standard CodeView screen will appear, as shown in Figure F-1.

As the figure shows, the program listing appears in a window in the upper part of the screen, called the "display window." The window at the bottom of the screen is called the "dialog window." It's here that you type instructions to CodeView. The line at the top of the screen, with the words "File", "Search", and so on, is the menu bar.

## Operating CodeView

CodeView offers an extremely versatile user-interface. You can use a mouse to select menu options, you can select menu options with the keyboard, you can use function keys, and you can type commands into the dialog window. Many operations can be invoked using several or all of these approaches. As a result, it can be confusing to figure out which method to apply to a given operation.

In this discussion we'll assume that you don't have a mouse. Without a mouse, the menu approach is less efficient, usually involving more keystrokes than other methods, so we'll describe all operations using function keys and

```
File View Search Run Watch Options Language Calls Help F8=Trace F5=Go
═══════════════════════════════════╡ badloop.c ╞════════════════════════════
1:
2:        /* badloop.c */
3:        /* sums the squares of numbers from 1 to 10 */
4:        main()
5:        {
6:            int count, countsq, total;
7:            for(count=1; count<=10; count++)
8:                {
9:                countsq = count * count;
10:               total += countsq;
11:               }
12:           printf("Sum of squares is %d", total);
13:       }



═════════════════════════════════════════════════════════════════════════════
Microsoft (R) CodeView (TM)   Version 2.10
Copyright (C) Microsoft Corp 1986.  All rights reverved.

>
```

Figure F-1. The CodeView Screen

commands typed into the command window. (The curious can experiment with the menus by holding down the [Alt] key and typing the first letter of a menu's name, then using the cursor keys to move down the menu's items, or left and right to different menus.)

## Moving the Cursor

We've seen that the CodeView screen has two parts: the display window and the dialog window. The cursor can be used in either window. You can move it back and forth with the [F6] function key. Try pressing [F6] and you'll see the cursor jump from one window to the other. Within either window you can move the cursor up and down using the cursor keys on the numeric keypad.

Another useful thing to know is that the display and dialog windows can be made larger and smaller (one expands as the other shrinks). [Ctrl] [G] makes the window bigger and [Ctrl] [T] makes it smaller. These commands work for whichever window the cursor is in. Expanding the dialog window can be useful when its contents get complicated.

## Running Programs from Within CodeView

Running a program from within CodeView is as easy as running it from DOS. Make sure that the cursor is in the dialog window, and then type "g" (or "G") for Go, followed by [Return]. A message will appear in the dialog window:

"Program terminated normally." That sounds promising, but where is the program's output? It's not in the display window, and it's not in the dialog window.

## The Output Screen

CodeView actually operates on two screens at the same time. The first was shown in Figure F-1. The second contains the output of the program being debugged. In a sense, this output screen is the "real" screen: the one you would see if you weren't using CodeView but merely running your program in the usual way from DOS. It's easy to switch to the output screen: simply press function key [F4]. Here's what you'll see:

```
C>cv badloop
Sum of squares is 5658
```

The first line shown above was placed on the screen when CodeView was called. (There may be other lines above it on the screen, of course.) The second line is the output generated by badloop.c. It's still the wrong answer: 5658 (or some other number). Press [F4] again to return to the display window.

Can you run the program again? Try typing "g". You'll get a message "restart program to debug." You must tell CodeView to start over at the beginning of the program. To do this, enter "l" (or "L") for Load.

## Tracing Through the Program

Let's trace through the program one line at a time. Make sure the program is initialized with "l". Then, to trace one program line, press the [F8] function key. The program line being executed will be shown on the screen in reverse video (or complementary colors, if you're using a color display). Each time you press [F8] the highlight moves down one line. Only lines that actually generate machine language code in the executable file are traced. Comments are skipped, as are variable declarations and statements with nothing but a brace. Note that the marked line is the statement *about to be executed*.

You can now see exactly where the program is going. It starts at the opening brace, executes the **for** statement, and then cycles through the loop over and over. Finally it comes out of the loop and displays the "Program terminated normally" message (this time on the display window instead of the dialog window).

There are actually two ways to step through a program. The Trace command described above will trace *into* functions. If your program calls a function (other than a library function), the steps of the function will be traced when it is reached. By contrast, the Step command (activated with the [F10] function key), steps *over* functions; it executes the function, but in one step. If you know a function works, this is the command to use. If you think it might harbor a bug, trace into it with Trace.

Using the Trace command showed that our program was going to the right places and executing the instructions in the right order. But the answer generated by the program is still wrong. We need to find out what the program's variables are doing as the program executes.

## Variables and Watch Statements

We can examine the values of variables by placing them in a "watch window" on the screen. To do this, we enter "w?" into the dialog window, followed by the variable (or expression) whose value we want to display.

There is a potential glitch here. To tell CodeView about a variable, the variable must be known to the program being debugged. The only way the program can know about the variable is if it has already been initialized in the program. So we must trace through the program far enough to initialize its variables.

To do this in badloop.c, enter "l" to initialize the entire program, then press [F8] twice. This will move the highlight to the **for** statement, executing the variable declarations on the way. Now the variables are known to CodeView. Enter the command

```
w? count
```

in the dialog window. You'll see a new window open at the top of the screen, containing the variable name **count** and its value (which could be anything, since **count** has not yet been initialized in the **for** loop). The new window is called the "watch window."

Follow the same procedure with the variables **countsq** and **total**. Figure F-2 shows what the screen should look like now.

Now when you trace through the program with the [F8] key you can see the values of the variables change right before your eyes. Executing the **for** statement sets **count** to 1. Executing the next statement sets **countsq** to 1. And then in the next statement **total** is set to . . . but what's this? Why is **total** set to 5658 (or some other number), when it should also be 1? Of course—we forgot to initialize it, so 1 is added to whatever garbage quantity was in **total** before. We've found our bug.

Other commands can be typed into the dialog window to manipulate watch statements. The command

```
>w
```

with no parameters will cause all the watch statements to be listed in the dialog window. Entering

```
>y 1 3
```

will cause watch statements 1 and 3 to be deleted. The watch window will shrink to accommodate the remaining variables. The command

```
>y *
```

```
File View Search Run Watch Options Language Calls Help F8=Trace F5=Go
                            ╡ badloop.c ╞
0)   count   :   15540
1)   countsq :   25
2)   total   :   22

3:        /* sums the squares of numbers from 1 to 10, prints result */
4:        main()
5:        {
6:            int count, countsq, total;
7:            for(count=1; count<=10; count++)
8:               {
9:               countsq = count * count;
10:              total += countsq;
11:              }
12:           print("Sum of squares is %d", total);
13:       }



>w? count
>w? countsq
>w? total
>
```

Figure F-2. The Watch Window

will delete all the watch statements. This will cause the watch window to disappear entirely.

## Breakpoints

Often when debugging you will want to run the program full speed, up to a certain point, and then stop it at a particular line so you can investigate things at your leisure. This might be true if your program contains a long loop, for instance; you wouldn't want to step through every cycle of the loop, you only want to see what will happen when the loop terminates. Breakpoints can accomplish this.

For example, suppose we want to see what the state of badloop.c is after the loop has been completed but before the **printf()** statement on line 12 has been executed. To do this, we install a breakpoint on line 12. A program must be initialized with the "l" command before a breakpoint can be installed, so make sure this has been done.

There are several ways to install a breakpoint. Here's one: in the dialog window, enter the command "bp" followed by a period and the line number where you want to install the breakpoint:

```
>bp .12
```

You'll see the indicated line appear in bold (or a different color) to indicate it contains a breakpoint.

Now when you run the program all the statements up to the **printf()** on line 12 will be executed. Line 12 will appear in reverse video, since this is the line about to be executed.

## Finding the Values of Variables or Expressions

Once you've stopped the program at a given point you can find the value of any variable or expression by typing a question mark followed by the expression. For instance, to find the value of the variable **count**, you can enter

```
>? count
```

The value (which should be 11) is printed out in the dialog window. You can also find the value of any C expression, such as

```
>? count * count
```

## Enabling and Disabling Breakpoints

You can set as many breakpoints as you like. To see which ones you've set, enter "bl". This will show you the breakpoints, listing first the number of the breakpoint (starting with 0), then the address (in hexadecimal segment-offset form), then the function and line number. In the case of the breakpoint installed above, the output is

```
>bl
0 e 3CB3:0038  _main:12
```

This shows that breakpoint 0 is installed in the 12th line of **main()**. The "e" following the breakpoint number indicates that the breakpoint is enabled.

You can disable one or more breakpoints by typing "bd" followed by a list of their numbers (separated by spaces). To disable our breakpoint on line 12, we would type

```
>bd 0
```

Now listing the breakpoints will show this one with a letter "d" for disabled:

```
>bl
0 d 3CB3:0038  _main:12
```

The breakpoint now will have no effect on program operation. However, it can be enabled again by entering "be" followed by its number:

```
>be 0
```

Breakpoints have another feature that can be helpful if you're having trouble debugging a loop. It's often useful to go through most of the loop at full speed, but stop just before the end to see what happens when the loop is exited. For example, in the badloop.c example, we might want to execute the loop eight times and then stop so we can trace through the last two iterations.

To do this, reset the program with the **l** command, deactivate any breakpoints you don't want set, and type:

```
>bp .10 8
```

This sets a breakpoint on line 10 in the middle of the loop, but specifies that it not stop the program until it has been passed eight times. Enter "g" to run the program. Line 10, where the program stopped, will be shown in reverse video. If you check the value of **count** you'll see that the loop has been executed eight times:

```
>g
>? count

8
```

Now you can trace through the remaining cycles of the loop to see what happens when it exits (presumably there will be no surprises in this simple example).

## The Iceberg

What we have said about CodeView in this appendix is only the tip of the iceberg. CodeView has many more features than we've covered, and the features we have covered have many options and variations we didn't mention. One of the most exciting aspects of CodeView is how easy it makes working with the assembly language version of a C program. This provides a powerful tool for studying assembly language and for learning how to use assembly language to optimize C programs.

We hope this summary will whet your appitite for further exploration of this powerful utility.

# G

## The QuickC Debugger

If you're writing in QuickC, you can use its built-in debugger. This appendix describes how to debug programs in the QuickC environment.

The QuickC debugger is simple yet powerful. It doesn't have all the bells and whistles of CodeView, but it incorporates the major features necessary for efficient debugging. You can single-step through programs, see variables change as the program runs, and execute sections of the program at full speed, stopping where you want.

We discussed in Chapter 1 how to correct syntax errors discovered by the QuickC compiler, so we won't cover that here. You might also want to refer to the first few pages of the CodeView appendix for some general thoughts on the debugging process.

## Single-Stepping

The first thing the debugger can do for you is slow down the operation of the program. One trouble with finding errors is that a typical program executes in a few milliseconds, so all you can see is its final state. By invoking QuickC's single-stepping ability you can execute just one line of the program at a time. This way you can follow where the program is going.

Here's a small example program:

```
/* errelse.c */
/* demonstrates single stepping */
main()
{
    int number, answer = -1;

    number = -50;            /* test value */
    if(number < 100)
       if(number > 0)
          answer = 1;
    else
       answer = 0;
    printf("answer is %d\n", answer );
}
```

Type the program and run it by selecting Start from the Run menu. Our intention in this program is that when **number** is between 0 and 100, **answer** will be 1; when **number** is 100 or greater, **answer** will be 0; and when **number** is less than 0, **answer** will retain its initialized value of – 1.

Unfortunately, when we run the program with a test value of – 50 for **number**, as shown, we find that **answer** is set to 0 at the end of the program, instead of staying – 1. What's wrong? (You may see the problem already, but bear with us.)

Perhaps we can understand where the problem is if we single-step through the program. To do this, press the [F10] key. (You can also use [F8]; it operates the same as [F10] unless functions are involved.)

When you first press [F10] you'll see the Compile window from the Run menu appear briefly. The program must be compiled with the Debug option set in this window, but this usually happens automatically when you start single-stepping. In some circumstances a window will appear with the message "Program must be compiled with debug option. Build with debug?" Press [Enter] or click on the "Yes" box.

Pressing [F10] the first time causes the opening brace of the program, following main( ), to be highlighted. Press [F10] again. The highlight will move to the next program line. (It skips over the declarations.) The line *about to be executed* is highlighted; in other words, pressing [F10] causes the highlighted line to be executed. The highlighted line is called the *currently executing line*. We'll shorten this to CEL.

Execute each line of the errelse.c program in turn by pressing [F10]. Eventually you'll reach the first **if** statement:

```
if(num < 100)
```

This statement is true (since **number** is – 50); so, as we would expect, the CEL moves to the second **if** statement:

```
if(num > 0)
```

This is false. Since there's no **else** matched with the second **if**, we would expect the CEL to move to the **printf()** statement. But it doesn't!  It goes to the line

```
answer = 0;
```

The screen when the CEL has reached this line is shown in Figure G-1.

Now that we see where the program actually goes, the source of the bug should become clear: the **else** goes with the last **if**, not the first **if** as the indenting would lead us to believe. So the **else** is executed when the second **if** statement is false, which leads to the erroneous result. We need to put braces around the second **if** or rewrite the program in some other way. We've sucessfully used the single-stepping feature to track down a bug.

In this short example, single-stepping may not be necessary to discover the bug, but in a more complex program, with multiple nested **if**s, loops, and

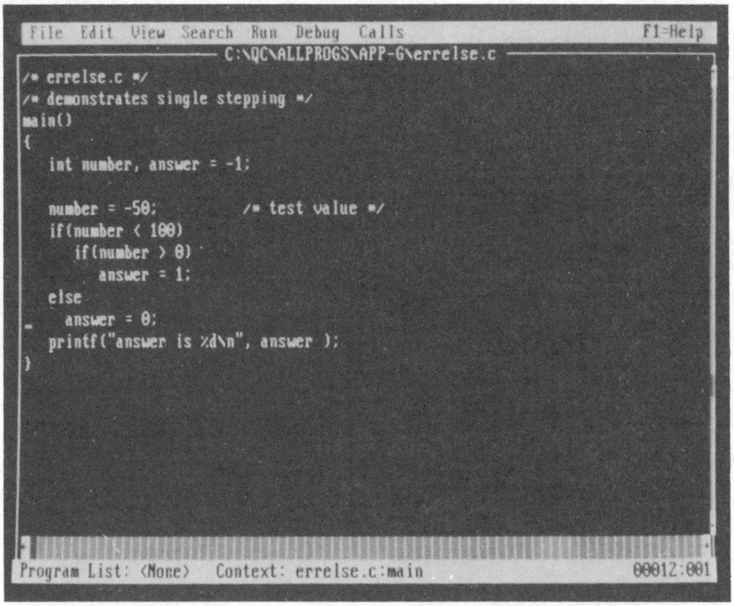

```
 File  Edit  View  Search  Run  Debug  Calls                      F1=Help
┌──────────────────── C:\QC\ALLPROGS\APP-G\errelse.c ──────────────────────┐
│/* errelse.c */                                                           │
│/* demonstrates single stepping */                                        │
│main()                                                                    │
│{                                                                         │
│    int number, answer = -1;                                              │
│                                                                          │
│    number = -50;              /* test value */                           │
│    if(number < 100)                                                      │
│        if(number > 0)                                                    │
│            answer = 1;                                                    │
│    else                                                                  │
│      answer = 0;                                                         │
│    printf("answer is %d\n", answer );                                    │
│}                                                                         │
│                                                                          │
└──────────────────────────────────────────────────────────────────────────┘
 Program List: <None>    Context: errelse.c:main                   00012:001
```

Figure G-1. The Currently Executing Line (CEL)

functions, it's often an essential technique. Try single-stepping through some programs containing loops and complex **if** statements.

## Resetting the Debugger

Suppose you've single-stepped part of the way through a program, and want to start over at the beginning. How do you put the CEL back at the top of the listing? Select Restart from the Run menu. The highlight on the CEL will disappear, and will reappear on the opening brace the first time you press [F10].

## Examining the Output Screen

You can examine the output screen (where the program's output goes) by pressing the [F4] key. In the errelse.c example the only output comes at the last line of the program, which you'll see anyway when you execute the closing brace of the program. So in this case there isn't much reason to use [F4]. But in most programs you'll want to switch back and forth between the program and the output screen. To return to your program from the output screen, press [F4] again (or any other key).

# Watch Expressions

Single-stepping is usually used with *watch expressions*. A watch expression is a sort of magic microscope that lets you see how the value of a variable changes *as the program runs*.

Here's a short example. This program is intended to calculate the factorial of a number entered by the user. It's similar to the factor.c program in Chapter 3, but it uses a **for** loop instead of a **while** loop.

```c
/* errloop.c */
/* attempts to calculate factorials */
/* demonstrates watchpoints */
main()
{
    long number, j, answer;

    printf("Enter number: ");
    scanf("%D", &number );
    answer = 1;
    for( j=0; j<number; j++ )
        answer *= j;
    printf("Factorial of %d = %ld\n", number, answer );
}
```

Unfortunately, no matter what number we enter when we run this program, it always prints the same result:

```
Factorial of 5 is 0
```

The factorial of 5 should be 120. Can we find the problem with the debugger? Single-stepping by itself isn't much help, as the program seems to go around the loop the correct number of times (5 in this case). Let's see if watch expressions can cast more light on the problem.

We'll assume that you've typed the program into the view window. Select Add Watch . . . from the Debug menu. A window will appear. Enter the variable name **number** in the box provided. You'll see a watch window appear at the top of the screen. This window will contain the line **number: <No debug information>**.

When you press [F10], the line in the watch window will change to **number: <Unknown identifier>**. Debug is now in effect, but the variable is unknown because we have not yet executed the program statement that declares it.

Set up watch expressions for **j** and **answer** the same way. Lines for these variables will appear in the watch window. You can put a variable into the watch window at any point in the program, and you can add as many variables as you want. You can enter two or more variable names at once by separating them with semicolons.

Single-step through the program, using the [F10] key. You'll see the CEL move down through the listing as before. You'll also see the values of the variables change in the watch window. When you've executed the program lines where the variables are declared, the watch window will change to something like this:

```
answer: 43234244L
j: -72319873L
number: 930986876L
```

The variables are declared, but have garbage values because they have not yet been initialized. When you execute the **scanf()** statement, the output screen will appear. Enter a small value, like 5. Continue single-stepping through the program. In the watch window you'll see **number** acquire the value 5, **answer** the value 1. When you enter the loop, **j** becomes 0.

When you execute the loop you'll see that the CEL does not appear to move; this is because there is only one statement in the loop. However, the program is going around the loop. You can tell this because the values in the watch window change. Figure G-2 shows the screen after several cycles through the loop.

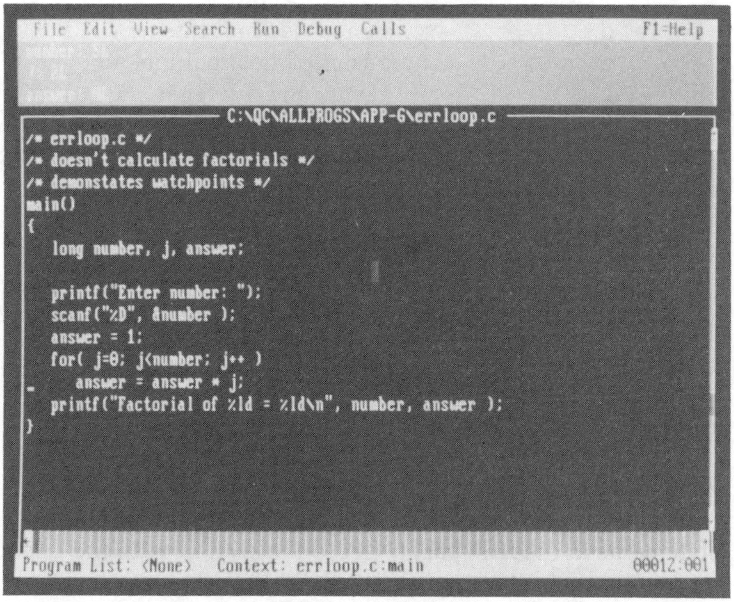

Figure G-2. The Watch Window and errloop.c

Can you figure out what the bug is? The variable **answer** is initialized to 1, but on the first cycle through the loop, it becomes 0, as you can see in the watch window. From then on it remains 0, since anything times 0 is 0. Why did it become 0? As we can also see in the watch window, **j** is 0 the first time through the loop, and the program multiplies **j** by **answer**. The bug is that we start **j** at 0 instead of 1. To fix this, we must change **j = 0** to **j = 1** in the **for** loop expression and **j < number** to **j < = number**. When we make these changes the program works correctly.

You can delete the last watch expression you entered by selecting Delete

Last Watch from the Debug menu, or you can delete all the Watch expressions with Delete All Watch.

Watch expressions can contain simple variables, array elements, structure members, structure-pointer members, and pointers. Arithmetic operators, as in **var1 + 3**, are not allowed, nor is pointer arithmetic, such as **\*(ptr + j)**.

Ordinarily, a variable is displayed as whatever data type it was declared. However, you can display a variable as a different type. Follow a variable name by a comma and and a single-letter format specifier. These specifiers, listed in Table G-1, are similar to those used in the **printf()** function. For example, entering **number,x** into the watch window would cause **number** to be displayed as a hex value, and **number,hd** would display it as a two-byte signed decimal number, using the lower two bytes even if it is a four-byte integer.

### Table G-1. QuickC Format Specifiers

| Format Specifier | Value Displayed As |
| --- | --- |
| d | signed decimal integer |
| u | unsigned decimal integer |
| x | hexadecimal integer |
| f | floating point |
| e | exponential notation |
| g | floating point or exponential |
| c | character |
| s | string |
| h | before integer specifiers: two-byte integer |
| l | before integer specifiers: four-byte integer |

# Breakpoints

It often happens that you've debugged part of your program but must deal with a bug in another section, and you don't want to single-step through all the statements in the first part to get to the section with the bug. Or you may have a loop with many iterations that would be tedious to single-step through.

Here's an example. This program attempts to average the integers from 0 to 499.

```
/* errbreak.c */
/* attempts to average first 500 integers */
/* demonstrates breakpoints */
main()
{
    int j, total=0, average;

    for( j=0; j<500; j++ )
        total += j;
    average = total / j;
```

```
        printf("average = %d\n", average );
    }
```

When we run the program, it says the average is –12. This doesn't look right; the average should be around 250. To figure out what's wrong, set up watch expressions for **j**, **total**, and **average**. Now try single-stepping into the loop. Everything looks good for the first dozen or so cycles; **j** starts at 0 and is incremented each time, and **total** starts at 0 and is increased by whatever **j** is. We could go on stepping through the loop, but 500 iterations is too time consuming. We really want to run the program full speed until the end of the loop and stop it there so we can check the values of the variables.

The way to do this is with a *breakpoint*. A breakpoint marks a line where the program will stop. You start the program in the usual way, and it executes all the statements up to the breakpoint, then stops. You can now use the watch window to examine the state of the variables at that point.

## Installing Breakpoints

To set a breakpoint, position the cursor on the appropriate line. In the errbreak.c program this is the line where the **average** is calculated. Now select Toggle Breakpoint from the Debug menu. The line with the breakpoint will be highlighted (differently from the CEL). You can also use [F9], a shortcut key, to install a breakpoint at the cursor position.

To run the program down to the breakpoint, select Start from the Run menu. All the instructions in the loop will be executed. The program stops on the line with the breakpoint, which becomes the CEL. Now look at the Watch expressions. The **total** variable is –6,322. A large negative number often results from the overflow of a positive number, so perhaps at this point we can guess that we've exceeded the capacity of signed integers. In fact the actual total is 499x250, or 124,750, which is far larger than the 32,767 limit. The cure is to use variables of type **long int**.

You can install as many breakpoints as you wish in a program. This is useful if the program can take several different paths, depending on the result of **if** statements or other branching constructs. You can block all the paths with breakpoints, and then see where the program stops.

You can remove a single breakpoint by positioning the cursor on the line with the breakpoint and selecting Toggle Breakpoint from the Debug menu (just as you did to install the breakpoint). The breakpoint highlight will vanish. You can remove all breakpoints in a program by selecting Clear Breakpoints.

## Go to Cursor

If you only need to install one breakpoint, you can take a shortcut approach. Position the cursor where you want the program to stop and press the [F7] key. This causes all the program lines up to the cursor position to be executed. Similarly, you can execute up to the line containing the mouse pointer by clicking the right-hand mouse button.

# Function Debugging

When one function calls another, certain complexities occur in the debugging process. In this section we'll see how the QuickC debugger handles these function-related situations.

## Trace Into versus Step Over

Suppose you're single-stepping through the **main()** function, and it calls another function, say **func()**. Do you want to single-step *into* **func()**, stepping through the lines of code that constitute the function, or do you want to step over it, treating it as a single line of code? The answer is, it depends: sometimes you want to single-step into a function, and sometimes you want to execute it as a single line of code.

This is the purpose of the [F10] and [F8] keys. Both provide single-stepping, but the [F10] key steps over any function it encounters, while the [F8] key traces into it. By selecting the appropriate key at each step you can determine whether you step over or trace into a particular function.

For example, consider the following example program.

```
/* errfunc.c */
/* demonstrates trace, step, call stack */
main()
{
    func1();
    func1();
}

func1()
{
    func2();
}

func2()
{
}
```

Try single-stepping through this program with the [F10] key. You'll see the CEL go from the opening brace of **main()** to the first **func1();** line, to the second **func1();** line, and then to the closing brace of **main()**. It never goes to the functions themselves.

Now use [F8] to trace into the functions. The CEL goes to the opening brace of **main()**, then to the call to **func1();**, then to the opening brace of **func1()** itself, then to the call to **func2();**, then to the opening brace of **func2()**, and so on. All the code will be traced into all the functions, no matter how deeply they are nested.

Even using the [F8] key you can't trace into QuickC library routines such as **printf()**. For a routine to be debugged, its source file must be available, and the source files for library routines are not included in the sytem. Also, these routines are presumably bug free, so there is no need to debug them.

## The Calls Menu

When tracing into several levels of functions it's easy to forget where you came from. You may know you're in a particular function, but you've forgotten which function called the one you're in.

QuickC gives you a handy way to see the whole chain of function calls that led to your present location in the program.

For instance, suppose you're single-stepping through the errfunc.c program, using the [F8] key to trace into every function. The **main()** function has called **func1()**, and **func1()** has called **func2()**. To see the function calls that have taken place up to this point, select the Calls menu. The result is shown in Figure G-3.

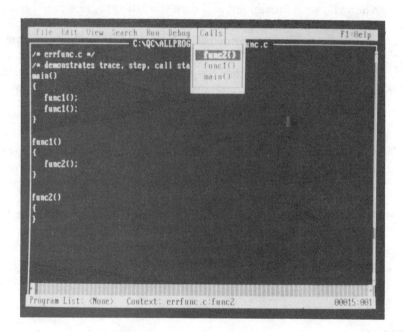

Figure G-3. The Calls Menu

It would be nice to watch new functions being added to and removed from the Calls menu as you single-stepped through a program, but this is not possible. You can't leave the Calls menu in the window as you single-step. Pressing [F8] when the Calls menu is on the screen results in petulant beeping from QuickC, but no action. This feature is quite useful in programs that have large numbers of nested functions, however.

If a call to a function has arguments, the values of the arguments will also be shown on the Calls menu.

You can display the line *immediately following* the line currently being executed in any of the functions shown in the Calls menu. (The line currently being executed is, except for the last function in the chain, a call to the next function.) To see the line, move the highlight to the desired function name and press [Enter]. The appropriate section of the function will appear in the Edit window. This makes it easy to move back and forth between the called function and the calling function.

In addition to seeing where the call to a function is, you can also start executing at the point following the call to the function. Select the function name from the Calls menu and start executing by pressing [F7]. This takes you to the cursor location, one line past the function call.

## Tracing and Swapping

When you set a breakpoint and then start the program running by selecting Start from the Run menu, the lines executed are not ordinarily highlighted. They are executed roughly in the normal way until the breakpoint is encountered.

It's possible to cause each line to be highlighted as it's executed. This is done by selecting the Trace On command from the Debug menu. The effect is that of a very fast typist repeatedly pressing the [F8] key. If the program is in a tight loop you can see the highlight flying around in the loop. The row number in the lower-right corner of the screen blurs, and the vertical scroll bar jiggles. Program operation also slows down markedly.

You can't halt the program from the keyboard or with the mouse, so be careful not to enter a long loop with Trace On set; you'll have to reboot. This option does provide an impressionistic view of where the program is going, however, and it can be helpful in some circumstances.

You can also cause the output screen to appear following the execution of each program line. The resulting rapid screen-switching makes both screens difficult to read, but again, in some circumstances this might be a useful feature, permitting you to keep an eye on both the screen and the program at the same time.

## Summary

Table G-2 summarizes the key combinations used for debugging in QuickC. We've covered the most important features of the QuickC debugging facility. You learned how to single-step through programs with the [F10] key and how to monitor the values of variables as the program runs, using watch expressions. You learned that [F10] steps over functions while [F8] traces into them and that a list of the function calls currently in use can be seen in the Calls menu.

## Table G-2. QuickC Debugging Key Combinations

| Key | Purpose |
| --- | --- |
| [F4] | Display output screen |
| [F7] | Execute to cursor |
| [F8] | Single-step: trace into functions |
| [F9] | Toggle breakpoint |
| [F10] | Single-step: step over functions |
| [Shift] [F2] | Delete last watch expression |

# H

# *The QuickC Editor*

If you're using QuickC as your development environment, you'll need to know how to operate the QuickC editor. Even if you're developing with the Optimizing Compiler you may want to write your source files with the QuickC editor. It's a simple but effective editor that is easy to learn.

This appendix shows you how to use the QuickC editor. We don't cover all its capabilities; the manuals that accompany the compiler do that. Rather we cover the important features, which should be enough to get you started and enable you to write the program examples in this book.

## Starting the Editor

The editor is part of the QuickC integrated programming environment. To start QuickC, type qc at the DOS prompt, as described in Chapter 1.

The cursor will be flashing in the upper-left corner of the view window. This is where you'll do your writing and editing.

Type a few sentences. Press [Enter] to go to the next line down. Use the backspace key to delete mistyped characters. You can move around the screen by pressing the cursor keys. To insert text, move the cursor to the desired place and type the new text. The previous text will shift right to make room.

One important difference between QuickC and a typical word processor is that QuickC has no automatic word wrap. When you reach the end of a line, the screen simply scrolls left to accommodate more characters. You can type up to 256 characters on a line (although it's not clear why you would want to; usually you want to see the entire line at once).

Another way QuickC differs from word processors is that you can move the cursor into the blank area to the left of text lines, or into blank lines, and start typing wherever the cursor is. This makes it easier to place material in columns (to line up comments, for example) without having to type a lot of spaces and tabs. Also, QuickC does not insert non-ASCII control characters into the file, the way such word processors as WordStar and WordPerfect do. These characters cannot be digested by the compiler, which requires a pure ASCII file.

# Getting Around the Menu System

Commands to QuickC let you load and save files, cut and paste blocks of text, and search for particular text strings and perform other actions. Most commands to the QuickC editor are made by selecting items from menus. You can see the names of the menus—File, Edit, View, and so on—in the *Menu bar*, the highlighted line at the top of the screen. You select an item from a menu with the keyboard or a mouse. Although you don't need a mouse to use QuickC, if you have one you'll find that it performs many operations more conveniently than the keyboard.

## Using the Mouse to Select Menu Items

If you have a mouse installed in your system, QuickC will automatically connect with it when you start the program. You'll see the mouse pointer—a small rectangle—in the upper-left corner of the screen. When you move the mouse, the pointer moves in unison on the screen.

To see the selections on a menu, move the mouse pointer to the name of the menu on the menu bar. For instance, move it to the word "Files." Now press the left mouse button. (The left mouse button is used for almost all actions in QuickC). The menu will "drop down" from the menu bar. You'll see a list of commands: Open, Merge, Save, and so on. To select one of these commands, hold the mouse button down and drag the pointer down the menu until the command you want is highlighted. Then release the button.

For example, suppose you've typed in a source file and you want to save it to disk. Place the mouse pointer on the File menu, press [Enter], and drag the pointer down to the Save as . . . option. Release the button and a window will appear. On the line provided, type the name you want to give your source file. There is a small box labelled "OK" in the window. When you've entered the file name correctly, move the mouse pointer to this box and press the mouse button once, quickly. This is called "clicking on" the box. The file will be saved and you'll find yourself back in the view window.

## Using the Keyboard to Select Menu Items

To see the contents of a menu using the keyboard keys, hold down [Alt] and type the first letter of the menu's name. For example, to see what's on the file menu, type [Alt] [F]. (You can use upper- or lowercase letters.) To select a particular item from the menu, press the letter that's highlighted in that particular item. In most cases this will be the first letter of the selection, but if there's a conflict it may be another letter.

For example, to save a file, select the file menu by pressing [Alt] [F]. Then press [A], which is the highlighted letter in the Save As . . . option. Type in the file name and then press [Enter]. The file will be saved. The [A] key is used for Save As . . . because the [S] key is assigned to the Save option.

When boxes appear in response to a command, you select the appropriate option by typing the letter that's highlighted in the appropriate box.

## Exiting from the Editor

Now that you know how to use the menus, you can exit from QuickC. Type [Alt] [F] to select the file menu, and press [X] to select the Exit option. Or, if you're using the mouse, drag the mouse pointer down to Exit. You'll find yourself back in DOS. If you haven't saved your file, a box will ask if you want to save it before exiting.

# Basic Editor Commands

At the heart of any editor are commands that move the cursor on the screen, scroll the screen, and insert and delete text. We've mentioned several of these already. Table H-1 provides a summary of the most useful of these commands. (The usage [Down] means the down cursor key, and so on.)

### Table H-1. Editor Commands

| Key | Moves the Cursor |
| --- | --- |
| [Left] | one character left |
| [Right] | one character right |
| [Down] | one line down |
| [Up] | one line up |
| [Ctrl] [Left] | one word left |
| [Ctrl] [Right] | one word right |
| [Home] | to beginning of line |
| [End] | to end of line |
| [Ctrl] [Home] | to beginning of file |
| [Ctrl] [End] | to end of file |

| Key | Scrolls |
| --- | --- |
| [PgUp] | up one screen |
| [PgDn] | down one screen |
| [Ctrl] [W] | up one line |
| [Ctrl] [Z] | down one line |

| Key | Insert and Delete |
| --- | --- |
| [Ins] | Toggles insert mode on/off |
| [Ctrl] [N] | Inserts blank line |
| [Backspace] | Deletes character to left of cursor |
| [Del] | Deletes character under cursor |
| [Ctrl] [T] | Deletes word |
| [Ctrl] [Y] | Deletes line |

When you have insert mode toggled off, you type over any existing text, obliterating it in the process. When the insert mode is toggled on (the default), what you type is inserted between the letters of existing text.

If you know the classic WordStar commands you'll find that you can substitute them for many of the commands shown above. In fact, you can use WordStar commands for most of the editing functions in QuickC.

### Using the Mouse to Move the Cursor

If you want to move the cursor more than a few characters, it's usually easier to use the mouse than the keyboard commands. Move the pointer to the desired location, and click the left mouse button. The cursor will jump to the new location.

# Block Commands

You can select a block of text—anything from a character to many pages—and perform various operations on it. Once it's selected, a block can be moved to a different place in the file, copied, deleted, or written to disk.

### Using the Mouse to Select Text

Selecting a block of text with the mouse is easy. First, position the pointer at the beginning of the block, as described above. To select the text, hold down the mouse button and drag the pointer to the end of the block. As you move the pointer, the selected text is highlighted. If you want to go below the bottom line of text, move the pointer to the bottom of the screen. The text will scroll upward.

When you've selected the text block, let go of the mouse button. The selected block will remain highlighted.

There is a shortcut to selecting a single word with the mouse: move the pointer to the word and "double-click" on it by quickly pressing the left-hand mouse button twice.

### Using the Keyboard to Select Text

To select text with the keyboard, move the cursor to the beginning of the block with the keyboard key commands. Now, hold down the [Shift] key, and use keyboard commands to move the cursor to the end of the block. For instance, you might hold down [Shift] and press [Down] until a paragraph is highlighted. You can use any of the common cursor control commands while [Shift] is being pressed.

### Operations on a Text Block

Once the block of text is selected, you can perform the desired operation on it.

To delete the block, select Clear from the Edit menu. The block is gone forever. If you want to replace marked text with new text, you don't need to use Clear; just start typing. The selected text will vanish, replaced with what you have just typed.

To move a selected block of text to another location takes two steps. First, select Cut from the Edit menu. This deletes the selected block of text, but saves it in an internal buffer called the ClipBoard. Now move the cursor to the place you want the block to go and select Paste from the Edit menu. The text block will reappear in the new location.

Copying a block of text is similar. Select Copy from the Edit menu. This writes the block to the ClipBoard, but does not delete it. Now move the cursor to the desired location and select Paste from the Edit menu. A copy of the text block will appear at the new location.

The Clear, Copy, Cut, and Paste operations can also be activated using key combinations rather than selections from the edit menu. Once you learn it, typing the key combination is faster than making a menu selection, but it's harder to remember. The block commands are summarized in Table H-2.

### Table H-2. Text Block Operations

| Edit Menu | Keyboard Shortcut | Action |
|---|---|---|
| Clear | [Del] | Deletes block |
| Copy | [Ctrl] [Ins] | Saves block in ClipBoard |
| Cut | [Shift] [Del] | Deletes block, saves it in ClipBoard |
| Paste | [Shift] [Ins] | Writes ClipBoard to cursor location |

## File Handling

Files are manipulated from the File menu. If you don't specify a file name when you invoke QuickC, the file being edited is called untitled.c. To save a file under a different name, select Save As . . . from the File menu. To save it under the name it already has, select Save. To insert a file from the disk into your file at the cursor position, select Merge . . . and enter the name of the file to be merged. To open a file previously saved to disk, select Open . . . and enter the file name. To start work on a new file, select New.

You can switch between two files by using Open . . . to open file A, and then using Open . . . again to open file B. (You can't exit from QuickC during this process.) Now if you're working on A, you can immediately shift to B by selecting Select Last File and vice versa. This is useful if you're comparing files, for example. The [F2] key provides a shortcut to Select Last File. Table H-3 lists the file-handling options.

### Printing Files

To print a file, select Print from the File menu.

### Table H-3. File-Handling Options

| File Menu | Action |
| --- | --- |
| New | Opens a new file |
| Open . . . | Opens named file |
| Open last file | Opens previous file |
| Merge . . . | Loads named file at cursor position |
| Save | Saves file, using current name |
| Save as . . . | Saves file, asks for new name |

## Searching and Replacing

To search for an arbitrary text string, select Find from the Search menu. When it prompts you, enter the string to be searched for. This command will find the first occurrence of the string. To find subsequent occurrences of the same string, select Repeat Last Find from the Edit menu or use the shortcut key [F3].

You can also select a block of text and search for it using the Selected Text option in the Edit menu. The block selected must all be on the same line. Again, to find subsequent occurrences of the same text, select Repeat Last Find or press [F3].

To perform a search and replace, select Change . . . from the Edit menu. Enter the string to be searched for, and the string to replace it, in the spaces provided. Table H-4 summarizes the search options.

### Table H-4. Search Commands

| Search Menu Commands | Keyboard Shortcut | Action |
| --- | --- | --- |
| Find | | Finds specified text |
| Selected text | [Ctrl] [\] | Finds selected block of text |
| Repeat last find | [F3] | Finds next occurrence |
| Change . . . | | Search and replace |

## Other QuickC Editing Commands

Here are some other useful commands you can give the editor.

### Place Markers

You can place a marker in your text and then return immediately to the marker. You could use this feature to return quickly to the place in the listing where variables were declared, for instance. You can set up to four markers, numbered 0, 1, 2, and 3. Type [Ctrl] [K], [0] to place marker 0, and [Ctrl] [Q], [0] to jump to marker 0.

## Matching Braces

Sometimes you can find an opening brace in a listing but lose sight of the closing brace that matches it. To find the closing brace, position the cursor on the opening brace and type [Ctrl] ] (the Ctrl key and either bracket key). The cursor will move to the closing brace. Pressing [Ctrl] ] again takes you back to the opening brace. This works with braces {}, brackets [], parentheses (), and angle brackets < >.

## Undo Command

If you've made an editing mistake and you're still on the line the mistake is on, you can restore the original line by selecting Undo from the Edit menu or by typing [Alt] [Backspace]. You can't undo a line once the cursor has moved to a different line, though, and you can't restore a line deleted with [Ctrl] [Y]. (If you think you might want to restore a line, delete it by selecting Cut from the Edit menu.)

## Read-Only Mode

If you want to browse through a listing, while being sure you don't alter it, you can select the Read Only option from the Edit menu. This locks out all insert and delete operations.

## DOS Shell

You can call up a copy of DOS from within the editor by selecting DOS Shell from the File menu. Once in DOS you can display directories, copy files, and so forth. To return to the place you left off in QuickC, type "exit" at the DOS prompt.

# *Graphics Functions Reference*

This appendix summarizes the Microsoft C graphics functions, grouping them into categories. For a more complete description, see Chapter 12. Most arguments in these functions are of type **short**, so data types are not indicated unless they are a type other than **short**.

## Configuration

```
_getvideoconfig(&config)          get video mode information
                                  returned in videoconfig struct

        struct videoconfig {    /* defined in graph.h */
          short numxpixels;     /* horiz pixels */
          short numypixels;     /* vert pixels */
          short numtextcols;    /* text columns */
          short numtextrows;    /* text rows */
          short numcolors;      /* actual colors */
          short bitsperpixel;   /* bits per pixel */
          short numvideopages;  /* video memory pages */
        };

_setvideomode(mode) set video mode
    _DEFAULTMODE     mode -1     restore screen to previous mode
    _TEXTBW40        mode  0     40x25   CGA   text
    _TEXTC40         mode  1     40x25   CGA   text, color
    _TEXTBW80        mode  2     80x25   CGA   text
    _TEXTC80         mode  3     80x25   CGA   text, color
    _MRES4COLOR      mode  4     320x200 CGA   graphics, 4 color
    _MRESNOCOLOR     mode  5     320x200 CGA   graphics, 4 gray
    _HRESBW          mode  6     640x200 CGA   graphics, B&W
    _TEXTMONO        mode  7     80x25   MA    text, B&W
    _MRES16COLOR     mode 13     320x200 EGA   graphics, 16 color
    _HRES16COLOR     mode 14     640x200 EGA   graphics, 16 color
    _ERESNOCOLOR     mode 15     640x350 EGA   graphics, B&W
    _ERESCOLOR       mode 16     640x350 EGA   graphics, 64 color
    _VRES2COLOR      mode 17     640x480 VGA   graphics, 2 color
    _VRES16COLOR     mode 18     640x480 VGA   graphics, 16 color
    _MRES256COLOR    mode 19     320x200 VGA   graphics, 256 color

_clearscreen(type)  clear screen, viewport, or window
```

```
type = _GCLEARSCREEN    clear screen
type = _GVIEWPORT       clear viewport
type = _GWINDOW         clear text window
```

## Coordinates

(Upper-left corner is 0,0 in graphics coordinates)

```
_getcurrentposition()    returns current logical position (CP)
                            returned in struct xycoords
_getlogcoord(x,y)        return logical coords of physical x,y
                            returned in struct xycoords
_setlogorg(x,y)          set logical origin to physical x,y
                            previous x,y in struct xycoords
_getphyscoord(x,y)       return physical coords of logical x,y
                            returned in struct xycoords


        struct xycoord  {   /* defined in graph.h */
            short xcoord;   /* x coordinate returned */
            short ycoord;   /* y coordinate returned */
        };
```

## Text

(Upper-left corner is 1,1 in text coordinates)

```
_settextcolor(color)            set text color (0-15)
color = _gettextcolor()         get text color (0-15)
_setbkcolor(long color)         set text background (0-8)
_settextposition(row,col)       set text position
                                    previous pos in struct rcoord

_gettextposition()              get current text position
                                    returned in struct rcoord

        struct rccoord  {       /* defined in graph.h */
            short row;          /* text row */
            short col;          /* text column */
        };

_outtext(char far *string)      output at current position, color
_settextwindow(r1,c1,r2,c2)     define text window
_wrapon(wrapOption)             clip or wrap line at window border
    _GWRAPON                    clip line at window border
    _GWRAPOFF                   wrap line at window border
```

## Viewports and Clipping

```
_setcliprgn(x1, y1, x2, y2)     define clipping region
_setviewport(x1, y1, x2, y2)    define graphics viewport
```

# Color

```
_setcolor(colorNumber)                    set color
color = _getcolor()                       get color at pixel x,y
long color = _getbkcolor()                get background color
_setbkcolor(long color)                   set background color
_selectpalette(paletteNumber)             select color palette
_remappalette(value, long color)          reassign value to color
_remapallpalette(&colors)                 reassign all values
        long colors[16];                  array of new values
```

## Pixel Values and VGA Constants

| Color | Pixel Value | Constant | VGA Value |
|---|---|---|---|
| Black | 0 | _BLACK | 0x000000L |
| Blue | 1 | _BLUE | 0x2a0000L |
| Green | 2 | _GREEN | 0x002a00L |
| Cyan | 3 | _CYAN | 0x2a2a00L |
| Red | 4 | _RED | 0x00002aL |
| Magenta | 5 | _MAGENTA | 0x2a002aL |
| Brown | 6 | _BROWN | 0x00152aL |
| Light gray | 7 | _WHITE | 0x2a2a2aL |
| Dark gray | 8 | _GRAY | 0x151515L |
| Light blue | 9 | _LIGHTBLUE | 0x3f1515L |
| Light green | 10 | _LIGHTGREEN | 0x153f15L |
| Light cyan | 11 | _LIGHTCYAN | 0x3f3f15L |
| Light red | 12 | _LIGHTRED | 0x15153fL |
| Light magenta | 13 | _LIGHTMAGENTA | 0x3f153fL |
| Yellow | 14 | _LIGHTYELLOW | 0x153f3fL |
| White | 15 | _LIGHTWHITE | 0x3f3f3fL |

## CGA Palettes

| | Pixel Value | | | |
|---|---|---|---|---|
| Palette | 0 | 1 | 2 | 3 |
| CGA 0 | Backgrnd | Green | Red | Brown |
| CGA 1 | Backgrnd | Cyan | Magenta | Light gray |
| CGA 2 | Backgrnd | Light green | Light red | Yellow |
| CGA 3 | Backgrnd | Light cyan | Light magenta | White |

# Drawing

```
_setpixel(x,y)                       set pixel to current color
color = _getpixel(x,y)               get color value of pixel
_moveto(x,y)                         move Current Position to x,y
_lineto(x,y)                         draw line from CP to x,y

_rectangle(fill, x1, y1, x2, y2)     draw rectangle
        fill = _GFILLINTERIOR            fill with current color
        fill = _GBORDER                 don't fill
_arc(x1,y1,x2,y2,x3,y3,x4,y4)        draw arc bounded by
                                        rectangle x1,y1,x2,y2
                                        from vector x3,y3 to x4,y4

_ellipse(fill,x1,y1,x2,y2)           draw ellipse bounded by
                                        rectangle x1,y1,x2,y2
        fill = _GFILLINTERIOR           fill ellipse
        fill = _GBORDER                 don't fill ellipse
_pie(fill,x1,y1,x2,y2,x3,y3,x4,y4)   draw pie-slice bounded by
                                        rectangle x1,y1,x2,y2
                                        from vector x3,y3 to x4,y4
        fill = _GFILLINTERIOR        fill pie-slice
        fill = _GBORDER              don't fill pie-slice
```

# Fill

```
_getfillmask(unsigned char far *mask)   set fill pattern array
_setfillmask(unsigned char far *mask)   get fill pattern array
_floodfill(x,y,boundaryColor)           fill inside area
_setlinestyle(unsigned short mask)      set line to bits of mask
unsigned short mask = _getlinestyle()   returns mask
```

# Storing Images in Memory

```
_getimage(x1,y1,x2,y2, char far *buff)   store image in buffer
_putimage(x,y, char far *buff, action)   get image from buffer
        action = _GPSET                     erase existing pixel
        action = _GPRESET                   invert new pixels
        action = _GAND                      point by point AND
        action = _GOR                       point by point OR
        action = _GXOR                      point by point XOR
long size = _imagesize(x1,y1,x2,y2)      bytes needed for image
```

# Cursor

```
_displaycursor(toggle)   restore cursor at exit from graphics
        _GCURSORON          restore cursor at exit
        _GCURSOROFF         leave cursor off at exit
```

# Pages

```
_setactivepage(page)        set page to accept graphics output
_setvisualpage(page)        set page to be displayed
```

# Answers to Questions and Exercises

## Chapter 1
## Answers to Questions

1. b and d

2. compiled, linked, and executed

3. a and c are both correct

4. functions

5. The parentheses following **main()** indicate that "main" is a function and provide a place to put arguments.

6. a and b

7. False: only the semicolon signals the end of a statement.

8. Here's what's wrong with the example:

   a. no parentheses following **main**

   b. parentheses used instead of braces around body of program

   c. "print" used instead of "printf"

   d. no parentheses surrounding **printf()**'s argument

   e. no semicolon at the end of the statement

   f. program statement not indented

9. On the left there is a string which will be printed; on the right is a series of constants (or variables) which will be placed in the string.

10. The output is:

    one

```
two
three
```

# Chapter 1
## Suggested Answers to Exercises

### Exercise 1

Here's one possibility, although there are others:

```
main()
{
    printf("Mr. %s is %d,", "Green", 42);
    printf("Mr. %s is %d.", "Brown", 48);
}
```

### Exercise 2

```
main()
{
    printf("%c, %c, and %c are all letters.", 'a', 'b', 'c');
}
```

# Chapter 2
## Answers to Questions

1. a, b, and c are correct.

2. character (**char**), integer (**int**), floating point (**float**), long integer (**long**), and double-precision floating point (**double**)

3. a, b, and d are correct; there is no type "double float," except in ice cream parlors. However, **long float** is the same as **double**.

4. True

5. four

6. −32768 to 32767

7. d

8. False: it can hold numbers 65,536 times as large.

9. b and c are correct

10. '\x41' prints 'A' and '\xE0'prints the Greek letter alpha.

11. *decimal*      *exponential*
    a. 1,000,000   1.0e6
    b. 0.000,001   1.0e−6
    c. 199.95     1.9995e2
    d. −888.88   −8.8888e2

12. *exponential*    *decimal*
    a. 1.5e6       1,500,000
    b. 1.5e-6     0.000,001,5
    c. 7.6543e3   7,654.3
    d. −7.6543e−3  −0.007,654,3

13. There's no address operator preceding the **years** variable in the **scanf()** function.

14. d

15. True

16. a and c

17. `number++;`

18. `usa += calif;`

19. '\t' is the tab character, '\r' is the return character which prints a carriage return (but no linefeed), not to be confused with the newline character, '\n', which prints both a carriage return and a linefeed.

20. d

21. False

22. b

23. a. 1 > 2       false
    b. 'a' < 'b'    true (the ASCII codes are compared)
    c. 1 == 2    false
    d. '2' == '2'   true

24. b

25. No. The begin-comment symbol ( /* ) can't be used within a comment.

# Chapter 2
# Suggested Answers to Exercises

## Exercise 1

```
/* age.c */
/* calculates age in minutes */
main()
{
    float years, minutes;
    printf("Please type your age in years: ");
    scanf("%f", &years);
    minutes = years * 365 * 24 * 60;
    printf("You are %.1f minutes old.\n", minutes);
}
```

## Exercise 2

```
/* square.c */
/* finds square of typed-in number */
main()
{
    float square, number;

    printf("Type in number to be squared: ");
    scanf("%f", &number);
    square = number * number;
    printf("Square is: %f", number);
}
```

## Exercise 3

```
/* box2.c */
/* draws 4x4 box */
main()
{
    printf("\xC9\xCD\xCD\xBB\n");    /* top line */
    printf("\xBA  \xBA\n");          /* two spaces in the middle */
    printf("\xBA  \xBA\n");          /* ditto */
    printf("\xC8\xCD\xCD\xBC\n");    /* bottom line */
}
```

# Chapter 3
# Answers to Questions

1. initialize, test, increment
2. d
3. semicolon
4. b
5. commas
6. a
7. False
8. b
9. deeply
10. value
11. a, b, c, and d are all correct
12. True
13. b
14. b
15. False: it causes a return to the beginning of the loop.

# Chapter 3
# Suggested Answers to Exercises

## Exercise 1

```
/* square.c */
/* prints out the square of the first 20 integers */
main()
{
    int n;
    for (n=1; n<21; n++)
        printf("The square of %2d is %3d\n", n, n * n);
}
```

## Exercise 2

```
/* charcnt2.c */
/* counts characters in a phrase typed in */
/* until period is typed */
main()
{
```

```
        int count=0;
        printf("Type in a phrase:\n");
        while ( getche() != '.' )
            count++;
        printf("\nCharacter count is %d", count);
    }
```

## Exercise 3

```
/* between.c */
/* tells how many letters between two letters */
main()
{
    char ch1, ch2;
    while (1)
        {
        printf("\n\nType first character: ");
        ch1 = getche();
        printf("\nType second character: ");
        ch2 = getche();
        printf("\nThere are %d characters between.", ch2-ch1-1 );
        }
}
```

# Chapter 4
# Answers to Questions

1. b and c are both correct

2. Yes, except for the keyword **then**, which doesn't exist in C.

3. False

4. c

5. a—there is no conditional expression following **else**.

6. Yes: the compiler doesn't care if you put multiple statements on one line, although it is more difficult to read.

7. False

8. b

9. d

10. b

11. No: colons must be used after the **case** statements, and **break** statements are needed after the **printf()** statements.

12. False: **break** statements are not used if two **case**s trigger the same set of statements.

13. No: variables, such as **temp**, cannot be used in **case** expressions.

14. d

15. 0

# Chapter 4
# Suggested Answers to Exercises

## Exercise 1

```
/* speed.c */
/* prints appropriate response to user's speed */
main()
{
   int speed;
   printf("Please type the speed you normally ");
   printf("travel in a 55 mph zone: ");
   scanf("%d", &speed);
   if ( speed > 75 )
      printf("I'm taking you to headquarters, buddy.");
   else
      if (speed > 65 )
         printf("I'm gonna hafta write you up, mac.");
      else
         if (speed > 55 )
            printf("I'll let you off with a warning, this time.");
         else
            if (speed > 45 )
               printf("Have a good day, sir.");
            else
               printf("Can't you get the lead out, buddy?");
}
```

## Exercise 2

```
/* checker2.c */
/* draws a checkerboard on the screen */
main()
{
   int x, y, z;
   for (y=1; y<=8; y++)                 /* stepping down screen */
      for (z=1; z<=3; z++)              /* 3 lines per square */
         {
         for (x=1; x<=8; x++)          /* stepping across screen */
            if ( (x+y) % 2 == 0 )      /* even numbered square? */
                                       /* print 6 rectangles */
               printf("\xDB\xDB\xDB\xDB\xDB\xDB");
            else
```

```
        printf("      ");        /* print 6 blank spaces */
    if (y * z < 24 )             /* print newline, */
        printf("\n");            /*    except on last line */
    }
}
```

## Exercise 3

```
/* linesX.c */
/* prints four crossed lines on screen */
main()
{
    int x, y;
    for (y=1; y<24; y++)             /* step down screen */
        {
        for (x=1; x<24; x++)         /* step across screen */
            if ( x == y )            /* NW-SE diagonal? */
                printf("\xDB");      /* print solid color */
            else if ( x == 24 - y )  /* SW-NE diagonal? */
                printf("\xDB");      /* print solid color */
            else if ( x == 12 )      /* vertical line? */
                printf("\xDB");      /* print solid color */
            else if ( y == 12 )      /* horizontal line? */
                printf("\xDB");      /* print solid color */
            else
                printf("\xB0");      /* print gray */
        printf("\n");                /* next line */
        }
}
```

## Exercise 4

```
/* linesX2.c */
/* prints four crossed lines on screen */
main()
{
    int x, y;
    for (y=1; y<24; y++)
        {
        for (x=1; x<24; x++)
            if ( x==y || x==24-y || x==12 || y==12 )
                printf("\xDB");
            else
                printf("\xB0");
        printf("\n");
        }
}
```

### Exercise 5

```
/* circle.c */
/* draws quarter circle on screen */
main()
{
    int x, y, rs;
    for (y=1; y<24; y++)
        {
        for (x=1; x<48; x++)
            {
            rs = x*x + y*y;
            if ( rs < 420 && rs > 380 )
                printf("\xDB");
            else
                printf(" ");
            }
        printf("\n");
        }
}
```

# Chapter 5
# Answers to Questions

1. All except b are valid reasons for using functions. Functions don't run faster than inline code or macros.

2. True

3. No: the call to the function must be terminated with a semicolon.

4. False: you can return from a function by simply "falling through" the closing brace.

5. `char foo(float, float);`
   or
   `char foo(float arg1, float arg2);`

6. No, the declarator at the start of the function should not be terminated with a semicolon.

7. a and c

8. False: functions commonly use local variables which are accessible only to the function in which they're defined.

9. b and c, although we won't learn about c until the chapter on pointers.

10. a, b, d, and e

11. No: the argument passed to the function is type **int** in the calling program but type **float** in the function.

12. a

13. many

14. d

15. c

16. c

17. substituted

18. No: you can't have spaces in the left-hand part of the statement (the identifier).

19. "EXP" is the identifier and "2.71828" is the text.

20. a and b are both correct.

21. a, b, and d

22. No: the macro expands into the incorrect

```
postage = rate*l + w + h
```

23. inserted

24. b, c, and d

25. INCLUDE

# Chapter 5
# Suggested Answers to Exercises

## Exercise 1

```
/* maxnum.c */
/* tells largest number in array typed in */
#include <stdio.h>              /* for printf() */
#define MAXSIZE 20              /* size of array */
int maxnum(int[], int);        /* prototype */
```

```
      void main(void)
      {
         int list[MAXSIZE];
         int size = 0;                  /* start at element [0] */
         int num;                       /* temp storage */

         do                             /* get list of numbers */
            {
            printf("Type number: ");
            scanf("%d", &list[size]);
            }
         while ( list[size++] != 0 );
         num = maxnum(list, size-1);    /* get largest number */
         printf("Largest number is %d", num);  /* print it */
      }


      /* maxnum() */
      /* returns largest number in array */
      int maxnum(int list[], int size)
      {
         int dex, max;

         max = list[0];                 /* assume 1st element largest */
         for (dex=1; dex<size; dex++)   /* check remaining elements */
            if ( max < list[dex] )      /* if one bigger, */
               max = list[dex];         /*    make it the largest */
         return(max);
      }
```

## Exercise 2

```
/* times.c */
/* calculates difference between two times */
#include <stdio.h>       /* for printf(), etc. */
float getsecs(void);     /* prototype */

void main(void)
{
   float secs1, secs2;    /* declare variables */

   printf("Type first time (form 12:22:55): ");
   secs1 = getsecs();
   printf("Type second (later) time: ");
   secs2 = getsecs();
   printf("Difference is %.0f seconds.", secs2-secs1);
}

/* getsecs() */
/* gets time from kbd in hours-minutes-seconds format */
```

```
/* returns time in seconds */
float getsecs(void)
{
    float hours, minutes, seconds;

    scanf("%f:%f:%f", &hours, &minutes, &seconds);
    return ( hours*60*60 + minutes*60 + seconds );
}
```

## Exercise 3

```
/* swapprog.c */
/* program to test swap function */
#include <stdio.h>          /* for printf(), etc. */
void swap(void);            /* prototype */
int num1, num2;            /* external variables */

void main(void)
{
    printf("Enter two integers: ");
    scanf("%d %d", &num1, &num2);
    printf("num1=%d num2=%d\n", num1, num2);
    printf("Swapping.\n");
    swap();
    printf("num1=%d num2=%d\n", num1, num2);
}

/* swap() */
/* exchanges values of two external variables */
void swap(void)
{
    extern int num1, num2;
    int temp;

    temp = num1;
    num1 = num2;
    num2 = temp;
}
```

## Exercise 4

```
    /* timesM.c */
    /* calculates difference between two times */
    /* uses macro */
    #define HMSTOSEC(hrs,mins,secs) (hrs*3600 + mins*60 + secs)

    main()
    {
        float secs1, secs2;    /* declare variables */
```

```
        float hours, minutes, seconds;
        printf("Type first time (form 12:22:55): ");
        scanf("%f:%f:%f", &hours, &minutes, &seconds);
        secs1 = HMSTOSEC(hours, minutes, seconds);
        printf("Type second (later) time: ");
        scanf("%f:%f:%f", &hours, &minutes, &seconds);
        secs2 = HMSTOSEC(hours, minutes, seconds);
        printf("Difference is %.2f seconds.", secs2-secs1);
   }
```

# Chapter 6
# Answers to Questions

1. c

2. d

3. type, name, size

4. No: brackets are used in array declarations, not parentheses.

5. The fifth element

6. b

7. d

8. No: use **j < MAX**, and **&prices[j]**.

9. No: must use brackets following the name.

10. c

11. d

12. **external, static**

13. c and d

14. sure

15. array[1][0]

16. address

17. a

18. a and c, which are the same thing.

19. False: the function doesn't move the values stored in the array.

20. c, although some other choices aren't clearly false.

21. string, character.

22. c

23. null '\0'.

24. **gets( )**

25. 9 (space must be left for the '\0' character).

26. True

27. a

28. **&string[5]**

29. You can't use assignment statements with strings.

30. **strlen(name)**

# Chapter 6
# Suggested Answers to Exercises

## Exercise 1

```
/* temp.c */
/* averages one week's temperatures */
/* prints them out along with average */
main()
{
    int temper[7];              /* array declaration */
    int day, sum;
    for (day=0; day<7; day++)      /* put temps in array */
        {
        printf("Enter temperature for day %d: ", day);
        scanf("%d", &temper[day]);
        }
    sum = 0;                    /* calculate average */
    for (day=0; day<7; day++)      /* and print temperatures */
        {
        printf("Temperature for day %d is %d.\n", day, temper[day]);
        sum += temper[day];
        }
    printf("Average is %d.", sum/7);
}
```

## Exercise 2

```
/* fltemp3.c */
/* averages arbitrary number of temperatures */
#define LIM 5
main()
{
    float temper[LIM];                 /* array declaration */
    float sum=0.0;
    int num, day=0;
    printf("Enter temperature for day 0: ");
    scanf("%f", &temper[0krt]);
    while ( temper[day++] > 0 )     /* put temps in array */
        {
```

```
        printf("Enter temperature for day %d: ", day);
        scanf("%f", &temper[day]);
        }
    num = day-1;                        /* number of temps entered */
    for (day=0; day<num; day++)      /* calculate average */
        sum += temper[day];
    printf("Average is %.1f", sum/num);
}
```

## Exercise 3

```
/* insert.c */
/* inserts a character into a string */
main()
{
    char charac;
    char string[81];
    int position;
    printf("Type string [Return], character, position\n");
    gets(string);
    scanf("%c %d", &charac, &position);
    strins(string,charac,position);
    puts(string);
}

/* strins() */
/* inserts character into string */
strins(str,ch,n)
char str[], ch;
int n;
{
    char scratch[81];                /* temporary space */
    strcpy( scratch, &str[n] );   /* save 2nd half in scratch */
    str[n] = ch;                     /* insert character */
    strcpy( &str[n+1], scratch ); /* shift 2nd half right */
}
```

## Exercise 4

```
/* rotate */
/* prints all possible rotations of a word */
#include <stdio.h>                /* for printf() */
#include <string.h>               /* for strlen() */
void rotate(void);                /* prototype */

char word[] = "medieval";
int length;

void main(void)
{
    int k;
```

```
    length = strlen(word);
    for (k=1; k<=length; k++)
        {
        rotate();
        printf("%d. Word=%s\n", k, word);
        }
}

/* rotate() */
/* rotates external string "word" one position */
void rotate(void)
{
    int j;
    char ch;

    ch = word[0];                  /* save first char */
    for (j=0; j<length-1; j++)     /* move other chars left */
        word[j] = word[j+1];       /*     one position */
    word[length-1] = ch;           /* put first char on end */
}
```

# Chapter 7
# Answers to Questions

1. b and c

2. a and c

3. True

4. False: we learned how to pass the addresses of arrays to functions in the last chapter.

5. False: when a value is passed to a function, the value itself (not its address) is stored in the function's memory space.

6. d

7. c

8. addresses, declare, indirection

9. b

10. Both a and d will work (provided they are known to the function where the reference is made).

11. c

12. *pointvar = *pointvar / 10;

13. b and d

14. In the function's memory space

15. ptrj = &j;

16. No: it should be **scanf("%d", ptrx);**

17. a

18. No: you can't increment an address, which is a pointer constant.

19. Print the array elements: "4  5  6".

20. 2

21. Print the addresses of the array elements.

22. Print the array elements: "4  5  6".

23. Almost: the second creates a pointer as well as an array.

24. The same amount, different amounts

25. "I come not to bury Caesar"

    "I come not to bury Caesar"

    "to bury Caesar"

26. 13 bytes: 11 for the string plus null character and 2 for the pointer to the string

27. False: every *row* of a two-dimensional array can be considered to be a *one-dimensional* array.

28. arr7[1][1], *(*(arr + 1) + 1)

29. d

30. *(*(arr7 + x) + y)

# Chapter 7
# Suggested Answers to Exercises

### Exercise 1

```
/* zerovars.c */
/* tests function which zeros three variables */
#include <stdio.h>                 /* for printf() */
void zero(int *, int *, int *);   /* prototype */

void main(void)
{
    int x=4, y=7, z=11;

    zero( &x, &y, &z );
    printf("x=%d, y=%d, z=%d.", x, y, z);
}

/* zero() */
/* puts zero in three variables in calling program */
```

```
void zero(int *px, int *py, int *pz)
{
   *px = 0;
   *py = 0;
   *pz = 0;
}
```

## Exercise 2

```
/* zeroarr.c */
/* tests function to zero array elements */
#include <stdio.h>                  /* for printf() */
void zero(int *, int);              /* prototype */
#define SIZE 5                       /* size of array */

void main(void)
{
   static int array[SIZE] = { 3, 5, 7, 9, 11 };
   int j;

   zero(array, SIZE);               /* call funct to add consts */
   for (j=0; j<SIZE; j++)           /* print out array */
      printf("%d  ", *(array+j) );
}

/* zero() */
/* zeros out elements of array in calling program */
void zero(int *ptr, int num)
{
   int k;
   for(k=0; k<num; k++)
      *(ptr+k) = 0;
}
```

## Exercise 3

```
/* zerostr.c */
/* tests function which puts null character in string */
#include <stdio.h>                  /* for printf() */
void zero(char *);                  /* prototype */

void main(void)
{
   char *phrase = "Don't test the river with both feet";

   printf("Phrase=%s.\n", phrase);
   zero(phrase);
   printf("Phrase=%s.\n", phrase);
}
```

```
/* zero() */
/* function to put null character at start of string */
void zero(char *str)
{
   *str = '\0';
}
```

## Exercise 4

```
/* mergarr.c */
/* adds elements of two arrays */
#define ROWS 4
#define COLS 5
main()
{
   int j, k;
   static int arr1[ROWS][COLS] =
                     { { 13, 15, 17, 19, 21 },
                       { 20, 22, 24, 26, 28 },
                       { 31, 33, 35, 37, 39 },
                       { 40, 42, 44, 46, 48 }  };
   static int arr2[ROWS][COLS] =
                     { { 10, 11, 12, 13, 14 },
                       { 15, 16, 17, 18, 19 },
                       { 20, 21, 22, 23, 24 },
                       { 25, 26, 27, 28, 29 }  };
   int arr3[ROWS][COLS];

   for(j=0; j<ROWS; j++)                /* add arrays */
      for(k=0; k<COLS; k++)
        *(*(arr3+j)+k) = *(*(arr1+j)+k) + *(*(arr2+j)+k);
   for(j=0; j<ROWS; j++)                /* print out new array */
      {
      for (k=0; k<COLS; k++)
         printf("%d ", *(*(arr3+j)+k) );
      printf("\n");
      }
}
```

# Chapter 8
# Answers to Questions

1. b and c

2. 256

3. 2

4. False: key combinations such as [Alt] [z] can be represented as well.

5. d

6. b and c

7. a, b, and c

8. a. The CONFIG.SYS file must be in the main directory and must contain the line DEVICE = ANSI.SYS. The ANSI.SYS file must be in the system.

9. d is the most correct, although a case could be made for c.

10. "\x1B[2J"

11. False: it can be moved immediately to any location.

12. bold, blinking, underlined, reverse video

13. "\x1B[C"

14. False: it causes an exit from the entire program.

15. num = atoi(str);

16. True

17. b and d

18. strcpy(str,"steeple");
    strcat(str,"chase");

19. a, c, and d

20. C>prog1 <f1.c >f2.c

# Chapter 8
# Suggested Answers to Exercises

## Exercise 1

```
/* backsp.c */
/* prints letters, backspaces with left arrow key */
#define C_LEFT "\x1B[D"                  /* move cursor left */
```

```
#define L_ARRO 75                        /* left arrow key */
main()
{
    char key;
    while ( (key=getch()) != 'X' )    /* read keyboard */
       if( key == 0 )                 /* if extended code, */
          {
          if( getch() == L_ARRO )     /* read second code */
             {                        /* if left arrow */
             printf(C_LEFT);          /* move cursor left */
             printf(" ");             /* print space over char */
             printf(C_LEFT);          /* reset cursor */
             }
          }
       else
          putch(key);                 /* not ext code, print char */
}
```

## Exercise 2

```
/* decihex.c */
/* translates decimal number into hexadecimal */
/* uses command-line arguments */
main(argc,argv)
int argc;
char *argv[];
{
    long num;
    if( argc != 2 )
       printf("Example usage: decihex 128");
    else
       {
       num = atol( *(argv+1) );
       printf("Hex=%x", num );
       }
}
```

## Exercise 3

```
/* braces.c */
/* checks if numbers of right and left braces are equal */
#define EOF '\x1A'
main()
{
    int left=0, right=0;
    char ch;
    while( (ch=getche()) != EOF )
       {
       if( ch=='{' )
          left++;
```

```
            if( ch=='}' )
                right++;
            }
        if (left != right)
            printf("\n\nMismatched braces\n");
    }
```

## Exercise 4

```
/* hiletter.c */
/* highlights letters in a phrase */
#include <stdio.h>              /* for printf(), etc. */
#include <conio.h>             /* for getch() */
#include <string.h>            /* for strlen() */
#define CLEAR  "\x1B[2J"       /* clear screen */
#define ERASE "\x1B[K"         /* erase line */
#define C_LEFT "\x1B[D"        /* move cursor left */
#define C_RITE "\x1B[C"        /* move cursor right */
#define START  "\x1B[2;1f"     /* cursor at start of line */
#define L_ARRO 75              /* left arrow key code */
#define R_ARRO 77              /* right arrow key code */
#define REVERSE "\x1B[7m"      /* reverse video attribute */
#define NORMAL "\x1B[0m"       /* normal attribute */

void display(char *, int);     /* prototype */

void main(void)
{
    char key, phrase[80];
    int curpos=0;              /* position of hilited char */

    printf(CLEAR);             /* clear screen */
    puts("Type phrase:");
    gets(phrase);
    while ( (key=getch() ) == 0 )  /* quit of not ext code */
        {
        key=getch();           /* get extended code */
        switch (key)
            {
            case L_ARRO :
                if ( curpos > 0 ) --curpos; break;
            case R_ARRO :
                if ( curpos < strlen(phrase)-1 ) ++curpos; break;
            }
        display(phrase, curpos); /* display phrase */
        }
}

/* display() */
/* displays phrase, highlight at cursor position */
```

```
void display(char *string, int position)
{
    int j;

    printf(START);                         /* cursor to line start */
    printf(ERASE);                         /* erase line */
    for(j=0; j<strlen(string); j++)        /* one letter at a time */
    {
        if ( j==position )                 /* if cursor position, */
            printf(REVERSE);               /*     reverse video */
        printf( "%c", *(string+j) );       /* print letter */
        printf(NORMAL);                    /* normal display */
    }
}
```

# Chapter 9
# Answers to Questions

1. same type, different types

2. False: arrays are more appropriate for elements of the same type.

3. b, c, and d are all correct

4. ```
   struct xxx
       {
       char string[10];
       int num;
       };
   ```

5. c

6. type, variable, value

7. `struct vehicle car;`

8. `jim.arms = 2;`

9. ```
   struct body
           {
           int arms;
           int legs;
           }jim;
   ```

10. Yes, at least in modern compilers.

11. a and b

12.
```
struct partners
    (
    struct body sandy;
    struct body pat;
    };
```

13. True (in modern compilers)

14.
```
struct book *ptrbook;
```

15. a and d. This expression will also work.

```
(*addweath).temp
```

16. a free section of memory

17. memory

18. next structure

19. False: the **sizeof()** function returns the size of a *data type*.

20. d

21.
```
union intstr
    {
    char string[10];
    int num;
    };
```

22. Read-Only Memory Basic Input/Output System

23. d

24. True

25. d

26. AX, BX, CX, DX

27. AH, AL, BH, BL, CH, CL, DH, DL

28. b and c

29. d

30. False: there is a ROM service routine that returns the memory size.

# Chapter 9
# Suggested Answers to Exercises

## Exercise 1

```
/* date.c */
/* demonstrates structure to hold date */
main()
{
    struct date
        {
        int month;
        int day;
        int year;
        };
    struct date today;

    today.month = 12;
    today.day = 31;
    today.year = 88;

    printf("date is %d/%d/%d",
                today.month, today.day, today.year );
}
```

## Exercise 2

```
/* date2.c */
/* demonstrates passing structure to function */
#include <stdio.h>                      /* for printf() */

struct date                    /* structure definition */
    {
    int month;                 /* structure members */
    int day;
    int year;
    };

void prindate(struct date mmddyy);     /* prototype (follows */
                                       /*      struct def) */
void main(void)
{
    struct date today;         /* structure variable */

    today.month = 12;          /* give values to */
    today.day = 31;            /*      structure variables */
    today.year = 88;
    prindate(today);           /* print date from structure */
}
```

```
/* prindate() */
/* prints date passed via structure */
void prindate(struct date mmddyy)
{
    printf("date is %d/%d/%d",
                mmddyy.month, mmddyy.day, mmddyy.year );
}
```

## Exercise 3

```
/* book.c */
/* demonstrates nested structures */
#include <stdio.h>                    /* for printf() */
#include <string.h>                   /* for strcpy() */

struct date                          /* structure for date */
    {
    int month;
    int day;
    int year;
    };

struct book                          /* structure for book */
    {
    char title[30];
    struct date duedate;
    };

void prinbook(struct book bk);       /* prototype */

void main(void)
{
    char *thistitle = "Day and Knight";
    struct book thisb;
    struct date today;

    strcpy(thisb.title,thistitle);   /* put title in struct */
    thisb.duedate.month = 12;        /* put date in struct */
    thisb.duedate.day = 31;          /* day */
    thisb.duedate.year = 89;         /* year */
    prinbook(thisb);                 /* print out structure */
}

/* prinbook() */
/* prints book info passed via structure */
void prinbook(struct book bk)
{
    printf("Title: %s\n", bk.title );
    printf("Due date: %d/%d/%d",
            bk.duedate.month, bk.duedate.day, bk.duedate.year );
}
```

## Exercise 4

```
/* position2.c */
/* demonstrates ROM 'cursor position' service */
#include "dos.h"
#define TRUE 1
#define CLEAR "\x1B[2J"              /* clear screen */
#define ERASE "\x1B[K"              /* erase line */
#define VIDEO 0x10
#define SETC 2
main()
{
    union REGS regs;
    int row=1, col=1;
    printf(CLEAR);
    while ( TRUE )
        {
        regs.h.ah = SETC;            /* 'set cur pos' service */
        regs.h.dh = 22;              /* row in DH */
        regs.h.dl = 0;               /* column in DL */
        int86(VIDEO, &regs, &regs); /* call video services */
        printf(ERASE);               /* erase line */
        printf("Type row and column number (form 10,40): ");
        scanf("%d,%d", &row, &col); /* get coordinates */
        regs.h.ah = SETC;            /* 'set cur pos' service */
        regs.h.dh = row;             /* row in DH */
        regs.h.dl = col;             /* column in DL */
        int86(VIDEO, &regs, &regs); /* call video services */
        printf("*(%d,%d)", row, col);    /* print coordinates */
        }
}
```

## Exercise 5

```
/* agent4.c */
/* maintains list of agents in memory */
/* can search for skills */
#include <stdio.h>                 /* for printf(), etc */
#include <conio.h>                 /* for getch() */
#include <string.h>                /* for strcmp(), etc */
#define TRUE 1
void newname(void);               /* prototypes */
void search(char *);
int instr(char *, char *);

struct personel                   /* define data structure */
    {
    char name [30];               /* name */
    int agnumb;                   /* code number */
    float height;                 /* height in inches */
```

```
        char skill[80];              /* special skills */
        };
struct personel agent[50];       /* array of 50 structures */
int n=0;                         /* number of agents */

void main(void)
{
    char ch, inskill[20];

    while (TRUE)
        {
        printf("\nType 'e' to enter new agent,");   /* print */
        printf("\n   'l' to list all agents, ");     /* selections */
        printf("\n   's' to search for skills: ");
        ch = getche();                               /* get choice */
        switch (ch)
            {
            case 'e':                  /* enter new name */
                newname(); break;
            case 'l':                  /* list all agents */
                search('\0'); break;  /*    (all contain '\0') */
            case 's':                  /* list agents with skill */
                printf("\nEnter skill to be searched for: ");
                gets(inskill);         /* get skill */
                search(inskill); break;   /* list those agents */
            default:                   /* user mistake */
                puts("\nEnter only selections listed");
            }  /* end switch */
        }  /* end while */
}  /* end main */

/* newname() */
/* puts a new agent in the database */
void newname(void)
{
    printf("\nRecord %d.\nEnter name: ",n+1); /* get name */
    gets(agent[n].name);
    printf("Enter agent number (3 digits): "); /* get number */
    scanf("%d", &agent[n].agnumb);
    printf("Enter height in inches: ");        /* get height */
    scanf("%f", &agent[n].height);
    fflush(stdin);                             /* clear buffer */
    printf("Enter skills (one line): ");       /* get skills */
    gets(agent[n++].skill);
}

/* search() */
/* search database for agents with listed skill */
void search(char *inskill)
{
    int j;
```

```
        if (n < 1)                              /* check empty list */
           printf("\nEmpty list.\n");
        for (j=0; j < n; j++)                   /* search list */
           if( instr(agent[j].skill, inskill) >= 0 )
                 {                              /* if agent has skill */
              printf("\nRecord number %d\n", j+1);   /* list agent */
              printf("   Name: %s\n", agent[j].name);
              printf("   Agent number: %03d\n", agent[j].agnumb);
              printf("   Height: %4.2f\n", agent[j].height);
              printf("   Skills: %s\n", agent[j].skill);
                 }
    }

/* instr() */
/* returns position of word in sentence */
int instr(char *sent, char *word)
{
    int n, slen, wlen;

    slen = strlen(sent);                /* length of sentence */
    wlen = strlen(word);                /* length of word */
    for(n = 0; n <= slen-wlen; n++) /* move along sentence */
                                        /* to wlen from end */
        if ( strncmp(sent+n, word, wlen) == 0 )
            return(n);                  /* match, return index */
    return(-1);                         /* no match, return -1 */
}
```

# Chapter 10
# Answers to Questions

1. a. 00000001,

   b. 11111000,

   c. 0001001000110100,

   d. 1111110000001010

2. b

3. False: the bitwise operators treat variables as sequences of bits.

4. c

5. mask

6. c

7. d (since the sign bit will be shifted in on the left)

8. combine

9. segment, offset

10. b

11. a and b are equivalent and both are correct

12. absolute

13. four

14. d

15. True

16. faster

17. b

18. False: the pointer must be typecast:

```
farptr = (int far *) 0xA1001234;
```

19. a, b, c, and d are all correct

20. True

21. c and d are both true

22. bits, groups of bits

23. a, c, and d are all correct

24. 0xB0000, 0xB0F9F

25. a, b, c, and d are all correct

# Chapter 10
# Suggested Answers to Exercises

## Exercise 1

```
/* exortest.c */
/* demonstrates bitwise EXCLUSIVE OR operator */
```

```
#define TRUE 1
main()
{
    unsigned char x1, x2;
    while(TRUE)
        {
        printf("\nEnter two hex numbers (ff or less, example 'cc 7'): ");
        scanf("%x %x", &x1, &x2);
        printf("%02x ^ %02x = %02x\n", x1, x2, x1 ^ x2 );
        }
}
```

## Exercise 2

```
/* bintohex.c */
/* converts binary number typed by user to hex and decimal */
#define TRUE 1
main()
{
    int count, ans;
    char ch;
    while(TRUE)
        {
        printf("Type binary number(terminate with spacebar):\n");
        count=0; ans=0;
        while( count++ < 16 )
            {
            if( (ch=getche()) == '0' )
                ans <<= 1;
            else if( ch == '1')
                ans = (ans << 1) + 1;
            else break;
            }
        printf("= %x (hex) = %u (dec)\n\n", ans, ans );
        }
}
```

## Exercise 3

```
/* ddraw.c */
/* moves cursor on screen,leaves trail */
/* uses direct display memory access */
#define COMAX 80
#define ROMAX 25
#define L_ARRO 75
#define R_ARRO 77
#define U_ARRO 72
```

```
#define D_ARRO 80
#define ACROSS 205
#define UPDOWN 186
#define BOX 219
#define TRUE 1
int far *farptr;
int col=40, row=12;                    /* insert position */
main()
{
    char ch;
    farptr = (int far *) 0xB0000000; /* start of screen mem */
    clear();                          /* clear screen */
    while(TRUE)
        {
        if ( (ch=getch()) == 0 )      /* if char is 0 */
            {
            ch = getch();             /* read extended code */
            switch(ch)
                {
                case R_ARRO: if(col<COMAX) ++col; ch=ACROSS; break;
                case L_ARRO: if(col>0)     --col; ch=ACROSS; break;
                case D_ARRO: if(row<ROMAX) ++row; ch=UPDOWN; break;
                case U_ARRO: if(row>0)     --row; ch=UPDOWN; break;
                default: ch=BOX;          /* rectangle at corners */
                }
            insert(ch);               /* insert char */
            }
        }
}
/* add clear() function from wpro1.c */
```

## Exercise 4

Start with wpro2.c. Add the following line to the **#define** section:

```
#define CTR_BK 127              /* [Ctrl] and backspace keys */
```

Add a line to the second **switch** section so it looks like this:

```
switch(ch)
    {
    case BK_SPC: if(col>0) delete(); break;
    case CTR_BK: if(col>1) delword(); break;
    default: if(length<COMAX) insert(ch,attr);
    }
```

Then add the following function:

```
/* delword */
```

```
/* deletes word to left of cursor position */
delword()
{                                            /* while not space, */
    while( (*(farptr+col-1) & 0xFF) != ' ' && col > 0 )
        delete();                            /* del char to left */
    if(col > 0)
        delete();                            /* delete space */
}
```

# Chapter 11
# Answers to Questions

1. resolution, text/graphics, number of colors, monitor type, display adaptor type, memory size, number of pages, memory starting address

2. d

3. 4, 8

4. b

5. ROM BIOS routine, direct memory access

6. blue, green, red, intensity

7. all four choices

8. 4

9. d

10. b

11. sixteen (including black)

12. a

13. False

14. b and c

15. color

16. a

17. On each bit plane, eight.

18. None is correct; a single bit plane cannot represent cyan.

19. bit

20. d

21. read

22. c

23. False

24. b

25. move

# Chapter 11
# Suggested Answers to Exercises

### Exercise 1

```
/* fillco.c */
/* fills screen with color */

main()
{
    char far *farptr;
    int j;
    char cocon;
    char color[20];
    printf("Type black, cyan, magenta or white: ");
    gets(color);
    switch (color[0])
        {
        case 'c': cocon = 0x55; break;
        case 'm': cocon = 0xAA; break;
        case 'w': cocon = 0xFF; break;
        default:  cocon = 0x00; break;
        }
    farptr = (int far *) 0xB8000000;
    for(j=0; j<0x3F3F; j++)
        *(farptr+j) = cocon;
}
```

### Exercise 2

```
/* conrect2.c */
/* draws concentric rectangle of different colors */
void rect(int, int, int, int, unsigned char);  /* prototypes */
void putpt(int, int, unsigned char);

void main(void)
{
    int z;
    for(z=50; z>=10; z-=10)
        rect(100-z, 100+z, 160-z, 160+z, (z/10)%4);
}

/* rect() */
/* draws rectangle on screen using putpt() */
void rect(int top, int bot, int left, int rite,
                                        unsigned char color)
{
    int x, y;
    for(y=top; y<=bot; y++)
```

```
            for(x=left; x<=rite; x++)
                putpt(x,y,color);
    }


/* putpt() */
/* displays point at location col, row */
#define BYTES 40                     /* (bytes per row) / 2 */
#define PIX    4                     /* pixels per byte */
void putpt(int col, int row, unsigned char color)
{
    int addr, j, bitpos;
    unsigned int mask=0xFF3F;        /* 11111111 00111111 */
    unsigned char temp;
    unsigned char far *farptr;       /* to hold screen address */
    farptr = (char far *) 0xB8000000;/* set ptr to screen addr */

    /* calculate offset address of byte to be altered */
    addr = row*BYTES + col/PIX;      /* calculate address */
    if(row & 1)                      /* if odd row number */
        addr += 8152;                /* use 2nd memory bank */

    /* shift two-bit color & mask to appropriate place in byte */
    color <<= 6;                     /* put color on left */
    bitpos = col & 0x03;             /* get lower 2 bits */
    for(j=0; j<bitpos; j++)          /* shift mask & color */
        {                            /*      to right */
        mask >>= 2;                  /*      bitpos times */
        color >>= 2;
        }

    /* put two color bits in screen memory location */
    temp = *(farptr+addr) & (char)mask; /* and off color bits */
    *(farptr+addr) = temp | color;      /* or on new color */
}
```

## Exercise 3

```
/* arrow.c */
/* draws arrow, which moves as directed by cursor keys */
#include <conio.h>          /* for getch() */
#define MAXC 320            /* horizontal resolution */
#define MAXR 200            /* vertical resolution */
#define RED 2               /* 2-bit color values */
#define BLACK 0
#define L_ARRO 75           /* cursor control keys */
#define R_ARRO 77
#define U_ARRO 72
#define D_ARRO 80
void drawarro(int, int, unsigned char);  /* prototypes */
void putpt(int, int, unsigned char);
```

```
void main(void)
{
    int x=160, y=100;                  /* starting location */
    int dx=4, dy=4;                    /* speed to move arrow */
    int nux=160, nuy=100;              /* new position */
    int ch;                            /* keyboard char */

    drawarro(x, y, RED);               /* draw initial arrow */
    while( getch()==0 )                /* exit if not ext code */
        {
        ch = getch();                  /* read extended code */
        switch(ch)                     /* change new coords */
            {
            case R_ARRO: nux = x + dx; break;
            case L_ARRO: nux = x - dx; break;
            case U_ARRO: nuy = y - dy; break;
            case D_ARRO: nuy = y + dy; break;
            }
        drawarro(x, y, BLACK);         /* erase old arrow */
        drawarro(nux, nuy, RED);       /* draw new arrow */
        x=nux; y=nuy;                  /* make old = new */
        }
}


/* drawarro() */
/* draws arrow 16x16 pattern. Upper-left corner at col, row */
void drawarro(int col, int row, unsigned char color)
{
    unsigned int mask;
    int x, y, dotpat;

    static unsigned int arro[16] =   /* picture of arrow */
                { 0x03FF, 0x01FF, 0x00FF, 0x007F,
                  0x00FF, 0x01FF, 0x03FF, 0x07F7,
                  0x0FE3, 0x1FC1, 0x3F80, 0x7F00,
                  0xFE00, 0x7C00, 0x3800, 0x1000 };

    for(y=0; y<16; y++)                /* each of 16 rows */
        {
        dotpat = arro[y];              /* pattern for this row */
        mask = 0x8000;                 /* one-bit mask on left */
        for(x=0; x<16; x++)            /* each of 16 columns */
            {
            if(mask & dotpat)          /* if part of pattern */
                putpt(col+x, row+y, color); /* draw dot */
            mask >>= 1;                /* move mask right */
            }
        }
}
```

```
/* putpt() */
/* displays point at location col, row */
#define BYTES 40                      /* (bytes per row) / 2 */
#define BANK 8192-BYTES               /* 2nd bank - one row */
void putpt(int col, int row, unsigned char color)
{
    int addr, j, bitpos;
    unsigned int mask=0xFF3F;         /* 11111111 00111111 */
    unsigned char temp;
    unsigned char far *farptr;        /* to hold screen address */
    farptr = (char far *) 0xB8000000;/* set ptr to screen addr */
    addr = row*BYTES + (col >> 2);    /* calculate address */
    if(row & 1)                       /* if odd row number */
        addr += BANK;                 /* use 2nd memory bank */
    color <<= 6;                      /* put color on left */
    bitpos = col & 0x03;              /* get lower 2 bits */
    for(j=0; j<bitpos; j++)           /* shift mask & color */
        {                             /*     2 bits right */
        mask >>= 2;                   /*      bitpos times */
        color >>= 2;
        }
    temp = *(farptr+addr) & (char)mask; /* AND off color bits */
    *(farptr+addr) = temp | color;      /* OR on new color */
}
```

## Exercise 4

```
/* bar.c */
/* draws bargraph; for EGA mode 14 (640x200) */
#include <conio.h>     /* for outp() */
#define BLUE 1         /* EGA colors */
#define GREEN 2
#define YELLOW 14
#define RED 4
#define IWHITE 15
void rect(int, int, int, int, unsigned char);  /* prototype */

int data[16] =                        /* height of bars */
    { 25,85,50,100,125,150,180,140,70,170,80,35,70,90,110,30 };
void main(void)
{
    int count;
    unsigned char color;

    for(count=0; count<16; count++)        /* once for each bar */
        {
        if(data[count]<40) color = BLUE;
        else if(data[count]<80) color = GREEN;
        else if(data[count]<120) color = YELLOW;
        else if(data[count]<160) color = RED;
```

```
            else color = IWHITE;
            rect(200-data[count],190,count*40,count*40+20,color);
            }
    }


/* rect() */
/* draws rectangular, mode 14 (640x200) */
/* rectangle must be integral number of bytes wide */
#define MAXB (640/8)                        /* bytes in a row */
void rect(int top, int bot, int left, int rite,
                                        unsigned char color)
    {
    unsigned char far *farptr;
    int row, byte;
    outp(0x3C4,2);                  /* set address in sequencer */
    outp(0x3C5,color);              /* set color in map mask */
    farptr = (unsigned char far *)0xA0000000;  /* ptr EGA mem */
    for(row=top; row<=bot; row++)
        for(byte=left/8; byte<rite/8; byte++)
            *(farptr + row*MAXB + byte ) = 0xff; /* set 8 pixls */
    }
```

## Exercise 5

```
/* ediag.c */
/* draws diagonal lines on screen.  Use mode 13 (320x200) */
/* uses EGA write mode 2 */
#include <conio.h>                    /* for outp() */
#define BLUE 0x01                     /* ega colors */
#define YELLOW 0x0E
#define RED 0x04
#define BLACK 0
void putpte(int, int, unsigned char);  /* prototype */

void  main(void)
    {
    int x;
    for(x=0; x<200; x++)
        {
        putpte(x,x,BLUE);             /* diagonal line */
        putpte(x,199-x,YELLOW);       /* diagonal line */
        putpte(x,100,RED);            /* horizontal  line */
        putpte(100,x,BLACK);          /* vertical line */
        }
    }

/* putpte() */
/* displays colored pixel at location col, row */
/* uses EGA write mode 2 */
#define MAXR 200                      /* rows */
```

```
#define MAXC 320                      /* columns */
#define PIX  8                        /* pixels per byte */
#define MAXB (MAXC/PIX)               /* bytes in a row */
void putpte(int col, int row, unsigned char color)
{
    static unsigned char table[8] = { 0x80, 0x40, 0x20, 0x10,
                                       0x08, 0x04, 0x02, 0x01 };

    char far *farptr;
    int addr, bitpos;
    unsigned char temp;

    farptr = (int far *) 0xA0000000; /* set ptr to EGA mem */
    outp(0x3CE,5);                   /* select mode register */
    outp(0x3CF,2);                   /*     set to mode 2 */
    outp(0x3C4,2);                   /* select map mask register */
    outp(0x3C5,0xF);                 /* activate all bit planes */

    addr = row*MAXB + col/PIX;       /* calculate address */
    bitpos = col & 7;                /* lower 3 bits are bitpos */
    outp(0x3CE,8);                   /* select bit mask reg */
    outp(0x3CF,table[bitpos]);       /* set bit to be changed */
    temp = *(farptr+addr);           /* read byte into latches */
    *(farptr+addr) = color;          /* send color to address */

    outp(0x3CE,8);                   /* select bit mask reg */
    outp(0x3CF,0xFF);                /* make all bits writeable */
    outp(0x3CE,5);                   /* select mode register */
    outp(0x3CF,0);                   /* set write mode 0 */
}
```

# Chapter 12
# Answers to Questions

1. Microsoft C library functions are more convenient.

2. Direct memory access is generally faster and more flexible.

3. GRAPHICS.LIB (or GRAPHICS.QLB in Quick C)

4. a and c

5. GRAPH.H

6. a, b, and d

7. a and b

8. False

9. d

10. GRAPHICS.LIB (or GRAPHICS.QLB in Quick C)

11. False

12. b

13.  _setvideomode()

14.  False

15.  b

16.  _setlinestyle()

17.  c

18.  b

19.  c

20.  a, b, c, and d

# Chapter 12
# Suggested Answers to Exercises

### Exercise 1

```
/* paint.c */
/* permits user to draw, using cursor */
#include <graph.h>
#define RIGHT 319                  /* screen edges */
#define BOT   199
#define ESC    27                  /* escape key */
#define L_ARRO 75                  /* cursor control keys */
#define R_ARRO 77
#define U_ARRO 72
#define D_ARRO 80
main()
{
   int x, y;
   char key;
                                           /* initialize graphics */
   if(_setvideomode(_MRES4COLOR)==0 )
     { printf("Can't set mode"); exit(1); }
   x = RIGHT/2;                         /* put dot in middle */
   y = BOT/2;
   _setpixel(x, y);
   while( (key=getch()) != ESC )       /* if [Esc], exit loop */
     {
      if( key == 0 )                   /* if extended code, */
         {
         switch( getch() )             /* read second character */
            {
            case L_ARRO: if(x > 0)    --x; break;  /* left */
            case R_ARRO: if(x < RIGHT) ++x; break;  /* right */
            case U_ARRO: if(y > 0)    --y; break;  /* up */
            case D_ARRO: if(y < BOT)   ++y; break;  /* down */
            } /* end switch */
```

```
                    _setpixel(x, y);                /* draw dot */
                }   /* end if */
            }   /* end while */
        _setvideomode(_DEFAULTMODE);            /* restore previous mode */
    }
```

## Exercise 2

```
/* coin2.c */
/* displays a coin rotating about vertical axis */
/* uses _getimage() and _putimage() */
#include <graph.h>
#include <malloc.h>
#define XC 160                          /* center of ellipse */
#define YC 100
#define RAD 50                          /* vertical radius */
#define N  8                            /* number of views */
#define DELAY 10000                     /* delay between views */

main()
{
    int xRad;                           /* horizontal radius */
    char *buff[N];                      /* pointers to buffers */
    long size;                          /* size of buffer */
    int j, k;
                                        /* set video mode */
    if(_setvideomode(_MRES4COLOR)==0 )
        { printf("Can't set mode"); exit(1); }
                                        /* get image size */
    size = _imagesize( XC-RAD, YC-RAD, XC+RAD, YC+RAD );

    for( j=0; j<N; j++ )                /* make and store */
        {                               /*     images of ellipses */
        xRad = j * RAD / (N-1) ;        /* find x radius */
        if( j==0 )   xRad = 1;          /* vertical line */
        _clearscreen(_GCLEARSCREEN);    /* get rid of old image */
                                        /* draw ellipse */
        _ellipse( _GBORDER, XC-xRad, YC-RAD, XC+xRad, YC+RAD );
        buff[j] = malloc(size);         /* get image memory */
                                        /* place image in memory */
        _getimage(XC-RAD, YC-RAD, XC+RAD, YC+RAD, buff[j]);
        }
    while( !kbhit() )                   /* draw ellipses */
        {                               /*     until keypress */
        for( j=0; j<N; j++)             /* increasing width */
            {                           /* draw image */
            _putimage( XC-RAD, YC-RAD, buff[j], _GPSET );
            for(k=0; k<DELAY; k++);     /* delay, erase image */
            _putimage( XC-RAD, YC-RAD, buff[j], _GXOR );
            }
```

```
        for( j=N-2; j>0; j--)              /* decreasing width */
            {                              /* draw image */
            _putimage( XC-RAD, YC-RAD, buff[j], _GPSET );
            for(k=0; k<DELAY; k++);        /* delay, erase image */
            _putimage( XC-RAD, YC-RAD, buff[j], _GXOR );
            }
        }  /* end while */
    _setvideomode(_DEFAULTMODE);           /* restore previous mode */
}
```

## Exercise 3

```
/* ezedit.c */
/* mini editor works in text window */
#include <graph.h>               /* needed for graphics */
#define LEFT   10                /* left side of window */
#define TOP     8                /* top of window */
#define RIGHT  50                /* right side of window */
#define BOT    21                /* bottom of window */
#define WIDTH  (RIGHT-LEFT+1)    /* width of window */
#define HEIGHT (BOT-TOP+1)       /* height of window */
#define ESC    27                /* escape key */
#define L_ARRO 75                /* cursor control keys */
#define R_ARRO 77
#define U_ARRO 72
#define D_ARRO 80
#define ALT_C  46                /* key combo for color change */
#define BACKS   8                /* backspace */


main()
{
    char key;                        /* keyboard char */
    int row, col;                    /* cursor row & column */
    char string[2];                  /* 1-char string */
    struct rccoord rc;               /* for text position */

    _clearscreen(_GCLEARSCREEN);     /* clear entire screen */
    _settextwindow(TOP, LEFT, BOT, RIGHT);  /* define window */
    row = HEIGHT/2; col = WIDTH/2;   /* cursor to middle */
    _settextposition(row, col);
    _setbkcolor(1L);                 /* set background color */

    while( (key=getch()) != ESC )    /* if [Esc], exit loop */
        {
        if( key == 0 )               /* if extended code, */
            {
            switch( getch() )        /* read second character */
                {
                case L_ARRO:         /* move cursor left */
```

```
                         if(col > 1)
                             _settextposition(row, --col);
                         break;
                     case R_ARRO:               /* move cursor right */
                         if(col < WIDTH)
                             _settextposition(row, ++col);
                         break;
                     case U_ARRO:               /* move cursor up */
                         if(row > 1)
                             _settextposition(--row, col);
                         break;
                     case D_ARRO:               /* move cursor down */
                         if(row < HEIGHT)
                             _settextposition(++row, col);
                         break;
                     case ALT_C:                /* change text color */
                         _settextcolor(getch()-'0');
                         break;
                 }  /* end switch */
             }  /* end if */
         else                               /* not extended code */
             {
             if(key==BACKS)                 /* if backspace */
                 {
                 if(col > 1)                /* and not at left edge */
                     {                      /* move TP left */
                     _settextposition(row, --col); /* move TP left */
                     _outtext(" ");               /* print blank */
                     _settextposition(row, col);  /* reset TP */
                     }
                 }
             else                           /* normal printing char */
                 {
                 *string = key;             /* make 1-char string */
                 *(string+1) = 0;           /* terminate string */
                 _outtext(string);          /* print character */
                 rc = _gettextposition();   /* get new cursor pos */
                 row = rc.row;              /* reset row and col */
                 col = rc.col;
                 }
             }
         }  /* end while */
     }
```

# Chapter 13
# Answers to Questions

1. standard I/O and system I/O

2. a, b, c, and d are all correct

3. file pointer

4. a and b

5. **fclose()**

6. d

7. False: a file that is written to but not closed may lose data when the program is terminated.

8. c and d

9. binary mode

10. a, c, e, and f

11. binary, unless using formatted I/O

12. c

13. False

14. d (not to be confused with c)

15. **fwrite()**

16. bytes

17. c and d

18. handle

19. a and d

20. **read()**

21. **setmode()**

22. c

23. True

24. b and d

25. pmode

26. system-level

27. d

28. C>encrypt <file1.txt >file2.txt

29. a and c

30. False

# Chapter 13
# Suggested Answers to Exercises

## Exercise 1

```
/* braces.c */
/* checks numbers of right and left braces are equal */
```

```c
#include <stdio.h>
main(argc,argv)
int argc;
char *argv[];
{
    FILE *fptr;
    char string[81];
    int left=0, right=0;
    char ch;

    if(argc != 2)                              /* check # of args */
        { printf("Format: C>type2 filename"); exit(); }
    if( (fptr=fopen(argv[1], "r")) == NULL)   /* open file */
        { printf("Can't open file %s.", argv[1]); exit(); }
    while( (ch=getc(fptr)) != EOF )            /* get char */
        {
        if( ch=='{' ) left++;                  /* count lefts */
        if( ch=='}' ) right++;                 /* count rights */
        }
    if (left != right)                         /* check if equal */
        printf("\nMismatched braces\n");
    else
        printf("\nBraces match.\n");
    fclose(fptr);                              /* close file */
}
```

## Exercise 2

```c
/* writedex.c */
/* writes strings typed at keyboard, to file */
/* prints offset for each phrase */
#include <stdio.h>
main()
{
    FILE *fptr;                         /* declare ptr to FILE */
    char string[81];                    /* storage for strings */
    fptr = fopen("textfile.txt","wb");  /* open file */
    while(strlen(gets(string)) > 0)     /* get string from keybd */
        {
        printf("Offset=%d\n\n", ftell(fptr) );  /* print offset */
        fputs(string,fptr);             /* write string to file */
        fputs("\n",fptr);               /* write newline to file */
        }
    fclose(fptr);                       /* close file */
}
```

## Exercise 3

```c
/* readdex.c */
/* reads strings from file */
```

```
#include <stdio.h>                    /* for fopen(), etc. */
#include <process.h>                  /* for exit() */
int table[4] = { 0, 29, 49, 79 };    /* for textfile.txt */
void rdex(int);                       /* prototype */

void main(void)
{
    int index;

    while(1)
        {
        printf("\n\nEnter index number (0 to 3) of string: ");
        scanf("%d", &index);                  /* get index */
        rdex(table[index]);                   /* print string */
        }
}

/* rdex() */
/* reads string from file at offset, displays it on screen */
void rdex(int offset)
{
    FILE *fptr;                              /* ptr to FILE */
    char string[81];                         /* stores strings */
                                             /* open file */
    if( (fptr=fopen("textfile.txt","rb"))==NULL )
        { printf("Can't open file."); exit(1); }
    if(fseek(fptr,(long)offset,0) != 0)    /* set file ptr */
        { printf("Can't put pointer there."); exit(0); }
    if( fgets(string,80,fptr) == NULL )    /* read string */
        { printf("Can't read string."); exit(0); }
    printf("%s",string);                     /* print string */
    fclose(fptr);                            /* close file */
}
```

## Exercise 4

Make appropriate changes to the interface part of the program, and add this routine:

```
/* delrec() */
/* deletes selected record */
delrec()
{
    int recno, j;
    printf("\nEnter record number to be deleted: ");
    scanf("%d", &recno);
    if(recno<1 || recno>n)
        { printf("Invalid record number.\n"); return; }
    for (j=--recno; j<n-1; j++)  /* write each structure */
        agent[j] = agent[j+1];   /*   over preceding one */
```

```
        n--;                            /* one less structure */
    }
```

## Exercise 5

```
/* concat.c */
/* concatenates two files to form a third */
#include "fcntl.h"                      /* needed for oflags */
#include "sys\types.h"                  /* needed for
sys\stat.h */
#include "sys\stat.h"                   /* needed for pmode */
#define BUFSIZ 4096                     /* buffer size */
char buff[BUFSIZ];                      /* buffer */
main(argc,argv)
int argc;
char *argv[];
{
    int inhandle1, inhandle2, outhandle, bytes;
    if(argc != 4)                       /* check arguments */
      { printf
        ("Format: C>concat source1.xxx source2.xxx dest.xxx");
        exit(); }
                                        /* open files */
    if( (inhandle1 = open(argv[1], O_RDONLY | O_BINARY)) < 0)
      {printf("Can't open file %s.", argv[1]); exit(); }
    if( (inhandle2 = open(argv[2], O_RDONLY | O_BINARY)) < 0)
      {printf("Can't open file %s.", argv[2]); exit(); }
    if( (outhandle = open(argv[3],
         O_CREAT | O_WRONLY | O_BINARY, S_IWRITE)) < 0)
      { printf("Can't open file %s.", argv[3]); exit(); }
                                        /* copy first file */
    while( (bytes = read(inhandle1,buff,BUFSIZ)) > 0)
      write(outhandle,buff,bytes);      /* add second file */
    while( (bytes = read(inhandle2,buff,BUFSIZ)) > 0)
      write(outhandle,buff,bytes);
    close(inhandle1);                   /* close files */
    close(inhandle2);
    close(outhandle);
}
```

# Chapter 14
# Answers to Questions

1. a, b, and c

2. linker

3. declared, **extern**

4. a and c

5. False: only modules containing functions referred to in the program are included.

6. c and d

7. b

8. **#define**

9. d

10. large

11. a and d

12. False: except that the stack segment can share the data segment.

13. b and c

14. /AL

15. d

# Chapter 15
# Answers to Questions

1. c and d

2. declared, **external**

3. c

4. created and destroyed

5. a and b

6. False: it is only visible from the point where it is defined onward.

7. **external static**

8. c

9. **enum fish gamefish;**

10. d

11. names

12. c

13. True

14. bytes of memory

15. a

# Index

### The Waite Group's
### C Primer Plus, Revised Edition
*Mitchell Waite, Stephen Prata, and Donald Martin*

This revised and expanded edition of a best-seller presents everything you should know to begin programming in the exciting C language, now used by over 80 percent of the software community. The book is organized for quick learning and encourages problem solving through questions and exercises.

The authors have updated the text with information on C++, AT&T's successor to C, which is used for object-oriented programming.

Topics covered include:

- Structure of a Simple C Program
- Variables, Constants, and Data Types
- Character Strings, *#define, printf( ),* and *scanf( )*
- Operators, Expressions, and Statements
- Input/Output Functions and Redirection
- Choosing Alternatives: *if, else,* Relational and Conditional Operators
- Storage Classes and Program Development
- The C Preprocessor
- Arrays and Pointers
- Character Strings and String Functions
- Structures and Other Data Delights
- The C Library and File I/O
- Bit Fiddling, Keywords, Binary Numbers, IBM® PC Music, and More

576 Pages, 7½ x 9¾, Softbound
ISBN: 0-672-22582-4
**No. 22582, $24.95**

### The Waite Group's
### Advanced C Primer ++
*Stephen Prata*

Programmers, students, managers, and hackers alike, will learn to master the C programming language. Anyone who knows the basics of C will learn practical C tips never before published. This indepth coverage gives you a rare and complete examination of video access ports, segmented memory, and registers.

*Advanced C Primer ++* takes the reader further than most C books on the market, showing how to manipulate the hardware of the IBM PC family of computers directly from C. Readers learn how to access routines in the Read Only Memory (ROM) of an IBM PC, how to use system calls in PC DOS from C and i/o ports, how to control the video screen, and to integrate assembly routines into C programs.

Topics covered include:

- Advanced C Programming
- Register and Bit Level System Control
- Hardware Operation for Beginners and Experienced Users
- Advanced Use of Pointers, Functions, Storage Classes, Arrays and Structures
- C Library Access
- Use of Assembly Language Modules
- Binary and Text File Input and Output

Includes chapter questions and answers.

512 Pages, 7½ x 9¾, Softbound
ISBN: 0-672-22486-0
**No. 22486, $24.95**

### The Waite Group's
### C++ Programming
*John Berry*

This new guide and tutorial is aimed at developers and intermediate-level students who already know the C language. It teaches the use of object-oriented programming skills and introduces the major features of the C++ language with explanations followed by practical examples that will work on both UNIX and MS-DOS systems.

The book includes quizzes, exercises, and key words and is ideal for self study or as a complete course.

Topics covered include:

- How the C++ Translator Works
- New Structure Operators and Data Types
- Input and Output Message Streams in C++
- Pointers and Reference
- Classes and Inheritance
- Function and Operator Overloading
- In-line Functions
- All About C++ Pointers
- Private and Public Structures
- The Operator Function
- Derived Classes

336 Pages, 7½ x 9¾, Softbound
ISBN: 0-672-22619-7
**No. 22619, $24.95**

### The Waite Group's
### Essential Guide to ANSI C
*Naba Barkakati*

An intermediate-level pocket guide for programmers, this book conforms to the American National Standards Institute's (ANSI) C draft and is the first book on the newly adopted standard for C. It provides a convenient and fast reference to all C functions, with examples for each, in a handy "shirt-pocket" size.

The book concentrates on the 146 functions in the ANSI C library and contains debugged real-world examples for every routine. Each function page includes a brief tutorial and states the purpose, syntax, example call, includes, returns, and "see also" references in alphabetical format.

Topics covered include:

- How to Use This Essential Guide
- Overview of ANSI C
- The ANSI C Preprocess, Language, and Library
- Streams and Files in C
- ANSI C File Routine Reference
- Process Control
- Variable-length Argument Lists
- Memory Allocation and Management
- Data Conversion and Math Routines
- Character Classification and Conversion
- String Comparison and Manipulation
- Searching and Sorting
- Time Routines

224 Pages, 4¼ x 8½, Softbound
ISBN: 0-672-22673-1
**No. 22673, $6.95**

**Visit your local book retailer or call**
**800-428-SAMS.**

| The Waite Group's | The Waite Group's | The Waite Group's | The Waite Group's |
|---|---|---|---|
| **Essential Guide to Turbo C®** | **Turbo C® Bible** | **Turbo C® Programming for the PC, Revised Edition** | **Inside the AMIGA® with C Second Edition** |
| *Naba Barkakati* | *Naba Barkakati* | *Robert Lafore* | *John Berry* |

**The Waite Group's**
**Essential Guide to Turbo C®**
*Naba Barkakati*

This user-friendly reference book explains all of the functions of the Turbo C library.

Compact and concise, the book covers all version 2.0 features including 8086 segments and offsets, paragraphs, code and data segments, heap, near and far data, and memory models. Each function is treated separately and provides a brief tutorial along with its purpose, syntax, example call, and references.

Topics covered include:

■ Overview of the Turbo C Language
■ The Turbo C Programming Environment
■ Process Control
■ Variable Arguments
■ Memory Allocation
■ Buffer Manipulation
■ Data Conversion
■ Math Functions
■ Character Classification and Conversion
■ String Manipulation
■ Searching and Sorting
■ Time and Date Functions
■ File and Directory Manipulation
■ Input and Output Routines
■ System Calls
■ Graphics Modes, Coordinates, and Attributes
■ Drawing and Animation
■ Combining Graphics and Text
■ Text Mode Routines

288 Pages, 4¾ x 8½, Softbound
ISBN: 0-672-22675-8
**No. 22675, $7.95**

**The Waite Group's**
**Turbo C® Bible**
*Naba Barkakati*

Clear and well-written tutorials point out the different purposes and appropriate uses of each Turbo C function to make programming more organized, complete, and powerful. The library routines are organized into functional categories with explanations that include the purpose, syntax, example call, includes, common uses, returns, comments, cautions and pitfalls, and cross-reference for that function.
Unique compatibility check boxes show portability with Microsoft C versions 3.0, 4.0, and 5.0; Microsoft QuickC, and the UNIX System V compilers.

Topics covered include:

■ Turbo C 1.0 Compiler Features and Options
■ Process Control
■ Variable-Length Argument Lists
■ Memory Allocation and Management
■ Buffer Manipulation
■ Data Conversion Routines
■ Math Routines
■ Character Classification and Conversion
■ String Comparison and Manipulation
■ Searching and Sorting
■ Time Routines
■ File and Directory Manipulation
■ Input and Output Routines
■ System Calls
■ Graphics Modes
■ Drawing and Animation
■ Combining Graphics and Text

950 Pages, 7½ x 9¾, Softbound
ISBN: 0-672-22631-6
**No. 22631, $24.95**

**The Waite Group's**
**Turbo C® Programming for the PC, Revised Edition**
*Robert Lafore*

This entry-level book moves quickly through the fundamentals of the latest version of Turbo C, using step-by-step, hands-on tutorials to show readers how to write useful and marketable C programs.

Based on the newest Turbo C compiler but compatible with Turbo C 1.0 and 1.5, it contains new information on the Turbo C graphics library, the graphics model, and Debugging Tracer, as it highlights ANSI C features. The language concepts are presented in an orderly, graded fashion to allow readers to move smoothly from simple topics to the more advanced.

Topics covered include:

■ Getting Started
■ C Building Blocks
■ Loops, Decisions, Functions
■ Arrays and Strings, Pointers
■ Keyboard and Cursor
■ Structures, Unions, and ROM BIOS
■ Memory and the Monochrome Display
■ Direct CGA and EGA Color Graphics
■ Files and Larger Programs
■ Advanced Variables
■ Appendices: Reference, Supplementary Programs, Hexadecimal Numbering, Bibliography, ASCII Chart, The Turbo C Debugger, Answers to Questions and Exercises

700 Pages, 7½ x 9¾, Softbound
ISBN: 0-672-22660-X
**No. 22660, $22.95**

**The Waite Group's**
**Inside the AMIGA® with C Second Edition**
*John Berry*

Everyone who has recently upgraded their AMIGA computer system, or is thinking about doing it, needs this revised edition of *Inside the AMIGA with C*. The book covers the AmigaDOS™ operating system in greater detail, and is compatible with the new AmigaDOS 1.2. Paying particular attention to the AMIGA 500, the book presents special AMIGA graphics features including sprites, Genlock, and blitter objects, with updated information on Intuition™.

Like the original book, code listings in each chapter are carefully constructed both as practical routines and as instructional examples for beginning to intermediate C programmers. The new edition features several new programs that demonstrate the use of color palettes and registers and a software toolkit that contains a library of C routines to create and manage screens, windows, input from gadgets, and control graphics.

Topics covered include:

■ The AMIGA Programming Environment
■ Using Intuition
■ Process Control and AmigaDOS
■ Drawing in Intuition
■ Animating the Sprites
■ Programming Sound
■ Artificial Speech
■ Programming with Disk Files

400 Pages, 7½ x 9¾, Softbound
ISBN: 0-672-22625-1
**No. 22625, $24.95**

**Visit your local book retailer or call**
**800-428-SAMS.**

## The Waite Group's Essential Guide to Microsoft® C

*Naba Barkakati*

This conveniently sized reference organizes and simplifies all 370 functions in the popular Microsoft C library. In a user-friendly format, it shows the many "hidden" routines available to programmers, providing instant access to the power of the Microsoft C 5.1 compiler. The book includes complete new ANSI features such as const, volatile and void prototypes and details 80x86 segments and offsets, paragraphs, code and data segments, near and far data, and memory models.

Topics covered include:

- Microsoft C 5.0 Compiler Features and Options
- Process Control
- Variable Arguments and Memory Allocation
- Buffer Manipulation
- Data Conversion and Math Functions
- Character Classification and Conversion
- String Manipulation
- Searching and Sorting
- Time and Date Functions
- File and Directory Manipulation
- Input and Output Routines
- System Calls
- Graphics Modes, Coordinates, and Attributes
- Drawing and Animation
- Combining Graphics and Text

304 Pages, 4¼ x 8½, Softbound
ISBN: 0-672-22674-X
**No. 22674, $7.95**

## The Waite Group's Microsoft® C Bible

*Naba Barkakati*

*Microsoft C Bible* provides a thorough description of the 370 functions of the Microsoft C library, complete with practical, real-world MS-DOS-based examples for each function. Library routines are broken down into functional categories with an intermediate-level tutorial followed by the functions and examples.

Included are two "quick-start" tutorials, complete ANSI prototypes for each function, extensive program examples, and handy jump tables to help enhance learning.

Topics covered include:

- Overview of the C Language
- Microsoft C 5.0 Compiler Features and Options
- Process Control
- Variable Length Argument Lists
- Memory Allocation and Management
- Buffer Manipulation
- Data Conversion Routines
- Math Routines
- Character Classification and Conversion
- String Comparison and Manipulation
- Searching and Sorting
- Time Routines
- File and Directory Manipulation
- Input and Output Routines
- System Calls
- Graphics Modes, Coordinates, and Attributes
- Drawing and Animation
- Combining Graphics and Text

824 Pages, 7½ x 9¾, Softbound
ISBN: 0-672-22620-0
**No. 22620, $24.95**

## The Waite Group's QuickC™ Bible

*Naba Barkakati*

This book, written for first-time programmers making the transition from Pascal or BASIC to C, is a complete, user-friendly reference to Microsoft's QuickC compiler.

The book shows how to accomplish such sophisticated procedures as using the environment and the PSP, provides complete details on video and graphics modes, and drawing and animation. It reveals little-known secrets of C programming, providing helpful, in-depth tips to make programming more organized and powerful. A pocket-size foldout reference card of all QuickC functions and commands is included, and unique compatibility boxes show portability with other compilers.

Topics covered include:

- Overview of the C Language
- Process Control
- Variable-Length Argument Lists
- Memory Allocation and Management
- Buffer Manipulation
- Data Conversion and Math Routines
- Character Classification and Conversion
- String Comparison and Manipulation
- Searching and Sorting
- Time Routines
- File and Directory Manipulation
- Input and Output Routines
- System Calls and Graphics Modes

900 Pages, 7½ x 9¾, Softbound
ISBN: 0-672-22632-4
**No. 22632, $24.95**

## The Waite Group's MS-DOS® Bible, Second Edition

*Steven Simrin*

This revised edition of the best seller is ideally targeted for the intermediate level user and programmer of the operating system, especially those who have upgraded to the new version 3.3. The comprehensive tutorial emphasizes the new features found in DOS 3.3 and provides expanded coverage of batch files, device drivers, memory management, and network commands.

The new expanded batch language, disk structure, terminate and stay resident programs (TSRs), and the Lotus-Intel expanded memory model 4.0 are highlighted. The new commands are explained in detail, and a unique "Information Jump Table" is included and enhanced for easy reference.

Topics covered include:

- Starting MS-DOS
- MS-DOS Files and Batch Files
- Directories, Paths, and Trees
- Installing a Fixed Disk
- Redirection, Filters, and Pipes
- EDLIN
- Extended Keyboard and Display Control
- Debug
- Link
- Disk Structure
- MS-DOS Device Drivers
- MS-DOS Commands
- Appendices: Undocumented Features; MS-DOS Interrupts and Function Calls; Practical Batch Files; ASCII Cross Reference Table

568 pages, 7½ x 9¾, softbound
ISBN: 0-672-22617-0
**No. 22617, $22.95**

### Visit your local book retailer or call
### 800-428-SAMS.

### The Waite Group's MS DOS® Developer's Guide, Second Edition

*John Angermeyer and Kevin Jaeger*

This new and expanded developer's guide covers the MS-DOS and PC-DOS™ operating systems up to Version 3.3, concentrating on techniques for developing application programs as well as memory resident programs and device drivers. The book is aimed at the serious programmer, developer, or "power user" with a significant understanding of MS-DOS.

Topics covered include:

- Structured Programming
- Program and Memory Management in the MS-DOS Environment
- TSRs
- EMS
- Real-Time Programming Under MS-DOS
- Installable Device Drivers
- Writing Programs for the Intel 8087/80287 Math Coprocessor
- LANs and MS-DOS
- Programming the Serial Port
- Programming the EGA and VGA
- Disk Layout and File Recovery Information
- Recovering Data Lost in Memory
- Differences Between MS-DOS Versions
- High-Level Languages
- Debugging

550 Pages, 7½ x 9¾, Softbound
ISBN: 0-672-22630-8
**No. 22630, $24.95**

### The Waite Group's Understanding MS-DOS®

*O'Day and Angermeyer*

MS-DOS is a very powerful and intricate operating system, with millions of users. This operating system can be explored by beginning programmers in a hands-on approach at the keyboard.

*Understanding MS-DOS* introduces the use and operation of this popular operating system for those with little previous experience in computer hardware or software. The fundamentals of the operating system such as EDLIN, tree structured directories and pathnames, and such advanced features as redirection and filtering are presented in a way that is easy to understand and use.

Topics covered include:

- Organizing Data and Files
- Redirecting Input and Output
- Using the Text Editor EDLIN to Create and Edit Files
- Special Function Keys and Key Combinations
- Creating Batch Files of Often Repeated Commands
- Create and Use Tree Structured Directories

240 Pages, 7 x 9, Softbound
ISBN: 0-672-27067-6
**No. 27067, $17.95**

### The Waite Group's Tricks of the MS-DOS® Masters

*John Angermeyer, Rich Fahringer, Kevin Jaeger, and Dan Shafer*

This title provides the personal user (not necessarily the programmer or software developer) with a wealth of advanced tips about the operating system and tricks for using it most successfully.

Also included are advanced tips on using popular software packages such as WordStar®

Topics covered include:

- Secrets of the Batch File Command Language
- Secrets of Pipes, Filters, and Redirection
- Secrets of Tree-Structured Directories
- Discovering Secrets: A Debugger Tutorial
- Secrets of DOS Commands
- Secrets of Files
- Secrets of Free and Low-Cost Software
- Secrets of Add-on Software, Boards, and Mass Storage
- Secrets of System Configuration
- Secrets of Data Encryption

568 Pages, 7½ x 9¾, Softbound
ISBN: 0-672-22525-5
**No. 22525, $24.95**

### The Waite Group's Discovering MS-DOS®

*Kate O'Day*

This comprehensive study of MS-DOS commands such as DEBUG, LINK, and EDLIN begins with general information about operating systems. It then shows how to use MS-DOS to produce letters and documents; create, name, and manipulate files; use the keyboard and function keys to perform jobs faster; and direct, sort, and find data quickly.

It features a command summary card for quick reference.

Topics covered include:

- Introduction to MS-DOS
- What is a Computer System?
- What is an Operating System?
- Getting MS-DOS off the Ground
- System Insurance
- Editing
- Filing
- Batch Files
- Paths
- Input/Output
- Hard Disks
- Appendices: Error Messages, Reference Card

296 Pages, 7½ x 9¾, Softbound
ISBN: 0-672-22407-0
**No. 22407, $19.95**

**Visit your local book retailer or call
800-428-SAMS.**

Dear Reader:

If you enjoyed this book, you may be interested in these additional subjects and titles from The Waite Group and Howard W. Sams & Company. Reader level is as follows: ★ = introductory, ★★ = intermediate, ★★★ = advanced. You can order these books by calling 800-428-SAMS.

| Level | Title | Catalog # | Price | |
|-------|-------|-----------|-------|---|

### C and C++ Programming Language

*Tutorial, UNIX & ANSI*

| | | | | |
|-------|-------|-----------|-------|---|
| ★ | C Primer Plus, Revised Edition, Waite, Prata, & Martin | 22582 | $24.95 | |
| ★★ | C++ Programming, Berry | 22619 | $24.95 | NEW |
| ★★★ | Advanced C Primer ++, Prata | 22486 | $24.95 | |

*Tutorial, Product Specific*

| | | | | |
|-------|-------|-----------|-------|---|
| ★ | Microsoft C Programming for the PC, Revised Edition, Lafore | 22661 | $24.95 | NEW |
| ★ | Turbo C Programming for the PC, Revised Edition, Lafore | 22660 | $22.95 | NEW |
| ★★ | Inside the Amiga with C, Second Edition, Berry | 22625 | $24.95 | NEW |

*Reference, Product Specific*

| | | | | |
|-------|-------|-----------|-------|---|
| ★★ | Microsoft C Bible, Barkakati | 22620 | $24.95 | NEW |
| ★★ | Quick C Bible, Barkakati | 22632 | $24.95 | NEW |
| ★★ | Turbo C. Bible, Barkakati | 22631 | $24.95 | NEW |
| ★★ | Essential Guide to ANSI C, Barkakati | 22673 | $7.95 | NEW |
| ★★ | Essential Guide to Turbo C, Barkakati | 22675 | $7.95 | NEW |
| ★★ | Essential Guide to Microsoft C, Barkakati | 22674 | $7.95 | NEW |

### DOS and OS/2 Operating System

*Tutorial, General Users*

| | | | | |
|-------|-------|-----------|-------|---|
| ★ | Discovering MS-DOS, O'Day | 22407 | $19.95 | |
| ★ | Understanding MS-DOS, O'Day & Angermeyer | 27067 | $17.95 | |

*Tutorial/Reference, General Users*

| | | | | |
|-------|-------|-----------|-------|---|
| ★★ | MS-DOS Bible, Second Edition, Simrin | 22617 | $22.95 | NEW |

*Tutorial/Reference, Power Users*

| | | | | |
|-------|-------|-----------|-------|---|
| ★★ | Tricks of the MS-DOS Masters, Angermeyer & Jaeger | 22525 | $24.95 | |

*Tutorial, Programmers*

| | | | | |
|-------|-------|-----------|-------|---|
| ★★ | MS-DOS Papers, Edited by The Waite Group | 22594 | $26.95 | NEW |
| ★★ | OS/2 Programmer's Reference, Dror | 22645 | $24.95 | NEW |
| ★★★ | MS-DOS Developer's Guide, Revised Edition, Angermeyer, Jaeger, et al. | 22630 | $24.95 | NEW |

### UNIX Operating System

*Tutorial, General Users*

| | | | | |
|-------|-------|-----------|-------|---|
| ★ | UNIX Primer Plus, Waite, Prata, & Martin | 22028 | $22.95 | |
| ★ | UNIX System V Primer, Revised Edition, Waite, Prata, & Martin | 22570 | $22.95 | |
| ★★ | UNIX System V Bible, Prata and Martin | 22562 | $24.95 | |
| ★★ | UNIX Communications, Henderson, Anderson, Costales | 22511 | $24.95 | |
| ★★ | UNIX Papers, Edited by Mitchell Waite | 22570 | $26.95 | |

*Tutorial/Reference, Power Users and Programmers*

| | | | | |
|-------|-------|-----------|-------|---|
| ★★ | Tricks of the UNIX Masters, Sage | 22449 | $24.95 | |
| ★★★ | Advanced UNIX—A Programmer's Guide, Prata | 22403 | $24.95 | |

### Macintosh

*Tutorial, General Users*

| | | | | |
|-------|-------|-----------|-------|---|
| ★ | HyperTalk Bible, The Waite Group | 48430 | $24.95 | NEW |

*Tutorial/Reference, Power Users and Programmers*

| | | | | |
|-------|-------|-----------|-------|---|
| ★★ | Tricks of the HyperTalk Masters, Edited by The Waite Group | 48431 | $24.95 | NEW |